POLITICAL ACTION

MASS PARTICIPATION IN FIVE WESTERN DEMOCRACIES

Samuel H. Barnes
Max Kaase

and

Klaus R. Allerbeck
Barbara G. Farah
Felix Heunks
Ronald Inglehart
M. Kent Jennings
Hans D. Klingemann
Alan Marsh
Leopold Rosenmayr

 SAGE PUBLICATIONS   Beverly Hills   London

For information address:

SAGE PUBLICATIONS, INC.
275 South Beverly Drive
Beverly Hills, California 90212

SAGE PUBLICATIONS LTD
28 Banner Street
London EC1Y 8QE, England

Printed in the United States of America

Library of Congress Cataloging in Publication Data

Main entry under title:

Political action.

    Includes bibliographical references and index.
    1. Government, Resistance to—Addresses, essays, lectures.   2. Democracy—Addresses, essays, lectures.
3. Political psychology—Addresses, essays, lectures.
4. Political sociology—Addresses, essays, lectures.
I. *Barnes*, Samuel Henry, 1931-   II. *Kaase,* Max.
JC328.3.P63   301.5'92'091722   78-19649
ISBN 0-8039-0957-8

CONTENTS

PREFACE

Political Action is the first cross-national volume from our eight-nation project. If, as someone once remarked, the goal of science is the education of the scientist, this project has come closer than most to achieving its goals. It is difficult to convey the immediate and long-term impact on participants of a collaboration such as this. If still less than a family, we have become more than a project: we are a scholarly community of fate, bound together by lasting friendships forged by the time, emotion, and physical and intellectual energies committed to the project, as well as by our willingness to accept collectively as well as individually the verdict of our peers on our work.

We have followed the equal partners format from beginning to end. Scholars from several countries met in Brussels in the spring of 1971, brought together by a common interest in understanding the waves of dissatisfaction and protest that seemed to be changing the politics of advanced industrial countries.

Some assumptions were shared from the beginning. Other agreements were reached only after extensive discussion at more than a dozen meetings over a period of several years. Consensus was quickly achieved on a number of points. Our focus of study would be advanced industrial democracies; extending further the range of countries was thought to increase the number of problems and to complicate intolerably the always vexing problems of cross-national measurement and conceptual equivalence. Our data base would be sample surveys of national populations. We wanted to generalize about nations; samples of subareas or subgroups such as students were inadequate. The use of aggregate and events data appeared promising, but the magnitude of the data collection and analysis effort required was deemed too large for a single project. Finally, we planned from the beginning that our joint analyses would be thematic rather than country-by-country. Individual country groups were encouraged to publish volumes dealing with their countries, and several are listed, along with other works deriving from this project, in the List of Publications at the end of this volume.

Extended discussions permitted clarification of theoretical foci, identification of salient previous work, evaluation of pretest results, and—finally—agreement on a core set of questions requiring, on the average, one hour to administer. Most countries added ten minutes of questions unique to the country.

Numerous and extended meetings enabled us to achieve agreement through consensus, with neither the formalities of democratic voting nor the leadership of intellectual godfathers or financial angels. These meetings made the project a cultural feast for the participants. We absorbed the viewpoints of other members, became familiar with all areas of the subject and not just our individual concerns, and learned about other cultures from the very best teachers. We also visited member countries, sampled national cuisines, drinks, and life styles, and experienced and exploited national variations in universities and research institutes.

The final set of countries reflects both our interest in obtaining a purposive sample of advanced industrial democracies and the hazards of fund raising. To join the project, each group had to find the means to administer the common core questionnaire to a national sample. The initial members of the team were from Germany, the United States, Britain, the Netherlands, and France. The French group dropped out after several meetings when it became apparent that funds for a French survey would not be forthcoming. Subsequently, an Austrian group joined the project; somewhat later, Swiss, Italian, and Finnish groups were also added. The first country to enter the field was Britain, with fieldwork in that country being completed very early in 1974. Germany, the Netherlands, Austria, and the United States completed their fieldwork by September of 1974. Fieldwork in Finland, Switzerland, and Italy took place in late 1974 and during 1975. Since the planning for the initial analyses was well underway prior to the entry of the latter three countries, the group decided to concentrate in this initial volume on the first five countries that had carried out their fieldwork together. A subsequent work will deal with all eight countries.

While the design and analysis were conceived and carried out jointly, the funding and execution of the fieldwork were the responsibilities of each national team. Samuel H. Barnes served as organizational coordinator for the project.

In Britain, leadership in launching the project was provided initially by Mark Abrams, then Director of the Survey Unit of the British Social Science Research Council (SSRC); he has been a supporter and mentor throughout the project. Funding was provided by the British SSRC, and fieldwork was carried out by Mary Agar Fieldwork Services Ltd. Abrams and Alan Marsh served as principal investigators on the British project.

German financing was provided by the Deutsche Forschungsgemeinschaft (DFG), and fieldwork was executed by the Gesellschaft fuer angewandte Sozialpsychologie (GETAS). German principal investigators were Klaus R. Allerbeck, currently of the University of Bielefeld, and Max Kaase and Hans D. Klingemann of the Zentrum fuer Umfragen, Methoden, und Analysen (ZUMA) and the University of Mannheim.

The Dutch study was funded by the University of Tilburg and fieldwork was executed by students selected and trained from throughout the country. The principal Dutch investigators were Philip Stouthard, Felix Heunks, and Cees de Graaf of the University of Tilburg.

Leopold Rosenmayr was the principal Austrian investigator; he was assisted by Anselm Eder, Inga Findl, Kathleen Stoffl, and Elfie Urbas. Austrian funding was provided by the Austrian National Science Foundation. Fieldwork was carried out by the Institut fuer Empirische Sozialwissenschaft (IFES) after special training and under supervision by the Austrian group, all of whom were members of the Institute of Sociology of the Social Sciences Faculty of the University of Vienna.

The American study was financed by the National Institute of Mental Health and the U. S. Army Research Institute; it was executed by the Survey Research Center of the Institute for Social Research (ISR). American principal investigators are Samuel H. Barnes, Ronald Inglehart, and M. Kent Jennings; Barbara G. Farah was an associate throughout the project. All are associated with the University of Michigan's Department of Political Science and the Center for Political Studies of the ISR.

As we pointed out above, project decisions were worked out at more than a dozen meetings of the group. We want to thank the organizations that hosted and financed these conferences of the group. The initial meeting in Brussels was supported by the European Communities Office of Information under the direction of Jacques-René Rabier; his support and enthusiasm were very important in launching the project and were greatly appreciated. Subsequent meetings were hosted by several institutions, including the Universities of Cologne, Geneva, Mannheim, Michigan, and Tilburg; the Villa Serbelloni and the Rockefeller Foundation; the Survey Unit of the British SSRC; the U.S. National Science Foundation, the DFG, and the Volkswagen Foundation; the Zentralarchiv fuer empirische Sozialforschung (ZA) at the University of Cologne, ZUMA at Mannheim, and the Center for Political Studies of the University of Michigan. The DFG also supported a two-month stay of Max Kaase in the United States for the purpose of working on the manuscript. The Deutscher Akademischer Austauschdienst (DAAD) enabled Samuel H. Barnes to spend a month in Mannheim in connection with the project. Without these opportunities for the group to discuss problems of design and analysis the project could not have gone forward; we are grateful to these institutions that have facilitated our meetings.

In a joint effort such as this, close attention must be paid to problems of comparability. The German group hosted us at a three-week data confrontation seminar funded by the DFG and held at ZUMA in Mannheim in the summer of 1975. At that time we were able to achieve agreement on our general analysis strategy as well as to create a large number of new variables that were utilized by the group in all subsequent analyses. Most of this technical work was carried out at ZUMA and at the Center for Political Studies.

Responsibility for additional data cleaning and for the preparation of the cross-national dataset—both for the five nations and, subsequently, the full eight nations—was assumed by the ZA at the University of Cologne. We are especially grateful to the ZA and in particular to Maria Wieken-Mayser, who has been responsible throughout for resolving data and documentation discrepancies among eight national studies, coordinating archiving efforts, and preparing a final codebook and data tape for distribution to the group and to the scholarly community. We want to thank her for her patience, good will, scholarly qualities, and continued support of our project. Distribution to the larger scholarly community of the codebook and datasets is the joint responsibility of the ZA and the Inter-university Consortium for Political and Social Research (ICPSR). We appreciate the assistance throughout the project of these two admirable organizations.

In addition, Kai Hildebrandt held major responsibility for the creation and documentation of the derived measures. He, along with Russell Dalton and Samuel Evans, provided the major part of the technical support that is so critical in a study of this magnitude and scope. Garland Montalvo typed many chapter drafts as well as the final manuscript; she also assisted the editors and the group with great skill, tact, and patience in the resolution of numerous problems large and small. We appreciate the assistance of these colleagues at Michigan.

A number of people have helped in various phases of the project in each of the countries. We especially want to thank Warren E. Miller, who has facilitated in this instance—as in others—the development of cross-national comparative research. His commitment to the project over a nine-year period has been unfailing. Rudolf Wildenmann of the University of Mannheim has been a valued and very helpful supporter. Extremely useful reactions to an early draft of the manuscript were offered by Philip E. Converse, Ted Robert Gurr, and Norman H. Nie. Their efforts are greatly appreciated.

This volume is a truly collaborative achievement. While particular individuals or groups of individuals wrote particular chapters, all of the volume has been subjected to vigorous criticism, debate, and revisions by members of the group. The final editing was the responsibility of the authors of this preface. But it is in truth a jointly authored work. We all shared its planning and execution. We share its achievements and its shortcomings as well.

Samuel H. Barnes, Ann Arbor
Max Kaase, Mannheim
March 12, 1979

Chapter 1

INTRODUCTION

SAMUEL H. BARNES and MAX KAASE

*T he waves of political protest that swept the advanced industrial democ-*racies in the late 1960s startled scholars as well as politicians. The empirical study of politics in democracies first flourished during an era of economic expansion and political tranquility. The baselines against which mass political action was measured were established in this period; the sudden rise in unconventional forms of politics, the decline in levels of trust in government, and increasing political sophistication, however measured, were phenomena demanding explanation, for they fit uneasily into the tentative picture of the political process being sketched out by a generation of empirical researchers.

Much of this early research dealt with the United States, but as replications and innovative studies were undertaken in other countries with similar social and political systems, the same familiar patterns were discernible. A body of literature arose that was extremely critical of what came to be called "classic democratic theory."[1] The criticism focused on what was viewed as a discrepancy between the assumptions of classic democratic theory and the findings of empirical research concerning the nature of democratic political systems. The "elitist" theorists, as they were often labeled, pointed out that mass publics, unlike elites, did not possess the levels of knowledge, commitment, and involvement assumed by the classical theory. It was a short step—though one not always taken by every theorist—to the viewpoint that extensive mass participation was undesirable and led to instability. Stable democracy resulted from well-socialized elites maintaining control over the political process, with elections as a check on abuse of office through the provision of competing sets of leaders and with mass inputs carefully channeled through elite-dominated institutions.

The 1950s and early 1960s were marked by an unprecedented period of economic growth and political stability in Western liberal democracies. But with both increasingly taken for granted, with constantly rising levels of education, and with a shift toward a postindustrial economic order, new strains made themselves felt on the political system. The theme of the day was no longer stability, but change, and this demand for change was supported not only by elites, but also by substantial segments of mass publics. The new political themes emphasized classic democratic ideals and their realization, such as equality, the rights of minorities, and the unfair advantages possessed by the upper middle classes.

Hand in hand with these sociopolitical processes went a major shift in emphasis within the social sciences, exemplified in political science by the postbehavioral critique of earlier empirical work. In particular, the assumptions of elitist and pluralist democratic theory were vigorously challenged. Empirical analysis had concentrated on conventional forms of political participation; protest behavior and its repression received little attention and even less endorsement. Either the conceptualizations were inadequate or the behaviors had no place, or perhaps both at once. However, these unconventional forms of political action seemed somehow related to other developments in society, but the nature of the linkages was not understood.

The striking lack of theoretical and empirical work on direct political action in the industrialized countries of the West was a challenge to social science. The study we report in this book is a response to this challenge. In 1971, social scientists from six countries, sharing curiosity over the determinants of the protest movements that had flooded Western democracies in the late 1960s, met for the first time to discuss a comparative empirical research project that would explore the phenomenon of political unrest. Whereas the waves of protest began to recede, the interest of those involved in the early planning of the project did not. In 1974, after a long period of theoretical and practical work, fieldwork was carried out for a comparative study of five Western democracies—Austria, Great Britain, the Netherlands, the United States, and West Germany. This book is the first of several reports on results of the study.

THE ORIGINS OF POLITICAL ACTION—
THEORETICAL PERSPECTIVES

A major problem that we faced was the poverty of available theory for guiding research. As we looked for guidance we found theoretical fragments, often deriving from other times and places, instead of operationalizable theory. While none of these fragments turned out to form a theoretical core for our research, several have influenced our thinking.

Numerous writers have proposed explanations of contemporary politics that revolve around the concept of postindustrial society.[2] We have admittedly been fascinated by much of this literature, though it places a high emphasis on the *economic* processes that characterize the change from industrial to postindustrial society. At this point the theory of postindustrial society can hardly be regarded as a coherent set of propositions from which concrete hypotheses amenable to empirical analysis can be deduced. Nevertheless, we have found it to be a highly stimulating heuristic device for reflections and speculations about the consequences of the secular trends addressed by that particular body of theory for the *political* order in advanced industrial societies. We have chosen the term "advanced industrial" as being more descriptive and less subject to normatively charged interpretations than postindustrial.[3] The role that rising levels of education and of technical and intellectual skills assume in these societies provides a direct and uncontroversial link to a primary concern of ours—the structure of political participation as a significant part of the political order in advanced industrial society.

Another strand of thought that has interested us is the concept of a hierarchy of needs, a notion associated with Abraham Maslow,[4] though it has been traced at least as far back as Karl Marx.[5] In Maslow's formulation, security needs—for nourishment and shelter—must be met before needs higher on the hierarchy, such as the need for esteem and belonging, become predominant.[6] The highest level on the need hierarchy is self-realization or self-actualization, the need to develop one's potential to the fullest; it becomes dominant only after the lower needs are met. These needs are rooted in human development and are formed early in life; all except self-actualization are deprivation needs that arise from what one lacks during the formative years of childhood, hence it is primarily those without such deprivation who can be expected to be motivated by the higher order needs.[7] As a consequence, it is very likely that the nature of the traditional political cleavages will be substantially altered as higher-level values increasingly affect political issues and are fed into the political process by an expanding highly competent and efficacious segment of the population capable of establishing and utilizing new channels of communication.

Perhaps the most widely utilized concept employed to explain political protest is relative deprivation.[8] We too make considerable use of it. There are several different research traditions that use the concept of deprivation and a rich theoretical literature has related deprivation to protest. The origins of the concept are to be found in psychological theories of frustration and aggression. Deprivation feelings derive from the frustrations that arise from people's inability to achieve desired values. Deprivation, in turn, leads to aggression or, in politics, violent or at least unconventional political action. As is clear from research on frustration and aggression, the former does not lead inevitably to the latter. Many personality, cultural, and situational variables intervene, so that frustration should be expected to lead to aggression only under particular conditions.

The operationalization of relative deprivation theory is complicated by the subjective nature of human expectations, and hence of deprivation. Deprivation can be relative to absolute standards of well-being; it can be relative to some internal conceptualization of an ideal situation; it can be relative to a less ideal notion of what one thinks is one's "just desserts" in a particular situation; it can be relative to one's own expected achievements in the future; and there are numerous other formulations. What is important is that specific value achievements must be measured by the individual against specific value expectations. And even if feelings of deprivation exist, personal and political resources and situational factors affect the probability that deprivation will lead to action.

The importance of these resource and situational factors is the reason why indicators of absolute deprivation—that is, quantitative measures of material well-being—have seldom been useful predictors of political protest. Those who are most deprived often lack the personal and material resources necessary for protest behavior; daily survival leaves them little time or energy for such activities. It has been argued that revolution occurs when change for the better is well underway and there are setbacks, rather than when things are at their worst. In Alexis de Tocqueville's words, "Evils which are patiently endured when they seem inevitable become intolerable when once the idea of escape from them is suggested."[9] Expectations rather than objective achievements are the determinants of political action. The study of expectations requires, in Davies' words, "the assessment of the state of mind—or more precisely, the mood—of a people."[10]

The "assessment of the state of mind" of a people is among the procedures at which survey research excels. But such research can also probe more difficult-to-measure determinants of behavior such as psychological and material resources and, with less certainty, situational factors as well. Situational factors can best be effectively encompassed by research designs that systematically identify and control for different political environments. However, our goal is to deal with national populations, hence we have used national samples.

One problem common to survey research and operationalizations influenced by its requirements is that in all relationships between attitudes and behavior, culture and context become crucial; yet they are extremely difficult to operationalize in a rigorous and parsimonious fashion. In the widest sense of the term, culture is everything that is not biologically determined and situations are potentially almost infinitely varied. But this need not lead to despair, for problems of this nature can be greatly simplified by aiming at theories and explanations of a more general nature. In fact, the multiplicity and variability of empirical sociopolitical phenomena under potential scrutiny can be reduced—and because of the need for functionally equivalent phenomena, even must be reduced—in order to arrive at theories that are general but still specific enough to be useful.

RESEARCH DESIGN

Our research design grows out of our theoretical interest in understanding the relationship between what people expect out of politics and what they do in politics. This is a subject that can be investigated in all political systems: we concentrate on advanced industrial societies. We start with assumptions similar to those of Alex Inkeles and David Smith, who—though they were writing about a different segment of the continuum of economic development—were guided by similar assumptions:

> We believe certain panhuman patterns of response persist in the face of variability in culture content. These transcultural similarities and the psychic properties of individuals provide the basis for a common response to common stimuli. On these grounds we concluded that men's very different cultures might nevertheless respond in basically the same way to certain of the relatively standard institutions and interpersonal patterns introduced by economic development and sociopolitical modernization.[11]

Our theoretical perspectives have led us to expect that aspects of advanced industrial society, including the great expansion of higher education, the changing composition of the labor force, and the growth of a separate youth culture, may have had similar impact in all of these countries. The waves of protest that swept Western democracies in the 1960s seem to be related to these underlying changes. In every country, there are specific national reasons for protest, ranging from concern for civil rights to opposition to war to dissatisfaction with the educational system to antiauthoritarian sentiments.

Nevertheless, the similarity of both actors and actions across national boundaries suggests more fundamental similarities in underlying processes.

Some of our reasons for concentrating on advanced industrial societies are theoretical; others are of a practical nature. There is an empirical basis for anticipating different patterns of relationships in different kinds of societies. The literature on domestic violence, which is theoretically close to our interest in protest, demonstrates that at low levels of economic development the relationship between development and violence is positive: the least developed societies have the lowest level of violence. At intermediate levels of development there is no relationship. At advanced levels, relationships are negative. The overall relationship between levels of economic development and levels of domestic violence is thus curvilinear.[12]

Types of domestic unrest are likely to differ substantially at different levels of economic development. Ted Robert Gurr refers to turmoil, conspiracy, and internal war.[13] Douglas A. Hibbs, Jr. distinguishes between collective protest (riots, antigovernment demonstrations, and political strikes) and internal war (armed attacks, deaths from political violence, and political assassinations).[14] Still other formulations are available. Some of these forms of violence are absent in the countries that we are studying; different levels of development seem to exhibit strikingly different patterns.

There is also evidence for assuming that patterns of domestic violence differ according to the institutional structure of the polity. The form of government and the existence of participation, civil liberties, and political pluralism have a major impact upon the structure of domestic violence. This leads us to concentrate not only on economically advanced countries but also on those with roughly similar democratic structures.

The thrust of our theoretical interests also encourages a focus on advanced industrial societies. The literature on postindustrial society posits the existence of many shared features. The Maslowian need hierarchy suggests that economically advanced democracies should exhibit a substantial proportion of those with higher order needs—an important aspect of our thinking about the sources of protest. Finally, the literature on deprivation leads to the conclusion that the nature of deprivation is likely to differ according to level of economic development; psychologically oriented measures of deprivation should be increasingly important as absolute material deprivation is progressively overcome.

This volume concentrates heavily on attitudinal and other data derived from individuals. We are aware of the very large impact that political structures have on individual attitudes and actions. By studying countries with relatively similar political structures we minimize the impact of systemic factors and amplify the importance of individual level factors. This point will become clearer in the light of the discussion that follows.

This research begins with several assumptions about the nature of social science research in general and research in comparative politics in particular.[15] We are concerned with general statements about social phenomena, and only comparative research can overcome what Frederick Frey calls the "spectre of parochialism."[16] Many students of foreign politics emphasize what is distinct about particular countries. We are strongly committed to the nomothetic approach, rather than the idiographic approach followed by many country and area specialists; only comparative research will enable us to "distinguish between those regularities in social behavior that are system-specific and those that are universal."[17]

Our overall research strategy can be characterized as a modified "most different systems" rather than "most similar systems" design. These labels, which derive from Przeworski and Teune, are easily misinterpreted. They write that the most similar systems design is "based on the belief that systems as similar as possible with respect to as many features as possible constitute the optimal samples for comparative inquiry."[18] Rather than study individuals, such designs focus "almost exclusively at the level of systems."[19] They continue, "The alternative strategy takes as the starting point the variation of the observed behavior at a level lower than that of systems. Most often this will be the level of individual actors, but it can be the level of groups, local communities, social classes, or occupations."[20] In this design, "systemic factors are not given any special place among the possible predictors of behavior." Przeworski and Teune note, however, that "the difference between the two strategies should not be overemphasized." They add that in the most different systems design, the first step is "to identify those independent variables, observed within systems, that do not violate the assumptions of the homogeneity of the total population. Although the samples are derived from different systems, they are initially treated as if the population from which they are drawn is homogeneous. If the subgroups of the population derived from different systems do not differ with regards to the dependent variable, the differences among these systems are not important in explaining the variable. If the relationship between an independent and the dependent variable is the same within the subgroups of the population, then again the systemic differences need not be taken into consideration.

"To the extent that general statements can be validly formulated without regard to the social systems from which the samples were drawn, systemic factors can be disregarded. . . . Whereas studies of concomitant variation require positive identification of relevant systemic factors, the 'most different systems' design centers on eliminating irrelevant systemic factors." Przeworski and Teune continue, "in the most different systems design, the question of at which level the relevant factors operate remains open throughout the process of inquiry. The point of departure of this design is the population of units at the lowest level observed in the study, most often individuals."[21] Thus, "to the extent that identifying the social system does not help predict individual characteristics, systemic factors are not important."[22] They add that "most recent comparative studies of political behavior seem to discover that relationships among individual attitudes are the same regardless of political system."[23] "The countries differ with regard to levels of education, class structure, and family socialization, but they do not differ as *systems* so long as their patterns of relationships are the same. Systems differ not when the frequency of the particular characteristics differ, but when the patterns of the relationships among variables differ."[24]

We have quoted at length from this work of Przeworski and Teune because it aptly describes the goals of the present research. However, the present volume falls short of their prescriptions in one important respect: we are not interested in exploring systemic variations. The analyses in this book focus upon patterns of relationships common to most if not all of the countries. In many cases, we could profitably explore the unexplained variance in individual countries. But we have chosen not to do so in a systematic manner in this volume. In a few cases, ad hoc treatments do utilize the insights of the researchers to discuss individual country variations. But these are not a principal goal of the research.

There is a second way in which we do not permit the system to have its full impact: we do not systematically use country as a dummy variable and hence as an independent variable. While all of our analyses are carried out within each country rather than on pooled data, and thus we are quite conscious of country differences, we do not concentrate on estimating the impact of country as an independent variable. Our reasons for adopting this strategy merit brief attention. The first reason is that country is a surrogate for variables that we have either not measured or have not included in our analyses. Consequently, to attribute an independent impact to country is simply to give a label to the unknown. A thorough analysis would require that we proceed to break down country into a number of structural and aggregate cultural variables. While this is possible, and will be pursued in further analyses, it is beyond the scope of the present volume. A second and related reason is that we focus on social-psychological variables. Compared with the more obviously political variables such as party organization, electoral laws, and institutional structure, psychological processes can be expected to be *relatively* invariate across political systems. We do not wish to overstate this point; for example, it is clear from our own analyses that a heavily psychological measure such as trust in government is greatly affected by a simple behavioral-structural variable such as having voted for the incumbent government or not. But we focus on measures at the individual level, regardless of their possible origins in group and other nonindividual level sources.

To summarize, our goal is to explore relationships among our independent and dependent variables that form similar patterns in all or most of the countries. We recognize that important country differences exist. In terms of the multiple regression model employed by Przeworski and Teune, our strategy results in a search for roughly similar slopes but without much concern for different regression intercepts. We believe that these differences would be greatly reduced through the introduction of additional variables, but it is not our purpose in this volume to do so.

Given our lack of concern in this volume with the impact of system, some readers may wonder why we did not eliminate system effects by standardizing each non-nominal variable within each country and thereby automatically setting all intercepts at zero. We had several lengthy debates within the group precisely on this point. Our decision not to standardize reflects our belief that the country differences remain important even if we do not deal with them extensively within our analyses. That is, we prefer to let them stand, easily visible, as reminders of differences between countries.

We have concentrated on Przeworski and Teune because their formulation provides a precise and parsimonious model for explaining what we have set out to accomplish. However, the same points can be understood in other formulations, including in particular the framework provided by Arend Lijphart. In a 1971 article he distinguished the comparative method from the statistical method, and in a 1975 restatement he noted that his comparative method was similar to Przeworski and Teune's "most similar systems" design.[25] He added that the "method of controlled comparison" of Eggan, the "specification" of Holt and Turner, and J. S. Mill's "method of difference" and "method of concomitant variations" are also variants of the same basic method of analysis.[26]

The "most different systems" design, on the other hand, belongs in the category of statistical analysis. Both the statistical and comparative methods of Lijphart and the most similar and most different systems designs of Przeworski and Teune are to be contrasted with Lijphart's "case study" method, which our design certainly does not employ. The important methodological point is that our study focuses on statistical analyses of individual-level relationships, and hence does not employ what in the increasingly codified vocabulary of comparative politics is called the comparative method. This is a study in comparative politics; in the rigorous terminology of the day it is not a "comparative" study, as it neither compares political systems as required by Lijphart nor focuses explicitly on analyses at two levels as required by Przeworski and Teune.

THE SAMPLE

Our theoretical interests led to a commitment to national representative samples of individuals.[27] As we have indicated, a weakness of much research on political action is its reliance on aggregate data to test propositions about the motivations of individuals. We are determined to deal with individuals, and this, of course, requires information about individual attitudes and behavior. A second weakness of much research is that even when it deals with individual behavior, the population sampled consists of students of a particular locale, inhabitants of a single city, or other restricted groups. We wish to generalize about mass publics, hence we need national samples.

We would have liked to have had data for treating contextual effects. We are keenly aware of the importance of context in molding actual behavior; indeed, this awareness, combined with the infrequency of the more extreme forms of behavior, leads us to focus on protest *potential* rather than *involvement*. But the implementation of a truly contextual design would have necessitated extensive aggregate data on the level of some meaningful contextual unit. These were not available and could not be collected within the constraints of a limited study, if at all. Moreover, there are extremely thorny theoretical and analytical problems in linking individual and aggregate information that are not yet thoroughly resolved.

From the beginning of our discussions of the project we have been interested in change in the parameters of expectations and action. Aggregate data could provide a baseline for evaluating change in some forms of political action. Data on recorded incidents of protest behavior, for example, would have permitted generalizations about changes in frequencies. However, the effort required would constitute an immense project by itself. And these data would still not be directly relevant for our primary interest in the roots of individual action. As a result, our interest in change remains largely implicit in this study except in two instances. The first is that we have utilized several questions that have been asked in previous surveys in at least some of the countries; we report on these earlier results where applicable. The second instance in which we deal with change is in our treatment of parents and children; in these analyses we are able to examine both generational differences (between older and younger cohorts) and lineage differences (between individual pairs of parents and children).

Two major practical considerations concerning the requirements of national survey research entered into our decision to restrict the study to these five countries. The first is the possibility of drawing a national sample and obtaining well-conducted interviews. In advanced industrial democracies these needs are easily met. We have used professional polling organizations in four of the countries. In the Netherlands the ease of sampling and compact nature of the country made the use of student interviewers feasible. The second requirement of survey research is somewhat more subtle, but experience suggests that the greater the range of educational levels existing in a country the more difficult it becomes to design an interview schedule equally well-adapted to all segments of the population. Questions used for educated urbanites may be unintelligible for illiterate peasants, for example, and the problem is exacerbated by the use of extensive open-ended questions and the investigation of complex issues. This problem exists in varying degrees in all studies; its importance is minimized by restricting the research to countries with high literacy rates.

The hazards of fund-raising played a major role in determining the final set. Each country's principal investigator or investigators assumed responsibility for raising funds for fieldwork and analysis in that country. At no time did any individual or country group assume responsibility for the project: we used an "equal partners" format throughout.[28]

Table 12 of the Technical Appendix provides basic information on the samples. They are all national samples of the population age sixteen and above.[29] In the United States, area sampling procedures were followed by the Survey Research Center, which executed the fieldwork; in other countries sampling was carried out from lists of the total population. Parent-child pairs were obtained in the following manner: when a youth sixteen through twenty fell into the sample a parent was interviewed, and when a parent of a youth of that age group fell into the sample the youth was interviewed as well. Thus the pairs referred to in Table 12 of the Technical Appendix represent two interviews, one of which is counted in the cross-section sample as well.

Our decision was to use our samples as unweighted. As the British had oversampled districts with a high percentage of middle-class households, we randomly eliminated a portion of the respondents from those districts, so that the result is an unweighted representative British sample as well.

Our concern throughout the book is to uncover similar patterns in the five countries when they exist and to understand the nature of the differences when these are uncovered. It is national patterns that we seek to understand.

PLAN OF THE BOOK

The structure of the present volume follows the logic of our theoretical concerns. Part I—chapters 2 through 6—introduces the theoretical origins of our conceptualization of political action, describes the measures employed, and presents the typology of action types. Part II—chapters 7 through 12, presents discussions of ideology and values. Part III—chapters 13 and 14—deals with personal satisfaction and deprivation and political satisfaction.

Part IV—chapters 15 and 16—explores relationships between parents and children. Chapter 17 concludes the volume.

From the beginning of our discussions, we have thought in terms of a division of labor based on substantive interests rather than on country by country concerns. This book reflects that division of labor. Individual chapters were written by the scholar or scholars who concentrated on that subject from a very early stage of the project. We achieved an agreement on design and measurement early in our project, but differences remain in such matters as working style, preferences for certain analytical techniques, and even idiosyncracies in the presentation and interpretation of data. We have sought to eliminate repetition and incompatibilities, but have not otherwise sought to impose uniformity. The present volume thus retains considerable variation in the individual chapters and reflects its multiple authorship. However, all chapters have been subjected to vigorous criticism by all authors. The result is a truly collaborative volume.

NOTES

1. More extensive documentation for the points made in this introduction will be provided in the chapters that take up these topics in detail. This debate has been widely documented. For an introduction see Jack Walker, "A Critique of the Elitist Theory of Democracy," *American Political Science Review,* 60 (June 1966), pp. 285-295; Peter Bachrach, *The Theory of Democratic Elitism,* Boston: Little, Brown, 1967.

2. Good introductions to the literature on postindustrial society include the following: Daniel Bell, *The Coming of Post-Industrial Society,* New York: Basic Books, 1973; Zbigniew Brzezinski, *Between Two Ages: America's Role in the Technetronic Era,* New York: Viking Press, 1971; M. Donald Hancock and Gideon Sjoberg, *Politics in the Post-Welfare State,* New York: Columbia University Press, 1972; Samuel Huntington, "Post-Industrial Politics: How Benign Will It Be?" *Comparative Politics,* 6 (January 1974), 163-191; the contributions to Leon Lindberg (ed.), *Politics and the Future of Industrial Society,* New York: David McKay, 1976; Theodore Roszak, *Where the Waste-Land Ends: Politics and Transcendence in Postindustrial Society,* Garden City, N.Y.: Doubleday, 1972; Donald Schon, *Beyond the Stable State,* London: Temple Smith, 1971; and Alain Touraine, *The Post-Industrial Society,* New York: Random House, 1972.

3. Leon Lindberg lists thirty terms that have been used in the literature to describe a roughly similar phenomenon: "Technetronic, postindustrial, postwelfare, postbourgeois, postcapitalist, postChristian, postcivilized, posteconomic, posthistoric, superindustrial, postmarket, consultative commonwealth, humanistic capitalism, temporary society, postmodern, postorganization, post-Protestant, post-Puritan, postscarcity, posttraditional, posttribal, postliterature, postmaterialist, promethean, friendly fascism, mature society, corporate state, garrison state, postliberal, service society," op. cit., p. 17. It is with some regret that we add advanced industrial to this list!

4. See Abraham Maslow, *Motivation and Personality,* New York: Harpers, 1954; and Jeanne M. Knutson, *The Human Basis of the Polity,* Chicago: Aldine, 1972.

5. Carlo Tullio-Altan notes that Marx made the basic distinction between physical needs and social needs, with the former—biological and natural—being the realm of necessity and the latter needs deriving from the human personality and, of course, being socially determined. *I valori difficili inchiesta sulle tendenze ideologiche e politiche dei giovani in italia,* Milano: Valentino Bompiani, 1974, p. 65.

6. The use of ranking techniques in operationalizing values was further developed by Milton Rokeach, *The Nature of Human Values,* New York: Free Press, 1973.

7. The value hierarchy is discussed by two members of our group in previous publications—Ronald Inglehart, "The Silent Revolution in Europe: Intergenerational Change in Post-Industrial Societies," *American Political Science Review,* 65 (December 1971), pp. 991-1017; and especially in *The Silent Revolution,* Princeton: Princeton University Press, 1977, Chapter 5; and Alan Marsh, "The 'Silent Revolution,' Value Priorities and the Quality of live in Britain," *American Political Science Review,* 69 (March 1975), pp. 21-30. See also Markku Haranne and Erik Allardt, *Attitudes Toward Modernity and Modernization: An Appraisal of an Empirical Study,* Helsinki: Research Group for Comparative Sociology, Research Report No. 6, 1974, p. 67.

8. The best general work remains Ted Robert Gurr's *Why Men Rebel,* Princeton: Princeton University Press, 1970. Numerous other relevant works are cited in various chapters of our present work.

9. *The Old Regime and the French Revolution,* New York: Harper Bros., 1956, p. 214.

10. "Toward a Theory of Revolution," *American Sociological Review,* 27 (February 1962), p. 18.

11. Alex Inkeles and David H. Smith, *Becoming Modern: Individual Change in Six Developing Countries,* Cambridge, Mass.: Harvard University Press, 1974, p. 12.

12. Ted Robert Gurr, op. cit., p. 11.

13. Ibid.

14. Douglas A. Hibbs, Jr., *Mass Political Violence: A Cross-National Causal Analysis,* New York: John Wiley, 1973, p. ix.

15. The general literature on methodologies and strategies in comparative politics is extensive. We have been particularly influenced by Roger W. Benjamin, "Strategy versus Methodology in Comparative Research," *Comparative Political Studies,* 9 (January 1977), pp. 475-484; Moshe M. Czudnowski, *Comparing Political Behavior,* Beverly Hills, Calif.: Sage, 1976; Frederick W. Frey, "Cross-Cultural Survey Research in Political Science," in Robert T. Holt and John E. Turner (eds.), *The Methodology of Comparative Research,* New York: Free Press, 1970, pp. 173-294; Robert T. Holt and John E. Turner, "The Methodology of Comparative Research," in Holt and Turner (eds.), op. cit., pp. 1-20; Arend Lijphart, "The Comparable-Cases Strategy in Comparative Research," *Comparative Political Studies,* 8 (July 1975), pp. 158-177; Theodore W. Meckstroth, " 'Most Different Systems' and 'Most Similar Systems': A Study in the Logic of Comparative Inquiry," *Comparative Political Studies,* 8 (July 1975), pp. 132-157; Stein Rokkan et al. (eds.), *Comparative Research Across Cultures and Nations,* Paris: Mouton, 1968; Stein Rokkan, "Cross-National Survey Research: Historical, Analytical, and Substantive Contexts," in Rokkan et al., *Comparative Survey Analysis,* pp. 5-55, Stein Rokkan, "Comparative Cross-National Research: The Context of Current Efforts," in Richard Merritt and Stein Rokkan (eds.), *Comparing Nations,* New Haven, Conn.: Yale University Press, 1966, pp. 3-25; Sidney Verba, "The Uses of Survey Research in the Study of Comparative Politics: Issues and Strategies," in Stein Rokkan et al. (eds.), *Comparative Survey Analysis,* pp. 56-106; Sidney Verba, "Cross-National Survey Research: The Problem of Credibility," in Ivan Vallier (ed.), *Comparative Methods in Sociology,* Berkeley, Calif.: University of California Press, 1971, pp. 309-356.

16. Frederick W. Frye, "Cross-Cultural Survey Research in Political Science," p. 190.

17. Allen D. Grimshaw, "Comparative Sociology: In What Ways Different From Other Sociologies," in Michael Armer and Allen D. Grimshaw (eds.), *Comparative Social Research: Methodological Problems and Strategies,* New York: John Wiley, 1973, p. 5.

18. Adam Przeworski and Henry Teune, *The Logic of Comparative Social Inquiry,* New York: Wiley-Interscience, 1970, p. 32.

19. Ibid., p. 35.

20. Ibid., p. 34.

21. Ibid., p. 36.

22. Ibid., p. 40.

23. Ibid., p. 43.

24. Ibid., p. 45.

25. Arend Lijphart, op. cit., p. 164.

26. Ibid.

27. For a detailed discussion of this topic see the Technical Appendix.

28. Commitments for the financing of the fieldwork in the five countries had been secured by 1973. Three other countries—Finland, Switzerland, and Italy—obtained funding and executed their fieldwork in 1975 and early 1976. Later volumes will include them. Attempts to raise funds for a French study were unsuccessful, though French colleagues were involved with the research project from the beginning. A similar lack of success with generating financial support caused the withdrawal of the Canadian contingent. Time constraints caused a Japanese group to withdraw.

29. The Austrian sample includes only respondents sixteen to seventy years.

Chapter 2

POLITICAL ACTION
A Theoretical Perspective

MAX KAASE and ALAN MARSH

INTRODUCTION

In chapter 1 we have described the historical and theoretical context of this study in general terms. In this chapter we will extend the previous discussion with particular emphasis upon political *action*. We prefer the term "political action" to the more commonly used "political participation" because it aligns far more closely with our theoretical concerns.

Following this introduction, we will place our study within the contemporary debate concerning participation and democracy and will state our own position in this debate. Then we will argue that empirical research has not kept pace with the growing theoretical emphasis upon noninstitutionalized, nonelectoral political action, an emphasis that reflects the prominence of protest in the mass politics of Western democracies during the 1960s. Finally—the core of this chapter—we will describe the elements of a microtheory of political action. We will argue that from a systemic perspective direct political action generally, and political protest in particular, do not necessarily assume antiregime properties; rather, it may form one element of an expanded repertory of political action. We will end this chapter with a presentation of the heuristic model that has guided much of the research reported in this volume.

DEMOCRATIC THEORY AND POLITICAL PARTICIPATION

If democracy is rule by the people, as we and many others maintain, then the notion of political participation is at the center of the concept of the democratic state. As a normative, prescriptive system of thought, contemporary democratic theory must reconcile the right of all citizens to determine what is in their best interest and their obligation to participate rationally and responsibly. This dualism is linked to contemporary confrontations between democratic citizenship theory and democratic elitist theory,[1] between revisionist and antirevisionist democratic theory,[2] and between institutionalist and participatory democratic theory.[3] These confrontations have been of enormous consequence not only for political science as an academic discipline but also for the concrete courses of political action taken by citizens and governments.

While we cannot neglect developments in democratic theory and practice in our empirical work, we are not normative theorists; rather, we are analysts who assess empirical phenomena and seek systematic explanations for them. Our concern is with attitudes and behaviors in advanced industrial societies: how do values, ideology, and personal and political satisfaction relate to political action in these societies? We emphasize the pattern of relationships because of our cross-sectional design, though cohort and parent-child analyses as well as cross-national comparisons will add a dynamic, processual element. And the emphasis on advanced countries means that we concentrate on countries that come close to being what Bell calls postindustrial societies in which more than 50 percent of the active labor force is employed in the tertiary sector of the economy.[4]

Both considerations are highly relevant for the theoretical context of our study. Our concerns are not with modernization theory and its concomitants of urbanization, industrialization, secularization, democratization, education, and mass media development.[5] We are not interested in evolutionary sequences in which political participation as a goal (or value) can be confronted with other competing goals such as socioeconomic development in order to assess its relative costs and consequences—if realized—for a society.[6] Nor are we concerned with the processes by which political participation as a citizen right had first to be established and then realized. Rather, our study deals with the structure and meaning of citizen political involvement in five advanced industrial societies operating within the framework of liberal democratic constitutions and procedures.

It has already been mentioned that our choice of countries is purposeful but also embraces an element of chance. In this sense, we cannot claim a full variation along the dimension of democratic industrialized societies. Hence, we cannot claim that our results are representative of the total set of such nations. We do not regard this to be a major disadvantage. In accordance with what Przeworski and Teune have—somewhat ambiguously—called a "most different systems design," our main emphasis, as was pointed out in chapter 1, is on the analysis of individual-level relationships.[7] Five countries provide an adequate test of the generality of the relationships found.

Over the last decade the concept, problems, and contingencies of political participation have gained increasing prominence in public and academic discussions. Bell even states that "the axial principle of the modern polity is *participation.*"[8] Today, the limitations on *institutionalized* citizen participation in decision-making, whether in politics or in industry, highlight the controversies of the day. This is somewhat ironic considering that the gap between preaching and practicing the principle of "one person, one vote" has, even in established liberal democracies, only quite recently been narrowed or fully closed.[9]

The constitutional right to free and equal participation for all has far-reaching effects for existing elite structures, elite circulation, interest aggregation, and interest representation. Therefore, it is hardly surprising that the question of what are and are not legitimate acts of political participation has been and will continue to be a matter of conflict in day-to-day politics. At first glance it may appear as if scholarly thinking about political participation were more coherent and united than views among those actively engaged in politics, but this is not so. Rather, the academic field is flooded with segmented and frequently contradictory fragments of theories of democracy—some prescriptive and some descriptive—that look at political participation from correspondingly different angles.[10] A good case in point is the current controversy about the desirability of high voter turnout. This discussion beautifully conveys the point that little can be said about the aggregate and individual meaning of any given act of political participation unless its institutional, structural, and individual conditions are explicitly specified.[11]

It is particularly important to keep in mind that political participation derives its meaning for the individual and for the political system from the interaction between political authorities and partisans as mediated through political institutions.[12] We will return to this point in greater detail later. This processual perspective is important because it inevitably results in a less static conceptualization of the role of both political behavior and political institutions.

We have mentioned before that political participation as a general societal value is universally accepted in liberal democratic ideology but that it is embedded in many different versions of democratic theory. Modernization theory alerts us to the fact that this value can only be achieved through high costs—economic and political as well as individual—and may in fact be too expensive a goal to strive for when other important goals such as national unity, socioeconomic development, and the like are at stake.[13] There can be no question, however, that the advanced industrial societies we are studying can afford this investment.

As a societal value, participation is linked in so many ways to democratic government—rationality, control, responsiveness, flexibility, legitimacy, conflict resolution, to name only a few—that it can justifiably be regarded as one of the central pillars of such government. The extent to which individual citizens decide to avail themselves of the opportunities opened up through the impact of this value on sociopolitical institutions is an altogether different problem. In his assessment of the state of research on public opinion and voting behavior, Converse applies cost-benefit analysis to the problem of the lingering vast differences in the ability of mass publics to take in, properly process, and retain political information even in the time of electronic mass media.[14] His elaboration on interest (or motivation) and cognitive capabilities as two core elements of information handling is also relevant for evaluating the likelihood that any given individual will participate actively in politics. Both motivation and cognitive stock have been shown by many scholars to be in part dependent on structural factors such as socialization practices in the home, formal education, organizational membership, and the like. This is often overlooked by those critics of broadened opportunities for political participation who refer to the potential threat to the rational political decision-making process originating, as they see it, from the lack of citizen competence in politics. This status quo oriented perspective overlooks the potential for change in modern democratic societies *provided this change is truly wanted.* In fact, many contemporary controversies about the proper forms of political participation remind us of the puzzle that confronted early researchers on democratic attitudes. In repeated empirical studies, researchers found that mass publics, unlike elites, were apparently unable to apply general democratic principles to concrete political situations.[15] Elitist theorists of democracy concluded from these results that elites were the true keepers of the democratic flame.[16]

The parallel between controversies about democratic attitudes and individual prerequisites for political participation can be carried even further. In both cases, it is doubtful that there exists a direct causal link between an abstract principle or value and concrete applications of it. We maintain that the meaning of abstract principles has to be defined and rendered concrete in sociopolitical processes. Moreover, the solutions emerging from such processes are timebound and therefore temporary.

These are some of the considerations that should be kept in mind as we set out to analyze political action and inclination toward political action in advanced industrial societies. Two more points need to be made. First, political protest and violence are, as has been widely noted, forms of political expression that even the more developed countries have exhibited throughout history. "Collective violence has flowed regularly out of the central processes of Western countries," Tilly observes. And he continues, "Men seeking to seize, hold or realign the levers of power have continually engaged in collective violence as part of their struggles. The oppressed have struck in the name of justice, the privileged in the name of order, those inbetween in the name of fear."[17] Whether violence and protest are, by necessity, also "normal" characteristics of advanced industrial societies is an altogether different question that is not so easily answered.

But the second point is by far more important to deal with. In the past, direct, noninstitutionalized political action has been conceptually and empirically linked to political protest, unrest, violence, and system change. This is reflected in the citizen's perception of many legal acts of voluntary political involvement, such as demonstrations, as illegitimate. By contrast, it is our contention that Western liberal democracies are experiencing a process of change in political culture exhibited by, among other things, the increasing inclination of the citizenry to participate in such acts. We believe that this shift in political values, which may well constitute a threat to the political status quo, does not in itself threaten the persistence of the liberal democratic order. We will return to this point later in this and in other chapters of the book.

SOME EMPIRICAL EVIDENCE
FROM MACROPOLITICAL RESEARCH

The extent to which advanced industrial societies of the West have experienced political violence and collective protest can be assessed, on the aggregate level at least, through data collected in macropolitical research. Research by Gurr and others has pointed out at least three distinctive types of uninstitutionalized conflict behavior in which individuals engage: turmoil, conspiracy, and internal war.[18] Of course, these are not evenly distributed among nations. In a methodologically sophisticated study, Hibbs analyzed the dimensionality of the conflict data gathered by the World Data Analysis Program at Yale University[19] and found two dimensions of conflict within societies—collective protest and internal war.[20] Among other indicators, "armed attacks" and "deaths from domestic violence" represent the internal war dimension; "anti-government demonstrations" and "riots" represent the collective protest dimension. These data give us a first clue about the structure of direct political action in the five countries we studied for a time period for which survey evidence is not available.[21] In the following paragraphs we present the results of a secondary analysis of the Taylor–Hudson data on 136 countries intended to establish the rank of our five countries on the two dimensions discovered by Hibbs. More recent data provided by Gurr will complement this analysis.

For a variety of reasons the implications of this analysis are tentative at best. One important substantive reservation we have is that the data do not extend beyond 1967, when direct action techniques had just begun their rise to prominence in the advanced Western polities. While this shortcoming does not destroy the utility of these materials as background information for our countries, it does prevent us from establishing a direct link between the macro indicators and the indicators in our own study. As a second reservation, Hudson and Taylor themselves are extremely cautious with respect to the intercountry validity of their data. Third, for various reasons, between 40 percent and 60 percent of the 136 countries report zero or close-to-zero occurrences on these indicators.

Crude and tentative as these data may be, they nevertheless offer some interesting insights into the prominence of major types of direct political action in the five countries. Thus, it can be stated that none of the five countries loads on the dimension of internal war. Political activities falling under this label simply do not occur there with sufficient frequency to warrant their consideration as part of the political culture. Even if the ranks for the United States may look impressive to some, these event data follow a pattern of geometrical increase that means that intermediate ranks do not point to substantial levels of the activity in question.[22] By contrast, on the dimension of collective protest, particularly as measured by the occurrence of antigovernment protest demonstrations, the five countries on the average rank considerably higher.

While this reading of the data appears uncontroversial, we still have to face the question of how well the interpretation would hold up had the time series been extended and had the social movements of the late 1960s and the explosion of political violence in Northern Ireland been permitted to have their full impact on the analysis. There is, of course, overwhelming and unequivocal empirical evidence supporting our claim that citizens in our five nations were very active in engaging in a broad variety of antigovernment demonstrations and related activities; this is, in fact, what our study is about.

In light of the Northern Ireland conflict, the small-scale war the Baader-Meinhof terrorists declared on Germany in the 1970s, and similar occurrences of hostage dramas and destruction of life and property by explosives planted by radicalized political gangs all over Western Europe and the United States, it seems justified to ask whether an absence of internal war can still be legitimately diagnosed for the period in which our study was conducted. Fortunately, Ted Gurr has made available to us data on rebellion and protest he has collected for eighty-seven nations covering the time periods from

Table 2.1: RANK OF COUNTRIES ON VARIOUS CONFLICT DIMENSIONS[1]

| | Internal War | | | | | | Collective Protest | | | | | |
| | Deaths From Domestic Violence | | | Armed Attacks | | | Riots | | | Antigovernment Protest Demonstrations | | |
	1953-1957	1958-1962	1963-1967	1953-1957	1958-1962	1963-1967	1953-1957	1958-1962	1963-1967	1953-1957	1958-1962	1963-1967
Number of Countries With Zero Occurrences (= ranks)[2]	60	52	54	62	52	49	62	55	57	78	75	74
Remaining Ranks	69	83	82	67	83	87	67	80	79	51	60	52
The Netherlands	+3	+	+	+	+	69	+	+	+	+	+	51
Britain	+	82	+	+	78	79	+	55	70	48	32	40
United States	67	81	70	45	55	61	64	59	33	46	28	15
Germany	+	+	80	58	79	82	56	70	73	36	56	30
Austria	+	+	+	+	62	+	+	44	+	33	+	+

SOURCE:: Douglas A. Hibbs, Jr., *Mass Political Violence*, New York: John Wiley, 1973.

1. The ranks are based on the per capita occurrence of the specified events averaged over five-year periods. Because of missing population data for the 1953-1957 period seven countries and for 1958-1962 period one country could not be rank-ordered.

2. "Zero occurrence" does not necessarily mean that no such event took place. Since the reported events are divided by population (in thousands) and multiplied by 100, low-event counts will occasionally show up as zero occurrence although five digits after the decimal point were permitted.

3. + indicates that the country belongs to those with "zero occurrence" of the event during the specified time period.

1961-1965 and from 1966-1970.[23] While even these records do not extend to 1974, the date of our study, they nevertheless permit a clue as to whether or not our cautious conclusions derived from the Taylor-Hudson data can be further substantiated. To be sure, the lack of convergence between the two data bases regarding the number of nations (136 against 76) and the indicators renders any direct and systematic comparisons impossible. But, even within these limitations, the data generally corroborate our prior conclusions that the countries in our study fall on the dimension of protest and not on the dimension of internal war, especially when we look at the 1966-1970 ranks.[24]

The situation in the United States in the late 1960s, however, clearly requires a qualification of this general statement. Whereas, in commenting upon the Taylor-Hudson data, we somewhat underemphasized the rank of the United States on the internal war dimension, the Gurr data for the 1966-1970 period indicate that something close to internal war—though spatially limited—indeed took place. But even at the climax of confrontations among the National Guard, police, and protesters in America the incidents of extreme violence were not able to challenge seriously the normal operation of the democratic process in this country. Also, there can be no question that by 1974 the tides of massive conflict had subsided, bringing the United States back to a state of normalcy on the internal war dimension again.

Table 2.2: RANK OF COUNTRIES ON VARIOUS CONFLICT DIMENSIONS

	Internal War (Conflict Deaths Per 10 Million)		Collective Protest[2] (Mandays of Turmoil Per 100 000)	
	1961-1965[1]	*1966-1970*	*1961-1965*	*1966-1970*
Number of Countries With Zero Occurrences (= ranks)	33	27	21	14
Remaining Ranks	54	60	66	73
The Netherlands	+	+	+	52
Britain	+	55	43	29
United States	45	33	27	9
Germany	+	58	42	42
Austria	+	+	24	+

1. The joint data base for the two periods is n = 87.
2. Excluded were antiforeign protest and private clashes.

All of these considerations, however, do not extend to the Northern Ireland conflict, which by 1977 had cost the lives of more than 1,700 people, about sixty of them on the British mainland. In a formal sense, we need not be concerned with Northern Ireland since no interviews for our study were conducted there.[25] But there is no question that it is a unit of the United Kingdom and therefore part of a democratic nation known and praised for its stability and tolerance of diversity. We cannot, of course, offer an "easy" explanation of this phenomenon, and we are well aware of the fact that the Irish Question at various points in British history has riven the political community, brought down governments, and disrupted the conduct of politics. The violence and intensity of this conflict clearly qualify for the label "internal war."

A first conclusion derived from consideration of these data is that there is nothing at all about advanced industrial societies that *guarantees* immunity from acts of warfare generated from internal political events, though the probability is very low. A second is that three of the five countries—Britain, the United States, and Germany—do indeed show substantial, antigovernment protest demonstrations, thus pointing to the fact that this type of political participation was apparently not at all alien to advanced Western industrial societies even before the sociopolitical movements of the late 1960s erupted at full strength. A third is—as we had hypothesized on theoretical grounds—that antigovernment demonstrations obviously cannot be readily interpreted as an unambiguous indicator of *system* instability.

While we do not want to overinterpret these results, we find that they confirm our expectations about the structure of political participation in Western political systems. In the 1960s, demonstrations occurred with sufficient and increasing frequency in the countries of our study (and certainly in other democracies such as France, Sweden, and Italy not covered here) to warrant consideration and inclusion in empirical studies of political participation. Still, as was mentioned before, cross-sectional or longitudinal survey data dealing systematically with attitudes toward direct political action in these countries are practically nonexistent in the literature for all of the 1960s and even the early 1970s.[26] Obviously, this lack of information not only ·reflects the initially more isolated, less general occurrence of these techniques, but also the *theoretical* preoccupation of the discipline with electoral types of political involvement. Unfortunately, there is no way to reconstruct attitudinal data on direct political action for this epoch. Moreover, the existing aggregate data on conflict do not, of course, lend themselves to reliable trend extrapolation or to the assessment of the meaning of protest activities for a given political system and its citizens at a particular point in time. Thus many of today's controversies about political participation are beyond the analytical potential of this cross-sectional survey study.

For example, we will not be able to determine whether or not participation enhances self-esteem and self-realization.[27] Neither will we be able to follow the long-term consequences of political participation on either the individual level—in terms of positive and negative reinforcement, satisfaction or dissatisfaction, lower or higher sense of efficacy and trust, and the like—or on the system level—in terms of following participatory inputs through concrete decision-making processes. What we will be able to analyze—from advanced industrial societies—are aspects of the structure and dimensionality of political actions that go beyond electoral and election-related forms.

REFLECTIONS ON A MICRO
THEORY OF POLITICAL ACTION

Systemic Conditions and the Meaning of Political Action

A theoretical preoccupation with segmented sociopolitical phenomena and a corresponding research methodology focusing on single points in time can be held responsible jointly, though not exclusively, for tendencies in empirical research to overinterpret findings and extrapolate them beyond their narrow contextual limits. A good example is the stimulation and support elitist democratic theory received in the late 1940s, 1950s, and early 1960s from the results of empirical research that indicated a considerable lack of political interest and involvement on the part of the average citizen. In addition, heavy reliance on nonhistorical research methodologies by those who study contemporary societies increases the chance that major systemic changes will go unnoticed. This will be so as long as their impact is not personally experienced or widely publicized through channels of communication such as the mass media. Scheuch, in a book on the governability or nongovernability of the Federal Republic of Germany, correctly observes that the percentage of individuals deriving their income from the primary sector of the economy has been reduced by 50 percent or more in Western countries during the last two decades without resulting in major sociopolitical conflicts.[28]

Changes in the occupational structure of the industrialized Western nations certainly are not the only ones worth noting. One change that can be unambiguously demonstrated with survey data and is of major importance with respect to the structure of political action is the increasing political involvement of the citizenry.[29] This politicization reflects secular trends such as the "educational revolution,"[30] the growth of an interventionist welfare state supported by a progressive income tax system, the decrease in the number of working hours, the technological time-saving upgrading in household appliances, and, as a major factor, the development of a widespread electronic mass communication network including, in particular, the diffusion of television.[31] A major factor in all these developments of course was an unprecedented rate of economic growth that not only made it possible to pay for these changes but also, and more importantly, reduced the potential large-scale income and wealth distribution conflicts to highly ritualized peaceful confrontations among pluralist corporate actors such as political parties, trade unions, and employer unions.[32]

The emphasis on political stability that characterizes this phase of economic growth is well embedded in notions of elitist democratic theory and can be easily understood in light of the apocalyptic experiences suffered by citizens in almost all industrialized Western countries during World War II. The high hopes of the 1950s for limited, peaceful conflicts are well summed up by Lipset, who wrote in 1961, "the democratic class struggle will continue, but it will be a fight without ideologies, without red flags, without May Day parades."[33] This conclusion sounded plausible enough against the background of economic well-being and undisturbed development in the postwar industrialized societies. The return of the ideologies, flags, and parades in the movements for civil rights, for peace in Vietnam, and for more participation constituted a definite challenge to the explanatory capabilities of social scientists. One challenge in particular was to discover why support for these movements was found overwhelmingly among the well-to-do classes.

One answer to this question lies in the structural changes we have described but cannot *systematically* integrate into our study and analysis design. An additional answer can be provided by Inglehart's theory of value change, which will be more thoroughly discussed in this and particularly in later chapters of the book.[34] Finally, an answer can be sought in the important relationship between democratic values that are so closely bound to concepts of participation, on the one hand, and concrete forms of political action, on the other. These latter are defined as legal or legitimate, or both, in a given society at a given point in time. Here it will be argued that the emphasis on *existing* political structures underestimates the actual impact of the substantive political philosophy of democracy, of political ideology as a constrained belief system, and of well-developed political cognitions upon processes of political change. These factors, as well as the structural changes we have mentioned above, add to the amount and intensity of systemic strain on the social and political order in advanced industrial societies.

A Systems Perspective of Political Action

As the standard definition based on Eastonian thinking goes, politics is a process that produces decisions about the production and distribution of scarce material and nonmaterial resources. Such a frame of reference points to the high conflict potential of this process. Its successful management has a direct bearing on the survival chances of any given political regime. In this sense, then, the institutionalization of adequate patterns of conflict management enables a polity to achieve its goals without facing the constant threat of self-destruction. Likewise, it remains strong against external threats.

Positions of influence in a political and social system at a given point in time testify to the economic, technological, organizational, and ideological resources that the actors in the system command. As a result, participation in conflicts that are regarded as legitimate—such as between employers and labor unions or between government and opposition—generally reflects the societal status quo. The extent to which competing groups have access to resources will change over time, so there will always be groups that have not yet gained access to channels of influence. Consequently, noninstitutionalized conflicts reflect a system state in which newly emerging interest cleavages have not been sufficiently recognized and therefore are not coopted into the regular bargaining processes. The result is inadequate representation of minorities. The failure to recognize this phenomenon is at the core of much criticism directed at pluralist democratic theory.

According to fundamental democratic principles, democratic societies, at the very least, guarantee individual citizens or social groups the chance to influence decisions by political authorities. To the extent that this principle is realized or believed to be realized, any recourse to collective political violence or the threat thereof is unnecessary. On the other hand, lack of system responsiveness might legitimately, though not necessarily legally, permit resort to various direct action techniques including the use of violence as the final point on a continuum of unconventional political behavior.

If we relate political actors and political authorities in such a dynamic model, we can then conceptualize political participation in any of its concrete forms as an interaction between political authorities and nonauthorities (or potential partisans, as Gamson prefers to call them) in which mutual expectations and eventual outcomes determine the dynamics of this interaction.[35] The core variables relevant to the process are the trust of the nonauthorities in the political authorities, the formers' trust in the nonpartisan nature of the institutions of the political system, the perceived success of attempts by nonauthorities to influence outcomes, the ability of authorities to change outcome decisions, and the authorities' definition of the situation in terms of its potential for social control. But, most important, the concrete nature of the exchange is determined by the responsiveness of the political actors, their chosen means of influence, and the repertory of political resources and activities that partisans command.[36]

The concept of political repertory defined as the sum of all political skills an individual has acquired through vicarious reinforcement and imitative learning will play an important role in the empirical analysis we shall present in the following chapters. It will permit us to consider jointly conventional and unconventional forms of political participation without an a priori limitation of our theoretical perspective. We regard the command of a political repertory as a prerequisite for citizens to express political demands.

Obviously, our approach to the understanding of political participation is an instrumental and rationalistic one. It assumes that a specific participatory act is selected as the precise means for the political actor to achieve certain goals at a minimal cost, goals that do not seem to be otherwise achievable because of the lack of responsiveness of the political authorities and institutions. It does not assume, however, that this calculation, which is *zweckrational* in Weber's sense, is carried out independently of all external social stimuli and structures of influence. Therefore, our approach is neither identical with nor similar to the concept of the rational individual "political man" who collects all available and necessary information and then makes up his mind accordingly—an ideal type that has been demolished by modern empirical research. Nor is our approach identical with that of the traditional "ruling elite" model, since we do not assume that the organizational structures necessary to pose a realistic threat to the governing elites must be based on traditional, well-established influence positions.

The establishment of complex and efficient mass communication systems has somewhat eased the organizational requirements for successful political inputs. The impact on political decision-making of the student movement in the middle and late 1960s is a good case in point. Even so, the importance of demand organization across time and space, for example, cannot be emphasized enough. With the exception of political terrorism, which must be regarded as a pathological concomitant of advanced industrial society, it is still the *collective* character of political action or the threat of such action that determines the sequence and character of interactions between partisans and political authorities.[37]

The overall view of political participation and political action we have presented thus far is basically of a functionalist nature. This is in line with conflict theorists such as Coser who, following a systems perspective, stresses the impact of extreme forms of societal involvement on the ability of sociopolitical systems to adapt successfully to structural challenges.[38] The importance of Gamson's similarly functionalist theoretical conceptualization is that it explicitly considers the actions and reactions of the state as a possible reason for the recourse by partisans to direct action techniques. These are actions that in the past have frequently been analyzed within the framework of political extremism or deviance.[39] One important factor in this one-sidedness was, in our opinion, the pluralist bias that confined people's actions to the *existing* political institutions, implicitly assuming that the process of interest aggregation and interest input into the decision-making structure was functioning properly.

This assumption has become less and less credible as the once homogeneous and well-structured hierarchy of political preferences diversified. This hierarchy was well embedded in the class cleavage and, to a lesser extent, in the religious cleavage, which, as Lipset and Rokkan once stated, have been the base for many of the existing Western party systems.[40] As the diversification process continues, the central role of political parties as a link between the populus and the political decision-making elites depends ever more heavily on diffuse, generalized support by citizens.

At this point, the distinction between *government trust,* or trust in the political authorities, and *system trust,* or trust in the political institutions and acceptance of the political philosophy of the political system, becomes very important. As Gamson has pointed out, trust as a general concept can be understood as a blank check issued by citizens on the assumption of system responsiveness. With citizen demands becoming more specific, the ability of political authorities—and this includes the political parties—to maintain government trust will increasingly depend not only on their general reactions but also on their reactions to specific, less institutionalized demands.

If this analysis is correct, it implies consequences for the dimensionality of the political space and the corresponding structure of political party systems in Western advanced industrial societies. While the Downsian model of a unidimensional party space has hardly ever been validated empirically,[41] it may, at least in the days of constrained demand organization, have served nevertheless as a useful analytical tool. But now slow changes can be observed in the hierarchical structure of the political space, and politics also becomes increasingly important for the average citizen, not only because educational levels and resulting cognitive capabilities are increasing, but also because the state, as we have mentioned before, has been rapidly enlarging its spheres of influence and responsibility. Both the hierarchical structure of the political space and the low level of citizen involvement in politics once permitted and even required that "normal" citizens develop general orientations toward the parties in order to reduce the complexity of the political process to a level congruent with their own capabilities and motivations to participate. On the other side, political authorities were happy, and even relieved, to reciprocate this demand for simplicity and provide straightforward pathways for participation. By contrast, it is now reasonable to predict that there will be an increasing tendency for citizens with particular demands to organize themselves outside the established political institutions in general and outside the existing parties in particular.[42]

The lack of empirical analyses of the development of political trust in four of the five countries in our study renders impossible generalizations based only on the observed decline in *government trust* in the United States.[43] Such a decline in government trust does not necessarily pose an immediate threat to the stability of the Western democratic polities as long as *system trust* remains at a high level. Variations in trust in government are a normal phenomenon in representative democracies; they reflect incumbency roles on the system level. But if trust in government substantially deteriorates because even those citizens who identify with the governing party or parties lose trust in "their" political authorities, then changes in system trust are also likely to occur unless the institutional make-up of the political system changes to meet the new demands.[44]

Much of this is speculation. Still the systemic perspective we have applied to political action is essential in order not to fall prey to a static conceptualization of the problem. In public perceptions, acts of unconventional political behavior are usually associated with social movements that at least try to transcend the sociopolitical structure of a given system. Many observers view the rise in noninstitutionalized political participation as an effort at transcendence of this nature; some view it with feelings of fear, others with feelings of hope. In spite of speculations about the imminent breakdown of the present social and political order, we have a less apocalyptic view of the future.

Elements of a Micro Theory of Political Action

This study was begun in 1971 with a strong interest in measuring and explaining dimensions of political action. We were especially concerned with unconventional political behavior, which can be defined as behavior that does not correspond to the norms of law and custom that regulate political participation under a particular regime. This interest is reflected in the following schematic representation of the core variables in the study. This figure is not meant to be a systematic specification of causal relationships among variables or blocks of variables. Rather, we see it as an heuristic device permitting a broad overview of the set of constructs that have been found to be theoretically or empirically useful for the explanation of political participation. In accordance with the "grand design" of our study, we have operationalized and measured all constructs referring to *individual actors*. In this chapter we will not try to link these constructs systematically in order to arrive at some kind of a causal model. This will be left to later chapters in the book. Our interest at this point lies in offering a concise description of the range of the project's research interests in the realm of political action.

The Main Dependent Variables: Conventional and Unconventional Political Participation. In most contemporary empirical research, political participation appears as a straightforward concept that is theoretically well grounded and amenable to empirical research without major obstacles. We do not intend to challenge this notion directly; it is, in fact, supported by a substantial body of good empirical research, especially on electoral behavior. Nevertheless, substantial criticism has been leveled at much of the empirical work on political participation on theoretical as well as ideological grounds. Voting behavior, which has been the focal point of some of the best empirical political science research done to date, has been branded irrelevant and misleading.[45] Quantitative participation research in general has been accused of being status quo oriented, too narrowly focused on only the *political* arena, and lacking a wider perspective with respect to the goal of democratization.[46]

Given our theoretical interest, the cross-national and cross-sectional character of our research design, and the limitations of empirical research in general, we have found these criticisms to be of little relevance for our research on political participation despite the validity of some of the charges. As it turns out, we can live quite comfortably with the broad standard definition offered in the literature, which refers to political participation as all voluntary activities by individual citizens intended to influence either directly or indirectly political choices at various levels of the political system.[47] However, this working definition entails one key element that requires qualification with regard to our own empirical research.

We have mentioned before that our interest in uninstitutionalized direct political action had to be reconciled with the cross-sectional, national representative survey design. This design is well suited for the measurement of institutionalized, "traditional" political acts such as voting and so on. However, it is much less adequate for measuring behaviors that occur irregularly, infrequently, and in specific, often local, contexts of mobilization. As the detailed discussion in the following chapter will show, the cross-national study design required and warranted a conceptual approach concentrating on protest *potential* in the five countries. In comparison, the measurement of the behavioral component of conventional political involvement did not incur major problems.

Another problem of great concern to us has been the dimensionality of the political action space. When Milbrath in 1965 postulated a unidimensional hierarchy of political involvement in the United States, he observed that

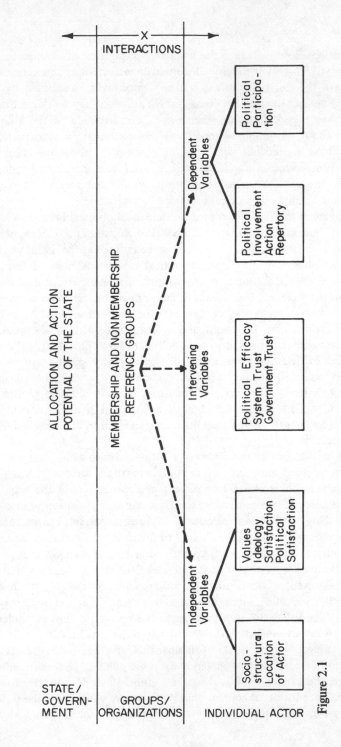

Figure 2.1

"demonstrations do not fit into the hierarchy of political involvement in the United States."[48] This hierarchy of conventional activities oriented exclusively toward the electoral process was not *empirically* established by Milbrath. It has been challenged by Verba and Nie, though their work can also be interpreted—as they themselves observe—as a confirmation of the Milbrath hypothesis about the unidimensionality of conventional political participation.[49] We have started out with a similar assumption about the unidimensionality of unconventional political participation. We understand this dimension as reflecting the lengths to which a given individual is prepared to go in the use of unconventional political means.

Two aspects of this dimension of unconventional political behavior require elaboration: these are its relationship to political violence and to conventional political participation. Political violence can be defined as the use of physical force against objects or persons for political reasons. Almost all forms of direct political action, including many conventional ones, are, at least potentially, prone to violence. One could, in fact, conceptualize these acts as the representation of an underlying continuum of violence proneness. As we have mentioned before, even if protest and violence are, historically speaking, "natural" concomitants of any sociopolitical development, their consequences are sufficiently unpleasant to explain why people are usually opposed to political violence. This is particularly true for the advanced industrial societies of the West, where many find it difficult to imagine situations in which violence could be a meaningful political resort. This evaluation is apparently shared with little disagreement by the mass publics in these countries.[50]

A study by Blumenthal and others of attitudes toward violence alerts us to the fact that we are dealing with a very complex attitude structure. According to their analyses, there exists a consistent perceptual bias in the way that violence-prone social groups think of specific actions as violent or nonviolent. Since they share with others rejection of "violence" as an abstract societal norm, such groups face the difficult task of justifying the fact that the direct action techniques they adopt are frequently violent or at least violence-prone. The cognitive dissonance that is bound to arise from this discrepancy in belief elements is resolved, as Blumenthal and others show, by a simple psychological trick: the respective social groups define "their" action repertory as "non-violent" and the actions of other (usually opposed) groups as "violent." Thus they are able to maintain their view that violence is fundamentally evil.

Another aspect of the work of Blumenthal and her colleagues is also relevant for the assessment of violence by mass publics. They were able to demonstrate the existence of two separate dimensions of attitudes toward violence: violence for social control, that is, repressive violence by the state or vigilantism to maintain the status quo, and violence for social change, that is, a set of beliefs that the sociopolitical changes deemed necessary can be brought about only by violent means.[51] We will deal later with both aspects of attitudes toward violence when we develop our measurement instruments.

The second question we raised concerned the relationship of unconventional to conventional political behavior. The former is rather closely related to what in colloquial as well as scholarly discourse is frequently referred to as protest behavior.[52] Our preference for the term "unconventional political behavior" reflects two considerations, one theoretical and one political.

As we have tried to demonstrate in our discussion of the systemic conditions of political involvement, there is every reason to assume that, in a middle- or long-range analysis of political action, concrete forms of participation may experience changes in the degree to which they are considered unconventional. These forms may be evaluated both according to their *legality*, that is, their conformity to positive legal norms relevant for a given type of behavior, and their *legitimacy*, that is, the extent to which a given population at a given point in time approves or disapproves them.[53] Although legality and legitimacy are not completely unrelated, for analytical purposes they must be kept separate to permit the analysis of lags or discrepancies between the two and of processes of change in political culture.[54]

The Main Independent Variables. The content of the two boxes labeled "independent variables" in Figure 2.1 surely has already alerted the reader to the fact that in this general overview of relevant theoretical constructs the concept of "independent variables" is used very loosely indeed. Clearly, what in a given analysis is regarded as an independent variable has to be determined theoretically. Consequently, our interest at this point is simply to point to blocks of variables that we regard as being the most important antecedents of political action.

The first such block includes variables locating individuals in the social structure of society. Three core elements of this structure have been proven time and again to be relevant for political participation. The first is social status, the position in which individuals find themselves *relative to others* with respect to education, income, and the like. The second element indicates the degree of integration into networks of secondary associations such as interest groups and comparable organizations.[55] The third is age, which is differentiated into the two components of generation and position in the life cycle.

The second block of variables is designed to measure sociopolitical values and is based on the conceptualization of value change proposed by Inglehart in 1971. Inglehart sets out to provide an explanation for the puzzling observation that members of the middle classes were heavily overrepresented in the protest movements of the late 1960s, and he begins with the psychological theory of a value—or need hierarchy proposed by Maslow.[56] Briefly summarized, this theory postulates that individual needs are hierarchically organized, and that satisfaction of each respective lower stage of the hierarchy leads to the activation of needs located one step higher in the hierarchy.

Without discussing this theory in any greater detail,[57] at least one general hypothesis related to the appearance of unconventional political behavior on the political scene can be formulated as follows: contrary to many expectations, satisfaction of the physical and safety needs, a goal that is now at least in sight in many advanced industrial societies, will not eliminate political conflict. Rather, the conflict in these societies will now shift to values related to the needs ranking higher on the need hierarchy, such as the feeling of belonging and self-actualization.

A third block of variables deals with the motivational and cognitive conditions that make it possible for citizens to orient themselves in the world of politics, and with their ideological commitments. We have already pointed out the extent to which a rational, means-end political calculus requires, in addition to the motivation to engage and act, the cognitive capabilities to assess adequately the contingencies of a given situation and then to make the relevant choices from the repertoire of political means available. This perspective is particularly relevant for analyses on the macro level of the political system. The reason is that increases in levels of mass political competence can, at least in the long run, lead to a reduction in the "pluralist bias" and ensure a more adequate consideration of noninstitutionalized interests. Unfortunately, after the pioneering work by Converse published in 1964, very little cross-national research has been done to provide firmer empirical grounds for estimating the cognitive capabilities of mass publics.[58] In our study, Klingemann made a substantial effort to overcome this lack of empirical data by adapting Converse's measurement approach in order to arrive at a cross-national indicator of level of conceptualization based on open-ended questions.[59]

This measure is complemented by indicators derived from two questions— one closed and one open—about self-placement on the ideological left-right dimension and the respondent's cognitive understanding of that dimension. On the one hand, these indicators will permit us to answer the questions of the extent to which mass publics are guided by ideological preferences and how these preferences are integrated by the existing party systems. On the other hand, these indicators will make possible an assessment of the left-right ideological balance in advanced industrial societies and its consequences for political action.

The fourth and final block of variables to be discussed is centered around the concept of relative deprivation. This concept is anything but new and was derived from work on reference group theory.[60] Relative deprivation has played a major role in macro conflict research where it was defined either as the "perceived discrepancy between men's value expectations and their value capabilities"[61] or the "discrepancy between present social aspirations and expectations, on the one hand, and social achievements, on the other."[62] Whatever the theoretical importance of relative deprivation, it certainly did not fare well in macropolitical empirical research. Thus Hibbs sums up his analyses—utilizing his operational definition of the relative deprivation concept—by stating that "the social mobilization-government performance and social mobilization-social welfare hypotheses do not provide powerful explanations of differences across nations in levels of mass political violence."[63]

Relative deprivation as a micro concept in survey research has only sparsely been used *systematically* in empirical studies in the past.[64] Therefore, it is not at all surprising that an examination of empirical research into unconventional political behavior in 1971 concludes, "there is considerable reason for rejecting the sociological and popular cliché that absolute or relative deprivation and the ensuing frustration or discontent or despair is the root cause of rebellion."[65] Still, a careful analysis of the operationalizations of such a complex concept 'as relative deprivation in the studies reanalyzed reveals that such a far-reaching conclusion is not at all warranted. Rather, it should be regarded as bad research policy that the unavailability of adequate data results in ex post operationalizations that are not grounded in the theory they are designed to assess and therefore do not provide a proper test of the construct.

One important factor that has to be considered explicitly is that relative deprivation can become politically relevant only as a collective property of one or more groups. In essence, a built-in feature of relative deprivation theory is that, in order to cross the threshold of awareness, deprivations have to be pinpointed and put into a common frame of reference through the activities of political elites in order to overcome the isolation of the individual. Here we see a direct link to the role that ideologies and political sophistication play in processes of political mobilization.[66]

Second, it must not be forgotten that even collective deprivations[67] have to be politicized, that is, fed into the political process. As Dahl writes, "to the dismay and astonishment of the activists who struggle to rouse a disadvantaged group to oppose its lot, the human psyche does not invariably impel those who are deprived of equality to seek it, or sometimes even to want it."[68] Dahl maintains that five conditions must be fulfilled for a successful process of politicization:

A) perception of deprivation;
B) high relevance for the individual and for the group;
C) evaluation of deprivation as illegitimate;
D) feelings of anger, frustration, resentment over it;
E) actual demand for removal of deprivation.[69]

There are two additional conditions that are missing in Dahl's formulation and that are crucial for the process of politicization. The first is that political authorities be held responsible for the condition of felt deprivation; the second is that the performance of the authorities in the respective areas of deprivation be negatively evaluated.

Both the requirements of a *collective* deprivation and of the politicization of the deprivation reveal once more the limits of a cross-sectional representative survey study design as long as its focal point is the explanation of *concrete acts of unconventional political behavior.* If relative deprivation theory is to be given a fair chance to explain political unrest, then a time lapse in which dissatisfaction precedes unrest must be assumed. In addition, there must be social actors who anticipate and define deprivation and push it over the threshold of individual awareness. Or it may happen that certain actors take up existing individual deprivations and organize as well as articulate them. There has to be an interaction over time between actors on different system levels to initiate the process of unrest. The process itself is strongly influenced by factors based on the societal value system as well as on organizational and structural properties of the participants in the conflict, and this is true notwithstanding the dynamics of the confrontation itself.[70]

Some Intervening Variables. Macropolitical conflict research has identified variables that determine whether a readiness for conflict behavior is indeed transformed into action: these variables include the coercive potential of the state,[71] subjective justifications for the respective behavior,[72] and the responsiveness of political authorities to citizen demands.[73] We will be dealing only with subjective individual perceptions of government and system responsiveness. Gamson's model for the exchange between political authorities and partisans assumes a central intervening role for political trust or, to use a more general term, legitimacy beliefs.[74] This interest in *processes* of influence exchange emphasizes the properties of the trust concept *as a variable.* According to Gamson, levels of public trust depend on the outcomes of influence efforts by potential partisans. We will not be able to deal with this dynamic perspective with our data; Gamson himself is also unable to support his theoretical approach empirically. Nevertheless, he provides some important conceptual differentiations that require separate and explicit operationalizations.

The first distinction refers to the Eastonian categories of input and output dimensions.[75] The theoretical equivalent of the input dimension is the perception by individuals of their ability to influence; its operationalization is the political efficacy scale.[76] The theoretical equivalent of the output dimension is trust, defined as the individual's perception of influence, or the probability that the political system will produce preferred outcomes even if left untended; its operationalization is the system responsiveness scale.[77]

The second distinction deals with four different aspects of political trust that, Gamson argues, are hierarchically organized along a specificity-generality dimension: (1) political authorities, (2) political institutions, (3) public philosophy, and (4) political community.[78] In this study only the first of these four steps in the hierarchy—*government* trust—has been adequately operationalized while measures of *system* trust—steps two, three, and four in the hierarchy—can at best be regarded as very rough approximations of the concept.[79]

SUMMARY

In this chapter we have developed the theoretical contours that have guided our research into conventional and unconventional forms of political participation in advanced industrial societies. It was necessary to discuss, at least in general terms, the relationship to democratic theories of participation as a political value or goal, and to speculate about the meaning that acts of unconventional political participation might have in a systemic analysis. In order to come to grips with the phenomenon of political protest, we had to pay particular attention to two serious problems.

First, popular and scholarly views of political protest have specified a conceptual frame of reference for the explanation of this phenomenon— theories of collective violence—that regard unconventional political behaviors as part of a scenario in which political stability is disrupted by aggressive social or political groups. While we do not deny the usefulness and validity of this approach *in general,* we argued that it is too one-sided for the analysis of the newly emerging participatory political culture of advanced industrial societies. This implies a culture characterized by the waning of broad socio-political movements for system change and an increase in limited, issue-based, and frequently regional ad hoc group actions that may well dissolve after the issue has receded. It is particularly important to note that in this theoretical perspective the emergence of direct action techniques does *not* in itself signal the end of stable liberal democracy (or the end of "Spaetkapitalismus" as certain German political philosophers have preferred to call it).[80]

Second, and not unrelated to this difference in theoretical emphasis just mentioned, we found that very little empirical cross-sectional evidence and even less longitudinal survey evidence is as yet available for mass publics nationally as well as cross-nationally on styles of political participation that go beyond institutionalized, electorally oriented activities. Thus, whereas the macrodata we have looked at do not contradict our basic contention of an increasing predisposition of mass publics toward direct political action techniques and thereby indicate a secular trend toward a different quality of political life, the critical evaluation of this research-guiding hypothesis grown out of the theory of value change will have to come from the data of our own study. Since we are following a new path in looking at political action in very broad terms, the cross-national design of the study is particularly useful in helping us, on the one hand, to avoid overinterpretations of our data and, on the other, to arrive at conclusions of more general validity. To describe a new set of relationships between social structure, social dispositions, and political action in one country is exciting but uncomfortable. The arm of chance is a long one. To find such a phenomenon replicated in four other nations simultaneously is exciting and reassuring.

NOTES

1. Dennis F. Thompson, *The Democratic Citizen*, Cambridge: Cambridge University Press, 1970, pp. 10ff.
2. Henry S. Kariel, (ed.), *Frontiers of Democratic Theory*, New York: Random House, 1970.
3. Juergen Habermas et al., *Student und Politik*. Neuwied: Luchterhand-Verlag, 1961.
4. Daniel Bell, *The Coming of Post-Industrial Society*, London: Heinemann, 1974, pp. 14ff. Germany and Austria are slightly less developed in this respect. In the following table we have included both Bell's figures which are based on a 1969 OECD publication, and the data contained in Eike Ballerstedt and Wolfgang Glatzer, *Soziopolitischer Almanach*. Frankfurt-New York: Herder and Herder, 1975, p. 93, on the percentage of labor force employed in the tertiary sector.

| Country | Percentage of Labor Force in Tertiary Sector | | | |
| | OECD | | Almanach | |
	Year	#	Year	#
The Netherlands	1969	49.8	1968	51.3
Britain	1969	49.7	1966	51.4
United States	1969	61.1	1971	60.8
Germany*	1969	41.4	1971	43.4
Austria	–	–	1971	42.1

*According to 1977 micro census data 50.1 percent of the active labor force were employed in the tertiary sector in Germany.

5. Samuel P. Huntington, *Political Order in Changing Societies,* New Haven: Yale University Press, 1968, p. 32.

6. Samuel P. Huntington and Joan M. Nelson, *No Easy Choice: Political Participation in Developing Countries,* Cambridge: Harvard University Press, 1976.

7. Adam Przeworski and Henry Teune, *The Logic of Comparative Social Inquiry,* New York: John Wiley, 1970, pp. 31ff.

8. Daniel Bell, *The Coming of Post-Industrial Society,* p. 12.

9. According to the handbook by Dolf Sternberger and Bernhard Vogel (eds.), *Die Wahl der Parlamente, Band 1, Europa,* Berlin: Verlag Walter de Gruyter, 1959, the active right to a free, direct, equal and secret vote was awarded to:

• The Dutch in 1917 (age limit: 25 years), the age limit was reduced to 21 years in 1956 (p. 867);

• The British in 1948 (age limit: 21 years); after the reform of 1928 a double vote for university graduates was still in effect (p. 634);

• the Germans in 1920 (age limit: 20 years) (p. 252);

• the Austrians in 1923 (age limit: 20 years) (p. 940).

The situation in America is considerably more complicated. May it suffice to note that the present Carter Administration is considering measures to ease voter registration to boost turnout that still substantially lags behind other Western democracies.

Another case in point is Switzerland where women obtained full national voting privileges only in 1971.

10. The discussion in Thompson, *The Democratic Citizen,* pp. 53ff., represents a more balanced, complex view on participation although it too suffers from the lack of formalization of the arguments.

11. See the discussion in Seymour M. Lipset, *Political Man,* Anchor Book Edition, New York: Doubleday, 1963, pp. 226ff.; furthermore Bernard Berelson, "Survival Through Apathy," in Henry S. Kariel (ed.), *Frontiers of Democratic Theory,* pp. 68ff. (reprinted from "Voting"), and Bernard Berelson, "Democratic Theory and Public Opinion," *Public Opinion Quarterly,* 16 (Fall 1952), pp. 313ff. A more recent statement is Manfred Kuechler, "Was leistet die empirische Wahlsoziologie", in Max Kaase (ed.), *Wahlsoziologie heute. Analysen aus Anlass der Bundestagswahl 1976,* Opladen: Westdeutscher Verlag, 1977, p. 153.

12. William A. Gamson, *Power and Discontent,* Homewood: Dorsey Press, 1968.

13. Samuel P. Huntington and Joan M. Nelson, *No Easy Choice,* pp. 159ff.

14. Philip E. Converse, "Public Opinion and Voting Behavior," in Fred I. Greenstein and Nelson W. Polsby (eds.), *Handbook of Political Science,* Vol. 4, Reading: Addison Wesley, 1975, pp. 93ff.

15. James W. Prothro and C. M. Grigg, "Fundamental Principles of Democracy: Bases of Agreement and Disagreement," *Journal of Politics,* 22 (Spring 1960), pp. 276ff.; Herbert McClosky, "Consensus and Ideology in American Politics," *American Political Science Review,* 58 (June 1964), pp. 361ff.

16. The facets of the problem are well described in Thomas R. Dye and I. Harmon Zeigler, *The Irony of Democracy,* Belmont: Duxbury Press, 1970.

17. Charles Tilly, "Collective Violence in European Perspective," in Hugh David Graham and Ted Robert Gurr (eds.), *Violence in America,* New York: Signet Books, 1969, pp. 4f.

18. Ted Robert Gurr, *Why Men Rebel,* Princeton: Princeton University Press, 1971, p. 11.

19. Charles Lewis Taylor and Michael C. Hudson, *World Handbook of Political and Social Indicators,* New Haven: Yale University Press, 1972. The data were made available

for secondary analysis through the Inter-university Consortium for Political and Social Research (ICPSR), Ann Arbor.

20. Douglas A. Hibbs, Jr., *Mass Political Violence*, New York: John Wiley, 1973, pp. 7ff.

21. Hibbs also includes political strikes in his collective protest measure and assassinations in his internal war measure. For an operational definition of the six indicators see Hudson and Taylor, pp. 59ff.

22. This assessment is also shared by Hibbs (p. 10) who used logarithmic transformations for all variables before beginning the substantive analysis.

23. A fuller analysis of these data can be found in Ted Robert Gurr, "Political Protest and Violence in the 1960's: The United States in World Perspective"; in Hugh David Graham and Ted Robert Gurr (eds.), *Violence in America: Historical and Comparative Perspectives,* Revised College Edition, Beverly Hills, Cal.: Sage Publications, 1979. We appreciate the permission of Gurr to use these data for our analyses.

24. In the Gurr data Northern Ireland is treated as a separate nation and not as part of the United Kingdom.

25. The British investigators felt they could not accept the responsibility of sending their interviewers down the Falls Road to ask people penetrating questions about their political beliefs.

26. Verba, Nie, and others in their seven-nation study conducted in the United States; Sidney Verba, Norman H. Nie and Jae-On Kim, "The Modes of Democratic Participation," *Comparative Politics Series,* Sage Professional Paper No. 01-013, Beverly Hills: Sage Publications, 1971; Sidney Verba et al., "The Modes of Participation," *Comparative Political Studies,* 6 (July 1973), pp. 235ff.; Jae-On Kim, Norman Nie, Sidney Verba, "The Amount and Concentration of Political Participation," *Political Methodology,* 1 (Spring 1974), pp. 105ff. The American part of the study is thoroughly analyzed in Sidney Verba and Norman H. Nie, *Participation in America,* New York: Harper & Row, 1972. In this book Verba and Nie state on page 3 that "our concern is with activities 'within the system'—ways of influencing politics that are generally recognized as legal and legitimate." This perspective is, of course, perfectly in order as long as the Verba-Nie data are not mistakenly interpreted as a complete representation of the structure of political action. This limitation is critically noted by Jerrold G. Rusk, "Political Participation in America: A Review Essay," *American Political Science Review,* 70 (June 1976), pp. 583ff. This criticism is even more strongly voiced by William R. Schonfeld, "The Meaning of Democratic Participation," *World Politics,* 28 (October 1975), pp. 141ff. For a similar point see Robert H. Salisbury, "Research on Political Participation," *American Journal of Political Science,* 19 (May 1975), p. 325.

27. The "participatory" side of the controversy has been taken by Carole Pateman, *Participation and Democratic Theory,* Cambridge: Cambridge University Press, 1970. The assumption of a positive causal relationship between participation and self-esteem has been challenged on empirical as well as theoretical grounds in Paul M. Sniderman, *Personality and Democratic Politics,* Berkeley: University of California Press, 1975, pp. 315ff. An interesting, unusual perspective on the problem has been unfolded by William Lafferty, "Participation and Democratic Theory: Reworking the Premises for a Participatory Society," *Scandinavian Political Studies* (Oslo), 10, 1975, pp. 53ff.

28. Erwin K. Scheuch, *Wird die Bundesrepublik unregierbar?,* Koeln: Arbeitgeberverband der Metallindustrie, 1976, pp. 28ff. That these enormous changes could be peacefully accommodated testifies to the adaptive capabilities of modern sociopolitical systems.

29. See Elisabeth Noelle-Neumann, "Wahlentscheidung in der Fernsehdemokratie," in Dieter Just and Lothar Romain (eds.), *Auf der Suche nach dem muendigen Waehler,* Bonn: Bundeszentrale fuer Politische Bildung, 1974, p. 186, for a table of survey marginals representative for the Federal Republic over a period of 21 years which show a 22 percentage point increase in the number of those indicating their interest in politics. For the United States see Warren E. Miller and Teresa E. Levitin, *Leadership and Change,* Cambridge: Winthrop Publishers, 1976, p. 229.

30. Philip E. Converse, "Change in the American Electorate," in Angus Campbell and Philip E. Converse (eds.), *The Human Meaning of Social Change,* New York: Russell Sage, 1972, pp. 322ff.

31. John P. Robinson and Philip F. Converse, "Social Change Reflected in the Use of Time," in Angus Campbell and Philip E. Converse (eds.), *The Human Meaning of Social Change,* pp. 17ff.

32. The relevance of such corporate agreements is stressed by Philippe C. Schmitter, "Associability and Governability," Paper presented at the Colloquium on "Overloaded Government" held at Florence from December 13 through December 16, 1976.

33. Seymour M. Lipset, *Political Man,* p. 445.

34. The first presentation was Ronald Inglehart, "The Silent Revolution in Europe: Intergenerational Change in Post-Industrial Societies," *American Political Science Review,* 65 (December 1971), pp. 991ff. See also his book, *The Silent Revolution: Changing Values and Political Styles Among Western Publics,* Princeton, N.J.: Princeton University Press, 1977.

35. This conceptualization closely follows William A. Gamson, *Ideology and Discontent,* op. cit.

36. It is important to note that our particular perspective is not meant to reflect the "classical" mass-elite model since partisans in conflict with political authorities may, of course, also be or recruit societal elites.

37. Ted Robert Gurr, *Why Men Rebel,* pp. 7ff; Klaus v. Beyme, "Politischer Extremismus im Lichte sozialwissenschaftlicher Radikalismusforschung," in Rudolf Wassermann (ed.), *Terrorismus contra Rechtsstaat,* Neuwied: Luchterhand Verlag, 1976, pp. 48ff.

38. Lewis Coser, *The Functions of Social Conflict,* New York: Free Press, 1956.

39. The set of studies on the authoritarian and dogmatic personality is a good case in point.

40. Seymour M. Lipset and Stein Rokkan, "Cleavage Structures, Party Systems, and Voter Alignments: An Introduction," in Seymour M. Lipset and Stein Rokkan (eds.), *Party Systems and Voter Alignments,* New York: Free Press, 1967, pp. 1ff.

41. Donald E. Stokes, "Spatial Models of Party Competition," in Angus Campbell et al., *Elections and the Political Order,* New York: John Wiley, 1966, pp. 161ff. (First published in 1963 in the *American Political Science Review.*)

42. A good example of this development is the conflict about the erection of numerous nuclear energy production plants in West Germany. This conflict has a clear government/antigovernment dimension on *both* the federal and state level thereby cutting across party lines. It threatens to erode government as well as system trust because only after violent actions all over West Germany had successfully stopped construction work on some of the sites did it become evident that major problems involved in the production of nuclear energy had not been sufficiently considered and adequately solved by the political authorities.

43. Arthur H. Miller, "Political Issues and Trust in Government: 1964-1970,"

American Political Science Review, 68 (September 1974), pp. 951ff. See also Jack Citrin's "Comment" and Miller's "Rejoinder" in the same issue of this Review.

44. This interpretation is corroborated by Miller's empirical analyses. See his "Political Issues and Trust in Government: 1964-1970," pp. 963ff., 1970ff.

45. This criticism has been frequently voiced by Murray Edelman. See his *The Symbolic Uses of Politics,* Urbana: University of Illinois Press, 1964; "Research Orientations: Some Pitfalls and Some Strategic Suggestions," in Henry S. Kariel (ed.), *Frontiers of Democratic Theory,* pp. 352ff.; *Politics as Symbolic Action,* Chicago: Markham, 1971.

46. Gisela Zimpel, *Selbstbestimmung oder Akklamation? Politische Teilnahme in der buergerlichen Demokratietheorie,* Stuttgart: Enke Verlag, 1972; Ulrich v. Alemann (ed.), *Partizipation–Demokratisierung–Mitbestimmung,* Opladen: Westdeutscher Verlag, 1975.

47. Sidney Verba and Norman H. Nie, *Political Participation in America,* New York, 1972, p. 2: "Political participation refers to those activities by private citizens that are more or less directly aimed at influencing the selection of governmental personnel and/or the actions they take."

Herbert McClosky, *International Encyclopedia of the Social Sciences,* Vol. 12, New York: Macmillan and the Free Press, 1972 (first 1968), p. 252: "Political participation will refer to those voluntary activities by which members of a society share in the selection of rulers and, directly or indirectly, in the formation of public policy." Samuel P. Huntington and Joan M. Nelson, *No Easy Choice,* p. 4: "We define political participation simply as activity by private citizens designed to influence governmental decision making."

Interestingly enough, Lester W. Milbrath in his book *Political Participation,* Chicago: Rand McNally, 1965, nowhere explicitly offers an operational definition of the term. Extrapolating from the text, political participation refers to "individual behavior as it relates to the political system" (p. 3).

48. Lester W. Milbrath, *Political Participation,* p. 18. However, in the new edition of "Political Participation" by Milbrath and Goel, Chicago: Rand McNally, 1977, p. 20, a different perspective now largely coherent with our own regarding the conventionality of certain political acts has been adopted in that the authors argue "that standards about "normality" and "legitimacy" differ from culture to culture and over time."

49. Sidney Verba and Norman H. Nie, *Participation in America,* pp. 60ff.

50. Monica Blumenthal et al., *Justifying Violence,* Ann Arbor: Institute for Social Research, 1972. See also Monica Blumenthal et al., *More About Justifying Violence,* Ann Arbor: Institute for Social Research, 1975, and the detailed discussion of our data in the following chapter.

51. Monica Blumenthal et al., *Justifying Violence,* pp. 26ff.

52. See as an example Jerrold G. Rusk, "Political Participation in America: A Review Essay," pp. 585, 588.

53. These two aspects of unconventionality are also differentiated in Muller's definition of political dissent behavior. See his "A Test of a Partial Theory of Potential for Political Violence," *American Political Science Review,* 66 (September 1972), p. 934. See also Max Kaase, "Bedingungen unkonventionellen politischen Verhaltens in der Bundesrepublik Deutschland," in Peter Graf Kielmansegg (ed.), *Legitimationsprobleme politischer Systeme, Sonderheft 7 der Politischen Vierteljahresschrift (PVS),* Opladen: Westdeutscher Verlag, 1976, pp. 184ff.

54. Legality and legitimacy were included as two separate dimensions in the British pretest. As one would expect, the two were positively correlated ($r = .30$), but the

weakness of the correlation indicates that the two, as we have argued on theoretical grounds, are by no means identical. For a detailed description of the British pretest analyses see Alan Marsh, "Explorations in Unorthodox Political Behavior: A Scale to Measure 'Protest Potential'," *European Journal of Political Research,* 2 (June 1974), pp. 107ff. It was decided to exclude the legality dimension from data collected in the main study because of our emphasis on legitimacy and—a very practical reason—because of the problem of very limited questionnaire space.

55. There is little point and also need to base these statements on literature references which are abundant. See the already mentioned books by Milbrath, *Political Participation,* Verba and Nie, *Political Participation in America,* and, as an example of a cross-national survey study, Gabriel Almond and Sidney Verba, *The Civic Culture,* Princeton: Princeton University Press, 1963.

56. Abraham Maslow, *Motivation and Personality,* New York: Harper & Row, 1954.

57. For a thorough presentation see Ronald Inglehart's chapters in this book.

58. Philip E. Converse, "The Nature of Belief Systems in Mass Publics," in David E. Apter (ed.), *Ideology and Discontent,* New York: Free Press, 1964, pp. 206ff.

59. These analyses are presented in the chapters by Hans D. Klingemann in this book.

60. One example is Robert K. Merton, *Social Theory and Social Structure,* New York: Free Press, 1949.

61. Ted Robert Gurr, *Why Men Rebel,* p. 13.

62. Ivo K. Feierabend, Rosalind I. Feierabend, and Betty A. Nesvold, "Social Change and Political Violence: Cross-National Patterns," in Hugh David Graham and Ted Robert Gurr (eds.), *Violence in America,* pp. 606ff. It is not at all necessary to rely exclusively on the term "relative deprivation." John P. Spiegel, "Theories of Violence: An Integrated Approach," *International Journal of Group Tensions,* 1 (1971), p. 83, speaks of the "clash between the ideal value pattern and the actual or operative patterns," addressing the problem of the inconsistency between political ideals and practice as a motivating force to political violence. However, the decisive factor here is the discrepancy between expectations and reality.

63. Douglas A. Hibbs, Jr., *Mass Political Violence,* pp. 61ff. Erich Weede, "Unzufriedenheit, Protest und Gewalt: Kritik an einem makropolitischen Forschungsprogramm," *Politische Vierteljahresschrift,* 16 (September 1975), pp. 409ff., also has little good to say about the validity of the relative deprivation concept in macropolitical research.

64. One of the first empirical studies using relative deprivation as a central variable was W. G. Runciman, *Relative Deprivation and Social Justice,* London: Penguin Books, 1966. See also Edward N. Muller, "A Test of a Partial Theory of Potential for Political Violence," and Bernard Grofman and Edward N. Muller, "The Strange Case of Relative Gratification and Potential for Political Violence: The V-Curve Hypothesis," *American Political Science Review,* 67 (June 1973), pp. 514ff.

65. Clark McPhail, "Civil Disorder Participation: A Critical Examination of Recent Research," *American Sociological Review,* 36 (December 1971), p. 1064.

66. The parallel between this argument and the classic Marxist notions of "Klasse an sich" and "Klasse fuer sich" are obvious.

67. In complex industrial societies a differentiation between collective violence and collective political violence, which is made by Gurr for good analytic reasons, seems superfluous since it is difficult to imagine a social conflict of some magnitude that will not also involve the political system.

68. Robert A. Dahl, *Polyarchy,* New Haven: Yale University Press, 1971, p. 95.

69. Ibid.

70. Well-known theoretical approaches to this problem are William Kornhauser, *The Politics of Mass Society*, New York: Free Press, 1959; Neil J. Smelser, *Theory of Collective Behavior*, New York: Free Press, 1963, and Ted Robert Gurr, *Why Men Rebel*, op. cit. These approaches have triggered widespread criticism. Examples of this criticism are Joseph Firestone, "Three Frameworks for the Study of Violence: A Critique and Some Suggestions for a New Synthesis." Research Paper No. 11, Center for Comparative Political Research, Binghamton, 1971; Anthony Oberschall, *Social Conflict and Social Movements*, Englewood Cliffs: Prentice-Hall, 1973; Terry Nardin, *Violence and the State: A Critique of Empirical Political Theory*, Comparative Politics Series, Sage Professional Paper No. 01-020, Beverly Hills: Sage, 1971.

71. Ted Robert Gurr, *Why Men Rebel;* Neil F. Smelser, *Theory of Collective Behavior.*

72. Ted Robert Gurr, *Why Men Rebel.*

73. William A. Gamson, *Power and Discontent.*

74. Ibid.

75. Ibid., p. 42.

76. The scale is documented in John P. Robinson, Jerrold G. Rusk, and Kendra B. Head, *Measures of Political Attitudes*, Ann Arbor: Institute for Social Research, 1968, p. 460.

77. William A. Gamson, *Power and Discontent,* pp. 42, 54. The scale is derived from the various attitude items used in studies of the Center for Political Studies, Institute for Social Research, Ann Arbor. For a critical review of the extended work on subjective political efficacy see George I. Balch, "Multiple Indicators in Survey Research: The Concept 'Sense of Political Efficacy'," *Political Methodology,* 1 (Spring 1974), pp. 1ff.

78. William A. Gamson, *Power and Discontent,* pp. 50ff.

79. This is particularly unfortunate since a recent analysis by Edward N. Muller and Thomas O. Jukam, "On the Meaning of Political Support," *American Political Scien Review,* 71 (December 1977), 1561-1595, has demonstrated the analytical usefulness of a differentiated approach to the measurement of political support as the most general label for a whole family of related concepts.

80. Juergen Habermas, *Legitimationsprobleme im Spaetkapitalismus,* Frankfurt: Suhrkamp-Verlag, 1973; Claus Offe, *Strukturprobleme des kapitalistischen Staates,* Frankfurt: Suhrkamp-Verlag, 1972.

Chapter 3

MEASURING
POLITICAL ACTION

ALAN MARSH and MAX KAASE

INTRODUCTION

The previous chapter outlined our theoretical focus upon extending the analysis of political behavior beyond conventional forms such as voting, party support, and participation in campaigns to embrace new political dimensions arising from an increased use of direct action and protest tactics. Such an intent arouses a hornet's nest of methodological difficulties of both a conceptual and a technical nature. In particular, to develop a measure of the extent to which ordinary people feel disposed to engage in political protest activities may seem, at first acquaintance, a rather unpromising idea. What could such a measure mean? After all, proportionately few people regularly take any active role in conventional forms of political engagement such as attending meetings or helping in elections even though such activities are

AUTHORS' NOTE: Parts of the first two sections of this chapter were published in Alan Marsh, *Protest and Political Consciousness*, Beverly Hills: Sage, 1977. It should be noted throughout this text that whenever comparisons are made between the results obtained in the cross-national study and those described in the British study published by Marsh, certain key variables, e.g., "protest potential," "political trust," and so on, though having the same name, were calculated with different algorithms. The reader interested in following up such comparisons should check these differences carefully. We gratefully acknowledge permission to reprint these sections.

well-embedded rituals of the political process sanctioned by law, custom, and habit.

In most Western nations, low rates of conventional party activity support a papier-mâché edifice of "political life" that receives wide and continuous coverage by news media. It should, of course; it affects everyone. Yet it is given attention out of all proportion to the numbers of ordinary people who participate at what is called the grass roots of politics.

It would seem to follow from this that unconventional forms of political action, though also widely reported, involve even fewer participants. It is suspected by many that protests are usually carried out by a stage army of mostly left-wing students of hirsute appearance who represent no one but themselves. This view we may call the rent-a-crowd theory of political protest. It is a popular view and can be found even among academic observers of modern politics. Indeed, it is commonly supposed that a consensus of opinion exists in most Western democracies that authorities should have a fairly free hand to contain political irregularities of these kinds.

At the risk of appearing to erect a straw man, it is worth stating that we believe this concept to be mistaken. In our view, actual involvement in protest behavior may be contingent upon strong and hence infrequent stimuli, such as the location of a new airport or an atomic power station, the passing of laws related to powerful moral dilemmas such as abortion, the opposition to war, and so on. But the *potential to participate*, the individual readiness to be mobilized, is an abiding property of a wide sector of the whole political community, whether currently active or not. It is this property of attitude wedded to individual behavioral intentions that we need to measure. We shall now examine the practical case for doing so.

First, it may be argued that aggregate levels of individual behavior and events need not reflect aggregate levels of individual *readiness* to behave in certain ways should the occasion arise. For example, most people's readiness to defend themselves against assault remains undiminished even though they are never attacked. Is it then largely a matter of opportunity? It is true that outside of concentrations of disadvantaged minority groups or the student community, protest itself is not very frequent. But one could also ask how many civil authorities in Europe or America could now, say, build a new expressway through an established neighborhood and remain confident that their scheme would go unchallenged. It would surely founder not merely by attracting opposition from a "freak fringe" but also from a broad front among the local population. Events of these kinds are not rare. In recent years such events have often exposed operational inadequacies in the capacity of the conventional political system to deal with such political needs, especially in its speed of response. At the same time, often to the dismay of authorities, the alleged consensus among the wider community of nonactivists for draconian antiprotest measures has been known to evaporate in favor of calls for a fair hearing for protesters with an apparently just case, or even for those with an unpopular case who have been handled too roughly. It is our belief that slowly but surely during the last few years, the *idea* of unconventional political participation as a legitimate resource of democratic citizenship has spread out into the wider political community. Just as the 1968 student rebellion took political scientists unawares, we believe similar types of behavior less flamboyant in style but more serious in total impact have become a significant part of the political repertory of many ordinary people in diverse sectors of society.

No one suspected that the students and the blacks would revolt in the 1960s because, among other reasons, no one had ever attempted, seriously and scientifically, to measure either their capacity for protest or their desire for *this* kind of political redress and for the kinds of satisfactions protest can bring, beyond those attainable through the conventional pathways of political action.[1] We do not suggest that for the wider community some political Armageddon lies imminent but unheralded. We do suggest that the lesson should be learned and the assessment of this new—or, as many scholars insist, this revived—component of political action should become as commonplace among the tools of behavioral political science as are measures of voting behavior and of party system support.

In one sense at least, it does not really matter whether or not those individuals found to be *inclined* toward direct action and protest techniques subsequently get involved in acts of protest. Unlike voting or even a positive response to the abiding presence of party political activity within the local community, the acts of unconventional political behavior that we call protest are by their very noninstitutionalized nature acts that occur only if special events external to the individual call them forth. In contrast, party activity and the opportunity to vote occur regularly and predictably.

What we wish to measure, then, is the individual propensity to engage in unconventional forms of political behavior as a means of political redress, namely—and in brief—the use of such tactics as petitions, demonstrations, boycotts, rent or tax strikes, unofficial industrial strikes, occupation of buildings, blocking of traffic, damage to property, and personal violence. This tendency we shall call "protest potential." The conceptual and methodological development of our measure of protest potential will be unfolded in considerable detail later in this chapter.

As the previous chapter made clear, we conceptualize unconventional political action as an element of behavior within the political community that remains connected to the more familiar elements of representative democratic politics. It follows, therefore, that we need also to measure the extent to which individuals will participate in conventional forms of political behavior. In so doing we step back upon ground far more familiar to behavioral political scientists. The common practice, for example, is quite simply to ask people how *often* they read about politics in newspapers, discuss politics with others, seek to influence voting, contribute to work on community problems, attend political meetings, contact politicians or public officials, or spend time actually working for a political party or candidate. We see no compelling reasons to deviate from this practice, and such a measure of conventional political participation will be developed below alongside our measure of protest potential.

An issue not touched upon earlier, but which receives detailed treatment below, concerns what one might call the logical counterpoise of protest behavior. The extent to which political protest is likely to occur in a given situation does not depend wholly upon the interaction between the protest potential of those involved and the strength of the political stimulus they experience. It depends also upon a complementary interaction between the will and the means to resist possessed by the authorities and the support such resistance receives from those other members of the community not of the same mind as the protesters on the particular issue, or even from the alleged "Silent Majority" that is presumed to be in favor of strict and tangible means of social control for its own sake. From a measurement point of view, we shall not be content merely to know who has a low protest potential. We shall also want to know who would go further and sanction the authorities' use of such actions as encouraging police violence against demonstrators, judicial punishment, the use of troops to break strikes, and the banning of all public protest demonstrations.

These three components of political action—protest potential, conventional participation, and repression potential—form the basic "parameters of license" for protest. One might, of course, be equally interested in explaining parameters of license for repression potential or even conventional participation in such a triadic conceptualization. Our interest, however, is firmly focused upon trying to explain protest potential as it exists within the wider political community. This idea of parameters of license is introduced in order to clear up one of the major conceptual difficulties underlying the notion of a general measure of protest potential. This difficulty concerns the old and difficult puzzle in behavioral research of the relationship between attitudes and behavior. Although we have stated clearly our belief that a measure of potential to protest has its own face validity regardless of the chance opportunity to engage in actual protest, we must discuss this puzzle before introducing the actual measures designed for this study.

ATTITUDES, BEHAVIOR, AND THE
PARAMETERS OF LICENSE FOR PROTEST

Political participation has been used as a kind of crucible test by researchers interested in the attitude-behavior problem. When participation of a conventional kind is used as the dependent variable, quite a high degree of correspondence between attitudes concerning voting, campaigning, and so on and actual behavior is found.[2]

Unconventional political behavior has produced far more equivocal results. Wicker's rather gloomy review of the problem[3] picks out, among others, the finding of Carr and Roberts of poor relationships between attitudes favoring participation in civil rights demonstrations and actual participation by black students.[4] He gives prominence also to the well-known series of experiments conducted by DeFleur and Westie[5] and Lynn[6] that showed that young female undergraduates who indicated support for civil rights and promised to participate in an NAACP publicity campaign tended to backslide when confronted with a real opportunity to do so.[7] Wicker summarizes his review of the literature: "Taken as a whole, these studies suggest that it is considerably more likely that attitudes will be unrelated or only slightly related to overt behaviors than that attitudes will be closely related to actions."[8]

McPhail surveyed much of the quantitative literature assembled to explain participation by citizens in civil unrest in North American cities.[9] He found that only about 8 percent of the attitude material collected explained a significant proportion of the variance (that is, more than 9 percent) in the propensity to engage in riot behavior and concluded that far more realistic measures involving situational factors were necessary if social scientists were ever to achieve greater accuracy in the prediction of behavior. This view is not uncommon, but many researchers in the field have experienced more success than McPhail. Spilerman, for example, concluded from his study of black protest behavior: "An explanation which identifies *disorder-proneness* as an attribute of the individual seems better able to account for the findings" (emphasis added).[10] In general terms, McClosky too is optimistic: "It is . . . clear . . . that the survey method does not restrict the political scientist to the study of opinions and attitudes. Used imaginatively, it permits him to learn something about overt political behavior as well."[11]

Our own pilot work took this problem into account and followed a promising line of development indicated by Fishbein's research.[12] He proposes a model for behavioral prediction that accepts, as we do, the proposition that conscious behavioral dispositions are the nearest approximation to actual behavior that we may hope to predict. His results indicate that real improvements in prediction will occur, provided that measures of respondents' conscious behavioral intentions are qualified systematically by (1) beliefs about the social norms related to that actual behavior (and not some vague class of behaviors), (2) a sense of positive or negative *affect* toward the behavior, and (3) judgements about the *utility* of such behavior. Some of the essential features of the pilot model have survived intact for use in the main study and will be explained more fully below.[13]

In our view a genuinely direct relationship between attitude and behavior is neither possible nor perhaps even a desirable research goal to strive for. It is probably naive to expect that, if only our questionnaire measures could achieve the right level of complexity, the behavior of individuals in a given social context and known physical surroundings could be calculated accurately from a knowledge of their related attitudes. Most modern researchers know this to be true, but even in the academic community a strong expectation remains that only a very high correspondence between attitude and behavior will validate a given measure.

Certainly there is room for and indeed need for improvement where specific behavioral outcomes in emotionally charged areas of human activity are important to predict. But we are as much concerned here with these "parameters of behavioral license" that may exist among the population regarding the use of protest methods as we are with the likelihood of action among specific individuals. These parameters of license are the boundaries between endorsement and censure that are extended by the general population to protest campaigners (or, as Gamson calls them, active partisans[14]) that place popular constraints upon the extent of their use of protest methods. It is against an estimate of that threshold of disapproval that active partisans will calculate the point at which they might forfeit public sympathy for their cause through the unpopular extremity of their methods. It is, of course, the same point at which the authorities will be likely to start feeling confident at exercising their (theoretical) monopoly on legitimate violence because they begin to feel the weight of public support as they move to oppose the protesters. This is not to say that either party is particularly skilled at this calculation. The "Committee of 100" in Britain in 1962 miscalculated the parameters of license extended to their Gandhian "direct action" techniques used during the latter stages of the Campaign for Nuclear Disarmament. At Kent State University a National Guard commander tragically miscalculated his own license to oppose students protesting about the United States forces' incursions into Cambodia.

In support of this notion of parameters of license, evidence is available that changes in mass public opinion will result in changes in protest behavior in the same direction. Skolnick shows how increasing disapproval of the war in Vietnam was accompanied by a surge of protest behavior.[15] It may be argued that both public and activists were responding independently to the same increasingly unpleasant accounts of the conduct of the war. Skolnick gives this possibility due weight but concludes that the slow but steady growth of negative public sentiment was a major factor in launching the protest movement notwithstanding public support for police control of demonstrations. The activists sensed a powerful body of disquiet, confusion, and a lack of confidence in official explanations for what Skolnick calls "the War with time to think." The American public had no Pearl Harbor to assist an easy identification of the "right" side and found it difficult to identify the "succession of strongmen, juntas and shadow governments" with a democratic ideal in need of defense from communism. Thus they were receptive to counterargument, or at least appeared so to activists who were thus encouraged to persist.

It would be interesting to know the extent to which this is genuinely a two-way process. Berkowitz conducted an ingenious experiment into the local impact of protest against the Vietnam war.[16] Samples of spectators and nonspectators of an antiwar protest in a small town in the United States were asked to sign a peace petition and to accept a peace button to wear. The spectator sample comprised people who were watching or walking past the demonstration; the nonspectators were a roughly matched quota sample of people in the same town who had not seen the demonstration at all. Of the total *approached,* more people signed and accepted buttons among the spectator sample than those approached elsewhere. This was not true of the total who, having been approached, actually stopped and responded "yes" or "no" to the interviewer's invitation to sign a petition and accept a peace button to wear. Thus, more people deftly avoided the interviewer's approach (interviewers wore peace-buttons themselves) when there was no *event* to provide a context for the approach. This indicates that the impact of the demonstration was due more to the attention-getting properties of the event than to its potential to change attitudes.

It would be unwise to dismiss the possibilities of a two-way establishment of parameters of license on the basis of a single experiment. Quite possibly the protest movement had an aggregate effect on public opinion over a longer period. But the linkage that seems most plausible is this: activists and public respond independently at first to the stimulus for protest conveyed by the media. A few activists respond, probably with scant regard for public opinion. Their response amplifies media coverage of the stimulus and the public responds first by restating their overall parameters of license for the techniques chosen by the activists and then by modifying those parameters somewhat by their perception of the justice of the protest. The enhanced visibility of the movement promotes recruitment especially from sympathizers who already had a high protest potential. The linkage is of course immensely more complex than that suggested but this states the main strands of the process.

Eisinger's analysis of racial differences in protest behavior in the United States also suggests a similar socially embedded attitude-behavior linkage. His analysis of community politics in Milwaukee indicates that black activists are sensitive to the support of their wider community. Unlike white activists, blacks enter protest "assured of the broad-based support of their political community," whereas whites incur rather higher social and psychological costs and are therefore more likely to be strongly committed.[17] This suggests that whites' parameters of protest are less generous than those provided for blacks and hedge the white activist around with social inhibitions. Blacks are provided with far more permissive models for aggressive political behavior and their legitimate political reference groups now include the emergent and sometimes insurgent black African nations. In contrast, the relevant models and reference groups for young whites are law-abiding, conciliatory, and consensual: the white congress and state legislature, the white middle-class pressure groups, and so on.

It is being proposed, then, that there exist in the population invisible boundaries of behavioral license that play an important role in regulating the behavior of active partisans in the political area. Thus protest potential may be conceived of as a property of both the individual and of the political community. That is to say, personal norms of behavior contribute to community norms as well. It would be unwise to maintain that this attitudinal threshold for behavior is entirely unaffected by the issue at stake or by chance involvement: people do get "swept up" in movements. But again our pilot work indicated that people give more weight to the mode of behavior than the issue in whose cause it is adopted.

Lipsky has spelled out this indirect process in protest movements. Protest *targets* consist, almost invariably, of some agent or institution of authority.[18] The target is influenced, constrained, or actually coerced by expressions and acts of dissent by activists. These expressions and acts are amplified and also modified by the news media and diffused through community reference groups. So too are any responses made by the authorities, especially repressive measures taken by police or other bodies. This information is compared (by those who think about such things) with the established, long-term norms (parameters) for behavior and thus emerges an "issue-norm" (our term, not Lipsky's) that is communicated back along similar routes to activists. Frequent revisions of issue norms may in turn change parameters. It is a very complicated process and impossible to study through many simultaneous foci. This is why our approach to the problem must be carefully defined.

So what is more important: to study the individual's propensity to engage in protest or to describe this peculiar species of community norms called "parameters of license"? While both are equally important, this cross-sectional study will have to retain its focus upon the individual. The phrase "a high protest potential" will refer to a readiness of *individuals* to pursue political goals by direct means. If for no other reason, a psychological approach demands such a focus; but it is a deliberately "soft" focus. Our introduction of a partially indirect conceptualization of the attitude-behavior relationship serves to emphasize that people do not become mobilized out of a political void. There is a constant interplay between the individual's attitudes and the community's norms.

By way of summary, then, we can pinpoint our approach to the measurement of protest potential as an example of social psychology applied in the field of political science. Whereas we retain the focus of measurement and analysis upon the *individual* and thus accept the measurement of subjective political consciousness as valid, we conceive of that individual consciousness as both a *part* and a *product* of the political community to which the citizen belongs. Thus the expression of an intention to behave in a certain manner has social and political causes and consequences that must be weighted in the analysis alongside the consequences for individuals. In the long run, to try to know *exactly* who might be mobilized in protest behavior is possibly of marginal interest, except perhaps to the authorities, compared with the knowledge of how protest potential becomes concentrated among certain kinds of people who occupy certain social locations and are shaped by critical configurations of social experience and basic psychological dispositions.

PROTEST POTENTIAL

Development Work

The common basis for attitude scale construction in survey research is that respondents *evaluate* one or more *stimulus objects* that reflect the focal attribute of the underlying *dimension* of attitude that one wishes to estimate. Evaluative judgments may be obtained for *subdimensions* that may reflect components of a complex underlying dimension. Protest potential is just such a complex dimension and one that is also reflected by several stimulus-objects, that is, by examples of several different *kinds* of protest behavior. Much protest behavior is highly idiosyncratic and unsuitable for use in this way. Because the measure is to be used in several different countries, both stimuli and evaluative dimensions need to be as universal as possible while still reflecting the actual range of tactics protesters employ. At the same time, the stimuli have to be clear, simple, and unambiguous. Careful pilot work was necessary, not merely to meet the technical demands of scaling procedures but also to overcome a concern about the feasibility of a measure of protest potential. This concern rested upon the fear that, when asked to evaluate their conscious behavioral intentions toward, for example, lawful demonstrations, respondents would reply, very reasonably, "Well, it depends on what issue is at stake . . . , on what my personal involvement is . . . , or on what I feel about the value of others involved," and so on. Would people demand a context for evaluation?

The pilot study was conducted in Britain and is fully described elsewhere.[19] The main elements of this pilot work were then replicated in other countries in the study. The salient details are as follows.

The stimulus objects to be used were chosen a priori to represent a range of protest behaviors familiar to most people. For ease and simplicity of presentation each behavior was printed on a small card as shown in Figure 3.1.

The evaluative dimensions to be employed were not introduced a priori but were evolved from a repertory grid study of a prepilot sample. These dimensions—or constructs as they can also be called—were approval, justification, effectiveness, behavioral intentions ("would do"), legality, individual-mass, violence, and self-punishment. Four groups consisting of fifty students, fifty young workers, fifty older middle-class respondents, and fifty older working-class respondents were asked to evaluate each behavior on each

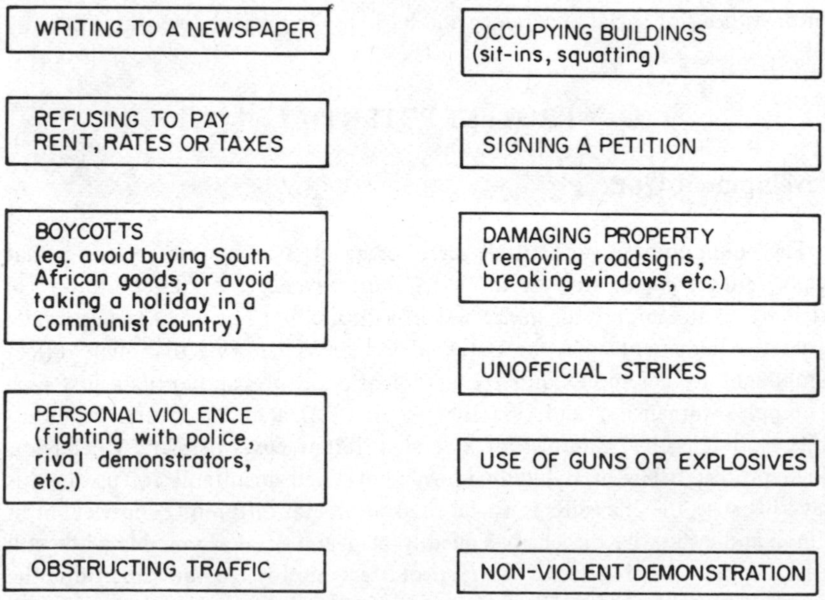

WRITING TO A NEWSPAPER	OCCUPYING BUILDINGS (sit-ins, squatting)
REFUSING TO PAY RENT, RATES OR TAXES	SIGNING A PETITION
BOYCOTTS (eg. avoid buying South African goods, or avoid taking a holiday in a Communist country)	DAMAGING PROPERTY (removing roadsigns, breaking windows, etc.)
	UNOFFICIAL STRIKES
PERSONAL VIOLENCE (fighting with police, rival demonstrators, etc.)	USE OF GUNS OR EXPLOSIVES
OBSTRUCTING TRAFFIC	NON-VIOLENT DEMONSTRATION

Figure 3.1

[66]

dimension. For the justification, effectiveness, and behavioral intention dimensions, these ratings were repeated for each of five hypothetical protest scenarios: a wage claim, an antiexpressway protest, an antidiscrimination campaign by blacks, a protest about an invasion of one country by the forces of another, and an anti-Common Market campaign—remember, all in a British context. Thus we hoped to detect whether different issue contexts would produce the predicted "it depends" effect.

A large amount of information was obtained quickly by the respondents sorting the cards onto a scale card designed as in Figure 3.2. This technique may appear to be unnecessarily brusque and to invite response-set. On the contrary, interviewers found that most respondents bent to their task with great interest. While shuffling cards around, they mused in a way that suggested a serious effort to place the cards in positions that accurately represented their views. Respondents were free to do so untroubled by the need to offer repeated responses to the interviewer as required by more conventional verbal procedures. In fact, the card sort provided many respondents with an ease of expression they may not otherwise have possessed. In cross-national attitudinal research the old maxim, "Least said the better," has a special force. Response-set was reduced by randomizing the order of evaluation from dimension to dimension.

The main results of this development study were twofold. First, different protest scenarios had very little impact upon the ratings given to each protest item on each of the three dimensions treated—justification, effectiveness, and behavioral intentions. Surprisingly—indeed, contrary to much attitude-behavior research—it was primarily the *principle* of the behavior that was evaluated rather than the issue-context in which it occurred. From a methodological point of view this result was excellent: any measure of protest potential developed from those items would be far more generalizable than might otherwise have been hoped.

Second, we found that underlying each of the subdimensions used was a very powerful single dimension of "positive-to-negative affect." This caused each of our very different target-groups to "line up" the items on a *single*

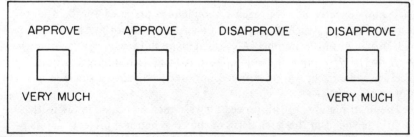

Figure 3.2

continuum from the relatively innocuous behaviors such as petitioning through increasingly severe forms of protest such as demonstrations, boycotts, strikes, occupations, blockades, damaging property, and violence. Students and workers, old and young, all possessed this same phenomenon of increasingly severe thresholds of protest, despite having themselves very different *levels* of behavioral intent. Many of the students would go all the way along the continuum, endorsing every item in sequence. Older workers rarely endorsed much beyond demonstrations. Everyone showed the same idea of a continuum, some merely going further along it than others. The juxtaposition of protest items and evaluative dimensions in effect posed the underlying question, "Think about political protest; how far are you prepared to go?" And respondents indicated, by their pattern of answers, "This far and no further." This is exactly the principle underlying the cumulative scaling procedures associated with the name of Louis Guttman.

Guttman scaling procedures have fallen into some disrepute in recent times. Those who now employ them must usually demonstrate very good reasons for doing so. Fortunately, we are able to meet stringent criteria to demonstrate the reliability of the various scales of attitudes toward protest behavior. Rarely do genuinely cumulative scales emerge as neatly from the data as did our protest potential scale. What this means, quite simply, is that items are first arranged in order from the most popular—petitions—through to the least popular—personal violence. If a truly unidimensional and cumulative scale exists, by knowing the "highest" item any respondent endorses— assuming the item scores to be dichotomized into approve-disapprove, or whatever dimension is used—then one also knows that the respondent endorses each of the items below that highest item and rejects every item above it. The coefficient of reproducibility (CR) measures the extent to which this is true throughout the sample. This statistic enjoys an indifferent reputation. While the normally accepted minimum CR value of .90 sounds quite stringent, it is in fact rather easy to obtain, especially when the two ends of the scale are marked by items having very skewed marginal distributions. Despite these shortcomings, cumulative scaling has definite advantages over the more common additive forms. Each point on the scale is labeled so one knows exactly how far each respondent is prepared to go in terms of concrete examples such as boycotts or strikes, and not just some arbitrary high, medium, or low number. Also isolated are those who would go nowhere at all. In the developmental study, Guttman-scaling techniques proved to be precisely the correct way to proceed in order to develop a single measure of protest potential.

The main features of this procedure were then replicated in Switzerland, a country included in the later stages of the cross-national project, Germany,[20] the Netherlands, the United States, and France, which is, alas, no longer with the project. In each country a very similar unidimensional *and* cumulative structure of attitudes toward these protest behaviors emerged.

Working concurrently with our pretest study, other researchers had arrived, quite independently, at a similar approach to the measurement of unconventional political behavior. Most closely related is Muller's work in Waterloo, Iowa, in which he presented very similar stimuli to his respondents but where each "threshold-point" on the scale is described in greater detail than in our study.[21] For example, his "Type III" threshold is described as follows: "Trying to stop the government from functioning by engaging in sit-ins, mass demonstrations, takeovers of buildings, and things like that."

Muller's scale traversed the distance from legal demonstrations to civil war ("Arming oneself in preparation for battles with government authorities such as the police or National Guard") and conformed to a unidimensional structure for both "approval" and "behavioral intentions," and these two dimensions he found sufficiently closely related to merit their inclusion in a combined scale.

O'Connor's study at the Universities of Essex, St. Andrews, and Montpellier also derived a unidimensional, cumulative structure from a ten-item scale of the extent to which students had attended a rally, petitioned, demonstrated (on campus, in town, or in the capital city), contributed to protest funds, had been arrested for civil disobedience, committed violence, and so on.[22]

The Main Project

The analysis of the pilot data determined the elements of the protest scales that were deployed in the cross-national questionnaire. The "use of guns or explosives" was dropped from the range of stimulus objects because it was almost impossible to find anyone—even the most radical of undergraduates—who would endorse their use. "Writing to a newspaper" was also dropped for exactly opposite reasons. The "non-violent demonstrations" item was changed to "lawful demonstrations." A new item, "painting slogans on walls," was added to the scale items. The card-sort technique was retained in the same form as in the pilot study.

Of the many subdimensions tested, three appeared clearly the most important. These are the following:

(1) "approval-disapproval": a generalized sense of positive-to-negative *affect*;
(2) "effective-ineffective": a *cognitive* dimension of perceived utility;
(3) "would do-would never do": that is, conscious *behavioral* intentions.

The questions asked were: "We would like to know how you feel about these things. Please place each of the little cards you have there on one of the parts of this card to show me." The card offered the following choices:

(1) "Whether, in a general way, you feel you approve strongly, approve, disapprove, or disapprove strongly"

(2) "The extent to which these actions may be *effective* when people use them in pressing for changes. Are they usually very effective, somewhat effective, not very effective, or not at all effective?"

(3) "Whether you have actually done any of these things on the cards *during the past ten years.* If not, the extent to which you feel you might do each of these things ["would do" or "might do"] or whether you would never, under any circumstances, do each of these things."

That these three dimensions should reflect the traditional social psychological formulation of the major components of attitude into affective, cognitive, and conative (action-related) elements is purely fortuitous but nonetheless gratifying.

Respondents were asked to indicate their views by sorting the protest example cards onto each of the three dimension-cards as before, but first they were asked to indicate whether there were any items they *failed to recognize.* This avoided the possibility that especially cooperative respondents would give ratings to objects about which they had no real ideas. Only the boycott item drew more than a few "Don't recognize" responses, and this mostly in mainland Europe where they averaged about 7 percent of each national sample. This result, simple enough in itself, is of more than methodological interest. It indicates support for our basic idea that a substantial level of consciousness about protest behavior has indeed permeated the wider political community. Everyone knows what protest behavior is, though not everyone will necessarily recognize it by that name.

Tables 2, 3, and 4 in the Technical Appendix show the distribution of views obtained from each national sample for each example of protest behavior on each of the three evaluative dimensions. Considering first the approval and behavioral dimensions, within each national sample, the following generalizations seem broadly true.

Petitions are universally acceptable means of protest, and lawful demonstrations are widely endorsed by substantial majorities. These two items appear to represent the first threshold of departure from conventional into unconventional political activity. It is important to note here that we consider petitions unconventional in the sense only that in at least three of the five countries—Britain, Germany, and Austria—there are sizable minorities who do not approve of and would under no circumstances sign petitions.

Whereas they lack the fullest possible endorsement by the mass publics of these countries, petitions are nevertheless so widely accepted and used that they constitute, as we will see shortly, the lowest, "easiest" point on all of the protest scales we constructed.

• The use of boycotts also receives widespread support, except in Austria, and is endorsed by between 35 percent and 50 percent of the respondents. Withholding rents and taxes as a form of protest is also accepted by quite large minorities, especially in the Netherlands. These two items—boycotts and rent strikes—form a second threshold representing an unequivocal entry into the use of protest methods.

• The occupation of adminstrative buildings or factory sit-ins receives limited support from quite significant minorities as does the practice of blocking traffic with an illegal street demonstration. Here we enter a third threshold of protest activity more commonly associated with a substantial commitment to direct action techniques or civil and political disobediance that often involves a deliberate infraction of the law. Not surprisingly, therefore, only about 15 percent of the people in our five-nation sample are seriously prepared to make a prior commitment to this kind of action. It is perhaps surprising that those figures are as high as they are. The obvious and remarkable exception to this are the Dutch respondents, of whom 42 percent approve of occupations and 22 percent of traffic blockades, while 25 percent and 14 percent, respectively, say they have done or would definitely do them.

• The position of "unofficial strikes" is more equivocal. In terms of "approval," such action is very unpopular, especially in Germany and, perhaps surprisingly, in Britain. Yet, in the face of their own disapproval, some people are prepared to contemplate taking such action and even more are prepared to admit that unofficial strikes can be effective.

• The ultimate threshold of protest activity in these five countries is clearly signalled by the universal condemnation heaped upon the use of personal violence, such as fighting with police or other demonstrators, and deliberate damage to property as a means of political protest. If further proof were needed, this result supports MacFarlane's view: "What we are normally confronted with in constitutional democracies is action directed not at the overthrow of the social system or the government but of particular government policies. Insofar as this requires widespread public support and approval for one's aims, it places a low premium upon violence."[2][3]

In view of the strong evidence that exists for very high rates of personal violence in American society and not least in American politics, compared with other countries in our study, it is perhaps surprising that the overwhelming majority who say they will never use violence is no smaller in America than in Europe. The level of positive support for damage and violence is so low that very little variance remains for survey analysis. Consequently, these items will play hardly any part in the analyses that follow.

One very surprising result was the similarly universal condemnation of "painting slogans on walls." Superficially, this activity seems harmless enough and sometimes amusing. We believed that it might even be acceptable to the majority because putting up posters and sloganizing is a common feature of political campaigns in both the orthodox and unorthodox spheres. The only reasonable conclusion to be drawn from this result is that most people regard the activity as a defacement of visual surroundings and thereby a public nuisance and many others may associate political daublings with graffiti other than the strictly political. Political activists, on the other hand, regard slogan-painting as immature, irresponsible, and ineffective. The technical outcome is that the item did not scale and will be excluded from future consideration in this analysis.

There are wide differences between countries. The Netherlands has by far the highest levels of approval and positive behavioral intentions toward protest, followed at some distance by the United States. Britain and Germany have similar and comparatively modest levels of protest potential, while among Austrians high protest potential is a rather rare phenomenon.

To discuss and analyze these differences item by item would be very unwieldly. Following the strategy developed in the pilot study, Guttman scaling procedures were again introduced to facilitate the development of a single cumulative score on the various dimensions of attitudes toward protest that might be assigned to each individual respondent on the basis of a consistent pattern of responses.

In each country, reliable Guttman scales were found for the remaining seven protest items for both the approval and behavioral intentions scores, in exactly the same way as was described above with respect to the pilot study. In all, three such Guttman scales were constructed:

(1) the protest approval scale (dichotomizing the "approval-disapproval" ratings);

(2) the would do protest scale (dichotomizing the behavioral intention ratings "have done/would do—might do/would never do"). This scale was designed to obtain the indicator closest to protest behavior since the scarcity of actual past participation in the majority of these direct action techniques we analyzed did not permit a scale solely based on past protest behavior;

(3) the might do protest scale (dichotomizing the behavioral intentions ratings "have done/would do/might do—would never do") to obtain a scale embracing all respondents who would, at least under extreme circumstances, consider engagement in the respective unconventional behaviors.

Guttman scales have a poor record for replication, both over time and cross-nationally, so this result was especially reassuring from a methodological point of view.

It was also found that the cumulative scores for approval were strongly correlated with the two behavioral intentions scales in each country as shown in Table 3.1.[24]

Considering the fact that both behavioral intentions scales are derived from the same set of questions it may appear surprising that they are only correlated at the .7 level. A look at Table 3 in the Technical Appendix reveals, however, that the inclusion or exclusion of the "might do" category involves quite substantial numbers of respondents, affecting the correlation between the two scales correspondingly. This is a consideration of some importance for the construction of our main dependent variable protest potential, to which we now turn.

We have pointed out before that our emphasis on protest *potential* takes into account theoretical, measurement-related, and practical considerations. In particular, it seemed desirable to develop a measure demanding a certain amount of cognitive constraint from respondents in order to guard against measurement artifacts and to comply as fully as possible with our attitude-behavior relationship model. The solution adopted to cope with these problems was to rely on the approval and behavioral intentions dimensions *at the same time* and to look for an algorithm to combine information on both to derive a single protest potential score. As a *theoretical* rationale, this strategy appears adequate to reliably assess protest potential. *Empirically*, the positive relationships between the approval and behavioral intention dimensions are sufficiently high, but also not too high, to justify combining the approval and behavioral intention scores into a single score. Unlike additive Likert-type scales or factor scores, however, this cannot be achieved simply by adding scores together, because the "labeling" advantage of cumulative scaling would

Table 3.1: INTERSCALE CORRELATIONS

Countries	Protest Approval vs. Would Do Protest		Protest Approval vs. Might Do Protest		Would Do Protest vs. Might Do Protest	
	$r =$	$N =$	$r =$	$N =$	$r =$	$N =$
The Netherlands	.58	1151	.57	1151	.73	1170
Britain	.53	1398	.56	1398	.71	1434
United States	.60	1618	.67	1618	.69	1643
Germany	.62	2216	.60	2216	.71	2249
Austria	.44	1270	.45	1270	.70	1331

be lost. A much better approach is to combine scores for each item and then recreate a single Guttman scale using the new dichotomized scores.

It is possible, either consciously or unconsciously, to adjust scale construction to favor an aggregate outcome. That is, a distribution of positive or negative views that is congruent with one's theoretical expectations, which in this case is that protest potential will be generally higher and more widespread than might be anticipated, especially in Europe. In order to guard against such manipulation, our scale construction procedures consequently *minimized* the possibility that positive scores would accumulate unless there was demonstrable proof that positive scores were appropriate.

The following demonstrates the options available in constructing a *protest potential scale* based on an evaluation of responses to both approval and behavioral intentions in regard to each of the seven protest activities.

(Potential) Participation	Approval				
	Approve Strongly	Approve	Disapprove	Disapprove Strongly	Don't Know
Have done	1	2	3	4	
Would do	5	6	7	8	
Might do	9	10	11	12	
Would never do	13	14	15	16	
Don't know					

In order to obtain a single yes or no score for each respondent and each protest activity, decisions had to be made in regard to three problems:

(1) the treatment of missing data,
(2) the definition of cutting points for both dimensions,
(3) the treatment of inconsistent response patterns.

The handling of missing data *for individual items* was easily determined. If a respondent had missing data on even one of the dimensions, a missing data value was assigned for that item. If a respondent had accumulated missing data for more than three of the seven activities scaled, a missing data value was assigned on the protest potential scale. If a respondent had one, two, or three missing data, the scaling algorithm provided a corrected score. (For a detailed discussion of the scaling algorithm see the Technical Appendix at the end of the book.)

The definition of the cutting points for each dimension did not pose major problems. For the approval dimension, the logical break was between the "approve" and the "disapprove" category. On the behavioral intentions dimension the "might do" category was the only one requiring some consideration. A glance at the marginals displayed in Table 3 in the Technical Appendix reveals that a decision to exclude this category would result in substantially reducing the number of those scoring "yes" on the various items in the scale (see also the Technical Appendix for the marginal distributions of the would do scale and might do scale). With our theoretical emphasis on the action repertory concept, that is, the willingness of individuals at least to consider seriously participation in acts of unconventional political behavior under extreme circumstances, the logical result was to include the "might do" responses in the pattern of answers indicating an affinity toward direct action techniques. We were, however, aware that these responses implied a reduced identification with these techniques. This point was consequently taken up in our reflections on the most difficult problem facing us: the treatment of inconsistencies between approval and behavioral intentions.

The inconsistencies we refer to involve those cells of the above diagram containing people who either approve of a given activity but would under no circumstances get involved in it (cells 13-14 of the diagram), or who did, would, or might get involved despite the fact that they disapproved of it (cells 3, 4, 7, 8, 11, and 12 of the diagram). Of those two sets of inconsistencies, the first (approval, yes; intention, no) was easily resolved in line with the theoretical emphasis on a behavior-repertory by scaling those respondents "no" because they clearly stated no inclination whatsoever toward actually participating in the respective activities. This left us with the group of respondents who indicated past behavior or behavioral intentions, but without approval. In this case, a point can be made for scaling such respondents "yes," this under the assumption that the behavioral inclination, especially in the repertory context, is more relevant for potential participation than the affective approval dimension. Whereas this argument might appear weak for the "might do—disapprove, strongly disapprove" respondents (cells 11 and 12), a strong case could be built for it with respect to the "do/would do—disapprove/strongly disapprove" respondents (cells 3, 4, 7, and 8).

In order to arrive at a solid base for the decision to be taken, we wondered what might bring people to engage in activities they disapproved or even strongly disapproved of. The first hypothesis refers to the manifest context of the questions. Although we have no systematic empirical evidence to back up this speculation, we are nevertheless inclined to argue that for a substantial number of respondents the discrepancy can be traced back to their implicit understanding of the questions as referring to an unusual *political* situation, such as a coup or the abolishment of civil liberties by an authoritarian regime. This is particularly likely in the German and Austrian cases, where the phrasing of the question particularly stressed the public and political context in which the activities were supposed to take place. Here we are probably facing a slight problem of indicator equivalence. If these speculations hold up, then we would not regard such respondents as commanding the political repertory we are trying to measure.

The second hypothesis with respect to this discrepancy was one we were able to test empirically. Our analysis first of all assumed that the lack of consistency between approval and behavioral intentions was caused by the assessment of the effectiveness of these direct action techniques. The argument here is that a citizen, though basically disapproving of such techniques, might nevertheless be willing to engage in them because they were felt to be highly effective. Following this argument, six groups of respondents were defined by combining the approval and behavioral intention ratings for each of the seven activities, as follows:

	Approval	*Behavioral Intention*
Group 1	Approve	Did/Would Do
Group 2	Disapprove	Did/Would Do
Group 3	Approve	Might Do
Group 4	Disapprove	Might Do
Group 5	Approve	Would Not Do
Group 6	Disapprove	Would Not Do

Our expectation was that, should there indeed be an indirect impact on the responses to both dimensions of the effectiveness assessments, the mean effectiveness ratings for each activity (scored four to one, very effective to not at all effective), in particular for Group 2 but also for Group 4, would be close to the respective effectiveness means of Group 1 and Group 3. However, this expectation was in no way borne out by the data. Rather, in every country and for every activity, the means followed an extremely consistent pattern: Group 1 and Group 3, with an average .2 lower mean, had by far the highest effectiveness means, thereby indicating that protest approval and high effectiveness ratings tend to go together.[25] By contrast, the mean effectiveness scores for Groups 2 and 4 were, on the average, between .6 and 1.0 lower than the means for Group 1. The extent to which the approval rating determines the effectiveness rating of the direct action techniques is further demonstrated in Group 5. Here the effectiveness ratings are slightly but consistently higher than those for Groups 2 and 4. The finishing touch to this analysis is provided by Group 6, that is, respondents who neither approve of nor are behaviorally inclined toward the direct action techniques in question. Consistently, for each activity and in each country, this group displays by far the lowest mean effectiveness rating among the six groups. As the result of this analysis, we can clearly state that the effectiveness dimension does not account for the disapproval-behavioral intentions discrepancy.

Our interpretation of these results is that the observed inconsistency is systematically related to a certain lack of familiarity with some of the direct action techniques we are studying. This interpretation is sustained by further empirical evidence. First, we observed that the variance of the effectiveness ratings for Group 2 (disapprove—did/would do) is, on the average, substantially higher than the variance for the consonant Group 1 (though this in part may be attributed to the small size of Group 2 and the resulting higher sampling error). Second, and more important, we found that the percentage of discrepancies in relation to the total number of respondents in the respective behavioral intentions categories substantially increases once we move beyond petitions, demonstrations, and boycotts.

In addition to these analyses encouraging a decision to resolve the observed approval-behavioral intentions discrepancies in favor of the affective approval dimension, we want to stress once again our theoretical emphasis on consistency in accordance with the Fishbein-Azjen model of behavioral predictions guiding our pretest work. Our concept of the political repertory that a citizen is able and, under certain circumstances, is likely to bring into the political process requires an operational approach that does not make it too easy for a citizen to be counted among those prone to direct action. *Given this theoretical framework and the empirical analyses just reported, it was decided that whenever discrepancies between the affective and conative dimensions toward direct-action techniques occurred these discrepancies would be resolved by assigning a negative response for the respective item.*

This is how the scaling algorithm for the protest potential scale finally looked:

(Potential) Participation	Approval Approve Strongly	Approve	Disapprove	Disapprove Strongly	Don't Know
Have done	yes	yes	no	no	
Would do	yes	yes	no	no	Missing
Might do	yes	yes	no	no	Data
Would never do	no	no	no	no	
Don't know	Missing Data				

Before discussing the resulting protest potential scale, it is useful to consider some of the consequences of the decision in favor of this particular scaling algorithm. The consistency requirement affects the critical categories of the behavioral intentions dimension—"have done/would do" and "might do" in different ways. As one would expect, the "have done/would do" category definitely indicates a strong commitment to the respective direct-action technique. This is not only reflected in the smaller number of respondents voicing an inclination toward such techniques, but also by the fact that the percentage of those affected by the consistency requirement is small for the three most common direct-action techniques—petitions, demonstrations, and boycotts. On the average, about 2 percent of each national sample and 10 percent of the behavioral intentions category are involved; somewhat more are involved for the other techniques—on the average, approximately 5 percent of each national sample and 30 percent of the respondents in the category. These numbers increase substantially, however, once we move to the "might do" category. Here, an average of 10 percent of each national sample and 60 percent of the respondents in the "might do" category are affected.

By comparison, we are dealing with much lower numbers when we consider those respondents who, though they approve of a given direct action technique, do not show any inclination to make use of it themselves. Thus, the effect of our scaling algorithm is to curtail the behavioral inclinations dimension, thereby reducing the variance this dimension can contribute to the protest potential scale. This is evident when we look at the correlations between the protest potential scale and the three other protest scales.

In every instance except for the might do protest scale in Austria, the protest potential scale is more strongly related to the affective than to the conative dimension of direct action. Whereas the differences in correlations do not look conspicuously high, it must be kept in mind that small changes in correlations at the absolute level of magnitude we are facing have a substantial impact with respect to the changes in explained variance; as one example, in the Netherlands protest potential and would do protest share 53 percent of the variance while protest potential and protest approval share 67 percent of the variance, a 14 percentage point difference, though the absolute difference in correlations is only .09.

Table 3.2: **CORRELATIONS OF PROTEST POTENTIAL SCALE**

	Approve Protest Scale		Would Do Protest Scale		Might Do Protest Scale	
	$r =$	$N =$	$r =$	$N =$	$r =$	$N =$
The Netherlands	.82	1149	.73	1149	.78	1143
Britain	.79	1398	.68	1398	.78	1398
United States	.90	1615	.69	1615	.79	1615
Germany	.91	2212	.72	2212	.73	2212
Austria	.72	1267	.67	1267	.75	1267

However, the larger impact of the affective dimension on the protest potential scale should not be misinterpreted as a lack of behavioral components in that scale. These components are clearly there, and we maintain that the scale has exactly the qualities we demanded: it provides us with a maximally reliable measure of behavioral predispositions with respect to direct-action techniques.

We now turn to the protest potential scale itself.[26] Table 3.3, Part A, shows the Guttman scales that emerged in each national sample. The ordering of the items is not always quite the same. In each country the first four points on the scale are identical, that is, "no protest," "petitions only," "lawful demonstrations," and "boycotts." "Rent strikes" occupy either the fifth or sixth point and "unofficial strikes" either the seventh or last, that is, the most extreme position. "Occupations" and "street blockades" are more problematic, occurring at points ranging from fifth to last. These idiosyncracies are caused by two factors. First, they are caused by random sample variation because of the low proportion of positive responses associated with each of the more extreme items, and, second, by systematic sample variation caused in turn by the differing functional equivalence of the stimulus-object from country to country. Is an "occupation" viewed as the same thing in the Netherlands as in the United States? No, it is not, for it probably does not have connotations of violence to the same degree in the Netherlands as it does in the United States. Nevertheless, the position taken here is that the *dimension* is certainly functionally equivalent from nation to nation and that protest potential scores should be assigned on a country-specific basis, item for item as they occur in each national sample as in Table 3.3, Part B.

We find the similarities between the national scales to be much more impressive than the differences. The presence in each country of a unidimensional cumulative scale reinforces our view that the idea of protest potential is indeed a universal phenomenon in Western democratic politics.

The highest levels of protest potential obviously exist in the Netherlands where 31 percent of the total population will venture beyond even demonstrations and boycotts into more extreme forms of protest. The Netherland's reputation as a "permissive" polity is plainly justified by these data, but it is also difficult to think of the Dutch as an "aggressive" group of people. This encourages us in the belief that we are measuring mature sociocentric political attitudes rather than idiosyncratic, egocentric sources of truculence and aggression. Further evidence for this is presented later (see chapter 5). The United States has as few people as the Netherlands who will go no further than signing petitions, though fewer Americans than Dutch will venture beyond the use of boycotts.

Germany and Britain have almost identical distributions, with, respectively, 40 percent and 45 percent inactive (compared with 30 percent among

Table 3.3: PROTEST POTENTIAL SCALE

A) *Rank Order of Items*

	1	2	3	4	5	6	7
The Netherlands	Petitions	Demonstrations	Boycotts	Occupations	Rent Strikes	Blockades	Unofficial Strikes
Britain	Petitions	Demonstrations	Boycotts	Rent Strikes	Blockades	Occupations	Unofficial Strikes
United States	Petitions	Demonstrations	Boycotts	Rent Strikes	Occupations	Unofficial Strikes	Blockades
Germany	Petitions	Demonstrations	Boycotts	Rent Strikes	Blockades	Unofficial Strikes	Occupations
Austria	Petitions	Demonstrations	Boycotts	Blockades	Rent Strikes	Unofficial Strikes	Occupations

B) *Guttman-Scale Scores*

	0 (No Protest)	1	2	3	4	5	6	7 (High)	CR	Percentage of Nonscalable Respondents	N =
The Netherlands	9	20	25	15	11	7	7	6=100%	.94	4	1149
Britain	23	22	25	15	7	3	2	3	.95	6	1398
United States	9	21	24	26	8	6	3	3	.96	6	1615
Germany	19	21	29	19	5	3	2	2	.97	5	2212
Austria	21	33	26	11	5	2	1	1	.97	20	1267

the American and Dutch), and they have 12 percent and 15 percent in the highly active categories. In Austria, however, high protest potential is a rare phenomenon, with 54 percent inactive and only 9 percent highly active.[27] Yet we should not focus too strongly upon those scoring high on the scale. In every country a large proportion—usually a majority—of the total population gives a commitment to the prospect of at least joining a lawful demonstration or even supporting a boycott. While only marginally unconventional, such a behavior is a strong act of protest for most people and its significance should not be underestimated. Moreover, as we shall see below, the strong behavioral emphasis of the protest potential measure tends to exclude nearly everyone over fifty from higher levels of protest potential; hence the levels of protest potential among that proportion of the population even marginally available for mobilization is really much higher than might have been expected. This is also supported by the fact that overall rates of approval tend to be higher than rates of behavioral commitment, indicating a more positive climate of opinion among those unable to participate for practical reasons of age, infirmity, remoteness of dwelling, family commitment, and so on.

Protest Potential and the Effectiveness of Protest

The "effectiveness-of-protest" scores did not conform to Guttman scale criteria. Careful inspection of the data (see Table 4 in the Technical Appendix for the marginal distributions) revealed that the *internal* structure of the effectiveness dimension contained subtle but important deviations from a true cumulative pattern. The most significant of these deviations involved people who regarded occupations, traffic blockades, and violence as *effective* and petitions and lawful demonstrations as *ineffective*, thus accumulating an unacceptably high number of "errors" in the response patterns. That a certain contempt for the effectiveness of "moderation" should form part of the attitude of "militants" would surprise no popular commentator on the subject. Rather than viewing this finding as some lamentable technical deficiency, it seems possible that this difference in attitude structure may tell us something.

The scaling model to which the effectiveness scores do conform is the additive Likert scale. The items are evenly correlated and in a factor analysis tap a strong common factor. This factor accounts for an average of 40 percent of the *total* variance in the five countries. Not unexpectedly, of the seven action techniques, only six load on this factor; of those, "demonstrations" regularly display the lowest loading though it never drops below .53. The second, much weaker factor, which accounts for an average 18 percent of the *total* variance, is primarily determined by "petitions" and, to a lesser extent, by "demonstrations." This finding reinforces our observation that, in effectiveness, both action techniques—but "petitions" in particular—follow a different rationale, a point to which we will return shortly.

Based on this analysis a mean effectiveness of protest index was constructed by using the full range of effectiveness ratings and computing a mean index of the effectiveness scores for six of the seven direct action techniques appearing in the protest potential scale, excluding petitions for reasons already hinted at above.

The reasoning that connects the belief in the effectiveness of an act—its "perceived utility," in theoretically precise terminology—to the performance of the same act rests in the widest sense upon learning theory. Specifically, the argument is derived from those aspects of learning theory that stress the power of positive reward ("reinforcement") to increase the likelihood of a repetition of the rewarded act in the future. This tendency will generalize to other examples of the class of behaviors to which the rewarded act may belong and will do so according to a lawfully decremental response-generalization curve. These are the two cardinal principles of operant conditioning theory. Thus if activists come to believe—and it need not be true—that participation in, say, a sit-in demonstration in government offices has proved to have a high utility in pressing political demands, then they will engage in more behavior of this kind in the future provided there is no marked decrement in related sources of motivation. Also, the high perceived utility of this act will generalize to similar acts like street blockades, factory occupations, picketing, or even boycotts—thus making their occurrence more likely. Although the sterner elements of the behaviorist school would not find it admissible, we feel reasonably confident that, in human beings, vicarious reward learning is a reality. To use one example, as one group of students wrests concessions from the university's disciplinary board by forceful means,

Table 3.4: **CORRELATION OF PROTEST POTENTIAL SCALE WITH MEAN EFFECTIVENESS OF PROTEST INDEX**

	$r =$	$N =$
The Netherlands	.65	1124
Britain	.47	1382
United States	.55	1591
Germany	.59	2169
Austria	.49	1226

so others will be persuaded of the effectiveness of such acts and be encouraged to do something similar.

Such straightforward Skinnerian hypotheses may seem too obvious to bear spelling out like this. The results of the analysis certainly appear uncontroversial. In each country, the belief that protest tactics are effective is strongly associated with a high protest potential (see Table 3.4). There seems at first glance nothing complex about such a relationship. Yet it merits some careful study. Those who score *high* on the protest potential scale believe that all the items on the scale are effective. They also believe that petitions are somewhat effective but *less* so than those scoring in the middle range of protest potential. Probably for different reasons, they share a certain skepticism about petitions with those who score *lowest* on the protest potential scale. Those scoring in the middle range of the scale tend to believe that occupations (but not blockades) are effective, even though they are not themselves prepared to go that far. Paradoxically, they are considerably *less* likely than are the more active protesters to believe that demonstrations are effective even though they endorse their use for themselves. Those scoring lowest on the protest potential scale are fairly agreed that none of the items is effective, save perhaps for petitions.

All this seems sensible. But considered on the aggregate level of analysis it gives rise to an apparent paradox: the majority of respondents tend to favor only the most moderate forms of protest. They also believe that petitions and demonstrations are *effective* means of protest and that occupations and strikes are not. If people are taking a very broad view, they may be correct to believe that a very rapid spread of extreme forms of political protest may become self-defeating by attracting more repression than concession, thus destabilizing the system for no tangible gain. Yet, within the short-term perspective that our respondents were asked to consider, petitions, at least by themselves, are simply not a very effective means of protest compared with more vigorous forms such as strikes. So why should 70 percent to 80 percent of respondents have said they believed that petitions were an effective means "of pressing for changes?" Far fewer people thought strikes effective; these, of course, were those people who endorsed their use.

The most likely explanation for what we have found is that, item-for-item, effectiveness scores do predict protest potential for action-prone citizens and that the scale effect emerges because those who disapprove of protest abandon objectivity to use their effectiveness evaluation to reinforce their negative views. To say "It doesn't do any good anyway" emphasizes their scorn. This result is akin to Blumenthal's finding that for many people "police beating students" is not "violence," because violence is a negative concept that they could not bring themselves to apply to an activity they strongly approved.[28] In the same way, the powerful affective dimension traversed by low-to-high protest potential conditions people's responses to what should be an uncomplicated cognitive evaluation. Such things, however, are rarely straightforward. To admit that an activity of which one disapproves is nonetheless effective implies a degree of informed ruefulness that does not come easily to most people. Only demonstrations and unofficial strikes attracted this view in any significant proportion of the samples, and this mostly in Britain and the Netherlands.

Conventional Political Participation

We included as conventional political participation primarily those acts of political involvement directly or indirectly related to the electoral process.[29] Consequently, our respondents were asked to report how often they read political views in the newspapers, discussed politics with friends, tried to convince friends to vote as they did, attended political meetings, contacted officials, or spent time working for a party or a candidate in an election. Following Verba and Nie, we also inquired about how often the interviewees contributed to political efforts to solve community problems.

Each national distribution of the frequency with which people claim to participate in conventional forms of political behavior is presented in Table 1 in the Technical Appendix.

The United States and Germany clearly show the highest levels of participation, though even in Germany these are not very high in absolute terms; the majority of respondents in both countries rarely go further than informing themselves about politics and discussing it with friends. In Austria, Britain, and the Netherlands, one may be forgiven for speculating a moment about how the business of representative parliamentary democracy is ever carried out. The "grass roots" of politics seem shriveled and starved of the nourishment of participation by the citizens. Only one-third of the Austrians and one-quarter of the Britons and the Dutch *ever* attend a political meeting and only 2 percent do so often. Only 7 percent of the Britons ever participate in an election campaign compared with 22 percent of German and 29 percent of American respondents. This replicates the finding of Almond and Verba that participation in America and Germany was more frequent than in Britain.[30]

A similar transformation was then applied to these seven items as was used for our various scales on attitudes toward unconventional political participation. The responses on each of the items were dichotomized: "often" and "sometimes" were scored "yes"; "rarely" and "never" were scored "no"; and these newly created dichotomized items were then submitted to Guttman scale analysis (see the Technical Appendix for the details of scale construction).

Table 3.5: CONVENTIONAL POLITICAL PARTICIPATION SCALE

A) Rank Order of Items

	1	2	3	4	5	6	7
	Read About Politics in Papers	Discuss Politics With Friends	Work on Community Problems	Contact Politicians or Public Officials	Convince Friends to Vote as Self	Participate in Election Campaign	Attend Political Meetings
The Netherlands							
Britain	Read	Discuss	Community	Contact	Convince	Attend	Campaign
United States	Read	Discuss	Community	Campaign	Contact	Convince	Attend
Germany	Read	Discuss	Convince	Attend	Campaign	Community	Contact
Austria	Read	Discuss	Attend	Convince	Community	Campaign	Contact

B) Guttman-Scale Scores

	0 (No Participation)	1	2	3	4	5	6	7 (High)	CR	Percentage of Nonscalable Respondents	N =
The Netherlands	29	21	30	8	5	2	1	4=100%	.95	1	1194
Britain	28	25	31	7	4	1	1	3	.95	2	1460
United States	16	18	24	12	9	8	7	6	.91	0	1713
Germany	23	32	17	9	5	4	4	6	.94	1	2295
Austria	34	23	22	7	4	3	2	5	.94	0	1577

The most important result of this analysis is that the seven items of conventional political involvement also form a single unidimensional and cumulative scale indicating "how far one will go" along the orthodox pathways of political involvement. Comparing the resultant scales cross-nationally some problems arise concerning the item ordering. In each country, "no participation," "read about politics in the newspapers," and "discuss politics with friends" form the first three points on the scale. From then on almost every possible sequence of activities occurs. This is due, even more so than in the case of the protest potential scale, to the very low number of positive responses given to the more active examples. No more than 6 percent of respondents in any country will engage in every aspect of conventional participation. But this also means that about 60 percent to 80 percent of respondents in each country are identified by the first three points on the scale. Thus it seems justifiable to use each national scale as a functionally equivalent score.

Before considering more substantive issues, it is worth noting that the unidimensional model of conventional political participation has been strongly challenged by the work of Verba and Nie in the United States.[31] They claim that a four-factor model is more appropriate. The quadrants they describe are: voting, campaigning, communal activity, and particularized contacting. Our data corroborate their findings in one particular. Voting did not "fit" the unidimensionality requirements in the various factor and Guttman scale analyses we performed before the final version of the scale was constructed. But this is a result that may also be arrived at quite easily by theoretical deduction. With reflection it becomes apparent that voting is a unique form of political behavior in the sense that it occurs only rarely, is highly biased by strong mechanisms of social control and social desirability enhanced by the rain-dance ritual of campaigning, and does not involve the voter in major informational or other costs. A similar assessment of the act of voting is presented by Verba and Nie, who write: "The regularity with which they [voting specialists] vote contrasted with the fact that they attempt to influence the action of government in no other way makes it appropriate to consider them 'voting specialists'."[32] As a consequence, we did not include "voting" in our conventional political participation scale.

But even without "voting," the American scale is certainly the weakest compared to the four European countries (CR = .91 compared to .94 in Germany and Austria and .95 in Britain and the Netherlands). If one dug vigorously enough into the factor structure of the American data, one would probably find traces of the Verba and Nie multifactor model; but, clearly, in Europe the unidimensional model is a fully appropriate way to proceed. It is possible that the tendency toward fragmentation of activity in America is associated with the multiple cleavages of ethnic, regional, and interest group pressures that characterize American politics and that contrast so strongly with the dominant class and religious cleavages that characterize the four European countries in our study.

Beyond this substantive interpretation, of course, there has to be kept in mind that Verba and Nie started out conceptually with a multifactor model that is reflected in the much broader set of activities they included in their study. In this sense, it was almost inevitable that they also ended up empirically with a multifactor model of conventional political participation.

Repression Potential

We will now conclude the development of measures reflecting our conceptualization of "parameters of license" for political action and consider the opposite boundary fence of protest potential: repression potential. Unlike protest and conventional participation, individual citizens can rarely be said to participate personally in repressive acts of social and political control. Political vigilantism can occur, of course. Hard-hatted manual workers have been known to intervene in student demonstrations, strike-breaking has always been common, and unpopular protest movements like pacifist organizations during wartime sometimes suffered a rough handling by outraged citizenry often with the winking collusion of the authorities. When Bertrand Russell was being beaten' by antipacifist rioters who broke up his meeting called to oppose conscription during World War I, one of his lady followers succeeded in securing police assistance for him only after pointing out that he was the brother of an Earl. Such opportunities, however much their prospect may be relished by those of a retributive disposition, are not common, and, more importantly, they can rarely be generated independently of a specific act of protest. The job is usually left to the authorities. Therefore, we have conceptualized repression potential as the tendency to grant authorities increasingly severe instruments of control to contain correspondingly severe challenges by protesters, strikers, or other unorthodox activists. Since allegiance to an authority figure is so obviously implied by such a tendency, we may say that, whereas protest is *un*orthodox political behavior and conventional participation is *orthodox,* repression potential is *super*orthodox political behavior. It is perhaps vicarious in character, but it must have a strong quasi-behavioral element for many people. The four questionnaire items chosen to represent this tendency are the following.

(1) the courts giving severe sentences to protesters who disregard the police;
(2) the police using force against demonstrators;
(3) the government using troops to break strikes;
(4) the government passing laws to forbid all political demonstrations.

Respondents were asked to indicate the extent to which they approved of each kind of event. The distributions obtained are given for each country in Table 5 in the Technical Appendix.

The scores obtained were dichotomized (approve very much + approve versus disapprove + disapprove very much) and submitted to the same Guttman scale procedure described for the protest potential scale and the conventional political participation scale (see the Technical Appendix for the details of scale construction).

Again, the results are positive and possess levels of reliability much more akin to the protest potential than the conventional political participation scale. The four items form a unidimensional and cumulative measure of "how far the government ought to go" in opposing unorthodox political action by others. The comparative results are given in Table 3.6.

Of the three political action scales, the repression potential scale has the most divergent cross-national item-ordering. In each nation, the legal sanctions of the courts are people's chosen first line of defense against politically disruptive behavior, except in the United States where the police are thrust into this role first and the courts are second. In the Netherlands and Britain, the police are placed second in line and in Britain and the United States the use of troops to break strikes and a total government ban on all demonstrations are less popular, in that order.

In Germany and Austria, the patterns are different. Although dissimilar in their rates of participation in both protest and conventional behavior, they are agreed that a total ban on all political demonstrations is preferable to the use of police or troops. This is a most interesting result. From one point of view it may be argued that this result arises from weaker democratic traditions in Germany and Austria. Whereas the strident public democracies of the United States, Britain, and the Netherlands have raised the right to demonstrate, even at the risk of a police baton, to an inalienable status, the citizens of Germany and Austria are apparently still willing to sign away their civil liberties in exchange for a quiet life. This argument has a certain intuitive appeal, but we believe, it indicates a superficial and ultimately a wrong conclusion. This apparent authoritarian lapse by German and Austrian respondents may certainly be associated with their modern political histories, but it is more likely to reflect a rejection of that historical experience than the acceptance of any continuing retributive tradition. First, one may note a certain logical consistency in that two kinds of legal sanction (courts and legal prohibition) are preferred before two kinds of official violence (police and troops). One then has to recall *whose* police and *whose* troops it was that have provided the model for the exercise of this kind of coercion by the regime on the streets of these countries. It may then be self-evident why Germans and Austrians might prefer first the courts and then the government

Table 3.6: REPRESSION POTENTIAL SCALE

A) Rank Order of Items

	Courts Punish Demonstrators	Police Use Force Against Demonstrators	Troops Used to Break Strike	Government Ban on All Political Demonstrations	N =
The Netherlands	Courts	Police	Troops	Ban	1194
Britain	Police	Courts	Troops	Ban	1460
United States	Courts	Ban	Police	Troops	1713
Germany	Courts	Ban	Troops	Police	2295
Austria					1577

B) Guttman-Scale Scores

	0 (No Government Action Sanctioned)	1	2	3	4 (All Government Actions Sanctioned)	CR	Percentage of Nonscalable Respondents
The Netherlands	47	23	13	12	5=100%	.94	6
Britain	12	15	28	27	18	.95	7
United States	18	16	28	20	18	.95	5
Germany	19	18	18	19	26	.93	5
Austria	17	20	14	21	28	.91	9

to blow the whistle, as it were, upon political developments that threaten to get out of hand before resorting to forces whose history is, to say the least, ambivalent.

On the aggregate level of comparison, there is little evidence to support a view that repression potential is inherently greater in Germany and Austria. Comparing Germany and Austria with the two most "traditionally" demo-cratic countries, Britain and the United States, we do find that 26 percent to 28 percent will go all the way with repressive measures compared with 18 percent. Combining those reaching point three on the scale, however, the figures in the four countries are very similar, ranging from 38 percent in the United States to 49 percent in Austria. At the other end of the scale, the four countries differ scarcely at all in the proportion that would sanction no counteraction against protesters. In fact, it is in Britain that this proportion is lowest at only 12 percent.

This result seems to dent Britain's reputation as a tolerant polity. On the other hand, it is possible to argue that in Britain the use of police against demonstrators or even the use of troops to provide essential services during the miners' strike—an issue current during the survey period—provides a far less draconian spectacle than the work of riot police or National Guardsmen elsewhere. British policemen are not always pleasant to demonstrators, but they are rarely armed and bodily harm is rarely suffered.[33]

Self-evidently, the key feature of Table 3.6 is the extraordinarily deviant case of the Netherlands. In measuring attitudes within relatively homoge-neous countries one seldom uncovers differences between countries as spec-tacular as this. Whereas in the other four countries between 12 percent and 19 percent will sanction no counteraction against unruly demonstrators, in the Netherlands this figure is 47 percent. Conversely, whereas between 38 percent and 49 percent of people elsewhere will sanction all or most of these repressive measures, only 17 percent will do so in the Netherlands. Recalling that the Netherlands also revealed the highest protest potential, though not at all the highest levels of conventional participation, we may say that what we have called the parameters of license for unconventional political behavior yawn wide in the Netherlands—far wider than they do in the other four countries.

Suspending judgment on whatever compositional effects may—and in fact do—contribute to this vast cross-national deviance until the next chapter, we feel that, like the Austrian and German item-ordering, this result too may have its origins in World War II. Forms of civil disobedience were linked in many people's experience with the Resistance Movement in the Netherlands. For example, it is said that when the Nazis ordered all Jews to wear a yellow Star of David on their sleeves to identify them in public, half the gentile population of Amsterdam emerged from their homes the following day wearing the yellow star armbands. Public resistance to authoritarian and repressive actions generally, and to those enacted by uniformed agents of political authority in particular, has achieved an extraordinarily high level of positive affect within the Dutch political value-system through this kind of association. It may even be argued that protest has been institutionalized in Dutch politics to an extent that it may weaken its conceptual status as unconventional behavior in that country.

The relationship between protest potential and repression potential is of course a negative one. Consistently in each country those who favor protest methods as a means of political redress tend also to disapprove of the use of repressive countermeasures by authorities, while those opposing protest tend to favor repression.

In the four European countries the magnitude of this relationship is a moderate one. This indicates a consensual opinion that many people are prepared to support moderate levels of protest behavior provided the authorities have sufficient resources to prevent things from "getting out of hand." This view is far more prevalent in the Netherlands than the marginal distributions would indicate. Also, many of those with a high protest potential concede that the normative framework of the law is a legitimate resource of society and are prepared to accept the lawful consequences of unlawful acts. Indeed, much of the literature on the philosophy of civil and political disobedience stresses that the acceptance of punishment for an unlawful act of protest is *part* of the protest itself.[34] It is a common political experience that some protesters in a moral cause will show a distinct eagerness to go to jail for their beliefs and thus draw greater public attention and sympathy to their campaign.

In the Blumenthal et al. study of attitudes toward violence among American men, two scales were used that bear close comparison with our protest and repression scales.[35] They called these "violence for social change"

Table 3.7: **CORRELATION OF REPRESSION POTENTIAL SCALE WITH PROTEST POTENTIAL SCALE**

	r =	N =
The Netherlands	-.33	1096
Britain	-.35	1329
United States	-.51	1564
Germany	-.35	2136
Austria	-.27	1185

(riotous public behavior) and "violence for social control" (severe police and National Guard actions against demonstrators, and so on). To their evident surprise, these two scales were only weakly related in the expected negative direction, having a gamma coefficient of only $-.2$. In our American sample, the negative correlation between the analogous protest and repression scales is actually much higher than in Europe ($r = -.51$, gamma $= -.51$). Blumenthal's survey team interviewed only men but this is not the source of the discrepancy between our findings and theirs. In the United States and in Europe there are no significant differences between the sexes on this measure. Since Blumenthal's scales measured attitudes toward more extreme kinds of behavior than ours, an even stronger negative correlation would be expected (especially using the nonparametric gamma statistic which detects "corner-correlations" between two variables having skewed distributions). The discrepancy is frankly mysterious, and we can only venture the opinion that our result conforms far more closely to good theoretical expectations than does the earlier finding. Given the traumatic political upheavals in the urban United States during the late 1960s and early 1970s, which far exceeded even the worst excesses of Berlin or Paris in May 1968, we should expect a sharper polarization of views among Americans when compared to Europeans, and this is what we find.

SUMMARY

The measures discussed in this chapter have provided us with empirical access to a wider repertory of political action than have previous studies of political behavior. Alongside familiar measures of the extent people will involve themselves in conventional or orthodox political behavior, we have operationalized a key feature of the modern political experience: the parameters of license for unconventional political action. These parameters consist of the boundaries of opinion within which potential actors may move, defined on the one hand by protest potential and on the other by repression potential. The individual propensity to protest is apparently much more widespread than actual behavior would suggest. The belief that protest can be effective is even more widespread. This leads us to believe that involvement in protest behavior is governed far more by local political opportunity than by consensual feelings of deference and loyalty to normative values of public order or to the institutions that enforce them. It is true that the more extreme methods cannot be described as enjoying any widespread legitimacy, but neither can it be said that extreme forms of repression enjoy much greater normative support in the five countries we have examined. The custodians of civil authority in Europe and the United States do not have carte blanche when confronted with unorthodox forms of political action. Nor are the legitimate pathways of political action laid down by tradition and practice any antidote to noisy and disrespectful forms of protest.

A summary of the relationships between each of our three measures of political action is perhaps best appreciated diagramatically and so Table 3.8 lays out the triadic configurations of protest potential, conventional participation, and repression potential for each country.

The most striking feature of this table is not the predictable negative relationship between protest and repression potential discussed above but the consistent range of modest but significant *positive* correlations between protest potential and conventional participation. How could this be? In all

Table 3.8: PROTEST POTENTIAL, CONVENTIONAL PARTICIPATION, AND REPRESSION POTENTIAL, BY COUNTRY (coefficient is r)

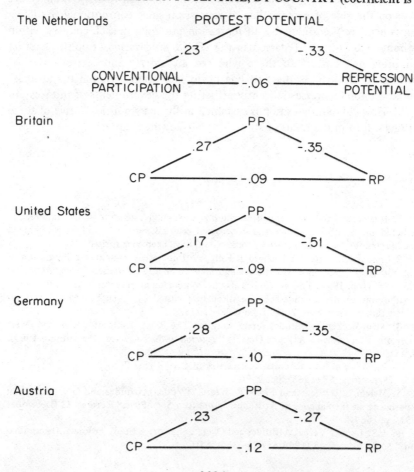

popular understanding of the subject, protest behavior implies a departure from the orthodox pathways of political redress. Protesters are supposed to be alienated from mainstream politics. That is why they protest, isn't it? A moment's thought might indicate that this is not necessarily so. In chapter 5 we apply to this important finding considerably more than a moment's thought. It provides the starting point for an analysis of political action that takes up the main theme of our theoretical introduction in chapter 2: an understanding of modern political behavior involves an understanding of the extent and diversity of the behavioral repertory of the participant citizen. For the moment we may summarize our view through a brief paraphrase of two concepts found useful by Blumenthal et al. Both protest and conventional political behavior clearly lie within a similar general sphere of "politics for social change" and in contrast to "politics for social control." Within the parameters of license for protest, conventional political activity actually lies more on the side of protest than of repression since conventional participation is *negatively* correlated with repression potential in each country within the range $-.05$ to $-.12$ (Pearsonian r's). This configuration of political action will bring no comfort to those who see an orderly and tightly governed political community as the first line of defense against the harsh and unexpected economic stresses currently afflicting the governments of the Western world. How this configuration is sustained in the mass politics of five of these nations will form the focus of study in the following chapters.

NOTES

1. It is at least arguable, of course, whether such an investigation would have clearly predicted the trouble that lay ahead because external stimuli would have remained unaccounted for, but at least fewer people would have been so surprised.

2. Charles R. Tittle and Richard J. Hill, "Attitude Measurement and Prediction of Behavior: An Evaluation of Conditions and Measurement Techniques," *Sociometry,* 30 (June 1967), pp. 199ff. This article has also been included in the interesting collection of contributions to the attitude-behavior discussion edited by Allen E. Liska, *The Consistency Controversy,* New York: John Wiley, 1975.

3. Allan Wicker, "Attitudes versus Actions: The Relationship of Verbal and Overt Behavioral Responses to Attitude Objects," *Journal of Social Issues,* 25 (Autumn 1969), pp. 41ff.

4. L. Carr and S.O. Roberts, "Correlates of Civil-Rights Participation," *Journal of Social Psychology,* 67 (1965), pp. 259ff.

5. Melvin L. DeFleur and Frank R. Westie, "Verbal Attitudes and Overt Acts: An Experiment on the Salience of Attitudes," *American Sociological Review,* 23 (December 1958), pp. 667ff.

6. L.S. Lynn, "Verbal Attitudes and Overt Behavior: A Study in Racial Discrimination," *Social Forces,* 43 (1964/65), pp. 353-364ff.

7. There exists an alternative and, to some, a sexist explanation of this finding. The women were asked, without warning, to fulfill a promise to be photographed with a "Negro of the opposite sex." It may be that those who declined were not welching on a promise but expressing a distaste for being photographed unprepared, irrespective of their racial attitudes.

8. Allan Wicker, "Attitudes versus Actions: The Relationship of Verbal and Overt Behavioral Responses to Attitude Objects," p. 65.

9. Clark McPhail, "Civil Disorder Participation: A Critical Examination of Recent Research," *American Sociological Review,* 36 (December 1971), pp. 1058ff.

10. Seymour Spilerman, "The Causes of Racial Disturbances: A Comparison of Alternative Explanations," *American Sociological Review,* 35 (August 1970), p. 645.

11. Herbert McClosky, "Survey Research in Political Science," in Charles Y. Glock (ed.), *Survey Research in the Social Sciences,* New York: Russel Sage, 1967, pp. 125ff.

12. Martin Fishbein, "Attitude and Prediction of Behavior," in Martin Fishbein (ed.), *Readings in Attitude Theory and Measurement,* New York: John Wiley, 1967, pp. 447ff.

13. For a detailed description of the pilot work see Alan Marsh, "Explorations in Unorthodox Political Behavior: A Scale to Measure 'Protest Potential'," *European Journal of Political Research,* 2 (June 1974), pp. 107ff.

14. William A. Gamson, *Power and Discontent,* Homewood: Dorsey Press, 1968.

15. Jerome H. Skolnick, *The Politics of Protest,* New York: Ballantine Books, 1969.

16. William R. Berkowitz, "The Impact of Protest: Willingness of Passersby to Make Antiwar Commitments at Anti-Vietnam Demonstrations," *Journal of Social Psychology,* 93 (June 1974), pp. 31ff.

17. Peter K. Eisinger, "Racial Differences in Protest Participation in an American City," *American Political Science Review,* 68 (June 1974), p. 604. The article is a considerably altered version of a paper presented at the Workshop on Political Behavior, Dissatisfaction, and Protest, First Joint Workshop Sessions of the European Consortium for Political Research (ECPR), Mannheim, April 1973, p. 38.

18. Michael Lipsky, "Protest as a Political Resource," *American Political Science Review,* 62 (December 1968), pp. 1144ff.

19. Alan Marsh, "Explorations in Unorthodox Political Behavior: A Scale to Measure 'Protest Potential'."

20. The German pretest results are reported in Max Kaase, "Political Ideology, Dissatisfaction and Protest," in Klaus v. Beyme (ed.), *German Political Studies,* Vol. 2, London: Sage, 1976, pp. 7ff.

21. Edward N. Muller, "A Test of a Partial Theory of Potential for Political Violence," *American Political Science Review,* 66 (September, 1972), pp. 928ff.

22. R.E. O'Connor, "Political Activism and Moral Reasoning: Political and Apolitical Students in Great Britain and France," *Journal of Political Science,* 4 (January 1974), pp. 53ff.

23. L.J. MacFarlane, *Political Disobedience,* London: Macmillan, 1971, p. 20.

24. Muller too found that his respondents' protest approval and behavioral intentions scales were positively correlated at r = .69. See Edward N. Muller, "A Test of a Partial Theory of Potential for Political Violence," p. 936.

25. This result is elaborated upon in the third section of this chapter.

26. In independent analyses not reported in this book with two exceptions (Tables 5.7 and 5.8) the British coauthor of this chapter has used a different scaling algorithm for the protest potential scale. See Alan Marsh, *Protest and Political Consciousness,* Beverly Hills: Sage, 1977, Appendix Four.

27. The percentage of Austrian respondents who could not be classified with respect to the protest potential scale exceeds that of the other four countries by a factor of three. This unfortunate situation is due to the fact that our Austrian colleagues introduced an "it depends" category not present in any of the other countries. This category had to be treated as missing data, thereby causing the high incidence of nonscaleable respondents.

28. Monica Blumenthal et al., *Justifying Violence,* Ann Arbor: Institute for Social Research, 1972.

29. Almost all of the activities we chose are part of Milbrath's hierarchy of political involvement. See Lester W. Milbrath, *Political Participation,* Chicago: Rand McNally, 1965, pp. 16ff. The item to measure community involvement was adapted from Sidney Verba and Norman H. Nie, *Participation in America,* New York: Harper & Row, 1972, p. 352.

30. Gabriel A. Almond and Sidney Verba, *The Civic Culture,* Boston: Little, Brown, 1965 (paper), pp. 53ff.

31. Sidney Verba and Norman H. Nie, *Participation in America,* pp. 56ff.

32. Ibid., p. 79.

33. This is an example of the ever-present problem of differing functional equivalence of stimulus objects from country to country, and it reinforces the strategy to consider the *dimension* as the functionally equivalent measure. While items may differ in intensity and in some qualitative aspects, the scale tends to measure the same thing in each country.

34. C. Cohen, *Civil Disobedience,* New York: Columbia University Press, 1971.

35. Monica Blumenthal et al., *Justifying Violence,* pp. 37ff.

Chapter 4

BACKGROUND OF POLITICAL ACTION

ALAN MARSH and MAX KAASE

INTRODUCTION

We have established in the preceding chapter measures of "political action": protest potential, conventional political participation, and repression potential. Each of our respondents now has a single scale-score representing his or her position on each of these behaviorally related dimensions of political attitude. We have also learned that those having high scores on the protest potential scale are more likely than not to have high rates of conventional participation, and that such activists are unlikely to endorse severe forms of political repression. Conversely, those who do favor draconian forms of repression are unlikely to be versatile political activists, especially if it involves behavior of an unconventional kind. While this configuration between scales is consistent across five nations, aggregate levels of participation differ widely. Our task in this chapter is to set each of these measured tendencies into the contextual social backdrop of each national sample provided by our measures of respondents' social characteristics.

The approach to this analysis will be very familiar to those even recently acquainted with the techniques of survey research. We shall simply—if manipulating a five-nation data set may ever said to be simple—take these three dependent variables and examine their relationship with other measures like the respondents' age, sex, amount of education, and so on. One may examine these relationships singly or in combination (e.g., "Do young working-class males have a higher protest potential than middle-aged middle-class women?"),[1] but we shall remain on familiar territory; unlike in the previous chapter, we shall not have much need of methodological innovation. Using conventional survey analysis procedures, we shall describe the social location of the dispositions toward political action that are measured by our new scales.

Readers will recall, however, having been primed by chapter 2 to expect a broadly sweeping analysis that includes the intervention of cognitive skills, political values, feelings of political disaffection, and so on. Our theoretical introduction often repeated the belief that such intervening variables act prismatically to mediate political behavior at the individual level; without their use conventional forms of analysis—such as described above—cannot be successfully interpreted. Quite so. But when handling the presentation of data from five separate countries, and when contemplating the application of a complex analytical model five times over, one must describe carefully the similarities and differences in the social contexts within which all this individual-level explanation of behavior is to occur. Otherwise, everyone—the researchers and their audience—will get lost very quickly.

Having set our measures into their social location in chapters 4 and 6, later chapters will advance into the detailed and systematic analysis of individual feelings, attitudes, perceptions, and values, and will examine how critical configurations of these thoughts, feelings, and beliefs shape political action. Thus, from a political-social psychological perspective this book shall, we hope, avoid a common error in survey research associated with political sociology, wherein such sensitive human characteristics as values and beliefs are swamped in the analysis of macrosocial processes such as educational background controlled by age, sex, and father's SES and anything else the researcher can think of. On the other hand, by first presenting the description of the systemic social context within which individual processes occur, we hope to avoid the other common error in survey research associated with social psychology of appearing to tear the individual out of this social context and so treat the lone respondent as the basic social unit. It is a principal aim of the study to explain why people act politically the way they do through an understanding of the way they think and feel about such things but we recognize at the same time that people are not mobilized out of a social and political void. The behavior and norms of their peers, their workmates, their coreligionists, their neighbors, and their stored social experience of a lifetime will all impinge on their deliberate and conscious thought that may lead them to choose one orientation to political action or another. It is this context we shall try to establish first.

Additionally, we have a second, similarly pedestrian but equally important, purpose in this chapter. This is to determine to what extent the very
wide variation in aggregate levels of political behavior that we found comparing country with country may be ameliorated by compositional effects.
That is to say, when a dependent variable is strongly associated with a
particular characteristic such as age, populations that differ in age composition will reveal a specious cross-national difference. For example, do the
Netherlands and Austria differ so much in levels of protest potential because
they have differently constructed populations? If so, *how much* of the
aggregate difference is due to these compositional effects, and to what extent
may they be controlled for in the analysis?

In this kind of cross-national survey analysis, clear presentation of data is
almost as important as analytical technique. In order to provide the reader
with a comparative framework at the outset, Table 4.1 sets down for each
national sample a summary analysis of the zero-order relationships between
most of the sociostructural variables we shall consider in this chapter and
each of our three measures of political action. (The statistic employed to
represent these relationships is the tau-beta correlation coefficient [tau-b],
which is a conservative nonparametric measure of association. Like the more
familiar parametric Pearson r correlation coefficient, tau-b ranges from +1.0
through −1.0, indicating the extent of a positive or negative association
between two variables.[2]

Obviously, it would be unwise to try to take in the broad sweep of this
analysis in one attempt. On the other hand, it would be tedious to proceed
through each finding one by one. As a device to impose both economy and
clarity upon the analysis we propose, first of all, to consider this analysis in
two sections. The first concerns those sociostructural variables that have an
immediately "personal" character, for example, age, sex, education, and
religion. For purely heuristic purposes, we shall call this the social domain.
The second area concerns those variables having to do directly with people's
economic activity and their relationship to the means of production, for
example, occupational status, income, and trade union membership. This we
shall call the economic domain. When these two stories are clearly told,
country by country, some integrated form of analysis can then be attempted.

POLITICAL ACTION AND THE SOCIAL DOMAIN

Age and Sexual Identity

It is inevitable that our attention should fall first upon the relationship
between political action and age. As we have asserted elsewhere,[3] no elabo-

Table 4.1: ZERO-ORDER SOCIOSTRUCTURAL CORRELATES OF POLITICAL ACTION, BY COUNTRY (tau-b)

	The Netherlands	Britain	United States	Germany	Austria
SOCIAL DOMAIN					
AGE					
Protest Potential	−.22	−.26	−.32	−.24	−.17
Repression Potential	.11	.19	.28	.19	.02
Conventional Participation	.00	.02	.03	−.11	.00
SEX					
Protest Potential	−.12	−.15	−.08	−.16	−.17
Repression Potential	.00	.14	.08	.03	.08
Conventional Participation	−.22	−.15	−.13	−.31	−.23
YEARS SCHOOLING					
Protest Potential	.17	.24	.26	.18	.23
Repression Potential	−.06	−.14	−.21	−.16	−.15
Conventional Participation	.26	.17	.26	.23	.19
TYPE OF SCHOOL					
Protest Potential	.14	.22	.27	.19	.23
Repression Potential	−.06	−.11	−.19	−.16	−.15
Conventional Participation	.26	.17	.26	.23	.19
RELIGIOUS ATTACHMENT					
Protest Potential	−.18	−.09	−.13	−.15	−.09
Repression Potential	.21	.10	.10	.15	.14
Conventional Participation	−.08	−.10	−.07	−.06	−.07
ECONOMIC DOMAIN					
OCCUPATIONAL PRESTIGE					
Protest Potential	.07	.12	.12	.10	.15
Repression Potential	−.01	.00	−.08	−.09	−.10
Conventional Participation	.20	.13	.19	.15	.12
FAMILY INCOME					
Protest Potential	.14	.23	.17	.15	.16
Repression Potential	−.03	−.09	−.11	−.08	−.09
Conventional Participation	.20	.13	.21	.21	.14
SELF-REPORTED SOCIAL CLASS					
Protest Potential	−.04	.04	.13	.03	.15
Repression Potential	.10	.10	−.09	−.02	−.04
Conventional Participation	.19	.14	.17	.16	.09
TRADE UNION MEMBERSHIP					
Protest Potential	.05	.14	.05	.10	.12
Repression Potential	−.05	−.17	−.12	−.07	−.12
Conventional Participation	.12	.11	.01	.15	.14

rate theoretical reasoning need herald the suggestion that protest potential will be associated with youthfulness. Young people enjoy the physical vigor, the freedom from day-to-day responsibilities of career and family, and have the *time* to participate in the pursuit of the energetic kinds of political activity implied by a high protest potential. Protest behavior is therefore held to be primarily an outcome of the joie de vivre of youth itself.

Moreover, young people are said to be somehow *naturally* vulnerable to strong and purist kinds of ideological motivation. Purist ideologies—be they the Young New Left of the late 1960s or the Young New Right of the late 1930s—breed impatience with the established traditional forms of obtaining political redress. This impatience impels politically conscious young people and their cohorts into a mood of revolt and thence onto the streets. Now that the new economic freedom of the twentieth century, among other things, has created a new constituency of "Youth," it should not be surprising that this process occurs. These movements are centered upon the great universities of the West, where the highest levels of ideology and freedom of expression intersect.[4] It is almost what is expected of them. As an old proverb has it: "He who is not a revolutionary at twenty has no heart. He who is still a revolutionary at forty has no head."

The key notion underpinning the "life-cycle" explanation of protest is simply the *fact* of generational conflict that is built into modern society. Seen from the point of view of the adolescent—especially when that view is sharpened by the vivid and uncompromising clarity that is given all of us at that age and so cruelly taken away somewhere around our twenty-first birthday—the normal channels of political communication are moss-strewn with elderly compromise. Old men—especially *men*—have all the power. Naturally, young people will resent this arrangement and, naturally, they will challenge it. Protest behavior provides an ideal medium for that challenge. So young people will have a high protest potential and, naturally again, they will reject authority's attempts to control protests and so uphold the complementary view of a low repression potential.

Yet, as we noted in our theoretical introduction, this "natural" and expected tendency for youth to protest—which people now believe commonplace—had certainly lapsed after the world had drifted through the politically still waters of the 1950s and early 1960s. Compared with their successors, compared with their now-grown children, compared even with their fathers in the 1930s, the youth of postwar Europe and America were a dull lot. True, one may trace many of the antecedents of modern mass youth phenomena among minority interests of the 1950s. The New Left, for example, started in England in 1956, followed in 1958 by the progenitor of the Peace Movement: the Youth Campaign for Nuclear Disarmament. Rock music, being the continual shouting of slogans in support of adolescence, was also well established.

Yet, an occasional preoccupation with "Beatniks," jazz, and rock n' roll scarcely amounted to a mass movement. En mass, the Fifties generation were quiet and conformist. Were they then somehow "unnatural?" No, of course they were not. They merely lived in a world that was *busy,* wholly preoccupied with rebuilding itself after the War. For the first time since the 1920s real progress was visible. Many of the injustices that gave rise to earlier protest movements in the 1930s—poverty, unemployment, poor housing, ill-health, and so on—all appeared to be melting away. One would not wish to deny that the "life-cycle" explanation of protest is plausible; it contains far too much good sense to be otherwise. It only *makes* sense, however, if it also takes account of social and political change. It is a fundamental hypothesis of this study that such a change has occurred in Western democracies; a change in attitudes and values, in political understanding, in satisfactions, and in political expression. These changes, as shall be described, have fueled, facilitated, and shaped radical changes in political behavior in the last ten to fifteen years. All this has little to do with the *fact* that, as always, a proportion of the population is young. When change brings protest, the young will protest the most. This is not the same thing as saying that the young protest because they are young. That is a "superstitious theory"; it describes everything and explains nothing.

What of youth and conventional political participation? We know there is a positive relationship between conventional and unconventional participation; but it is modest enough in magnitude to admit many exceptions, and many of those exceptions may be young. The all-round political versatility that our theoretical basis compels us to seek may well be something that, while certainly a property of young people rather than old, may not be associated with the very youngest of our respondents. In other words, while we expect protest and repression potentials to increase and decrease respectively as a linear function of youthfulness, we expect an accompanying degree of participation in conventional political activities to be curvilinearly related to age even though biased toward the young end of the age range.

The correlation coefficients reported in the first lines of Table 4.1 confirm our hypothesis with respect to protest and repression potential. Naturally, the hypothesized curvilinear relationship between age and conventional participation cannot be reliably tested by a linear correlation coefficient, but the largely neutral relationships between age and conventional participation shown in the table at least do not directly contradict the hypothesis. Below we will turn to an adequate examination of this hypothesis.

A partial exception to this finding appears in Austria where the youth-protest connection is weakest (tau-b = .17, compared with an average of .26 elsewhere) and the youth-antirepression relationship is nonexistent (tau-b = .02, compared with an average of .19 elsewhere).

If Youth Protest is a natural state, what is "unnatural" about Austria? Perhaps not unnatural but certainly unfamiliar, is that Austria has, at the time of writing, a busy and highly successful socialist government and, compared with a turbulent and traumatic past, there are more personal wealth and security than anyone in Austria really expected. This state of affairs is still possibly a welcome novelty even to younger Austrians who are not anxious to rock a newly stabilized, well-provisioned national boat. A vessel of state that is, moreover, moored very close to the communist fleet. Austria's orientation toward socialist Europe—and the Third World, too, for that matter—is sufficiently cooperative to draw the sting from any incipient Left youth movement Austria may yet possess. It would be wise, however, to suspend speculation of this kind until we have examined more of the evidence.

First, we will take a closer look at the all-important youth-protest relationship. In Figure 4.1 we have taken as a sort of "key number" the proportion of respondents scoring "high" on the protest potential scale, i.e., at points four through seven, and plotted this proportion across the age range of each national sample divided into twelve five-year age groups. The magnitude of the tau-b correlation reported in Table 4.1 is, of course, reflected in the steepness of the descent of this line from left to right, that is, from young to

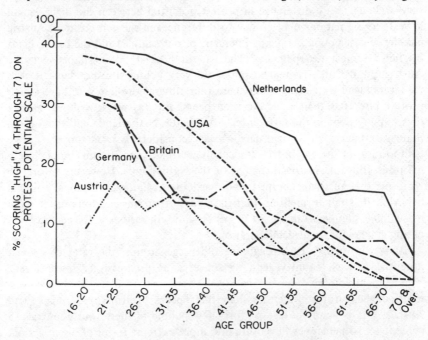

Figure 4.1: PROTEST POTENTIAL BY AGE BY COUNTRY

old. It follows that this line is shallowest in the case of Austria and drops most steeply in the case of the United States. This latter finding is unsurprising perhaps in a nation that first took seriously the idea of a generation gap, and whose political system seems most readily to have found room for a generational age-axis alongside all the other multiple cleavages of race, sex, region, religion, and class that characterize American politics.

An instructive way of looking at Figure 4.1 is to estimate the extent to which the very wide aggregate difference in protest potential we observed between nations is ameliorated by having controlled for the powerful effects of age. Looking first at our younger respondents—those less than twenty-six years old—we find that four nations, the Netherlands, United States, Germany, and Britain, are not at all dissimilar in their rates of protest potential. Among young people in these four countries, between 30 percent and 40 percent are prepared to use unconventional and sometimes illegal forms of political action. They also show correspondingly low levels of repression potential.

The great exception to this finding is the case of the Austrian youth, among whom a high protest potential is less than half as common as it is among young people in the other four nations. We speculated earlier that the very wide aggregate difference in protest potential between the highest- and lowest-scoring nations may be due to differences in age composition. Austria has the fewest young people (18 percent of our sample) and the Netherlands by far the most (36 percent). The gap in protest potential between the Austrians and Dutch is greatest among the very youngest respondents: Dutch teenagers (aged sixteen to twenty) are four times more likely to have a high protest potential than their Austrian peers. But, as we saw above, among these young people, the difference between the Netherlands and the United States, Germany, and Britain narrows very considerably even though the age composition of these countries (especially Germany and Britain) more closely resembles that of Austria than that of the Netherlands. However, before we write off the Austrians completely as participants in unconventional political behavior, it is fair to mention that the young Austrians can still muster quite respectable numbers (about 50 percent) who will seriously consider participating in a lawful street demonstration.

As we move upward through the older age groups, the rates of protest potential in each country tend to converge at progressively lower levels. Young to middle-aged Americans (aged twenty-six to forty) show a consistently higher protest potential than their peers in Britain, Germany, and Austria, but beyond the age of forty few people in these four countries (5 percent to 10 percent) will venture into more extreme forms of direct action.

However, the generalization about the middle age ranges does not hold in the Netherlands. Right up through the age range, even to the oldest respondents, the Dutch sample contains at least twice as many people who have a high protest potential than do the other, increasingly convergent, national samples. This difference is particularly noticeable in the forty to fifty-five age range, where the percentage of committed protesters is three times that in other countries.

This result reinforces the idea expressed in the previous chapter that protest activities are associated by many Dutchmen with the Resistance Movement during World War II. The greatest cross-national difference between the Netherlands and the other four countries taken together occurs among those whose social and political attitudes were formed when they were teenagers during the war: the forty to forty-five age group. Naturally, at that time antiauthoritarian sentiments were rife and were constantly reinforced by allied propaganda. This age cohort probably internalized the idea that active resistance to a political authority is prima facie a democratic act worthy of support almost regardless of the issues it reflects. It is intriguing to note that in Britain a similar upward peak in protest potential is noticeable among the forty to forty-five age group. After all, the British and Dutch shared the same propaganda sources at that time.

This result also disposes of one other worry regarding the Dutch survey. Whereas in the other four countries interviewing was carried out by professionals, the Dutch respondents were interviewed by paid but hitherto inexperienced students. This might have had the result of encouraging younger respondents to boast of a high protest potential to a student interviewer who evidently belonged to a class of people whose own high protest potential was a matter of daily reportage. This faintly perverse social-desirability effect among certain subgroups is common in survey research. Schuman, for example, found that black American respondents were far more likely to give attitude responses that were hostile to whites if they were interviewed by another black.[5] We expected a similar effect. We have now established, however, that it is not the young but the middle-aged Dutchmen who really deviate from cross-national norms, and it is much too fanciful to suggest that *they* do so merely to impress a student interviewer. On the other hand, the very low repression potential found throughout the Dutch sample may have been depressed still further by this source. Some of those who privately believed that political dissenters should be firmly dealt with were perhaps unwilling to say so to a guest in their house who appeared a likely person to place himself in the way of such action.

Perhaps the principal value of Figure 4.1 is that it emphasizes very effectively just *how much* protest potential there is now available for mobilization in Western political communities. Surveys always oversample older people. So when the over-fifties are taken out of consideration, the sheer amount of protest potential present among that section of the population that is any way *available* for such mobilization may be seen more clearly. If we consider only the under-forties—which is probably more realistic in terms of the actual mobilization of activists—one realizes that nearly half the Dutch, a third of the Americans, and at least a quarter of the Germans and British (if rather fewer Austrians) are all seriously committed to the idea of using unconventional and even some illegal forms of political protest. These figures imply the presence within Western political communities of a substantial and widely spread constituency for radical political action.[6]

The most efficient way of opening up this analysis further to include the other two dimensions of political action, repression potential and conventional participation, is to include simultaneous consideration of the second important aspect of the social domain: sex and sexual roles. This may appear an unnecessarily complicated step. The reason for it is quite simple: as we shall see below, whereas age best predicts protest and repression potential, conventional participation is more heavily influenced by sex. Put together they produce a powerfully descriptive "first mapping" of the social location of political action.

From a theoretical point of view, what should we expect of the impact of sexual identity upon political action? It is a matter for continuing debate whether or not men are innately more aggressive than women or whether they are simply more likely to be socialized into adopting aggressive roles and a more belligerent outlook than are women. There is no doubt that Western cultural values expressed in child-rearing styles have consistently rewarded controlled aggression in male children and encouraged contrastingly passive and nurturant traits in female children.[7] If protest potential is linked to individual aggression, then we should expect men to have a higher protest potential than women. It should be remembered, though, that we have in no way demonstrated that individual aggression is directly linked to protest potential. It remains for the moment merely a reasonable assumption, but one upon which we should not place too much weight.

It is more parsimonious to think of sex roles and political behavior in terms of socially determined *availability* for mobilization. What are accepted as the "normal" demands of the modern nuclear family tend to ensure that men remain more available for participation in political action, even after early marriage. Young wives, even those formerly active, are not only likely to be significantly inhibited from participation in unconventional political acts by their domestic lifestyles, but also by traditional beliefs discouraging their involvement.

Since we postulate circumstantial rather than attitudinal reasons for a lower protest potential among women, it does not follow that their lower propensity to protest will be accompanied by a correspondingly higher repression potential.

With respect to conventional political participation, we may refer to a wealth of empirical evidence that women are far less likely than men to participate in the workings of party politics, and that this is especially true of women in continental Europe.[8]

The summary analysis in Table 4.1 shows the above hypothesis to be broadly true. In Europe, though less so in the United States, protest potential is positively associated with being male, but at a low order of magnitude. Except in Britain, and then only marginally so, repression potential does not increase correspondingly among women. Conventional participation is strongly associated with being male in Germany, convincingly so in Austria and the Netherlands, less so but still significantly in Britain and the United States.

To achieve the contextual mapping spoken earlier, Table 4.2 shows the distribution of protest potential scores (trichotomized 0-1/2-3/4-7) separately for men and women within each of three age groups: 16 through 29, 30 through 49, and 50 and over. Table 4.3 repeats this analysis for repression potential scores (trichotomized 0-1/2/3-4), and Table 4.4 does the same for conventional political participation (again trichotomized 0-1/2-3/4-7).

Tables 4.2 and 4.3 show precisely how age and sex interact powerfully to describe the extensive parameters of license for protest that exist among young men. In the Netherlands and the United States, 90 percent of young men will use some kind of direct political action from demonstrations onward. In Britain and Germany, 75 percent to 80 percent will do so, and even in Austria 70 percent will go to moderate levels of protest. In each country no more than about half of the sample of young men will endorse any repressive measure beyond the nationally determined "first step." Young women too are really not very far behind their male peers, to the extent that women under thirty tend to have as high a protest potential and a lower repression potential than men aged thirty through forty-nine. This similarity is due more to the surprisingly high protest potential of the latter group than to low levels among young women. It is among the middle-aged that sex differences are greatest. Between 70 percent and 80 percent of middle-aged men will consider at least joining a lawful demonstration or supporting a boycott, except in Austria where it is 58 percent, and the proportion of those who will go further into even illegal forms of protest is only about one-third lower than the same proportion among much younger men. Among middle-aged women, rates of protest and repression potential are, respectively, much lower and higher than those among their menfolk in Britain, Austria, and Germany, but in the Netherlands and the United States these differences are still not very great. Age remains the key explanation.

These results may then be contrasted with the quite different pattern presented in Table 4.4 for conventional political participation. Age has very

Table 4.2: PROTEST POTENTIAL BY AGE, BY SEX, BY COUNTRY

	Protest Potential	16-29		30-49		50 & over	
		Men	Women	Men	Women	Men	Women
The Netherlands	Low (0, 1)	10%	27%	22%	31%	39%	50%
	Medium (2, 3)	43	41	41	35	45	35
	High (4-7)	47	32	37	34	16	15
	(n =)	(197)	(217)	(177)	(185)	(190)	(199)
Britain	Low (0, 1)	26	30	30	47	48	65
	Medium (2, 3)	42	45	48	43	41	29
	High (4-7)	32	25	22	10	11	6
	(n =)	(133)	(165)	(215)	(212)	(290)	(362)
United States	Low (0, 1)	9	30	20	27	45	51
	Medium (2, 3)	54	30	60	51	50	43
	High (4-7)	37	40	20	22	5	5
	(n =)	(209)	(267)	(245)	(287)	(245)	(345)
Germany	Low (0, 1)	20	22	27	46	43	58
	Medium (2, 3)	47	56	58	46	50	39
	High (4-7)	33	22	15	8	7	3
	(n =)	(194)	(198)	(457)	(427)	(397)	(539)
Austria	Low (0, 1)	31	48	42	61	52	71
	Medium (2, 3)	58	41	42	32	41	25
	High (4-7)	11	11	16	7	6	4
	(n =)	(117)	(138)	(238)	(298)	(185)	(287)

Table 4.3: REPRESSION POTENTIAL BY AGE, BY SEX, BY COUNTRY

	Repression Potential	16-29		30-49		50 & over	
		Men	Women	Men	Women	Men	Women
The Netherlands	Low (0, 1)	76%	75%	70%	72%	64%	62%
	Medium (2)	13	14	16	9	15	8
	High (3, 4)	11	11	14	19	21	30
	(n =)	(199)	(210)	(179)	(181)	(193)	(161)
Britain	Low (0, 1)	45·	39	29	19	27	17
	Medium (2)	27	31	37	28	28	23
	High (3, 4)	28	30	34	53	45	60
	(n =)	(137)	(160)	(211)	(210)	(287)	(359)
United States	Low (0, 1)	53	52	29	35	25	18
	Medium (2)	28	23	42	27	33	20
	High (3, 4)	19	25	29	38	42	62
	(n =)	(211)	(275)	(246)	(293)	(244)	(349)
Germany	Low (0, 1)	62	57	39	35	22	31
	Medium (2)	16	16	24	17	20	15
	High (3, 4)	22	27	37	48	58	54
	(n =)	(190)	(200)	(449)	(432)	(395)	(538)
Austria	Low (0, 1)	48	36	45	33	38	30
	Medium (2)	10	13	14	12	16	16
	High (3, 4)	42	51	41	55	46	54
	(n =)	(128)	(158)	(265)	(348)	(205)	(339)

little impact upon rates of participation except that in most countries other people (especially the middle-aged) tend to have marginally *higher* rates of participation than those under thirty. The curvilinear relationship we speculated about earlier—that conventional participation would be noticeably concentrated among the middle-aged—is not borne out generally and appears only slightly among men in the United States and Germany.

The dominant influence on conventional participation is, as we have said, membership in the male sex, and Table 4.4 illustrates the intriguing fact that this male dominance increases as the average national participation rate increases. That is to say, as we move from the least participatory nations to the highest, i.e., from Britain and the Netherlands, through Austria to Germany and the United States, the male dominance of conventional politics becomes more pronounced. In Germany, it amounts almost to a male stranglehold on party politics. In Britain, on the other hand, the dominant influence is clearly one of universal apathy. The really deviant group in the whole analysis is British men. Of those men under thirty in Britain, only 2 percent ever involve themselves in conventional politics beyond the level of polite conversation and sometimes helping out in community work, compared with between 15 and 32 percent elsewhere, and more than half of them do no more than glance at the political sections of the newspapers. Older men in Britain are scarcely more active (nor are older Dutchmen), and their participation rates trail those of comparable groups in Germany and the United States by a factor of two or three to one.

Recall for a moment our partial support for Verba and Nie's multifactor model of political participation.[9] We found that the propensity to vote did not align with our scale of increasing involvement in conventional party-related activities. So it is interesting to note that this apparently total apathy for conventional political involvement in Britain, and the nearly similar state in the Netherlands and Austria, is not reflected in turnout at elections. In Britain, for example, in February 1974 nearly 80 percent of the electorate turned out to favor their chosen candidate with a cross on the ballot paper.[10] This is a higher rate of voting than is commonly achieved in many other countries, especially in America.

If we now take a pace back from the close scrutiny of these three tables, the most compelling generalization that strikes one is that among the whole of the Dutch sample, among most of the British sample, among young people just about everywhere, and most especially among young women, direct action is a more popular idea than conventional forms of political involvement. It is not possible to make a precise empirical judgment about this. The scales are different, and the items that compose each have a different value and weight. Yet to anyone experienced in this kind of research, we feel this would appear a reasonable statement. This finding does not necessarily

Table 4.4: CONVENTIONAL PARTICIPATION BY AGE, BY SEX, BY COUNTRY

Conventional Participation	16-29		30-49		50 & over	
	Men	Women	Men	Women	Men	Women
The Netherlands						
Low (0, 1)	40%	61%	36%	56%	43%	64%
Medium (2, 3)	46	29	46	37	44	31
High (4-7)	15	10	18	7	13	5
(n =)	(202)	(222)	(187)	(191)	(200)	(179)
Britain						
Low (0, 1)	55	60	41	58	43	63
Medium (2, 3)	43	33	46	35	44	28
High (4-7)	2	7	13	8	13	9
(n =)	(142)	(166)	(220)	(220)	(303)	(391)
United States						
Low (0, 1)	39	45	17	34	27	40
Medium (2, 3)	35	38	37	35	39	34
High (4-7)	26	17	46	31	34	26
(n =)	(215)	(280)	(255)	(303)	(260)	(380)
Germany						
Low (0, 1)	40	59	32	65	48	73
Medium (2, 3)	28	26	34	25	26	20
High (4-7)	32	15	34	10	26	7
(n =)	(199)	(210)	(458)	(447)	(406)	(575)
Austria						
Low (0, 1)	50	66	43	64	43	31
Medium (2, 3)	33	27	36	25	34	58
High (4-7)	17	8	21	11	23	11
(n =)	(139)	(166)	(279)	(371)	(227)	(394)

contradict our earlier finding that protest potential and conventional participation tend to occur coterminously. However, these results do foreshadow
the idea that a well-tuned political versatility—the extended political repertory, discussed earlier—is not likely to be very common among older respondents, the youngest, and women.

Education

These bare demographic patterns determined by age and sex point to
social availability as an important element in the explanation of political
action, but this would be a sterile path to follow, leading only to static
descriptions. As we said earlier, the kinds of explanations we seek have a
dynamic quality concerned with people's thoughts, values, and beliefs. So, as
the next step in establishing a relevant social context, we should ask: "What is
the most important element in people's social experience that shapes the
context of these mental qualities we wish to explore?" The first answer—
certainly from a psychologist—would have something to do with the quality
of people's most intimate relationships, especially those of childhood. These
broader socialization issues will be treated in the detail they deserve in
chapters 15 and 16 which examine the results of the special parent-child pair
data. The second answer—which comes most readily from political scientists
who have worked with survey data—concerns the quality of a person's
education.

Why should education affect political involvement? There is a wealth of
empirical data to show that it does, especially in the sphere we have
designated conventional participation. Every major survey of political behavior has determined that the more education a person has received, and the
better the quality of that educational experience, the more likely it is that he
or she will at some time or other become involved in party political activities.
The consensual explanation for this phenomenon is that education provides
the cognitive skills necessary to find one's way around the confused miasma
that surrounds politics, if not actually teaching such skills directly. Moreover,
the experience of higher forms of education will tend to break down people's
natural tendencies to oversimplify their view of the world. This gives them
easier access to those mental skills that translate individual grievances, group-
interests, and even broader political needs into the forms of political action
appropriate to the resolution of those needs.[11]

Alternatively, it would be prudent not to be oversold on the idea of a
strong linear relationship between better education and increasing political
involvement. After all, most educators would argue that overall standards of
education have improved considerably during the past thirty years or so;
certainly far more people have experienced *more* education than formerly.
Yet political participation in terms of party membership and even voting

turnout have in many countries fallen during the same period. In Britain, for example, we noted that young people—by far the best educated generation that country has yet produced—noticeably shun conventional participation. It should always be borne in mind that people do not *have* to excel in IQ tests to be able to function politically. As Moorhouse and Chamberlain point out, "It is not necessary for men, certainly not the mass of men, to encompass society intellectually before they set about changing it."[12] Nevertheless, it may well help.

This last point brings us to some difficulties in conceptualizing the relationship between education and protest potential. Conventional participation we know about, but it may be argued equally that direct political action is the last resort of the inarticulate. Does it not follow, perhaps, that those whose lack of education excludes them from the articulate subtleties of party politics are also those who will most readily take to the streets? If one cannot get one's way through reasoned argument, then why not shout and throw stones? For example, were the blacks of Watts, Detroit, and Miami in 1967-1968 responding only to white oppression or to their own difficulties in working through the system? In a liberal academic environment, one can get into trouble posing such questions as these, but they have some intuitive appeal. As we have discussed earlier, the image of the protester as a desperate member of an ill-informed rabble dies hard. Where this argument encounters most trouble, however, is that everyone also knows that much modern political protest is actually undertaken by students and by obviously well-educated members of modern pressure groups like the environmentalist movement, women's liberation, and others bent on radical reform. Is there then perhaps a curvilinear relationship between education and protest potential—an alliance of the articulate "agitator" and his ill-informed but politically frustrated "followers?" This too is an appealing argument that has much currency among popular observers of contemporary politics.

On the other hand, we have committed ourselves to the idea of political protest as a new component of a modern political versatility. If, as we maintain, the widening of the citizen's political action repertory reflects the rise of a new sophistication in mass political participation, then it follows that protest is not the expression of inarticulate rage nor even the result of simple folk being persuaded to follow self-interested agitators. It follows, in fact, that protest in its modern expression is just as much a product of high levels of awareness generated by good education as is conventional political participation.

With respect to the theoretical relationship between education and repression potential, we are surely on safer ground. As one of us has written before: "The suppression of dissent in the political community offers a cognitively simple solution to the vexing complexities of modern politics which appeals, to be candid, to the cognitively simple."[13] Therefore, the ill-educated will be most likely to embrace the kinds of political suppression implied by the more extreme forms of government action described in the repression potential scale, especially those involving the use of troops and government bans.

The empirical solutions to these arguments are not easy to obtain in a cross-national survey because it proves extremely difficult to construct a measure of low-to-high education that is comparatively valid from country to country. Drawing upon the work by Hans Dieter Klingemann (see also the Technical Appendix), in this section we field two measures of education: the number of years of schooling received and the type of school attended. Although, as Klingemann demonstrates, the second of these measures is the most efficacious measure to use, the figures given in Table 4.1 show that at this level of analysis largely identical results are obtained using the two measures.

We find, in essence, that the "widening political repertory" hypothesis is the most parsimonious explanation of the results. Each of the tau-b correlation coefficients describing the relationship between the two measures of political action (protest and conventional participation) and the two measures of education (years schooling and type of school) are positive though of moderate size. There is also a remarkable consistency in these measures of association from country to country. The following diagram summarizes the magnitude and the consistency of these relationships.

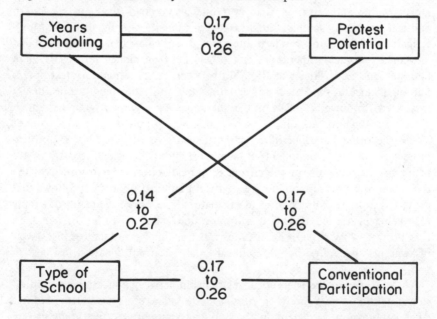

RELATIONSHIPS BETWEEN POLITICAL ACTION AND EDUCATION

Increasing education, therefore, is *equally* associated with increasing participation in both conventional political activities and with increasing levels of
protest potential. There are no important cross-national differences in this
result, save to observe that consistently the strongest relationships are found
in the United States where the "most" education and the "most" participation tend to coincide.

Since our special interest is in protest potential and the association
between education and protest is still the most contentious to interpret, the
actual percentage figures for the relationship between the type of school the
respondent attended and protest potential are laid out in Table 4.5.

Table 4.5 indicates that, like "age," the education variable goes quite a
long way toward ameliorating some of the cross-national differences in
protest potential noted earlier, especially when comparing Austria with the
other countries. Although no one is quite batting in the same league as the

Table 4.5: PROTEST POTENTIAL BY TYPE OF SCHOOLING RECEIVED

	Protest Potential		Primary Only	Secondary, High School	University, College	(tau-b)
The Netherlands	Low	0	11%	4%	0%	
		1	22	13	17	
		2	26	24	24	
		3	14	22	18	
	High	4-7	28	37	42	(.14)
Britain	Low	0	29	13	5	
		1	24	21	5	
		2	23	29	30	
		3	12	18	34	
	High	4-7	12	20	26	(.22)
United States	Low	0	19	5	4	
		1	31	20	11	
		2	25	25	19	
		3	18	28	35	
	High	4-7	8	21	31	(.27)
Germany	Low	0	23	11	5	
		1	23	18	12	
		2	28	34	33	
		3	18	21	27	
	High	4-7	8	17	24	(.19)
Austria	Low	0	26	10	6	
		1	35	32	6	
		2	23	30	44	
		3	9	16	18	
	High	4-7	7	13	27	(.23)

Dutch intelligentsia (*none* of whom has a protest potential score of zero), we can see that Austrian students and graduates (many of them older graduates) are attracted to protest behavior to a similar extent as their counterparts in Britain, Germany, and even in America. The Austrians still have some tendency more than others to stop short at demonstrations. So *some* of the apparent political lethargy of the Austrian sample can be explained simply in terms of their lack of a large proportion of young people and especially of a large body—even perhaps an adequate "critical mass"—of young intellectuals.

Table 4.5 is also an important illustration to the reader that tau-b coefficients that appear rather modest in magnitude in Table 4.1 may reflect quite large and significant aggregate differences between groups for whom the statistic is calculated. In the United States, for example, a tau-b coefficient of .27 summarizes a relationship between protest potential and education wherein only 15 percent of college-educated people will go no further than signing a petition while 66 percent of them will go further even than street demonstrations, compared with 40 percent of those having only primary education who will go no further than signing petitions and only 26 percent who will contemplate action beyond demonstrations. Similarly wide differences are evident for every country save the Netherlands. Still, the pervasiveness of protest potential in the Netherlands is clearly evident. Even Dutchmen with no more than primary education show a higher protest potential than well-educated people elsewhere.

Something else we need to know is the extent to which the association between education and political action exists independently of the relationships we have described for age and sex. This is necessary because we know that in each national sample better educated people tend to be disproportionately young and male. Young men are, for whatever reason, more prone to protest than other groups. So is this the "cause" of the results for education? An analysis was conducted breaking down the education tables for each of three age groups and both sexes in each country.

Such an analysis generates too indigestible a feast of tables to set before the reader, and, anyway, we shall take up this problem again in a wider context at the end of this chapter. If they may be taken on trust for the present, the results are fairly straightforward. Except among young Dutchmen, education still influences participation independently of age and sex. The results do contain a few surprises. In particular, we find that, except in the United States, young and even middle-aged female college students and graduates, unlike their sisters elsewhere, have a *higher* protest potential than male students and graduates. This may have something to do with the concentration of the female intelligentsia among those studying or who are skilled in the arts and humanities,[14] but it may also have much to do with the radical mood that has undoubtedly seized young women in their position since about 1970. We shall have reason to return to this topic in later chapters, not least because we also find that, particularly in Germany, their conventional political participation levels fall *well below* those of their male peers. This, it may be said, tells its own story; but it is a story that will become more intriguing as we proceed to higher levels of analysis.

Another reason for refraining from laying out all this information explicitly is that, except in the United States, the numbers of college-educated people present in national random samples are really too small to be disaggregated this way. Yet if anyone should remain in doubt that students and the political community of the academic world provide one fountainhead of direct political action in modern societies, they may be referred again to the British study referenced before.[15] There, in chapter 8, the results of a special subsample of 300 university and polytechnic students are analyzed. Even compared with members of the British national sample of the same age, the students' protest potential is twice as high, with 53 percent scoring at the highest point on the scale, and only 1 percent at the lowest. Yet, interestingly, and despite their very high levels of political disaffection measured in other ways, these British students still maintained very high levels of conventional participation that correlated positively ($r = .41$) with their protest potential—a much stronger relationship than that among the British national sample ($r = .26$). (It was also fascinating to note that young British women students too had as high a protest potential as the male students.)

These results all tend to confirm that the political repertory approach is the correct way to proceed. At the same time, the warning should be repeated that it is unwise to become oversold on education as an "explanation" of political action. We still have to learn how it works, and it should be borne in mind that, within the European samples especially, the "intelligentsia" is still a relatively small group. *It is true that the majority of the best educated are prone to political action but by no means the majority of all of those prone to political action received the best education.*

Our straightforward hypothesis that better education and the enlightenment it is supposed to bring will decrease the support given to repressive action by the authorities is only partially confirmed by the results given in Table 4.1. If the term may be allowed, the results are consistently equivocal. Years of schooling are negatively related to repression potential in the range of $-.06$ and $-.19$. The trouble with posing scientifically formed hypotheses in political science is that scientific naivete can look like real political naivete. These results are a terse reminder that of course not all well-educated people will become politically active in a "liberal" direction. It is evident, looking closer at the data, that less well-educated people do favor repression potential to a greater extent, but the "cognitive simplicity" spoken of earlier is likely to have sources other than sheer lack of education.

Religion

Another important aspect of the social environment that shapes people's beliefs and values is institutionalized religion. There are places, even in the modern industrial world, where religion still has a direct and profound impact upon politics. The example of Northern Ireland scarcely needs spelling out again. One needs only to scan the names of even present-day European political parties to observe their religiously influenced origins. Those parties anxious to declare themselves "Christian" usually meant "Protestant," and of the Right too. Those catering to Catholic interests are often careful to say so (e.g., the Dutch KVP) even though they too are of the Right. Even when labels disappear, assumptions remain. A favorite jibe of the Left in Britain is to describe the Anglican Church as "the Conservative Party at prayer." In the United States, specifically religious interest groups tend to exercise their influence within one or both the two major parties. That they do so effectively any Democratic mayor of New York, for example, will be happy to confirm. When religious cleavages intersect with ethnicity, the influence can be powerful. The Jews provide only one example, the Catholic Irish are probably a better one.

Yet we are not dealing here with the relationship between religion and partisan choice. For the present, we need to know only the extent to which religious affiliation may affect rates and styles of political participation as measured by our three scales. And there are problems even with this.

Religion, at least in terms of sectarian affiliation, is an impossibly difficult notion to compare cross-nationally—as though British Anglicans, for example, had any basic similarity to Austrian Lutherans merely on the grounds that they are both "Protestant" Christian sects. Indeed, in none of our five nations do "Protestant" or Catholic respondents manifest any systematic differences in their political participation rates. The results do indicate, however, that those professing no religious affiliation at all do have a notably higher protest potential accompanied by a correspondingly lower repression potential and have even a higher conventional participation rate.

This finding leads us to suppose that the more important dimension is not sectarian affiliation but the extent of a respondent's subjective sense of religiosity. Our respondents had been asked to state whether they regarded themselves as "very religious," "fairly religious," "not very religious," or "not at all religious." As may be seen in Table 4.1, intense religious feelings quite strongly inhibit political activity in both the conventional and unconventional spheres. The relationship with protest potential, of course, is dependent upon age. Religiously inclined people tend to be older and, hence, less inclined to protest, but it is not so in the case of conventional participation, which we know already is equally a characteristic of young and old. For many people, and especially the old, it may be that church attendance and participation in the spiritual life of the community is in some sense an alternative, even exclusive, activity compared with political participation. It provides a different "life." Despite larger numbers of old people among the religious, it is still surprising to see that repression potential is linked to religiosity. A taste for political repression is not an obvious corollary of a Christian way of life. But the statistical relationship is moderately strong.

Race

For the purposes of this overview, race is defined as white or nonwhite; this latter category includes blacks, Indians, Orientals, and Chicanos. No one, least of all the authors, would bother to defend such a dichotomy as an adequate description of ethnic origin. It will, however, provide us with a glimpse of whether rates of political activity or choice of participation styles among members of racial minorities actually do differ from whites to the extent that may be expected. The involvement of members of such minorities

Table 4.6: POLITICAL ACTION AND RACE

	The Netherlands		Britain		United States	
	White	*Non-White*	*White*	*Non-White*	*White*	*Non-White*
Protest Potential						
Low (0, 1)	29%	40%	45%	44%	30%	29%
Medium (2, 3)	40	29	40	36	50	41
High (4-7)	31	30	15	20	20	30
(n =)	(1158)	(39)	(1438)	(32)	(1526)	(189)
tau-b	.02		.00		.07	
Repression Potential						
Low (0, 1)	70	69	36	60	31	64
Medium (2)	13	6	28	16	29	16
High (3, 4)	17	25	46	24	40	20
(n =)	(1158)	(39)	(1438)	(35)	(1526)	(189)
tau-b	.03		.10		.18	
Conventional Participation						
Low (0, 1)	50	59	53	41	33	45
Medium (2, 3)	39	32	37	52	37	29
High (4-7)	11	9	10	7	30	26
(n =)	(1158)	(39)	(1438)	(32)	(1526)	(189)
tau-b	.04		.01		.04	

in the political protest movements of recent times has been considerable. Does it also reflect a high, generalized protest potential among such minorities as was found for the student community and the intelligentsia?

It is possible to operationalize this variable in only three countries in this study: the Netherlands (mostly migrants from the former Dutch East Indies), Britain (migrants from the West Indies and the Indian subcontinent), and, of course, the United States. ("Guest workers" in Germany, some of whom are of non-European origin, were excluded from the survey because they do not enjoy citizen status.)

Table 4.6 shows that in the Netherlands and Britain those few members of nonwhite ethnic minorities included in our samples do not show a greater protest potential than members of the majority group, but in the United States there is some tendency for blacks to be more militant than whites.

With respect to repression potential, nonwhites in all three countries show very low levels compared with those of whites. In the Netherlands, this is no lower than the remainder of the Dutch sample. It could scarcely be otherwise, given the widespread rejection of repressive action in that country. In Britain, especially among West Indians, and in the United States these levels of repression potential are about half those found for whites. Thus blacks may well identify themselves as members of a group that has suffered disproportionately on occasion from the repressive actions of police and troops, and so express rejection of their use upon others. Despite this, their rates of conventional political participation do not differ significantly from those of whites.

POLITICAL ACTION AND THE ECONOMIC DOMAIN

The emergence of the industrial class system has determined many of the basic functions and features of political life in the developed world, especially in Europe. Class conflict is to varying degrees endemic to modern politics. The *idea* of class provides the medium through which many people orient themselves toward the political system and guides their choice of party. To identify oneself as a worker *tends* (for it is by no means an infallible process) to suggest a disposition toward politics that best seeks a remedy for the exploitation of one's own labor. Conversely, to identify one's interests with those of the professional and managerial classes tends to suggest support for those political elements most likely to perpetuate the rewarded status of currently elite groups. The worker may favor a faction that advances his interests by means of reappropriation, by redistribution, or by enlisting more benevolent patronage. The manager may favor an authoritarian or a liberal regime. Whatever the chosen remedy, class provides for many the first prism through which the political world is viewed. So class is properly regarded by political scientists as a key element of any scientific explanation of political behavior.

The preeminence of class as an explanatory concept needs no further introduction or elaboration at this point. It leaves us, however, with two problems. First, how do we develop a single measure of class that is valid cross-nationally? Second, the dominant influence of class explanations of politics, given by others in the literature, suggests that, like religion, class may have relevance for predicting people's partisan choice but has not too much to say regarding their participation style and behavioral repertory. It is *style* and *repertory* that interest us.

Regarding the first problem, the short answer is probably that we do not develop a single measure of class. Definitions of class are legion. They vary from a Marxist approach, based on the individual's relationship to the means of production, to the amazingly complex assemblies of occupational groups and subgroups well-loved by government census offices.

Whatever the practical or ideological basis of the measure used, just about everyone will agree that class is a multifaceted concept that contains a number of key elements. Principal among these elements are:

(1) the *nature* of the occupation to be classified, especially whether the work is manual or nonmanual;
(2) the disposable income received for the work, especially relative to the rewards received by others, and;
(3) the social and economic status generated by the employment and rewards, especially in terms of the power it confers over others.

For any occupation, the balance of these three elements contributes to a national hierarchical score to determine whether the respondent is rated a member of a higher or lower class group. Note that the resulting measure would always be categorical because the ideal of a continuously graded attribute of class makes no sense.[16] This is so because, although some of the contributory elements of class may be conceived of as continuously graded (income, power, status, and so on), their changing *balance* results in categorical anomalies. For example, many skilled manual workers command a greater income than junior nonmanual grades who nonetheless enjoy supervisory status over others. Who then is in the higher class?

It is possible to cope with these problems within a single national occupational system, but to attempt an equivalent hierarchical grading across five nations is a very unpromising idea. Far better, we believe, is to retain the key elements of class in a disaggregated form and so achieve cross-nationally valid levels of measurement while drawing our conclusions about class inferentially. We have been greatly aided in this attempt by the work of Donald Treiman, who has developed a cross-national measure of what is conceptually the most difficult aspect of class, namely status or, as Treiman prefers, occupational prestige. It is this measure that will concern us first.[17]

Occupational Prestige

As Treiman describes, "there have been some eighty-five studies of occupational prestige conducted in nearly sixty countries throughout the world."[18] Typically, such studies invite random samples of the population "to *rank* a set of occupational titles with respect to their prestige or social standing." Usually, they are done in a series of subsets and the results are aggregated to form a series of average prestige scores for each occupation that may be standardized in some way to provide a *quasi*-continuous scale of *relative* prestige. From these eighty-five studies, Treiman created a single Standard International Occupational Prestige Scale. Note that this concept of prestige is wider than work-based status and is all the more useful for that. It includes, for example, the idea of higher status attaching to nonmanual work.

Each of our respondents has received a score on this scale. For example, a civil engineer merits a score of 70, a bank clerk 48, a garage mechanic 43, and a laborer 19. Since not everyone has a job, and it would make no sense to exclude, say, housewives from consideration and even less sense to lump them all together in one category, we shall concentrate upon the occupational prestige of the head of the household. In practice, this means that wives take on their husband's occupational prestige—a procedure we would not try to defend on ideological grounds but simply as a commonly adopted expediency.

What impact should occupational prestige have upon political action? As far as conventional political participation is concerned, we should reasonably expect that higher status individuals will have higher participation rates. If for no other reason, such people will be better educated, and we know already that higher levels of education are associated with increased participation. The same is true for protest potential, though less unequivocally. More generally speaking, we may also argue that, since our five nations are to some degree meritocratic, many respondents who are awarded high prestige scores will have "earned" them by upward social mobility-striving that may or may not be associated with education. In itself, such personal efficacy and resourcefulness are as likely as education to be reflected in a willingness to reach out for the levers of political power when necessary—though, again, one suspects that such levers will be of a conventional kind rather than the self-constructed, unconventional variety.

One element running counter to these trends will be the fact that, even if they are heads of their own households, many young people will have a low prestige score through sheer lack of seniority in a career that may eventually bestow high status. Their youth announces them as potential protesters while at the same time suppresses their prestige scores.

Balanced against these speculations is the theoretical dilemma that, whereas traditional theory would expect the greatest protest potential to be encountered among the oppressed—i.e., those with low prestige—common sense and practical observation suggest that unconventional political behavior is most often carried through by young people from middle-class backgrounds. Such people are certainly most likely to participate in conventional activities. Conversely, a paradox runs in the other direction, that whereas high prestige suggests a utilitarian interest in good social control achieved through political repression, in fact the most retributive views are most often found among those lower in social class.

The tau-b correlations reported in Table 4.1 indicate some support for the above hypothesis. Protest potential and, more especially, conventional political participation are both positively associated with higher occupational prestige of the head of household. However, as Tables 4.7 and 4.8 show, in terms of actual percentage distributions these relationships are not impressive in their magnitude. In the case of conventional participation, particularly in the Netherlands and United States, members of high occupational prestige families are about twice as likely to have a high rate of participation as those with low prestige. For protest potential, it is far more a case of high prestige reducing the possibility that people will have very low scores than of accelerating their potential participation in more extreme forms of protest. Repression potential scores, which are not shown, are left more or less unaffected by prestige.

So while we have replicated the common finding that higher status—middle class—people are overrepresented among conventional political activists, we have not really found the same for unconventional activists. This is so despite the fact that education, which we and others have shown is the fuel behind increased middle class participation in politics, is *equally* strong as a predictor of conventional *and* unconventional political behavior. This strongly suggests that the neutral relationship between prestige and protest is due to an influx of lower status and probably *working class* people into the ranks of more committed potential protesters. Put another way, we have found that, whereas conventional activists, while also well-educated, may almost equally be drawn from households having high or low status. Inferentially, this points to the possibility of surprisingly high levels of protest potential among better educated and hence possibly *younger,* skilled manual workers.

Table 4.7: PROTEST POTENTIAL BY OCCUPATIONAL PRESTIGE OF HEAD OF HOUSEHOLD

	Protest Potential	Occupational Prestige				
		Low 1	2	3	*High* 4	*(tau-b)*
The Netherlands	Low 0	16%	8%	7%	4%	
	1	19	22	22	18	
	2	24	22	26	26	(.07)
	3	10	17	15	18	
	High 4	31	30	30	34	
	(n =)	(196)	(289)	(353)	(258)	
Britain	Low 0	27	27	18	11	
	1	22	25	19	19	
	2	25	20	29	29	(.13)
	3	13	13	17	22	
	High 4	13	14	17	19	
	(n =)	(332)	(390)	(249)	(198)	
United States	Low 0	11	9	9	4	
	1	25	28	18	15	
	2	23	23	25	24	(.12)
	3	22	23	28	33	
	High 4	19	17	20	24	
	(n =)	(327)	(431)	(453)	(441)	
Germany	Low 0	24	20	13	14	
	1	24	21	21	18	
	2	24	31	33	34	(.10)
	3	18	18	19	21	
	High 4	10	10	14	14	
	(n =)	(465)	(691)	(515)	(385)	
Austria	Low 0	28	22	15	10	
	1	37	31	35	30	
	2	19	28	27	33	(.15)
	3	10	10	14	14	
	High 4	6	9	9	13	
	(n =)	(320)	(420)	(248)	(187)	

Table 4.8: CONVENTIONAL POLITICAL PARTICIPATION BY OCCUPATIONAL PRESTIGE OF HEAD OF HOUSEHOLD

	Conventional Participation	Occupational Prestige				
		Low 1	2	3	High 4	(tau-b)
The Netherlands	Low 0	37%	37%	27%	16%	
	1	24	23	22	15	
	2	27	25	33	37	(.20)
	3	6	8	9	10	
	High 4	6	8	9	22	
	(n =)	(206)	(301)	(367)	(265)	
Britain	Low 0	27	34	21	15	
	1	30	25	26	19	
	2	30	28	35	37	(.13)
	3	5	6	9	11	
	High 4	9	7	10	18	
	(n =)	(340)	(416)	(257)	(200)	
United States	Low 0	26	18	15	7	
	1	20	20	17	13	
	2	20	26	26	23	(.18)
	3	10	14	12	14	
	High 4	24	22	29	43	
	(n =)	(335)	(436)	(461)	(448)	
Germany	Low 0	30	26	19	10	
	1	33	31	32	29	
	2	15	17	17	19	(.15)
	3	7	8	11	14	
	High 4	15	18	20	27	
	(n =)	(483)	(721)	(526)	(396)	
Austria·	Low 0	40	39	29	14	
	1	22	21	21	29	
	2	19	19	25	33	(.12)
	3	7	7	7	7	
	High 4	12	13	19	16	
	(n =)	(403)	(547)	(288)	(215)	

Income

Conceptually, income is a pleasingly uncomplicated element of class. As defined to our respondents, it is the amount received after deductions at source. Truly, there are cross-national variations in the relationship between disposable income and the social wage; i.e., money is recycled through government to provide, say, health care, in one country whereas it is left to individuals to care for their own health in others. But, being a genuinely continuous variable that may be treated as a percentile value, income relative to domestic distributions is a perfectly valid cross-national measure. Again, we have taken household income as the appropriate measure.

In this case, as Table 4.1 shows, we find more definite results than those for occupational status. The higher the respondent's family income the more likely it is that he or she will have high scores on both the conventional and unconventional participation scales and, this time, more or less equally so. Also there are some indications that higher income actually depresses repression potential a little.

Does this mean that the most hardnosed element of class—money—is the measure that really counts in determining the political outcomes of economic status? It is possible, of course, and it recalls aptly our earlier discussions of the theoretical difficulties of incorporating in our general explanation the protests of the students—the sons and daughters of the rich—in the 1960s and early 1970s. Here surely is some proof.

On the other hand, this finding might equally reflect support for the speculations above concerning the young skilled workers. As mentioned in our example of the nonlinear categorical nature of class, skilled workers in most of the countries of our surveys quite often receive substantially more than allegedly higher status nonmanual grades. Many of the manual jobs assigned low status in the Treiman scheme quite clearly command very high wages, especially in countries like the United States, the Netherlands, and Germany. This would be an equally parsimonious explanation of the findings and a more congruent one as well.

Another possibility—that the finding is due simply to the higher earnings of men who, anyway, have higher participation scores—is helpfully eliminated by using the household measure. There are too few single-woman households to make that difference. A further possibility—that the effect is due mainly to the low income of the oldest respondents—will be considered with others below.

Self-Reported Social Class

We spoke earlier of the *idea* of class. By this we mean rather more than the concept of class as simply some kind of political interest group. But probably we mean less than Marxist theorists who speak of class consciousness as a realization by the workers that they are members of an exploited majority. We leave aside also all the cultural aspects of class celebrated by sociologists. We mean, as we outlined earlier from a political scientist's point of view, that people located in different sectors of the social economy perceive and possess different interests. Whenever resources are less than abundant—which is most of the time for most commodities—such interests conflict. Systematically, these conflicts occur and are resolved through the political representation of socioeconomic class groups.

On the other hand, we have just demonstrated that the key element of the model—the *objective* measurement of class—has few implications for participation styles. When age and education are accounted for, it has probably very few indeed. But we should not be too dismayed about this apparent failure. The theoretical model laid out in chapter 2 emphasized the conscious politicization of social and economic roles before their impact upon political behavior may adequately be assessed. Now we can apply the first and simplest test of this hypothesis. If objective class does not influence participation much, perhaps subjective class will. It may be that, in order for class membership to affect participation, such membership should at least be acknowledged and articulated by the members. Accordingly, our respondents were asked to say which social class they felt they belonged to. Those declining to assign themselves voluntarily were asked whether they felt themselves to be "working class," "middle class," or "upper middle class."[19] The intention was to test whether the *idea* of class was more important than the fact of class; the two measures often differ.[20]

The analysis of subjective social class demonstrated first that we were right to be suspicious of the possibility of a universally valid popular idea of class. As Table 4.9 demonstrates, class identity varies considerably from country to country.

These results support a common belief that Britain remains the last true proletarian polity in Western Europe, while status-striving is widespread in Germany and America. However, reference back to Table 4.1 will show that subjective class identity has even less impact upon choice of participation, or upon repression potential, than do our objective class measures. There is no consistent relationship with protest potential and, though there is a positive relationship with conventional participation, it only weakly mirrors the objective measures provided by prestige and income.[21]

Table 4.9: SUBJECTIVE SOCIAL CLASS BY COUNTRY

	"Working Class"	"Middle Class"	"Upper Middle Class"	
The Netherlands	39	51	10	(=100%)
Britain	65	32	3	
United States	39	44	17	
Germany	34	57	9	
Austria	48	45	7	

The results for the relationship between subjective social class and repression potential are frankly uninterpretable. In Germany and Austria, subjective class is neutrally related to repression potential; in the United States, a weak negative relationship exists; in Britain and Holland, the relationship is similarly weak but runs in the opposite, positive, direction.

Obviously, the subjective mediation of social roles into political action will have more complex and mature antecedents than crude notions of class.

Trade Union Membership

A clearer aspect of the way economic behavior will affect political behavior beyond simply the choice among party candidates lies in the role of secondary groups. Farmers join farmers' pressure groups, businessmen form trade and industry associations, workers join unions. Entry into these organizations is a socializing experience. Unfortunately, we do not have sufficient farmers and businessmen in our sample to test whether active entry into their representative pressure groups will modify their individual political behavior; but we have quite enough workers.

Rates of trade union membership differ somewhat in the five countries of our study, varying from 15 percent and 17 percent in Germany and the United States to 26 percent and 27 percent in Britain and Austria. The expectations we attach to trade union membership are quite straightforward. If, for no better reason than the presence of "strikes" in our scale, we should expect trade union members (and former members now retired) to have a higher protest potential than nonmembers. Likewise, the item implying the use of troops to break strikes will depress repression potential among trade unionists.

The results in Table 4.1 indicate only weak support for these hypotheses. Expectations are upheld at rather modest levels of association in the two most unionized countries—Britain and Austria—but only very inconsistently elsewhere. We should expect stronger results than those reported. In Britain especially (where the contrast between unionists and nonunionists still amounts only to a difference of 21 percent *versus* 13 percent of those scoring highest on the Protest Potential Scale), the scene of political and social protest shifted perceptibly toward the industrial sphere during the early 1970s. In the period immediately following the British survey, the Conservative Government suffered an electoral defeat largely brought about by industrial action by the miners and their allies in the labour movement. This result does not necessarily imply that a popular image of union militancy is a false one. It implies merely that potential protest among even unionized workers is matched in strength by potential protest in other sectors of the community, much as we have described above.

INTEGRATION AND CONCLUSIONS

Survey research works through measures of association. Survey researchers tell their story in a "this-goes-with-that-and-so-it-follows-that" style of exposition. Seldom can they say, "this-causes-that." This style is often difficult to follow because, even if the authors are good at their craft, the things that "go with" the thing one is trying to explain also "go with" each other. Low income goes with low protest potential but so does increasing age, and the old are poor. Higher social class goes with high conventional political participation but so does higher education, and the rich buy better schooling. So what is "causing" what? The problem of correlated predictor variables is called multicollinearity, and it has at least two important consequences for results obtained from multivariate analysis procedures like multiple regression analysis: it influences the magnitude and the size of regression coefficients, and it increases their standard errors.[22] Obviously, both consequences are undesirable because they render substantive interpretations of the coefficients questionable.

Fortunately, in the regression analyses we are about to present we will not be greatly troubled by multicollinearity. Based on simulated data, Opp and Schmidt were able to show that the critical value of a correlation between predictors is about .6.[23] This value is nowhere even approached among our predictors: of the six independent variables selected for regression analysis, only age and education (average r = .27), education and occupational prestige (average r = .43), and sex and trade union membership (average r = .33) are correlated at any level of significance.

Regarding the choice of variables to be entered into the regression, we naturally capitalized on the heuristic order imposed upon this chapter and tested first the impact of the three most important elements of the social domain: age, sex, and education. Then, in a second equation, we looked at the same three variables, but added religiosity and the two least interdependent elements of the economic domain: occupational prestige and trade union membership. (One may readily see in this context the futility of including, say, prestige and income together.)

The unbracketed figures provided under each column heading in Tables 4.10 through 4.12 are beta coefficients that measure, in standardized units, the increment that may be expected in the dependent variable for each increment in the independent variable. In brackets, we also give the unstandardized B regression coefficients. The relative magnitude of both coefficients is a rough guide to the importance of a given variable for the variance explained in the dependent variable when all other independent variables in the regression are held constant. The reason why we present both coefficients is that they serve different purposes. The unstandardized coefficients are invariant across populations even if variances and covariances between populations vary; they "give us the laws of science."[24] Therefore, the Bs should be used for the comparison of different populations (and countries). On the other hand, the unstandardized coefficients directly reflect the scale upon which a variable has been measured. This scale is, however, usually not homogeneous across variables. Thus, in order to be able to assess the *relative* impact of a given variable *within any one population* the standarization of the variables is required.[25]

In addition to the regression coefficients, we also supply as summary measures for the explanatory power of the set of independent variables the multiple-correlation coefficient (R) and its square (R^2) indicating the total amount of explained variance in the dependent variable.

Once more, this dual analysis repeated for three kinds of political action over five nations generates a mass of numbers that is not easy to summarize. Overall, though, the result is fairly clear.

Protest potential is the most "explicable" variable. Age (dominantly), sex, and education jointly provide an explanation of between 11 percent (in Austria) and 22 percent (in the United States) of the total variance in protest potential scores. Except in the Netherlands, where religiousness seems to have particular importance, only 1 percent to 2 percent explained variance is added by the inclusion of religiousness and the two economic domain variables. Only in Britain does trade unionism retain any independent predictive powers for protest potential, and occupational prestige scarcely at all. This is an important result in that we can state with increasing confidence that, despite the expected association with higher education, protest potential is not only found among better educated young people—especially young men from the middle classes—but also among better educated young people from working class homes and occupations.

The results for repression potential provide a mirror image of those for protest potential but at lower levels of explained variance, ranging from 6 percent in Austria to 16 percent in the United States. This is surprising in that very behaviorally specific measures like protest potential are often *less* easily analyzed in this way than more generalized attitudes of the kind that make up the repression scale. The answer is probably that, whereas most old people reject protest *behavior* on practical grounds, liberally minded older people in the samples are still free to express their distaste for repressive measures when they are used on the young.

The patterns for conventional participation are somewhat different and are of the kind to be expected from the foregoing analysis. The dominant role of age in the protest/repression explanation is taken over in the interpretation of sex (i.e., maleness) and higher education. In the Netherlands and Britain especially, occupational prestige retains good independent predictive power

Table 4.10: MULTIPLE REGRESSION ANALYSIS OF PROTEST POTENTIAL SCALE[+]

Countries	Age		Sex		Education		Religiousness		Trade Union Membership		Occupational Prestige		R	R^2
The Netherlands	-.23	(-.02)	-.11	(-.42)	.16	(.11)							.35	.12
Britain	-.30	(-.03)	-.15	(-.53)	.12	(.10)							.39	.15
United States	-.35	(-.03)	-.06	(-.21)	.21	(.11)							.47	.22
Germany	-.29	(-.03)	-.13	(-.41)	.17	(.12)							.40	.16
Austria	-.17	(-.01)	-.12	(-.32)	.21	(.15)							.33	.11
The Netherlands	-.19	(-.02)	-.09	(-.34)	.15	(.11)	.17	(.34)	-.03	(-.13)	.01	(.00)	.39	.15
Britain	-.28	(-.03)	-.12	(-.41)	.10	(.09)	.03	(.06)	-.09	(-.34)	.06	(.01)	.41	.16
United States	-.33	(-.03)	-.04	(-.13)	.20	(.10)	.12	(.20)	-.04	(-.12)	.04	(.00)	.48	.23
Germany	-.25	(-.02)	-.09	(-.29)	.18	(.12)	.12	(.22)	-.06	(-.24)	.01	(.00)	.42	.18
Austria	-.16	(-.01)	-.11	(-.29)	.16	(.12)	.07	(.11)	-.03	(-.09)	.09	(.01)	.34	.12

[+]Education was operationalized by the years a respondent had spent in school. This variable is described in detail in the Technical Appendix. Entries are standardized (beta) and, in parentheses, unstandardized (b) regression coefficients.

Table 4.11: MULTIPLE REGRESSION ANALYSIS OF REPRESSION POTENTIAL SCALE[+]

Countries	Age		Sex		Education		Religiousness		Trade Union Membership		Occupational Prestige		R	R²
The Netherlands	.15	(.01)	.02	(.04)	-.04	(-.02)							.17	.03
Britain	.23	(.02)	.13	(.33)	-.04	(-.02)							.28	.08
United States	.31	(.02)	.07	(.18)	-.15	(-.06)							.39	.15
Germany	.21	(.02)	-.01	(-.03)	-.16	(-.10)							.29	.08
Austria	.02	(.00)	.06	(.18)	-.15	(-.12)							.17	.03
The Netherlands	.11	(.01)	-.02	(-.05)	-.05	(-.02)	-.20	(-.26)	.06	(.19)	.01	(.00)	.27	.07
Britain	.21	(.01)	.08	(.19)	-.05	(-.03)	-.05	(-.07)	.12	(.35)	.02	(.00)	.31	.10
United States	.30	(.02)	.04	(.11)	-.14	(-.06)	-.07	(-.10)	.08	(.21)	-.02	(.00)	.40	.16
Germany	.17	(.01)	-.05	(-.15)	-.16	(-.10)	-.13	(-.22)	.07	(.26)	-.03	(.00)	.32	.10
Austria	.01	(.00)	.02	(.06)	-.11	(-.09)	-.13	(-.24)	.09	(.29)	-.04	(.00)	.24	.06

[+]Education was operationalized by the years a respondent had spent in school. This variable is described in detail in the Technical Appendix. Entries are standardized (beta) and, in parentheses, unstandardized (b) regression coefficients.

Table 4.12: MULTIPLE REGRESSION ANALYSIS OF CONVENTIONAL POLITICAL PARTICIPATION SCALE[+]

Countries	Age		Sex		Education		Religiousness		Trade Union Membership		Occupational Prestige		R	R²
The Netherlands	.09	(.01)	−.18	(−.61)	.26	(.15)							.31	.10
Britain	.11	(.01)	−.14	(−.45)	.18	(.14)							.23	.05
United States	.13	(.01)	−.14	(−.59)	.36	(.24)							.38	.14
Germany	−.07	(−.01)	−.29	(−.17)	.22	(.19)							.41	.17
Austria	.05	(.01)	−.22	(−.87)	.13	(.13)							.28	.08
The Netherlands	.06	(.01)	−.16	(−.54)	.18	(.10)	−.02	(−.04)	−.08	(−.33)	.17	(.02)	.36	.13
Britain	.09	(.01)	−.13	(−.42)	.13	(.10)	−.11	(−.19)	−.10	(−.35)	.12	(.02)	.29	.08
United States	.11	(.01)	−.15	(−.64)	.31	(.21)	−.09	(−.20)	.01	(.04)	.09	(.01)	.40	.16
Germany	−.07	(−.01)	−.27	(−.10)	.19	(.17)	−.01	(−.02)	−.06	(−.03)	.07	(.01)	.42	.17
Austria	.05	(.01)	−.21	(−0.82)	.10	(.11)	.02	(.05)	−.05	(−.20)	.05	(.01)	.29	.08

[+]Education was operationalized by the years a respondent had spent in school. This variable is described in detail in the Technical Appendix. Entries are standardized (beta) and, in parentheses, unstandardized (b) regression coefficients.

to raise conventional participation even after sex and education have been accounted for. This finding may reflect the connection suggested earlier between the efficacious and entrepreneurial attitudes of upwardly socially mobile people and a tendency toward political action. If, despite perhaps a poor education, one acquires a status worth defending, one is also likely to be the sort of person who includes active political reflexes among one's public skills.

The findings of chapter 3 led us to believe that modern political activism was by no means the sole property of politically exotic extremists. There was simply too much protest potential around for this to be true, and protest potential showed convergent links with conventional political participation. This tendency toward a modern political versatility was tempered, it is true, by quite substantial amounts of repression potential but, again, the overall impression was one of a surprisingly permissive climate of opinion (even leaving the Netherlands aside for a moment), encouraging political activism to flourish.

This chapter has strengthened and elaborated these impressions. It is, of course, still true that, if one wishes to meet a protest-prone political activist, then the shortest route to a successful chance interview is through the bar of the students' union at the nearest university. This is the route taken by most journalists who need a "filler" on the current scene in extremist politics. In this way, the student-dissident-protest image has been constantly reinforced in the public mind. Yet the evidence presented above suggests strongly that the young student interviewed in this way is not *typical* of the kind of person now likely to be mobilized in unorthodox political behavior. Such a person will be young, certainly, but not necessarily a youth. We found that a good education accelerated the will to protest, but a *degree* was not an essential qualification for entry into activism. Nor is protest potential even predominantly a middle class characteristic. Overall, men are more ready than women to be mobilized, but *young* women have an impressive political potency that, unlike the even-handed versatility shown by men, is pointed sharply in the direction of protest methods. Indeed, this evidence dispels any wonder that may linger about the success of the feminist politics now snapping at the flanks of conventional party systems.

The feminist movement is one of a number of new political forces to emerge since the peace movement of the 1960s demonstrated, quite literally, that protest was a potent and even a legitimate pathway toward political redress. As this realization has spread out into the wider political community—and this chapter has shown that it *has* spread out widely—so similar movements have fed upon it. The environmentalist movement, the consumer movement (Naderism), the participation movement, and a thousand and one campaigns for and against a range of things so diverse that conventional politics finds them increasingly difficult to encompass—all these flourish in the widening parameters of license for protest and generalized political activism. Compared to the 1960s, the 1970s may appear increasingly tame. The widespread violence of Watts, Detroit, the Chicago Convention, the Sorbonne, Rome, even Prague, all appear to have given way to renewed apathy and, consequently, to acts of terrorism by increasingly isolated and pathological extremist groups.

What really appears to have happened—what is really significant—is that what was extremism in the 1960s is becoming the legitimacy of the 1970s. In passing from the vanguard to the masses, political protest has obviously been modified, toned-down. On the way, it has picked up increased connections with conventional politics. Even the common safeguards to public order have been retained. Yet this very diffusion, far from diluting the idea of protest, may surely have increased its potency to contribute to political change. The governments of our five nations, and probably the governments of most similar nations, now have to contend with a polity full of young, well-educated men and women who do not accept that their political efficacy is bounded by officially sanctioned channels of representative democracy. They have a wider political armory to deploy, and seem very willing to use it. It is this crucial idea of political versatility, of a widening of the citizen's political action repertory, of the *balance* between conventional and unconventional political action, that will claim our attention in the following chapter.

NOTES

1. Yes, of course they do.

2. An issue of major concern for the presentation of cross-national data and comparative analyses is the choice of the correct measures. Ronald Schoenberg, "Strategies for Meaningful Comparison," in Herbert L. Costner (ed.), *Sociological Methodology 1972,* San Francisco: Jossey-Bass, 1972, p. 4, seems to sum up the state of the art in writing that "it is simply not legitimate to compare standardized measures across different samples since any difference in such measures may just as likely be attributable to differences in variances as to differences in effects." Whereas we see no basis for disagreement with this statement *on statistical grounds,* we are nevertheless at a loss with regard to the choice of an appropriate nonstandardized nonparametric coefficient. Three reasons convinced us that we could and should stay with a "normal" coefficient like tau-b for nonparametric analyses: our emphasis is strictly on description and not on formal causal analysis; well-established alternatives to standardized nonparametric correlation coefficients are not at hand; and the "normal" coefficients are widely used in comparative social research. For parametric analyses like regression analysis, results are presented using both the standardized (beta) and nonstandardized (b) regression coefficients.

3. Max Kaase and Alan Marsh, "The Matrix of Political Action." Paper read to the 10th World Congress of the International Political Science Association, Edinburgh, Scotland, August 1976.

4. For a lucid, if somewhat romanticized discussion of this point, see Richard Flacks, *Youth and Social Change,* Chicago: Markham, 1971.

5. Howard Schuman, *Black Racial Attitudes,* Ann Arbor: Institute for Social Research, University of Michigan, 1974.

6. Radical with a small "r," of course. As will be made clear in later chapters, the radical left is by no means the most important source of protest potential.

7. There must be literally hundreds of references to support the point. As good and short a summary as any is to be found in Roger Brown, *Social Psychology,* New York: Free Press, 1966, pp. 167-172.

8. See the analysis of Gabriel A. Almond and Sidney Verba in *The Civic Culture,* Princeton: Princeton University Press, 1963, pp. 387ff., where they show this cross-nationally and attribute lower political participation rates of women, among many factors, to their lower educational attainment. See also Giuseppe DiPalma, *Apathy and Participation,* New York: Free Press, 1970. Our own analyses indicate that in all five countries women with elementary and secondary education are still well below the male rates of unconventional and conventional political involvement. Only university-educated women have been able to substantially bridge that gap. Details of this analysis are unfolded later in the chapter.

9. Sidney Verba and Norman Nie, *Participation in America,* New York: Harper & Row, 1972, pp. 56ff.

10. It is fair to add that in a second General Election of that year (October 1974), the turnout fell to a more familiar 72.3 percent.

11. The best contemporary account of this process is given by Paul Sniderman, *Personality and Democratic Politics,* Berkeley: University of California Press, 1975.

12. J.M. Moorhouse and C.W. Chamberlain, "Lower Class Attitudes to Property: Aspects of the Counter-Ideology," *Sociology* 8 (September 1974), p. 398.

13. Alan Marsh, *Protest and Political Consciousness,* Beverly Hills: Sage, 1977, p. 130.

14. Ibid., ch. 8.

15. Ibid.

16. Reading the literature of nineteenth- and early twentieth-century England leaves one with the impression that some societies achieve so finely calibrated a notion of class, from low-to-high, that everyone theoretically can occupy a unique point on the continuum, but it is not a practical idea for scaling purposes.

17. Donald J. Treiman, "Problems of Concept and Measurement in the Comparative Study of Occupational Mobility," *Social Science Research* 4 (1975), pp. 183ff.

18. Ibid., p. 193.

19. Here we are following a tradition of measurement first defined in Richard Centers, *The Psychology of Social Class,* Princeton: Princeton University Press, 1949.

20. See David Butler and Donald Stokes, *Political Change in Britain,* New York: St. Martin's, 1969, especially ch. 4.

21. In the British study, Alan Marsh, *Protest and Political Consciousness,* pp. 85-87, pursued this idea to a complicated logical end, involving an analysis of political action by the intersection of objective and subjective social class. No significant results were found.

22. Karl-Dieter Opp and Peter Schmidt, *Einfuehrung in die Mehrvariablenanalyse,* Hamburg: Rowohlt, 1976, p. 169.

23. Ibid., p. 171.

24. Hubert M. Blalock, *Causal Inferences in Nonexperimental Research,* Chapel Hill: University of North Carolina Press, 1961, p. 51.

25. Opp and Schmidt, *Einfuehrung in die Mehrvariablenanalyse,* pp. 120ff., offer a good introduction to the rationale for selectively using standardized and unstandardized regression coefficients.

Chapter 5

POLITICAL ACTION REPERTORY

Changes Over Time and a New Typology

MAX KAASE and ALAN MARSH

INTRODUCTION

In the previous two chapters we have developed and analyzed two scales intended to measure respondents' reported conventional political participation and their potential unconventional political participation. In addition, we have dealt with attitudes toward repressive political action by the state. In this chapter we will be concerned only with changes in subjective political competence and the relationship between conventional and unconventional political involvement. Competence is a core concept in the study by Almond and Verba of political culture.[1] It is theoretically and empirically related to the notion of political repertory we discussed in chapter 2 in that both competence and repertory assume that citizens have acquired through social learning qualifications that will help them to respond to political needs and demands to achieve the goals they strive for.[2]

The basic hypothesis underlying this chapter is that conventional and unconventional political involvement—as operationalized before—are not mutually exclusive but rather operate jointly and thereby constitute what we will call a political action repertory. We will approach this analysis on two different tracks. First, we will study the development of subjective political competence over time. This analysis will be based on time-series data and should yield interesting results regarding core questions of this research project, such as the politicization of mass publics and the emergence of new styles of political action in the 1960s and 1970s in the industrialized democracies of the West. Second, and entirely within the conceptual and empirical realm of our project, we will construct and validate a political action repertory typology. In so doing, we will investigate the nature of the relationship between conventional and unconventional political action.

THE ANALYSIS OF
SUBJECTIVE POLITICAL COMPETENCE

The scarcity in the 1950s and early 1960s of those acts of political participation that we have termed unconventional and the corresponding lack of scholarly interest in their analysis have resulted in a shortage of longitudinal bases for comparison that would permit us to evaluate our own data more effectively. Fortunately, *The Civic Culture* study by Almond and Verba contains a set of questions explicitly designed to measure the subjective political competence of individuals on the local as well as on the national level of the political system. That study's concern with the extent to which individuals believe they can exert influence is well in line with our interest in the political action repertory citizens possess as one part of their overall political resources. Our theoretical perspective is not entirely congruent with that of Almond and Verba, and their scheme for coding these open-ended questions reflects their specific research interests. Nevertheless, we will be able to compare, for three of our five countries (Britain, the United States, and Germany), how the overall sense of subjective competence and the role of direct action techniques may have changed in those countries between 1959-1960 and 1974.[3]

Comparisons of this kind are by no means straightforward. There are at least five sources of potential noncomparability of open-ended questions over time: coding procedures, the use of precodes, coding unreliability, sampling frames, and interviewer quality.[4] Of these five points, we will only address ourselves to the first two in some detail, assuming that the other three are sufficiently known and well covered in the methodological literature.

A good example of problems in longitudinal analysis based on open-ended questions is a socialization research result mentioned by Schuman.[5] In a study of changes in child-rearing practices between 1952 and 1971, a theoretically intriguing initial result was that changes had indeed occurred in the direction of a more permissive and physically warm relationship between mother and child. Since this result was achieved via comparison of open-ended questions, Schuman decided to code the 1951 data anew in 1972-1973 to check the validity of the substantive conclusions. The result of this analysis was that the observed longitudinal change turned out to be almost completely an artifact of divergent coding.

The second point of concern is the use of precodes in the Almond-Verba study. Nowhere in *The Civic Culture* is it mentioned that the subjective local and national competence questions are not full-fledged open-ended questions but rather questions with precodes coded by the interviewers during field work.[6] Although reliable empirical evidence with respect to the use of precodes in open-ended questions is not available, we nevertheless suspect that the obtained response patterns are not completely independent of the available precodes even if, as is the case with the Almond-Verba study, an "other response" category is available. By contrast, in this study no precodes were used.

With these reservations in mind, one may justifiably ask whether systematic comparisons between the Almond-Verba data and our own make any sense at all. While this point would seem well taken, it can also be argued that, if appropriate caution is taken, the scarcity of cross-national time series data alone warrants a closer look at these sets of information. Moreover, the importance of adding a dynamic perspective to the analysis whenever possible left us with no alternative choice, as no other data from earlier periods were available in more than one country.

We will approach this analysis with a clear and limited focus. There are three topics to be investigated. First, we are interested in the percentage of people who claim they cannot do anything about a local regulation or a national law they consider unjust or harmful. This should prove to be a relatively reliable indicator, less affected by the potential sources of bias discussed above. Second, we want to know to what extent people in 1974 name unconventional political activities, which—as Almond and Verba show— were scarcely salient in 1959-1960.[7] The third inquiry deals with the overall concept of political repertory. The analysis we will present is based on the assumption that our concept of political repertory can be operationalized *with respect to this particular set of questions* and by the *number of responses* a given individual has provided for the questions.

In 1959-1960 and in 1974, representative samples in five countries were asked the following two questions. (1) Suppose a regulation were being considered by (specify most local government unit—town, village, and the like) which you considered very unjust or harmful, what do you think you could do? (If needed) Anything else? (Take down full response.) In 1974, the interviewer probe was extended. Interviewer prompt: If necessary say "anything else?" If respondent answers: "Nothing alone" or "Wouldn't do anything by myself" or similar, probe firmly: say, "What do you think you might be able to do with others' help?" And, "Who else might you act with?" (2) Suppose a law were being considered by the (appropriate national legislative body as specified) which you considered to be very unjust or harmful, what do you think you could do? (If needed) Anything else? (Take down full response.) In 1974 the interviewer probed as in question 1 above.[8]

Before we begin to describe and evaluate the findings a note of caution is in order. It would be tempting to analyze stability and change in citizen competence in greater detail, and we will do this to a certain extent later in the chapter when we will be looking at these data according to education, sex, and age of our respondents. But a thorough comparison requires consideration of substantive and methodological problems we are not able to tackle here because of limited space and a different thrust in our analysis. We will therefore only briefly mention three of the most important problems and then proceed with our analysis. First, a simple comparison of the competence marginals is potentially misleading because they only represent the overall balance of stability and changes having occurred in particular subgroups of the population. Second, differences in sampling frames, coding rules and the like may influence the data in ways not amenable to systematic control. Third, before observed changes or stability are attributed to political characteristics of the respondents or their environment, the impact of population factors (like the numerical strength of age cohorts) and compositional effects (like changes in the percentage of well-educated people among given age cohorts) would have to be accounted for. Compositional effects are even more important for cross-national than for longitudinal comparisons because of the widely varying distributions between countries of relevant structural variables like education and age.[9]

Of the three substantive questions we wanted to examine, the first is whether and to what extent changes in the overall level of local and national competence had taken place between 1959-1960 and 1974. Table 5.1 presents, in correspondence with Almond and Verba, the national totals for those respondents who felt capable of doing something about an unjust or harmful local regulation or national law.

We have decided to present these data in two formats: in parentheses are the percentages reported by Almond and Verba,[10] and the other columns contain percentages computed after the elimination of missing data (don't knows and refusals); our analysis will refer to these percentages. This adjustment is necessary for a direct comparison because of the widely varying number of missing data across time and countries. From these data we can see that, though vast changes in *local* competence have not occurred, the *direction* of the changes has brought Britain, the United States, and Germany much closer together than was the case in 1959-1960. The Netherlands too fall into this group, while Austria even in 1974 is on a substantially lower level than Germany was in 1959.

Table 5.1: FERCENTAGE OF RESPONDENTS WHO SAY THEY CAN DO SOMETHING ABOUT AN UNJUST OR HARMFUL LOCAL REGULATION OR NATIONAL LAW, 1959-1960 AND 1974

	Local Regulation						National Law					
	1959-60		1974		1974 ÷ 1959-60 % differences		1959-60		1974		1974 ÷ 1959-60 % differences	
Country	(%)*	%	(%)	%			(%)	%	(%)	%		
The Netherlands	(–)	–	(62)	71	(–)	–	(–)	–	(43)	53	(–)	–
Britain	(78)	81	(64)	74	(–14)	–7	(62)	66	(57)	66	(–5)	0
United States	(77)	82	(71)	77	(–6)	–5	(75)	78	(78)	82	(+3)	+4
Germany	(62)	67	(67)	70	(+5)	+3	(38)	40	(56)	59	(+18)	+19
Austria	(–)	–	(43)	48	–	–	(–)	–	(33)	41	(–)	–

SOURCE for 1959-1960 data: Gabriel Almond and Sidney Verba, *The Civic Culture*, Princeton: Princeton University Press, 1963.
*Percentages in parentheses are based on all respondents. Percentages not in parentheses are computed excluding missing data.

[141]

With respect to subjective *national* competence, the picture is more complicated. One finding by Almond and Verba still holds in 1974, though with some qualifications: the level of national competence is below that of local competence. Two important modifications, however, deserve particular attention.

For one, the American data show an increase in national and a decrease in local competence. Thus, in 1974, more United States citizens felt nationally competent than felt locally competent. That the United States sample is by far the most nationally competent, at least in subjective terms, can be explained, in our judgement, only by the particular political and institutional structure of that country. The United States has many more elective offices and, by comparison with the European countries (in particular Germany, Austria, and the Netherlands), lacks centralized party systems and proportional representation, which render members of parliament less dependent on their local constituencies.[11] Britain's middle-of-the-road position further supports this interpretation.

Also, there is a very substantial increase in German national political competence. We will abstain at this point from offering any substantive interpretation of this increase, though it seems worth pointing out that even in 1959 the German population already ranked higher than the United States and Britain on various measures of political cognition.[12]

Tables 5.2 and 5.3 contain the data on local and national competence necessary to answer the other two questions we had formulated above with regard to changes in:

(1) the occurrence of unconventional political action techniques, and
(2) the overall political repertory.[13]

The extent to which unconventional action techniques have found their way into the self-professed political repertory of citizens between 1959-1960 and 1974 is the next item on our agenda. However, the evaluation of the data presented above has to be preceded by some remarks on the equivalence of coding categories. This equivalence problem is not so much a result of different coding schemes as such, since in the 1974 study we tried to be as true as possible to the Almond-Verba study. Rather, the problem is that, in 1959-1960, "petitions," which we have used as the "easiest" activity in our protest potential scale, were lumped together with activities like writing letters, which we have labeled "conventional." For 1959-1960 there is no way to disentangle this "mix." Therefore, we were forced to exclude "petitions" from the "unconventional political action" category when rearranging the 1974 data. While in 1974 an average 13 percent of respondents in the five

Table 5.2: LOCAL SUBJECTIVE COMPETENCE: 1959-1960 AND 1974

	Britain			United States			Germany			The Netherlands	Austria
	1959 %	1974 %	1974 ÷ 1959 % difference	1960 %	1974 %	1974 ÷ 1960 % difference	1959 %	1974 %	1974 ÷ 1959 % difference	1974 %	1974 %
What can a citizen do about a local regulation considered unjust or harmful?											
Unconventional political action, like demonstrations	0.2	7.1	+6.9	0.5	6.9	+6.4	0.7	7.8	+7.1	19.0	2.9
Total percentage of responses*	115.8	123.6	+7.8	123.7	166.7	+43.0	111.4	133.8	+22.4	137.9	114.0
(N =)	(911)	(1268)		(910)	(1524)		(889)	(2167)		(1009)	(1353)

SOURCE for 1959-1960 data: Gabriel Almond and Sidney Verba, *The Civic Culture*, Princeton: Princeton University Press, 1963.
*Respondents with missing data on the presented variables were excluded from the analysis. Percentages add up to more than 100 percent because of multiple responses.

Table 5.3: NATIONAL SUBJECTIVE COMPETENCE: 1959-1960 AND 1974

	Britain			United States			Germany			The Netherlands	Austria
	1959 %	1974 %	1974 ÷ 1959 % difference	1960 %	1974 %	1974 ÷ 1960 % difference	1959 %	1974 %	1974 ÷ 1959 % difference	1974 %	1974 %
What can a citizen do about a national law considered unjust or harmful?											
Unconventional political action, like demonstrations	—	4.3	+4.3	0.3	3.6	+3.3	1.9	9.5	+7.6	16.5	5.9
Total percentage of responses*	110.9	117.9	+7.0	124.9	147.2	+22.3	106.8	124.4	+17.6	122.0	111.7
(N =)	(903)	(1244)		(926)	(1570)		(890)	(2151)		(939)	(1244)

SOURCE for 1959-1960 data: Gabriel Almond and Sidney Verba, *The Civic Culture*, Princeton: Princeton University Press, 1963.
*Respondents with missing data on the presented variables were excluded from the analysis. Percentages add up to more than 100 percent because of multiple responses.

countries have indeed named "petitions" as one means of political influence, it is impossible to extract the precise number of those respondents who named "petitions" in 1959-1960. This limitation in comparability reduces the category of unconventional political behavior to the more demanding acts of direct action such as demonstrations, protest meetings, boycotts, and the like.

An additional problem in comparability with 1959-1960 is created by the fact that Almond and Verba included violent actions, riots, rebellion, internal war, and political murder in a single category together with protest demonstrations. Aside from the fact that this combination of activities sheds an interesting light on the theoretical conceptualization of protest in the peaceful 1950s, it fortunately poses less of a practical problem than one might first expect, since, at that time, this category was chosen by less than 1 percent of the citizens in the United States, Britain, and Germany. This is, above and beyond the practical consideration, a point of substantial relevance to us since it corroborates our proposition that in the late 1950s direct action techniques were practically nonexistent *among mass publics* as perceived means of political influence.

By contrast, as Tables 5.2 and 5.3 indicate, there is now an average 7 percent of respondents *in these three nations* who would be willing to apply unconventional political means to influence specific political outcomes either on the local or national level. When, in line with the reasoning underlying the protest potential scale, we add petitions to this category in 1974, it brings the respective share up to approximately one-fifth of the population who *consciously* include direct action techniques in their political repertory.

That this percentage is *substantially higher* in the Netherlands and *lower* in Austria is very much in line with the analysis we have presented in the previous two chapters. Looking at these results from a different angle, it can also be safely stated that, while unconventional political behavior has entered the political repertory of some citizens, it has in no way replaced and will not, we speculate, replace the more conventional means of political participation.

We will now address the third topic sketched out earlier in the chapter: the breadth of the overall political repertory citizens in the five countries possess. Given the set of questions we are dealing with, we decided to tackle this question by looking at the number of activities a given individual spontaneously offers as those he or she would be willing to apply in case of an unjust or harmful regulation or law. This indicator, at least with respect to its measurement properties, is probably the most fragile bridge we cross. The number of responses to open-ended questions is dependent on the type and quality of interviewers, on the interview situation, on the respondent, and certainly also on the respective interview schedule itself, in terms of both quality and length.

While we keep these potential shortcomings of the data and earlier methodological reservations in mind, the results nevertheless indicate that a substantial rise in overall competence on both the local and national level over the last fifteen years has indeed occurred. Three country-specific observations deserve special mention. For one, the increase in both local and national competence in Britain is much lower than in Germany and the United States. This is a result for which we do not have a ready substantive interpretation. Second, the Netherlands—at about the level of Germany—and Austria, with by far the smallest overall repertory, follow a pattern familiar from previous results and thereby add plausibility to this particular analysis. Finally, we are surprised by a stunning increase in national competence in the United States. We will focus some additional attention on this result as we now proceed with our analysis and will try to qualify our analyses by bringing in education, sex, and age as three sociostructural variables known from the literature and our chapters 3 and 4 to be an important part of the explanation of varying rates of political competence and participation.

In *The Civic Culture,* Almond and Verba had already extensively discussed the impact of education and, with somewhat less emphasis, that of sex on subjective political competence. Within the focus of our own work we have reanalyzed the Almond-Verba data, but have also added "age" because of its importance for direct political action, as we were able to demonstrate in chapter 4. To conserve space we will not present these data in detail; the following paragraphs will summarize the most salient findings.

As in 1959-1960, education still is an excellent predictor of political competence.[14] Not only does the number of respondents who feel unable to influence local or national political outcomes monotonically *decrease* with increasing education, but also the number of activities a respondent has in his repertory monotonically *increases* with education. This may come as a surprise to those expecting an increase in political participation to reduce existing inequalities in opportunities for participation. In fact, quite the contrary is true. Changes in total responses from 1959-1960 to 1974 show that the higher the education, the higher the *increase* in repertory.[15] This result conforms to the principle that Converse artfully describes as "them what has, gets," referring to the relevance of cognitive capacities and capabilities for acquiring, processing, and retaining political information.[16]

A little earlier in the chapter we had already mentioned the problem of compositional effects for comparative analysis. Education is an exemplary variable to demonstrate such effects. In *The Civic Culture,* which dealt with Britain, the United States, Germany, Italy, and Mexico, Almond and Verba had raised the question: "which are greater, educational or national differences" in subjective local competence?[17] Their tentative conclusion was that the same educational groups across these five nations resemble each other at least as much as different educational groups within nations. Their finding becomes less ambiguous, however, when only Britain, the United States, and Germany are considered: the within-country educational differences clearly outweigh the across-country differences in magnitude. We will look at our data as crudely as they did at theirs by just calculating percentage point differences across educational levels within nations and within educational levels across nations. The results for the three countries already studied in 1959-1960 support and even further accentuate the earlier finding that education has a heavier impact on competence than does nationality. The Netherlands follows the same pattern, but Austria is a deviant case. There, the level of competence among those with elementary education is an average 25 percentage points lower than in all other nations, and this difference is only substantially reduced when we reach the level of university education.

In the next chapter we will approach the problem of systematic country comparisons much more thoroughly. But even with the crude analysis approach we have chosen here it is apparent that the *overall level* of political competence in a given country depends not exclusively but very strongly on the average educational attainment in that country.

In one aspect the data do not conform to our expectations. In chapter 4 we had emphasized the role of formal education for the propensity to engage in direct action techniques. Thus, we had expected the same pattern to emerge in the answers to these open-ended questions. This, however, is clearly not the case. Why not? We speculated that responses to open-ended questions depend more on active learning experiences than did responses to closed-ended questions. We further reasoned that some of the items from which the protest potential scale is built entail labor conflict and civil disobedience techniques where learning occurs among a broader spectrum of social groups than just the better educated. Thus we finally concluded that if the learning hypothesis were true this should show up in a *lower* correlation between education and *actual* direct action participation than between education and protest *potential*. Consequently, we constructed a six-item Guttman scale of actual protest participation (compared with the protest potential scale we excluded petitions because they are also not included in the unconventional action category of the open-ended questions) and looked at its correlation with education. However, except in Britain, this correlation is not appreciably lower (in fact, in Germany and the Netherlands it is even slightly higher) than that with protest potential so we appear to be wrong about this.

Differences in repertory due to sex that had existed in Britain and the United States in 1959-1960, when *The Civic Culture* surveys were taken, have disappeared by 1974. Whether this can be regarded as a consequence of the Women's Liberation Movement is an open question, though these differences were certainly overwhelming in 1959-1960. The German female repertory "deficit," in 1974 as in 1959, mainly reflects the different educational composition of the sexes; as education increases, the sex differences decrease. Nevertheless, it comes as a surprise that although the percentage of better educated women has appreciably increased from 1959 to 1974, in Germany the gap between the sexes in overall competence has in fact widened and not narrowed. In the Netherlands women also feel somewhat less competent than men, whereas the Austrians display very few sex differences in the matter, this mostly because the overall competence level is so low that there is hardly room for such differences to materialize.

The analysis of age differences in competence has to start with the acknowledgement that limitations in case numbers, particularly with regard to the original Almond-Verba data, have forced a theoretically unsatisfactory age group classification upon us. We may use only three categories. Thus we will not be able to thoroughly check whether the curvilinear relationship between age and participation reported in the literature[18] also holds for political competence. Within these limitations, our data can lend support at least to the "slow down" tail of the hypothesis.[19] That is to say that, consistently, in all countries and at both points in time, the oldest citizens are the ones feeling least competent and having the most limited political repertory. However, contrary to 1959-1960, in 1974 in all countries except the United States—and even there the difference between the first two age groups is small—the youngest respondents have the fullest repertory, though they by no means also universally have the lowest percentage of noncompetents.

Among the three countries where a longitudinal analysis is possible, age-related changes in the size of repertory are most striking in Germany, where the youngest age group has increased its repertory by almost twice the margin of the following age group. The data further indicate that unconventional political acts, even though seldom volunteered, cannot be regarded as an exclusive prerogative of the young, though there is a slight tendency in that direction in the Netherlands, Germany, and Austria. As with education it has to be pointed out that the results of the open-ended questions do not agree with the great impact of youthfulness on protest potential we were able to demonstrate in chapter 4.

Although our hypothesis as to why this is so was not supported in the case of education, we decided to check whether age and actual direct action participation are correlated at a lower level than age and protest potential. This time, we struck gold. In all five countries, actual direct action participation correlates at substantially lower values with age than protest potential. In our view, this result indicates that *participation* in direct political action has a lesser element of youthfulness than *attitudes* toward such participation, thereby reflecting the more complex set of potential situations driving citizens into direct political action.

The most important conclusion to be derived from the analysis of age and competence is that younger people are now brought into the political process at an earlier age and at higher rates than in the 1950s and early 1960s. This is not only a side-effect of increasing levels of education among the young. A remaining mystery is the tremendous increase in American local competence repertory over the last fourteen years (almost 43 percentage points), concentrated particularly in the upper educational strata.

Let us summarize the core results of the analyses presented in this chapter to this point.

(1) Insofar as the data permit us to judge, the level of subjective local and national competence has remained fairly stable in Britain and the United States. In Germany we have observed a substantial increase in national competence. Whereas the level of both local and national competence in the Netherlands is comparable to that in Britain and Germany, Austria falls substantially lower on both accounts. In national competence the United States citizens are, as in 1960, far above all other countries surveyed.

(2) Depending on country and systemic level, between 60 percent and 80 percent of the population—except in Austria—show a sense of subjective political competence as operationalized. This in itself is by no means a trivial result if the Almond-Verba argument still holds that feelings of subjective competence are related to the level of satisfaction with the political system.[20]

(3) As in the 1950s, education is still an important determinant of subjective political competence.

(4) Independently of education we have observed a thrust toward more political competence among the young.

(5) A new set of political activities has been added to the citizen's political repertory—a set that had little salience even among the most highly educated strata of the societies examined in the earlier years.

However, neither the percentage of "direct action" responses nor the way these responses behaved in our analysis concurred with our expectations and with the analyses based on standardized indicators. We will return to this point in a later section of this chapter

THE RELATIONSHIP BETWEEN CONVENTIONAL AND UNCONVENTIONAL POLITICAL ACTION: A THEORETICAL PERSPECTIVE

Special care has been taken in conceptualizing types of political involvement in order *not* to present the concept of unconventional political behavior as some kind of *opposite* to orthodox or *conventional* political behavior. Active partisans will signal their discontent and demands for redress of political grievances through a mixture of political methods. For example, a demonstration may end in a lobby of the legislature, or an unofficial strike may occur to provoke the intervention of officials. This view of protest tactics was, of course, not the one that dominated public debate after the surprising revival of direct action techniques in the 1960s epitomized in the outbursts of students and blacks. Striving for cognitive simplicity, many observers on the scene ascribed the growth of protest movements to the breakdown of orthodox politics. The rise of alternative methods of political involvement was blamed on increasing popular contempt for establishment politics. The point has only recently been grasped that these alternatives need not be mutually exclusive. In this sense, we hold that theoretical positions on this matter have now matured to a point where they align with political reality.

The impression of mutual exclusivity has arisen because orthodox politicians and authorities are so often the *target* of protest. But one of Turner's conditions for defining "credible protest" designed to provoke ameliorative action by some target group draws attention to the subtle differences between persuasion and coercion as protest tactics.[21] Protest by persuasion is designed to arouse sympathy, protest by coercion is to arouse fear, and both can be used in combination to obtain an optimal result. However alienated and extreme a protest may appear, if it retains the aim of enlisting the *help* of existing authorities, the activists involved cannot have rejected the relevance of conventional politics for the cure of their grievance. Indeed, much direct action arises not because citizens have rejected conventional politics but because the protesters believe conventional politicians have rejected or excluded them. Thus, our contention is that direct action tactics are designed to *augment* political leverage against an unresponsive system, not to install an alternative administration. While revolutionaries may use protest to try to foment prerevolutionary conditions, revolutionaries have proved only rarely to be the instigators and almost never the beneficiaries of protest movements.

Wilson, writing in 1961, underlined his material bargaining theory with what then seemed an uncontroversial statement: "Protest action, involving such tactics as mass meetings, picketing, boycotts, and strikes, rarely finds enthusiastic participants among upper-income and higher-status individuals."[22]

By 1968, other theorists in the United States had to accommodate the uncomfortable fact that one of the most privileged groups in the country had not merely joined the blacks' struggle, but had reduced to an embattled confusion major institutions of the very system that was designed to ensure their own future privilege, namely, university students.[23] Developing his own frame of reference and, among other relevant literature, also reviewing Wilson's influential article, Lipsky agrees that "protest represents an important aspect of minority group and low income group politics."[24] But he hastens to add: "Groups which seek psychological gratification from politics, but cannot or do not anticipate material political rewards, may be attracted to militant protest leaders."[25]

It would be difficult to deny that direct political action can have its own intrinsic gratification. For example, Driver dryly describes the contraction of the mass appeal of the British Campaign for Nuclear Disarmament after the Cuba crisis as a process whereby "demonstrations began to be left to people who happened to enjoy them."[26] Despite this, for us the essentially instrumental character of protest remains theoretically uppermost and gives rise to the hypothesis that some kind of *positive* relationship will exist between the preparedness to engage in conventional and in unconventional political behavior.

Given the obvious importance for political theory this hypothesis holds, it is surprising that so little relevant evidence has accumulated. The evidence that does exist is supportive. Aberbach and Walker found that unconventional *and* conventional political behavior among blacks was contingent upon distrust of political authorities, with remedies being sought through both kinds of activity.[27] A study in the San Francisco Bay Area found a similar effect, with a positive correlation between a conventional participation index and a protest participation index of .39 (tau-b).[28]

Even more impressive is Muller's result from a pretest study of German farmers, workers, and intellectuals. Correlations between his indices of aggressive political behavior and conventional political behavior were .36 (tau-b) and .70 (gamma). Muller describes the relationship in detail: "Those who show no participation in conventional activity are virtually certain not to participate in aggressive activity; those who participate in conventional activity are unlikely to participate in aggressive activity; but practically all of those who participate in aggressive activity also participate in conventional activity."[29]

Table 5.4: CORRELATION OF
CONVENTIONAL POLITICAL
PARTICIPATION SCALE
AND PROTEST POTENTIAL
SCALE

	r =	N =
The Netherlands	.23	1144
Britain	.27	1389
United States	.17	1613
Germany	.28	2207
Austria	.23	1265

What can our study contribute to this discussion? At the end of chapter 3 we briefly reported the correlations between the two relevant variables, the protest potential scale and the conventional political participation scale. In Table 5.4 we repeat those correlations that unequivocally sustain our own hypothesis and findings from other studies: in each country conventional and unconventional political participation are *positively* correlated.

Though consistently positive, the magnitude of these correlations is not staggering. But the two modes of participation do impinge on a common political universe and the choice of one certainly does not exclude the choice of the other. They are convergent but they are only somewhat convergent. It is a common experience of the real political world that ad hoc groups tend to utilize political weapons found among their party and interest-group contacts as well as those they may forge for themselves in the form of direct action techniques. Rusk, in his review article on *Participation in America,* returns several times to one principal critical focus: that Verba and Nie omitted protest behavior from their study, and thus may present an inadequate or even distorted view of the whole gamut of modern political behavior.[30] By choosing to study protest behavior and protest potential, our focus is drawn inexorably forward to the study of modern political versatility.

THE POLITICAL ACTION REPERTORY TYPOLOGY: AN OPERATIONALIZATION

Our analytical perspective is certainly not shared by those who claim that the increasing noninstitutionalized political participation of mass publics beyond electoral activities signifies the breakdown of liberal democracy and the beginning of a transition toward a socialist political and economic order. A careful analysis of the assumptions upon which this judgment is based reveals that the structure of political participation in any given polity is implicitly regarded by those critics as a reflection of varying levels of system affect: high conventional participation and low unconventional participation are seen as concomitants of high system affect, and vice versa. However, this is exactly the notion challenged in our theory and data.

As we move from speculation to analysis our focus of concern shifts, in line with the data in our hands, from systemic to individual-level phenomena. What does a positive individual-level correlation between the protest potential scale and the conventional political participation scale mean in statistical and in substantive terms? Obviously, statistically speaking the respondents are distributed over the matrix space defined by the two scales such that in each segment (or quadrant) of that space some respondents will be found. Needless to say, their exact location and clustering are determined by the joint distribution of the two scales. In substantive terms, the conclusion has to be that while both types of involvement tend to co-occur or not to occur at all, there are also respondents who tend to rely more or less exclusively either on conventional or on direct action politics. Any analysis strategy permitting us to single out these respondents operationally as distinctive types would then enable us to analyze clusters or types of political involvement according to their sociodemographic and political characteristics. This, in turn, would enable us to answer much more precisely questions about the impact of the emergence of direct action techniques on political repertories and about the meaning and consequences of direct political action for the political process in Western advanced industrial societies.

Of the various analysis strategies available for the attainment of our objective, we decided to choose the typological approach. In our view, this approach has the advantage of conceptual clarity and analytical ease, as will become immediately apparent from the following description of how the political action repertory typology was constructed.[31] It is based on the two eight-point Guttman scales of protest potential and conventional political participation. In Figure 5.1 the full eight by eight matrix is displayed. It was mentioned in chapter 3 that both scales have country-specific variations in item order, starting with scale position three for the conventional political participation scale and with scale position four for the protest potential scale. Therefore, an "idealized" item ordering was chosen for representation that conforms with the "average" item ordering in the five countries.[32]

This figure contains the five-fold typology of political action to be used in all further typology analyses. It is necessary here to discuss the rationale behind decisions taken in arriving at this typology. Particularly important are the rules adopted to set scale cutting points.

The figure indicates that initially a tripartite division of each scale into low (0-1), medium (2-3), and high (4-7) had been considered, with the cutting points taking into account the distribution of our respondents over the scale. However, a nine-fold typology is difficult to analyze as well as interpret. And we were also aware that the cutting points, in particular on the conventional scale, did not necessarily reflect a *theoretical* perspective. Therefore, we ran preliminary analyses with the nine types in order to establish a similarity/dissimilarity pattern among them. Various measures of political interest were used as a "check." This was especially meaningful since we were simultaneously interested in validating our typology[33] This analysis revealed a sufficient amount of similarity in all countries in the distribution profiles for Types IIa and IIb, IIIa and IIIb, IVa and IVb, and Va and Vb to warrant the decision in favor of the final five-fold typology of political action repertory:

    I: Inactives
    II: Conformists

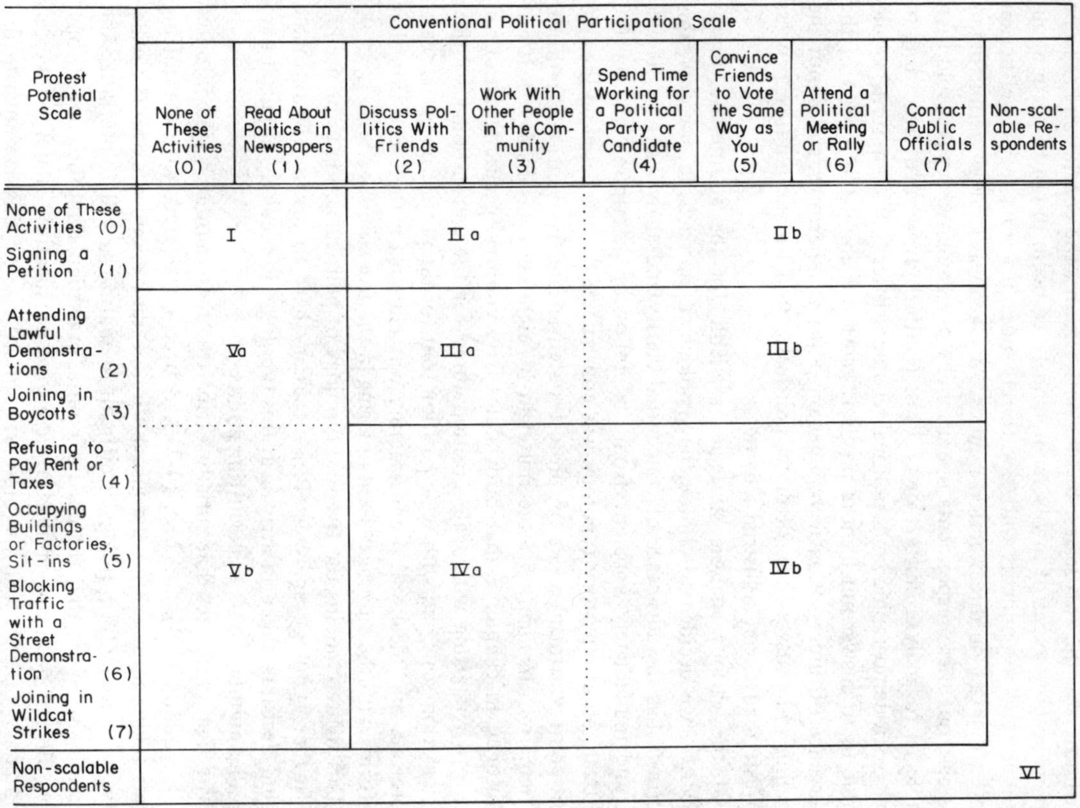
Conventional Political Participation Scale
Protest Potential Scale
None of These Activities (0)
Read About Politics in Newspapers (1)
Discuss Politics With Friends (2)
Work With Other People in the Community (3)
Spend Time Working for a Political Party or Candidate (4)
Convince Friends to Vote the Same Way as You (5)
Attend a Political Meeting or Rally (6)
Contact Public Officials (7)
Non-scalable Respondents
None of These Activities (0)
Signing a Petition (1)
Attending Lawful Demonstrations (2)
Joining in Boycotts (3)
Refusing to Pay Rent or Taxes (4)
Occupying Buildings or Factories, Sit-ins (5)
Blocking Traffic with a Street Demonstration (6)
Joining in Wildcat Strikes (7)
Non-scalable Respondents
I
II a
II b
V a
III a
III b
V b
IV a
IV b
VI

Figure 5.1

III: Reformists
IV: Activists
V: Protesters

Of the five substantive groups, the *Inactives* are an unequivocal category. At most they will read about politics in the newspapers and perhaps sign a petition if asked. Many of them do not even do either of these. The *Conformists* will go further along the route of conventional participation. Some of them even participate in campaigns. But they will not embrace direct political action. The *Reformists*, too, will participate conventionally, but they will also enlarge their political repertory to embrace legal forms of protest, demonstrations, or even boycotts. The *Activists* enlarge their repertory to the fullest extent, some of them to include even nonlegal forms of protest. Finally, the *Protesters* are similar to the Reformists and Activists in their commitment to protest behavior. But they differ from the previous groups in that they do not participate in conventional forms of political activity. Under certain circumstances, Protesters will demonstrate, strike, even occupy buildings, but they neither contact officials nor show up on the hustings.

Table 5.5 shows the distribution of each national sample on the five categories of the typology.[34] A particular advantage of the way the full matrix was collapsed into the five action types is that country-specific differences in *the order of the items*, a problem that may have concerned some readers, become irrelevant. This is so because the cutting points for the typology involve only such items that have been identically rank-ordered in each of the five countries, even though each scale was independently computed.

Table 5.5: TYPOLOGY OF POLITICAL ACTION REPERTORY

Types	The Netherlands	Britain	United States	Germany	Austria
Inactives	17.9=%	30.1	12.3	26.6	34.9
Conformists	11.1	15.4	17.5	13.5	19.2
Reformists	19.8	21.9	36.0	24.6	20.9
Activists	19.3	10.2	14.4	8.0	5.9
Protesters	31.9	22.4	19.8	27.3	19.1
(N =)	(1144)	(1389)	(1613)	(2207)	(1263)
Percentage of Nonclassified Respondents	5	6	6	4	20
(N =)	(1203)	(1483)	(1719)	(2307)	(1584)

Since the action repertory typology is frequently employed in later chapters of this book, certain properties and potential limits need attention. First, "voting" as the most frequently used indicator of "normal" political involvement is absent from this typology, for reasons discussed in chapter 3.

The second point concerns an important and unavoidable property of the typology: the underlying scales are composed of indicators that differ in their closeness to actual behavior. The conventional political participation scale is based on seven items indicating frequency of engagement in specified acts of political participation. It is, therefore, a behavioral indicator. By contrast, the protest potential scale, however painstakingly it has been conceptualized and operationalized, is nevertheless an indicator of *intentions* and not of manifest activity.

On the other hand, this problem should also not be overemphasized. If the approval ratings of the individual unconventional activities are seen as legitimacy indicators for those acts, then it may well be argued that social desirability, or opinion climate, would even underestimate somewhat the willingness of individuals to profess propensity to unconventional political behaviors.[35]

The extent to which one may be willing to grant behavioral properties to the typology cannot be determined on the basis of the empirical evidence available. Even if it is questionable to expect that there is *necessarily* a strong link between past and future behaviors, the concept of a stock of capabilities, a repertory, has to assume—on the basis of concepts from learning theory—that such a link, or at least processes of imitative learning, exist. It is in this sense that the political action repertory typology should be viewed as only slightly distorted in favor of the unconventional side of the coin.

The distortion stems from the greater distance of the protest potential scale from actual past behavior. But the measurement properties of the typology are not the only problems that merit special attention. In addition, the marginal distributions of the typology have to be approached with a clear understanding of the algorithm from which the typology was derived. Whereas no alternative exists to the conventional political participation scale in the measurement instruments derived in the study, there are various substitutes available for the protest potential scale, particularly the would do protest scale, which bears a more direct emphasis on the conative dimension. This varying emphasis is clearly visible in the marginal distributions of the two scales: the number of respondents ranging high on the would do protest scale is substantially smaller than the number of respondents ranging high on the protest potential scale (see the Technical Appendix for the marginals).

Thus, substituting the would do protest scale for the protest potential scale in constructing the typology affects the marginal distributions of the typology accordingly in shifting the balance from the Protesters to the

Inactives and from the Activists to the Reformists as well as from the Reformists to the Conformists. While these changes in the relative strength of the five types are by no means trivial substantively, extensive analyses we conducted (but do not report in the book) have convinced us that the structure of the *relationships* between the types and other variables is not effected noticeably by the substitution of the protest potential scale for the would do protest scale. Both these relationships and the marginal distributions of the typology in the five countries will be left to the following chapter. Next, we will validate the typology in relating it to the Almond-Verba questions on subjective political competence discussed before.

POLITICAL ACTION AND POLITICAL COMPETENCE: A VALIDATION

The data presented thus far clearly indicate that in advanced industrial societies direct political action techniques do not in fact bear the stigma of deviancy. Nor are they seen as antisystem-directed orientations. Therefore, one should expect that respondents with a fuller repertory will be more politically involved in many ways. This expectation is well in line with assumptions of Almond and Verba, which they were able to sustain empirically: "A subjectively competent citizen, therefore, is more likely to be an active citizen."[36] While the unidirectional causality of the argument is open to controversy, it does point to a line of inquiry to be followed in order to validate and derive a better understanding of the typology we have developed.

In a manner similar to the way the local and national competence questions were used to assess the beliefs of mass publics with regard to their opportunities for political influence, we will now look into the relationship between political action types and their local and national subjective political competence. In particular, it may be hypothesized, both for local and for national competence, that: (1) the level of competence monotonically rises from Inactives to Activists. We were uncertain what to expect from the Protesters in this respect, but speculated that their level of subjective competence was high because of their emphasis on direct action; (2) the reliance on unconventional political means is concentrated among Activists, Protesters, and, to a lesser degree, Reformists;[37] (3) The repertory of political means, operationalized as the number of responses per question, also monotonically rises from Inactives to Activists. Since Protesters by definition do not rely on conventional means of political involvement, we expected a somewhat limited repertory with somewhat more emphasis on direct action techniques.

Table 5.6: SUBJECTIVE LOCAL AND NATIONAL COMPETENCE: Selected Categories[a]

	Political Action Repertory Typology				
	Inactives	Conformists	Reformists	Activists	Protesters
1. No Competence[b]					
The Netherlands	56 (74)=%	33 (63)	23 (37)	10 (27)	30 (46)
Britain	41 (46)	23 (30)	11 (23)	14 (19)	28 (37)
United States	54 (48)	24 (13)	11 (8)	11 (8)	26 (20)
Germany	50 (63)	35 (44)	15 (25)	11 (16)	25 (38)
Austria	63 (76)	50 (56)	35 (42)	18 (23)	49 (48)
2. Direct Political Action[c]					
The Netherlands	8 (7)	10 (5)	19 (16)	31 (30)	22 (18)
Britain	8 (4)	10 (6)	5 (5)	13 (8)	5 (3)
United States	3 (1)	7 (1)	6 (3)	13 (11)	8 (4)
Germany	3 (4)	6 (8)	8 (13)	23 (25)	10 (10)
Austria	2 (4)	4 (4)	2 (7)	13 (16)	5 (11)
3. Political Repertory[d]					
The Netherlands	113 (106)	123 (111)	147 (124)	161 (144)	137 (122)
Britain	108 (106)	124 (114)	137 (126)	141 (140)	122 (116)
United States	120 (112)	150 (139)	185 (157)	201 (183)	168 (136)
Germany	113 (109)	130 (118)	149 (137)	170 (159)	136 (124)
Austria	108 (105)	115 (112)	121 (119)	131 (125)	115 (115)

a. Ns for this table are all respondents with valid information on both variables. Ns are not reported here. Percentages in parentheses refer to *national* competence, other percentages refer to *local* competence.

b. Percentages of respondents claiming they do NOTHING against a *local* regulation or *national* law they considered unjust or harmful.

c. Percentage of respondents naming direct political actions among those they would consider in order to fight a harmful or unjust regulation or law.

d. Total percentage of responses to the question regarding what a respondent could do to counteract a harmful or unjust regulation or law.

[158]

Starting out with political competence we can observe that in each of the five countries surveyed it is indeed strongly related to the political repertory commanded by an individual. Three additional comments are in order. First, even in the least-involved category, the Inactives, about one-half of the citizens in that category feel that, if necessary, they have political means available—however limited or small—to act against a *local* regulation they deem unjust or harmful. Except in Britain and the United States the Inactives feel much less competent toward influencing an unjust or harmful law under consideration by their *national* legislature. Furthermore we find that, while there are certain country-specific differences, both the Reformists and the Activists are politically highly competent. And, finally, Protesters feel less politically competent than might have been expected. Surprisingly, they resemble the Conformists much more than the Reformists and Activists, to whom they are closer on the protest potential scale. The inclination to direct political action, we had observed before, emerges only weakly in the answers to the open-ended Almond-Verba questions. Thus, for strictly statistical reasons we would not expect a succinct pattern of increasing frequency in direct action tactics as we move from Inactives to Protesters. This expectation is basically borne out by the data. Nevertheless, it is worthwhile mentioning that the Activists are the category with the highest prominence of direct action. This is what one might expect because Activists range high on the protest potential scale; but it then certainly comes as a surprise that Protesters ranging equally high on that scale volunteer substantially fewer direct action responses to the open-ended questions than the Activists. Apparently, the exclusive reliance on direct action does not necessarily lead to a conceptual preoccupation with unconventional politics.

Lastly, the results regarding the breadth of the political repertory of each action type fully correspond with the expectation of a monotonic increase from Inactives to Activists; this increase can be observed in each country without exception. It reinforces the distinction between Reformists and Activists. Indeed, the Protesters' repertory is, as we had anticipated, more limited than that of Reformists and Activists. In this sense, they take a middle-of-the-road position between those who are not involved at all and those who are substantially involved in politics.

The results referring to the Protesters deserve some additional comments. The Protesters are a theoretically especially intriguing category. If they conscientiously reject conventional politics—as one might be inclined to believe—then they can well be regarded as the epitome of the political revolutionary who is alienated from the traditional societal processes and structures. But we would expect this to show up very clearly in the way that they relate to the sphere of politics, and the preliminary analyses presented do not corroborate these expectations. This is a puzzle that we will set out to solve in the following chapter.

THE BOUNDARIES OF POLITICAL ACTION

In this chapter, we have been able to show that direct political action techniques have made their way into the political repertory of citizens. It also became apparent that a discrepancy exists with respect to the measurement of individual leanings toward unconventional political behavior by open-ended questions, on the one hand, and standardized, well-structured procedures on the other. This discrepancy needs clarification. Fortunately, at least some clarification can come from the British part of the study, where an additional question asked whether and under what circumstances disobeying an unjust law would be considered justified.

These data shed an interesting light on our previous discussion. Disobeying an unjust law certainly is not the most conventional of actions. Nevertheless, the majority of Britons who have an opinion on the matter are willing to do just that—a surprisingly high number even if the way the question is phrased ("Are there ever times?") clearly signals that extreme circumstances had to be considered by the respondents. How does this finding square with the results derived from the Almond-Verba questions on subjective political competence?

Not only does the distribution of responses in favor of and against lawbreaking support the concept of "repertory" in that the Reformists and particularly the Activists more than the other action types can conceive of situations where it might be justified to disobey a law. But, more importantly, these data point to a factor likely to suppress "unconventional" responses to the Almond-Verba questions: their "legalistic" phrasing, the redress they take to the conventional, well-established procedures of getting a regulation through the city council or a law through the legislature.

Suppose the question had been as follows: "Assuming your Council wished to build a new road through your local park and you felt this was very unjust or harmful, what do you think you could do about it?" Would it have yielded the same low number of "unconventional" answers received using the Almond-Verba questions? It seems reasonable to expect that the kind of personal competence relevant to the adoption of direct action techniques would come through in response to the hypothetical stimulus we just described. And it would come through in a way that it does not when people respond to questions about laws and regulations, MPs and Councillors.

There is further supportive evidence. British respondents who indicated willingness to disobey a law "in special times" were asked in a follow-up

Table 5.7: POLITICAL ACTION REPERTORY TYPOLOGY: Britain

Do you think there might ever be times when people might be justified in disobeying laws to protest things they find very unust or wrong? What times are these?	Inactives	Conformists	Reformists	Activists	Protesters
Yes, times specified	28=%	38	56	67	43
Yes, but no time specified	14	10	14	14	17
No	47	46	25	18	33
Don't know	11	6	5	1	7
(N =)	(367)	(285)	(326)	(136)	(258)

question: "What times are these?" Those who could answer the question at all responded as seen in Table 5.8.

If the first three code categories are regarded as "political" responses, then for the Reformists and the Activists political answers outweigh the nonpolitical ones at a rate of almost two to one. The other three participation types show a more balanced ratio. This result permits a qualified answer to the question of whether and to what extent the Almond-Verba questions on subjective political competence underestimate the willingness of citizens to employ unconventional political techniques to achieve political goals.

A little less than one-third of the British sample is willing to disobey a law for *political* reasons of which the pursuit of civil liberties is the most prominent. This figure is substantially higher than the one-fifteenth of the

Table 5.8

	Political Action Repertory Typology: Britain				
	Inactives	*Conformists*	*Reformists*	*Activists*	*Protesters*
It is justified to disobey a law in order to . . .					
Protect civil liberties	13=%	17	31	28	13
Pursue industrial action	15	10	17	19	19
Pressure authorities for improvements	12	19	16	22	17
Resist unreasonable authority	17	14	17	9	13
Total "political" responses	57	60	81	78	62
Protect individual property, family, standard of living	41	37	27	33	46
Other responses	20	13	9	13	16
Total "nonpolitical" responses	61	50	36	46	62
Total	118	110	117	124	124

NOTE: Respondents could give more than one answer.

sample who spontaneously named unconventional political activities in response to the open-ended questions on subjective political competence. This result indicates that the Almond-Verba questions do indeed substantially underestimate the magnitude of readiness to bring direct action techniques to bear on the political process. This is well in line with the higher estimates of proneness to direct political action derived from our analysis of the action repertory typology. It also explains why we were unable to detect the expected increase in open-ended direct action responses among those with better education. After all, those would have been the respondents most likely to react correctly to the "legalistic" content of the questions by referring to institutionalized measures of political influence.

SUMMARY

This chapter has addressed itself to the core theoretical proposition that the conventional and unconventional dimensions of political participation are neither independent nor negatively related to each other.

In a first step we were able to go back to the Almond and Verba 1959-1960 data for three of the five countries of our study in order to show that:

(1) the overall political repertory had broadened considerably by 1974, and
(2) unconventional, direct action types of political influence had found their way into the repertory of a wider segment of the population.

In the second stage of analysis we developed a political action repertory typology, combining both conventional and unconventional aspects of political participation. This typology emphasizes that a considerable portion of the public in five advanced industrial societies has already accepted direct action techniques without abandoning conventional types of political involvement. This corresponds well with the initial theoretical proposition guiding this part of our research.

The latter section of this chapter validated the action typology in a comparison with the Almond-Verba competence indicators, while at the same time qualifying the usefulness of the Almond-Verba questions for the assessment of predispositions toward unconventional political action. The validation procedure was least successful regarding the Protesters, who deviated from initial expectations in that they are less direct-action prone and less politically competent than hypothesized.

NOTES

1. Gabriel A. Almond and Sidney Verba, *The Civic Culture,* Princeton: Princeton University Press, 1963.

2. The concept of "repertory" corresponds—though in a more limited sense—to Dahl's "resources." Dahl—as we—stresses the fixed character of resources, at least in a short- or middle-range perspective. See Robert A. Dahl, *Who Governs,* New Haven: Yale University Press, 1961, pp. 226ff. The idea of resources also plays an important role in social indicator research and studies of the quality of life. As one example, see Erik Allardt, "Dimensions of Welfare in a Comparative Scandinavian Study," *Acta Sociologica,* 19 (March 1976), pp. 227ff.

3. Whereas interviewing in Britain and Germany took place in the summer of 1959, the American part of the study was done in March 1960.

4. This difficulty confronts not only longitudinal but also cross-national studies and is therefore relevant for us beyond the limited focus of this particular analysis. In our study, the British, German, and Austrian fieldwork was done by commercial market research institutes. The American data were collected by the University of Michigan Institute for Social Research. The fieldwork for the Dutch study was organized by our Dutch colleagues who recruited a group of student interviewers to conduct the interviews.

5. Howard Schuman, "Old Wine in New Bottles: Some Sources of Response Error in the Use of Attitude Surveys to Study Social Change." Paper prepared for the Research Seminar Group in Quantitative Social Science at the University of Surrey, April 4, 1974.

6. The Zentralarchiv fuer Empirische Sozialforschung at the University of Cologne, the German academic social science data archive, holds a copy of the original German questionnaire of the study showing the precodes. We assume that the questionnaire design was not handled differently in the other four countries.

7. Almond and Verba, *The Civic Culture,* pp. 191, 203.

8. The wording of the 1959-1960 Almond-Verba questions was taken from the ICPSR Codebook, Study No. ICPSR 7201, pp. 24, 27. All analyses of the Almond-Verba data reported later in the chapter were computed with the ICPSR-OSIRIS versions of the study. It is important to note that all comparative analyses with respect to the Almond-Verba questions employ the age range of their study, that is, eighteen years and older. Thus respondents aged sixteen and seventeen were excluded from the 1974 data in these analyses.

9. According to our data, the number of persons with only primary education in Germany has been reduced by 14 percentage points between 1959 and 1974.

10. Almond and Verba, *The Civic Culture,* p. 185.

11. This interpretation is further corroborated by the emphasis that Americans, more than any other nationality, place on the act of voting as a reflection of personal competence.

12. Almond and Verba, *The Civic Culture,* pp. 89, 94, 96. The level of political conceptualization in the five countries will be discussed by Hans D. Klingemann in chapters 8 through 10 of this book.

13. We have mentioned before that Almond and Verba used a precoded scheme to classify the responses of their interviewees. In 1974 the responses were obtained by truly open-ended questions and coded according to a newly developed coding scheme that nevertheless had built into it the intention to compare our results with those obtained in 1959-1960. The more numerous 1974 coding categories were recoded to fit the

1959-1960 coding scheme. Also, the reader is alerted to the fact that in our study the set of questions adopted from Almond and Verba was located in the questionnaire before any of the questions and items on conventional as well as unconventional political action were asked. This is important here because otherwise a contamination through learning during the interview could not be completely ruled out.

14. These data are not presented in tabular form in order to save space.

15. Respondents with university education in Germany do not follow this pattern. Considering, however, that the German results in 1959 are only based on twenty-five respondents, we are inclined to conclude that the German 1959 total in this group was probably artificially inflated.

16. Philip E. Converse, "Public Opinion and Voting Behavior," in Fred I. Greenstein and Nelson W. Polsby (eds.), *Handbook of Political Science,* Vol. 4, Reading: Addison Wesley, 1975, pp. 96ff.

17. Almond and Verba, *The Civic Culture,* p. 205.

18. As one example, see Sidney Verba and Norman H. Nie, *Participation in America,* New York: Harper & Row, 1972, pp. 138ff., although we feel uneasy about their considering age and position in the life cycle as equivalent operationally.

19. Slight traces of curvilinearity with regard to age and competence can be detected in Britain and the United States, thereby sustaining our suspicion that the division in only three age categories may indeed hide this particular type of relationship.

20. Almond and Verba, *The Civic Culture,* pp. 241ff.

21. Ralph H. Turner, "The Public Perception of Protest," *American Sociological Review,* 34 (December 1969), pp. 815ff., in particular p. 816.

22. James Q. Wilson, "The Strategy of Protest: Problems of Negro Civic Action," *Journal of Conflict Resolution,* 5 (September 1961), p. 296.

23. Kenneth Kenniston, *Young Radicals,* New York: Harcourt Brace Jovanovich, 1968, pp. 14ff.

24. Michael Lipsky, "Protest as a Political Resource," *American Political Science Review,* 62 (December 1968), p. 1144.

25. Ibid., p. 1148.

26. Christopher Driver, *The Disarmers,* London: Hodder& Stoughton, 1974, p. 148.

27. Joel Aberbach and Jack L. Walker, *Race in the City,* Boston: Little, Brown, 1973.

28. Cited from Edward N. Muller, "Behavioral Correlates of Political Support," *American Political Science Review,* 71 (June 1977), p. 454.

29. Ibid., p. 456.

30. Jerrold G. Rusk, "Political Participation in America: A Review Essay," *American Political Science Review,* 70 (June 1976), pp. 583ff., in particular pp. 584ff.

31. Typologies are an established instrument of scholarly inquiry although Giovanni Sartori, *Parties and Party Systems,* Cambridge: Cambridge University Press, 1976, pp. 293ff., an avid spokesman for the classificatory mode of analysis, correctly observes that for the last two decades this mode has increasingly been regarded as obstructive to quantitative political science. A more recent example of typological analysis is the "new politics" typology by Warren E. Miller and Teresa F. Levitin, *Leadership and Change,* Cambridge: Winthrop Publishers, 1976. A typology of conventional political participation was developed by Verba and Nie, *Participation in America,* pp. 56ff.; and Blumenthal et al., *Justifying Violence,* Ann Arbor: Institute for Social Research, 1972, pp. 179ff., combined the dimensions of violence for social control and violence for social change to arrive at their Violence Typology. But typologies such as ours combining the dimensions of conventional and unconventional political involvement have as yet rarely

been presented in the literature. The first such typology was created in 1974 for Switzerland by Charles Roig and published in Dusan Sidjanski, Charles Roig, Henry Kerr, et al., *Les Suisses et la Politique: Enquête sur les Attitudes d'Electeurs Suisses,* Bern und Frankfurt: Lang Verlag, 1975, pp. 170ff. Closest to our own work is a typology combining two additive indices of aggressive political behavior and conventional political behavior. This typology was developed in 1975 by Edward N. Muller, "Behavioral Correlates of Political Support," pp. 454ff.

32. This "idealized" item ordering was derived from scales that were based on the pooled but unweighted data from all countries. Whereas this approach would not be acceptable for substantive analysis and is therefore not used anywhere in the book, in this case it seemed appropriate since the interest is in providing overall, average information with respect to the item ordering.

33. The data are reported in Max Kaase and Alan Marsh, "Pathways to Political Action, Part II: Further Explorations," Paper presented at the Workshop on Political Behavior, Dissatisfaction, and Protest, Fourth Joint Workshop Sessions of the European Consortium for Political Research (ECPR), Louvain-La-Neuve, April 1976, p. 11.

34. The Technical Appendix reports the complete nine by nine matrices of the two combined scales. The tables represent the country-specific ordering of items for each scale.

35. For a very interesting use of the concept of opinion climate in electoral research see Elisabeth Noelle-Neumann, *Oeffentlichkeit als Bedrohung,* Freiburg/Muenchen: Verlag Karl Alber, 1977.

36. Almond and Verba, *The Civic Culture,* p. 182.

37. We are aware of the fact that the low overall level of occurrence of unconventional political means in the open-ended questions limits this analysis very much.

Chapter 6

DISTRIBUTION OF POLITICAL ACTION

MAX KAASE and ALAN MARSH

INTRODUCTION

The political action repertory typology developed in the preceding chapter focuses on styles and skills that individual citizens bring to bear on the political process. In this chapter we will first compare the distribution of repertory types across countries. This will enable us to get a better picture of the role political participation plays as one segment of political culture in the five nations.[1] Analogous to the way we looked at the social location of political action in chapter 4, we will then try to determine the social characteristics of the five repertory types and their similarities across countries. This analysis should yield a better understanding of the meaning of specific types of political action in advanced industrial societies, particularly with regard to the Protesters, that is, those respondents who feel exclusively inclined toward direct action techniques. Finally, in this chapter we will address ourselves once again to the question of country differences in participatory culture. On this occasion, however, our emphasis will be less descriptive.

POLITICAL ACTION REPERTORY IN
COMPARATIVE PERSPECTIVE

To compare, country by country, the rate of active citizen involvement in politics is no easy task. Specific institutional arrangements, organizational structures, and citizen attitudes jointly shape the profile of political participation in each country. The result of any empirical comparison across countries will also depend on the completeness and the accuracy of the measurements taken of the participatory space. Thus, caution must be exercised when countries appear to be more or less participatory compared to other countries. A simple example may demonstrate this difficulty. Clearly, voting is one of the most important acts of political participation in liberal democracies. But which votes should we consider—votes for community, state, or national elections? What about referenda? And what about the election of public officials that is customary in the United States but not, let us say, in Germany? If, for example, we concentrate our attention on national elections we will find that the United States is the *least* participatory of our five nations. On the other hand, data from empirical studies show that the United States has a very participation-oriented citizen culture on the local level of government.[2] Thus, voting is apparently ill-suited as an *overall* indicator of the extent to which citizens are actively involved in the political process. We could continue this discussion but the point is sufficiently well established that any comparison, in absolute terms, between countries must be well aware of the limitations it necessarily carries.

With these limitations in mind we shall now set out to look at the way our five countries fare regarding the political action repertory of their citizens. We will summarize the distribution of the typology in a slightly different format than previously so that the data are more closely tailored to examine our claim that a mixed political repertory, combining propensities for conventional and unconventional participation, has come to characterize the participatory culture of advanced industrial societies (see Table 6.1).

Looking first at the Inactives—those who are least likely to contribute any initiative to the political process—it becomes apparent that political apathy, by a wide margin, is lowest in the United States. Interestingly, the high levels of overall involvement reflect a rather balanced contribution of both the dimensions of conventional and unconventional politics. In concrete terms, Americans engage more in lawful demonstrations and particularly in boycotts than their counterparts elsewhere, and they more often talk politics with their friends. The lack of political apathy emerging from this analysis is well in line with results of high levels of subjective local and national political competence we reported in the preceding chapter. There is no question that

Table 6.1: **POLITICAL ACTION REPERTORY TYPOLOGY RESTRUCTURED: The Modes of Political Action**

	The Netherlands	Britain	United States	Germany	Austria
A. *Modes of Political Action*					
None					
(Inactives)	18=%	30	12	27	35
Only Conventional					
(Reformists)	11	15	18	13	19
Mixed Mode (Reformists					
and Activists)	39	33	50	33	27
Only Unconventional					
(Protesters)	32	22	20	27	19
(N =)	(1144)	(1389)	(1613)	(2207)	(1265)
B. *Lack of Involvement in:* *					
Unconventional Politics	9=%	23	9	18	21
Conventional Politics	29	28	· 16	23	34

*Percentage of scalable respondents with "0" value on the respective scale.

the United States can be characterized as a fully developed participant political culture.[3]

Expressed as an aggregate percentage difference, the Dutch seem almost as active in politics as the Americans. A closer look at the data reveals, however, that there are important differences in involvement between the two. First of all, the Netherlands display a surprising lack of engagement in conventional politics. The only reason why this is not reflected in the percentage of Inactives is that it is more than outweighed by their apparent preoccupation with direct action politics. This orientation of the Dutch citizenry—and this is a second important distinction between the Netherlands and the United States—has two specific characteristics. First, it extends to direct action tactics like the occupation of buildings while the Americans hold back from this degree of protest, and, second, it is based much more heavily on potential than actual participation. In this sense, the Netherlands could at least be described as a *potential* participant culture. This conclusion is corroborated by the data on civic competence where the Dutch are at par with Germany and below Britain and the United States on local and below all three on national competence.

Both Britain and Germany show roughly equal but clearly higher rates of political detachment than the United States and the Netherlands: more than one-fourth and less than one-third of the citizens do not actively engage in politics. Whereas the Austrian respondents at first sight seem not to be substantially lower in political involvement, it has to be kept in mind that the Austrian sample excludes respondents beyond the age of seventy, thereby artificially inflating the number of politically involved people, although the rate is not known precisely. Thus, of the five countries in our study it is Austria where political apathy is by far the highest.

Moving from detachment to attachment it is, of course, problematic to deduce from the ratio of conventional, through mixed mode, to unconventional involvement whether the mixed mode will be the political style of the future. It seems safe to state, though, that in terms of sheer numbers and—as we shall see shortly—from the sociodemographic characteristics of the Conformists everywhere, an exclusive reliance on conventional politics is a minority choice and will probably remain so.

The mixed mode repertory corresponds most closely to our theoretical approach of increasing political versatility. Not unexpectedly, in the United States this political style dominates all the other styles we have distinguished. Thus, our statement that America is a truly participant culture can be further differentiated by observing that a marriage of conventional and unconventional participation has taken place to an extent that precludes any doubts with regard to the "within-system" status of direct action techniques. The picture in the other countries is less clear. In three of them though (that is, except Austria) the integration of direct action techniques into the political repertory nevertheless has proceeded to a point where the mixed mode category is the most frequent one of the four modes described in Table 6.1.

Before moving to the Protesters one qualification of these results and their interpretation is in order. Since the Reformists and Activists were merged to arrive at the mixed mode category, it is important to keep in mind that, except in the Netherlands, the Reformists contribute much more to the mixed mode category than the Activists (see Table 5.4 for details). Thus, for most of the citizens with a mixed mode repertory their command of direct action techniques presently does not extend beyond petitions, demonstrations, and boycotts. On the other hand, compared with the level of political involvement commonly thought appropriate to citizens in Western democracies, this is still a potent political stance.

The challenge to mixed mode political action derives from the Protesters. It does not come as a surprise that they are most frequent in the Netherlands, the country with a strong inclination toward direct action techniques. It does come as a surprise, however, that in all five countries Protesters constitute at least about one-fifth of the population. Even reminding ourselves again that the protest potential scale measures mostly behavioral inclinations and little reported action, the number and sociodemographic properties of Protesters in each of the countries deserves particular attention.

Table 6.2 summarizes the differences in the five action types between the five countries. The measure we have chosen for this presentation is an index of percentage dissimilarity proposed by Duncan, Cuzzort, and Duncan.[4] The index is used to compute pairwise percentage point differences between the countries that are summed and then divided by two.

Despite the fact that the countries in this study all fall into the category of advanced industrial societies, only Britain and Germany have comparable rates and structures of political involvement. The other three countries display specific characteristics that separate them from each other: a high level of overall political involvement in America and a low level in Austria, and a high level of involvement in unconventional politics in the Netherlands. How can these differences be explained? We will turn to this question once we have analyzed the sociodemographic profile of the five action types.

A SOCIODEMOGRAPHIC PROFILE OF THE POLITICAL ACTION REPERTORY TYPES

The description of the sociodemographic location of the five action types will largely follow the analysis presented in chapter 4 of the three action scales. Obviously, this description cannot avoid a certain amount of redundancy since the two scales jointly constituting the typology have already been thoroughly examined before. On the other hand, the differences in social location of the protest potential scale and the conventional political participation scale are such that an analysis of the five action types will provide by no means fully predictable results.

The Baseline Model of Political Participation

In their analysis of conventional political participation in America in the late 1960s, Verba and Nie applied a so-called "baseline model" for explanation. This baseline model starts out from the strong positive bivariate relationship found between a summary measure of socioeconomic status and an

Table 6.2: DISSIMILARITY INDEX OF POLITICAL ACTION REPERTORY TYPOLOGY*

Political Action Repertory Typology	Pairwise Percentage Point Differences for All Countries									
	The Netherlands: Britain	The Netherlands: United States	The Netherlands: Germany	The Netherlands: Austria	Britain: United States	Britain: Germany	Britain: Austria	United States: Germany	United States: Austria	Germany: Austria
Inactives	-12	5	-9	-17	18	4	-5	-14	-22	-8
Conformists	-4	-6	-2	-8	-2	2	-4	4	-2	-6
Reformists	-2	-16	-5	-1	-14	-3	1	12	15	4
Activists	9	5	11	13	-4	2	5	6	8	2
Protesters	9	12	5	13	2	-5	3	8	1	8
Dissimilarity Index	18	22	16	26	20	8	9	22	24	14
Average Dissimilarity	19									

*Same Ns across types apply for each country.

[172]

overall political participation scale. But it also holds for three of the four subscales of political involvement Verba and Nie developed: campaign activity, voting, and communal activity. Only the fourth mode—particularized contacting—was found to be hardly correlated ($r = .07$) with socioeconomic status.[5]

In subsequent analyses Verba and Nie amended the bivariate model to include civic attitudes as an intervening variable and analyzed the effects of additional variables like membership in voluntary associations. These analyses, however, leave the basic model intact permitting them to summarize their findings as follows: "The standard socio-economic model of the process of politicization works in America, resulting in an overrepresentation of upper-status groups in the participant population."[6]

As Verba and Nie themselves are quick to point out, this general finding does not come as a surprise. In fact, the literature on political participation abounds with corroborating results, and the data we have presented on the correlates of conventional political participation are well in line with this literature. But Verba and Nie had not studied unconventional political behavior, and neither theory nor data regarding political participation in the 1960s provided sufficient reason to believe that the Verba-Nie baseline model also extended to direct action politics. Thus, our finding that, on the average, both the conventional and unconventional modes of political involvement are equally—and positively—related to one important determinant of social status—education—was certainly not self-evident.[7]

The detailed analysis of the action types will now permit us to qualify whether the socioeconomic baseline model—that is, the heavily biased recruitment of political activists from upper social strata—applies equally well to the three repertory types that are medium to high on protest potential: Reformists, Activists, and Protesters. While the answer to this question is our core interest we will, of course, also look at the way age and sex are related to the repertory types.

Sociodemographic Correlates of the Political Action Types

In order to minimize an overlap of content with chapter 4 we will concentrate our presentation on a graphic display linking the five action types with age, sex, and education. The entries into the plots are unstandardized percentage point differences representing, for each type and for each category of the respective independent variable, the deviation from the marginal distributions of the action type. Thus, to take one example from the Netherlands, a national average of 18 percent Inactives combined with 12 percent Inactives among the sixteen to twenty-nine age category results in an entry of

-6 in the plot.[8] Consequently, the zero line reflects the national average for each age group and country. In discussing these results for the five action types we will also bring in information derived from analyses not documented here. Our approach will be strictly descriptive, and the main emphasis is not yet on comparisons between the countries.

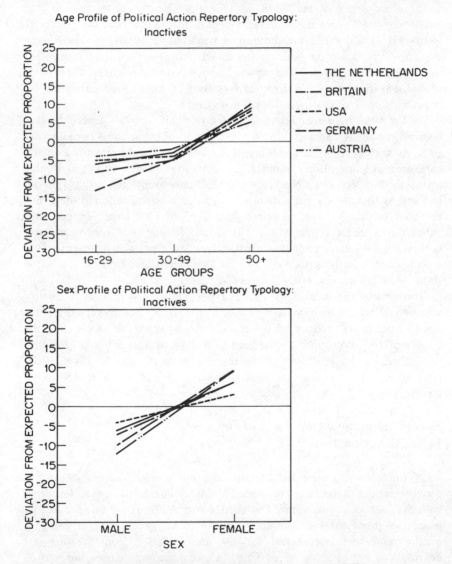

Figure 6.1: **SOCIODEMOGRAPHIC PROFILE OF INACTIVES**

Education Profile of Political Action Repertory Typology:

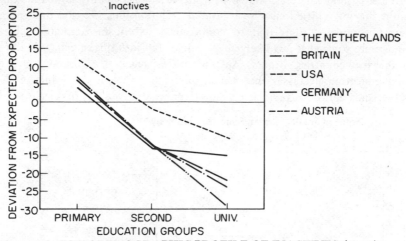

Figure 6.1: **SOCIODEMOGRAPHIC PROFILE OF INACTIVES (cont.)**

The Inactives. Very much in line with the socioeconomic baseline model, the formal level of education (as the one indicator we have chosen to represent the left side of the model) determines to a large extent whether or not a respondent is politically active: the lower the formal education of the respondents, the less active they are in politics.[9] Furthermore, political passivity increases linearly with age, and seemingly it is also much more a female than a male characteristic.[10] However, the female lack of involvement reflects to a large extent the substantially lower level of their educational attainment. But even though the sex differences in political detachment are much reduced as education increases, there nevertheless remains a female deficit in political involvement. This deficit clearly points to the total set of systemic conditions preventing women's full integration into the world of politics: traditional sex roles, lower status, family obligations, and the like.

Beyond the bivariate relationships we were particularly interested in the impact of education controlling for age, and for age and sex at the same time. These analyses yielded identical results across the five countries; again, not unexpectedly, low levels of educational achievement in every instance strongly lower the probability that a citizen will get involved in politics.[11]

The Conformists. Whereas the pattern of relationships between our set of independent variables and political apathy is unequivocal and very similar across countries, we are facing a more complex situation with respect to the Conformists. The one trait common to all countries is that political conformism is moderately associated with increasing age—hardly a breathtaking result. Staying a little longer with bivariate relationships, we find that sex is almost completely unrelated to conformism except in Germany, where women are somewhat *less* likely than men to fall into this category. In three of the five countries—Britain, Austria, and especially the United States—a good education decreases the chance of being a Conformist, while in the Netherlands and Germany this has no effect whatsoever. On first sight these

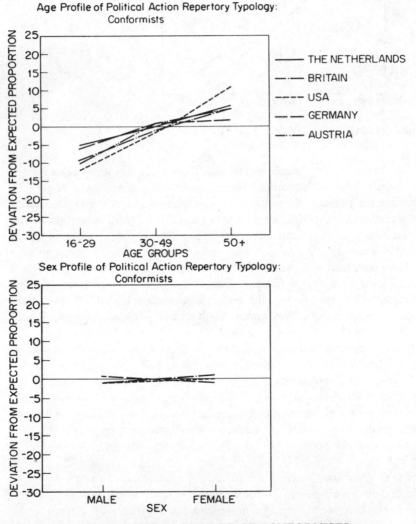

Figure 6.2: SOCIOPOLITICAL PROFILE OF CONFORMISTS

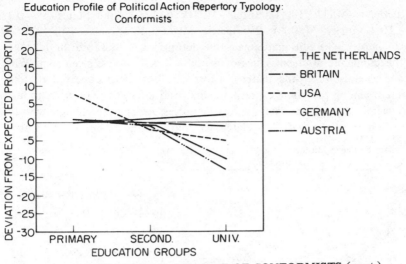

Education Profile of Political Action Repertory Typology: Conformists

THE NETHERLANDS
BRITAIN
USA
GERMANY
AUSTRIA

Figure 6.2: SOCIOPOLITICAL PROFILE OF CONFORMISTS (cont.)

latter results may be puzzling since conformism is a form of political involvement and should therefore be *positively* related to higher levels of education. However, conformism is the model of political involvement of the older citizens, and this more as a generational than a life cycle effect since the forms of political involvement regularly offered and rewarded by the political systems in the past were almost exclusively of the conventional type. Moreover, the educational opportunities offered to the older generation in their youth were far fewer than those available now. Thus education should have a different effect depending on age, and this is what we do indeed find. In all countries, among the sixteen to twenty-nine year old age group, education is negatively correlated with conformism (the gammas for the countries are: the Netherlands, −.28; Britain, −.57; United States, −.25; Germany, −.07; Austria, −.42). Among those fifty years and older, the correlation—except in the United States (−.11) where a broader set of political activities was available much earlier than in the European countries—is positive (the Nertherlands, .31; Britain, .12; Germany, .18; Austria, .05). Consistent with this analysis is that in all countries the thirty to fifty year old age group holds an intermediate position.

A further differentiation of the oldest age cohort according to gender adds another facet to the picture. In all countries among the old with higher education, women are more likely than men to be Conformists, though, once again, the gamma correlation in the United States remains in the negative (the

Netherlands—M:.11, F:.51; Britain—M:.10, F:.13; United States—M:—.13, F:—.10; Germany—M:.06, F:.29; Austria—M:—.09, F:.14).

Undoubtedly, traditional female role definitions encouraged the takeover of the dominant political values of a political system at a given time. With female liberation on the march, results certainly were expected to look different among the youngest respondents. And different they were, though they were not at all consistent across countries. Among the younger women, education is now negatively related to conformism, except in the United

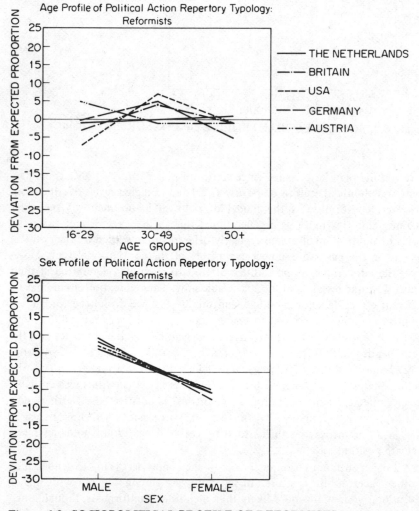

Figure 6.3: **SOCIOPOLITICAL PROFILE OF REFORMISTS**

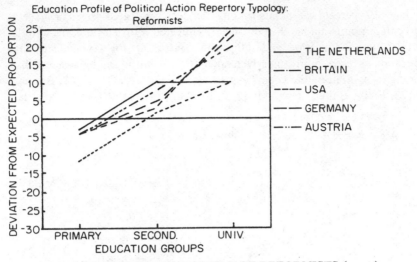

Figure 6.3: **SOCIOPOLITICAL PROFILE OF REFORMISTS (cont.)**

States where the gamma is .00. This corresponds to the results regarding young men for four of the five countries; only in Germany was a slightly positive correlation obtained. It is remarkable that in Britain and Austria the negative correlation between better educated women and conformism is even slightly stronger than for the men. The complete set of gammas for the five countries is as follows: the Netherlands—M:−.53, F:−.09; Britain—M:−.51, F:−.59; United States—M:−.59, F:.00; Germany—M:.09, F:−.28; Austria—M: −.40, F:−.44.

The Reformists. As we move away from political passivity to political involvement, the weight of higher education makes itself felt like a counterpoise to the way lower education favors passivity. The uniformity of the relationship across countries indicates that these effects are apparently achieved by processes that operate in functionally equivalent ways despite the differences in the makeup of national educational institutions. Clearly, reformism as a political style that integrates conventional political behavior with limited but uncontroversial direct action techniques follows the socioeconomic baseline model very closely.

Almost like a mirror image to the Inactives, women are poorly represented among Reformists. Naturally, one factor accounting in part for this difference is the lower level of education of women. But these data also once again testify to the enormous deficit less educated women have to overcome in political involvement; the gap between men and women is reduced from an average 19 percentage points among the least educated to an average 6 percentage points among the most highly educated. Furthermore, the correlations between education and reformism controlling for sex indicate that education is even more directly related to reformism among women than among men in all of the countries (the Netherlands–M:.21, F:.41; Britain–M:.28, F:.38; United States–M:.22, F:.33; Germany–M:.27, F:.32; Austria–M:.20, F:.51).

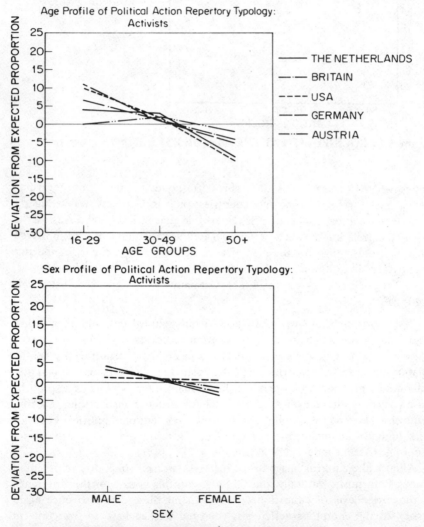

Figure 6.4: SOCIOPOLITICAL PROFILE OF ACTIVISTS

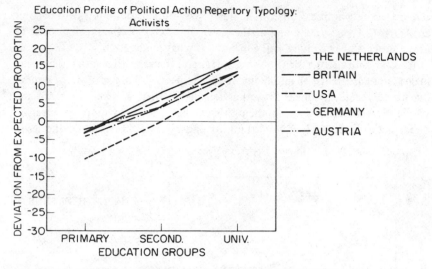

Figure 6.4: **SOCIOPOLITICAL PROFILE OF ACTIVISTS (cont.)**

The age profile of the Reformists deserves special attention. In three of the five countries—Britain, the United States, and Germany—a slightly curvilinear relationship exists, in that respondents belonging to the middle age category are more likely than younger or older respondents to be Reformists. It seems that the particular combination of political abilities Reformists possess concurs most nearly to the start up-slow down model of political socialization where, for different reasons, of course, both the young ("start up") and the old ("slow down") are less participatory than those of medium age.[12] In light of the high uniformity in relationships across countries observed to this point, it is surprising that the Netherlands and Austria do not follow the curvilinear pattern established for the other countries. In both cases, age is practically unrelated to reformism.

The Activists. Activists resemble Reformists in many ways: they are much better educated than average and the group contains more men than women. This reinforces the validity of the socioeconomic baseline model for a more advanced stage of political involvement encompassing controversial direct action tactics as well as conventional participation. Nevertheless, there are two interesting ways in which the two types differ.

First of all, in all countries activism as a political style declines steeply and linearly with increasing age, except in Austria where this decline does not begin before the age of fifty. Clearly, to be young has a lot to do with the willingness to apply somewhat more extreme unconventional methods to achieve desired political outcomes. But to be young is not enough to become an Activist. To be young and at the same time to be well educated, or to be in the process of becoming well educated, is what really counts.

Second, and at first sight quite surprisingly, the sex differential in favor of males is much smaller than one might have expected. This result is, of course, due to the fact that male as well as female Activists are well educated *and* young, thereby predisposing them, as we have seen, to more extravagant direct action tactics. It is important to understand, though, that the lesser

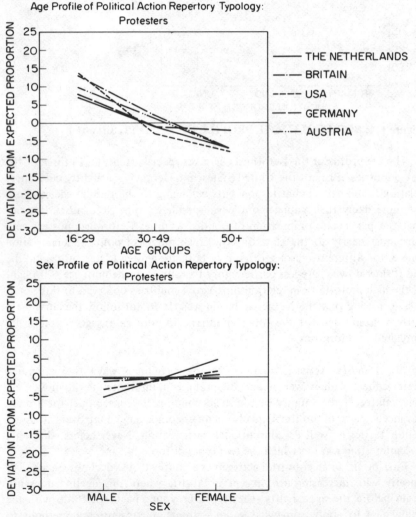

Figure 6.5: **SOCIOPOLITICAL PROFILE OF PROTESTERS**

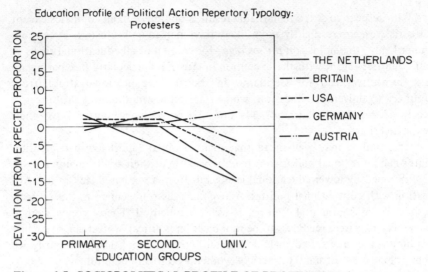

Figure 6.5: **SOCIOPOLITICAL PROFILE OF PROTESTERS (cont.)**

impact of sex is of a purely compositional nature. Among the Activists with elementary education, women are still 25 percentage points below their average, and only in the highest educational echelon is this difference reduced to 4 percentage points. Thus, we are once again confronted with the result that a poor education, while hampering political involvement both by men and women, still discourages and disadvantages women to a much greater extent.

The Protesters. Protesters, as we had defined them, possess a political portfolio limited to direct action techniques. Are the Protesters the harbingers of massive changes in the political order of liberal Western democracies to be expected in the future? This was the question we had asked ourselves when we designed the political action repertory typology. While a full answer to this question will have to await further analysis, the sociodemographic profile of the Protesters offers at least some additional insights beyond the tentative result arrived at in chapter 5, which was that—somewhat surprisingly—they do not excel in political competence.

A first indication of why this is so is that in three of the five countries—the Netherlands, the United States, and Germany—education is negatively correlated with being a Protester. Only in Austria does a very slight positive relationship exist, while Britain is even characterized by a curvilinear relationship: respondents with elementary and university education both are less likely than average to be Protesters.

With respect to sex, a remarkable result is obtained. In all countries except Austria women are slightly *more* likely than men to be Protesters. Even more remarkably, this holds—*on the average*—for women of all educational ranks in all countries—again with the exception of Austria. Particularly fascinating are the respective data for Germany: in the three educational strata, from primary to university education, women are represented among Protesters in each educational stratum 4, 11, and 23 percentage points above their expected share.

This finding may well mean that many women report low participation rates in conventional politics not merely because of their traditional inactivity conditioned by lower educational levels, but from a sex-based lack of identification with conventional politics. Active male discouragement in this respect, especially in continental Europe, is well documented. There, young women generally declare a readiness to be mobilized in political protest activity while shunning the grey-suited male-dominated world of "politics." Obviously we have discovered substantial traces of women's political liberation.[13]

One result regarding the Protesters holds in each of the five countries: they are much younger than the population as a whole. The relative youth of this group supports notions of availability and ready mobilization—with or without political goals—that have been put forward in the literature.[14]

In particular, the finding that Protesters possess at least an average and mostly a below-average education reinforces our belief in the usefulness of the action typology. At the same time it also points to the limits of the socioeconomic baseline model. Without the typology it would have been impossible to distinguish on theoretical grounds between propensities for direct action tactics that are prima facie indistinguishable. By contrasting, in particular, Activists and Protesters it was possible to demonstrate that the latter have apparently acquired their direct action repertory through processes other than that of formal cognitive development. Whatever the Protesters' particular learning experience may have been, it was unlikely to have been shaped decisively by their socioeconomic background.

Sociodemographic Correlates of the Political Action Types: A Summary

We will conclude the sociodemographic analyses of the action typology with a brief discussion of the results of a multiple regression analysis involving the set of three independent variables used before—age, sex, and education— to summarize and substantiate our previous findings. Because of the dichotomous nature of the dependent variables the application of ordinary least square estimation techniques is not without methodological problems.[15] Fortunately, the econometric literature provides a strategy that permits a control over the effects of dichotomous dependent variables on the regression coefficients.[16] The results of these analyses matched the results of the normal standard regressions—both with respect to the multiple correlation coefficient R, the b's, and the beta weights—to an extent that made it acceptable and meaningful to report only the latter results.[17]

Table 6.3: **SELECTED SOCIODEMOGRAPHIC INDICATORS AND POLITICAL ACTION REPERTORY TYPES***

Political Action Repertory Types and Countries	Age		Sex		Education		R	R²
Inactives								
The Netherlands	.12	(.00)	.13	(.10)	−.18	(−.02)	.30	.09
Britain	.12	(.00)	.13	(.12)	−.15	(−.04)	.26	.07
United States	.14	(.00)	.09	(.06)	−.22	(−.02)	.31	.10
Germany	.19	(.00)	.17	(.15)	−.17	(−.03)	.35	.12
Austria	.07	(.00)	.17	(.17)	−.16	(−.04)	.28	.08
Conformists								
The Netherlands	.18	(.00)	.01	(.00)	.05	(.00)	.16	.03
Britain	.18	(.00)	.02	(.01)	.01	(.00)	.18	.03
United States	.24	(.00)	.00	(.00)	−.04	(.00)	.26	.07
Germany	.07	(.00)	−.04	(−.03)	.01	(.00)	.08	.01
Austria	.12	(.00)	−.04	(−.03)	−.06	(−.01)	.14	.02
Reformists								
The Netherlands	.06	(.00)	−.13	(−.11)	.15	(.02)	.20	.04
Britain	.03	(.00)	−.12	(−.10)	.14	(.03)	.18	.03
United States	.06	(.00)	−.11	(−.11)	.19	(.03)	.22	.05
Germany	−.05	(.00)	−.17	(−.15)	.15	(.03)	.26	.07
Austria	−.02	(.00)	−.14	(−.11)	.16	(.03)	.24	.06
Activists								
The Netherlands	−.09	(.00)	−.10	(−.08)	.14	(.02)	.23	.05
Britain	−.14	(.00)	−.09	(−.05)	.05	(.01)	.19	.03
United States	−.20	(.00)	.00	(.00)	.15	(.02)	.28	.08
Germany	−.16	(.00)	−.12	(−.07)	.14	(.02)	.28	.08
Austria	−.04	(.00)	−.07	(−.03)	.14	(.02)	.18	.03
Protesters								
The Netherlands	−.19	(.00)	.08	(.08)	−.13	(−.02)	.20	.04
Britain	−.21	(.00)	.02	(.03)	−.01	(.00)	.21	.04
United States	−.25	(.00)	.06	(.05)	−.14	(−.02)	.25	.06
Germany	−.09	(.00)	.10	(.09)	−.07	(−.01)	.15	.02
Austria	−.16	(.00)	.01	(.01)	.00	(.00)	.16	.03

*Education was operationalized by the years a respondent had spent in school. This variable is described in detail in the Technical Appendix. Entries are standardized (beta) and, in parentheses, unstandardized (b) regression coefficients.

It is important to note for the interpretation and evaluation of these coefficients that, as we mentioned before, the average intercorrelation of $-.27$ in the five countries between education and age—the higher the age, the lower the education—does not cause multicollinearity concerns.

In substantive terms, these results corroborate the previous findings that:

- political inactivity is most frequent among the old, women, and the less well educated;
- conformism is the political style of those older citizens who do participate;
- reformism is prevalent among males, the middle-aged, and the better educated;
- activism is prevalent among the young, males, and the better educated;
- protest is very much the political style of the young and less educated— men and women equally.

While the regression analysis does not contribute much additional information to the picture we have already developed, and does not reveal some of the less obvious relationships that were unveiled through the multivariate table analyses, there are nevertheless some important points to be learned here.

The first point concerns the fact that the b's and the beta weights within types and across nations show an encouraging uniformity. They clearly corroborate the visual impression conveyed by the figures presented in the previous section that the countries are very similar in the way that the independent variables are related to the action types. Of course, deviations occur, but if they are substantial enough not to arouse suspicions of sampling error and the like, they convey information about deviations from generality in a given country. To give one example: that Activists in the United States are equally likely to be male or female, but are predominately male elsewhere, certainly reflects a real, observable difference between contemporary America and the four European democracies we have studied. The uniformity across countries is documented not only by the regression coefficients indicating the impact of a given independent variable relative to the other variables in the equation, but also in the multiple correlation coefficients (the Rs). This part of the analysis shows that the Conformists—as we had observed before—are the type least comparable across nations and also least likely to be accounted for with the set of three variables we have been working with throughout this section. While R^2 is generally higher for the other four types, it may nevertheless strike some as disappointingly low. What must be kept in mind, however, is that for purely mathematical reasons alone the chance of R^2 reaching high values is substantially reduced when the dependent variable is a dichotomy.

A global criticism that could be voiced against these analyses is that they are restricted to only three of the much broader available set of independent sociodemographic variables. That this decision was deliberate has already been mentioned. Beyond reasons of substance there were also practical considerations involved: difficulties of presentation within the scope of this book; the problem of missing observations as in the case of income, where about one-fourth of the respondents did not provide valid answers; the need for variables that made sense cross-nationally; and—last but not least—the fact that many of the variables eligible for consideration share part of the variance with the variables we have selected.

This last point is sustained empirically through a second regression analysis in which—in addition to age, sex, and education—occupational prestige of head of household (Treiman score)[18], trade union membership as a dichotomous variable, and religiosity are included. In the majority of cases, the inclusion of these three variables hardly affected the Rs at all, in some cases even *deflated* them because of an increase in missing observations through the new variables that reduced the overall number of cases available for analysis. In passing it may be noted here that in the Netherlands and Germany religiosity is indeed positively related to conformism, thus increasing the respective Rs by a statistically significant margin.

Finally, a word of caution should be added regarding the considerable impact that we have attributed to formal education as a condition for political participation. Our emphasis is—in terms of regression analysis—an emphasis on slopes, because slopes indicate how much participation is boosted by moving from a lower to a higher educational category. However, in a longitudinal analysis—which we unfortunately do not have—slopes can stay constant although the level of politicization *in the system as a whole* rises. This would be indicated, again in terms of regression analysis, as a change in intercepts. In Germany, for example, Noelle-Neumann has attributed the overall rise in political involvement over the last twenty years mainly to the impact of television.[19] If one agrees with the argument, this would be a picture-book example of such a global effect reflected in the intercept, though in this case there is reason to believe that such a trend also influences the slope that describes the relationship between education and political participation.

Some Conclusions

In many ways the analyses presented so far in this chapter have reiterated and reinforced findings that are well established in the literature on political participation. In particular, the sociodemographic profile of those respondents who had no active engagement in politics exhibits very familiar characteristics. Here is an instance in which the validity of the socioeconomic baseline model has found firm corroboration. It must be understood, however, that the emphasis on repertory has a built-in bias toward steady systematic involvement and is, almost by definition, not capable of capturing the ad hoc type of participation that is generated by processes of organizational or situational mobilization.

The data from this study leave little doubt that exclusive reliance on conventional, electorally oriented participation has become a minority style. If one shares our willingness to discard a life cycle interpretation of the relationships that we found, conventional participation will in the long run be supplemented by at least some direct action tactics. This broadened political repertory may deeply change the character of the political process in advanced industrial Western democratic societies.

The marriage of conventional and unconventional political participation resulting in a broad political repertory in practically all of the countries we have studied has, in varying degrees, come to dominate their participatory culture. We have found that a high level of formal education is an important condition for this marriage. This finding provides empirical support for our initial speculation that the rise of direct action techniques in advanced industrial societies does not derive from a strong sense of deprivation among the underprivileged. Furthermore, we have not discovered any evidence suggesting that Reformists and Activists bear any unreconcilable grudge against the political and social order of the societies in which they live.

We are able to confirm the validity of the socioeconomic baseline model of participation for the Reformists and Activists. This may come as a surprise and a disappointment to many of those who believe that the (re)emergence of direct action politics in the last decade or so might reduce some of the bias in political influence hurting the lower social classes. But there is no question that direct action techniques *in the early 1970s* were primarily a vehicle for sustaining and enhancing the influence of the middle classes on political decision-making. Whether the influence was used for the benefit of the middle classes themselves, for the underprivileged, or for all of society is a question that *in this context* is of only peripheral significance.

The one major unknown in our equation is the Protesters. Except for their youth the profile of this group is rather inconclusive. We conducted a number of analyses beyond the sociodemographic investigation reported here.[20] One such result, however, deserves special mention. After what we found in chapter 5 concerning the political competence of Protesters, it is no longer surprising but nevertheless fascinating that analyses with two distinctively separate indicators of political motivation clearly and unanimously indicate that Protesters have very little interest in what is usually called politics.[21] On the other hand, we will have to ask ourselves what being a Protester means when this political style is so obviously disconnected from the "normal" political input process. Needless to say, this question will be taken up again later in the book after more concepts have been developed and brought to bear on the data. For the moment it is important to underscore the contribution the use of the typology has made to our understanding of, especially, the protest dimension of political participation. In chapter 4 we struggled to explain the indeterminate character of the relationship between some of the social correlates of protest potential and conventional participation. We now know we were dealing with three quite different types of people scoring high on that single protest scale—Reformists, Activists, and Protesters—and with three quite different types of conventional campaigners: Conformists, Reformists, and Activists. The typology is more than a summary device; it paints a new and different picture of political participation.

COMPARING COUNTRIES: A METHODOLOGICAL NOTE AND SOME RESULTS

In analyzing the marginal distributions of the action typology earlier in the chapter we had stated as a question why, despite the similarity in economic, social, and political structure, the five countries display such differences in their participatory culture. In this context a consideration by Przeworski and Teune regarding the role that countries as analytical units should play in cross-national analysis is relevant.[22] They argue—and we are in agreement with the basic thrust of this argument—that the main emphasis in the social sciences should be on building general theory. For this purpose, however, countries have to be represented as values on variables amenable to empirical quantitative analysis, and not as constructs in their own right. The existence of residual country effects not accounted for by theoretically derived variables is only an indication of the fact that one has not proceeded far enough with respect to proper theory-building.

This position may well be regarded as somewhat unrealistic in the light of the broad range of conceptual, statistical, and empirical problems facing quantitative comparative social science research. Still, it is a position well-suited to suggest ways for coming to grips theoretically and empirically with systematic country comparisons.

A straightforward approach to comparative analysis would be the pooling of data from all countries surveyed. "Country" could then be used either as a categorical variable or a set of dummy variables. For reasons stated earlier in the book, this strategy has been ruled out. Thus country by country comparisons, based on analyses of individual countries, were the logical choice. In our chapters, these comparisons have taken two forms, each involving specific statistical techniques and summary measures: the analysis of bivariate or multivariate *relationships* and the analysis of univariate or multivariate *distributions.*[23]

Both types of analysis have to be considered in their own right, and which of the two is chosen depends on the focus of interest of the researcher. The difference between them can be demonstrated with a hypothetical example from regression analysis. Let us assume that we analyze two countries and find identical slopes when two variables are regressed against each other. Does this imply that the means, variances and consequently the location of distributions of those variables in the two countries are also identical? Obviously not. In fact, they can be quite different.

An illustration from the literature will substantiate the argument. Converse and Dupeux, in a comparative analysis of France and the United States, find large differences in the frequency of newspaper reading among the two countries.[24] In their subsequent analysis they argue that the differences in levels of education between the two countries determine the differences in level of newspaper reading and that the slopes are very similar. They conclude: "The capacity to move cross-national differences out to the marginals in this fashion not only strengthens [the] presumption of common causal factors, but also is a reassuring anchor in the unknown waters of cross-national research where the basic comparability of the data must be held to special question."[25]

The increasing thrust in the social sciences on explanation and prediction necessarily leads to a strong emphasis in cross-national research on relationships versus distributions.[26] This emphasis is clearly reflected in our own work and has also dominated the discussion in this chapter so far. A thorny problem in comparing relationships across countries, however, is the confounding effect of varying marginal distributions in both the dependent and independent variables.[27] Since, in particular, correlation and, to a more limited extent, regression coefficients are accordingly affected, cross-national comparisons aimed at discovering "a common nucleus of association"[28] between variables suffer from an unknown bias. In the following, we will therefore try to assess the extent to which our results pertaining to the sociodemographic correlates of the political action repertory types in the five countries must be corrected once this bias has been removed.

In 1968 Mosteller used a procedure originally suggested by Deming and Stephan that permits the standardization of bivariate and multivariate contingency tables.[29] This result is achieved by an iterative procedure in which the cells of the table are converted into probabilities changing between row and column totals until—at least with square tables—equal marginal distributions of both row and column variables are obtained. In the special case of square tables, row and column percents each sum to 100 percent. With unequal numbers of row and column variable categories the algorithm necessarily produces either row or column totals that are different from 100. This particular aspect of iterative fitting, however, is not relevant for our purpose to standardize distributions across samples because the format of tables and therefore the iterated marginals are, of course, identical in all of the countries.

This approach—while not without drawbacks, as has recently been noted in the literature[30]—is obviously appropriate for the problem we want to solve. Interestingly enough, Mosteller himself, as a demonstration of its capabilities, applied the procedure to a comparison of social mobility rates between Britain and Denmark.

We employed the iterative fitting technique with a certain amount of uneasiness because it had not been widely used before.[31] In addition, we were once again faced with the problem of selecting the appropriate summary measures of association to assess the results of our statistical operations. The analysis covered the five dichotomized action types and, as independent variables, the same we had used in the second section of this chapter, namely age, sex, and education.[32] The summary measures we decided to use were the classical ordinal correlation coefficients tau-b and gamma. While we do not know of any analyses in the literature where these coefficients were applied jointly with the iterative fitting algorithm, we nevertheless saw no obvious methodological pitfalls preventing us from this application. How did we expect the coefficients to change after the standardization? In strictly algebraic terms we knew that they would be different since the only measures invariant to scale transformations are the ones exclusively based on the cross-product ratio for 2 x 2 tables or all 2 x 2 subtables in an I x J table.[33] This is not the case for tau-b and gamma. In substantive terms we expected that, given the prior similarity in strengths of association that had emerged from the plots and the regression analysis, standardization would smooth the remaining differences between countries and make the correlations even more compatible. Table 6.4 presents the results of this analysis.

We do not intend to enter into a substantive discussion of these coefficients once more. Rather, we start out with two general comments. First of all, a quick glance down the columns of the table indicates—not surprisingly— that the overall similarity of relationships across countries we had earlier diagnosed also emerges from the analysis of ordinal measures of association. Second, and equally unsurprising because of the exclusion of tied pairs from calculation, gamma often takes on substantially higher values than tau-b. This fact may hardly seem worth mentioning except that, and this is a first result of the standardization analysis, the numerical value of tau-b is, on the average, more influenced by the predictors than is that of gamma. The explanation for this phenomenon is that the standardization technique by

Table 6.4: SOCIODEMOGRAPHIC CORRELATES OF POLITICAL ACTION REPERTORY: Before and After Standardization of Marginals

Countries and Sociodemographic Variables		INACTIVES		CONFORMISTS		REFORMISTS		ACTIVISTS		PROTESTERS	
		Before	After	Before	After	Before	After	Before	After	Before	After
		Standardization		Standardization		Standardization		Standardization		Standardization	
The Netherlands											
Age*	tau-b	.14	.18	.13	.21	.02	.03	-.13	-.18	-.12	-.13
	gamma	.32	.31	.35	.35	.05	.05	-.27	-.30	-.22	-.22
Sex	tau-b	.15	.20	.00	.00	-.15	-.19	-.11	-.14	.10	.11
	gamma	.38	.38	.00	.00	-.37	-.37	-.28	-.28	.21	.21
Education	tau-b	-.18	-.37	.02	.05	.13	.14	.16	.21	-.11	-.18
	gamma	-.70	-.59	.07	.08	.33	.24	.38	.35	-.28	-.31
Britain											
Age	tau-b	.14	.14	.15	.27	.00	.03	-.14	-.22	-.18	-.21
	gamma	.27	.24	.38	.44	.01	.05	-.38	-.38	-.36	-.36
Sex	tau-b	.14	.16	.02	.03	-.12	-.15	-.09	-.15	.02	.02
	gamma	.31	.31	.06	.06	-.29	-.29	-.30	-.30	.04	.04
Education	tau-b	-.22	-.40	-.04	-.22	.14	.25	.13	.24	.04	-.03
	gamma	-.53	-.64	-.11	-.37	.32	.42	.36	.40	.10	-.05
United States											
Age	tau-b	.15	.21	.24	.34	.04	.05	-.22	-.34	-.20	-.25
	gamma	.41	.36	.53	.56	.07	.09	-.52	-.55	-.43	-.42
Sex	tau-b	.11	.17	.01	.02	-.12	-.13	-.02	-.02	.06	.08
	gamma	.33	.33	.03	.03	-.25	-.25	-.04	-.04	.15	.15

Table 6.4: SOCIODEMOGRAPHIC CORRELATES OF POLITICAL ACTION REPERTORY: Before and After Standardization of Marginals (cont.)

Countries and Sociodemographic Variables		INACTIVES Before Standardization	INACTIVES After Standardization	CONFORMISTS Before Standardization	CONFORMISTS After Standardization	REFORMISTS Before Standardization	REFORMISTS After Standardization	ACTIVISTS Before Standardization	ACTIVISTS After Standardization	PROTESTERS Before Standardization	PROTESTERS After Standardization
Education	tau-b	-.23	-.47	-.11	-.18	.15	.19	.20	.36	-.07	-.14
	gamma	-.60	-.72	-.26	-.27	.28	.32	.51	.57	-.17	-.24
Germany											
Age	tau-b	.19	.25	.07	.15	-.07	-.05	-.19	-.37	-.06	-.09
	gamma	.39	.41	.17	.25	-.14	-.09	-.57	-.59	-.12	-.16
Sex	tau-b	.21	.24	-.04	-.06	-.20	-.23	-.15	-.29	.11	.12
	gamma	.46	.46	-.12	-.12	-.44	-.44	-.53	-.53	.24	.24
Education	tau-b	-.21	-.42	.00	-.01	.14	.23	.18	.32	-.05	-.18
	gamma	-.54	-.66	.01	-.01	.31	.39	.54	.52	-.11	-.31
Austria											
Age	tau-b	.07	.08	.12	.22	-.04	-.06	-.04	-.08	-.14	-.20
	gamma	.14	.13	.28	.36	-.09	-.11	-.17	-.14	-.31	-.33
Sex	tau-b	.22	.24	-.01	-.02	-.18	-.22	-.10	-.21	.00	.00
	gamma	.45	.45	-.04	-.04	-.42	-.42	-.41	-.41	-.01	-.01
Education	tau-b	-.19	-.41	-.04	-.26	.16	.23	.16	.37	.01	.06
	gamma	-.43	-.65	-.12	-.43	.37	.39	.54	.60	.04	.10

* Age was collapsed to three categories: 16—29 years, 30—49 years, 50 years and older.

definition affects skewed distributions, as in the case of education, much more than it does more balanced distributions. However, at this point we are above all interested in the question of the effects of standardization of marginals on the correlation similarity profiles of the countries. A table with 300 entries permits only the most superficial inspection. We therefore decided to use the dissimilarity index again, only this time based not on percentages but rather on the correlation coefficients of Table 6.4 in order to assess better the consequences of the standardization procedure.

Each entry into the table is the *average* dissimilarity of a given correlation—for example, age and Inactives—between two countries. Obviously, this presentation stresses the central tendency of the values as opposed to their dispersion. Therefore, when necessary, we will bring in additional information regarding specific country differences.

A first—and somewhat surprising—result is that in only five out of the thirty comparisons (five types x three variables x two measures of association) the standardization makes the countries more similar. Not considering the special case of the 2 x 2 table (sex and types) where the standardization does not affect the gammas at all, in the remaining twenty instances the dissimilarity index is—usually very slightly—increased by the standardization. We conclude from these analyses that whatever similarities or differences in relationships between countries exist are not created by unequal marginal distributions of the independent and dependent variables in the five countries.

Next we will look at the same data with a particular emphasis on the dissimilarities between them. For the Inactives all previous results of analyses are left intact after standardization. With the exception of education the same is true for the Conformists. The higher dissimilarity index for education is due exclusively to two countries, Britain and Austria, where the standardization noticeably increases the negative correlation between education and conformism, thus making these two countries more similar to the United States. These three countries are now clearly separated from the Netherlands and Germany, where the lack of relationship prevails even after standardization.

With regard to the Reformists the standardization does not significantly alter the structure of relationships. However, this is not the case for the Activists, the type least numerous in the five countries. Age is much less related to activism in Austria than in the other four countries. This result is only slightly accentuated by the standardization. A similar pattern exists with regard to sex, except that this time the United States can be identified as the major source of dissimilarity. Before and after standardization sex is practically unrelated to Activism, whereas in all other countries women are less Activist than men. Since this difference becomes even more pronounced after

Table 6.5: DISSIMILARITY INDICES: Correlations Between Three Sociodemographic Variables and the Political Action Repertory Typology (before and after standardization of marginals*)

		INACTIVES	CONFORMISTS	REFORMISTS	ACTIVISTS	PROTESTERS
AGE						
tau-b	Before	.02	.04	.03	.04	.03
	After	.04	.04	.03	.07	.04
gamma	Before	.07	.08	.06	.10	.08
	After	.07	.07	.05	.11	.07
SEX						
tau-b	Before	.03	.01	.02	.03	.03
	After	.02	.02	.03	.06	.03
gamma	Before	.04	.04	.05	.11	.07
	After	.04	.04	.05	.11	.07
EDUCATION						
tau-b	Before	.01	.03	.01	.02	.04
	After	.07	.08	.03	.04	.06
gamma	Before	.06	.07	.02	.05	.10
	After	.03	.14	.04	.06	.11

*Table entries are average country dissimilarities between correlations. Dissimilarities were calculated based on correlations in Table 6.4.

the standardization, it can also be held accountable for most of the *increase* in dissimilarity. The most prominent and coherent characteristics of the Protesters—their youth—is everywhere preserved after the standardization. Other previously uncovered relationships survive very well, though it may be worthwhile to mention that the negative relationship to education is even more visible now than before.

We started this part of our analysis by emphasizing relationships versus distributions and concentrated on the search for a common nucleus of associations independent of marginal distributions. The summary conclusion seems justified that beyond certain country differences that had already emerged before, no basic alteration in the structure of relationships resulted. This is indeed a satisfying outcome, since it indicates that the similarities and differences between countries that we have found are clearly not statistical and compositional artifacts.

As a final consideration in this part of our analysis we now return to the univariate distributions of the action typology and raise the question of the extent to which the distribution differences reflect compositional effects or substantive differences in participatory culture. It is important to understand that this question is different from the one asking about the similarity in predictive relationships across countries, in that it tries to quantify how similar participation would become if certain relevant sociodemographic characteristics were equally distributed in all countries studied. This is a relevant consideration since a brief look at the age and sex distributions in the five countries indicates convincingly the extent to which they differ on those two variables. Demographers have traditionally been concerned with this kind of problem, and standardization procedures are available from the literature.[34] We decided to choose a straightforward approach in that certain marginals should be physically adjusted through a standard weighting procedure. The importance of sex and age as two cross-nationally fully equivalent variables that emerged from the work in this chapter made those two prime candidates for standardization. The significant impact of age and sex on all five repertory action types made us believe that the weighting would indeed result in a substantial reduction of the typology differences across nations.

The samples in the five countries were consequently weighted according to a six-category variable combining sex and age as follows: (1) male 16 through 29 years; (2) male 30 through 49 years; (3) male over 49 years; (4) female 16 through 29 years; (5) female 30 through 49 years; (6) female over 49 years. The distribution to which all samples were standardized was the total of the five samples.[35] We obtained the results shown in Table 6.6.

The weighting produced intuitively meaningful results. As one example, the relative youth of the Dutch sample led us to expect that the percentage of Inactives would rise after a standardization to an older average population,

Table 6.6: POLITICAL ACTION REPERTORY TYPOLOGY: Before and After Standardization of Joint Age/Sex Distribution

	Before Standardization					After Standardization				
	The Netherlands	Britain	United States	Germany	Austria	The Netherlands	Britain	United States	Germany	Austria
Inactives	17.9=%	30.1	12.3	26.6	35.0	20.0=%	29.5	12.7	26.2	34.6
Conformists	11.1	15.4	17.5	13.5	19.2	12.1	14.7	18.6	13.1	19.0
Reformists	19.8	21.9	36.0	24.6	20.9	19.3	22.0	36.7	24.1	21.5
Activists	19.3	10.3	14.4	8.0	5.9	17.9	10.6	13.5	8.4	5.9
Protesters	31.8	22.4	19.9	27.3	19.0	30.6	23.2	18.5	28.2	19.1

and it did indeed rise a little more than two percentage points. But, all in all, the expectations we had that the countries would become clearly more similar in participatory culture did not materialize. What little effect the weighting had did not consistently bring the five countries closer together; only a slight reduction in the dissimilarity index was achieved, and the most noticeable individual effect concerned just the group of the Inactives.

It would have been tempting to broaden the analysis and use other variables such as education for the weighting. We decided against this because we were uncertain of the usefulness of the approach and because we did not expect major new results to emerge.

SUMMARY

The comparative analysis of the action typology indicated substantial differences in the frequency with which the types occur in the five countries. The American population was found to be the most active politically and the Austrian the least active politically. The high level of political involvement in the Netherlands reflects more than in any other country the preference of the Dutch for direct action techniques. While these differences exist and in this sense are very real, it was found that the structure of relationships between the action types and a set of sociodemographic variables was quite similar and remained very stable even after certain statistical techniques tailored to cope with the problem of unequal marginal distributions of variables across the countries were applied. Thus the conclusion seemed warranted that political action in the countries we have studied emerges from uniform sociopolitical processes.

The sociodemographic analysis of political action started out with the socioeconomic baseline model of political participation. This model postulates a heavy overrepresentation of the resourceful upper middle class in the input side, and this was found to be true for Reformists and Activists who command means of unconventional as well as of conventional political participation. However, the validity of the model did not extend to the Protesters, the action type that relies exclusively on direct action tactics.

NOTES

1. Gabriel A. Almond and Sidney Verba, *The Civic Culture,* Princeton: Princeton University Press, 1963, pp. 13ff., clearly see political participation as a less prominent element of political culture compared to the attitudes individuals hold toward the input and output aspects of the polity and the political process.
2. Ibid.

3. Ibid., p. 19.

4. Otis Dudley Duncan, Ray P. Cuzzort, and Beverly Duncan, *Statistical Geography*, New York: Free Press, 1961, p. 83. The index takes the form $ID = 1/2 \sum_{i=1}^{k} |X_i - Y_i|$, where k are the types in the typology. A set of five countries results in ten sets of differences that are each summarized in the form of this index.

5. Sidney Verba and Norman H. Nie, *Participation in America,* New York: Harper & Row, 1972, pp. 125ff., especially pp. 135ff.

6. Ibid., p. 336.

7. Because of the difficulties regarding indicator equivalence it was decided by the research group that a composite score of the respondent's socioeconomic status should not be developed.

8. We have decided against standardizing the entries in order to keep as close a relationship to the "real" data as possible. Additionally, percentagizing within demographic categories provides some basic standardization. A different approach to a similar problem was chosen by Verba and Nie, *Participation in America,* p. 26.

9. While it is clear that education is just an indicator for a complex set of properties such as cognitive ability, access to resources, integration into networks of primary and secondary communication, and so on, it nevertheless represents this set in a very convenient summary way.

10. A similar result is reported by Roig for Switzerland. See Dusan Sidjanski, Charles Roig, Henry Kerr et al., *Les Suisses et la Politique: Enquête sur les Attitudes d'Electeurs Suisses, 1971,* Berne and Frankfurt: Verlag Herbert and Peter Lang, 1975, p. 179.

11. In the terminology of regression analysis in this analysis we are looking primarily at the slopes of a regression equation with education as the independent variable. The different *levels of involvement* between the sexes would be represented by the intercepts of the equation. The intercepts could be regarded as the sums of all other factors beyond education which have an impact on the involvement rate.

12. Verba and Nie, *Participation in America,* pp. 138ff.

13. This result is corroborated by Eisinger's Milwaukee analysis where he finds that, after controlling for participation in conventional political behavior, "exclusive protestors . . . of both races are considerably younger than those who take part in both protest and electoral activity." See Peter K. Eisinger, "Racial Differences in Protest Participation in the American City," paper presented at the Workshop on Political Behavior, Dissatisfaction and Protest, First Joint Workshop Sessions of the European Consortium for Political Research (ECPR), Mannheim, April 1973, p. 26. Unfortunately, this part of Eisinger's analysis has been omitted from the version of the article published in the *American Political Science Review,* 68 (June 1974), pp. 592ff.

14. In an unpublished paper for the 1970 meeting of the International Sociological Association in Varna, Bulgaria, Philip E. Converse, and Roy Pierce, "Basic Cleavages in French Politics and the Disorders of May and June, 1968," p. 19, make some interesting comments about potential female participation in the May disorders that are directly relevant to our discussion:

One finds the expected differential by sex: men were more likely to participate than women by about a 5:3 margin, despite their minority status in the electorate. However, there is an additional item of interest where the sex differential is concerned. Our questions about demonstration participation permitted people to indicate that they wanted to participate, even if circumstances did not actually permit. Very many women were inhibited in one way or another from doing so. If all who went out of their way to tell us that they had wished to participate had actually gone into the streets, women would have outnumbered men four to three.

In a footnote, they add; "Interestingly enough, the great bulk of these inhibited women were also under thirty years of age. Women over thirty were more likely to have participated if so inclined." An abbreviated version of the article was published in German as "Die Mai-Unruhen in Frankreich," in Klaus Allerbeck and Leopold Rosenmayr (eds.), *Aufstand der Jugend?* Muenchen: Juventa, 1971, pp. 108ff.

15. One property of dichotomous variables is that they can be interpreted as mathematical expectations or probabilities with a range between 0 and 1, where the population mean would equal the probability of drawing a certain action type after an infinite number of draws. One problem in regressions with dichotomous dependent variables derives from the fact that the error term E_i in the regression equation has a discrete and *not* a normal distribution. Thus the application of the usual tests of significance is not possible. Next, heteroskedasticity of the error term leads to inefficient estimators of alpha and beta. In addition, the predicted values of the dependent variable do not necessarily stay within the 0-1 range, which is required for the probability interpretation of the dependent variable. See Arthur S. Goldberger, *Econometric Theory,* New York: John Wiley, 1964, pp. 248ff., and Jan Kmenta, *Elements of Econometrics,* New York: Macmillan, 1971, pp. 425ff.

16. This procedure was pointed out to us by Gregory Markus, Center for Political Studies, Institute for Social Research, the University of Michigan. Our thanks go to him and to Samuel Evans who did the computer work. The algorithm involves the derivation of a variance-covariance matrix from the estimated values of the dependent variables using ordinary least square techniques. This variance-covariance matrix is then used as a transformation weight for the independent and dependent variables in a second regression.

17. The similarity of results regarding Rs and beta weights by both procedures did not come as a surprise since these estimators are unbiased even in the case of the nontransformed regression analysis. See Jan Kmenta, *Elements of Econometrics,* p. 427.

18. The occupations that had been coded according to the standard occupational code of the International Labor Organization (ILO) were converted into occupational prestige scores following an algorithm by Treiman. For a detailed description of the procedure see the Technical Appendix.

19. Elisabeth Noelle-Neumann, "Wahlentscheidung in der Fernsehdemokratie," in Dieter Just and Lothar Romain (eds.), *Auf der Suche nach dem muendigen Waehler,* Bonn: Bundeszentrale fuer Politische Bildung, 1973, pp. 161ff.

20. Max Kaase and Alan Marsh, "The Matrix of Political Action," Paper presented at the 10th World Congress of the International Political Science Association, Edinburgh, August 1976.

21. We take up this theme again in our conclusions to chapter 17.

22. Adam Przeworski and Henry Teune, *The Logic of Comparative Social Inquiry,* New York: John Wiley, 1970, pp. 26ff.

23. Ibid., p. 39ff.

24. Philip E. Converse and Georges Dupeux, "Politicization of the Electorate in France and in the United States," in Angus Campbell, Philip E. Converse, Warren E. Miller, and Donald E. Stokes, *Elections and the Political Order,* New York: John Wiley, 1966, pp. 269ff., especially pp. 273ff.

25. Ibid., p. 276.

26. Adam Przeworski and Henry Teune, *The Logic of Comparative Social Inquiry*, p. 43; see also Sidney Verba, "Cross-National Survey Research: The Problem of Credibility," in Ivan Vallier (ed.), *Comparative Methods in Sociology*, Berkeley: University of California Press, 1971, p. 327, where he argues that of both techniques "the comparison of processes or the pattern of relationship among variables . . . is . . . much more interesting" and "increases the credibility of comparisons."

27. The impact of sampling error and measurement error—a very complex problem in *comparative* survey research—will not be considered here. In particular, it will be assumed that equivalent measurement across nations was achieved.

28. Frederick Mosteller, "Association and Estimation in Contingency Tables," *Journal of the American Statistical Association*, 63 (March 1968), p. 8.

29. Ibid., pp. 1ff., especially pp. 6-8. This algorithm was first proposed by W. Edwards Deming and Frederick F. Stephan, "On a Least Square Adjustment of a Sampled Frequency Table When the Expected Marginal Totals are Known," *Annals of Mathematical Statistics*, 11 (1940), pp. 427ff.

30. Yvonne M.M. Bishop et al., *Discrete Multivariate Analysis: Theory and Practice*, Cambridge, Mass.: MIT Press, 1975, pp. 97ff., in particular p. 101.

31. Not too many applications of the procedure are reported in the literature. We are not aware of analyses of cross-national data with this approach, probably due to the scarcity of cross-national survey studies. A somewhat different use of Mosteller's method—fitting a given table to a new set of specific marginals—is made by Robert Axelrod, "Where the Votes Come From: An Analysis of Electoral Coalitions 1952-1968," *American Political Science Review*, 66 (March 1972), pp. 11ff., and David Butler and Donald Stokes, *Political Change in Britain*, New York: St. Martin's, 1969, pp. 283ff.

32. Similar analyses were conducted with other sociodemographic variables known to be related to political involvement, such as, for example, trade union membership, occupation, and income. Not surprisingly—since these variables are also related to the three independent variables we picked—the results of these analyses were quite similar to those reported in the text.

33. Yvonne M.M. Bishop et al., *Discrete Multivariate Analysis: Theory and Practice*, pp. 392ff.; Frederick Mosteller, "Association and Estimation in Contingency Tables," pp. 3ff.

34. Yvonne M.M. Bishop et al., *Discrete Multivariate Analysis: Theory and Practice*, pp. 131ff.

35. Ibid., p. 133. The percentages for the six categories were: 10.9, 17.0, 17.0, 12.8, 18.7, 23.5.

Chapter 7

IDEOLOGICAL CONCEPTUALIZATION AND VALUE PRIORITIES

RONALD INGLEHART and HANS D. KLINGEMANN

INTRODUCTION

Thus far, our primary concern in this book has been to develop effective measures of certain distinctive forms of political action. Let us now turn to the question, "What makes given individuals use given modes of political participation?" In this and the next five chapters, some possible answers will be suggested and tested empirically. We will focus on two sets of factors: one's level of political cognition and one's value priorities. One's cognitive level and one's values are important both independently and in their interaction. In order to be *able* to engage in political action, an individual must possess at least a certain minimum of political knowledge. And in order to be *motivated* to act, an individual must want to change the way things are going, either to attain goals that would otherwise not be realized or to protect values that seem threatened. Thus, cognitive and evaluative factors both have crucial roles in shaping an individual's readiness to engage in political action, though their relative importance and interaction vary according to the nature of the action under consideration.

Conventional participation takes place within the framework of the established order. Although to be effective certain cognitive skills and material resources are required, the use of conventional means of political participation is affected only modestly by one's basic values. To undertake the relatively unconventional political actions involved in the upper levels of the protest potential scale, however, not only requires cognitive skills but calls into question certain basic values; an individual's value priorities play a crucial role in 'determining whether or not one engages in unconventional political activities. We would expect the propensity to engage in new forms of political participation to characterize persons with values at odds with the prevailing order. In short, we would expect conceptual level to be of paramount importance in relation to conventional political action; while value cleavages (in conjunction with one's conceptual level) would have their most important impact on protest potential. We believe that both of these factors have contributed to the rise of a new style of political action in recent years. Let us briefly sketch out the reasons why we think this is so.

IDEOLOGICAL CONCEPTUALIZATION, POSTMATERIALIST VALUES, AND THE NEW POLITICS

In their influential book, *The Civic Culture,* Almond and Verba developed the concept of "subjective political competence" and argued that it may be a prerequisite to democratic politics; only insofar as the citizen feels that he is capable of influencing political decision makers is he apt to play a participant role rather than that of an obedient "subject" or a politically irrelevant "parochial."[1] The authors demonstrate that the more educated a person is, the likelier he is to have a sense of "subjective political competence" and, therefore, be a political participant. Numerous other studies in various countries have established this point: citizens of higher socioeconomic status are more apt to participate in politics.[2] Results reported in the preceding chapters confirm these findings to a certain degree.

But is this relationship due to social status itself, or to the development of cognitive skills—a process that has been referred to elsewhere as cognitive mobilization?[3] Are those of higher status likelier to take part in politics (1) because of their greater capacity to process political information and their better knowledge of how to press their demands; *or* (2) because they have better social connections, more money, and because officials defer to the upper classes?

It seems likely that wealth and personal connections are relevant. However, if we are interested in long-term changes, cognitive variables are particularly interesting. By definition, there will always be upper, middle, and lower socioeconomic strata. But pronounced changes have occurred in absolute levels of education, information, and political sophistication, and they may be changing the nature of the political process.

As will be demonstrated in chapter 9 the better educated segments of Western publics show relatively high levels of political conceptualization; characterized by their ability to interpret politics in terms of broad unifying abstractions, these people might be described as having a high level of *objective* political competence, or an *"ideological"* conceptualization of politics.

The term "ideology" has caused much discomfort among social scientists. Different researchers offer differing definitions. The history, multiple meanings, and operational shortcomings of the concept have been discussed over an extended period of time.[4] The term is retained here in spite of its fearsome past in order to link our present inquiry with a specific research tradition. The foundation for that tradition is provided by Campbell et al. and by Converse.[5] These scholars employ the concept of political ideology in a specific way to denote well-defined groups within the general population. This line of inquiry is carried forth in the American context by Field and Anderson, Pierce, Klingemann and Wright, and Nie et al.[6]

Consistent with Converse we define an ideological mode of thought as a coherent world view, a comprehensive system of political beliefs in which political ideas are central.[7] The coherence or constraint of a belief system of this type is normally derived from a few principles such as, for example, equality or freedom. This definition of ideological conceptualization does not take into account normative or epistemological characteristics of the concept of ideology. Rather, it stresses the idea of a frame of reference, a taxonomy, that allows for a specific type of processing politically relevant information.

Our focus is on mass publics. Thus, we are concerned neither with a "sociology of knowledge" analysis of political thought, per se, nor with an analysis of the "theory class"—the creative political thinkers.[8] Rather, we are concerned with political ideologies only insofar as they reveal a certain breadth of social diffusion. We are looking at the impact of political ideas from the consumer's point of view. It is implicit in our conceptualization that political ideology be seen as a cultural product, propagated through organizational channels and learned by individuals who use it in their comprehension of the political world.

If certain central elements of political ideologies are consciously taken over by an individual, and come to integrate his or her comprehension and evaluation of politics, that person may be said to have an "ideological" conceptualization of politics. By central elements we mean the overarching principles of a world view. Such concepts as "the common ownership of the means of production," "defense of individual freedom before the power of the state," "the preservation of the traditional social and political order," are samples of items in this set of central elements. Terms symbolized through such concepts as "left," "middle," "right," "socialism," "liberalism," or "conservatism" are also incorporated.

Which political ideologies will be encountered among people in the nations under study, and how intensively these ideologies will be held, is an empirical question. But we do not expect to find radical differences across countries with regard to the types of ideological concepts employed by mass publics. The ideological models that have been widely propagated thus far have fairly consistently been organized around the left-right, or liberal-conservative dimension. The permanent theme of ideological controversy is much the same as that considered by Lipset et al. By "Left" we shall be referring to opposition to a more or less hierarchical social order, and an orientation favoring changes leading to greater uniformity of social and political condition.[9] The intensity with which value patterns of these types are held by the populations under investigation should covary with rising levels of ideological conceptualization of politics.

People in their everyday political life employ the type of political knowledge discussed above in order to aid their understanding and evaluation of a broad range of political events and situations. Conscious application of such concepts by individuals leads to a relatively high degree of consistency and is a characteristic of an ideological mode of thought. It must be borne in mind, however, that consistency can be produced by forces other than consciously held ideologies. Socialization in a specific subculture, for example, may equally produce a consistent pattern of beliefs. Many may know "what goes with what," but only few may be able to say "why." Despite its high level of consistency of beliefs, we would not characterize the former as an ideological conceptualization; consciousness of overarching principles—at least to a certain degree—is also required.

Ideological thinking fulfills essentially two complementary functions, one *cognitive* and the other *evaluative.* The first function of ideology in this sense is to help an individual order, retain, and understand political information. Once learned, an ideologically organized belief system should serve as an efficient means to aid understanding and storage of political information. It permits people to locate and make sense of a wider range of information than would be possible without such organization. News can be put in context, and thus given additional meaning.[10] The central principles of an ideology provide an explanatory base that allows an individual to understand a single case or instance of political stimuli as part of a whole. Day to day political events can thus be put readily in order. The overarching principles of the world view, as well as the implied contextual knowledge, can be brought to the interpretation of political situations with the result that a given case is describable and understandable with minimal effort. Converse has discussed the impact of prestored information like this on the intake of new information in terms of a cost-benefit analysis: "the more political information one already has, the lower the costs of acquiring and, perhaps more important, retaining new information."[11] Thus, we expect people having high levels of ideological conceptualization to be politically knowledgeable. And this should be true for knowledge about modes of political action, too. Political ideologies, political values, also help one to make political judgments. The superordinate values of a certain ideology determine whether a political situation or a political event is experienced as favorable or unfavorable, good or bad. One is informed not only about the situation, but one also knows the direction in which the situation ought to develop. The corresponding discrepancy between "is" and "ought" can serve as an essential source of political motivation, which should increase with the increasing centrality of ideas within the political belief system. In this sense political ideologies can be a major stimulus to political action. When modes of political action are controversial, ideological orientation may provide guidance as to which forms of political participation should be applied in order to gain political influence. Thus, we would expect that new forms of political action that are normatively not well supported within the population will be avoided by those groups of the population that are oriented toward the status quo.

Their high level of political skills puts the ideologues more nearly on a par with those in positions of political authority. Consequently, they should be relatively apt to engage in elite-challenging, as distinct from elite-directed, forms of participation. This distinction is important. Let us explore it briefly.

We suggest that participation springs from two fundamentally different processes, one being an older elite-directed mode of political participation, the other a newer elite-challenging mode. The institutions that mobilized mass political participation in the late nineteenth and early twentieth century—labor union, church, and mass political party—were typically hierarchical organizations in which a small number of leaders or bosses led a mass of disciplined troops. They were effective in bringing large numbers of newly enfranchised citizens to the polls in an era when universal compulsory education had just taken root and the average citizen had a low level of political skills. But while these organizations could mobilize large numbers, they usually produced only a relatively low qualitative level of participation—generally not going much beyond mere voting.

Elite-challenging participation is capable of expressing the individual's preferences with far greater precision than the old. It is a more issue-oriented form of participation, less likely to be based on established bureaucratic organizations than on ad hoc groups. It aims at attaining specific policy changes, rather than simply supporting those leaders identified with a given group. And, partly because it *is* issue-specific, this mode of participation requires relatively high levels of cognitive skills.

Given types of participation seem to be linked with specific skill levels. For example, if we take one's formal education as an indicator of political skills, we find that sheer literacy seems sufficient to produce high levels of voting, in the Western context. And the bulk of Western citizens reached this threshold generations ago. In recent decades the proportion of the population in most Western countries receiving secondary and higher education has tripled or even quadrupled. This may have important political consequences. Bare literacy alone may be sufficient to produce a high rate of voting, but to enter the ranks of the Activists—the group with the fullest political action repertory—seems to require at least a secondary education, if not a university education. Why? The reasons are fairly evident. Today most national officials have a university-level education. The citizen with a primary school education is hardly on a footing of equality with them—not merely in terms of social graces, but in regard to essential organizational techniques and even for figuring out whom he should contact in order to articulate a specific griev- ance. As a result, he is likely to depend on some kind of broker who purports to serve his interests *in general.*

But at high levels of economic development, traditional kinds of organiza- tional involvement become less essential and less effective. Rising levels of education apparently tend to move people *out* of such established elite- directed organizational networks as labor union and church and the urban political machine. Both union membership rates and church attendance have been falling in most Western countries. Similarly, the big city machines seem to be losing their grip.

Partly this may be due to rising conceptual and organizational skill levels among the mass public. Political participation remained relatively dependent on permanently established organizations as long as most people lacked organizational skills. Today, ad hoc organizations can be brought into being in response to any current political issue because the public has an unpre- cedentedly large leavening of potential counterelites. Effective boycotts, demonstrations, and similar activities can be organized and publicized by skillful amateurs, acting outside of established channels.

The "new" mode of political participation tends to be far more issue- specific and more likely to function at the higher thresholds of participation than was true of traditional elite-directed politics. It is new in that it relies less heavily on a permanent—and hence relatively rigid—organizational infra- structure. It is new in that it is apt to employ relatively disruptive "unconven- tional" forms of political participation. And it is new in that it depends on exceptionally high levels of ideological conceptualization among mass publics, and on value orientations that seem to have emerged only recently. In the following chapters we will provide empirical evidence in support of these assertions.

But before we do so, we must introduce a complementary theme. For mass publics do not automatically rise up to engage in elite-challenging activities simply because they possess the necessary skills to do so; substantial effort and risks may be involved. One is apt to engage in such activities only if one perceives important differences between one's own goals and those pursued by the elites in power. It is not just a question of cognitive skills, but of affective and evaluative factors as well: elite-challenging action is likely to take place when one knows how to cope with elites *and* wants something different from what the elites want.

Needless to say there are innumerable reasons why one may oppose a given set of elites (including the fact that one simply wants their jobs). But in the current historical context, certain groups seem more apt to reject the values underlying the established order than others. More interesting still, political protest potential does *not* seem to be concentrated mainly among the traditional social base of the Left—the economically deprived—but among relatively affluent groups. Results reported in the preceding chapters demonstrated that the upper socioeconomic strata are relatively apt to participate in conventional political activities. There is nothing new in this finding. It fits in well with social class interpretations of politics: the wealthier groups participate more because they are part of the establishment—they have better contacts and more resources. But another finding was presented as well: in the mid-1970s, the upper socioeconomic groups also showed a higher *protest* potential. This finding can hardly be attributed to one's linkages with the establishment. Though the phenomenon of protest amidst affluence has become well-known in recent years, its explanation is by no means simple. Clearly, it goes beyond the bounds of straightforward economic determinism. And it seems linked with another phenomenon that has been touched on in previous chapters. For as we have just seen, despite the relative rarity of manifest protest in the mid-1970s, people showing a high potential for unconventional protest were surprisingly widespread—especially among the younger generation. We believe that, in part, this reflects an intergenerational shift in basic value priorities. If so, the rules of the game governing acceptable political behavior may be undergoing important changes throughout the West. Let us examine the hypotheses that point to intergenerational changes in value priorities.

Two basic concepts lead to the expectation of intergenerational value change. The first is the idea that all human beings have a variety of needs, some of which are closely related to physical survival, while others are relatively remote.[12] In the former group are the needs for food, shelter, and clothing, and for protection against violence. At an intermediate level are the needs for belonging and love—which are virtually survival needs for the human infant and which relate to survival of the species insofar as procreation is involved. Relatively remote from survival are the needs for esteem, self-expression, and realization of one's intellectual and esthetic potential. As long as survival seems threatened, the physiological needs tend to take top priority in human behavior; but the other needs remain a potential source of motivation.[13] Given some respite from the struggle for survival, even the most impoverished society seeks to create beauty and to understand the nature of the universe. Thus art and religion (or science or quasi-religious ideologies) seem to be universal, a part of every known culture.

Though hungry people may have little time to pursue higher-order needs, the entire spectrum of needs persists, ready to emerge when circumstances permit it. If this concept is valid, it has implications that seem significant in the light of recent history. For during the past few decades, Western nations have attained real per capita income levels far higher than anything known prior to World War II. Partly as a result of this economic growth, but also as a consequence of social welfare legislation, unprecedentedly large segments of Western publics have experienced an unprecedentedly high level of economic security. One might expect a shift toward greater emphasis on noneconomic goals as a result.

This expectation must be interpreted in connection with our second main concept: this is that certain basic orientations, developed during one's pre-adult years, tend to persist throughout later life. The literature of social science is full of illustrations of this tendency as it applies to one's orientations toward sex, religion, politics, and many other things. The young are far more malleable than the old. Consequently, we would not expect one's basic value priorities to change overnight. Those who were shaped by the Great Depression or the two world wars during their formative years will probably tend to give a high priority to economic and physical security throughout their lives. The impact of postwar prosperity would become manifest only gradually, as those who were socialized during the postwar era enter the adult population. We would expect these younger groups to give higher priority to the need for belonging, self-expression, and the quality of life than older groups. As this transition takes place, the materialist consensus would tend to break down, perhaps giving rise to conflicts reflecting a disparity of basic value priorities.

The political implications of these hypotheses are significant. First, they imply that rising prosperity would not bring an end to political conflict, as the "End of Ideology" thesis seemed to promise—even though this thesis was partially correct, in that rising prosperity apparently *did* bring a decline in *traditional* forms of social class conflict. What this thesis failed to anticipate, however, was that new grounds for conflict are likely to emerge, as new goals come to the fore. Though the attainment of prosperity might bring satisfaction to those who gave top priority to materialist goals, this achievement itself would prepare the way for the gradual emergence of new (or newly important) bases of political cleavage. There are indications that this has already taken place to some extent, as is suggested by widespread indications of an increased emphasis on self-realization, protecting the environment, the quest for ethnic identity, and the reaction against hierarchical and impersonal forms of organization. Above all, there is now widespread suspicion of what was once universally accepted, on both Left and Right, as the incontrovertible manifestation of virtue and progress: economic growth.

In chapters 11 and 12 we will present detailed evidence in support of the conclusion that a set of nonmaterial or "Postmaterialist" values have attained top priority for a young, well-educated, and highly articulate minority that has emerged as a significant element of the adult population of Western nations in recent years. For this group, politics is no longer oriented primarily along traditional religious or social class cleavages but according to a set of New Politics issues that tends to pit the Postmaterialists against the Materialist majority.

Because established elites and institutions have only begun to come to grips with the issues they raise, the Postmaterialists feel an acute need to press for political change. This fact helps clarify some of the findings presented in previous chapters. For example, it was noted that the demographic characteristics of Reformists and Activists were virtually indistinguishable. What *does* differentiate these two types is their commitment to different value priorities. While the Reformists are predominantly Materialists, the Activists are, among all the action types, the Postmaterialist group par excellence. This fact also helps account for the rather surprising relationship found between protest potential and socioeconomic status. For despite their relatively favored economic status, Postmaterialists are heavily change-oriented. Western societies remain predominantly Materialist and their policies reflect the prevalence of Materialist priorities. Consequently, the Postmaterialist minority frequently find themselves overruled on matters of crucial importance to them. As a rule, we would expect those with Postmaterialist values to be relatively dissatisfied with their political systems at any given moment, and ready (and able) to seek change through any effective means—whether conventional or unconventional.

CONCLUSION

In this chapter we have outlined two important processes that we believe have been slowly transforming the preconditions for political action among

Western publics: these are a rising level of political conceptualization and the emergence of a small but highly significant group holding Postmaterialist value priorities. We hypothesize that it is the presence of ideological conceptualization of politics, rather than education or higher status occupations in themselves, that is primarily responsible for the relatively high levels of political activity shown by individuals with relatively high socioeconomic status. We hypothesize, moreover, that individuals with Postmaterialist values will tend to show high rates of political participation—and will be *particularly* apt to show a high potential for unconventional political protest. If, as we argue, Postmaterialists have emerged in growing numbers since World War II, it could explain the shift from protest based on the working class to protest based on the young and relatively affluent during the peak years of postwar prosperity.

We have dealt only with our general theoretical framework thus far. In chapters 8 through 10 we will develop empirical measures of one's level of ideological thinking. In chapters 11 and 12 we will undertake a more detailed exploration of changing value priorities and then proceed to examine the relationships among values, levels of ideological conceptualization, and the various types of political action, controlling for the effects of related variables such as education, political interest, age, and income.

NOTES

1. Gabriel A. Almond and Sidney Verba, *The Civic Culture,* Princeton: Princeton University Press, 1963.

2. Lester W. Milbrath and M.L. Goel, *Political Participation,* Rand McNally, 1977; Sidney Verba and Norman H. Nie, *Participation in America,* New York: Harper & Row, 1972.

3. Ronald Inglehart, *The Silent Revolution,* Princeton: Princeton University Press, 1977, ch. 11.

4. Karl Mannheim, *Ideology and Utopia.* New York: Harcourt Brace Jovanovich, 1954; David M. Minar, "Ideology and Political Behavior," *Midwest Journal of Political Science,* 5 (1961), pp. 317-331; Robert E. Lane, *Political Ideology,* New York: Free Press, 1962; John Plamenatz, *Ideology,* London: Pall Mall, 1970.

5. Angus Campbell, Philip E. Converse, Warren E. Miller, and Donald Stokes, *The American Voter,* New York: John Wiley, 1960; Philip E. Converse, "The Nature of Belief Systems in Mass Publics," in David A. Apter (ed.), *Ideology and Discontent,* New York: Free Press, 1964, pp. 206-261.

6. John O. Field and Ronald E. Anderson, "Ideology in the Public's Conceptualization of the 1964 Election," *Public Opinion Quarterly,* 33 (1969), pp. 380-398; John C. Pierce, "Party Identification and the Changing Role of Ideology in American Politics," *Midwest Journal of Political Science,* 14 (1970), pp. 25-42; Hans D. Klingemann and William E. Wright, "Levels of Conceptualization in the American and German Mass Public: A Replication," paper presented at the Workshop on Political Cognition, Univer-

sity of Georgia, Athens, Georgia, May 24-25, 1974; Norman H. Nie, Sidney Verba, and John R. Petrocik, *The Changing American Voter,* Cambridge, Mass.: Harvard University Press, 1976.

7. Philip E. Converse, "The Nature of Belief Systems in Mass Publics," in David A. Apter (ed.), *Ideology and Discontent.*

8. Daniel Bell, *The End of Ideology,* New York: Free Press, 1960.

9. Seymour M. Lipset, Paul F. Lazarsfeld, Allen H. Barton, and Juan Linz, "The Psychology of Voting: An Analysis of Political Behavior," in Gardner Lindzey and Elliot Aronson (eds.), *Handbook of Social Psychology,* Reading, Mass.: Addison-Wesley, 1954, p. 1135.

10. Philip E. Converse, "The Nature of Belief Systems in Mass Publics," in David A. Apter (ed.), *Ideology and Discontent,* p. 214; Robert E. Lane, *Political Ideology,* p. 353.

11. Philip E. Converse, "Public Opinion and Voting Behavior," in Fred I. Greenstein and Nelson W. Polsby (eds.), *Handbook of Political Science,* Vol. 4, Reading, Mass.: Addison-Wesley, 1975, p. 97.

12. We focus here on only one dimension of human values—a Material/Nonmaterial dimension. For an attempt to explore the entire range of human values and their political implications, see Milton Rokeach, *The Nature of Human Values.* New York: Free Press, 1973; Harold Lasswell, *Psychopathology and Politics* New York: Viking, 1960.

13. The classic argument for the existence of a need hierarchy underlying human behavior was made by Abraham Maslow, *Motivation and Personality,* New York: Harper & Row, 1954. For applications of this concept, see James C. Davies, *Human Nature and Politics,* New York: John Wiley, 1963; Amitai Etzioni, *The Active Society,* New York: Free Press, 1968; Robert Lane, *Political Thinking and Consciousness,* Chicago: Markham, 1970; Jeanne M. Knutson, *The Human Basis of the Polity,* Chicago: Aldine, 1972.

Chapter 8

MEASURING IDEOLOGICAL CONCEPTUALIZATIONS

HANS D. KLINGEMANN

There is *no easy way to agree on a conceptual definition of ideology.* Measures of ideological cognition suitable for cross-national research are even harder to come by. Empirical statements about the ideological conceptualization of politics and its effects on political action can be no better than the measuring instruments and operationalization procedures on which they are based. Thus it is of prime importance to lay out in detail how the indices have been constructed in this particular study.

Three different measures of ideological cognition will be described in this chapter. The first one focuses on the *active use of an ideological mode of thought.* The second taps the more passive dimension of ideological knowledge, testing for the *recognition and understanding of an ideological mode of thought.* The third, constructed from these first two, is an index that describes different stages or *levels of ideological conceptualization.* This index will be used as the main measure for the ideological mode of thought in the analyses presented in the following chapters.

Faced with the choice of developing fixed scales or using open-ended interviewing we opted for the latter method. A main part of our interest was in the saliency of ideological political concepts in Western advanced society. This ruled out the use of conventional scales because not much is reliably known about the types of political knowledge across several countries. Thus any attempt to construct closed-ended questions would have had to rely largely on pure guesswork or would have required an impossible amount of development and testing in each country. Our choice of open-ended questions links our inquiry to a well-established research tradition that, as far as cross-sectional surveys are concerned, has been developed mainly by scholars at the Institute for Social Research of the University of Michigan. We will draw heavily on their experience and exploit their results for a body of baseline information, at least for some of the countries under investigation.

THE ACTIVE USE OF AN IDEOLOGICAL MODE OF THOUGHT IN POLITICS

It is difficult to demonstrate empirically the extent to which ideological concepts are spontaneously at hand for the interpretation of political phenomena. The task is especially difficult if one wishes to employ a nationwide sample survey in order to make representative statements for an entire population. National surveys do not yield the type of in-depth information obtainable from small, exploratory studies. National surveys must compromise and rely upon rather short answers to open-ended questions as a substitute for the richer body of data that can be produced in long experimental sessions.[1] Thus the goal of representative results certainly has its price.

When using an open-ended question, the respondent is called upon to articulate a position and to structure it in his or her own words. No response alternatives are presented by the researcher; the respondent must select the frame of reference that best fits his or her conception of the question posed. Relying upon previous research, we assume that individuals choose that frame of reference that has proved in the past to be most efficient for solving similar problems of interpretation and evaluation.[2]

Data collected through open-ended questions are especially sensitive to the quality and skill of interviewers. This problem is particularly relevant in cross-national survey research where we can safely assume that the variance of interviewer performance between countries will be somewhat larger than the variance within each of the national field staffs. The interviewers participating in this study were specially trained and received detailed instructions that were standardized across the participating countries on how to record answers. We must admit that interviewer effects are not eliminated by these methods. However, this is the best method available for ensuring comparability, if, for reasons of expense, one cannot employ tape-recorded interviews.

In order to discover whether and to what extent ideological concepts are spontaneously employed for understanding and evaluating politics, the respondents were asked, early in the interview, to discuss positive and negative aspects of certain political parties. Political parties were chosen as stimulus objects because the usual respondent in each country is at least familiar with the labels and because these parties fulfill similar functions in the respective political systems. Moreover, this approach had already been tested on a national level.[3] Since our research interest is not in parties as such, the number of parties to be evaluated could be limited. To ensure a certain degree of stimulus equivalence, the main nonextremist "left" system party and the main nonextremist "right" system party were chosen. There was no ambiguity concerning which stimuli to choose for Austria, Britain, the United States, and Germany. For the Netherlands, the Partij van de Arbeid was an obvious choice, too. The selection of the Dutch Volkspartij voor Vrijheid en Democratie was guided by the fact that its supporters located themselves very much in the same region of a left-right self-anchoring scale as did the supporters of the Conservatives in Britain and the Christian Democrats in Germany.[4] Table 8.1 gives both an overview of the selected political parties and the exact wording of the question used.

Table 8.1: POLITICAL PARTIES USED AS STIMULUS OBJECTS

Countries	Nonextremist "left" system party	Nonextremist "right" system party
The Netherlands	Partij van de Arbeid	Volkspartij voor Vrijheid en Democratie
Britain	Labour Party	Conservative Party
United States	Democratic Party	Republican Party
Germany	Sozialdemokratische Partei	Christlich Demokratische Union/Christlich Soziale Union
Austria	Sozialdemokratische Partei	Österreichische Volkspartei

In Germany the Christlich Soziale Union has been used as the stimulus object in Bavaria only.

Question wording:
Now, I'd be interested in knowing your opinions of what you feel are the good and bad aspects of the political parties in the (United States).
Let's start with the (Democratic Party).
What do you like about the (Democratic Party)? (Probe fully)
What do you dislike about the (Democratic Party)? (Probe fully)
And what about the (Republican Party)? What do you like about the (Republican Party)? (Probe fully)
What do you dislike about the (Republican Party)? (Probe fully)

It cannot be taken for granted that the spontaneous utilization of ideological concepts can be tapped either generally or exhaustively by this measurement approach. This would be assured only if further stimulus objects of different kinds were included. Field and Anderson[5] and Nie et al.[6] have shown that the use of additional stimulus objects indeed has consequences for the choice of frames of reference. These authors have demonstrated, for the United States, that the presentation of presidential candidate names in addition to political party labels noticeably influenced the active use of ideological concepts in some years (1964, 1968, 1972). In other years, however, such an effect was not observed (1952, 1956, 1960). The American research shows that political parties draw more ideological responses than do the respective presidential candidates. In this study we use political parties as stimulus objects. This must be borne in mind when we speak of an active use of an ideological mode of thought and compare our results with those of previous studies.

When relying on the open-ended question as a data-gathering device, adequate coding of the free responses becomes a major concern. Here the survey researcher faces many of the same problems as the content analyst.[7] Content analysis of this sort stands or falls with its coding categories. The mix of categories controls all further analytical possibilities.

In coping with these problems we developed a classification scheme that coded the *type* of concepts used as well as the *evaluation* (positive or negative) of the concepts employed by the respondent. The classification scheme was designed to provide a comprehensive description of modes of political conceptualization in general. It offered seven main categories to distinguish between broad classes of concepts and each category was further subdivided. The original classification scheme for coding types of concepts consisted of sixty categories. None of these original categories was allowed to be changed by the participating research teams, nor could new major categories be added; but the teams were urged to add country-specific subcategories if necessary. Coding was done under the supervision of the national research teams. The coders were supplied with uniformly employed coding rules. Moreover, we attempted, through thorough documentation of uncertain coding decisions, to arrive at optimal comparability in coding. Nevertheless, coding is a significant source of error; but our procedures could have been improved upon only by adopting semiautomatic coding at prohibitive costs in time and money.

Although knowledge of at least the labels of the nonextremist main "left" and "right" system parties could be taken for granted, a considerable proportion of respondents did not feel in a position to make any favorable or unfavorable comments about either of the parties. This proportion ranged from a high of 28 percent in the Netherlands to a low of 6 percent in

Germany, with the United States (13 percent), Austria (17 percent), and Britain (18 percent) ranging in between. We label those respondents that could not put forth any spontaneous judgment of the political objects as "noncognizers." The high rate of nonresponse in the Netherlands may be due to the fact that, unlike in the other countries, the two parties chosen as stimulus objects got only about 42 percent of the valid votes cast in the 1972 General Election. And it may be that those respondents who never considered one of these political parties as a political alternative simply did not know any components of the parties' image. The low proportion of nonresponses in Germany fits earlier results reporting a relatively high level of political knowledge there.[8]

The use of *ideological concepts* in comparison to the other major types of political concepts is indicated in Table 8.2. The proportion of respondents who used at least one ideological concept was lowest in Britain, the United States, and Austria.

The use of *social group concepts* was much more frequent and stable across countries. About 40 percent of the respondents tried to understand and evaluate the political parties within this frame of reference.

In all nations under study, the *"nature of the times concepts"*, especially those denoting levels of governmental competence and specific domestic policies, were used most often. Except for Germany, there was little use of foreign policy concepts. A large proportion of the foreign policy references in Germany dealt with the theme of "Ostpolitik," which, at the time of data collection, was a matter of vigorous public debate.

Concepts related to specific *politicians* were found especially in the United States and Germany. The portion of respondents who used this type of concept is double that detected in the other countries. Concerns about Nixon in the United States and Brandt in Germany surely contributed to this result.

The purely *affective judgment* of the parties in terms of "good" and "bad" without any other reference to substantive concepts is widespread in all nations.

In this analysis, our interest lies with ideological concepts—that is, concepts abstracted from particular events or persons. Thus we will not deal separately with respondents who reacted solely in terms of specific social groups, politicians, or the "nature of the times" issues; these respondents will be grouped together as "nonideological conceptualizers."

The classification scheme allowed for a coding of *different types of ideological concepts*. Coders were urged to be generous and to classify a concept as ideological if it revealed an act of abstraction and referred to some sort of broader theory of the political and social order. The objective was to cast the net as widely as possible. However, it turned out empirically that ideological concepts were taken almost exclusively from the pool of argu-

Table 8.2: BROAD TYPES OF CONCEPTS ACTIVELY USED TO EVALUATE POLITICAL OBJECTS

Types of Concepts	The Netherlands		Britain		United States		Germany		Austria	
	Proportion of respondents using type of concept at least once	Type of concept as a proportion of the total number of concepts used	Proportion of respondents using type of concept at least once	Type of concept as a proportion of the total number of concepts used	Proportion of respondents using type of concept at least once	Type of concept as a proportion of the total number of concepts used	Proportion of respondents using type of concept at least once	Type of concept as a proportion of the total number of concepts used	Proportion of respondents using type of concept at least once	Type of concept as a proportion of the total number of concepts used
Ideological concepts	36% (438)	21% (799)	21% (319)	8% (442)	21% (355)	7% (623)	34% (778)	9% (1125)	20% (311)	8% (503)
Social group concepts	40 (483)	21 (803)	41 (602)	17 (906)	40 (689)	19 (1565)	45 (1037)	13 (1679)	39 (623)	16 (1000)
Nature of the times concepts	50 (604)	37 (1398)	59 (876)	35 (1857)	64 (1099)	36 (2989)	86 (1974)	53 (6626)	71 (1132)	52 (3171)
I: Party organization and competence concepts	31 (371)	16 (629)	35 (521)	13 (708)	49 (845)	20 (1682)	66 (1516)	22 (2734)	49 (770)	25 (1539)
II: Domestic policy concepts	32 (382)	18 (672)	38 (563)	19 (1006)	34 (586)	12 (1037)	53 (1223)	20 (2467)	51 (811)	26 (1602)
III: Foreign policy concepts	6 (67)	2 (97)	8 (122)	3 (143)	11 (196)	3 (270)	42 (970)	11 (1425)	2 (29)	0 (30)
Politicians and party leaders	15 (181)	6 (226)	18 (267)	7 (352)	40 (688)	15 (1278)	38 (886)	11 (1395)	16 (253)	6 (397)
Intrinsic values	32 (385)	15 (578)	65 (972)	34 (1807)	46 (800)	22 (1811)	49 (1130)	13 (1600)	42 (.1664)	16 (964)
N	1201	3804	1483	5364	1719	8266	2307	12425	1584	6035

ments related to the left-right or liberal-conservative dimension. Only a very small portion of respondents in Germany, Austria, and the Netherlands referred to the religious domain. In Britain and the United States there was no indication at all of a religious dimension. In at least some of the European countries, political conflict has traditionally been organized to a large extent along the lay-clerical axis; thus we had expected to find somewhat more overt concern about such matters.

The dominance of the left-right, liberal-conservative dimension does not come as a surprise. Similar findings have been reported for the United States and Germany.[9] This terminology has long been part of the political culture of the European countries and the United States. It is heavily used by political elites and the media, and serves as a convenient shorthand for labeling political objects and complex political situations. We encountered concepts that were expressed in radical left terms or reactionary right terms, as well as concepts using the terminology of the established, reformist left and the status quo oriented, liberal right. Thus, although orientation toward political and social change was the common theme, the tone of the arguments was varied. Radical left terms stressed the class struggle, equality, and the revolutionary character of left ideology in general. The notions of increased equality, a more just distribution of income and wealth, social progress, and reform were characteristic of terms denoting the established, reformist left. Reactionary right terms included references to capitalism, the profit motive, class society, and the reactionary tendencies contained in such views. Status quo oriented, liberal right terms brought out the preservation of individual freedom, the need for incentives to increase economic performance, the protection of free enterprise, and care for tradition. As a general result, there are few differences in the content of the left-right, liberal-conservative, dimension, as defined by the mass publics of the five nations.

The distribution of these types of ideological concepts is presented in Table 8.3. If we look at the distribution based on the *total number of ideological concepts,* we find a clear dominance of the more moderate ideological concepts in all of the countries. Concepts related to the radical left varied between 7 percent in the Netherlands, 14 percent in Britain, and 13 percent in Austria and the United States. Only Germany stands out with 32 percent. The smallest portion of ideological concepts was related to the reactionary right, reaching a relative high of 11 percent in Austria and a low of 4 percent in Britain, with Germany (7 percent), the Netherlands (6 percent), and the United States (5 percent) ranging inbetween.

It should be borne in mind, however, that these figures refer to the distribution of *types* of ideological concepts. Thus, it would be wrong to conclude that there is a high affinity for radical left concepts in Germany. Rather, such concepts are overwhelmingly negatively evaluated in that

Table 8.3:   TYPES OF IDEOLOGICAL CONCEPTS AS A PERCENTAGE OF
TOTAL IDEOLOGICAL CONCEPTS USED

Types of ideological concepts	The Netherlands		Britain		United States		Germany		Austria	
Concepts related to the radical left	7 %	(56)	14%	(64)	13%	(83)	32%	(358)	13%	(67)
Concepts related to the reformist left	36	(292)	36	(161)	42	(261)	30	(334)	36	(182)
Concepts related to the liberal, status quo right	44	(353)	41	(180)	38	(237)	19	(219)	24	(122)
Concepts related to the reactionary right	6	(49)	4	(18)	5	(33)	7	(77)	11	(56)
Concepts related to the religious domain	4	(36)	–	–	–	–	12	(133)	11	(53)
Concepts not classifiable in these terms	2	(13)	4	(19)	2	(9)	0	(4)	5	(23)
Total number of ideological concepts (N)	799		442		623		1125		503	

NOTE: For the exact operational definition cf. note 10, this chapter.

country, and the high proportion of arguments of this type may be a reflection of the pronounced anticommunism that has long been prevalent there. As is shown in Table 8.4, ideological concepts of both the radical left type and of the reactionary right type are negatively evaluated in all of the countries. The highest proportion of positive evaluations of radical left concepts was found in Britain (39 percent) and the Netherlands (36 percent); the highest proportion of positive evaluations of reactionary right concepts was encountered in the United States (58 percent), Britain (44 percent), and Austria (39 percent).

In this first step of our analysis we have located that portion of the respondents who are broadly sensitive to politics in terms of ideological concepts. And we are able to demonstrate that ideological concepts used by

Table 8.4: POSITIVE EVALUATION OF TYPES OF IDEOLOGICAL CONCEPTS

Types of ideological concepts	The Netherlands		Britain		United States		Germany		Austria	
Concepts related to the radical left	36%	(56)	39%	(64)	14%	(83)	5%	(358)	25%	(67)
Concepts related to the reformist left	94	(292)	97	(161)	67	(261)	89	(334)	95	(182)
Concepts related to the liberal, status quo right	73	(353)	83	(180)	73	(237)	58	(219)	74	(122)
Concepts related to the reactionary right	6	(49)	44	(18)	58	(33)	16	(77)	39	(56)
Concepts related to the religious domain	80	(36)	–	–	–	–	73	(133)	79	(53)

NOTE: For the exact operational definition cf. note 10, this chapter.

mass publics are overwhelmingly related to a moderately defined left-right, liberal-conservative dimension. The active use of a *single* ideological concept of this sort may itself indicate the notion of a continuum along which the respondent gauges political objects. In a strict sense, however, awareness of that dimension *as a continuum* is more explicitly defined when a respondent refers to it in terms of both left *and* right concepts, thus cutting the continuum at least at two points. When we require of ideologues that they actively use both left and right concepts, the proportion of *ideologues* becomes small indeed.[11] It ranges from 4 percent in Britain and Austria up to 9 percent in the Netherlands, with Germany and the United States both with 7 percent inbetween.

As might be expected, the proportion of *near-ideologues* is consistently larger than that of ideologues. The proportion of near-ideologues is highest in the Netherlands (27 percent) and Germany (26 percent), and fairly similar, but lower, in Britain (17 percent), Austria (15 percent), and the United States (13 percent). Thus, in the European nations, the proportion of near-ideologues is three to four times as great as that of the ideologues. In the United States, by contrast, it is only twice as great.

In order to qualify as an ideologue or near-ideologue a positive orientation toward the ideological concepts used is not required. It is sufficient that ideological concepts be spontaneously at hand. In a later chapter we will distinguish between different ideological camps by using indicators of value orientation that are measured independently.

The proportions of ideologues and near-ideologues imply a clear numerical dominance of *nonideological modes of conceptualization of politics* in all the nations studied. This larger group includes four-fifths of the population in Austria, Britain, and the United States. In Germany and the Netherlands roughly two-thirds are in the nonideological set.

It has already been noted that our measurement approach links us into the research tradition of the Institute for Social Research. The classical analyses of this research group deal with the 1956 presidential election study and with a follow-up survey of the same sample in 1960.[13] We have mentioned, too, that we build on these studies substantively as well as technically. In particular, we use nearly identical rules to define the *ideologues* and the *near-ideo-*

Table 8.5: ACTIVE USE OF AN IDEOLOGICAL MODE OF THOUGHT IN POLITICS: Distribution of Types

Types	The Netherlands		Britain		United States		Germany		Austria	
Ideologues (left and nonleft concepts used)	9%	(105)	4%	(54)	7%	(124)	8%	(174)	4%	(61)
Near-Ideologues (left or nonleft concepts used)	27	(327)	17	(255)	13	(226)	26	(603)	15	(238)
Non-Ideologues total	64	(769)	79	(1174)	80	(1369)	66	(1530)	81	(1285)
nonideological conceptualizers	36	(436)	61	(910)	66	(1138)	60	(1382)	64	(1013)
noncognizers	28	(333)	18	(264)	14	(231)	6	(148)	17	(272)
N		1201		1483		1719		2307		1584

NOTE: For the exact operational definition cf. note 12, this chapter.

logues. Thus, we are able to compare our results with the results of this important baseline research.[14] In addition to the 1956-1960 data, Klingemann and Wright have presented evidence related to the 1968 United States presidential election and the German Bundestagswahl in 1969.[15] Field and Anderson, Pierce, and, above all, Nie et al. have generated further results based on secondary analysis of surveys carried out by the Survey Research Center/Center for Political Studies, at the University of Michigan, for all presidential elections from 1952 to 1972.[16] Although the operationalization of the ideologues and the near-ideologues is not directly comparable, it is so similar that developmental trends can be compared.[17]

In the base year 1956, the proportion of ideologues among enfranchized American citizens was 2.5 percent.[18] This result, more than any other, has been the focal point of debate over some basic assumptions of democratic theory. Obviously, this portion of idea-oriented critizens has changed. The figure rose to 5.2 percent in 1968, and the 1974 result indicates a further increase, bringing the ideologues up to 7.5 percent. Due to somewhat different definitional criteria, the portion of ideologues reported by Nie et al.[19] and Field and Anderson[20] is consistently higher, but the general trend line leads to a similar and clear conclusion: the proportion of ideologues in the United States has increased over the past generation.

A different trend is visible in the case of the near-ideologues. The proportion of near-ideologues varied between 9 percent in 1956 and 15.1 percent in 1968, while falling slightly to 13.2 percent in 1974. Clearly, the 1974 drop may well be due to the absence of a presidential election campaign in that year compared to 1956 or 1968. However, it may well also indicate that more people qualified for the near-ideologue category at the height of the politicization of the American electorate in the 1960s than in the quieter days of the post-Vietnam era. The pattern discovered by Field and Anderson and Nie et al. differs very little from the one given above. In Germany two points in time can be compared. The proportion of ideologues among the population of voting age was 4.2 percent in 1969 and went up to 7.4 percent in 1974. The proportion of near-ideologues grew as well, from 20.2 percent in 1969 to 26.5 percent in 1974.

Thus there is steady change in the active use of ideological concepts in these two countries, with the results of our 1974 surveys being on the high side; but there certainly is no sweeping change.

We can summarize our initial findings as follows.

(1) It is demonstrable empirically in cross-national comparison that the stratum of ideologues, defined as people who actively use the left-right or the liberal-conservative dimension to understand and evaluate political phenomena, amounts consistently to less than one-tenth of

Table 8.6: IDEOLOGUES AND NEAR-IDEOLOGUES IN THE UNITED STATES AND GERMANY: A Cross-Time Perspective

| | United States | | | | Germany | |
	1956	1968	1974	1969	1974
Ideologues	2.5% (44)	5.2% (81)	7.5% (117)	4.2% (32)	7.4% (161)
Near-Ideologues	9.0 (158)	15.1 (235)	13.2 (205)	20.0 (153)	26.5 (577)
N	1762	1557	1555	766	2176

SOURCES: United States 1956, Campbell et al., 1960. United States 1968 and Germany 1969, Klingemann and Wright, 1974. The distributions for the United States 1968 and Germany 1969 have been slightly modified to fit the originally published 1956 data. In order to hold the age limitations constant (21 years and older), we have excluded those respondents from the 1974 surveys who were younger than 21 years.

the population. The confirmation of the minority position of a strictly defined "idea class" is in harmony with all prior empirical research.

(2) Cross-time comparisons that are possible for the United States and Germany indicate a moderate but steady rise of the ideologues up to 1974.

(3) The number of near-ideologues, defined by more generous criteria, is uniformly larger, but still does not exceed 27 percent in any of the five countries.

The measure that we have described and employed here deals with the active use of an ideological mode of thought. Before considering the potentially disproportionate influence of idea-oriented citizens, however, more scrutiny should be given to another state of ideological knowledge.

RECOGNITION AND UNDERSTANDING OF AN IDEOLOGICAL MODE OF THOUGHT

Our measure of active ideological thinking was designed to tap the saliency of ideological concepts in mass publics. The assumption was that saliency indicates a high centrality of ideology as a steering mechanism for political information processing. Results have shown that only a relatively small segment of the population in the countries under study gives ideological concepts high centrality in political belief systems. However, this finding does not necessarily define the limits of potential ideological communication. It is possible that many more people are able to understand politics in ideological terms, but they may give these concepts a rather low centrality. This would be a public which, when mobilized by an ideologically oriented elite, could be expected to understand the argument and act according to the inner logic of an ideological schema.

In this section we are going to suggest a measure of *recognition and understanding of an ideological mode of thought* in politics that relaxes the saliency component and stresses rather the aspect of passive ideological knowledge. Technically we rely on a combination of one closed-ended and two open-ended questions, thus capitalizing on the fact that people can recognize more objects (or concepts) when they are directly presented than they can readily recall on the basis of indirect cues.[21] The closed-ended question asked for recognition of political symbols with culturally well-established ideological connotations. The open-ended questions were designed to measure whether, indeed, the ideological implications of these political symbols were known. Thus, the respondents were asked to elaborate in their own words on the substantive meaning of certain symbols. Of course, all the technical problems of open-ended questions, discussed previously in relation to the measurement of active ideological thinking, also hold for the open-ended questions used here.

The political symbols "left" and "right" were employed as stimulus objects. On the one hand, these symbols have relatively unambiguous ideological connotations. On the other hand, it was evident from the number of empirical studies that the terms "left" and "right" were widely known, at least in the European countries.[22] In the most recent comparative study it could be demonstrated for nine European countries that more people were willing to locate their political views along a left-right self-anchoring scale than were prepared to report identification with any of the political parties of the respective systems.[23] One might argue for the United States that the culturally more familiar terms "liberal" and "conservative" should have been used as stimulus objects. For reasons of strict comparability, however, we did not replace the symbols "left" and "right" with "liberal" and "conservative." It has been shown that an American student population had no difficulty in responding to the concepts "left" and "right."[24] The same results might not be expected when questioning a representative cross-section of the American population. The poorly educated, in particular, may be less familiar with these symbols than their European counterparts. Later, we will put these speculations to an empirical test.

We considered the left-right terms as having been recognized if the respondents were ready to locate their own political position somewhere on a left-right self-anchoring scale. The scale, which the interviewer presented to the respondent, consisted of ten horizontally ordered boxes. No numbers or other cues were provided except the words "left" and "right" at the end points of the ten-point scale.[25] The scale has no explicit midpoint so that, in some of our later analyses, respondents could be classified as either placing themselves more to the left or more to the right. Furthermore, we did not want to reinforce the known tendency of the less well-informed respondents to put themselves in a middle position when in doubt under the pressure of the interview situation.[26]

Respondents who recognized the left-right dimension were then asked two follow-up questions about the meaning of the terms "left" and "right" in politics. Table 8.7 presents the scale as well as the wording of the question.

The classification scheme that guided coding contained thirty-one categories, including all of the country-specific additions. The understanding of the terms "left" and "right" was dealt with separately. For each symbol, up to three responses could be coded. In this analysis, we will rely upon the first response. Care was taken to ensure reliable coding results.

As was the case with our measure of active ideological thinking, we consciously tie the measurement of the recognition and understanding of an

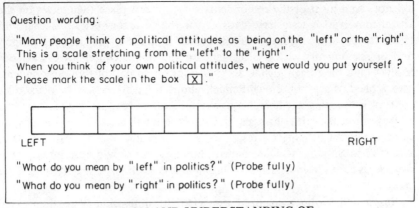

Question wording:

"Many people think of political attitudes as being on the "left" or the "right". This is a scale stretching from the "left" to the "right". When you think of your own political attitudes, where would you put yourself ? Please mark the scale in the box ☒ ."

LEFT   RIGHT

"What do you mean by "left" in politics?" (Probe fully)
"What do you mean by "right" in politics?" (Probe fully)

Table 8.7: RECOGNITION AND UNDERSTANDING OF AN IDEOLOGICAL MODE OF THOUGHT: The Measurement Instrument

ideological mode of thought to a specific research tradition. This measure was proposed, though in modified form, by Converse.[27] Thus here too we are in a position to cite some baseline results.

Recognition of the terms "left" and "right" was high in the European countries. It was highest in Germany (92 percent), and lowest in Austria (75 percent), with the Netherlands (90 percent) and Britain (82 percent) ranging inbetween. In 1973 these proportions were quite similar in Germany (93 percent), the Netherlands (93 percent), and Britain (82 percent)—the three countries out of the set of five for which comparable data are available from a cross-national study.[28] Thus, there is not much fluctuation over time with respect to the recognition of the left-right dimension. The relatively low figure for Austria may be due in part to a slight difference in wording that inadvertently intruded in the questionnaire despite efforts to achieve strict cross-national consistency. However, there is no way of evaluating this possibility because no earlier measurement is reported for Austria. As was expected, the American survey showed the lowest recognition rate (68 percent). In 1976, when the same question was asked again, the recognition rate was slightly higher (74 percent; CPS 1976 National Election Study). A comparison of these results with data generated by a similar self-anchoring scale that used the culturally well-known terms "liberal" and "conservative" is possible for the years 1972 and 1976. In these cases the recognition rate was 71 percent in 1972 and 67 percent in 1976 (CPS 1972 and 1976 National Election Studies). Thus, it seems as if there is not much of a difference with respect to the terms left-right and liberal-conservative as stimulus objects. However, the liberal-conservative question in both cases offered the answer category "have not thought much about it" whereas the left-right question did not. And most of the respondents who did not place themselves on the liberal-conservative scale have chosen just that category (1972: 21 percent; 1976: 26 percent). Without the difference in question wording the proportion of respondents with a placement on the liberal-conservative scale certainly would have been higher. In 1976 more than half of those respondents who replied "have not thought much about it" when asked to place their political views along the liberal-conservative scale were quite willing to choose a location on the left-right scale.[29] Thus without this difference in question wording one might expect a response rate to the liberal conservative scale of about 80 to 85 percent. Our concern, however, is not with response rate but with cross-cultural equivalence, a problem that will be discussed in a later paragraph.

Respondents who recognized the left-right dimension were then asked what they understood by "left" and "right" in politics. A sizeable proportion of those respondents either *could not give any meaning* of the terms *or* else completely *reversed* their *meaning*. Thus left was interpreted as "conservative," "entrepreneurs," and so on, whereas right was thought to mean "communists," "workers," and so on. The proportion of these respondents ranged from 20 percent in the Netherlands to 9 percent in Germany, with Britain (19 percent), the United States (15 percent), and Austria (13 percent) ranging inbetween. The answers of the respondents who could discuss the meaning of the terms were easily classifiable into three broad types.

Some respondents referred to social and political change, a particular organization of state and society, or linked "left" and "right" to the ideological movements of our times at least in some nominal sense. We considered them as having an *ideological understanding* of the terms, though the definition again is very generous indeed.

In the next cluster of responses we found a group of people who either equated the terms in a most direct way with *political parties* or, in fewer instances, with *social groups* such as "workers" or "the rich."

The last type of respondent tried to cope with the problem by linking "left" and "right" to purely affective or moralistic states. Thus, "left" was bad, dishonest, or untrustworthy, whereas "right" was seen as good, honest, trustworthy, or it was the other way around. We have labeled these responses as an *idiosyncratic or affective understanding* of the presumably ideological symbols.[30]

Understanding of each of the terms "left" and "right" was coded into a separate variable. There were slight differences in all of the countries, but all point to the fact that "left" was understood more often and in more ideological terms as well. Understanding of one of the terms showed a high degree of association with understanding of the other: coefficients (tau-b) range from .88 in the United States and Britain to .61 in Germany, with

Austria (.81) and the Netherlands (.74) in the middle positions. Thus there is a high probability that the respondents do not alter their types of explanation when switching from the meaning of "left" to the meaning of "right." For our final variable—recognition and understanding of an ideological mode of thought—we have combined the information obtained from the two open-ended questions.[31]

The resulting distribution reveals an interesting pattern. From the point of view of cross-national comparison, the differences and similarities between the European countries on the one hand and the United States on the other are most rewarding. The proportion of respondents who understood both "left" and "right" in ideological terms was highest in Germany (30 percent) and the Netherlands (27 percent); it was lowest in Britain (11 percent), with Austria (21 percent) ranging inbetween. However, the United States did not trail behind the European countries. Rather, around a quarter of the American population was able to define both "left" and "right" in ideological terms—a higher proportion than in Britain and Austria.

In America in most of the cases the terms "left" and "right" were related to the liberal-conservative dimension, with a tendency to see left and right at the extremes of the liberal-conservative continuum, thus extending that dimension a bit. Thus, a more general ideological orientation seems to allow for an ordering of culturally less familiar political symbols without any great difficulty. This interpretation is further supported by results obtained from the CPS 1976 Presidential Election Study. There was a clear tendency for respondents from the extreme liberal to the conservative position to see their political views more in the middle region of the left-right scale, reducing the association between the two scales to a gamma of .49.

European respondents who could not supply an ideological meaning to the terms tended to equate "left" and "right" with party names or social groups, as we have already mentioned. This was not the case in the United States; the respective category is almost empty. Lacking a traditionally predefined pattern of relationships between politically relevant objects and the left-right labels, American respondents who could not elaborate on them in ideological terms resorted to an affective-moralistic interpretation of the good-bad, honest-dishonest type. This, in turn, is an almost empty category in the European countries. The most comparable European country in this respect is Britain, in which the terms "labour" and "conservative" are much more familiar for labeling political parties or social groups than the terms "left" and "right." This finding points again to the conceptual value of the difference between "knowledge by proxy" and the more genuine ideological knowledge of the "what goes with what and why" type.[32]

Our results qualify the expectation of a widespread ideological understanding of the left-right dimension. If we are willing to include in what we might

Table 8.8: RECOGNITION AND UNDERSTANDING OF AN IDEOLOGICAL MODE OF THOUGHT IN POLITICS

Types of Understanding	The Netherlands		Britain		United States		Germany		Austria	
High ideological recognition and understanding	27%	(324)	11%	(171)	24%	(410)	30%	(699)	21%	(341)
Low ideological recognition and understanding	21	(251)	12	(174)	10	(173)	26	(599)	18	(281)
Nonideological recognition and understanding	52	(626)	77	(1138)	66	(1136)	44	(1009)	61	(962)
Type I Political parties or social groups	19	(235)	30	(448)	2	(38)	24	(553)	18	(288)
Type II Idiosyncratic or affective	3	(32)	10	(143)	16	(279)	3	(57)	5	(73)
Type III Wrong or no understanding	20	(243)	19	(275)	15	(262)	9	(218)	13	(207)
Type IV No recognition	10	(116)	18	(272)	33	(557)	8	(181)	25	(394)
N	1201		1483		1719		2307		1584	

NOTE: For the exact definition of the categories cf. note 31, this chapter.

call the ideological public those respondents who understood at least one of the symbols in ideological terms we can define the potential for successful ideological communication in its broadest sense. Messages of this type could count on a slight understanding of about half the German (56 percent) and Dutch (48 percent) populations. In Austria (39 percent) and the United States (34 percent) the proportion varies around one-third of the population. And in Britain (23 percent) about a quarter of the population would be reached.

In two of the countries, the United States and Britain, similar analyses have been carried out before. Converse offers results based on a 1960 ISR/CPS survey, in which 37 percent of the American electorate could supply no meaning to the liberal-conservative distinction, 46 percent could give some meaning, and only 17 percent related some broad ideological concepts to these terms.[33] When one compares the latter proportion with that found in 1974, one can conclude that there has been an increase in the ideological understanding of political symbols similar to the case with the active use of ideological concepts.

Butler and Stokes, in their 1963 British survey, asked if the political parties were seen in the frame of reference provided by the left-right dimension.[34] Among the respondents who said that they thought of the political parties in these terms only 2 percent could give a fully elaborated, dynamic interpretation; 14 percent had a partially elaborated static interpretation in mind; another 4 percent tried at least a nominal ideological interpretation of left-right symbolism; whereas 20 percent had only a minimal recognition of the terms.[35] Although the definition of the categories does not allow for any direct comparison, it appears justified to conclude that there has been an increase in the portion of respondents with an ideological understanding of the left-right symbols since 1963 in Britain, too.

LEVELS OF IDEOLOGICAL CONCEPTUALIZATION IN POLITICS

The preceding sections described the potential for ideological understanding as well as the saliency of an ideological mode of thought. We are now going to combine both aspects of ideological thinking into a summary measure. This index, "*levels of ideological conceptualization*," will then serve us in the further analysis as a general indicator of ideological thinking. The relationship between the *active use of ideological concepts* and the *ideological understanding of political symbols* is interesting in two respects. First, we can check whether active use of ideological concepts also implies their understanding. Second, the relation of active to passive ideological knowledge is worth exploration.

Table 8.9 shows how ideologues, near-ideologues, and nonideologues substantively understand the political symbols "left" and "right." As would be expected, active ideological thinking is a rather good predictor of the degree to which these terms were understood in an ideological sense. In Britain about a third of the ideologues discussed "left" and "right" in terms of political or social groups, thus leaving a relatively smaller portion for an ideological interpretation (63 percent). In all of the other countries, however, about four-fifths of the ideologues immediately put "left" and "right" in an ideological context. There is a steep gradient from the ideologues to the nonideologues with respect to recognition and understanding of ideological thinking. This gradient is most pronounced in Britain, Austria, and the United States, where the terms have lower currency than in Germany or the Netherlands. The more these labels have penetrated the political culture, the more the ideological content of the terms trickles down to the rank and file. All in all, the active use of ideological concepts implies with high probability that there will also be ideological understanding of political symbols. This agrees with the finding indicated by Converse in 1964.[36]

We will now turn to the second aspect of the relation between both indicators for ideological conceptualization and ask the question: to what degree is active use of ideological concepts conditioned by the availability of the more passive ideological knowledge? In all the countries under study we have found more respondents who could recognize political symbols and interpret them in an ideological context than there were people who actively used ideological concepts for the judgment and evaluation of political objects. This suggests that passive ideological thinking may be viewed as an antecedent to its more active form.

Table 8.10 shows that the probability of active ideological thinking grows with the increasing recognition and understanding of an ideological mode of thought. The chance that respondents who understand both "left" and "right" in ideological terms will use such terms actively amounts to 57 percent in Britain and the Netherlands, 44 percent in the United States, 43 percent in Germany, and 33 percent in Austria. Among those respondents with a low ideological recognition and understanding of "left" and "right," this portion varied between 43 percent in the Netherlands and 24 percent in the United States. Thus the ideological potential at the time of the survey was not nearly exhausted in any of the nations under study. The conditions under which this potential can be developed in such a way that active usage will result must remain unspecified. However, we believe that the ideological segment will expand from within this group of people whose cognitive limitations are lowest and may be overcome in shorter periods of time, rather

Table 8.9: RELATION OF RECOGNITION AND UNDERSTANDING TO ACTIVE USE OF AN IDEOLOGICAL MODE OF THOUGHT

Country	Recognition and understanding	Active use of an ideological mode of thought in politics				
		Ideologues	Near-Ideologues	Nonideological conceptualizers	Noncognizers	Total
THE NETHERLANDS	High ideological understanding	59% (62)	37% (122)	24% (103)	11% (37)	27% (324)
	Low ideological understanding	18 (19)	28 (90)	23 (99)	13 (43)	21 (251)
	Understanding in terms of political parties or social groups	15 (16)	24 (78)	25 (110)	9 (31)	20 (235)
	Understanding in idiosyncratic or affective terms	1 (1)	0 (3)	4 (18)	4 (12)	3 (32)
	Wrong or no understanding	4 (4)	8 (26)	16 (70)	43 (143)	20 (243)
	No recognition	3 (3)	3 (10)	8 (36)	20 (67)	10 (116)
	N	105	327	436	333	1201

Table 8.9: **RELATION OF RECOGNITION AND UNDERSTANDING TO ACTIVE USE OF AN IDEOLOGICAL MODE OF THOUGHT** (cont.)

Country / Recognition and understanding	Active use of an ideological mode of thought in politics				
	Ideologues	Near-Ideologues	Nonideological conceptualizers	Noncognizers	Total
BRITAIN					
High ideological understanding	40% (22)	30% (75)	7% (68)	2% (6)	11% (171)
Low ideological understanding	24 (13)	20 (51)	11 (99)	4 (11)	12 (174)
Understanding in terms of political parties or social groups	31 (17)	32 (80)	33 (302)	19 (49)	30 (448)
Understanding in idiosyncratic or affective terms	2 (1)	8 (21)	12 (105)	6 (16)	10 (143)
Wrong or no understanding	–	5 (13)	21 (187)	28 (75)	18 (275)
No recognition	3 (2)	5 (14)	16 (149)	41 (107)	18 (272)
N	55	254	910	264	1483

Table 8.9: RELATION OF RECOGNITION AND UNDERSTANDING TO ACTIVE USE OF AN IDEOLOGICAL MODE OF THOUGHT (cont.)

Country	Recognition and understanding	Active use of an ideological mode of thought in politics				
		Ideologues	Near-Ideologues	Nonideological conceptualizers	Noncognizers	Total
UNITED STATES	High ideological understanding	71% (88)	41% (92)	19% (210)	9% (20)	24% (410)
	Low ideological understanding	10 (12)	13 (30)	10 (120)	5 (11)	10 (173)
	Understanding in terms of political parties or social groups	2 (2)	2 (4)	2 (27)	2 (5)	2 (38)
	Understanding in idiosyncratic or affective terms	3 (4)	11 (26)	20 (223)	11 (26)	16 (279)
	Wrong or no understanding	11 (14)	11 (26)	16 (178)	19 (44)	15 (262)
	No recognition	3 (4)	22 (48)	33 (380)	54 (125)	32 (557)
	N	124	226	1138	231	1719

Table 8.9: RELATION OF RECOGNITION AND UNDERSTANDING TO ACTIVE USE OF AN IDEOLOGICAL MODE OF THOUGHT (cont.)

	Active use of an ideological mode of thought in politics				
Country / Recognition and understanding	Ideologues	Near-Ideologues	Nonideological conceptualizers	Noncognizers	Total
GERMANY					
High ideological understanding	49% (86)	36% (214)	27% (368)	21% (31)	30% (699)
Low ideological understanding	29 (50)	30 (178)	25 (350)	14 (21)	26 (599)
Understanding in terms of political parties or social groups	14 (24)	26 (160)	25 (353)	11 (16)	24 (553)
Understanding in idiosyncratic or affective terms	5 (8)	2 (11)	3 (37)	1 (1)	2 (57)
Wrong or no understanding	2 (4)	3 (20)	12 (165)	19 (29)	9 (218)
No recognition	1 (2)	3 (20)	8 (109)	34 (50)	8 (181)
N	174	603	1382	148	2307

Table 8.9: RELATION OF RECOGNITION AND UNDERSTANDING TO ACTIVE USE OF AN IDEOLOGICAL MODE OF THOUGHT (cont.)

Country	Recognition and understanding	Active use of an ideological mode of thought in politics				
		Ideologues	Near-Ideologues	Nonideological conceptualizers	Noncognizers	Total
AUSTRIA	High ideological understanding	59% (36)	32% (76)	20% (201)	10% (28)	21% (341)
	Low ideological understanding	21 (13)	24 (57)	18 (187)	9 (24)	18 (281)
	Understanding in terms of political parties or social groups	11 (7)	25 (59)	19 (188)	12 (34)	18 (288)
	Understanding in idiosyncratic or affective terms	2 (1)	5 (13)	5 (52)	3 (7)	5 (73)
	Wrong or no understanding	–	5 (13)	15 (150)	16 (44)	13 (207)
	No recognition	7 (4)	9 (20)	23 (235)	50 (135)	25 (394)
	N	61	238	1013	272	1584

than from among those who do not show any signs of linking into the ideational world of politics at all. In associational terms (gamma), the relationship between the two variables is strongest in Britain (.66) and the United States (.63). It is lowest in Germany (.29), and on a medium level in the Netherlands (.50) and Austria (.45).

The coefficients reflect differences in the ability of the nonideologues to discuss the terms left and right in an ideological frame of reference and the willingness to place their views on the left-right scale. This is especially true for Germany. A more detailed analysis reveals that the rather high degree of ideological understanding of the left-right dimension by nonideologues in Germany is due to the fact that the term "left" triggers almost twice as many ideological comments as is the case in the rest of the countries. These comments mostly relate to the communist movement, an ideological current that is overwhelmingly negatively evaluated. Thus our combined measure catches a lot of ideologues of the anticommunist type in Germany.

In the preceding discussion we have treated the active use of an ideological mode of thought as the dependent variable, and we have looked at the distributions that resulted for the different levels of the independent variable—recognition and understanding of ideological thinking. This implies that we are controlling for the marginal distributions of the independent variable, which are different for the different countries under investigation. However, the marginal distributions of the dependent variable are also different between countries and this may have an effect on the relationships, irrespective of the effect generated by the particular independent variable.

One can determine the size of this "country" effect by use of an analysis technique proposed by Goodman.[37] To this end the data are arranged in a three-dimensional table. The nationality of the respondent is thus conceived of as an additional independent variable. One can now predict the distribution of the dependent variable, active ideological thinking, by assuming an effect of the mean only. This corresponds to the hypotheses that the fifteen groups, as represented in our three-dimensional table, will not differ in the active use of an ideological mode of thought. This null hypothesis can be examined by use of a chi-square test. The resulting values can be viewed as analogues of the total variance of the dependent variable in a variance or regression analysis. In the same way one can now use either one of the two independent variables—recognition and understanding of an ideological mode of thought and nationality—for the prediction of the actual distribution of the dependent variable. Using the corresponding chi-square values, a measure of determination can be calculated that indicates the percentage reduction in the total variance. In our case a variance reduction in the above described sense of .77 is produced when using the variable recognition and understanding of an ideological mode of thought; for the variable nationality there is a

Table 8.10: RELATION OF THE ACTIVE USE OF TO RECOGNITION AND UNDERSTANDING OF AN IDEOLOGICAL MODE OF THOUGHT

Country	Active use of an ideological mode of thought	Recognition and understanding of an ideological mode of thought			Total
		High ideological recognition and understanding	Low ideological recognition and understanding	Nonideological recognition and understanding	
THE NETHERLANDS	Ideologues	19% (62)	7% (19)	4% (24)	9% (105)
	Near-Ideologues	38 (122)	36 (90)	18 (115)	27 (327)
	Nonideologues	43 (140)	57 (142)	78 (487)	64 (769)
	N	324	251	626	1201
BRITAIN	Ideologues	13 (22)	8 (13)	2 (20)	4 (55)
	Near-Ideologues	44 (75)	29 (51)	11 (128)	17 (254)
	Nonideologues	43 (74)	63 (110)	87 (990)	79 (1174)
	N	171	174	1138	1483
UNITED STATES	Ideologues	21 (88)	7 (12)	2 (24)	7 (124)
	Near-Ideologues	23 (92)	17 (30)	9 (104)	13 (226)
	Nonideologues	56 (230)	76 (131)	89 (1008)	80 (1369)
	N	410	173	1136	1719
GERMANY	Ideologues	12 (86)	8 (50)	4 (38)	7 (174)
	Near-Ideologues	31 (214)	30 (178)	21 (211)	26 (603)
	Nonideologues	57 (399)	62 (371)	75 (760)	66 (1530)
	N	699	599	1009	2307
AUSTRIA	Ideologues	11 (36)	5 (13)	1 (12)	4 (61)
	Near-Ideologues	22 (76)	20 (57)	11 (105)	15 (238)
	Nonideologues	67 (229)	75 (211)	88 (845)	81 (1285)
	N	341	281	962	1584

reduction of .26.[38] The country-effect on the distribution of active ideological thinking is thus substantially smaller than the effect of passive ideological knowledge. However, the country-effect (that is, all the situational and structural variables that are not specified) is nonetheless significant. In order to show the degree to which there is a similar nucleus of association between active ideological thinking and the passive recognition and understanding of ideological stimuli, we therefore have to remove the country-effect.

Mosteller has discussed a simple method by which this can be done and he has demonstrated its usefulness with an example from cross-national research.[39] By means of row and column multiplications it is possible to standardize a two-way table so that one gets uniformly distributed marginals on each side. The resulting numbers can be interpreted as transitional or conditional probabilities. There are, of course, limits to this technique, as Goodman and Bishop et al. have pointed out.[40] For our purposes, however, an approximate representation of that nucleus of association will suffice. Thus we have standardized our set of five tables separately to have row totals as well as column totals equal to 100. Results are presented in Figure 8.1. The similarities of the conditional probabilities across countries are quite evident. The dissimilarities between the bivariate distributions of the ten possible pairs of countries are, on the average, reduced by a factor of 3, from 19.35 to 6.48.[41] Thus, we assume that there is a similar nucleus of association, as Mosteller has defined it, in the countries under investigation.

Up to this point we have shown that "recognition and understanding of an ideological mode of thought" is more widely disseminated than the "active use of an ideological mode of thought." It has also been demonstrated that active ideological thinking, as a rule, implies underlying passive ideological knowledge.[42] And we have discussed the nature of the association between the two variables, concluding that it is quite similar across countries when eliminating the country-effect. This evidence suggests that passive ideological knowledge is antecedent to and a correlate of active ideological knowledge. Conceptualizing the relationship between these two variables in this way speaks for the utility of combining both indicators into a single index. The categories of this new variable should represent different levels or different degrees of command of an ideological conceptualization of politics. For the combination of the two indicators we have used the rule as specified in Table 8.11.

The numbers entered in the matrix denote the categories of the newly constructed variable. Categories 1 to 4 divide into four groups the respondents who have actively used at least one ideological concept and understood at least one of the symbols "left" or "right" in ideological terms. The categories 1 and 2, *high* and *middle levels of ideological conceptualization* of politics, contain respondents who actively employ an ideological frame of

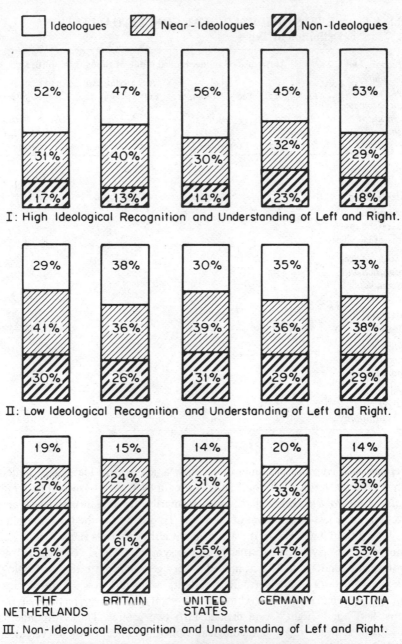

Figure 8.1: **RECOGNITION AND UNDERSTANDING OF AN IDEOLOGICAL MODE OF THOUGHT AND ACTIVE USE OF IDEOLOGICAL MODE OF THOUGHT (controlling for country-specific effects)**

Table 8.11: LEVELS OF IDEOLOGICAL CONCEPTUALIZATION: Definition of Types

Recognition and understanding of an ideological mode of thought in politics	Active use of an ideological mode of thought in politics			
	Ideologues	*Near-Ideologues*	*Nonideological Conceptualizers*	*Noncognizers*
	Left and nonleft terms used	*Left or nonleft terms used*	*Other than ideological concepts used*	*No evaluation of stimulus objects*
High ideological recognition and understanding Left and right understood in terms of ideology	1	2	3	4
Low ideological recognition and understanding Left or right understood in terms of ideology	2	3	4	4
Nonideological recognition and understanding	3	4	5	5
Wrong or no understanding, no recognition	4	4	5	6

reference and who, at the same time, show a substantive ideological understanding of the terms "left" or "right." Categories 3 and 4—*low* and *very low levels of ideological conceptualization*—primarily describe respondents who have a more or less passive level of ideology. To qualify for the lowest level of ideological thinking (level 4), it was sufficient either to use a single ideological concept or to give one of the political symbols, "left" or "right," an ideological connotation. This is, indeed, a very generous definition of ideological knowledge of some sort. Respondents who did not use ideological concepts spontaneously and who had no ideological understanding of the terms "left" and "right" were divided into two groups. Those respondents who used at least one nonideological political concept when evaluating political objects or who gave a nonideological interpretation of the left-right dimension were placed at level 5. The bottom level 6 consists of respondents who were both nonconceptualizers and who displayed a wrong interpretation of the terms "left" and "right" or did not recognize the left-right dimension at all. For our further analysis we collapse categories 5 and 6 because our main interest is in the difference between the various levels of ideological and the *nonideological conceptualization* of politics.

The resulting distribution of respondents over this scale in each of the nations is illustrated in Figure 8.2. There are systematic differences between all countries. However, three general conclusions are possible that are important within the framework of the debate on the nature of belief systems in mass publics.

(1) The nonideological conceptualization of politics in every case is the modal category.
(2) A considerable proportion of the population in each of the five nations has the capability for ideological thinking, if one sets the definition widely and does not demand a high degree of active use of ideological concepts.
(3) On the other hand, when one demands relatively sophisticated ideological knowledge and a high degree of active use of ideological concepts, the proportion of the population that can fulfill these criteria is uniformly very small.

The largest portion of respondents with a high level of ideological conceptualization never exceeds 5 percent of the total population. The lowest proportion is encountered in Austria (2 percent) and Britain (1 percent). These values agree in their size with those presented by Converse. When one recalculates the corresponding results from Converse[43] the value is 4 percent for the United States in the late 1950s—a figure that is quite comparable to the result as obtained in 1974.[44] The thesis that there is an extraordinarily thin layer of respondents with high ideological competence is thus supported on a cross-national scale.

This simple finding rules out an explanation of mass political action at the individual level that relies exclusively on an elaborated political ideology as we have defined it. However, it fits more convincingly a pattern of explanation that Converse[45] and Converse and Pierce[46] have proposed to come to grips with "Abolition and the Rise of the Republican Party," the "Mass Base of the Nazi Party," or the "Disorders of May and June, 1968, in France." Their model is of the elite-mass interaction type. It assumes effects of political ideas on elites, whereas mass behavior is seen more as an echo, not a voice. "The broad contours of elite decisions over time can depend in a vital way upon currents that are loosely called the history of ideas. But, of any direct participation in this history of ideas and the behavior it shapes, the mass is remarkably innocent."[47] And in this sense the "End of Ideology" is still with us.

When the defining criteria are set more broadly, of course, a far larger estimated value for the ideological potential of the societies under study is

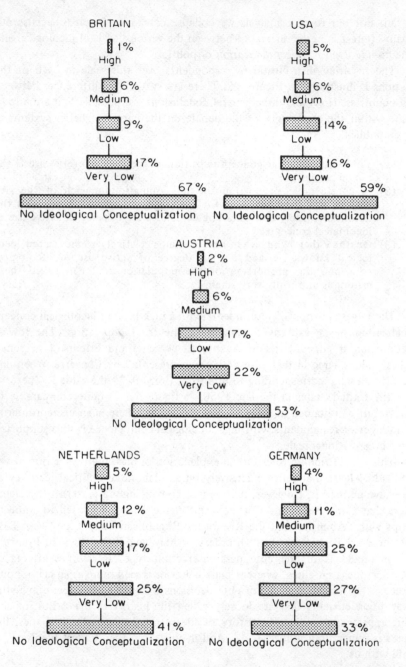

Figure 8.2: LEVELS OF IDEOLOGICAL CONCEPTUALIZATION IN POLITICS

found. When it comes to the range of the total ideological potential, Germany (67 percent) and the Netherlands (60 percent) stand clearly in the lead. Austria (47 percent) and the United States (41 percent) follow at a considerable distance. The ideological potential is more modestly developed in Britain, including one-third of the respondents.

When looking at the situation from this angle, the simple elite-mass model, however, does not hold up very well either. It seems that a more differentiated stratification model of ideological sophistication would fit advanced industrial society better. We cannot claim, with the instrument of a mass survey, to identify political elites in the normal sense of the term. And it is true that the "elites" below the level of positional elites that we may detect in this manner are still a small fraction of the population. However, they seem to be numerous enough, especially when it comes to the question of political influence. Different strata of ideologues may well operate in politically significant spheres where they can exert power by their capacity to locate and legitimize more efficient means of participation. In this sense, political ideas seem to be a road to political action today.

Nie et al. have defended the thesis that, at various points in time, the measured proportion of people who actively use ideological concepts will be affected by situational factors.[48] Public debate carried on in ideological terms would serve to stimulate the active use of an ideological frame of reference. This thesis acquires additional support in the light of our results. That group of persons that can mobilize elementary ideological knowledge in the short-run is relatively large in all five nations. This reinforces the idea of situationally conditioned elasticity of ideological reaction. Lacking adequate data, we cannot present any relevant analyses along these lines at this point in time. We are in a position, however, to discuss selected social-structural and motivational correlates of the levels of ideological conceptualization and to demonstrate the complex interrelations between ideological knowledge, values, and types of political participation.

One aspect of our measure should be stressed again before going on to further analyses. The indicator is meant to locate respondents who, in differing degrees, show signs of command of an ideological terminology. No effort has been made to distinguish ideological value communities; this problem will be taken up in a later chapter. Thus, it is perfectly in line with this measure that among respondents with an ideological frame of reference are some "anti"-ideologues. The proportion of respondents who spontaneously discuss political objects in ideological terms but affectively reject these concepts is rather low among those qualifying for a high level of ideological conceptualization. It is highest in Germany (15 percent) and Austria (11 percent); it is almost negligible in Britain (4 percent) and the United States (1 percent), and nonexistent in the Netherlands (0 percent).

The proportion of anti-ideologues is considerably higher among respondents qualifying for a medium level of ideological conceptualization. Germany (42 percent) and to a lesser degree Austria (33 percent) again take the lead while Britain (29 percent), the United States (26 percent), and the Netherlands (25 percent) trail behind.

For the remaining two categories—low and very low levels of ideological conceptualization—a strict check is not possible. However, there is a clear tendency for German respondents to display an anti-ideological orientation.[49] That is, they use ideological concepts to understand and evaluate politics, but simultaneously reject the very same ideological concepts in affective terms. This is the typical pattern of anticommunism, an ideological orientation that has a long tradition in the Western world and especially in Germany.

NOTES

1. Robert E. Lane's research on political ideology provides an excellent example of the latter type. The length of the transcripts of his conversations with fifteen men from Eastport varied from 154 pages to 322 pages. See Robert E. Lane, *Political Ideology,* New York: Free Press, 1962.

2. Robert Axelrod, "Schema Theory: An Information Processing Model of Perception and Cognition," *American Political Science Review* 67 (December 1973), pp. 1248-1266.

3. Angus Campbell, Philip E. Converse, Warren E. Miller, and Donald Stokes, *The American Voter,* New York: John Wiley, 1960; Hans D. Klingemann and William E. Wright. "Levels of Conceptualization in the American and the German Mass Public: A Replication." Paper presented at the Workshop on Political Cognition, University of Georgia, Athens, May 24-25, 1974.

4. Ronald Inglehart and Hans D. Klingemann, "Party Identification, Ideological Preference, and the Left-Right Dimension Among Western Mass Publics," in Ian Budge, Ivor Crewe, and Dennis Farlie (eds.), *Party Identification and Beyond,* London: John Wiley, 1976, p. 253.

5. John O. Field and Ronald Anderson, "Ideology in the Public's Conceptualization of the 1964 Election," *Public Opinion Quarterly* 33 (Fall 1969), p. 388.

6. Norman H. Nie, Sidney Verba, and John R. Petrocik, *The Changing American Voter,* Cambridge, Mass.: Harvard University Press, 1976, pp. 112-113.

7. Bernard Berelson, *Content Analysis in Communication Research,* New York: Free Press, 1952, p. 147; Ole R. Holsti, "Content Analysis," in Gardner Lindzey and Elliot Aronson (eds.), *Handbook of Social Psychology.* Reading, Mass.: Addison-Wesley, 1968, p. 644.

8. Almond and Verba have generated an indicator of political knowledge within the framework of their 1959-1960 cross-national surveys. Their index consisted of two questions. In the first the respondent was asked to name national party leaders; in the second the respondent was asked to name cabinet positions. Results show that 69 percent of the German respondents could produce four or more such names or positions. In the United States this amounted to 65 percent, and in Britain to 42 percent. These results correspond in their ranking very much with those obtained in our 1974 surveys.

See Gabriel Almond and Sidney Verba, *The Civic Culture,* Princeton: Princeton University Press, 1963, p. 93.

9. Campbell, Converse, Miller, and Stokes, *The American Voter,* pp. 222-223; Philip E. Converse, "The Nature of Belief Systems in Mass Publics," in David Apter (ed.), *Ideology and Discontent* (New York: Free Press, 1964), p. 216; Klingemann and Wright, "Levels of Conceptualization," pp. 5-13.

10. The exact grouping of ideological concepts can be obtained from the author: Dr. Hans D. Klingemann, ZUMA, 68 Mannheim 1, B2, 1, West Germany.

11. The terms "ideologues" and "near-ideologues" are taken from Campbell et al., *The American Voter,* pp. 216-265.

12. Ideologues are defined by their active use of left *and* right ideological concepts. Near-ideologues are defined by their active use of left *or* right ideological concepts.

Both types of concepts have been defined broadly. For pragmatic reasons we consider concepts that are related to the religious domain as right concepts. Thus the label "nonleft" would have been more appropriate to designate what we will call "right" in our further analysis. Liberal concepts, which occurred as country-specific codes in Britain and the Netherlands, have been grouped with "right" concepts also. The exact grouping can be obtained from the author (see note 10, above).

The formal rule for defining the variable "active use of an ideological mode of thought in politics" is as follows: ideologues (coded 1) used at least one left and one right term; near-ideologues (coded 2) used at least one left but no right term or at least one right but no left term; nonideological conceptualizers (coded 3) used neither left nor right terms though they did evaluate the parties; noncognizers (coded 4) did not evaluate the parties.

13. Campbell et al, *The American Voter,* pp. 216-265; Philip E. Converse, "The Nature of Belief Systems in Mass Publics," pp. 206-261.

14. We must keep in mind, however, that we are relying on political parties as stimulus objects only. In 1956 the presidential candidates served as additional stimulus objects. The analyses of Field and Anderson and Nie et al. show, however, that in 1956 the candidates did not contribute much to the overall proportion of the ideologues and near-ideologues. See Field and Anderson, "Ideology in the Public's Conceptualization of the 1964 Election," pp. 380-398; Nie, Verba, and Petrocik, *The Changing American Voter,* pp. 110-122.

15. Data for the 1968 presidential election study were kindly supplied by the Inter-university Consortium for Political and Social Research, Ann Arbor, Michigan. Data for the 1969 Bundestag election were generated by Hans D. Klingemann and Franz Urban Pappi, University of Cologne. In both cases the levels of conceptualization variable was coded from the original interview protocols by Hans D. Klingemann and William E. Wright. Here, too, neither presidential candidates nor candidates for chancellor were used as stimulus objects in addition to the political parties (Democrats, Republicans; Social Democrats, Christian Democrats, and Free Democrats). Klingemann and Wright, "Levels of Conceptualization."

16. Field and Anderson, "Ideology in the Public's Conceptualization of the 1964 Flection," pp. 380-390; John C. Pierce, "Party Identification and the Changing Role of Ideology in American Politics," *Midwest Journal of Political Science.* 14 (February 1970), pp. 25-42; Nie, Verba, and Petrocik, *The Changing American Voter,* pp. 110-122.

17. A thorough description with respect to operationalization is given by Field and Anderson, p. 386, and Nie, Verba and Petrocik, pp. 373-375.

18. Campbell et al., *The American Voter,* p. 249.

19. Nie, Verba, and Petrocik, *The Changing American Voter,* pp. 112-113, 115.

20. Field and Anderson, "Ideology in the Public's Conceptualization," p. 388.

21. Converse, "The Nature of Belief Systems," p. 219.

22. Emeric Deutsch, Denis Lindon, and Pierre Weill, *Les familles politiques,* Paris: Les Editions de Minuit, 1966; David Butler and Donald Stokes, *Political Change in Britain,* London: MacMillan, 1969; Samuel H. Barnes, "Left, Right and the Italian Voter," *Comparative Political Studies,* 4 (July 1971), pp. 157-175; Samuel H. Barnes and Roy Pierce, "Public Opinion and Political Preferences in France and Italy," *Midwest Journal of Political Science,* 15 (November 1971), pp. 643-660; Philip E. Converse and Roy Pierce, "Basic Cleavages in French Politics and the Disorders of May and June, 1968." Paper prepared for presentation at the session on "Social Structure and Political Alignments" of the Seventh World Congress of Sociology held at Varna, Bulgaria, 1970; Giacomo Sani, "A Test of the Least Distance Model of Voting Choice: Italy 1972," *Comparative Political Studies,* 7 (July 1974), pp. 193-208; Philip E. Converse, "Some Mass-Elite Contrasts in the Perception of Political Spaces," IPSA Round Table, Paris, 1975; Ronald Inglehart and Dusan Sidjanski, "The Left, the Right, the Establishment and the Swiss Electorate," in Budge, Crewe, and Farlie (eds.), *Party Identification and Beyond,* pp. 225-242; Inglehart and Klingemann, "Party Identification, Ideological Preference," pp. 243-273.

23. Inglehart and Klingemann, Ibid., p. 249.

24. Jean A. Laponce, "Note on the Use of the Left-Right Dimension," *Comparative Political Studies,* 3 (January 1970), pp. 481-502.

25. In the Austrian survey, however, an additional explanation was given, stating: "The outerpoints on this scale mean 'extreme left' and 'extreme right'." The additional explanation using the term "extreme" was only given in the *wording of the question.* The *visual scale* that was presented to the respondent *was exactly the same* as in the other four countries. However, the additional explanation may have biased the results in the Austrian case.

26. Deutsch, Lindon, and Weill, *Les familles politiques,* p. 21.

27. The set of questions Converse relied on was as follows:

Would you say that either one of the parties is more conservative or more liberal than the other?

If yes: Which party is more conservative?

What do you have in mind when you say that the Republicans (Democrats) are more conservative than the Democrats (Republicans)?

If no: Do you think that people generally consider the Democrats or the Republicans more conservative, or wouldn't you guess about that?

If answer to the question above: What do you have in mind when you say the Republicans (Democrats) are more conservative than the Democrats (Republicans)?

Responses to this set of questions were summarized in the variable: Recognition and understanding of the terms "conservatism" and "liberalism." The five categories of this variable were defined as follows: stratum I = recognition and proper matching of label, meaning, and party and a broad understanding of the terms "conservative" and "liberal"; stratum II = recognition and proper matching but a narrow definition of terms (like "spend-save"); stratum III = recognition but some error in matching; stratum IV = recognition and an attempt at matching but inability to give any meaning for terms; stratum V = no apparent recognition of terms (does not know if parties differ in liberal-conservative terms and does not know if anybody else sees them as differing).

Converse, "The Nature of Belief Systems." In 1967 Converse applied this type of measure again in France. Here he first used a closed-ended left-right self-anchoring scale and the following open-ended follow-up question.

On oppose souvent partis de gauche et partis de droite. A votre avis en quoi consistent les differences les plus important entre la gauche et la droite?

Eleven percent of the French respondents could be said to have an explicitly ideological frame of reference according to this survey; Converse, "Some Mass-Elite Contrasts."
28. Inglehart and Klingemann, "Party Identification, Ideological Preference," p. 248.
29. The exact figures are as follows:

Liberal-Conservative Scale

Left-Right Scale	Placement of Political views		Haven't much thought about it		Don't know, No answer	
Placement of political views	96%	(1301)	54%	(321)	28%	(42)
Don't know, no answer	14%	(205)	46%	(273)	72%	(106)
Total	100%	(1506)	100%	(594)	100%	(148)

The scales can be found in the ICPSR Codebook of the 1976 Presidential Election Study on pages 143 and 173.

30. The exact construction of these broader groupings may be obtained from the author (see note 10, above).
31. The following categories are used to construct the variable "Recognition and understanding of an ideological mode of thought in politics":

Understanding of left

Understanding of right	Political ideology	Political parties and social groups	Idiosyncratic, affective underst.	Wrong or no understanding	No recognition
Political ideology	1	2	2	2	–
Political parties and social groups	2	3	4	4	–
Idiosyncratic and affective understanding	2	4	5	6	–
Wrong or no understanding	2	4	6	7	–
No recognition	–	–	–	–	8

1 = High ideological recognition and understanding
2 = Low ideological recognition and understanding
3 = High recognition and understanding in terms of political parties and social groups
4 = Low recognition and understanding in terms of political parties and social groups
5 = High recognition and understanding in idiosyncratic or affective terms
6 = Low recognition and understanding in idiosyncratic or affective terms
7 = Wrong or no understanding
8 = No recognition

For the subsequent construction of our index levels of ideological conceptualization we have collapsed the categories as follows: 3 to 6, 7 to 8.

32. For an elaboration of this difference see Converse, "The Nature of Belief Systems," p. 212.

33. For the operationalization see note 27.

34. The exact question formulation was as follows:

Do you ever think of the parties as being on the left, the center, or to the right in politics or don't you think of the parties this way?

If yes: What do you have in mind when you say that a party is to the left or right?

See Butler and Stokes, *Political Change in Britain,* p. 475.

35. Ibid., p. 211.

36. Converse, "The Nature of Belief Systems," p. 224.

37. Among his numerous writings see: Leo A. Goodman, "How to Ransack Social Mobility Tables and Other Kinds of Cross-Classification Tables," *American Journal of Sociology,* 75 (July 1969), pp. 2-40; Leo A. Goodman, "The Multivariate Analysis of Qualitative Data: Interactions Among Multiple Classifications," *Journal of the American Statistical Association,* 65 (March 1970), pp. 226-256; Leo A. Goodman, "The Partitioning of Chi-Square, the Analysis of Marginal Contingency Tables, and the Estimation of Expected Frequencies in Multidimensional Contingency Tables," *Journal of the American Statistical Association,* 66 (June 1971), pp. 339-344; Leo A. Goodman, "A Modified Multiple Regression Approach to the Analysis of Dichotomous Variables," *American Sociological Review,* 37 (February 1972), pp. 28-46.

38. In this analysis we are using Table 8.10. The following hypotheses are tested:

Hypothesis	Chi-square	Degrees of freedom
1. The active use of an ideological mode of thought is independent of both the recognition and understanding of an ideological mode of thought and nationality	959.57	28
2. The active use of an ideological mode of thought is dependent on nationality but not on recognition and understanding of an ideological mode of thought	705.43	20

Hypothesis	Chi-square	Degrees of freedom
3. The active use of an ideological mode of thought is dependent on recognition and understanding of an ideological mode of thought but not on nationality	222.99	24

In this case H_1 is our null hypothesis. The reduction of the variation in chi-square is calculated as follows:

$$r^2 = \frac{x(H_1) - x(H_{2\,(1)})}{x(H_1)}$$

Chi-squares are maximum-likelihood chi-squares. For the analysis we have used the program ECTA.

39. Frederick Mosteller, "Association and Estimation in Contingency Tables," *Journal of the American Statistical Association,* 63 (March 1968), pp. 1-28.

40. Goodman, "How to Ransack Social Mobility Tables"; Yvonne M.M. Bishop, Stephen E. Feinberg, and Paul W. Holland, with the collaboration of Richard J. Light and Frederick Mosteller, *Discrete Multivariate Analysis: Theory and Practice,* Cambridge, Mass.: MIT Press, 1975, p. 101.

41. The index of dissimilarity is suggested by Otis Dudley Duncan, Ray P. Cuzzort, and Beverly Duncan, *Statistical Geography,* New York: Free Press, 1961, p. 83. In our case it has been calculated on the base of the 3 x 3 tables relating recognition and understanding of an ideological mode of thought to the active use of an ideological mode of thought. The formula is as follows:

$$\Delta = \frac{1}{2} \sum_{i=1}^{k} |x_i - y_i|$$

Applying this formula we obtain these coefficients for the following country-pairs:

Country Pairs	Original Distribution	Distribution, Controlled for the Country Effect
The Netherlands Britain	26.20	8.32
The Netherlands United States	19.80	3.75
The Netherlands Germany	10.84	6.69
The Netherlands Austria	17.08	3.76
Britain United States	12.57	8.06
Britain Germany	33.81	9.47

Country Pairs	Original Distribution	Distribution, Controlled for the Country Effect
Britain		
Austria	16.32	7.91
United States		
Germany	27.09	8.13
United States		
Austria	9.34	2.95
Germany		
Austria	20.40	5.75
$\overline{x}$	19.35	6.48

42. There are, of course, respondents who do not fit this pattern. However, we are inclined to attribute this to the insufficiencies of our measurement instruments.

43. Converse, "The Nature of Belief Systems."

44. Ibid., p. 224. The figure results from a combination of the following cells in Table 3: Stratum I x ideologue plus near-ideologue. The recalculated n is 58 : 1325 = 4.4 percent.

45. Ibid., pp. 249-254.

46. Converse and Pierce, "Basic Cleavages in French Politics."

47. Converse, "The Nature of Belief Systems," p. 255.

48. Nie, Verba, and Petrocik, *The Changing American Voter*, p. 121.

49. The following table gives the proportion of "anti-ideologues" per level of ideological conceptualization. "Anti-ideologues" are defined as respondents who actively use ideological concepts but evaluate all ideological concepts used negatively.

Levels of ideological conceptualization	The Netherlands %	n	Britain %	n	United States %	n	Germany %	n	Austria %	n
High	−	(62)	4	(22)	1	(88)	15	(86)	11	(36)
Medium	25	(141)	29	(88)	26	(104)	42	(264)	33	(89)
Low*	24	(110)	25	(72)	23	(39)	45	(210)	20	(70)
Very low*	25	(122)	43	(133)	25	(122)	44	(217)	25	(111)

*Respondents who do not actively use ideological concepts are excluded.

Chapter 9

THE BACKGROUND OF IDEOLOGICAL CONCEPTUALIZATION

HANS D. KLINGEMANN

*P*olitical ideologies are' cultural products that have to be learned by individuals. The development of a "political theory," the acquisition of an abstract, generalized orientation toward politics, requires structural opportunity and individual motivation. In this chapter we focus on education and political interest as determinants of ideological conceptualization. The decision to concentrate on this limited set of variables is based both on the findings of earlier research and on our own theoretical orientation.

Campbell et al. argue that ideological levels of conceptualization of politics are dependent on the more general capacity to cope with the abstract, which, by a number of routes *in the education process*—selection, development of intellectual capacities, and indoctrination—leads to differences in political concept formation.[1] They add that there are important *motivational components* as well. The empirical data presented by these authors show that political involvement is a potent determinant of levels of conceptualization in its own right. The general importance of these two factors has not been challenged by subsequent research work. However, the *relative weight* of education and motivation for the prediction of levels of conceptualization has become a matter of considerable debate. Nie, Verba, and Petrocik in *The Changing American Voter* have undertaken the task of replicating measures of ideological conceptualization in America from 1952 to 1972.[2] Within this time period their analyses indicate that the strata of ideologues and near-ideologues have increased by a factor of 2.7.[3] In addition, Nie and Andersen have demonstrated that the degree of average belief consistency over a range of political issues has also increased within the same period of time by a factor of 2.7.[4] Furthermore, these changes did not depend as much on aggregate changes in education as had been assumed in the earlier literature.[5] Rather, motivational and situational factors seemed to have gained relatively greater explanatory power. By introducing the concept of passive ideological knowledge we might find a plausible vehicle for these developments: citizens who employ ideological knowledge do not employ this taxonomic system in every situation. Rather, ideological knowledge will be activated in different ways in response to variations in the context of political conflict.

Before we turn to a detailed analysis of education and motivation as determinants of levels of ideological conceptualization, we will briefly describe in more general terms the social-structural correlates of levels of ideological thinking. As can be seen from Table 9.1, indicators of social status—occupational prestige, income, subjective social class, and, above all, education—show the strongest relationships to ideological thinking: the higher one's social status, the greater the likelihood of an ideological conceptualization of politics.

The same is true for males in contrast to females and, as far as the United States is concerned, for whites as compared to blacks. Age is unrelated to ideological thinking; and so, with the exception of Austria, is the religious dimension. The importance of social status indicators—especially education—is well in line with the earlier research. However, as we have already pointed out, we do not want to discuss the more general socioeconomic model here.[6] Rather, we concentrate on the specific role of education. It should be borne in mind, though, that education is strongly correlated with this broader set of variables.[7]

We have probed more deeply into the relation of ideological thinking to age because we had expected to find a positive association between the two variables. This expectation is based on the assumption of gradual political learning.[8] The longer one is exposed to politics the more likely one is to develop an efficient frame of reference for political information processing. However, this expectation was not supported by our data.

We hypothesized that the lack of a fit of the gradual learning model in our case might be due to the nontrivial negative relationship between education and age.[9] On the average, young people are better educated than old people. Given the strong positive association of ideological thinking with education, the different educational composition of age cohorts might well result in the cancelling out of the effect of age. Thus, we have controlled for education. However, we were still unable to detect a sizeable positive relation between ideological thinking and age.[10] The learning of an ideological mode of thought

Table 9.1: SOCIAL-STRUCTURAL CORRELATES OF LEVELS OF IDEOLOGICAL CONCEPTUALIZATION OF POLITICS

	The Netherlands		Britain		United States		Germany		Austria	
	gamma	N	gamma	N	gamma	N	gamma	N	gamma	N
Education (type of school)	.55	1201	.48	1436	.60	1704	.33	2288	.48	1583
Occupational prestige of head of household (Treiman scores)	.37	1179	.33	1231	.30	1686	.14	2138	.23	1459
Family income (Quartiles)	.29	938	.32	1155	.35	1402	.17	2004	.22	1019
Subjective social class	.33	1112	.30	1377	.44	1657	.24	2275	.30	1498
Membership in voluntary organizations	.27	1201	.42	1483	.28	1719	.15	2307	.26	1484
Sex (1=female, 2=male)	.36	1201	.30	1483	.17	1719	.21	2307	.36	1584
Age (5 year interval)	-.03	1201	-.03	1469	-.11	1718	-.03	2307	.05	1583
Race (1=black, 3=white)	—		—		.34	1715	—		—	
Religious affiliation (1=catholic, 2=other)	.21	1193	-.09	1458	.01	1691	.03	2303	.34	1582
Church going frequency (1=never, 5=high)	.00	852	.09	1456	-.06	1630	.00	2156	-.11	1487
Religiousness (1=not very, 4=very)	-.02	1172	.03	1454	-.03	1689	.02	2144	-.13	1569

NOTE: Levels of ideological conceptualization 1=nonideological conceptualization – 5 high ideological conceptualization; type of school 1=primary and related schools_compulsory education) – 3=universities and related schools; occupational prestige 14=low – 78=high; social class 1=working class – 3=upper middle class; membership in voluntary associations 0=no – 1=yes.

obviously does not follow the pattern of a gradual learning model or one of its variants.[11] It seems as if a certain critical mass of education and political involvement can induce an ideological conceptualization of politics at every age.

EDUCATION AND LEVELS OF
IDEOLOGICAL CONCEPTUALIZATION

The expansion of a general school system—continually broadening the age groups encompassed—can be conceived of as simultaneously the precondition and the consequence of advanced industrial society.[12] Differences in educational achievement are a primary explanation for variations in individual political competence.[13] Numerous empirical findings support this assumption. Ideological conceptualization can be thought of as a specific component of political competence—a component that stresses the cognitive aspect of political capabilities. Thus the level of ideological thinking should increase with the progressive acquisition of increased education. Table 9.1 shows that this is the case in all of the countries under investigation.

In this discussion we ask the questions of how the *conditional probabilities* differ and whether or not the *nuclear association* between education and ideological thinking varies across countries that in many ways are different with respect to the educational background of their respective populations. There are basically two options when it comes to the old problem of cross-national comparison of education. One can rely simply on years spent in classroom as an indicator. Or, alternatively, one can try to develop some kind of typology of schools. We have chosen the latter, more complicated course because, according to our judgment, we cannot safely assume that the education *systems* are equivalent in the countries under study.

Development of the school systems was historically different in these countries, resulting in a multiplicity of schools and programs. We rely on a broad typology that combines:

(1) primary and related schools (low level),
(2) secondary and related schools (middle level), and
(3) universities and related schools (high level).

Details and reasons leading to this particular grouping are presented in the Technical Appendix.

The distribution of the population across the three types of schools differs among countries. The differences among the European nations, however, are far less marked than the difference between the United States on the one hand and the European countries on the other.[14]

In the United States 19 percent of the respondents indicate some higher education. The corresponding value for the Netherlands is 8 percent, for Germany 5 percent, for Britain 5 percent, and for Austria 2 percent. The available official statistics corroborate, in their general ordering, the proportions as estimated by our surveys.[15] The proportion of respondents who have completed middle level schools is at least twice as large in the United States as it is in any of the other nations (53 percent). In the Netherlands this proportion is lowest at 15 percent; in Britain (26 percent), Austria (26 percent), and Germany (25 percent) this proportion is about a quarter of the respondents.

Correspondingly, of course, the difference with respect to the population with only primary education is even larger between the United States and the European countries. While in the United States this proportion amounted to 28 percent it averaged 70 percent in the European nations.

The measure of the association between types of education and levels of ideological conceptualization of politics (gamma) varies between .60 for the United States and .32 for Germany. In chapter 8 we emphasized the relatively high proportion of "anti-ideologues" in Germany; we thought that this might explain the rather low association of ideological thinking with education in that country. Thus we grouped these "anti-ideologues" with the nonideologues and then recalculated Table 9.1. The result was that all coefficients were of a lower size in all of the countries, including Germany. This finding indicates that the differing proportion of "anti-ideologues" does not cause the differences in the coefficients presented in Table 9.1.

The coefficient summarizes the bivariate relationship between the two variables. However, at this point we are more interested in conditional probabilities. Thus we would conclude from an inspection of the association coefficients that the total relationship is most similar between the United States and the Netherlands. But the conditional probabilities show that, with respect to respondents having only primary education, the distribution of levels of ideological conceptualization is most similar between the United States and Britain. We will first discuss similarities and dissimilarities between countries with respect to these conditional probabilities.

Figure 9.1 shows the high proportion of ideological thinking among respondents with higher education. In the United States (77 percent) and Britain (80 percent) this proportion turns out to be slightly lower than in the Continental European nations. This proportion is most marked in Austria (92 percent).

The differences between the Anglo-Saxon nations on the one hand and Germany and the Netherlands on the other become more accentuated within

Table 9.2: DISTRIBUTION OF RESPONDENTS PER TYPE OF SCHOOL BY COUNTRY

Type of School	The Netherlands		Britain		United States		Germany		Austria	
University and related schools	8%	(94)	5%	(78)	19%	(331)	5%	(127)	20%	(38)
Secondary and related schools	15	(179)	26	(380)	53	(903)	25	(564)	26	(414)
Primary and related schools	77	(928)	68	(978)	28	(470)	70	(1597)	71	(1131)
N	1201		1436		1704		2288		1583	

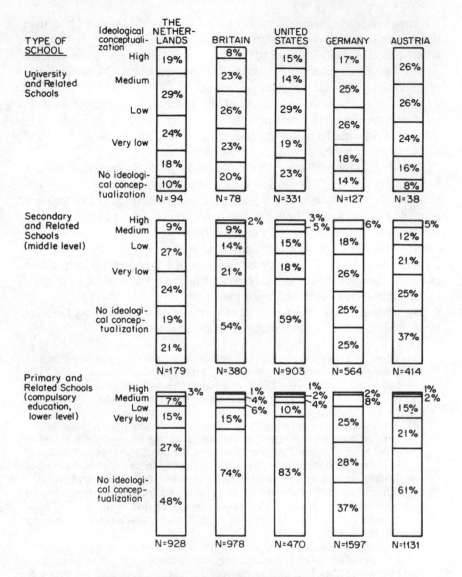

**Figure 9.1: LEVELS OF IDEOLOGICAL CONCEPTUALIZATION
IN POLITICS AND EDUCATION (type of school)**

the groups of respondents with middle or lower levels of education. In Britain the proportion of respondents with no ideological knowledge at all among the lower educated was 74 percent; in the United States the corresponding proportion was 83 percent. In Germany (37 percent) and the Netherlands (48 percent) this proportion was markedly lower.

The systemic pairwise comparison of the distribution of levels of ideological conceptualization between countries, holding education constant, indicates the similarities between the United States and Britain on the one hand and Germany and the Netherlands on the other.[16]

This result, however, does not mean that the nuclear association between education and levels of ideological conceptualization also has to be different. In order to settle that question, we have to take into account that the marginal distributions of both the independent and the dependent variables are different across countries. These country-specific effects can be removed by applying the Mosteller technique described in chapter 8. Results are presented in Figure 9.2. They clearly speak to the fact that we can assume a rather similar *nuclear association* between education and levels of ideological conceptualization in all the nations under study.[17]

The results of our analysis of the influence of education on levels of ideological conceptualization can be summarized as follows:

(1) There is a positive association between education—measured in system-specific terms—and levels of ideological conceptualization. The higher the level of education, the higher the probability of an ideological mode of thought. This holds in different measure for each of the nations under study.

(2) When one controls for type of education in each nation, thus taking into account the different distribution of the independent variable, there is an obvious difference between the conditional probabilities of levels of ideological conceptualization between the United States and Britain on the one hand and Germany and the Netherlands on the other. The difference stems from the fact that the proportion of respondents with an ideological conceptualization in the Anglo-Saxon nations is, within each category of education, lower than in Germany and the Netherlands.

(3) This difference, however, is not due to a genuinely different effect of education on ideological thinking. When the joint marginal effects are controlled a rather similar nuclear association between the two variables is clearly visible across countries.

POLITICAL MOTIVATION AND LEVELS OF IDEOLOGICAL CONCEPTUALIZATION

Besides education, political motivation has been found to be a main corollary of levels of conceptualization. The higher the political motivation,

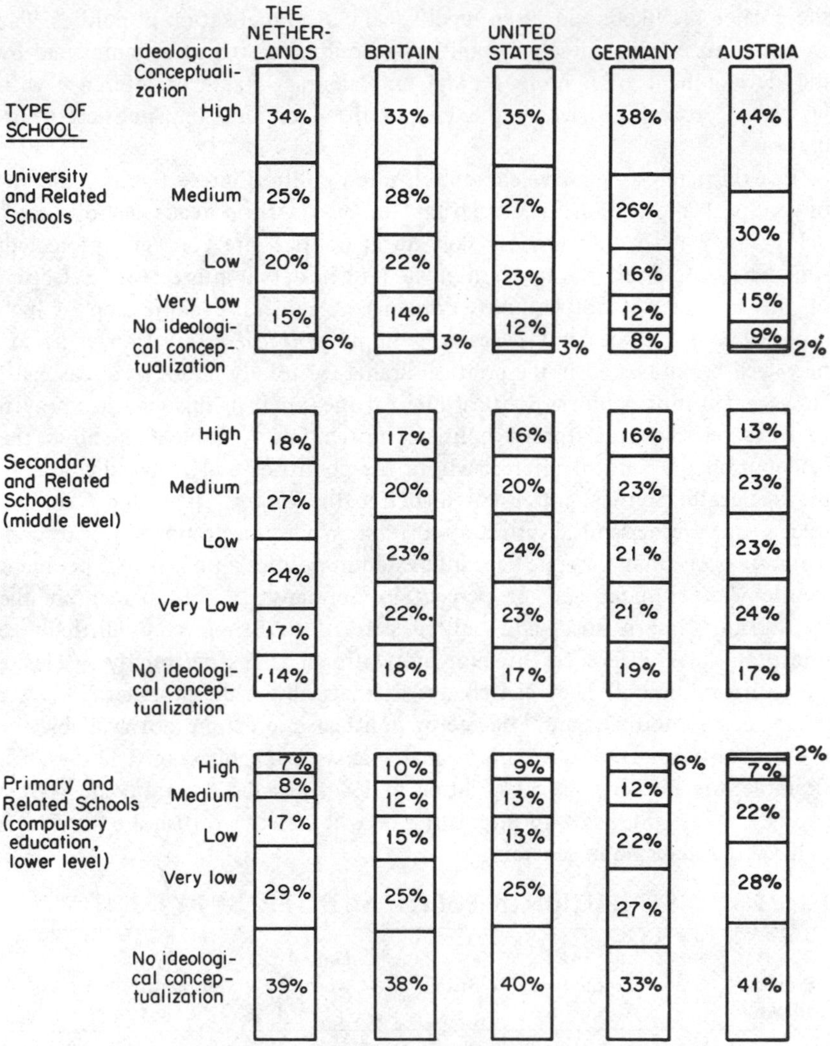

TYPE OF SCHOOL	Ideological Conceptualization	THE NETHER-LANDS	BRITAIN	UNITED STATES	GERMANY	AUSTRIA
University and Related Schools	High	34%	33%	35%	38%	44%
	Medium	25%	28%	27%	26%	30%
	Low	20%	22%	23%	16%	15%
	Very Low	15%	14%	12%	12%	9%
	No ideological conceptualization	6%	3%	3%	8%	2%
Secondary and Related Schools (middle level)	High	18%	17%	16%	16%	13%
	Medium	27%	20%	20%	23%	23%
	Low	24%	23%	24%	21%	23%
	Very Low	17%	22%	23%	21%	24%
	No ideological conceptualization	14%	18%	17%	19%	17%
Primary and Related Schools (compulsory education, lower level)	High	7%	10%	9%	6%	7%
	Medium	8%	12%	13%	12%	22%
	Low	17%	15%	13%	22%	2%
	Very low	29%	25%	25%	27%	28%
	No ideological conceptualization	39%	38%	40%	33%	41%

Figure 9.2: **LEVELS OF IDEOLOGICAL CONCEPTUALIZATION IN POLITICS AND EDUCATION (controlling for country-specific effects)**

the greater the likelihood of an ideological conceptualization of politics. The readiness to expose oneself to political stimuli seems to be accompanied by the development of a more general and abstract frame of reference with which to process efficiently the greater flood of incoming political information.

For this analysis we have chosen self-rated political interest as an indicator of political motivation. The relevant survey question reads as follows:[18] "How interested would you say you are in politics—are you very interested, somewhat interested, not much interested, or not at all interested?" Selection of this indicator is not without problems. A subjective expression of high political interest does not necessarily imply *political* motivation; a person may well be interested in the political drama for totally unpolitical reasons.[19] However, in most studies, political interest measured in this way has proven to be a reliable indicator of political motivation.[20] Table 9.3 shows the distribution of political interest within the countries under investigation. In the aggregate, political interest is higher in the United States and Germany than in the Netherlands, Austria, or Britain. While the proportion of respondents who say that they are very interested in politics amounts to 24 percent in the United States and 22 percent in Germany, it is 14 percent in the Netherlands and Austria, and only 9 percent in Britain. It is difficult to interpret these differences because motivational states are relatively elastic and situation-bound. They can change dramatically in the short term.[21] Data measuring a "normal times" degree of political interest are not available for these countries. Thus, we cannot really answer the question whether, for example, the British political situation in 1974 just did not motivate people enough to find politics very interesting or whether the British are much less politically interested in general.

Table 9.3: **DISTRIBUTION OF POLITICAL INTEREST BY COUNTRY**

Political Interest	The Netherlands		Britain		United States		Germany		Austria	
Very interested	14%	(169)	9%	(138	24%	(410)	22%	(516)	14%	(225)
Somewhat interested	43	(516)	35	(521)	45	(761)	41	(942)	39	(623)
Not much interested	23	(273)	32	(467)	22	(377)	21	(484)	27	(423)
Not at all interested	20	(235)	24	(345)	9	(160)	16	(360)	20	(311)
N		1193		1471		1708		2302		1582

The association between political interest and levels of ideological conceptualization is positive, as expected. However, the degree of association differs across countries. The gamma coefficient varies between .55 in the Netherlands and .27 in Germany, with the measures for Britain (.52), Austria (.49), and the United States (.40) being on the higher side.[22] The size of these coefficients is about the same or slightly higher than the association between education and levels of ideological conceptualization in the Netherlands, Britain, and Austria, while in the United States and Germany political interest has a somewhat lower predictive power.

In our discussion of the relationship between education and ideological thinking we have already pointed out that a comparison of conditional probabilities can yield additional insights. Figure 9.3 shows the distributions of levels of ideological thinking for three different states of political interest. A comparison across countries reveals similarities between these conditional distributions with respect to the United States and Britain, on the one hand, and the three Continental European countries, on the other. In the two Anglo-Saxon countries the proportion of respondents with a nonideological conceptualization of politics is notably higher on each level of political interest than is the case for Germany, the Netherlands, and Austria.[23]

The result is similar, though less pronounced, to the one we found for education. However, in this case, too, we have to ask ourselves if this difference between the two groups of countries results from a genuinely different effect of political interest on levels of ideological thinking. By application of the Mosteller technique we can give an approximate answer to this question. Figure 9.4 shows that the picture becomes much more similar across all the countries if we assume an equal distribution of marginals for political interest and levels of ideological conceptualization. Thus, we would infer that the thesis of a genuinely different *nuclear association* does not hold up very well.[24]

We can summarize our results as follows:

(1) Political motivation and levels of ideological conceptualization are positively associated. The higher the political motivation, the greater the likelihood of ideological thinking. This holds with differing degrees of association for all countries under investigation.

(2) A comparison of the distributions of levels of ideological conceptualization across countries—conditioned by the degree of political motivation—shows similarities between the two Anglo-Saxon countries on the one hand and the three Continental-European countries on the other. In the United States and Britain, the proportion of respondents with a nonideological conceptualization of politics is higher than in the Netherlands, Germany, and Austria.

(3) This difference, however, cannot be explained by a genuinely different effect of political motivation on levels of ideological thinking.

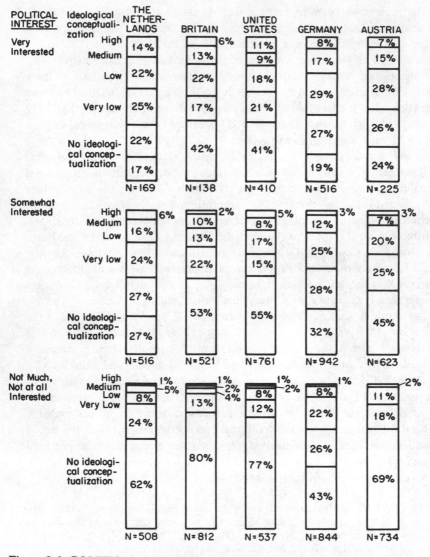

Figure 9.3: POLITICAL INTEREST AND LEVELS OF IDEOLOGICAL CONCEPTUALIZATION

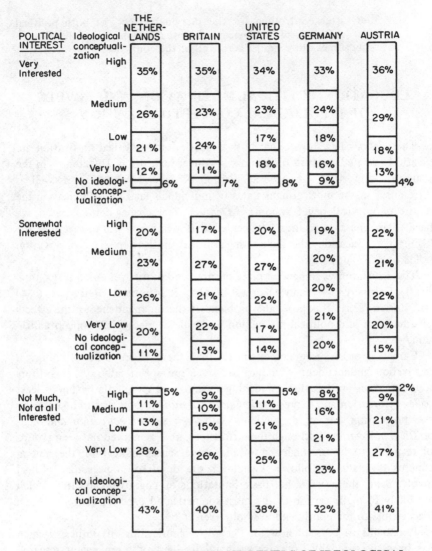

Figure 9.4: **POLITICAL INTEREST AND LEVELS OF IDEOLOGICAL
CONCEPTUALIZATION OF POLITICS**
(controlling for country-specific effects)

Rather, after controlling for the marginal effects of both political interest and levels of ideological conceptualization, the nuclear association becomes quite similar across all of the countries.

EDUCATION, POLITICAL MOTIVATION, AND LEVELS OF IDEOLOGICAL CONCEPTUALIZATION

The analysis has shown that both education and political motivation are positively related to levels of ideological conceptualization. Differences in the structural opportunity for the acquisition of general knowledge as well as differences in the motivational states of individuals lead to differences in the nature of political belief systems. As earlier research has demonstrated, we have to assume a covariation between education and political motivation: the higher the education, the higher the political motivation. This observation holds true for our study, too.

The association is somewhat more pronounced in the Netherlands (gamma = .50), Germany (.49), and Austria (.49) than it is in the United States (.34) and Britain (.28). This poses the problem of the independence of the effects of education and political motivation on levels of ideological conceptualization.

Campbell et al. have demonstrated that there is an effect of political motivation independent of education.[25] More specifically, these authors found that the proportion of ideologues among respondents having at least *college education* and expressing *low political motivation* was still higher than the proportion among respondents with *high school education and high political motivation*. Although the differences are less marked between groups of respondents having high school and grade school education, the general conclusion reads as follows: "whatever the depth of a person's political involvement, there are rather basic limitations on cognitive capacities which are likely to make certain of the most sophisticated types of content remain inaccessible to the poorly endowed observer."[26]

It remains to be seen how the "cognitive limitations" hypothesis, which has been discussed by Converse again in the light of more recent research findings, holds on a cross-national scale.[27] In Figure 9.5 we present the relevant evidence. Even a first glance shows that there are, indeed, independent effects of both education and political motivation on levels of ideological conceptualization. As the first-order gamma coefficient of Table 9.4 indicates, a spurious correlation can be safely excluded.

We have tested for the relative weight of education and political motivation country by country, using log-linear contingency table analysis as proposed by Goodman.[28] Results prove that neither education nor political motivation *alone* can satisfactorily predict the distributions of levels of ideological conceptualization as given in Figure 9.4.[29] Rather, we find that—with the exception of Britain—an additive model seems to be adequate.[30]

In Britain we encounter a particular interaction between higher education and high political motivation producing a rather *low* proportion of high or medium levels of ideological conceptualization. In the other education groups

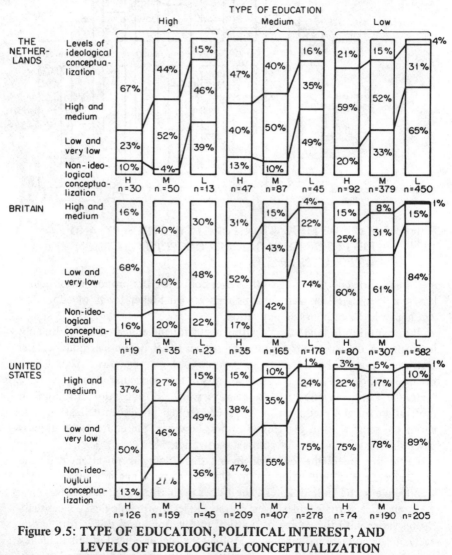

Figure 9.5: TYPE OF EDUCATION, POLITICAL INTEREST, AND LEVELS OF IDEOLOGICAL CONCEPTUALIZATION OF POLITICS

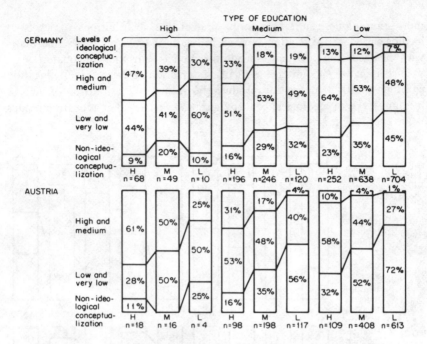

Figure 9.5: TYPE OF EDUCATION, POLITICAL INTEREST, AND LEVELS OF IDEOLOGICAL CONCEPTUALIZATION OF POLITICS (cont.)

in Britain, and generally in all of the other countries, the proportion of higher levels of ideological conceptualization rises with higher levels of education *and* higher levels of political motivation.

It is tempting to relate the deviating result for the educated and politically interested in Britain to the pragmatic image of the British upper middle class. However, it must be stressed that we are not on very firm ground here because of the small number of respondents in this particular group.

In the European countries the relative weight of education and political motivation for the prediction of levels of ideological conceptualization is of about the same size. In the United States, however, the educational effect is twice the size of the effect of political motivation.[31]

Given the use of the log-linear model, this finding is not affected by the greater variance of education in the United States. Thus education plays a greater role in the United States than it does in the European countries.

In all the countries under investigation the level of ideological conceptualization varies with the degree of political motivation. And this is true *within* each of our educational groupings. Among the higher educated this tendency is—with the exception of the Netherlands—less pronounced. Even with only low political motivation, the higher educated, as a rule, interpret politics in an ideological fashion. However, among respondents with medium or lower education, the importance of political motivation for the likelihood of the development of an ideological frame of reference grows. The lack of structural opportunity to learn is compensated to a certain degree by individual political motivation. The data presented by Campbell et al. have supported the thesis that cognitive limitations cannot be easily overcome by political motivation alone.[32] This hypothesis holds, by and large, on a cross-national scale. However, this analysis also shows that there are no strict boundaries as far as the medium and lower levels of education are concerned. High political motivation among the low education group is a sufficient condition for a level of the more active types of ideological conceptualization that is higher than the one encountered among respondents with a medium level of education and a low level of political motivation. Similarly, respondents with medium levels of education and high or medium levels of political motivation on the average reach levels of ideological conceptualization that are characteristic of respondents with high education and low political motivation.

In general, however, the analysis shows that the active state of ideological knowledge is relatively better predicted by education than by political motivation. For reasons that we have already discussed, Britain does not follow this pattern in the same way. Political motivation, on the other hand, is a relatively better predictor for active and passive states of ideological knowledge taken together. This finding holds for all countries with the exception of the United States. The result is important because it qualifies our distinction between active and passive states of ideological knowledge. It does not suggest that both states represent a similar degree of ideological reflection. Rather, the finding adds plausibility to the assumption that the active use

Table 9.4: **POLITICAL INTEREST AND LEVELS OF IDEOLOGICAL CONCEPTUALIZATION (controlling for education)**

Countries	Political interest and levels of ideological conceptualization (zero-order gamma)		Political interest and levels of ideological conceptualization, controlled for education (first-order gamma)	
The Netherlands	.58	(1193)	.53	(1193)
Britain	.53	(1424)	.50	(1424)
United States	.43	(1693)	.35	(1693)
Germany	.32	(2283)	.26	(2283)
Austria	.54	(1581)	.47	(1581)

NOTE: The variables are scored as can be seen from Figure 9.4. Compare note 29 (this chapter) for calculation of first-order gamma.

indicates a higher degree of command of an ideological frame of reference than does passive ideological knowledge. The conceptualization of the variable as *levels* of ideological thinking thus seems to be justified. In this context the deviation of the American case finds an explanation. In Europe the politically interested citizen is quite familiar with the terms left and right—at least in a nominal way—the stimuli we mainly rely on when defining the passive ideological knowledge. In the United States, however, it is reasonable to assume that it is more a matter of education than of political culture whether or not a respondent is able to infer the ideational background of these terms.

Whenever we speak of active and passive ideological knowledge we have to take into account that these two states of ideological conceptualization are different. The more active state implies a higher ideological reflection than does the more passive state of ideological knowledge. This should not be forgotten as we now turn to the attitudinal and behavioral consequences of an ideological conceptualization of politics.

NOTES

1. Angus Campbell, Philip E. Converse, Warren E. Miller, and Donald Stokes, *The American Voter,* New York: John Wiley, 1960, pp. 250-251.
2. Norman H. Nie, Sidney Verba, and John R. Petrocik, *The Changing American Voter,* Cambridge, Mass.: Harvard University Press, 1976.
3. Ibid., p. 115.
4. Norman H. Nie with Kristi Andersen, "Mass Belief Systems Revisited: Political Change and Attitude Structure," *Journal of Politics,* 36 (August 1974), pp. 540-591.
5. Herbert McClosky, "Consensus and Ideology in American Politics," *American Political Science Review,* 58 (June 1964), pp. 361-382; Philip E. Converse, "Change in the American Electorate," in Angus Campbell and Philip E. Converse (eds.), *The Human Meaning of Social Change,* New York: Russell Sage Foundation, 1972, p. 322.
6. Sidney Verba and Norman H. Nie, *Participation in America,* New York: Harper & Row, 1972, pp. 18-22.
7. The relation of education (type of school) to socioeconomic variables of this type is as follows:

	The Netherlands		Britain		United States		Germany		Austria	
	Gamma	*N*	*Gamma*	*N*	*Gamma*	*N*	*Gamma*	*N*	*Gamma*	*N*
Occupational Prestige of Head of Household	.55	(1146)	.51	(1206)	.46	(1673)	.47	(2120)	.48	(1458)

(continued)

	The Netherlands		Britain		United States		Germany		Austria	
	Gamma	*N*	*Gamma*	*N*	*Gamma*	*N*	*Gamma*	*N*	*Gamma*	*N*
Family Income (Quartiles)	.52	(938)	.49	(1131)	.48	(1391)	.49	(1996)	.50	(1019)
Subjective Social Class	.71	(1112)	.60	(1346)	.54	(1642)	.75	(2256)	.63	(1498)

NOTE: The definition of these variables is as given in Table 9.1.

8. Verba and Nie, *Participation in America*, p. 148.
9. The relationship between education (type of school) and age is as follows:

	Gamma	N
The Netherlands	−.18	1201
Britain	−.32	1426
United States	−.26	1703
Germany	−.25	2288
Austria	−.12	1582

10. Coefficients of association are as follows:

Country	University and Related Schools		Secondary and Related Schools		Primary and Related Schools	
	Gamma	*N*	*Gamma*	*N*	*Gamma*	*N*
The Netherlands	−.15	94	.09	179	.01	928
Britain	.01	78	.15	377	.01	971
United States	.00	331	−.03	903	.03	469
Germany	.08	127	−.01	564	.01	1597
Austria	.02	38	.07	413	.08	1131

The first-order partial gammas for the table above are as follows:

The Netherlands	−.01
Britain	−.03
United States	−.02
Germany	−.01
Austria	−.08

11. Most of these variants are of the "start up"-"slow down" type. See Lester Milbrath, *Political Participation*, Chicago: Rand McNally, 1965, pp. 134-135, Verba and Nie, *Participation in America*, pp. 138-148.

12. Oskar Anweiler, Friedrich Kuebart, Ludwig Liegle, Hans Peter Schaefer, and Rita Suessmuth, *Bildungssysteme in Europa*, Weinheim and Basel: Beltz, 1976, p. 15; Daniel Bell, *The Coming of Post-Industrial Society*, New York: Basic Books, 1973, p. 165ff.

13. Gabriel Almond and Sidney Verba, *The Civic Culture*, Princeton: Princeton University Press, 1963.

14. The coefficient of dissimilarity is calculated as suggested by Otis Dudley Duncan, Ray P. Cuzzort, and Beverly Duncan, *Statistical Geography*, New York: Free Press, 1961, p. 83. For more details compare note 41 in chapter 8.

The coefficients are as follows:

Country-Pairs	Coefficient of Dissimilarity
The Netherlands—Britain	11.56
The Netherlands—United States	49.69
The Netherlands—Germany	9.79
The Netherlands—Austria	11.25
Britain—United States	40.52
Britain—Germany	1.77
Britain—Austria	3.34
United States—Germany	42.22
United States—Austria	43.86
Germany—Austria	3.11

15. An O.E.C.D. report of November 1974 gives the following figures:

United States (1970)
(attended postsecondary education, age 14 and above)   20.3%

The Netherlands (1960)
(completed postsecondary education, active population, age 14 and above)   5.2%

Austria (1971)
(completed postsecondary education, age 14 and above)   2.1%

Germany (1970)
(completed postsecondary education, age 15 and above, total population having left school)   5.3%

Britain, no data available

See Organization for Economic Cooperation and Development, Secretariat, *Inequalities in the Distribution of Education Between Countries, Sexes, Generations, and Individuals,* Report, 1974, SME/CA/74.91. (mimeo)

16. The coefficients of dissimilarity are as follows:

Country-Pairs	Mean Coefficient of Dissimilarity
The Netherlands—Britain	79.15
The Netherlands—United States	91.95
The Netherlands—Germany	28.95
The Netherlands—Austria	44.35
Britain—United States	27.50
Britain—Germany	78.60
Britain—Austria	54.45
United States—Germany	92.30
United States—Austria	67.75
Germany—Austria	45.25

The dissimilarity is lowest among the higher educated and highest among the lower educated (high education: 14.32; middle level education: 22.99; low level education: 23.70).

17. The coefficients of dissimilarity reduce as follows:

Country-Pairs	Mean Coefficient of Dissimilarity
The Netherlands—Britain	20.80
The Netherlands—United States	22.25
The Netherlands—Germany	23.65
The Netherlands—Austria	30.95
Britain—United States	8.85
Britain—Germany	22.10
Britain—Austria	31.25
United States—Germany	24.35
United States—Austria	29.60
Germany—Austria	24.25

18. The wording of the question was slightly different in the different countries. In the text we have given the version as used in the United States and Britain. In the other countries the question was asked as follows:

The Netherlands:
Sommige mensen volgen regelmatig wat er gaande is bij de regering en di politiek, terwiji anderen daar niet zo in geinteresseerd zijn. Hoe is dat nou met U? Bent U zeer geinteresseerd in de politiek, of matig of weinig of helemaal niet?

Austria:
Wie wuerden Sie eigentlich Ihr Interesse an Politik einstufen? Sind Sie: sehr interessiert, einigermassen interessiert, wenig interessiert oder ueberhaupt nicht interessiert?

Germany:
Wie stark interessieren Sie sich fuer oeffentliche Angelegenheiten und Politik? Sind Sie: sehr interessiert, etwas interessiert, nicht sehr interessiert oder uber-haubpt nicht interessiert?

19. Duncan R. Luce, "Analyzing the Social Process Underlying Group Voting Patterns," in Eugene Burdick and Arthur J. Brodbeck (eds.), *American Voting Behavior*, New York: Free Press, 1960, p. 341; Campbell et al., *The American Voter*, p. 245.

20. Franz Urban Pappi, *Wahlverhalten und politische Kultur*, Meisenheim am Glan: Hain, 1970.

21. Philip E. Converse, "Public Opinion and Voting Behavior," in Fred I. Greenstein and Nelson W. Polsby (eds.), *Handbook of Political Science*, Vol. 4, Reading, Mass.: Addison-Wesley, 1975, p. 94.

22. The categories "not much interested" and "not at all interested" have been collapsed for all our subsequent analyses.

23. Pairwise comparison across countries shows the following figures:

Country-Pairs	Mean Coefficient of Dissimilarity
The Netherlands–Britain	69.7
The Netherlands–United States	68.3
The Netherlands–Germany	37.0
The Netherlands–Austria	41.3
Britain–United States	23.6
Britain–Germany	82.0
Britain–Austria	41.6
United States–Germany	84.5
United States–Austria	42.6
Germany–Austria	44.9

24. The dissimilarity coefficient reduces to the following values:

Country-Pairs	Mean Coefficient of Dissimilarity
The Netherlands–Britain	17.4
The Netherlands–United States	22.8
The Netherlands–Germany	32.6
The Netherlands–Austria	17.7
Britain–United States	19.6
Britain–Germany	28.3
Britain–Austria	24.5
United States–Germany	20.6
United States–Austria	19.6
Germany–Austria	28.4

25. Campbell et al., *The American Voter*, p. 252.
26. Ibid., p. 255.
27. Converse, "Public Opinion and Voting Behavior," p. 100.
28. Goodman, "The Multivariate Analysis of Qualitative Data."
29. The partial gamma was calculated as proposed by James A. Davis, "A Partial Coefficient for Goodman and Kruskal's Gamma," *Journal of the American Statistical Association*, 62 (March 1967), p. 191.

$$\text{Partial gamma} = \frac{\sum_i (P_i - Q_i)}{\sum_i (P_i + Q_i)}$$

Note: P = concordant pairs
Q = discordant pairs
i = subtables of the n-dimensional contingency table

30. For the 3 (political interest) x 3 (education) x 3 (levels of ideological conceptualization) tables (Figure 9.5) we have tested the following hypotheses:

Hypothesis 1   The distribution of levels of ideological conceptualization is independent of political interest and education.
Hypothesis 2   The distribution of levels of ideological conceptualization depends on political interest.
Hypothesis 3   The distribution of levels of ideological conceptualization depends on education.

Hypothesis 4   The distribution of levels of ideological conceptualization depends in an additive way on political interest and education.

This corresponds to the hypotheses 3, 2, 2, and 1 in Goodman "The Multivariate Analysis of Qualitative Data," p. 234. The probability for likelihood ratio chi-square (P) is .000 in all countries for the first three hypotheses. For H_4, P is .29 in the Netherlands, .002 in Britain, .34 in the United States, .23 in Germany, and > .50 in Austria.

31.   If we regard H_1 as the null hypothesis, we obtain for H_2 and H_3 the following reduction of the chi-squares:

	Political Interest H_2	Education H_3
The Netherlands	.69	.47
Britain	.56	.47
United States	.38	.77
Germany	.57	.63
Austria	.67	.54

The reduction of the variation in chi-square is calculated as proposed by Leo Goodman, "A Modified Multiple Regression Approach to the Analysis of Dichotomous Variables," *American Sociological Review*, 37 (February 1972), pp. 42-44. For details see note 38 of chapter 8.

32.   Campbell et al., *The American Voter*, p. 252.

Chapter 10

IDEOLOGICAL CONCEPTUALIZATION AND POLITICAL ACTION

HANS D. KLINGEMANN

Social scientists have generated a sizeable body of evidence that a high level of political sophistication as a rule implies a high degree of participation in the political process. Thus we also expect to find in this study that *the inclination toward political action increases with increasing levels of ideological conceptualization.* The general hypothesis should hold for two reasons. First, ideological knowledge enhances one's understanding of the interdependence of political phenomena. There is a clearer perception of the diverse opportunities for attaining political objectives through various forms of political activity. Second, political ideologies help to make political judgments. The concept of political ideology implies a high degree of value consciousness. And the superordinate values of a certain ideology determine whether a political situation or a political event is experienced as good or bad, desirable or undesirable.

This general thesis, however, needs qualification. We cannot safely assume that knowledge of possible means of participation necessarily results in its use. Rather the overarching principles of a particular world view may well intervene in a supporting or restraining manner. This aspect of the relationship between political sophistication and political action has rarely been stressed in the literature, largely because most of the research deals with forms of political participation that are accepted as clearly legitimate. And, indeed, in the case of conventional political participation it should not make much difference whether one's political belief system is dominated by a "pro change" or by a "pro status quo" type of value orientation.

Unconventional means of political participation, on the other hand, are controversial and value laden. Some value communities find them more acceptable than others. *We would expect a greater readiness for the advocates of change in the direction of greater equality to incorporate new means of political participation into their action repertory than we would expect for the defenders of the status quo.*

This consideration has consequences for the relationship between unconventional political participation, operationalized in this study as protest potential, and our measure of levels of ideological conceptualization. This latter measure does not express the direction—the substantive or value component—of ideological thinking. Rather, it stresses the strength component—the structural aspect—of the political belief system. People of differing value orientations may well exhibit similar levels of ideological conceptualization. And this turns out to be the case empirically.[1] However, if under this condition it is true that respondents holding pro change values are more inclined to use new participation modes than those holding pro status quo values, then we have to expect a lower association between protest potential and ideological thinking than between the latter variable and conventional participation.

We have postulated that value orientations that in a broad way revolve around the general theme of political, economic, and social change are systematically related to the degree of acceptance of new modes of political participation. However, the level of value consciousness is not equally developed across the populace. People differ in their capacity to infer the culturally defined implications of value positions. The concept of ideology, by its very definition, includes the notion of a high degree of value consciousness: related values should go together. A high level of constraint is considered to be characteristic of the ideologue's belief system. Thus the degree of value consciousness should also turn out to be of a high relevance for the determination of behavioral dispositions. This leads to the expectation that the effect of value orientation on protest potential varies in a systematic way with varying levels of ideological conceptualization. *The higher the level of ideological thinking, the greater will be the effect of value orientation on protest potential.*

We will put these considerations to an empirical test.

THE RELATIONSHIP BETWEEN
IDEOLOGICAL CONCEPTUALIZATION OF POLITICS
AND MODES OF POLITICAL PARTICIPATION

Empirical evidence for the thesis that the rate of *conventional political participation* is positively influenced by the degree of political sophistication has already been summarized in the literature.[2] We are not going to repeat the discussion here. A result reported by Converse will serve as a general orientation to the magnitude of that relationship.[3] Converse demonstrates, while relying on very similar operationalization procedures, that respondents with a pronounced ideological comprehension of politics attain a score on a scale of conventional political participation that is nine times higher than the score reached by those with a rather weakly developed political consciousness.[4] We also find, as expected, that the inclination to participate in conventional political action increases with rising levels of ideological conceptualization.

In the European countries we find, on the average, about 6 percent nonparticipants among respondents with high or medium levels of ideological thinking. This proportion increases to 19 percent among respondents with low or very low levels of ideological conceptualization and reaches 49 percent among respondents who conceptualize politics in nonideological terms. The respective proportions in the United States are considerably lower: 1 percent, 6 percent, and 25 percent. The roots of this difference may lie in the fact that the degree of participation as required by the institutional set-up of the political system, especially at the local level, is much higher in the United States than in the European countries.

The relationship between conventional political participation and levels of ideological conceptualization can be conveniently summarized by means of the gamma coefficient. Table 10.1 shows the range of these coefficients across countries. The highest associations are found in Britain (.48) and the Netherlands (.47). The relationships are still quite high in Austria (.42) and the United States (.39), but lower in Germany (.27).

These coefficients are lower in all countries under investigation than the association between conventional political participation and political interest. This finding is quite plausible. On the one hand, there are respondents who are ideologically knowledgeable but who are not motivated enough to participate at a high rate. This type comes close to the "inside dopester" as described by Riesman and Glazer.[5] On the other hand, we have presented evidence that ideological thinking is, after all, found in only a small part of the population. Moreover, nonideologues, when appropriately motivated, have an inclination to participate as well. Nevertheless, even granting this

Table 10.1: IDEOLOGICAL CONCEPTUALIZATION OF POLITICS AND CONVENTIONAL POLITICAL PARTICIPATION

Conventional Political Participation

Countries	Ideological conceptualization (zero-order gamma)		Political interest (zero-order gamma)		Ideological conceptualization, controlled for political interest (first-order gamma)	
The Netherlands	.47	(1194)	.72	(1186)	.28	(1186)
Britain	.48	(1460)	.68	(1448)	.34	(1448)
United States	.39	(1713)	.59	(1702)	.28	(1702)
Germany	.27	(2295)	.63	(2291)	.19	(2291)
Austria	.42	(1577)	.68	(1575)	.27	(1575)

NOTE: The variables are scored as follows: protest potential: 0 = no activity − 7 = 7 activity − 7 = 7 activities; ideological conceptualization of politics: 1 = nonideological conceptualization − 5 = high level of ideological conceptualization; political interest: 1 = not much or not at all interested − 3 = very interested.

general pattern, there is a genuine effect of ideological conceptualization that is not washed out by controlling for different degrees of political interest. The respective first-order gamma coefficients are presented in Table 10.1. The percent reduction of the initial zero-order association between conventional political participation and levels of ideological conceptualization ranges between about 30 percent and 40 percent.

In order to check whether or not we can assume a similar nucleus of association between conventional political participation and levels of ideological conceptualization across countries, we have again applied the Mosteller technique. We find that the assumption holds quite well. The average dissimilarity index between all possible pairs of countries is reduced from 61.5 to 17.5[6] Hence, when controlling for country-specific effects, a rather similar effect of ideological conceptualization on conventional political participation emerges.

Our general finding thus supports the hypothesis that the degree of ideological sophistication is positively related to the rate of conventional political participation and that the association is similar across countries.

We have postulated that the association between protest potential and levels of ideological thinking should be less pronounced. This should be so because we assume that a pro-change value orientation supports the inclination to use new means of participation while a pro status quo value orientation does not. And this tendency should be stronger with rising levels of value consciousness. However, our measure of ideological thinking does not differentiate between these value communities. Rather, there is a mix of these value orientations within each of the levels of ideological conceptualization. The hypothesized effects of value orientations on protest potential run counter to each other and the general magnitude of the association is thereby suppressed. Indeed, the increase in protest potential is much smaller across different levels of ideological conceptualization than was the case for conventional political participation. And this is true for all countries under investigation.

As shown in Table 10.2, gamma coefficients are, on the average, about three-quarters of the magnitude encountered for conventional participation. Differences between countries are less pronounced. The strongest association holds for the United States (.36), the weakest is found in Germany (.23).

The average size of these coefficients is somewhat larger than those found for the relationship between protest potential and political interest. This is in clear contrast to the finding with respect to conventional political participation. Similarly, the reduction of the zero-order association between levels of ideological conceptualization and protest potential when controlling for different degrees of political interest is much smaller than was the case for conventional political participation. Obviously, protest potential is determined by a more complex mechanism. Value orientation might be the intervening variable. Country-specific factors account for most of the difference in the relationship between protest potential and levels of ideological conceptualization. The average dissimilarity index reduces from 55.3 to 20.4

Table 10.2: IDEOLOGICAL CONCEPTUALIZATION OF POLITICS, PROTEST POTENTIAL, AND POLITICAL INTEREST

	Protest Potential		
Countries	Ideological conceptualization (zero-order gamma)	Political interest (zero-order gamma)	Ideological conceptualization, controlled for political interest (first-order gamma)
The Netherlands	.26 (1149)	.25 (1141)	.20 (1141)
Britain	.32 (1398)	.22 (1387)	.26 (1387)
United States	.36 (1615)	.13 (1607)	.34 (1607)
Germany	.23 (2212)	.21 (2208)	.20 (2208)
Austria	.29 (1267)	.36 (1266)	.19 (1266)

NOTE: The variables are scored as follows: protest potential: 0 = no activity − 7 = 7 activities; ideological conceptualization of politics: 1 = nonideological conceptualization − 5 = high level of ideological conceptualization; political interest: 1 = not much or not at all interested − 3 = very interested.

if one looks at the standardized distributions.[7] Thus, as was the case for conventional political participation, we can assume a rather similar nucleus of association between protest potential and levels of ideological conceptualization across countries.

Although we have found a positive association between protest potential and ideological thinking, the overall size of the relationship suggests that value orientations have to be taken into account for a more adequate explanation.

VALUE ORIENTATIONS, MODES OF POLITICAL PARTICIPATION, AND LEVELS OF IDEOLOGICAL CONCEPTUALIZATION

We have postulated that value orientations that in a broad way revolve around the general theme of political, economic, and social change are systematically related to the degree of acceptance of new modes of political participation. Values that support change in the direction of greater equality should increase approval of new and thus unconventional means of political participation. Values that support traditional stratification systems should suppress the willingness to try out unconventional participation modes that, as far as legitimacy is concerned, are still controversial.

We have argued further that the strength of this relationship should vary with the degree of conscious organization of values. And we have hypothesized that value consciousness—the degree of constraint between related value positions—should covary with levels of ideological conceptualization. We shall discuss these problems in the following sequence:

(1) the relation of modes of participation to value orientations;
(2) the relation of levels of constraint between value positions to levels of ideological conceptualization; and
(3) the relation of participation modes to value orientations at various levels of ideological conceptualization.

In chapter 8 we have briefly inquired into value orientations when building the measure of an active use of an ideological mode of thought. We have demonstrated that the ideological concepts as encountered in the open-ended responses were almost exclusively related to a moderate version of the change versus status quo theme of the left-right, liberal-conservative dimension. Open-ended responses of this type that could be used as indicators for value orientation are, however, not in high currency and thus not available for the larger part of the samples. We must rely then on other scales and indices that, at least for respondents with higher levels of ideological thinking, may be considered as components of a change versus status quo dimension. Three such measures are available:

(1) a left-right self-anchoring scale;
(2) an index to measure the degree of Materialism and Postmaterialism; and
(3) an index to measure the political importance of social equality.

The left-right self anchoring scale has been elaborated earlier.[8] The respondents were asked to place themselves along this dimension; they were free to define the specific content of the left-right continuum in the way that would best fit their own conceptions.

The Materialism/Postmaterialism index is described in detail in chapter 11. It is based on the assumption of a hierarchy of values. One speaks of a Materialist orientation when economic or security needs or the need to maintain order are given a higher priority than needs expressing a desire for self-realization or more political participation. Respondents who rank the latter goals higher are labeled Postmaterialists.[9]

The index of the political importance of social equality combines attitudes toward the importance of social equality with an evaluation of the government's responsibility to work toward achieving social equality in various areas. The specific issues we used here were (1) guaranteeing equal rights for men and women, (2) providing equal rights for ethnic or racial minorities (colored immigrants in Britain, racial minorities in the United States, and guest-workers in Austria, Germany, and the Netherlands), and (3) trying to even out differences in wealth. When questions of social equality are deemed to be unimportant and the government is not seen as having responsibility for dealing with such matters, the response is viewed as indicating low political importance of social equality.[10]

The bivariate relationships between these value indicators and the scales of conventional participation and protest potential as discussed in detail in chapter 3 are presented in Table 10.3.[11] The associations between conventional political participation and both the left-right self-anchoring scale and the index of political importance of social equality are practically zero in all of the countries.

In Germany, Austria, and the United States there is a rather moderate association between the Materialist/Postmaterialist value orientation and conventional political participation, indicating that a Postmaterialist orientation is supportive of conventional participation. This may be so because the desire for more political participation is one of the components of the Materialist/Postmaterialist index that defines the Postmaterialist end of the scale. This finding is very much in line with our reasoning. The participation modes that

Table 10.3: POLITICAL VALUE ORIENTATION AND MODES OF POLITICAL PARTICIPATION

	Relation of Conventional Political Participation to:						Relation of Protest Potential to:					
	L–R S		M – PM		PISE		L–R S		M – PM		PISE	
Countries	gamma	N	gamma	N	gamma	N	gamma	N	gamma	N	gamma	N
The Netherlands	.05	1080	.13	1132	.07	1158	.33	1041	.31	1101	.26	1120
Britain	-.04	1197	.04	1400	.05	1393	.13	1165	.18	1348	.12	1352
United States	-.02	1157	.03	1669	.02	1672	.21	1116	.22	1585	.22	1589
Germany	.11	2116	.22	2252	.04	2264	.24	2054	.26	2176	.14	2191
Austria	.05	1187	.17	1483	.05	1532	.07	997	.20	1214	.01	1247

NOTE: L–R S = left-right self-anchoring scale; M – PM = index Materialism-Postmaterialism; PISE = index political importance of social equality. The participation scales were scored 0 = no activity – 7 = 7 activities. A right, materialistic, or low political importance of social equality position received a low score.

are incorporated in the conventional political participation scale are all perceived as legitimate means of political action by the overwhelming part of the population.

In contrast, the relationships between the diverse value orientations and protest potential are, on the average, three times as robust. A Postmaterialist orientation is found to be consistently associated with protest potential. In general, however, even the coefficients for the Materialist/Postmaterialist index are of a quite modest order. They range from .31 in the Netherlands to .18 in Britain. Particularly low coefficients are found for the left-right scale and the social equality index in Austria.

This is certainly no glaring support for the hypothesis that value orientations serve as a steering mechanism when it comes to the selection of new and unconventional means of political participation. However, as compared to conventional political participation, the coefficients point to the fact that leftists, Postmaterialists, or social equalitarians exhibit a higher tendency to incorporate new modes of political participation in their action repertory than do rightists, Materialists, or those people who rank social equality low.

The general theme of the relation of value orientation to political participation will be taken up in a much broader perspective in chapters 11 and 12. In the present context our focus is more limited. As we have already pointed out, we want to test (1) whether or not a higher level of ideological conceptualization also implies a higher level of value consciousness, and (2) whether for this reason we might expect a systematic variation of the impact of value orientation on modes of political participation when controlling for the level of ideological conceptualization.

In our discussion we have assumed that in a broad way all three scales that have been used as indicators for value orientation revolve around the general theme of political or social change. If this is true, then a left self-location, a pro-social equality orientation, and a Postmaterialist position should go together; and, similarly, a right self-location, a position that ranks social equality low, and a Materialist orientation should be related. And, most importantly, these relationships should be stronger for higher levels of ideological thinking. This poses the general problem of attitudinal constraint in mass publics.

When operationalizing our measure of ideological conceptualization in politics, we have consciously avoided reliance on measures of attitudinal constraint. The main reason for that decision lies in the fact that it would otherwise have been very difficult to distinguish between ideology and ideology by proxy.[12] An ideological belief system, as we have defined it, should be more genuinely supported by ego, whereas an ideology by proxy is more of a social reflection of aspects of the state of a subcultural system. While the ideologues know what goes with what *and why,* the ideologues by proxy know what goes with what by repeating what political elites articulate at a given point in time. In the latter case a high level of attitudinal constraint would be a misleading indicator for an ideologically organized belief system sui generis. However, a level of constraint among related idea elements is still expected among respondents with a high level of ideological conceptualization—a level of constraint at least as high as for those with lower levels.

Previous research on attitude consistency has focused primarily upon comparisons between elites and masses, on the one hand, and on variations of attitudinal constraint within the population across time, on the other. Results of the comparisons between elites and masses lead to the conclusion that political elites at a given point in time, at least on the national level, exhibit, on the average, a higher measure of attitudinal consistency than nonelites. Converse reports coefficients for elites for the United States in 1958 that are nearly double those of the general population.[13] The same author has found similar results for France for the period 1967 to 1973. The relationship between a series of domestic and foreign policy position issues and the left-right self-placement of the respondents was much higher for candidates for the French National Assembly than for the French electorate.[14] Based upon their analyses in the American Leadership Project, Barton and Parsons provide a similar summary conclusion that the political belief systems of elites are substantially more structured than is the case for nonelites.[15] However, Luttbeg reports only modest differences between community elites and the general population with respect to community issues.[16] The latter result seems to suggest that the degree of attitudinal consistency varies with differing degrees of centrality of particular issue areas—a thesis that is further supported by the results of studies by Aberbach and Walker, and Klingemann and Wright.[17] A consistent organization of more diverse issue areas of varying individual centrality, however, is to be found only among those respondents who have high levels of ideological conceptualization.[18]

Nie and Andersen have investigated the development of attitudinal consistency over time among the American population. They obtain relatively low figures for the degree of constraint during the politically "calm" years of 1956, 1958, and 1960. However, for the somewhat more politically turbulent times—1964, 1968, 1971, and 1972—the occurrence of such consistency is considerably more frequent. In the first period, the average degree of association (gamma) between policy items is about .15 as contrasted to an average of .39 in the more recent period.[19] This latter value—for the general population—is roughly the same as that found among candidates for the American Congress in 1958. We are not aware of research comparing the attitudinal consistency of elites and masses in the period between 1964 and 1972. Our thesis would be that the differences between elites and masses, though at different levels, would persist.

The static character of our data base as well as the lack of comparable issue items in our study preclude a dynamic analysis that precisely compares our findings to those reported in previous research. The same holds true for possible comparisons between political elites and nonelites. A cross-section survey does not reach elites comparable with those targeted in the earlier works.

We are, nevertheless, engaged in the same general problem area when we try to examine the relationship between attitudinal constraint and levels of ideological conceptualization of politics. It is obvious that we cannot expect value consciousness at the level likely to appear in elite populations. Yet, the existence of a positive correlation that systematically varies with levels of ideological conceptualization would place in question the simple elite/nonelite distinction and would speak for moving toward a more differentiated conceptualization of political stratification along cognitive lines—a concept put forth in more general terms by Key.[20] This refinement would also put us in a position to make more sense out of a differing relevance of values to the modes of political participation. If we now turn to our own data we see from Table 10.4 that for the general population the level of constraint between the three value scales is modest at best. As in most of the comparable analyses, we have summarized the strength of the relationship between the scales by means of the gamma coefficient.[21] If one takes the mean coefficient as an indicator, the results obtained range from .29 in the Netherlands, through .20 in Germany, .18 in Britain, .14 in the United States, to a low of .08 in Austria. The general level of these coefficients does not differ appreciably from that reported in the previous literature for the politically "calm" times, as far as national cross-section surveys are concerned, with Austria being an exception.

In order to decide whether the degree of constraint varies positively with levels of ideological conceptualization, we have calculated the corresponding coefficients separately for the following three groups of respondents:

(1) respondents with a high or middle level of ideological conceptualization;
(2) respondents with a low or a very low level of ideological conceptualization; and
(3) respondents with a nonideological conceptualization of politics.

The results are presented in Table 10.5. The pattern that is produced supports our thesis nicely: the degree of interdependence between value positions revolving around the theme of social and political change rises with increasing levels of ideological conceptualization. And this is true on a cross-national scale. In only two out of the entire set of fifteen relationships does the rank order of the coefficients deviate from theoretical expectations (Table 10.5).

Table 10.4: LEVEL OF CONSTRAINT AMONG THREE VALUE ORIENTATION SCALES IN THE GENERAL
POPULATION

Value Orientation Scales	The Netherlands		Britain		United States		Germany		Austria	
	gamma	N	gamma	N	gamma	N	gamma	N	gamma	N
L–R S : M–PM	.32	1035	.17	1173	.12	1147	.26	2095	.13	1149
L–R S : PISE	.30	1056	.22	1176	.13	1147	.13	2106	.08	1173
M–PM : PISE	.26	1114	.14	1365	.16	1645	.20	2238	.04	1461
x̄	.29		.18		.14		.20		.09	

NOTE: L–R S = left-right self-anchoring scale; M–PM = index Materialism-Postmaterialism; PISE = political importance of social equality.

Respondents with high or medium levels of ideological conceptualization show mean coefficients that match those known from elite research, with Austria again being an exception.[22] A high degree of segmentation between the value scales is clearly visible among respondents with a nonideological conception of politics.

In the Netherlands, Britain, and the United States, among those respondents with high or medium levels of ideology, the strongest relationship between the individual scales can be observed with respect to the left-right scale and the index of political importance of social equality. In Germany and Austria, on the other hand, the largest coefficients are obtained between the left-right scale and the index measuring a Materialist/Postmaterialist value

Table 10.5: **LEVEL OF CONSTRAINT AMONG THREE VALUE ORIENTATION SCALES**

		Levels of Ideological Conceptualization					
Countries	Value Orientation Scales	High and medium		Low and very low		Non-ideological Conceptual-ization	
		gamma	N	gamma	N	gamma	N
THE	L−R S : M−PM	.52	197	.30	481	.16	357
NETHERLANDS	L−R S : PISE	.54	202	.35	484	.09	370
	M−PM : PISE	.44	196	.32	482	.09	436
	x̄	.50		.32		.11	
BRITAIN	L−R S : M−PM	.37	106	.25	358	.09	709
	L−R S : PISE	.60	109	.31	362	.12	705
	M−PM : PISE	.32	105	.19	371	.09	889
	x̄	.38		.25		.10	
UNITED	L−R S : M−PM	.38	189	.13	462	−.01	496
STATES	L−R S : PISE	.40	191	.12	463	.03	493
	M−PM : PISE	.36	189	.13	509	.13	947
	x̄	.38		.13		.06	
GERMANY	L−R S : M−PM	.41	347	.25	1156	.17	592
	L−R S : PISE	.27	349	.15	1165	.00	592
	M−PM : PISE	.26	346	.19	1170	.20	722
	x̄	.31		.20		.12	
AUSTRIA	L−R S : M−PM	.18	118	.14	568	.11	463
	L−R S : PISE	.17	125	.11	579	.01	469
	M−PM : PISE	.00	118	.07	581	.04	762
	x̄	.12		.11		.05	

NOTE: L−R S = left-right self-anchoring scale; M−PM = index Materialism-Postmaterialism; PISE = index political importance of social equality.

orientation. The Materialist/Postmaterialist orientation does not emerge as a totally independent dimension. Rather, it can well be conceived of as a new idea-element that gradually becomes a part of the old change versus status quo value dimension. We take this analysis, in general, to lend support to the hypothesis that value consciousness rises along with rising levels of ideological conceptualization. Given this result we can proceed to our final problem.

Our primary interest in this chapter is in whether the impact of value orientations on the choice of means to attain political objectives differs depending on the level of ideological conceptualization. We have already demonstrated that, as far as the general population is concerned, there is no association between value orientation and conventional participation, whereas we did find a moderate association between value orientation and protest potential. A pro-change orientation was supportive of the use of protest potential, while a pro status quo orientation was not. A higher value consciousness, as indicated by the higher levels of ideological conceptualization, should not affect the general finding that there is not much of a relationship between conventional political participation and value orientation. These means are commonly accepted as legitimate and this should be true whatever the degree of value consciousness. The relationship of protest potential to value orientation, in contrast, should be affected by the degree of value consciousness. The higher the degree of ideological conceptualization, the more pronounced these relationships should be. And here we can proceed from the fact that measures of value orientation are, for all practical purposes, uncorrelated with ideological conceptualization.[23] Table 10.6 summarizes the coefficients that are relevant to the key proposition.

One can readily see that there are only modest differences across the various levels of ideological conceptualization in the relationship between values and conventional political participation. There is a tendency for somewhat tighter relationships in the set of respondents with high or medium levels of ideological thinking, as compared to those further down the ideology scale. The coefficients are noteworthy in Germany (.24) and the Netherlands (.17) between conventional political participation and a Materialist/Postmaterialist orientation among the respondents scoring higher on ideology. Similarly, the relationships between the political importance of social equality and conventional political participation in Britain (.33) and Austria (.22), or with the left-right self-anchoring scale in Germany (.20) and the United States (.10), should be mentioned. Overall, however, these associations are not particularly strong, suggesting that the effect of value consciousness is modest in structuring the linkages between value orientations and conventional political participation. This finding is well in line with our general argument.

Table 10.6: VALUE ORIENTATION AND MODES OF POLITICAL PARTICIPATION WITHIN GROUPS OF DIFFERENT LEVELS OF IDEOLOGICAL CONCEPTUALIZATION OF POLITICS

	Relation of Conventional Political Participation to:						Relation of Protest Potential to:					
	L-R S		M-PM		PISE		L-R S		M-PM		PISE	
Country	gamma	N	gamma	N	gamma	N	gamma	N	gamma	N	gamma	N
Levels of ideological conceptualization:												
I. High and medium												
Netherlands	.09	203	.17	197	.10	202	.50	198	.51	192	.53	197
Britain	.31	110	.22	106	.33	109	.51	108	.21	104	.40	108
United States	.10	192	.03	189	-.01	191	.41	189	.46	186	.55	188
Germany	.20	350	.24	347	.09	349	.35	337	.39	334	.28	336
Austria	.02	125	.12	118	.22	125	.16	114	.16	108	.13	114
Levels of ideological conceptualization:												
II. Low and very low												
Netherlands	.01	497	.10	492	-.02	494	.35	482	.33	481	.27	481
Britain	.00	362	.11	370	.10	374	.28	355	.29	363	.21	368
United States	-.05	467	.01	513	.06	515	.23	456	.26	501	.22	502
Germany	.11	1174	.20	1176	.04	1185	.25	1143	.25	1144	.15	1156
Austria	.10	588	.15	587	.07	601	.08	494	.23	499	-.01	510
III. Nonideological conceptualization												
Netherlands	.03	380	-.01	443	.08	462	.18	361	.12	428	.09	442
Britain	-.05	725	-.01	924	.03	910	.04	702	.13	881	.06	876
United States	-.05	498	.02	967	.01	966	.15	471	.14	898	.17	899
Germany	.06	592	.19	729	.05	730	.16	574	.18	698	.10	699
Austria	.03	474	.10	778	.05	806	.08	389	.11	607	-.02	623

NOTE: L-R S = left-right self-anchoring scale; M - PM = index Materialism-Postmaterialism; PISE = index political importance of social equality. The participation scales were scored 0 = no activity - 7 = 7 activities. A right, materialistic, or low political importance of social equality position received a low score.

On the unconventional side of the ledger, in contrast, the hypothesized interaction effect is abundantly clear. The higher the level of ideological conceptualization, and thus value consciousness, the more pronounced is the link between value orientations and protest potential. And this is true for all the countries under investigation. Respondents with a pro-change value orientation and with high or medium levels of ideological conceptualization are inclined to possess high protest potential. Respondents with a more status quo value orientation tend to reject protest activities. With lower levels of ideological conceptualization this relationship diminishes. The pattern is most clear in the American and Dutch cases and least so in Austria.[24] This result is again very much in line with our hypothesis.

A search for systematic differences in the connection between protest potential and the specific value indicators across different levels of ideological conceptualization proved fruitless. It might have been reasonable to hypothesize a change in importance from the "old" left-right to the "new" Materialist/Postmaterialist values along with higher levels of ideology. However, the results do not justify such an interpretation.

As a summary, two major conclusions are warranted, which hold within the framework of our value consciousness interpretation of levels of ideological conceptualization.

(1) The relationship between value orientations and conventional political participation is modest, indeed, and there is no major alteration of this relationship within different levels of ideological conceptualization of politics. Thus, there is a normative consensus between the different political value communities about the usage of such means of influence.

(2) The relationship between value orientation and protest potential is more pronounced. Respondents who endorse political and social change are more inclined than those who favor the status quo to score high on the scale of protest potential. This relationship is decisively influenced by levels of ideological conceptualization. The higher the levels of ideological conceptualization, the more is the selection of such means guided by the particular value orientation.

ACTION REPERTORY, LEVELS OF IDEOLOGICAL CONCEPTUALIZATION, AND VALUE ORIENTATIONS

In chapter 5 it was argued that conventional political participation should not be seen merely as an alternative to unconventional political participation. Rather, the idea of an action repertory has been stressed. This means that particular mixes of conventional and unconventional types of activity characterize different population groups.

Our focus will be on the five types represented in the action repertory typology. Thus, we are going to add an additional facet to the more comprehensive discussion of the correlates of the action repertory typology represented in chapter 6.

Two questions will be addressed: first, we want to look at the proportion of ideologues among the action types; second, the general value orientation of those ideologues will be described.

Although with different degrees of strength, both conventional and unconventional political participation were positively associated with levels of ideological conceptualization. Thus, we expect to find a relatively high proportion of ideologues among the Activists and the Reformists—those types that are defined by a broad repertory of means of participation. This proportion should decrease for the Conformists and the Protesters—respondents who only use one segment from the full range of possible forms of political influence. And the proportion of ideologues should be lowest among the Inactives, who are least involved in the political process.

As Table 10.7 shows, these expectations are uniformly supported in all countries under investigation. In addition, we can observe that the percentage of respondents with high or medium levels of ideological conceptualization is larger among the Activists than among the Reformists. A similar finding applies, although on a lower general level, for the proportion of the ideologues among the Conformists and the Protesters. Here the Conformists have a larger portion of ideologues. Among the Inactives, higher levels of ideological thinking are almost nonexistent.

In the light of the earlier analyses, this result is hardly surprising. The second question, however, is more interesting: do the ideologues who differ with respect to their action repertory also differ in their general value orientations?

The size of the ideologue population within each of the action repertory types does not permit a detailed analysis. Thus, with respect to value orientation we have very broadly distinguished between respondents tending to be more change-oriented and those respondents inclined to support the status quo. We have grouped those respondents together who tend, *on the average,* more in one than in the other direction.[25] The value orientation of the respective groups within a specific action repertory type is given as the proportion of respondents tending to support a left, postmaterialistic, or social equality position. Results are presented in Table 10.8.

Except for the Protesters, the covariation between action type and value orientation points in the expected direction. In general, results are more pronounced at higher levels of ideological conceptualization. This, in turn, supports the value consciousness hypothesis.

Table 10.7: LEVELS OF IDEOLOGICAL CONCEPTUALIZATION WITHIN ACTION REPERTORY TYPES

Countries	Levels of Ideological Conceptualization	Action Repertory Types									
		Activists		Reformists		Conformists		Protesters		Inactives	
		%	N	%	N	%	N	%	N	%	N
The Netherlands	High	17	37	7	15	3	4	1	5	–	–
	Medium	17	38	23	52	10	12	8	28	3	7
	Low	23	50	26	59	28	36	12	44	8	17
	Very low	22	49	23	53	33	42	28	100	22	44
	Nonideological	21	47	21	48	26	33	51	187	67	137
			221		227		127		364		205
Britain	High	4	6	4	11	1	2	–	–	1	3
	Medium	13	18	12	36	6	14	3	8	3	10
	Low	20	29	16	49	10	21	7	23	3	14
	Very low	19	27	25	78	18	39	16	49	9	39
	Nonideological	44	62	43	130	65	138	74	231	84	352
			142		304		214		311		418
United States	High	11	25	8	46	3	8	2	8	–	–
	Medium	10	24	9	55	5	14	3	9	–	–
	Low	23	54	21	119	9	26	13	41	1	2

Table 10.7: LEVELS OF IDEOLOGICAL CONCEPTUALIZATION WITHIN ACTION REPERTORY TYPES (cont.)

Countries	Levels of Ideological Conceptualizations	Action Repertory Types									
		Activists		Reformists		Conformists		Protesters		Inactives	
		%	N	%	N	%	N	%	N	%	N
	Very low	24	55	19	113	13	38	12	37	10	20
	Nonideological	32	74	43	247	70	196	70	225	89	177
			232		580		282		320		199
Germany	High	10	18	7	38	1	3	3	17	1	8
	Medium	19	33	16	86	12	35	12	74	4	25
	Low	30	52	33	178	25	75	25	149	19	110
	Very low	28	50	23	126	31	92	25	150	31	179
	Nonideological	13	23	21	115	31	93	35	213	45	265
			176		543		298		603		587
Austria	High	11	8	4	11	2	5	3	7	0	1
	Medium	24	18	11	29	5	13	4	10	3	12
	Low	27	20	30	79	21	52	12	30	11	50
	Very low	15	11	27	70	26	62	25	60	18	81
	Nonideological	24	18	28	75	46	111	56	134	68	298
			75		264		243		241		442

Table 10.8: VALUE GROUPS WITH DIFFERENT LEVELS OF IDEOLOGICAL CONCEPTUALIZATION OF POLITICS WITHIN ACTION REPERTORY TYPES

Countries	Levels of Ideological Conceptualization	Action Repertory Types				
		Activists	Reformists	Conformists	Protesters	Inactives
The Netherlands	High and medium	87% (70)	46% (67)	13% (15)	72% (32)	14% (7)
	Low and very low	72 (94)	39 (110)	22 (73)	51 (133)	35 (48)
	Nonideological	59 (37)	37 (43)	29 (28)	48 (134)	32 (91)
Britain	High and medium	83 (23)	54 (46)	31 (16)	12 (8)	18 (11)
	Low and very low	70 (53)	49 (121)	28 (56)	44 (66)	28 (46)
	Nonideological	63 (52)	49 (97)	42 (112)	55 (162)	49 (236)
United States	High and medium	83 (48)	35 (99)	23 (22)	47 (17)	– –
	Low and very low	73 (98)	40 (214)	27 (52)	45 (71)	40 (15)
	Nonideological	68 (44)	43 (136)	41 (44)	55 (106)	44 (68)
Germany	High and medium	86 (51)	61 (74)	37 (14)	50 (90)	12 (32)
	Low and very low	77 (99)	55 (298)	34 (161)	44 (286)	29 (277)
	Nonideological	73 (15)	62 (106)	48 (83)	48 (165)	34 (190)
Austria	High and medium	62 (26)	63 (35)	41 (17)	59 (17)	23 (13)
	Low and very low	60 (30)	59 (145)	45 (103)	48 (79)	32 (117)
	Nonideological	47 (15)	44 (63)	49 (70)	54 (87)	44 (145)

NOTE: Cell-entries are the proportion of "pro-change" value orientation (as defined in this chapter) per group.

Ideologues who are Activists are change-oriented. This proportion is lowest in Austria, with 60 percent, while it ranges between 70 and 87 percent in the other countries. The Activists use both conventional and unconventional modes of political participation. Earlier we argued that the latter should have a higher currency among ideologues of the change-oriented type. Thus this result does not contradict our general thesis.

Ideologues who are Conformists exhibit a status quo orientation, which, on the average, amounts to 70 percent. Reliance on normatively well-supported legitimate means of political participation is consistent with a general status quo orientation. Ideologues who are Reformists come from both camps of value orientation. The chances of being more change or more status quo oriented are about equal. Since the action repertory of the Reformists is defined as comprising all legal forms of participation, this result, too, is plausible. The relatively few numbers of high- or medium-level ideologues among the Inactives are overwhelmingly status quo oriented. This tendency, however, becomes less pronounced for the ideologues with low or very low levels of conceptualization among the Inactives and for the nonideologues within the very same group. Thus, as far as the ideologues are concerned, this segment of the "inside dopesters" tends to be on the conservative side in all of the countries.

According to our general hypothesis regarding the relation between value orientation, modes of political participation, and ideology, we would expect the ideologues among the Protesters to be change-oriented. A status quo orientation should not be very prominent here. Forms of political participation that are not yet part of the established order should not be used by the more status quo oriented. As far as the ideologues among the Protesters are concerned, this thesis is not supported by our data. Rather, status quo orientation as well as change orientation is found equally in this group. A plausible explanation of this rather unexpected finding might be that, as far as the ideologues are concerned, these are of the more radical type. And if it comes to the more radical right ideologue, history has shown that they are well prepared to use unconventional means of activity in order to stop change in the direction of greater equality.[26]

We have tested this hypothesis with negative success. On neither scale did we find the ideologues among the Protesters occupying the extreme positions. Rather, their mean placement was not very different from the overall placement of the population as a whole. The puzzle cannot be solved; the small number of ideologues in the group simply does not allow for more detailed analyses.

The general finding, however, indicates that action repertory, value orientation, and ideological thinking hang together in a systematic way. Ideologues among the Activists are overwhelmingly change-oriented; ideologues among the Conformists, on the other hand, are mostly of the status quo type, while ideologues who are Reformists represent both change and status quo value orientations.

Thus, the overall conclusion of this chapter seems to be well founded: ideologically structured political belief systems do give values more weight in the selection of modes of political action.

NOTES

1. In no instance have we found a clear domination of either a pro-change or a pro status quo orientation within the categories of the index of levels of ideological conceptualization.

2. Lester W. Milbrath (with M. Goel), *Political Participation,* Chicago: Rand McNally, 1965, 1977; Herbert McClosky, "Political Participation," *International Encyclopedia of the Social Sciences,* Vol. 12, New York: MacMillan, 1968, pp. 252-265.

3. Philip E. Converse, "The Nature of Belief Systems in Mass Publics," in David Apter (ed.), *Ideology and Discontent,* New York: Free Press, 1964, p. 225.

4. The participation scale used by Converse consisted of the following items: party membership, campaign contributions, attendance at political rallies, other party work, attempts to convince others through informal communication, and displaying buttons or stickers. A total score of 15 was possible.

Respondents who were defined as (1) level of conceptualization = ideologue *and* recognition and understanding of the terms conservatism and liberalism = stratum I, had a mean score of 3.8. Respondents who were defined as (2) level of conceptualization = no issue content *and* recognition and understanding of the terms conservatism and liberalism = stratum V, had a mean score of .4.

5. David Riesman and Nathan Glazer, "Criteria for Political Apathy," in Alvin Gouldner (ed.), *Studies in Leadership,* New York: Harper & Row, 1950, p. 537.

6. The index of dissimilarity has been calculated according to the formula as described in note 41 of chapter 8.

7. See note 6 above.

8. See Table 8.7.

9. Index construction is described in the Technical Appendix. Marginals are given there, too.

10. Scale construction is described in the Technical Appendix (Social Equality Agenda Mean).

11. Details of scale construction for the conventional political participation and protest potential scales are given in the Technical Appendix.

12. Converse, "The Nature of Belief Systems in Mass Publics," pp. 93-111.

13. Ibid., pp. 228-229. A similar terminology should not obscure the fact that the operational definitions of elite and nonelite are very different in different studies. The results reported by Converse relate to candidates for the United States' Congress on the one hand and a national cross-section sample survey on the other hand.

With respect to the elite, the average gamma was .31; with respect to the nonelite, the average gamma was .17. See Norman H. Nie and Kristi Andersen, "Mass Belief Systems Revisited: Political Change and Attitude Structure," *Journal of Politics,* 36 (August 1974), p. 566.

14. Philip E. Converse, "Some Mass-Elite Contrasts in the Perception of Political Spaces," Paris: IPSA Round Table, 1975, pp. 27, 29.

15. Allan H. Barton and R. Wayne Parsons, "Measuring Belief System Structure," *Public Opinion Quarterly*, 41 (Summer 1977), pp. 176-177.

Barton and Parsons report measures of constraint for the following elite groups: large corporation presidents, labor leaders, higher civil servants, politically appointed federal officials, mass media leaders, voluntary association leaders, Democratic and Republican congressmen and party officials, large corporation vice-presidents and military leaders in 1971-1972. The nonelite sample consisted of members, officers and staff of District Council 37, the New York City branch of the American Federation of State, County and Municipal Employees.

Barton and Parsons used as a measure of attitudinal consistency the mean of a respondent's standard deviation across a set of items. The lower the standard deviation the higher the attitudinal consistency.

For the elite a figure of .44, for the nonelite, a figure of .77 was obtained.

A more detailed description of the statistical procedure can be found in note 21.

16. Norman R. Luttbeg, "The Structure of Beliefs Among Leaders and the Public," *Public Opinion Quarterly*, 32 (Fall 1968), pp. 398-403.

Luttbeg has used cross-section samples of two communities in Oregon (Eugene and Springfield). The elite population of these two communities was selected by the reputation technique. Data were gathered in 1959 (compare notes 7 and 8 in Luttbeg, 1968). Factor analysis reveals a similarly structured attitudinal organization among elites and nonelites. With respect to the elite, the first 5 factors explain 74 percent of the variance; with respect to the population the figure was 65 percent.

In a later article Luttbeg compared local and state findings, concluding that public issues of statewide importance show little evidence of an underlying pattern of organization. "Apparently only at the local level does the public retain any such ideological yardsticks by which new issues are judged." Norman R. Luttbeg, "The Structure of Public Beliefs on State Policies: A Comparison with Local and National Findings," *Public Opinion Quarterly*, 35 (Spring 1971), pp. 114-116.

17. Joel D. Aberbach and Jack L. Walker, "The Meanings of Black Power: A Comparison of White and Black Interpretations of a Political Slogan," *American Political Science Review*, 64 (June 1970), pp. 367-388; Hans D. Klingemann and William E. Wright, "Levels of Conceptualization in the American and the German Mass Public: A Replication." Paper presented at the Workshop on Political Cognition, University of Georgia, Athens, Georgia, May 24-25, 1974.

Aberbach and Walker report a high degree of consistency among blacks with respect to black ideology. Klingemann and Wright show a higher mean association with respect to segregation issues for "group benefit" oriented respondents than for ideologues.

18. Klingemann and Wright, 1974. They show that the level of constraint *between* issue domains is greatest for the ideologues. The analysis is based upon the ISR/CPS 1968 Presidential Election Study.

19. Nie and Andersen, "Mass Belief Systems Revisited," p. 566.

20. V. O. Key, *Public Opinion and American Democracy*, New York: Knopf, 1961, pp. 182-202.

21. Barton and Parsons, "Measuring Belief System Structure," p. 165.

Barton and Parsons have suggested an alternative measure for attitudinal constraint. Its application depends on two assumptions: (1) the items or scales should belong to a single dimension, at least in broad terms. In our case we would have to assume a pro-change versus pro status quo dimension. (2) Numbers have to be attached to the positions indicated by the items or scales. In our case we have assigned the scores 1 to 10 to the left-right self-anchoring scale and the index Materialism/Postmaterialism, and the scores 2, 4, 6, 8, 10 to the index of political importance of social equality. Low scores indicate the pro status quo; high scores the pro-change orientation.

The measure of consistency can be calculated from the following matrix:

Respondent	Attitude scales			Mean score of respondent across items	Variance around the mean score of respondent
	1	2	3		
1	x_{11}	x_{12}	x_{13}	x_1	$\bar{v}_1$
2	x_{21}	x_{22}	x_{23}	x_2	$\bar{v}_2$
3	x_{31}	x_{32}	x_{33}	x_3	$\bar{v}_3$
.					$\bar{v}_i$
.					
N	x_{n1}	x_{n2}	x_{n3}	x_n	v_n

NOTE: $\bar{v}_i$ = Variance of respondents means.

Thus, in our case, in the first step the mean score of a respondent across the three scales is calculated. If the scores are close together, the variance will be small, indicating high value consistency, and vice versa. As Barton and Parsons demonstrate, this way of calculation avoids some of the pitfalls of correlation-type measures.

Because their method is attractive, we have calculated attitude consistency this way, too. Results do not differ much from those obtained by using the gamma coefficient.

These are the means of the individual respondents' variance across the three scales for the following groups:

Levels of ideological conceptualization

Countries	High and medium		Low and very low		No ideological conceptualization	
	$\bar{V}$	N	$\bar{V}$	N	$\bar{V}$	N
The Netherlands	1.78	196	2.39	471	2.49	349
Britain	1.80	105	2.35	355	2.60	688
United States	2.07	189	2.49	458	2.75	489
Germany	2.54	346	3.01	1149	3.29	584
Austria	2.55	118	2.61	560	2.81	458

22. We cannot really decide whether this is a genuinely Austrian phenomenon, because some questions—as we have already mentioned—have been asked slightly differently. We have already mentioned the differences in question formulation with respect to the left-right self-anchoring scale.

23. The association coefficients are as follows:

Countries	L–R S		M – PM		PISE	
	Gamma	N	Gamma	N	Gamma	N
The Netherlands	.10	1085	.17	1138	.07	1164
Britain	.10	1211	−.01	1416	.00	1404
United States	.01	1162	.07	1671	.01	1675
Germany	.00	2126	.12	2263	−.04	2274
Austria	−.02	1190	.15	1487	.05	1535

The low association coefficients hide the fact that high level ideologues have, on the average, a high proportion of a left, postmaterialistic, or pro-social equality value orientation as compared to the total sample.

24. Again we have to point to measurement problems in Austria. Unlike in the other countries, two additional answer alternatives were presented to the respondent as far as questions are concerned which were needed for the construction of the index of Protest Potential: (1) kommt auf die Situation an, und (2) kann mich nicht entscheiden. These categories are quite populated and result in a relatively high number of nonscalable cases.

This difference from the other countries might have affected the results. In addition, the argument of note 22 must be considered, too.

If one would, however, compare ratios of the squared gamma coefficients, then the association is clearer in Britain than in the United States or the Netherlands. While weaker, the ratios for Austria are still roughly those expected and very much like those in Germany.

25. For our tentative grouping we have relied on the following three scales: the left-right self-anchoring scale, the index of materialism/postmaterialism, and the index of political importance of social change. In a first step we have calculated the mean position of each respondent on these scales, using the scores as described in note 21. The sample mean for all the respondents was used to separate the "pro-change" oriented respondents from the "status quo" oriented respondents.

26. Hans D. Klingemann and Franz Urban Pappi, *Politischer Radikalismus*, Muenchen: Oldenbourg, 1972.

Chapter 11

VALUE PRIORITIES AND SOCIOECONOMIC CHANGE

RONALD INGLEHART

INTRODUCTION

As we have demonstrated in chapters 3-6 there are striking differences in the propensities for political action of different age groups. In particular, the young show a markedly higher potential for "unconventional" political behavior than the old. Or, in slightly different terms, certain types of behavior that are "unconventional" for older groups are normal and acceptable for younger groups.

Such a finding would have been interesting, though scarcely surprising, during the student protest era of the late 1960s. It is far less obvious and even more interesting that, despite the virtual disappearance of manifest youth protest in the mid-1970s, the potential for unconventional political action of younger groups in Western nations remains markedly higher than that of older groups. Why?

There are a variety of explanations. For example, the fact that the young tend to be physically more energetic and have more free time than the old might, quite plausibly, account for a higher level of physical *activity*. But we are not dealing solely with differences in activity here: certain basic orientations of the respective age groups also seem to differ.

One of the central ideas that gave rise to the present research project was a hypothesis of intergenerational change in the value priorities of Western publics. This hypothesis implies the existence of persistent differences in the basic goals of different age cohorts—differences that lead them to accept different styles of political action. The distinctive value priorities of the respective cohorts are in turn attributed to differences in their formative experiences. Shaped by gradual changes, these intergenerational differences may have long-term consequences for mass political behavior.

In this chapter we will outline the hypotheses that led us to anticipate intergenerational differences in value priorities. We will then explore the origins of age-linked value differences, in an effort to determine to what extent they seem linked with long-term factors.

An individual's values do not work in a vacuum, however. For reasons outlined in the previous chapter, one's level of ideological thinking should also constitute an important influence on political action. Given the relatively high educational levels of the younger cohorts, one might expect them not only to have distinctive value priorities, but to show relatively high levels of ideological thinking as well. Consequently, in chapter 12 we will examine the impact of one's values and one's level of ideological thinking on both conventional and unconventional forms of political action. These two factors are only part of the story: their impact is conditioned by the institutional setting and socioeconomic circumstances of a given society. We will not attempt to deal with such macropolitical variables in the present analysis. But, as we will demonstrate, one's values and political skills seem to be key influences on an individual's potential for political action.

VALUE PRIORITIES AND CHANGES IN THE BASES OF POLITICAL CONFLICT

Each phase of economic and technological development is characterized by distinctive political conflicts that reflect the demands and challenges most salient in that era. As Marx suggested, the windmill was linked with a given mode of production and a distinctive type of politics, and the steam engine with another; the computer-directed assembly line may be associated with yet another type of politics that is still emerging.

There are reasons. The windmill symbolizes the technology of a predominantly agrarian society in which man is manifestly dependent on nature: the mill works if and when the winds blow, just as one's crops grow *if* there is enough but not too much rainfall and provided one isn't afflicted by blight or locusts. In such a setting, prosperity or misfortune seem largely beyond human control and one tries to adjust to the flow of events through acceptance of the will of God, Nature, or Fate—or through actions intended to appease superhuman powers. Magical or religious explanations of the world are predominant and religious cleavages tend to be the principal basis of political conflict.

With the coming of industrialization, production moves indoors into a man-made environment where the universe seems increasingly subject to human volition. The steam engine can be run any time, in fair or foul weather, provided one stokes it with fuel; the factory can run night or day with the aid of artificial lighting. Similarly, workers tend to be treated as appendages of their machines, to be driven at maximum capacity with minimum outlay. But in this setting, not only the *rate* of production, but the division of its fruits are manifestly subject to human manipulation. Economic production comes to be seen less as a struggle against nature than as a struggle of man against man—of propertyless and often starving worker against factory owner. Thus, social class conflict becomes the mode of politics that distinguishes industrial society. The distribution of the economic surplus is all the more likely to be called into question because it does not correspond to any long-familiar "natural" basis, for it is visibly increasing and manifestly manipulable. Economic issues take the center of the stage and materialist values become ascendant: the cultural hero becomes the Captain of Industry in capitalist societies, or the Stakhanovite in socialist settings.

Though they differ radically in many respects, both agrarian society and industrial society have one thing in common: they are societies of economic scarcity. Thus, most of humanity, throughout most of history, has had to worry about starvation—and even today, a majority of the world's population lives on or near the brink of hunger. In 1973, for example, over half of the world's population lived in countries with annual gross national products of less than $175 per person. Though it is difficult for a Westerner to conceive of surviving on this scale, it reflects modest *gains* over what has generally been the lot of most of humanity. In stark contrast, however, another portion of the world's population—the 20 percent living in the advanced industrial societies of the Western world and Japan—had attained a level of prosperity that was literally unprecedented in human history: they had annual gross national products ranging from $2,000 to nearly $6,000 per person.[1] Even controlling for inflation, the poorest of these countries enjoyed a standard of living far higher than anything the richest of them had known a generation earlier. This extraordinary level of prosperity reflects the remarkable period of economic growth that these nations have experienced since World War II. And it gives rise to the possibility that there have been shifts in value orientations, leading a substantial segment of these populations to hold world views significantly different from those prevailing in industrial or preindustrial societies.

Let us outline the reasons why we might expect this to take place. The basic idea, in a nutshell, is that people have a variety of needs and give most attention to those they feel are in short supply. The generation born after World War II, having been raised during a period of unprecedented prosperity, might tend to give relatively high priority to nonmaterial goals; their parents and grandparents, having experienced hunger and turmoil during their formative years, remain likely to emphasize economic and physical security.[2]

The advanced industrial societies of today, unlike any other large polities in modern history, are not pervaded by almost universal want. This fact could lead to a gradual shift in goal orientations—a process in which universal but often latent needs for belonging, esteem, and realization of one's intellectual and esthetic potential become more prominent, possibly along the lines of the need hierarchy described by Maslow.[3] While we see economic development as conducive to this change, the process is not one of simple economic determinism. Instead, it seems that the influence of economic factors rises at first, and then reaches a point of diminishing returns. Once the process of industrialization has encouraged people to see the world as manipulable by human effort, their goals may be (largely) determined by economic factors—as long as they continue to live under conditions of economic scarcity. But as the people of a given society reach progressively higher levels of economic security, we believe their preferences may come to be constrained less and less by economic variables and more and more shaped by noneconomic factors: the principle of diminishing marginal utility would lead us to expect a gradual shift in values and goals as a society approaches a state of widespread affluence. In other words, the richer you get, the less riches count. Marx and Engels themselves were aware of such a possibility, as is suggested by their observation that the first needs are those for food and drink, shelter and clothing; but as soon as one need is satisfied, new needs arise.[4] As a practical matter, Marx was mainly concerned with societies that were accumulating the capital needed for industrialization under conditions of severe economic scarcity—for not even the most advanced economies of his era had yet moved beyond that phase. But it is clear that Marx was aware that under given circumstances noneconomic motivations could become important or even paramount, and even in his discussion of societies of scarcity he showed considerable concern with the noneconomic costs of industrialization, such as alienation from one's work. Indeed, it has been argued that the concept of the human need hierarchy originates with Marx, rather than with Maslow.[5]

Regardless of its origins, in its simplest form the idea of a need hierarchy underlying human behavior would probably command almost universal assent. The fact that unmet physiological needs take priority over social, intellectual, or esthetic needs has been demonstrated all too often in human history. Starving people give top priority to obtaining food, and people deprived of water will go to almost any length to obtain it. The generalization is probablistic rather than deterministic, for there are rare heroic exceptions;

but it seems clear that there is a strong tendency for physiological needs to take precedence over "higher" needs. Directly related to physiological survival, a set of "safety" needs exists that seems almost equally basic, except for the fact that starving people will risk their lives in order to obtain food.

The rank ordering of human needs becomes less clear as we move beyond those needs directly related to survival. Needs for affiliation seem to be basic and almost universal, perhaps because human survival depends on being cared for by others as an infant, and in varying degrees may depend on membership in a group even as an adult. But the social needs also include a whole spectrum of goals such as prestige and self-esteem that have only a remote relationship to human survival. Accordingly, they play an important role in the behavior of some individuals, but seem relatively minor concerns to others. While Lasswell[6] is no doubt correct in viewing such things as deference and rectitude as basic values, it is difficult to say precisely where they fit on a detailed need hierarchy. The problem becomes even more complex when we deal with intellectual and esthetic values. The hierarchy proposed by Maslow seems plausible enough, but there is little empirical evidence in support of any specific detailed ordering. What *does* seem reasonably clear, however, is that there is a basic distinction between the needs for physiological safety and sustenance, on one hand, and the social, moral, intellectual, and esthetic needs, on the other hand.

This fundamental distinction between a set of goals directly related to material well being and a set of nonmaterial goals seems particularly useful for analysis of contemporary social cleavages. For, as was suggested earlier, we might expect to find substantial differences between those born before and after 1945 in the relative emphasis placed on material and nonmaterial (or Postmaterialist) goals. For the formative years of the older age groups, in virtually all Western societies, were characterized by the presence of widespread economic and physical insecurity; the postwar generation has been brought up without direct exposure to war and in comparatively affluent circumstances.

In the following section we will provide empirical evidence that substantial differences do indeed exist between the value priorities of older and younger generations in Western countries. A set of "Materialist" priorities (as we term them) tends to prevail among older respondents, while a "Postmaterialist" type becomes increasingly widespread as we examine progressively younger groups. But for present purposes we are primarily interested in the impact these value types may have on political action. What does the presence of Materialist or Postmaterialist value priorities imply?

In the first place, we would expect individuals with Postmaterialist priorities to have a somewhat greater potential for political participation in *general*. As Knutson suggests, people whose basic physical needs are unfulfilled are apt to spend their psychic energies coping with their immediate environment and have little remaining energy to devote to social or political activities.[7] They *may*, under extreme conditions, engage in food riots or (given proper leadership and a favorable setting) take part in revolutions. But under the circumstances prevailing in contemporary Western Societies, economic deprivation rarely reaches such extremes. The less-favored groups seem likely to be preoccupied with the demands of daily living, without being so desperate as to feel they have nothing to lose but their chains. On the other hand, people whose material needs have been met so regularly that they take them more or less for granted may attempt to fulfill unmet needs for belonging or affiliation or esteem through political participation. This is by no means the only way such needs can be met, of course, but under certain circumstances it can be a salient and attractive alternative.

But there are specific *types* of political action that seem particularly likely to attract people with Postmaterialist values. For if our hypotheses about value change are correct, they imply that Postmaterialists have only recently emerged in significant numbers. Even now they probably constitute a relatively small proportion of the population of Western societies. Consequently, Postmaterialists are relatively likely to be at odds with the type of society in which they live. For the arrangements and institutions of industrial society are based on Materialist assumptions. On the whole, Western nations have been reasonably successful in achieving economic growth during the past couple of decades—they have provided outputs of the type most valued by Materialists. But they have given relatively little emphasis to attaining Postmaterialist goals. As Abrams has pointed out, until the 1960s such phrases as "Quality of Life" were almost completely absent from the vocabulary of politicians and social scientists.[8] Western political systems have had many decades in which to move toward resolution of the socioeconomic conflicts that grew out of industrialization. The way was frequently rough and marked by violence, but through a variety of forms of social legislation these conflicts have moved toward peaceful coexistence. The lifestyle conflicts of advanced industrial society are still relatively raw and unsettled. Because their most highly valued goals remain far from attainment, the Postmaterialists are likely to seek radical, far-reaching changes in society and to be willing to employ disruptive elite-challenging techniques to bring them about.

Postmaterialists seem all the more willing to employ unconventional political protest techniques because they are relatively unconstrained by a concern to maintain economic and physical security—things that, by definition, they value less highly than the rest of the population. We would expect the Materialists, conversely, to be relatively at home with the existing social pattern and substantially more alarmed by activities that threaten to upset the applecart of advanced industrial society.

There is nothing *inherent* in Postmaterialist values that makes one politically dissatisfied: it depends on the relationship between one's values and the setting in which one lives. In a society where Postmaterialist concerns are given relatively great attention (such as, perhaps, Sweden or Denmark), Postmaterialists may not be particularly unhappy with their society or political system. If Materialist concerns were relatively neglected, strongly Materialist types might constitute the group most likely to engage in political protest; it is simply a question of probabilities. But most Western societies remain predominantly Materialist and their policies reflect the prevalence of Materialist priorities. There is a strong likelihood that the Postmaterialist minority will find themselves being overruled on matters that are important to them. Consequently, as a general rule we would expect those with Postmaterialist values to be relatively unhappy with their political systems at any given moment, and relatively apt to engage in political protest. If, as we argue, Postmaterialists have emerged in growing numbers since World War II, this fact could help explain the shift from protest based on the working class to protest based on the young and relatively affluent during the peak years of postwar prosperity.

MATERIALIST AND POSTMATERIALIST VALUES

We hypothesize that individuals with Postmaterialist values have emerged in increasing numbers during the years since World War II; that they now constitute a sizeable share of the youth and young adults in Western Europe and the United States; and that these individuals have a particularly high potential for unconventional political protest activities.

In order to test these hypotheses, we must be able to measure the relative priority one gives to Materialist versus Postmaterialist values. The surveys carried out in 1974 included a battery of questions designed to tap this dimension. The items were developed in a series of previous studies sponsored by the European Communities, with data gathered in a series of cross-national surveys executed from 1970 through 1976.[9] Since our hypotheses deal with a process of long-term change, in this chapter we will employ data from these other surveys as well as the 1974 surveys in order to provide a certain amount of temporal perspective on the changes.

In earlier explorations of value change we employed a four-item index of Materialist/Postmaterialist value priorities. This index was simple and parsimonious but inherently rather limited: a mere four items are a slender basis by which to measure a major dimension of human values. In subsequent surveys we developed a more reliable indicator based on a broader pool of twelve items. These items are designed to tap a variety of types of both material and nonmaterial goals, with the respondent being asked to select the ones he would give top priority. The following set of questions was used to measure Materialist/Postmaterialist priorities in our 1974 surveys:

In politics it is not always possible to obtain everything one might wish. On this card, several different goals are listed.

If you had to choose among them, which would be your *first* choice?

Which would be your *second* choice?

Which would be your *third* choice?

The goals listed were:
A. MAINTAIN ORDER IN THE NATION
B. GIVE PEOPLE MORE SAY IN THE DECISIONS OF THE GOVERNMENT
C. FIGHT RISING PRICES
D. PROTECT FREEDOM OF SPEECH

On these cards are some goals and objectives people say our country as a whole should concentrate on. Of course, all of these are important to all of us in one way or another, but which *three* are *most* important to you personally?

And from these three goals, which one, for you, is most important?

next most important?

third most important?

Please look at the rest of the cards and tell me which are the *three least* important?

Now which of these three is least important?

next-to-least important?

third least important?

The goals offered in this second group were:

A. MAINTAIN A HIGH RATE OF ECONOMIC GROWTH
B. MAKE SURE THAT THIS COUNTRY HAS STRONG DEFENSE FORCES
C. GIVE PEOPLE MORE SAY IN HOW THINGS ARE DECIDED AT WORK AND IN THEIR COUNTRY
D. TRY TO MAKE OUR CITIES AND COUNTRYSIDE MORE BEAUTIFUL
E. MAINTAIN A STABLE ECONOMY
F. FIGHT AGAINST CRIME
G. MOVE TOWARD A FRIENDLIER, LESS IMPERSONAL SOCIETY
H. MOVE TOWARD A SOCIETY WHERE IDEAS ARE MORE IMPORTANT THAN MONEY

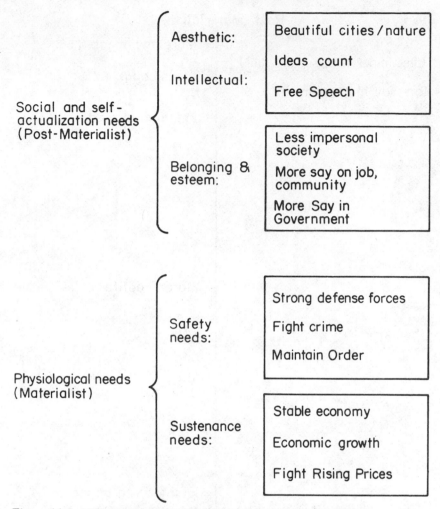

Figure 11.1: ITEMS USED TO MEASURE VALUE PRIORITIES, NEEDS INTENDED TO TAP

Figure 11.1 indicates the *type* of need each item was intended to tap, on a continuum ranging from those most directly related to physiological survival to "higher-order" needs, relatively remote from survival. This continuum of needs is based on the work of Maslow.[10] Our expectation was that emphasis on the six Materialist items would tend to go together empirically, forming one cluster, with the Postmaterialist items forming another distinct cluster. Insofar as this proved to be the case, we could use these items to identify individuals having either a relatively Materialist or Postmaterialist set of value

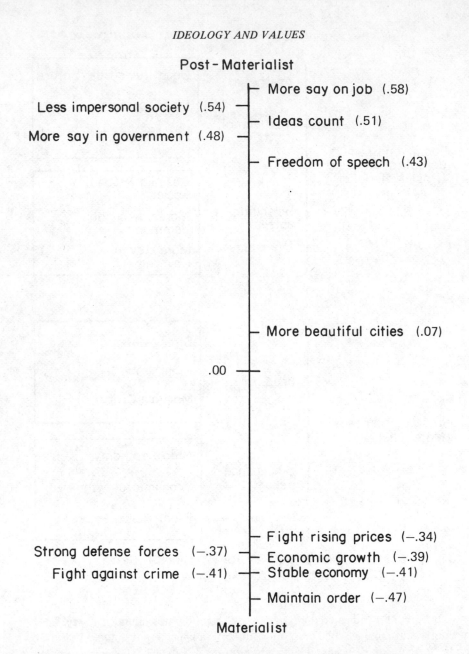

Figure 11.2: THE MATERIALIST/POSTMATERIALIST FACTOR

priorities. In order to test our expectation we performed conventional factor analyses on the rankings of these goals within each available national sample.

Figure 11.2 shows the results from a set of surveys carried out in the nine European Community countries plus the United States in 1973, under the sponsorship of the Commission of the European Communities.[11] Our expectations are confirmed to a remarkable degree. All six of the Materialist items cluster together at the negative pole. And five of the six Postmaterialist items form a cluster at the opposite pole. A single item—the one concerning "more beautiful cities"—does not fit into either cluster. This is not an isolated anomaly. Analyses of the data from all ten countries show precisely the same pattern: in every case, the six Materialist items form one cluster and five of the six Postmaterialist items form another cluster. A single item—always the one concerning "more beautiful cities" fails to fit into either cluster. The latter item does not behave as anticipated; but responses to the eleven other items live up to expectations with remarkable consistency. Furthermore, this consistency cannot be attributed to such common sources of spurious correlation as response set: the items were asked in a forced-choice format which gives no clue to the "right" answer.

In the 1973 surveys, the respondents ranked all twelve items in a common pool. But in the 1974 surveys—the basis of most of our analyses—our respondents ranked first a four-item pool and then an eight-item pool, as indicated above. This raises potentially serious problems of ipsivity. Our items reflect rankings, not absolute scores; this is crucial to operationalizing our hypothesis but it means that the rankings are not independent. It would make factor analysis entirely inapplicable with a very small pool of items. With only two items, for example, the rank of the first item automatically determines the rank of the second, generating a -1.0 correlation between them. With three items, one would expect negative correlations of about .5. With a pool of four items, this effect is still important: the choice of the first item leaves only three possibilities, and random answering would generate negative correlations of about .3 between *all four* items—so that only two of them would load on the first factor: whichever two items had the strongest negative correlation would define the two poles of the first factor, forcing the other two items onto a second factor. With a pool of eight items, the degree to which one item's rank determines that of another becomes fairly small: there are seven degrees of freedom. Table 11.1 shows the results of factor analyses of the value priorities items for each of the five nations surveyed in 1974. The results are quite similar to those from the 1973 surveys. These analyses are based on rankings from one group of eight items and another group of four items. As a consequence, there is a tendency for all of the items in a given group to be negatively correlated with each other, particularly in the case of the four-item group. Accordingly, the nonindependence of our rankings tends

Table 11.1: **THE MATERIALIST/POSTMATERIALIST DIMENSION, 1974**
(loadings of value priorities items on unrotated first factor) *

Goal:	The Netherlands	Britain	United States	Germany	Austria
Ideas count	.65	.38	.56	.58	.70
Less impersonal society	.54	.37	.53	.54	.68
Freedom of speech	.40	.00	.45	.46	.51
More say on job	.53	.62	.42	.44	−.14
More say in government	.55	.69	.44	.57	−.03
More beautiful cities	−.01	.00	.12	−.01	.06
Stable economy	−.25	−.39	−.39	−.20	.02
Fight crime	−.62	−.35	−.50	−.53	−.33
Strong defense forces	−.47	−.41	−.47	−.46	−.40
Maintain order	−.63	−.59	−.41	−.58	.15
Fight rising prices	−.26	−.12	−.45	−.43	−.60
Economic growth	−.43	−.46	−.43	−.35	−.58

*Missing data excluded from these analyses.

to spread the items over several dimensions, diminishing the amount of variance that can be explained by the first factor. Nevertheless, as our empirical results show, this effect is dominated by an even stronger tendency for Materialist items to be chosen together, on one hand; and for Postmaterialist items to be chosen together, on the other hand. In the 1973 surveys all twelve items were ranked in a common pool, so that the problem of nonindependent items was relatively minor; this may explain why the dimensional structure shown in Figure 11.2 is more coherent than the one shown by the 1974 data. Nevertheless, the fit between expectations and reality is reasonably good for *both* the 1973 and 1974 surveys. We have encountered one puzzling anomaly with the item concerning "more beautiful cities," but there seems to be little question that the other eleven items tap a Materialist/ Postmaterialist dimension.

Thus far, we have dealt with items designed to tap one specific aspect of an individual's value priorities—the Materialist/Postmaterialist dimension. Where does this dimension fit in the context of one's global outlook—one's *overall* value priorities? Rokeach has developed a battery of items that seems tailor-made to help answer this question.[12] His items are intended to be exhaustive, rather than intensive. Rokeach concludes that his pool of items taps all major areas of human concern with little duplication; and he has provided an impressive array of evidence in support of this conclusion. Accordingly, the Rokeach Terminal Values Survey was included in the American version of our 1974 questionnaire. If it does provide an exhaustive inventory of one's value priorities, some of its items should tap the Materialist/Postmaterialist dimension. The Rokeach battery is worded as follows:

> On the next page are 18 values listed in alphabetical order. Your task is to arrange them in order of their importance to *you*, as guiding principles in *your* life. Each value is printed on a gummed label which can easily be peeled off and pasted in the boxes on the left-hand side of the page. Study the list carefully and pick out the one value which is the most important to you. Peel it off and paste it in Box 1 on the left.
>
> Then pick out the value which is second most important for you. Peel it off and paste it in Box 2. Then do the same for each of the remaining values. The value which is least important goes in Box 18.
>
> Work slowly and think carefully. If you change your mind, feel free to change your answers. The labels peel off easily and can be moved from place to place. The end result should truly show how you really feel.

The items are:

A COMFORTABLE LIFE (a prosperous life)
AN EXCITING LIFE (a stimulating, active life)
A SENSE OF ACCOMPLISHMENT (lasting contribution)
A WORLD AT PEACE (free of war and conflict)
A WORLD OF BEAUTY (beauty of nature and the arts)
EQUALITY (brotherhood, equal of opportunity for all)
FAMILY SECURITY (taking care of loved ones)
FREEDOM (independence, free choice)
HAPPINESS (contentedness)
INNER HARMONY (freedom from inner conflict)
MATURE LOVE (sexual and spiritual intimacy)
NATIONAL SECURITY (protection from attack)
PLEASURE (an enjoyable, leisurely life)
SALVATION (saved, eternal life)
SELF-RESPECT (self-esteem)
SOCIAL RECOGNITION (respect, admiration)
TRUE FRIENDSHIP (close companionship)
WISDOM (a mature understanding of life)

Factor analysis of the twelve item Materialist/Postmaterialist battery plus the eighteen-item Rokeach battery reveals a complex and interesting structure. As we would expect, a number of dimensions are needed to capture the configuration of responses. But the Materialist/Postmaterialist dimension remains clearly recognizable, and several of Rokeach's items show substantial loadings on it. Table 11.2 gives results from a second factor analysis, based on the eleven items showing significant loading in Table 11.1, plus the related Rokeach items. In the Materialist cluster we find Rokeach's items "A Comfortable Life" and "Family Security"—two values having an obvious linkage with economic security. Also located in this cluster is an item relevant to the safety needs, "National Security." In the Postmaterialist cluster we find "Equality" and "Inner Harmony," plus a pair of items relating to the intellectual and esthetic needs—"Wisdom" and "A World of Beauty." Ironically enough, the item that we had designed to tap the esthetic needs failed to show the expected empirical relationships—but the item developed by Rokeach *does*. Analysis of the responses to our own item concerning "more beautiful cities" revealed a quite unexpected tendency for this item to be linked with emphasis on "The fight against crime." Inclusion of the word "cities" in this context seems to evoke a concern with safety among some respondents; in a latent way, the Cities are unbeautiful because they are dangerous.[13] Rokeach's item makes no reference to cities and apparently evokes esthetic concerns in unmixed form—and consequently falls into the Postmaterialist cluster precisely as the Maslovian hypothesis suggests it should. In short, the anomalous results obtained with this item seems to

Table 11.2: **MATERIALIST/POSTMATERIALIST FACTOR IN THE UNITED STATES, 1974 (loadings of eighteen items on unrotated first factor)***

Goal:	Loadings: (16%)
Ideas count	.58
Less impersonal society	.51
Freedom of speech	.46
WORLD OF BEAUTY	.32
WISDOM	.32
EQUALITY	.30
More say on job	.30
More say in government	.27
INNER HARMONY	.27
Maintain order	−.28
Stable economy	−.30
FAMILY SECURITY	−.37
Economic growth	−.42
Fight rising prices	−.42
NATIONAL SECURITY	−.43
Fight crime	−.45
COMFORTABLE LIFE	−.46
Strong defense forces	−.50

*Rokeach items appear in all capital letters.

reflect imperfect formulation of the "esthetic" alternative, rather than disconfirmation of this aspect of Maslow's model.

INDEX CONSTRUCTION

The foregoing analyses indicated that with the one exception noted our battery of values items does indeed seem to tap a Materialist/Postmaterialist dimension. Our next step, therefore, was to construct an index that uses one's choices among these items to provide a broad-based and effective measure of one's value priorities. The first step was to add up how many of the six Materialist items each respondent had given top priority—either as one of the *two* most important goals in the initial group of four items in the question above, or as one of the *three* most important goals in the subsequent group of eight items. We thereby obtained a Materialism Index on which each respondent received a score ranging from "0" to "5," depending on how many Materialist items were given high priority among these five choices. In similar fashion we next constructed a Postmaterialism index based on how many of the Postmaterialist items were given high priority (there were only five of the latter, since our analyses indicated that a concern with "more beautiful cities" occupied a neutral, position on the Materialist/Postmaterialist dimen-

Table 11.3: CONSTRUCTION OF VALUE PRIORITIES INDEX*

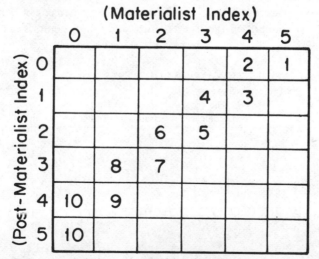

(Materialist Index)

(Post-Materialist Index)	0	1	2	3	4	5
0					2	1
1				4	3	
2			6	5		
3		8	7			
4	10	9				
5	10					

*In subsequent cross-tabulations, those with scores from 8 to 10 on this index are labeled Postmaterialists; those with scores of 4 through 7 are considered mixed; and those with scores from 1 to 3 are labeled Materialists. Cases with 2 or more incomplete rankings are treated as missing data; thus the blank cells above contain cases.

sion). Finally we combined these two indices as indicated in Table 11.3, to produce an index of Materialist/Postmaterialist value priorities with scores ranging from "1" through "10." The distribution of the resulting value types in each of our five nations is shown in Table 11.4. For convenience in such cross-tabulations as these, we have collapsed our ten-category index into a simpler array of four types: those with scores from "1" through "3" on our index had given priority to Materialist goals on *all five* of their top choices; or four Materialist items and the neutral item; or four Materialist items and one Postmaterialist item. In short, they had a Materialist/Postmaterialist ratio of *at least* four to one. We label this group the "Materialists." At the other end of the spectrum, those with scores of "8" through "10" have a similarly overwhelming preference for Postmaterialist goals, and they are given the label "Postmaterialists."

A variety of mixed combinations are also possible. For example, a score of "4" reflects the fact that the respondent chose three Materialist items and one Postmaterialist item (the remaining choice could be either missing data or the neutral item); while a score of "5" reflects a choice of three Materialist items and two Postmaterialist items. Those with scores of "4" or "5" are labeled as a "Mixed (Materialist)" type. Similarly, those with scores of "6" or "7" are labeled "Mixed (Postmaterialist)" types.

As Table 11.4 indicates, Materialists tend to be more common than Postmaterialists—in keeping with our hypothesis that Postmaterialists have only begun to emerge in sizeable numbers since World War II, they still constitute a minority of the total population. The Postmaterialists are least common in Austria, where they constitute less than 5 percent of the sample. They are most common in the Netherlands, where they comprise 21 percent of the sample.

Table 11.4: DISTRIBUTION OF VALUE TYPES

Index Scores:	The Netherlands	Britain	United States	Germany	Austria
1−3 Materialist	19%	30%	39%	56%	41%
4−5 Mixed (Materialist)	31	38	31	28	37
6−7 Mixed (Postmaterialist)	29	25	20	11	18
8−10 Postmaterialist	21	8	10	6	5
	100%	101	100	101	101

ATTITUDINAL AND DEMOGRAPHIC CORRELATES
OF THE VALUES INDEX

We have constructed an index of value priorities that enables us to classify our respondents as "Materialists," "Postmaterialists," or in various interme- diate categories. Our theoretical framework implies that this indicator taps a relatively deep-rooted and basic aspect of one's outlook. If this is the case, we would expect this indicator to be integrated into the respondent's structure of attitudes—that is, various other attitudes should show constraint in keeping with one's values. In the 1974 surveys our respondents rated a number of social problems as "very important," "important," "fairly unimportant," or "completely unimportant." Not all of these problems seem relevant to the Materialist/Postmaterialist dimension, but some of them do seem to tap related concerns. For example, our respondents were asked to indicate how much importance they attached to the problem of "guaranteeing neighbor- hoods safe from crime." We would certainly expect Materialists to show greater concern with this problem than Postmaterialists—and our expectation is well-founded, as Table 11.5 indicates. Though almost everyone regards this as an important problem, a substantially higher percentage of Materialists than Postmaterialists rate it as *"very* important"; there is a consistent and monotonic pattern, with the Materialists exceeding the Postmaterialists by at least 19 percentage points in every nation and a spread of fully 40 percentage points in the most pronounced case (Germany). There is nothing surprising about this result; it merely illustrates a certain internal consistency in the attitudes of our respondents.

But now let us turn to another item that shows no obvious connection in terms of face content with the Materialist/Postmaterialist dimension. Our respondents also rated the importance of "guaranteeing equal rights for men and women." The battery of twelve items on which our values index is based contained no item that touched directly on this subject. But our hypotheses hold that the Postmaterialists *are* Postmaterialist because they have satisfied

Table 11.5: EMPHASIS ON "GUARANTEEING NEIGHBORHOODS SAFE FROM CRIME" BY VALUE TYPE: Percentage Rating the Problem as "Very Important"

	The Netherlands	Britain	United States	Germany	Austria
Materialist	86%	81%	84%	89%	89%
Mixed (Materialist)	78	77	78	83	85
Mixed (Postmaterialist)	66	72	74	72	78
Postmaterialist	51	62	60	49	69

Table 11.6: EMPHASIS ON "GUARANTEEING EQUAL RIGHTS FOR MEN AND WOMEN" BY VALUE TYPE: Percentage Rating the Problem as "Very Important"

	The Netherlands	Britain	United States	Germany	Austria
Materialist	35%	21%	32%	36%	32%
Mixed (Materialist)	40	27	35	40	39
Mixed (Postmaterialist)	47	25	41	47	33
Postmaterialist	60	38	60	61	41

the safety needs. Being relatively secure in this respect, they would presumably have less need for a hierarchical authority structure, and place more emphasis on the belonging needs. Hence, Postmaterialists might tend to view the attainment of an egalitarian social structure as relatively important. This also proves to be the case, as Table 11.6 shows. While the overall percentage that rates equal rights for women as "very important" is considerably smaller than the percentage that is concerned with safety from crime, there is a consistent tendency for Postmaterialists to give this problem a higher rating. The tendency is weakest in Austria and strongest in the United States, where Postmaterialists are nearly twice as likely as Materialists to rate equal rights for women as "very important."

Finally, let us examine responses to another social problem that implicitly pits a Materialist value against the desire for an egalitarian social structure. Our respondents rated the importance of "trying to even out the differences in wealth between people." In this case there is an additional complication. For as our hypotheses imply (and as evidence presented below confirms) the Postmaterialists tend to be recruited from the wealthier social strata: they thus have a personal stake in *avoiding* "evening out differences in wealth." On the other hand, they presumably are more concerned with maximizing a sense of community and social solidarity than the Materialists are. This might lead

Table 11.7: EMPHASIS ON "TRYING TO EVEN OUT DIFFERENCES IN WEALTH BETWEEN PEOPLE" BY VALUE TYPE: Percentage Rating the Problem as "Very Important"

	The Netherlands	Britain	United States	Germany	Austria
Materialist	28%	23%	16%	31%	39%
Mixed (Materialist)	37	36	20	40	40
Mixed (Postmaterialist)	40	37	23	40	34
Postmaterialist	52	40	30	52	40

them to give greater emphasis to egalitarian goals. Which consideration prevails? Table 11.7 gives the answer. In four of the five countries, the Postmaterialists are substantially more apt to view a more equal distribution of wealth as "very important"—by margins of almost two to one. In the fifth case (Austria) there is virtually no difference between Materialists and Post-materialists on this score. Just as the dimensional structure of the Materialist/ Postmaterialist items was relatively weak in our Austrian sample, it seems that, in a sense, the Postmaterialists are less Postmaterialist there than elsewhere. On the whole, however, we may conclude both from evidence examined here and elsewhere that our values indicator enables us to predict a respondent's attitudes on a wide range of questions.[14]

Let us put our values indicator to another kind of test. The value-change hypothesis underlying this indicator generates a number of predictions, two of which relate to one's age group or generation-unit. The first such prediction is that the young should be likelier to have Postmaterialist value priorities than older respondents, many of whom experienced economic insecurity and physical danger during their formative years. The second prediction is that the age group differences should be largest within the populations of countries that have experienced large amounts of change between the formative periods of younger and older generations. More specifically, we predicted (1) that the age-related differences should be most pronounced in Germany, which in recent decades has experienced both rapid economic growth and a shift from a past filled with repeated devastation to its present social and political stability; and (2) that these differences should be smallest in Great Britain, which already held a position of relative prosperity and military security at the start of the twentieth century, but made relatively much smaller gains between then and 1974. Prior to World War I, the German per capita income was about 60 percent of the British—then the richest national-ity in Europe. In 1974, the mean German income level was almost double that of the British.

Let us note that these are genuine predictions, published several years before the present surveys were carried out.[15] Table 11.8 presents data that enable us to test these predictions. As we see, both expectations are supported by the evidence, here as in previous tests. In each of the five countries the younger age groups are far less apt to fall into the Materialist value type and much more likely to be Postmaterialists than older respondents are. In Britain, for example, nearly half of the oldest group are Materialists, while only 2 percent can be classified as Postmaterialists; among those less than thirty years old, Materialists are less than *half* as numerous and Postmaterial-ists more than *six times* as numerous as they are among the oldest group.

The relationship between values and age is even stronger in most of the other countries. For, as we predicted, evidence of changing value priorities is

Table 11.8:   VALUE PRIORITIES BY AGE COHORT, 1974: Percentage
Falling into Materialist or Postmaterialist Category*

Ages	The Netherlands		Britain		United States		Germany		Austria	
	Mat.	Pmat.	Mat.	Pmat.	Mat.	Pmat.	Mat.	Pmat.	Mat.	Pmat.
16–29	11%	28%	21%	13%	28%	17%	32%	15%	25%	9%
30–39	18	27	27	8	38	11	50	8	41	6
40–49	21	13	25	9	49	4	56	5	44	3
50–59	26	17	29	10	45	8	64	2	40	1
60–69	23	11	40	6	51	3	65	1	52	3
70+	38	11	46	2	42	4	74	2	–	–
gamma =	.21		.18		.20		.29		.18	

*Value types are based on each respondent's choice among twelve goals. Those who chose four or more of the six "Materialist" goals among their top five choices are classified here as Materialists. Those who chose four or more of the five "Postmaterialist" goals are classified as Postmaterialists. All other combinations are classified as "Mixed" except that cases with two or more missing rankings are treated as missing data. Gammas are based on the full ten-category value priorities variable, rather than the collapsed version shown here.

strongest in West Germany and relatively weak in Great Britain. The oldest German age group shows an immense preponderance of Materialists over Postmaterialists; among the youngest cohort we find something closer to an even balance.

Direct intergenerational comparisons based on data from parent-child pairs interviewed in each of the five countries further confirms this finding. In Chapter 15 we measure the size of the "generation gap" in each country by calculating the percentage of children who are more Postmaterialist than their parents, *minus* the percentage of parents who are more Postmaterialist than their children. We find a "generation gap" that ranges from a low of only 3 percentage points in Britain, to 26 points in the United States, 28 points in Austria, 31 points in the Netherlands, and 52 points in Germany. This last figure reflects the fact that in Germany, 62 percent of the "children" (ages sixteen to twenty) were more Postmaterialist than their parents, while only 10 percent of the parents were more Postmaterialist than their children (the remaining 28 percent being at identical levels).

VALUES AND FORMATIVE AFFLUENCE

Our hypotheses imply that the younger respondents in these countries are relatively Postmaterialistic because they spent their formative years (that is, their first twenty years or so) under conditions of relatively great economic security.

The data make it clear that the predicted relationship between age and values *does* exist. But there are various other possible explanations for this finding. The most obvious one would be that there is something inherent in youth itself that encourages one to emphasize nonmaterialistic values: one might argue that people are more naive and have fewer responsibilities when they are young, so that the observed pattern simply reflects an aspect of the human life cycle, rather than an ongoing historical change.

This life cycle interpretation seems fairly plausible and may account for our findings to some extent. The fact that the relative size of the generation gap seems to reflect the rate of economic change experienced by a given nationality tends to undermine any interpretation that relied on life cycle effects exclusively, but it seems worthwhile to probe more deeply into the origins of Materialist/Postmaterialist value priorities.

If Postmaterialist values reflect "formative affluence" (our shorthand term for economic and physical security during one's formative years), we might expect to find a higher proportion of Postmaterialists among our relatively wealthy respondents. Granted, virtually all members of the younger generation have been spared some of the harrowing events experienced by virtually all members of the older age groups, such as World War II and the Great Depression; nevertheless, the impact of these events was probably milder on the wealthier than on the poorer respondents. Those who rank in the upper economic strata *today* did not necessarily rank there during their formative years, but there undoubtedly is a fairly strong correlation between one's economic level now and in the past: we would expect some tendency for wealthier respondents to be less materialistic.

Analysis of value types according to family income provides modest but reasonably clear confirmation for this expectation. Among those in the lowest income quartile, only 24 percent have predominantly Postmaterialist values (scores from "6" to "10" on our values index); among those in the highest income quartile, 33 percent are predominantly Postmaterialist, across the five nations as a whole.

A breakdown according to the occupation of the head of household shows a similar modest but consistent relationship in the expected direction, as

Table 11.9: VALUE PRIORITIES BY OCCUPATION, HEAD OF FAMILY (percentage predominantly Postmaterialist)

	The Netherlands	Britain	United States	Germany	Austria
Nonmanual	54%	32%	30%	24%	30%
Manual	46	32	29	•14	20
Farm	38	28	22	5	15

Table 11.9 demonstrates. In the Netherlands, for example, only 38 percent of those living in farm households are predominantly Postmaterialistic, as compared with 54 percent of those from families headed by a person with a nonmanual occupation. Since farm families have the lowest mean incomes and those with nonmanual occupations have the highest, the relationship is in the expected direction—not only in the Netherlands but in each of the other four countries as well—though the relationships are generally not very strong.

One's education is another indicator of economic status, and analysis of our results by education shows a similar pattern (see Table 11.10): the more highly educated are more apt to be Postmaterialists. The relationship of value type with education is somewhat stronger than the relationship with occupation. There are several possible explanations for this fact. One would be that the process of education itself tends to encourage Postmaterialist values—either because they are emphasized in the school curriculum, or because those who receive higher education are exposed to a milieu containing a higher proportion of Postmaterialists. But there is another possible interpretation: education could be a somewhat stronger predictor of value type because it gets closer to the key causal factor, which is *formative* affluence. The occupation of the head of the household is a reasonably good indicator of one's *current* economic level. But one's education is an indicator of how prosperous one's *parents* were. It is correlated with current income as well—needless to say—but, particularly in Europe, whether or not one went to secondary school is strongly influenced by the socioeconomic status of one's parents. Thus we have two related but confounding influences mingled here. Let us try to separate them.

One way in which we attempted to obtain a measure of formative affluence was based on the following question: "Would you say that, when you were growing up, your family was financially well off, fairly well off, had some financial difficulties, or was their life really difficult?"

The responses to this question provide little support for the formative affluence hypothesis. Those who report that their family was well-off when they were growing up are somewhat more likely to be Postmaterialist than those who say their family had financial difficulties, but the relationship is

Table 11.10: VALUE PRIORITIES BY RESPONDENT'S EDUCATION
(percentage predominantly Postmaterialist)

	The Netherlands	Britain	United States	Germany	Austria
Primary School	41%	25%	27%	10%	16%
Secondary	49	36	25	14	25
Higher	64	37	36	32	33

weak in all five countries surveyed. Shall we reject the hypothesis? Not necessarily. For this item provides a very "soft" indicator of formative affluence, as becomes apparent when we cross-tabulate it with more concrete indicators of one's early economic level, such as the respondent's report of his father's occupation or education. A surprisingly large number of people who appear to be from objectively lower-status backgrounds report that their families were "well-off"—while substantial numbers of people from higher-status backgrounds report that their families "had some financial difficulties." Moreover, there is little correlation between the individual's age group and his report of how "well-off" his family was—although we *know*, with certainty, that the older cohorts were brought up under far more difficult circumstances than the younger ones. The problem, of course, is that this question provides no clear yardstick by which to judge whether one's family was "well-off" or "had some financial difficulties." The categories employed here are highly subjective and, accordingly, can bend and stretch a great deal from one person to another. In a sense, even the Rockefellers encounter "some financial difficulties," though not of a kind that raises the question whether they will have enough to eat. A person's occupation or level of education, on the other hand, can be described in reasonably concrete and specific terms that mean pretty much the same thing to everybody: a lawyer is a lawyer and a carpenter is a carpenter, though whether one considers them "well-off" may depend on one's standards of reference. Consequently, we might expect to obtain a more accurate indicator of formative affluence from the respondent's answer to such questions as the following: "During your early youth—let's say when you were between ten and eighteen years old—what was your father's main occupation? What sort of work did he do?" Or "What was the highest grade of school your father completed?"

When we turn to these more concrete measures, the evidence in support of the formative affluence hypothesis becomes dramatically stronger. Our British data do not provide a measure of one's father's occupation during the respondent's early youth. We do have such a measure for each of the four other national samples, however. Let us combine this with a measure of the respondent's father's education level to produce an index of the father's socioeconomic status. If the father had a manual occupation and no more than a primary school education, he is coded as having a "lower" socioeconomic status. If the father had a nonmanual occupation and a secondary or higher education, he is coded as having "higher" socioeconomic status. Those with other occupational and educational combinations are coded as having "intermediate" socioeconomic status. The socioeconomic status of the respondent himself (or herself) was also coded following the same procedure but utilizing the occupation of the head of the respondent's *present* household and the respondent's own education.

Table 11.11: VALUE PRIORITIES BY RESPONDENT'S SOCIOECONOMIC STATUS (by respondent's father's socioeconomic status)*

Socioeconomic Status	The Netherlands		United States		Germany		Austria	
	Status of Respondent	Status of Respondent's Father	Status of Respondent	Status of Respondent's Father	Status of Respondent	Status of Respondent's Father	Status of Respondent	Status of Respondent's Father
Lower	45%	47%	25%	25%	12%	13%	18%	20%
Medium	47	53	30	30	18	22	25	28
Upper	65	60	31	38	45	36	34	42
Gamma:	.19	.16	.03	.16	.28	.30	.20	.24

NOTE: Question on father's socioeconomic status not asked in Britain.
*Percentage predominantly Postmaterialist: i.e., scoring 6 to 10 on values index.

Now let us compare the two respective indices of socioeconomic status as predictors of the respondent's value type. Table 11.11 shows the results. In the Dutch sample, 45 percent of the respondents ranking "low" in socioeconomic status selected predominantly Postmaterialist goals—as compared with 65 percent of the Dutch respondents with "high" socioeconomic status. The full cross-tabulation of values by respondent's status yields a gamma coefficient of .19. When we tabulate value type by respondent's father's status, we obtain 47 percent Postmaterialists among the "lower" status Dutch respondents and 60 percent Postmaterialists among the "upper" status Dutchmen— with a gamma coefficient of .16. Thus, in the Dutch case, the respondent's own socioeconomic status is a slightly stronger predictor of the respondent's values than is the respondent's father's socioeconomic status (or SES). This is far from surprising. Normally, one would certainly expect an individual's own current characteristics to give a far stronger explanation of his current attitudes than the status of some *other* person—particularly since our measure of father's SES is based on recall data reporting the characteristics of another individual at a time that may lie several decades in the past. It follows that our indicator of the father's SES is almost certainly contaminated by a good deal more error in measurement than our indicator of the respondent's own current SES. It is therefore rather surprising to find that in the Dutch case, one's *father's* SES is almost as good a predictor of one's values as is the individual's *own* SES. What is even more surprising, however, is the fact that in each of the other three countries for which we have data, the father's SES is a *stronger* predictor of the respondent's values than is the respondent's own SES. This is an unusual and remarkable finding—and it confirms previous results based on 1971 data.[16] It tends to support the conclusion that one's values reflect the conditions experienced during one's formative years—perhaps several decades ago—at least as much, if not more, than one's recent experiences.

We find significant linkages between indicators of formative economic security and value types—and a crucial part of these linkages seems to reflect events that took place in the fairly distant past. As we hypothesized, changes in the degree of affluence experienced during one's *formative* years may account for the rising proportion of Postmaterialists among the younger age groups.

VALUES AND AFFLUENCE: AGGREGATE ANALYSES

The formative affluence hypotheses deal with intergenerational value change, and, ultimately, the only conclusive way to demonstrate that this type of change is taking place would be by measuring these publics' value priorities at a series of points spread across several decades. We do not, of course, dispose of such data but, as indicated earlier, we do have access to a series of relevant surveys carried out from early 1970 through late 1976. These surveys, most of which were sponsored by the European Communities, employed a four-item battery of value priorities questions identical to the first set of four items included in our 1974 surveys. With this modest battery it is possible to construct an index of Materialist/Postmaterialist value priorities that correlates strongly with the index described in this chapter. Two of the four items in this set have Materialist polarity, while the other two are Postmaterialist. Accordingly, our four-item index classes as "Materialists" those whose top two choices are both Materialist items; conversely, those whose top two choices are Postmaterialist items are categorized as "Postmaterialists"; and those who give top priority to one Materialist and one Postmaterialist item are coded as "Mixed."

At the present writing, this four-item index had been employed in representative national surveys carried out in thirteen different nations at a number of different time points; data from a grand total of thirty-eight national samples were available for analysis.[17] We propose to draw on this vast body of data in order to gain a cross-temporal and cross-national perspective that is particularly valuable for present purposes.

Table 11.12 summarizes the distribution of value types across the entire set of thirty-eight national surveys. Only the percentages falling into the two "pure" polar types are shown in this table (if one wishes to ascertain the percentage falling into the "Mixed" category, one can simply subtract these figures from 100). Since the basis of this simpler four-item values index is also available in our 1974 surveys, these results are included in Table 11.12.

One of the first expectations one would bring to this array of data is that the richer nations would show a higher proportion of Postmaterialists (and a lower proportion of Materialists) than poorer nations. Is this true?

As a first step in providing an answer, in Table 11.12 we have ranked the thirteen nations according to the ratio of Materialists to Postmaterialists. We combine data from several different years in doing so. We will examine changes across time presently but, for a first approximation, it seems justifiable to collapse results from a period of a mere six years or so. Our hypotheses imply that we are dealing with *intergenerational* value change. If they are correct, the true levels should not vary greatly over a relatively brief period. As we see, Materialists outnumber the Postmaterialists in every case, but there is a wide range of cross-national variance: at one extreme (Sweden), the former outnumber the latter by less than two to one; at the other extreme (Japan), we find a ratio of more than nine to one.

It is interesting to note that Sweden ranks in first place as the most Postmaterialist country for which we have data. For Sweden ranks above the

Table 11.12: DISTRIBUTION OF VALUE TYPES, 1970-1976 (polar types, based on original four-item values index)

	1970		1971-1972		1973		1974		1976		Mean		Ratio M:P–M
	Mat.	P–M	Mat.	P–M	Mat.	P–M	Mat.	P–M	Mat.	P–M	Mat.	PM	
Sweden	31%	13%	31%	15%	25%	14%	—	—	31%	17%	31%	17%	1.83
Belgium	25	12	35	10	35	10	—	—	30	14	29	14	2.07
United States[a]	30	17	36	9	31	13	27%	14%	—	—	31	12	2.65
The Netherlands	—	—	34	11	31	13	26	17	32	14	31	11	2.82
Switzerland[b]	—	—	34	11	35	12	—	—	—	—	34	11	3.09
France	37	11	44	11	32	8	—	—	41	12	39	12	3.25
Britain	36	8	—	—	32	8	24	10	27	8	32	9	3.56
Italy	33	12	46	8	40	9	—	—	41	11	40	10	4.00
Germany	42	10	44	10	42	8	52	9	41	11	42	10	4.20
Denmark	—	—	—	—	42	7	—	—	37	10	40	9	4.44
Ireland	—	—	—	—	36	8	—	—	47	6	42	7	6.00
Austria	—	—	—	—	—	—	40	6	—	—	40	6	6.66
Japan[c]	—	—	46	5	—	—	—	—	—	—	46.5	5	9.20

a. The first two American surveys shown were actually carried out in May 1972 and December 1972.
b. The Swiss survey was carried out in the first half of 1972.
c. The Japanese survey was carried out in the spring of 1972.

United States in this respect although she ranked second in per capita income in 1950 and only reached economic parity with the United States in the 1970s. This fact tends to support the interpretation that not sheer wealth per se but rather a sense of economic and physical *security* is the most crucial precondition for a Postmaterialist outlook. It seems possible that Sweden's long-established and advanced social welfare policies may have contributed to a relatively widespread sense of economic security—while American social institutions were somewhat less conducive to a sense of security, even at higher absolute levels of income.

Leaving such detailed comparisons aside, however, our basic question is: do the more affluent nations show relatively higher proportions of Post-materialists? Yes. Even if by "more affluent" we simply use the cross-national rankings based on gross national product per capita *when the surveys were carried out,* there is a fairly clear tendency for the richer nations to be less Materialist.

But is the ranking according to *current* economic level the appropriate test of our hypothesis? Clearly, the answer is no. For the formative affluence hypothesis holds that a given individual's values are most heavily shaped by the level of economic security experienced during his preadult years. For the average member of an adult national sample, this would refer to the economic conditions prevailing twenty-five years or more before the survey was carried out. Accordingly, we would expect the distribution of value types in given nations to reflect their relative economic levels two or three decades *earlier.*

When we use the national rank orderings in gross national product per capita from 1950, 1955, 1960, 1965, 1970, and 1975 to predict the ratio of Postmaterialists to Materialists shown in Table 11.12, we find that the rank ordering for 1950 provides the best prediction of the value distributions twenty to twenty-six years later.[18] The data for 1955 provide the second best explanation; the rankings from the 1960s come next; and the data from 1975 provide the weakest explanation of all. We find here a phenomenon that is strikingly similar to one we found at the individual level: in both cases, relative affluence is linked with the presence of Postmaterialist values; but there is a time lag of approximately one generation between economic changes and their maximum impact on the prevailing values of an adult national sample.

Figure 11.3 depicts the relationship between the ratio of Materialist to Postmaterialist values in given nations in 1970 to 1976, and their economic levels in 1950. As is evident, there are a number of deviant cases. Belgium, the Netherlands, and Italy are more Postmaterialist than we would expect on the basis of prior economic levels alone, while Denmark and the United States are less so. Nevertheless, the overall fit is very good. Seven of the thirteen nations are located either exactly on the regression line or within one rank of it. The

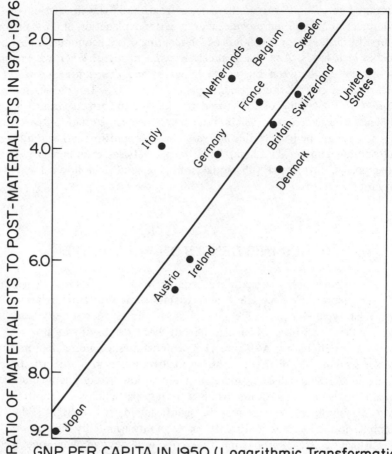

Figure 11.3: DISTRIBUTION OF VALVE TYPES BY ECONOMIC LEVEL (20 to 26 years before surveys)

correlation between our values indicator and each country's per capita gross national product in 1950 in constant dollars is .67—significant at the .018 level. On the whole, the empirical results come remarkably close to theoretical expectations.

Nevertheless, the fit between economic level and value type is capable of further improvement. For our theoretical framework argues that a shift toward Postmaterialist values occurs because economic gains reach a point of diminishing marginal utility for those whose basic value orientations are being formed.

As Dalton suggests, Postmaterialist values "increase rapidly as basic economic needs are met, and then more slowly as affluence approaches a saturation level."[19] If this is the case, a logarithmic transformation of our economic variable should provide an even better explanation of cross-national value distributions, for it will reflect the tapering off of economic impact as it reaches high levels. And this is precisely what happens. When we calculate the correlation between our values indicator and the *natural logarithm* of each nation's gross national product per capita in 1950. This correlation rises from its former value of .67 (based on the untransformed Gross National Product) to a remarkable .83—in other words, we can explain 69 percent of the variance on the basis of this one variable. This confirms earlier findings by Dalton using another data base:[20] the linkage between economic growth and value change involves a substantial time lag, and it follows a curve of diminishing returns.

OTHER INFLUENCES ON VALUE TYPE

Two variables play the central roles in our theoretical framework: age and affluence. Nevertheless, certain other variables show substantial relationships with value type, and it may be appropriate to discuss them briefly here. The first of these variables, which had already been dealt with in a variety of contexts, is nationality. As Figure 11.3 demonstrates, economic factors alone do not account for all of the cross-national variation in the distribution of values on the Materialist/Postmaterialist dimension. A considerable amount remains to be explained, and while it is not particularly relevant to our present analytic interests, it may be significant in its own right. Why, for example, do the Belgians consistently show an unwarrantedly high proportion of Postmaterialists—a proportion that goes well beyond what one would expect on the basis of their economic position alone? Is it due to problems of imperfect equivalence of the questions from one language to another? Perhaps. This type of question raises epistemological issues that are extremely difficult to resolve.

One can, of course, attribute it to the Belgian national character, or (more fashionably) to the Belgian political culture—but this, of course, is no explanation at all until one provides further information concerning *why* Belgium's historical heritage or cultural or social or political institutions lead to this result. What we have said of the Belgians applies, in large part, to the Dutch as well. Ironically enough, popular stereotypes of both the Dutch and the Belgians depict them as thrifty and narrowly Materialistic, among other things. Our data accord rather poorly with this image. It seems neither necessary nor appropriate to provide an explanation for such cross-national deviant cases here; we simply call attention to their existence and potential significance.

Table 11.13: VALUE PRIORITIES BY VOTE, LAST ELECTION
(percentage predominantly Postmaterialist)

Voted for:	The Netherlands	Britain	United States	Germany	Austria
"Left" parties*	63%	35%	37%	21%	24%
"Center" parties	64	38	–	19	16
"Right" parties	37	26	22	11	21
Gamma:	−.40	−.23	−.31	−.31	−.11

*The parties of the "Left" are: Netherlands − Socialists, Radicals, Communists, Democrats, 1966 and Pacifist Socialists; Britain − Labour; United States − Democrats; Germany − Social Democrats and Communists; Austria − Socialists, Communists and MLPO. The "Center" includes: Netherlands − Democratic Socialists, 1970; Britain − Liberals and Nationalists; Germany − Free Democrats; Austria − FPO, DFP, and EFP.

Another variable that shows strong relationships with value type is one's political party preference. As Table 11.13 shows, in each of our five countries those who prefer the parties of the Left are more apt to be Postmaterialists than those who prefer the Right. We do have an explanation for this finding: we regard it as an *effect* of holding given value priorities, rather than a cause. For the reasons set forth earlier in this chapter, within the current sociopolitical context Postmaterialists are likelier to desire major social changes than are Materialists—and insofar as the parties of the Left are likelier to favor the desired changes (which, of course, is not always the case) Postmaterialists tend to support the Left.

This finding is anything but obvious—indeed, it runs directly counter to traditional expectations, for Postmaterialists tend to come from the middle and upper socioeconomic strata—the traditional base of support for the *Right*. In *spite* of these traditional alignments, Postmaterialists tend to support the Left—a fact which clearly is more compatible with the view that they support the Left because they are Postmaterialists, rather than the other way around. We will return to this topic with additional evidence in Chapter 12, in our discussion of the consequences of holding given values.

Religion also has interesting linkages with value type. As we see in Table 11.14, those who profess no religion are markedly more Postmaterialist than those who do—but, apart from this, Postmaterialism seems to increase slightly with more frequent church attendance. Union membership and sex are also linked with value type: as Table 11.14 demonstrates, union members are more apt to have Postmaterialistic priorities than nonmembers, and men are somewhat more Postmaterialistic than women. Neither of the latter variables retains much independent association with value type, however, when we control for other factors in multivariate analyses (not shown here). These relationships are interesting and a description of the Materialist and Post-

Table 11.14: VALUE PRIORITIES BY VARIOUS SOCIAL BACKGROUND VARIABLES (percentage predominantly Postmaterialist)

	The Netherlands	Britain	United States	Germany	Austria
I. By Church Attendance					
Attend every week	42%	31%	26%	17%	21%
Attend almost every week	42	35	30	11	19
Attend once or twice. monthly	53	33	30	11	20
Attend a few times yearly	40	30	28	14	22
Never attend	45	34	32	27	31
No religion	66	57	58	15	32
II. By Union Membership					
Respondent is union member	54	35	30	22	26
Respondent is not union member	46	31	29	16	22
III. By Sex					
Male	50	35	29	21	28
Female	49	30	30	14	19

materialist value types would be incomplete without noting them; but, unlike the special case of partisan preferences, they are not of central theoretical significance and do not show particularly strong empirical relationships with the value priorities of Western publics.

CHANGES IN THE DISTRIBUTION OF VALUE TYPES ACROSS TIME

We will close this chapter by considering a topic we have neglected so far, but one that has particularly significant implications: changes in the distribution of value types over time. In this discussion we will focus primarily on data from the six nations in which our original four-item values index has been administered across a relatively broad time span—to be specific, as early as 1970 and as recently as late 1976. These surveys provide the only data base in which measures of Materialist/Postmaterialist value priorities are available over a reasonably lengthy period; furthermore, these data are particularly interesting because a major recession took place during this period.

Early 1970 was a period of high prosperity and full employment throughout Western Europe. There had been almost unbroken economic expansion for two decades. The years 1971-1975 were a period of exceptionally severe inflation; in 1973, prices were rising at rates nearly four times as high as during the 1960s. Following the 1973 oil embargo, a major recession occurred. Real income declined, unemployment rose sharply, and economic growth came to a halt. These factors clearly had an impact on the attitudes of Western publics. In December of each year, a national sample of the German public is asked, "Is it with hopes or with fears that you enter the New Year?" In December 1969, just before our first survey, confidence was near an all-time high: 63 percent felt hopeful. There was a marked deterioration of confidence in subsequent years. By December 1973, only 30 percent of those sampled expressed hope; confidence among the German public was at its lowest point since 1950.[21] In early 1974, American consumer confidence also reached the lowest level ever recorded.[22] This collapse of confidence was widespread. In 1974, 84 percent of the Italian public felt that the economic situation had become worse during the previous year, while only five percent felt it had improved. The outlook was almost equally gloomy in the Netherlands, Belgium, and France.[23]

If such conditions persisted for long, we would expect them to reshape the priorities of Western publics in a Materialist direction. But the question is, "*How* long?" If our items really do tap an individual's basic value priorities, they should be reasonably resistant to short-term forces.

Let us examine changes in the distribution of value types in the six countries for which we have data from as early as 1970 (see Table 11.15). There is no sign of a dramatic decline in the distribution of Postmaterialists from 1970 to 1976: it shows a slight decrease in Italy and the Netherlands, no change in Britain and Belgium, and a slight increase in Germany and France. Four of the six nations show at least small increases in the Materialist percentage, however. The net change is in the direction one would expect under conditions of economic insecurity, but compared with the calamitous shifts in consumer confidence observed during this period it seems almost incredibly small.

One of our two key hypotheses holds that younger respondents are relatively malleable. Accordingly, we would expect them to show more

Table 11.15: CHANGES OVER TIME IN DISTRIBUTION OF VALUE TYPES* (based on four-item index used in Feb./March 1970, Sept./Oct. 1973, and Nov. 1976)

	Britain			Germany			France			Italy			Belgium			The Netherlands		
	1970	1973	1976	1970	1973	1976	1970	1973	1976	1970	1973	1976	1970	1973	1976	1970	1973	1976
Materialist	36%	32%	37%	43%	42%	41%	38%	35%	41%	35%	40%	41%	32%	25%	30%	30%	31%	32%
Postmaterialist	8	8	8	10	8	11	11	12	12	13	9	11	14	14	14	17	13	14

*Figures for 1970 are from "The Silent Revolution in Europe," *American Political Science Review* (December 1971), p. 995; 1973 and 1976 figures are from European Community surveys.

change than older groups. Table 11.16 enables us to determine if this was actually the case. This table is based on combined results from the six surveys carried out at each time point; thus the percentage shown for given age groups in given years is based on about a thousand cases and generally a good deal more. This is important: since the observed changes over time are small, and real change might be swamped by normal sampling error when dealing with small percentage bases.

Among the six nations as a whole, the *overall* distribution of value types was virtually unchanged from 1970 to 1976. But this net result conceals two underlying processes that largely offset each other: (1) the youngest category became noticeably more Materialist and less Postmaterialist. In 1970, 20 percent of the youngest group were Materialists; this figure rose to 25 percent by 1976. Conversely, in 1970, 24 percent of the youngest group were Postmaterialists; this figure fell to 20 percent in 1976. Thus there was a net shift toward Materialism of 9 percentage points. This is the largest shift found among any age group. As hypothesized, the young seem most affected by current conditions. (2) The *next* youngest category moved in the *opposite* direction! Originally composed entirely of people born before 1945, population replacement brought large numbers of people from the postwar generation into its ranks as time went by. Although these people themselves became somewhat more Materialist as they went through the recession, their cohort was so much *less* Materialist than the one they replaced that the process of population replacement more than offset the impact of the recession on this age category: it shows a net shift of five points toward the *Post*materialist pole. The four older groups were relatively unchanged by the recession. Figure 11.4 shows the changes from 1970 to 1976 in graphic form. As a glance at this graph reveals, the largest gap between age groups in 1970 was the one between the two youngest categories. We attributed this gap to

Table 11.16: VALUE SHIFTS FROM 1970-1976

Ages	1970		1973		1976	
	Mat.	Postmat.	Mat.	Postmat.	Mat.	Postmat.
15–24	20%	24%	21%	20%	25%	20%
25–34	31	13	28	13	29	16
35–44	35	12	35	9	35	11
45–54	36	9	39	7	39	8
55–64	45	7	43	6	47	6
65 and over	48	3	45	4	52	5
Total:	35	12	34	10	37	12

NOTE: Combined results from the six European nations are shown in Table 11.15.

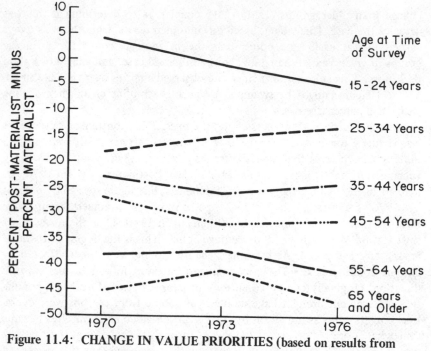

Figure 11.4: CHANGE IN VALUE PRIORITIES (based on results from combined six-nation samples)

whether one was born before or after 1945, viewing World War II as a major watershed in the formative experiences of Western publics.

But, as we noted, this gap could also be interpreted as a reflection of transitions in the human life cycle: in 1970, those born in 1945 were in their mid-twenties—the age at which many people marry, start families, begin their permanent occupations, and otherwise "settle down." Conceivably, such events might cause them to become more Materialist.

This life cycle interpretation does not fare very well in longitudinal perspective, however. For by 1976, those who were born in 1945 became thirty-one years old. And interestingly enough, in 1976 the gap between the two youngest groups had dwindled to only eight points. The largest gap had followed the postwar generation into their early thirties and now lay between the second and *third* youngest groups. In order to uphold a life cycle interpretation, one would need to argue that the process of "settling down" now took place several years later in 1976 than it did in 1970. An ingenious person could probably think up reasons why the life cycle had suddenly shifted by several years, but the credibility of such an effort would be difficult to uphold. The youngest group did, indeed, become significantly more Materialist during the Recession years—a fact that by itself might be attributed to either the impact of short-term forces, or to life-cycle processes. But the next youngest group moved in exactly the *opposite* direction—it became *less* Materialist, running contrary to life cycle expectations. The remaining groups shared little or no net change. Clearly, a life cycle interpretation alone does not seem capable of explaining this pattern.

The implications of these findings are important. First, it seems significant that the overall distribution of Postmaterialists was not significantly diminished by the worst recession since the 1930s. Our value types seem reasonably stable in the aggregate. Given age cohorts did become more Materialist, but the net impact of the Recession was largely offset by countervailing processes of population replacement. With a revival of prosperity, it would seem reasonable to anticipate growth in the number of Postmaterialists.

Second, we have seen evidence that the heavy concentration of Postmaterialists among the younger cohorts reflects one's early experiences and is—at least in important part—a matter of generational chance, rather than a life cycle phenomenon. If, as we hypothesize, Postmaterialist values lead to unconventional forms of political action, it suggests that the age-linked character of this behavior may also reflect generational change: the potential for unconventional protest may become more widespread with gradual population replacement. We will examine these possibilities in the following chapter.

NOTES

1. Based on Agency for International Development estimates.

2. For a more detailed presentation of this hypothesis and a mass of supporting evidence not presented here, see Ronald Inglehart, *The Silent Revolution: Changing Values and Political Styles Among Western Publics,* Princeton: Princeton University Press, 1977.

3. See Abraham H. Maslow, *Motivation and Personality,* New York: Harpers & Row, 1954. Other investigations that have applied Maslow's work to political analysis include: James C. Davies, *Human Nature and Politics,* New York: John Wiley, 1963; Robert E. Lane, *Political Thinking and Consciousness,* Chicago: Markham, 1970; Jeanne M. Knutson, *The Human Basis of the Polity,* Chicago: Aldine, 1972.

4. See Marx and Engels, "The German Ideology," in Lewis Feuer (ed.), *Marx and Engels; Basic Writings,* Garden City: Anchor, 1959, p. 249.

5. See Carlo Tullio-Altan, *I valori difficili: inchiesta sulle tendenze ideologiche e politiche dei giovani in Itulia,* Milan. Bompani, 1974.

6. See Harold D. Lasswell, *Psychopathology and Politics,* New York: Viking, 1960.

7. See Knutson, 1972.

8. Mark Abrams, "Subjective Social Indicators," *Social Trends,* 4 (1973).

9. These surveys have been carried out under the direction of Jacques-Rene Rabier, special advisor to the Commission of the European Communities, with fieldwork executed by the affiliates of the Gallup chain in most cases; in Belgium and Luxem-

bourg, the Brussels branch of International Research Associates was responsible for field work. For details on each of the respective surveys, see Rabier's *Euro-Barometre* reports, published twice yearly by the Commission of the European Community in Brussels.

10. See Maslow, 1954.

11. As noted above, these surveys were carried out under the direction of Jacques-Rene Rabier. Fieldwork took place in September and October 1973; the survey organizations and number of interviews for the respective countries were as follows: France, IFOP, N = 2227; Belgium, INRA, N = 1266; The Netherlands, Nederlandse Stichting voor Statistiek, N = 1464; Germany, Gesellschaft für Marktforschung, N = 1957; Italy, DOXA, N = 1909; Luxembourg, INRA, N = 330; Denmark, Gallup Markedsanalyse, N = 1200; Ireland, Irish Marketing Surveys, N = 1199; Great Britain, Social Surveys, Ltd., N = 1933. I wish to thank Jacques-Rene Rabier for enlisting my participation in the design of these surveys and for making the data available. Interested scholars can obtain data from all of the European Community surveys from the Inter-university Consortium for Political and Social Research at the University of Michigan or from BASS, University of Louvain. -

12. See Milton Rokeach, *Beliefs, Attitudes, and Values: A Theory of Organization and Change,* San Francisco: Jossey-Bass, 1968.

13. See Inglehart, *The Silent Revolution,* chapter 2.

14. Ibid., chapters 2, 7, 8, 12.

15. See Inglehart, "The Silent Revolution in Europe: Intergenerational Change in Post-Industrial Societies," *American Political Science Review,* 65 (December 1971), pp. 991-1017.

16. See Inglehart, *The Silent Revolution,* chapter 3.

17. Except as noted below, these data are from the surveys carried out in 1974 in the five nations that this book focuses upon, and (for other years) from the European Community surveys directed by Jacques-Rene Rabier. The additional American data are from a Survey Research Center Economic Behavior survey carried out in May 1972 and described in Burkhard Strumpel (ed.), *Economic Means for Human Needs,* Ann Arbor, Mich.: Institute for Social Research, 1976, chapter 1; from the Center for Political Studies Presidential Election Survey; from a survey sponsored by the European Community Information Service and carried out by the Gallup Organization in spring 1973. The Swiss data are from a survey carried out by the University of Geneva and the University of Zurich; see Dusan Sidjanski et al., *Les Suisses et la Politique,* Berne: Lang, 1975. Japanese data are from Joji Watanuki, *Japanese Politics: Changes, Continuities and Unknowns,* Tokyo: Sophia University Institute of International Relations, 1973. The Swedish data are from Hans L. Zetterberg, *Arbeta, Livsstil Och Motivation,* Stockholm: Arbetsgivareforeningen, 1977, p. 19.

18. Time series data on gross national product per capita for 1950-1965 are from Charles L. Taylor and Michael C. Hudson, *World Handbook of Political and Social Indicators, II,* New Haven, Conn.: Yale University Press, 1971. Japanese data for 1950 were not available, so we extrapolated backward from the figures for 1955, 1960, and 1965, obtaining an estimated per capita GNP of $250 for 1950.

19. See Russell J. Dalton, "Was There a Revolution? A Note on Generational Versus Life Cycle Explanations of Value Differences," *Comparative Political Studies,* 9 (January 1977), p. 468.

20. Ibid.

21. Institut fur Demoskopie, annual greeting card (Allensbach, December 1973).

22. See *ISR Newsletter,* 2 (Summer 1974), p. 2.

23. See Commission of the European Communities, "Information Memo: Results of the Sixth Survey on Consumers' Views of the Economic Situation" (Brussels: April 1974).

Chapter 12

POLITICAL ACTION

The Impact of Values, Cognitive Level, and Social Background

RONALD INGLEHART

INTRODUCTION

In the preceding chapter we argued that the value priorities of Materialists and Postmaterialists predispose them toward distinctive rates and types of political action. In this chapter we will analyze empirical evidence concerning whether and to what extent this is true. In order to do so, we must examine the impact of values in the context of certain cognitive and social background characteristics that also are related to political action. For as has been shown in chapters 8 and 9, relatively high levels of ideological cognition and awareness seem conducive to *both* conventional and unconventional forms of political action. Moreover, as has been pointed out earlier, the Reformists and Activists are characterized by very different mean ages and educational levels from the Conformists and Inactives. We know that Postmaterialists are younger, more affluent, more educated—and, no doubt, have higher levels of Left-Right cognition—than Materialists. Consequently, any attempt to assess the impact of values on political action must sort out the effects of these related variables. As one might expect, the relationships are complex and vary both cross-nationally and according to the type of political action under consideration. Nevertheless there is a coherent pattern which, we believe, can best be interpreted on the basis of the two following hypotheses: (1) conventional forms of political participation are primarily shaped by cognitive and status-related variables; (2) unconventional political participation and repression potential are more heavily influenced by the individual's age and value priorities. Thus the cognitive and evaluative factors that have been discussed in the past several chapters play complementary roles; each contributes to shaping one's propensity for political action but each plays the dominant role in certain types of action and a secondary role in other types of action. Figure 12.1 depicts these relationships.

The upper half of this figure deals with unconventional protest potential. It can also be taken to represent repression potential—in some respects, a

1. Protest Potential

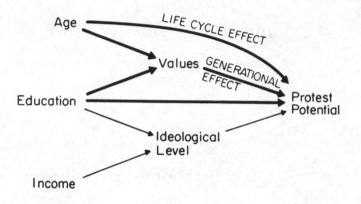

2. Conventional Political Participation

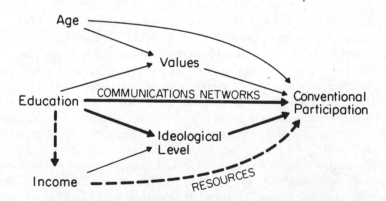

Figure 12.1: THE ROOTS OF POLITICAL ACTION: Ideal-Type Models

mirror image of protest potential. A heavy arrow is used to depict the relationship between the individual's values and his propensity for unconventional political participation, in keeping with our hypothesis that one's values play a particularly important role in shaping this type of political action. In the preceding chapter, we suggested a number of reasons why we would expect this to be the case. They might be summarized as follows:

(1) Materialists tend to be preoccupied with satisfying immediate physiological needs and their derivatives. Postmaterialists feel relatively secure about these needs and have a greater amount of psychic energy to invest in more remote concerns. This may lead to involvement in a wide variety of activities, among which politics is one possibility.

(2) As a recently emerging minority whose highest priorities tend to be slighted, Postmaterialists are apt to be relatively disaffected from the established social order.

(3) The disruption and property damage that may result from unconventional political action may seem less negative to Postmaterialists, since they threaten things they value less than Materialists do.

In short, the Postmaterialists have a larger amount of psychic energy available for politics; they are less supportive of the established social order; and, subjectively, they have less to lose from unconventional political action than Materialists. But while the first point would be conducive to higher rates of participation in *any* kind of political action, the second and third points are particularly conducive to *unconventional* political protest. We would expect Postmaterialist values to give some impetus to conventional participation but to have their greatest impact on unconventional political action.

One's age would also be especially relevant to unconventional political participation, partly because the young tend to be Postmaterialists—hence the heavy arrows from age via values to protest potential. But we might also expect the young to be relatively apt to engage in protest activities simply because the more demanding of these activities can be physically rather strenuous: disrupting traffic or occupying buildings can make demands on one's time and stamina that the young can withstand better than the old regardless of one's basic values. Thus our figure presents *two* heavy arrows from age to protest potential, a direct path reflecting the fact that, because they are at a stage in the human life cycle where their leisure time and physical vigor are at a maximum, young adults can more readily participate in protest activities than older adults; and an indirect path, reflecting the fact that at this point in history, young adults belong to a generation that is much likelier to have Postmaterialist values than older adults. Neither of these factors is as applicable to conventional forms of political action as it is to protest potential. Indeed, most of the existing literature indicates that there is a curvilinear relationship between age and conventional political participation, with the young, if anything, somewhat *less* likely to take part in conventional politics than those of middle age.[1] Accordingly, the arrows connecting age and values to conventional participation in the lower half of Figure 12.1 are relatively light, indicating that we would anticipate comparatively weak linkages.

Cognitive and status-linked variables seem likely to play predominant roles in regard to conventional participation. As we have seen in earlier chapters, the more educated show relatively high rates of both conventional and unconventional political action. But education is a complex variable. It can be an indicator of at least four different things each of which has different implications.

For one, it can be viewed as an indicator of formative affluence: in all Western societies, those who receive more education tend to come from wealthier families than those who receive less. We expect this aspect of education to be particularly important in relation to protest potential, by way of the linkage between education and value type—hence the heavy arrow between these two variables in the upper half of Figure 12.1.

Three other aspects of education seem likely to have their most significant impact on conventional participation. Education is an indicator of one's *current* affluence; the more educated tend to earn higher incomes than the less educated, and it requires little imagination to think of reasons why financial resources might give one privileged access to conventional political participation. Insofar as this is true, the impact of education on participation would be via the heavy dotted arrows shown in the bottom half of Figure 12.1. There is no reason to believe that wealth per se would be conducive to political *protest*, however, hence the absence of a corresponding path in the upper half of this figure. But education is not important solely because of its linkages with values and with income. Perhaps the most obvious consequence of education is that it increases one's cognitive skills. One learns how to deal with abstractions in general and, in doing so, to some extent, one learns how to cope with the relatively remote and abstract politics of a large, complex society: how to deal with government bureaucracies, how to express oneself in writing, and other skills and information that enhance the likelihood of having effective access to the political process. In chapters 8 and 9, we developed a measure of one's level of ideological thinking that should provide a reasonably good indicator of the presence or absence of such political skills. As we have demonstrated, the possession of these skills seems conducive to any type of political action, but they seem particularly crucial for dealing with the complex bureaucracies that are the organs of government in advanced industrial societies. Accordingly, the linkage between education and conventional participation via ideological level is indicated by a pair of heavy arrows.

In addition to formative affluence, current affluence, and cognitive skills, education is also an indicator of one's integration into distinctive communications networks: the more educated tend to move in a different milieu from the less educated. In general, their personal contacts are likely to be with individuals who are better informed and more influential, and they tend to be exposed to more extensive and more cosmopolitan mass media. On the whole, this should be conducive to higher rates of political participation. We do not have an adequate indicator of the individual's communication networks, but—insofar as the effects of the three other types of linkages are controlled for by their respective indicators—the direct path from education to political action may provide an estimate of the maximum importance of communications effects. We have sketched out a descriptive overview of the linkages anticipated between two types of political action and a group of social background variables, and indicated why and how we believe these variables are significant. Now let us turn to the empirical evidence.

VALUES AND POLITICAL ACTION

One of our central hypotheses is that Postmaterialists are apt to be relatively disaffected from the social order that prevails in most Western nations. Postmaterialists tend to be change-oriented and relatively ready to engage in unconventional political protest. Is this true empirically?

One obvious but interesting indicator of Postmaterialist support for change is the fact that they tend to vote for the political parties of the Left. But voting patterns are an ambiguous and highly situation-specific indicator of basic propensities. One might expect Postmaterialists to vote for the Left if given parties of the Left are seen as more favorable to Postmaterialist priorities than those of the Right. It is conceivable that at a given time and place a traditionally conservative party might be seen as most favorable to Postmaterialist goals; and while the former seems unlikely, one can readily envision situations in which there might be no clear-cut difference between the positions of the major parties. Accordingly, the strength of the relationship between values and reported vote in the most recent national election varies widely from country to country, ranging from a gamma coefficient of .11 in Austria to a high of .40 in the Netherlands—where a recent major realignment of political parties associated with a veritable cultural revolution seems to have made the Materialist/Postmaterialist dimension a major basis of political cleavages. Somewhat similarly, the American presidential election of 1972 presented the electorate with a choice between two candidates who represented manifestly different positions in regard to a number of relevant issues; but in most American elections the candidates tend to compete for the middle ground, minimizing the perceived distance on major issues.

Furthermore, one's values are by no means the only influence on electoral behavior; previous research has emphasized the importance of a host of other variables, among which long-term partisan loyalties (often inherited from one's parents or grandparents) have repeatedly been found to be crucial.[2] An individual's value priorities may play a minor role in electoral choice—and it is even conceivable that the linkage between values and vote is completely spurious, with the fact that one was raised in a milieu that favored the Left (for example) giving rise to a preference for the party or parties of the Left *and* for Postmaterialist values.

Fortunately, the data from the five nations surveyed in 1974 contain a variable that enables us to sort out this question of causality to some extent. Our respondents were asked what political party their father generally preferred when they were growing up. Table 12.1 shows the percentage who reported that they had voted for a party of the Left in the most recent national election according to value types, controlling for paternal party preference.[3] As the data demonstrate, there is a disproportionate tendency—frequently a strong one—for those Postmaterialists who were raised in a family that supported the Right to shift their own vote to the Left. In the Netherlands, for example, among those whose fathers supported the Right, only 16 percent of the Materialists voted for the Left in the most recent elections, but fully 55 percent of the Postmaterialists did so. In Britain, the figures are 11 percent among the Materialists and 37 percent among the Postmaterialists; in the United States, they are 14 percent and 46 percent, respectively. A similar pattern appears in Germany and Austria: those with Postmaterialist values are relatively apt to shift to the Left despite the conservative impact of family background.

The converse phenomenon appears among those who were raised in families that favored parties of the Left. Although most of those who were raised in this milieu continue to support the Left themselves, defection to the Right is far more common among Materialists than among other value types.

An individual's value priorities seem to have a substantial impact on electoral behavior, even when we control for family background. And the overall relationship is in the predicted direction: Postmaterialists—despite their relatively privileged economic position—are disproportionately apt to shift to the Left. But the pattern is highly variable from one national setting to another, reflecting the fact that the positions taken by given candidates and parties at given times can drastically affect the relevance of Materialist or Postmaterialist values. Interesting though it is, voting behavior can provide only an indirect and imperfect test of our hypothesis that Postmaterialists

Table 12.1: **VOTE IN LAST ELECTION BY VALUE TYPE,
CONTROLLING FOR POLITICAL PREFERENCE OF
RESPONDENT'S FATHER (percentage of respondents
who voted for the left)**

	During Respondent's Youth, Respondent's Father Voted for Party of the:			
	Left		Right	
1. *The Netherlands*				
Materialist	70%	(30)	16%	(93)
Mixed (Materialist)	78	(40)	19	(163)
Mixed (Postmaterialist)	85	(48)	27	(122)
Postmaterialist	88	(59)	55	(77)
2. *Britain*				
Materialist	60	(110)	11	(105)
Mixed (Materialist)	77	(148)	20	(92)
Mixed (Postmaterialist)	81	(82)	33	(57)
Postmaterialist	59	(32)	37	(19)
3. *United States*				
Materialist	28	(232)	14	(139)
Mixed (Materialist)	41	(86)	15	(30)
Mixed (Postmaterialist)	54	(95)	12	(57)
Postmaterialist	63	(49)	46	(28)
4. *Germany*				
Materialist	69	(210)	16	(324)
Mixed (Materialist)	66	(130)	31	(121)
Mixed (Postmaterialist)	67	(49)	28	(68)
Postmaterialist	78	(32)	58	(24)
5. *Austria*				
Materialist	74	(129)	26	(179)
Mixed (Materialist)	85	(148)	22	(126)
Mixed (Postmaterialist)	77	(83)	29	(56)
Postmaterialist	64	(22)	56	(9)

tend to be less supportive than Materialists of the social and political arrangements that prevail in their societies.

Our respondents were asked to indicate where their political ideas fell on a ten-point scale ranging from "Left" to "Right." In all five nations, the Postmaterialists showed a pronounced tendency to place themselves on the Left half of this scale, while Materialists were far more likely to place themselves on the Right. Figure 12.2 illustrates this pattern for each of our five nations. Theoretically, one's self-placement on this scale should reflect

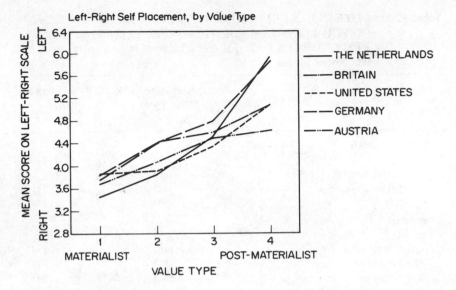

Figure 12.2: **LEFT-RIGHT SELF-PLACEMENT, BY VALUE TYPE**

one's underlying ideological position in a more direct and less situation-bound fashion than would be true of the way one votes in a given election. Insofar as this is the case, our results show that Postmaterialists not only tend to support the *parties* of the Left, but also tend to take a Leftist, or change-oriented, ideological position in regard to contemporary political issues. But, unfortunately, not even this evidence is entirely unambiguous. For the labels "Left" and "Right" have been a staple part of political discourse for many decades, particularly in European politics. To some extent, identification with the "Left" undoubtedly *does* reflect an ideology of opposition to the existing sociopolitical order, which is what interests us at present. But, as Inglehart and Klingemann have demonstrated, in many European countries (particularly those with multiparty systems) the terms "Left" and "Right" have become stereotypes for specific groups of parties. Through long usage, these labels have become partly assimilated to established party loyalties that owe their origins to religious or social class ties, or to political leanings transmitted from one's parents, rather than to one's response to current issues.[4]

Insofar as Left-Right self-placement is contaminated with a party identification component, it would not necessarily be an indicator of one's attitude toward social change, or of one's potential to engage in political protest. We must try to distinguish between these two components of the Left-Right dimension, one based on long-term partisan loyalties and the other on one's attitude toward current issues. Each person interviewed in our five national samples was asked to indicate how friendly or unfriendly his feelings were toward various groups in his society (see Technical Appendix). Our objective was to develop indices of each respondent's attitudes toward the major political parties and various other groups associated with a change-oriented or establishment-oriented position on key current issues. The list of groups that were rated in each of the five nations appears in the left-hand column of Table 12.2.

In measuring our respondents' attitudes toward these groups, an important concern was to remove a general "response-set" tendency from the ratings, that is, a pronounced tendency for some individuals to give *all* groups consistently high or low ratings. For example, one respondent might consider "50" a poor rating and therefore use primarily the 50-100 range. In contrast, another might consider 50 a high rating and therefore use the 0-50 range in evaluating the various social groups. To remove this "response-set" tendency the average rating across all groups was computed for each respondent. This, presumably, was the reference standard actually used by each respondent. Each respondent's mean score was then subtracted from the rating of each group. Thus for each respondent some groups are evaluated negatively (below the respondent's average) while other groups are evaluated positively. These adjusted ratings were then used in constructing factor score indices. Factor analysis of these ratings revealed a consistent pattern, with two basic dimensions underlying responses in each of the five nations studied. As Table 12.2 indicates, there was a Left-Right partisanship factor in each country, based on ratings of the most important conservative party in that nation and the rating of the most important party on the Left side of the political spectrum. Ratings of key institutions considered to be linked with the respective political parties also have significant loadings on this factor, which simultaneously taps one's *partisan* loyalties and one's sympathies in the longstanding opposition between labor and management. In the three countries where major parties of the Right are church-related, one's rating of the clergy also loads on this factor, forming part of the cluster containing management and the more conservative political party.

The cleavages between labor and management, and between religious and secular publics, have been part of the political scene for many decades. To a large extent they seem to have merged with the traditional Left-Right (or liberal-conservative) dimension underlying Western politics, so that one's loyalties tend to lie with one set of groups or another in a predictable and by now institutionalized pattern.

But new issues and new groups have become politically salient in recent years. One's reaction to these groups forms the basis of a second major dimension of sociopolitical cleavage. One tends to sympathize with the

Table 12.2: LEFT/RIGHT PARTISANSHIP AND ESTABLISHMENT/ANTI-ESTABLISHMENT ATTITUDES (factor analysis using Varimax rotation; based on group affect scores)*

Ratings of:	The Netherlands		Britain		United States		Germany		Austria	
	Left/Right (22%)	Establ./ Anti-Est. (20%)	Left/Right (18%)	Establ./ Anti-Est. (18%)	Left/Right (14%)	Establ./ Anti-Est. (24%)	Left/Right (23%)	Establ./ Anti-Est. (19%)	Left/Right (22%)	Establ./ Anti-Est. (17%)
Left Party	.75		.80		.70		.75		.81	
Labor Unions	.66	.32	.75		.58		.64		.71	
Big Business	−.59	.31	−.54		−.37	.39	−.63		−.39	
Right Party	−.78		−.76		−.74		−.81		−.82	
Clergy	−.52	.39		.51		.58	−.67		−.64	
Police		.69		.61		.72		.76		
Civil Servants		.54		.37	.30	.46		.57		.65
Small Business	−.34			.36		.37		.48		.57
Minority Group		−.31								
Women's Liberation		−.68		−.44		−.57	.41			−.37
Student Protesters		−.45		−.70		−.76		−.71		−.71
Revolutionary Groups		−.69		−.67		−.71		−.71		−.67

*The scores on the feeling thermometer were adjusted for response set by subtracting the individual's mean rating for *all* groups from his rating of any given group. Figures in parentheses are the percentage of the total variance explained by the given factor. All loadings above .30 are shown.

women's liberation movement, student protesters, and revolutionary groups, on one hand, or with the police, civil servants, and other elements of the established social order (including the clergy, in Britain and the United States, which do not have Christian Democratic political parties), on the other. Interestingly enough, one's position on this "establishment/anti-establishment" dimension is largely unrelated to one's partisan loyalties. The two dimensions seem to reflect both a traditional Left-Right cleavage, with an infrastructure based on the polarization between labor and management, and a New Politics dimension, based on one's reaction to groups that have become politically prominent much more recently.

In the United States, the establishment/anti-establishment dimension is the more important of the two dimensions in terms of explained variance, while in the four European countries the socioeconomic Left-Right partisanship dimension is of equal or greater importance. Moreover, in the United States, one's self-placement on the ten-category Left-Right ideology scale tends to be linked with the establishment/anti-establishment dimension, while in Europe it correlates more strongly with the Left-Right partisanship dimension. As Inglehart and Klingemann suggested, in most European countries the terms "Left" and "Right" have become largely assimilated to established party loyalties (that may originally have been linked with social class), while in the United States these terms have a stronger tendency to refer to a New Politics dimension based on support or opposition to the current establishment. In the United States, while Big Business *is* linked with the Right pole of the partisanship cluster, it is *also* seen as part of the establishment cluster. Among the European countries, Big Business tends to be seen simply as part of the Right partisanship cluster—except in the Netherlands, where traditional political alignments have recently broken down in spectacular fashion. In general, crystallization of attitudes along a New Politics dimension seems most advanced in the United States and the Netherlands, and least advanced in Austria.

We have argued that the New Politics reflects, in part, the growing salience of the Materialist/Postmaterialist dimension. Accordingly, we would expect it to be more strongly correlated with our value priorities indicator than is the traditional partisan loyalties dimension, and this proves to be the case. Postmaterialists do tend to support the parties of the Left rather than those of the Right. But the varimax factor analyses shown in Table 12.2 separate out the older and newer *components* of political cleavage. Value priorities prove to be much more highly correlated with the establishment/anti-establishment dimension than with the partisan dimension: across the five nations, values explain over twice as much variance in scores on the former dimension as they do with the latter dimension. And the correlations are in the expected direction: Materialists give relatively high ratings to establishment institutions, while Postmaterialists tend to sympathize with non-establishment groups.

Figure 12.3 illustrates the relationship between value type and support or opposition to the establishment. The pattern is pronounced and consistent across the five nations: Materialists are far more supportive of the established order than Postmaterialists. Let us emphasize that this relationship cannot be attributed to the partisan predispositions of the respective value types: the dependent variable has been constructed in a manner that makes it uncorrelated with political partisanship.

Figure 12.4 shows the relationship between values and scores on the partisanship dimension. While there is some tendency for Postmaterialists to favor the Left, by comparison with Figure 12.3 the slopes are shallow and the pattern inconsistent.

Miller and Levitin have identified a set of issues that were associated with the New Politics in the United States in the early 1970s.[5] On the basis of responses to a set of twelve questions dealing with topics ranging from the rights of the accused to student protest and the use of marijuana, they were able to categorize those interviewed in the CPS 1972 election survey as "New Liberals" (those who were consistently favorable to New Politics themes), "Centrists," and a "Silent Minority" (those who were consistently hostile to the New Politics). A secondary analysis of their data further demonstrates just how strongly the New Politics reflected the presence of Materialist or Postmaterialist values—and the relative *weakness* of the linkage between these values and established party identification. To illustrate the latter point: among those classified as "Materialists" (on the basis of the original four-item values index included in the CPS survey), 38 percent of the Materialists identified with the Democratic Party, as compared with 38 percent of the Mixed types and 46 percent of the Postmaterialists—giving a total spread of only 8 percentage points between the Materialists and Postmaterialists. The

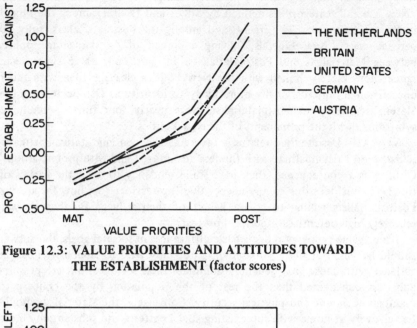

Figure 12.3: **VALUE PRIORITIES AND ATTITUDES TOWARD THE ESTABLISHMENT (factor scores)**

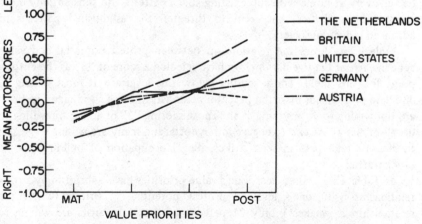

Figure 12.4: **VALUE PRIORITIES AND PARTISAN ATTITUDES**

relationship between values and orientations toward the New Politics was vastly stronger than this: among the Materialists, only 16 percent fell into the "New Liberal" category as defined by Miller and Levitin; among the Mixed types, the figure was 24 percent; and among the Postmaterialists, fully 60 percent were "New Liberals," giving a spread of 44 percentage points between Materialists and Postmaterialists. In short, our value types seem much more closely linked with the New Politics cleavage than with older ones. Though only marginally more likely to identify as Democrats than the Materialists were, the Postmaterialists were nearly four times as likely to sympathize with the proponents of the New Politics.

Very well. Despite their relatively favored socioeconomic status, Postmaterialists tend to sympathize with the less advantaged and with protest groups. Perhaps as a consequence, they have some tendency to favor the parties of the Left. But does this go any deeper than lip service? Just how far are the Postmaterialists willing to go on behalf of their values? Do they show a relatively high potential for political protest?

If our value typology reflects basic differences in societal goals, the answer should be yes. For the Postmaterialists not only tend to emphasize goals at variance with those that generally dominate their societies, but are presumably less constrained than the rest of the population by the concern to maintain economic and physical security. Conversely, the Materialists should be relatively at home with the existing social pattern, and substantially more alarmed by activities that seem to threaten the established patterns of advanced industrial society.

Table 12.3 shows the relationship between protest potential and value type in each of the five nations. We have selected a score of "3" as the cutting point for this table. Those scoring below this level are at most willing to circulate petitions or march in peaceful demonstrations; a good many of them are not willing to do anything at all. Those scoring "3" or above are willing to do all of the above *and* to engage in boycotts; and many are willing to go still farther—to take part in rent strikes, illegal occupation of buildings, or to block traffic.

As Table 12.3 makes clear, one's value priorities have a surprisingly strong relationship with one's level of protest potential. In Britain (where the relationship is weakest), only 21 percent of the Materialists are willing to engage in boycotts or go beyond them in protest against some form of perceived political injustice; among the Postmaterialists, 55 percent are willing to do so. The linkage between values and protest potential is particularly strong in the Netherlands, where we find only 27 percent of the Materialists ranking high on protest potential—as compared with 74 percent of the Postmaterialists. In all five countries for which we have data, the Postmaterialists are far readier to engage in political protest than the Materialists.

Table 12.3: PROTEST POTENTIAL BY VALUE TYPE*

	The Netherlands	Britain	United States	Germany	Austria
Materialist	27%	21%	38%	23%	17%
Mixed (Materialist)	38	30	46	30	19
Mixed (Postmaterialist)	47	33	50	43	24
Postmaterialist	74	55	72	74	48

*Percentage scoring "3" or higher on protest potential scale.

Conversely, the Materialists are much more likely to support the repression of political dissent. The repression potential scale developed for this project is based on support for actions ranging from "The courts giving severe sentences to protesters who disregard police" to a government ban on *all* public protest demonstrations. The resulting scale varies somewhat from country to country, but for purposes of Table 12.4 we dichotomize between respondents scoring "3" or above, and those scoring lower, dividing our samples into two groups of roughly equal size, with the former highly supportive of repressive policies and the latter much less so. As Table 12.4 demonstrates, Materialists tend to fall into the former group in each of the five nations and the relationship is consistently strong. In our *weakest* case (Britain), Materialists are more than twice as likely to score high on repression potential as are Postmaterialists. In the Netherlands and Germany the Materialists are respectively six times and seven times as likely to score high on repression potential as the Postmaterialists!

Presumably for the reasons suggested above, the relationship between values and conventional political participation is much weaker. Table 12.5 presents cross-tabulations comparable to those in the two preceding tables. The Postmaterialists are more active than Materialists in every country, but a

Table 12.4: REPRESSION POTENTIAL BY VALUE TYPE*

	The Netherlands	Britain	United States	Germany	Austria
Materialist	32%	56%	47%	56%	57%
Mixed (Materialist)	23	44	37	39	49
Mixed (Postmaterialist)	10	40	32	21	41
Postmaterialist	6	23	15	8	15

*Percentage scoring "3" or higher on repression potential scale.

Table 12.5: CONVENTIONAL POLITICAL PARTICIPATION BY VALUE
TYPE*

	The Netherlands	Britain	United States	Germany	Austria
Materialist	50%	40%	68%	43%	38%
Mixed (Materialist)	33	44	65	55	43
Mixed (Postmaterialist)	48	48	63	64	57
Postmaterialist	67	64	76	83	59

*Percentage scoring "2" or higher on conventional political participation scale.

really strong association between values and conventional participation is
found only in Germany, while in the United States the linkage is quite weak.

Clearly, one's value priorities have a powerful relationship with one's
orientation toward both political protest and the repression of such protest.
But, as we argued at the start of this chapter, values are only part of the
story. They are related to whether one favors protest or repression; they help
determine the *direction* in which one moves, if one acts at all. But the
presence or absence of cognitive skills has a great deal to do with whether or
not one acts.

VALUES, LEVEL OF CONCEPTUALIZATION, AND POLITICAL ACTION

To measure one's level of political skills and consciousness is no easy task.
In chapters 8, 9, and 10 we explored the extent to which our publics make
active use of an ideological mode of thought in politics, and their recognition
and understanding of an ideological mode of thought. On the basis of these
two measure, we were able to classify our respondents according to their
degree of ideological conceptualization, with high level ideologues at one
extreme and nonideological types having a complete absence of the ability (or
inclination) to generalize about politics at the other extreme. This analysis of
ideological cognition is interesting in its own right. But the "levels of
ideological conceptualization" variable also offers a promising means to help
explain the presence or absence of protest potential. For the nonideological
types, regardless of their values, seem unlikely to engage in conventional or
unconventional political action. On the other hand, those with a highly
developed ability to deal with political abstractions should be relatively likely
to engage in any form of political activity. Whether they engage in protest or
in conventional activities would depend on the relationship between their
values and the society in which they live.

Our expectation is that those who have Postmaterialist values *as well as* a high level of conceptualization will show the highest level of protest potential. Table 12.6 tests this hypothesis. It proves to have a strong empirical foundation. In the United States, for example, among Materialists who showed no understanding whatever of the political meaning of "Left" and "Right," only 31 percent rank high on protest potential; among Postmaterialists with a high level of conceptualization (those scored as high or medium on level of ideological conceptualization) fully 88 percent show a high protest potential. As Table 12.3 demonstrated, protest potential in the United States ranged from a low of 38 percent to a high of 72 percent when tabulated by value priorities alone. As subsequent analyses will demonstrate, the two variables combined explain substantially more variance than they do singly. The same is true in each of the four other countries.

Table 12.6: PROTEST POTENTIAL BY VALUE TYPE, CONTROLLING FOR LEVEL OF CONCEPTUALIZATION

| | Ideologues and Near-Ideologues | | | |
	Postmaterialist	*Mixed (pm)*	*Mixed (mat)*	*Materialist*
The Netherlands	(89)%	54%	47%	24%
Britain	*	*	46	(56)
United States	88	81	73	50
Germany	77	56	40	27
Austria	(62)	43	40	(47)

| | Mentions Groups or Sheer Affect Only | | | |
	Postmaterialist	*Mixed (pm)*	*Mixed (mat)*	*Materialist*
The Netherlands	74	52	42	27
Britain	71	47	40	27
United States	81	68	61	47
Germany	74	41	40	24
Austria	(46)	28	24	18

| | Incorrect or No Understanding of "Left" and "Right" | | | |
	Postmaterialist	*Mixed (pm)*	*Mixed (mat)*	*Materialist*
The Netherlands	49	41	31	28
Britain	44	26	25	16
United States	55	36	33	31
Germany	*	35	21	20
Austria	*	13	11	14

NOTE: Percentage scoring "3" or higher on protest potential scale
( ) indicates fewer than thirty cases.
 * indicates fewer than twenty cases.

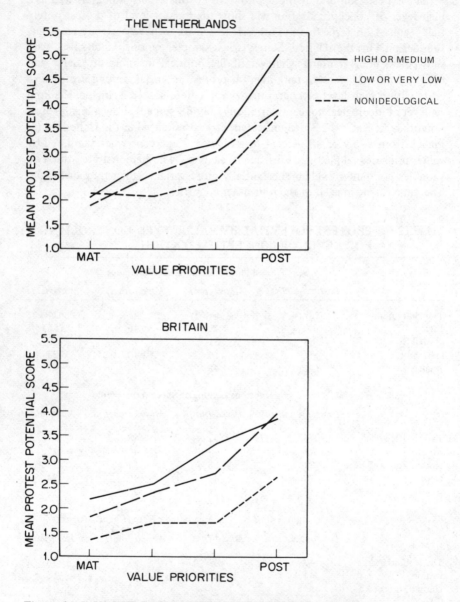

Figure 12.5: **VALUE PRIORITIES AND PROTEST POTENTIAL BY LEVELS OF CONCEPTUALIZATION**

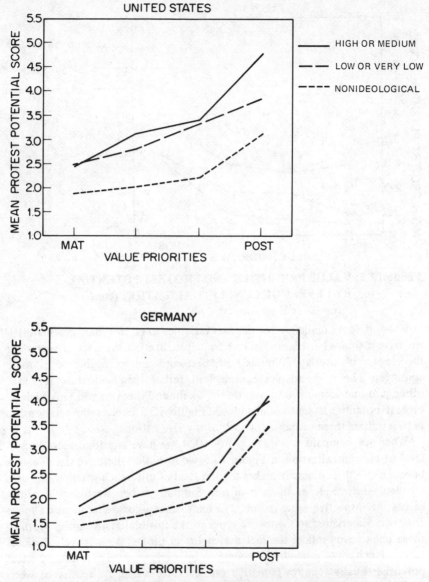

**Figure 12.5: VALUE PRIORITIES AND PROTEST POTENTIAL
BY LEVELS OF CONCEPTUALIZATION (cont.)**

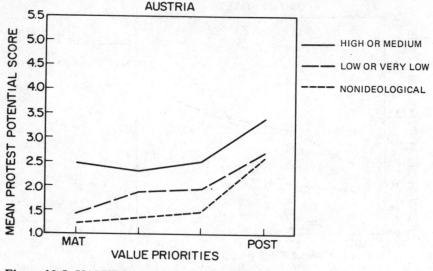

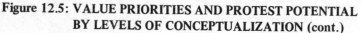

**Figure 12.5: VALUE PRIORITIES AND PROTEST POTENTIAL
BY LEVELS OF CONCEPTUALIZATION (cont.)**

There is some tendency for the two variables to go together: Postmaterialists have a somewhat higher level of conceptualization than Materialists. But the degree of overlap is modest at best and almost negligible in some countries. The two variables complement rather than substitute for each other, and their combined impact on the likelihood that one will rank high on protest potential is substantial indeed. Figure 12.5 depicts the relationship between these three variables for each of the five nations.

When we compare the three groups that we have stratified according to level of conceptualization in Figure 12.5 we note that there are sizeable gaps between the three lines: it makes a good deal of difference whether one uses an ideological mode of thought or not. Similarly, when we follow the lines across the respective value groups, the lines generally rise sharply as we move from the Materialists to the mixed types to the Postmaterialist group. Both of these phenomena reflect the fact that political protest is a relatively difficult form of behavior, generally discouraged by society. A high level of protest potential usually requires *both* that one perceive a strong disparity between one's own values and the way things are, *and* a highly developed political consciousness. Protest can conceivably occur almost anywhere—but the likelihood is strongly enhanced when both conditions are met. Thus, the mean score on our protest potential scale rises from about 3.0 to more than 4.5 as we follow

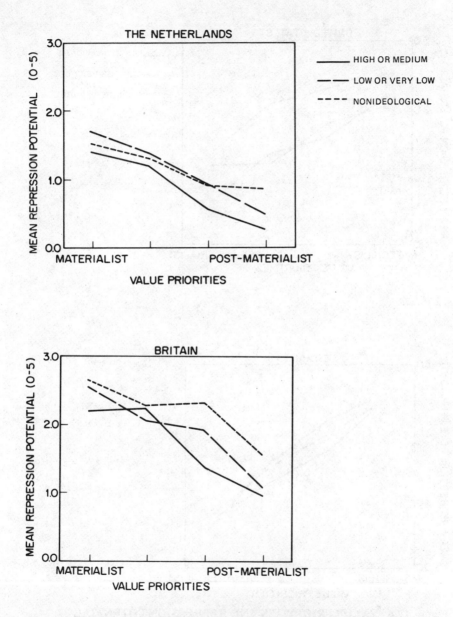

**Figure 12.6: VALUE PRIORITIES AND REPRESSION POTENTIAL
BY LEVELS OF CONCEPTUALIZATION**

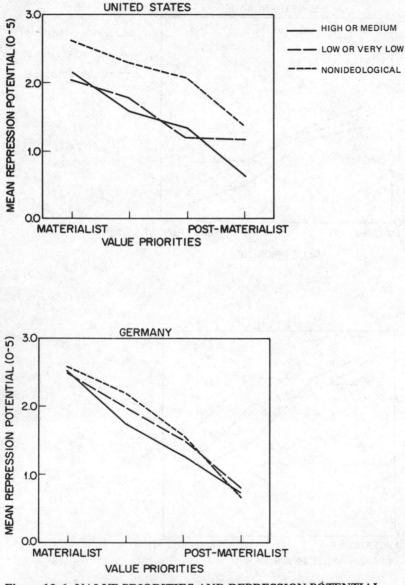

Figure 12.6: VALUE PRIORITIES AND REPRESSION POTENTIAL BY LEVELS OF CONCEPTUALIZATION (cont.)

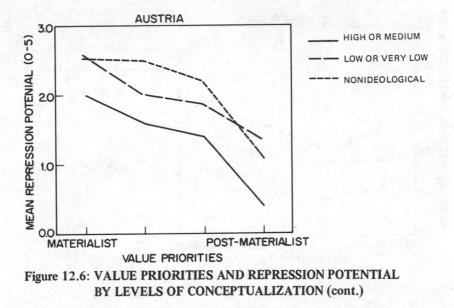

Figure 12.6: VALUE PRIORITIES AND REPRESSION POTENTIAL
BY LEVELS OF CONCEPTUALIZATION (cont.)

the category of high or medium-level ideologues from the mixed value types to the Postmaterialist value type. Similarly, among those with a low or very low level of ideological conceptualization, we witness a jump from a mean protest potential score of about 2.5 among those with mixed values, to a mean score of almost 4.0 among the group that is a step higher on both variables.

Figure 12.6 shows the relationship of values and level of conceptualization to repression potential in our five nations. These graphs are virtually a mirror image of Figure 12.5: the Materialists give far more support to repression than the Postmaterialists, and those with high or medium levels of ideological conceptualization give substantially less support than those with nonideological levels. The latter point is worth emphasizing because it is far from self-evident. One might conceivably argue that those with high ideological levels would be relatively apt to support *either* protest or repression, depending on whether they were of the Left or Right. But, as the evidence indicates, this is not the case. Respondents with high or medium levels of ideological conceptualization are significantly less likely to support the repression of political dissent than are those with nonideological levels. This is especially true of those who lean toward the Left; but even among partisans of the Right, respondents with high or medium levels tend to be less repressive than those with nonideological levels. As Putnam found to be the case with political elites, an ideological mode of thought is not necessarily conducive to

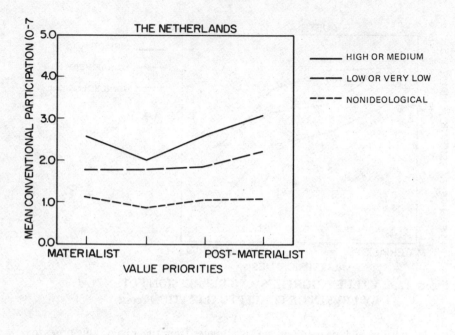

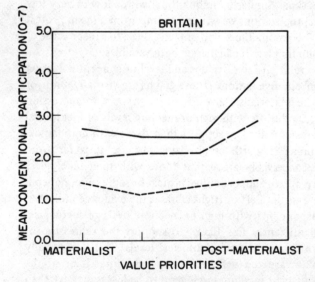

**Figure 12.7: VALUE PRIORITIES AND CONVENTIONAL
PARTICIPATION BY LEVELS OF CONCEPTUALIZATION**

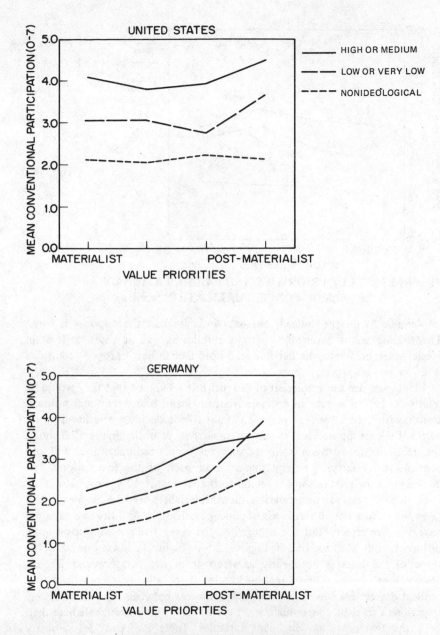

**Figure 12.7: VALUE PRIORITIES AND PARTICIPATION BY
LEVELS OF CONCEPTUALIZATION (cont.)**

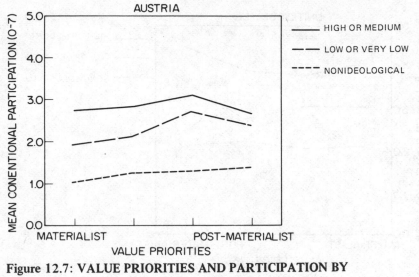

Figure 12.7: **VALUE PRIORITIES AND PARTICIPATION BY
LEVELS OF CONCEPTUALIZATION (cont.)**

intolerance of dissent—indeed, our data indicate that the *opposite* is true.[6]
The finding seems applicable to mass publics as well as elites, at least in
Western democracies (whether it would hold true in East European countries
is, of course, uncertain).

Ideologues are not intolerant of dissent. But we argued that they would be
relatively apt to engage in *both* conventional and unconventional political
action, with their value type playing a major role in deciding whether they act
within the existing political system or *against* it, or both. Figure 12.7 shows
the relationship between value type, level of conceptualization, and our
conventional political participation scale in each of the five nations. The
direction of the relationships is similar to that in Figure 12.4: Postmaterialists
show higher rates of participation than Materialists, and ideologues higher
rates than those with lower levels of conceptualization. And the two variables
have additive effects. But the *strength* of the respective relationships is quite
different from what we find in Figure 12.5 or Figure 12.6. On one hand, the
slope of the lines is not nearly as steep as in the two previous figures:
conventional political participation is related to value type, but only to a
modest degree. On the other hand, the *distances* between lines are relatively
large: one's level of conceptualization plays a more important role here than
with the two previous dependent variables. Table 12.7 provides summary
statistics to compare the strength of the relationships among these variables in
each of our five national samples. It demonstrates (1) that value type and

level of conceptualization have about equally strong relationships with protest potential; (2) that value type has the more powerful linkage with repression potential; but (3) that one's level of conceptualization generally has far more impact on conventional political participation. One's value type has a great deal to do with whether one supports or opposes the established social order. Except in Germany, it has only a modest connection with one's rate of conventional political activity. On the other hand, high levels of political skills and consciousness are highly conducive to both conventional and unconventional political activity.

MULTIVARIATE ANALYSES

We have found strong and cross-nationally consistent relationships between values, level of conceptualization, and protest potential. We were led to anticipate these relationships by hypotheses about causal connections. But the presence of these relationships does not, of course, demonstrate causality. There are a variety of alternative ways in which one could account for the existence of these relationships, most of them based on the notion of spuriousness. Thus values and protest potential might be related simply because Postmaterialists are younger and better educated than those with other value priorities. If, by controlling for age or education, or both, we eliminated the relationship between values and protest potential, we would have demonstrated the spuriousness of the latter relationship. We would then be left with the problem of explaining *why* the young and better educated are more apt to protest—and to do so is not quite as easy as it might seem at first glance. One has heard enough about student protest in recent years that it may seem intuitively obvious to assume that well-educated youth have some inherent tendency to act against the established social order, but even a brief examination of recent history makes it clear that this is simply not true. The literature of the 1950s and early 1960s takes just the *opposite* premise for granted—finding not only that university students were apolitical, conservative, and conformist during that period, but, furthermore, taking it to be intuitively obvious that this would *necessarily* be the case, since they come from economically favored backgrounds and accordingly are imbued with conservative values. To be sure, their relative youth and education would provide students with the energy and skills to be disproportionately *active*— but the *direction* of their activity would presumably be in support of the system that guarantees their economically favored position: they would rank low on protest potential but high on conventional political participation and, in some circumstances, repression potential.

Table 12.7: RELATIVE IMPACT OF VALUES AND POLITICAL SKILLS*

	Value Type	Level of Conceptualization
The Netherlands		
Protest Potential	-.34	-.28
Repression Potential	.37	.14
Conventional Participation	-.13	-.49
Britain		
Protest Potential	-.20	-.34
Repression Potential	.26	.18
Conventional Participation	-.04	-.50
United States		
Protest Potential	-.24	-.37
Repression Potential	.29	.30
Conventional Participation	-.03	-.40
Germany		
Protest Potential	-.33	-.24
Repression Potential	.39	.13
Conventional Participation	-.27	-.30
Austria		
Protest Potential	-.23	-.32
Repression Potential	.26	.20
Conventional Participation	-.16	-.42

*Cell entry is gamma. Negative sign indicates that Postmaterialists are *more* apt to protest and to take part in Conventional political activities; they are *less* supportive of Repressive activities.

It is worth remembering that the dominant mode of student activism in France, Germany, and Italy in the 1930s was Monarchist or Fascist. There are good logical grounds for assuming a *negative* connection between education and protest potential in a society completely imbued with Materalist values.

On the other hand, under contemporary circumstances, our hypotheses imply that the younger and better-educated groups should have a relatively high concentration of Postmaterialists—and evidence in chapter 10 supports this expectation. This raises *another* alternative interpretation—what might be termed the "Campus Fad" explanation of student protest: that students show relatively high levels of protest potential simply because they live in a milieu that is supportive of protest, and not because of any value differences rooted in the students themselves.

We would certainly expect social learning processes to be at work within the student subculture, as they are nearly everywhere else. There probably *is* a tendency for aspects of a Postmaterialist world view to be communicated to anyone who lives in the student milieu. But we should not overestimate the importance of this influence. Our British colleagues interviewed a supplementary sample of 286 British students drawn from twelve universities and twelve Polytechnical institutes. They find that protest potential does *not* simply reflect the fact that one lives in a student milieu. For even among this sample entirely composed of students, the individual's value priorities seem to play a crucial role, with Postmaterialists showing a high level of protest potential and Materialists showing a low level (see Table 12.8). The relatively high potential for protest among students seems to reflect the fact that they have: (1) an exceptionally high concentration of Postmaterialists and (2) relatively high cognitive levels. Protest is not something inherent in their milieu.

Let us now try to sort out the impact of one's value priorities and level of ideological thinking from the other social background variables discussed at the start of this chapter. Our hypotheses imply causal sequences that can best be analyzed by means of path analysis. Accordingly, Figure 12.8 presents a set of models of the effects of values, cognitive level, age, education, and income on protest potential and on conventional political participation in each of the five nations.[7]

The multiple correlation is shown for each model, and it may be worthwhile to preface our discussion with a comment about the amount of variance explained by the five predictors. Our models show multiple correlations ranging from .36 to .52: clearly, we have not accounted for all or even most of the variance in political action. Indeed, for one accustomed to dealing with statistical data aggregated at the national level, these would probably seem distressingly low multiple correlations. We must bear in mind that these models are based on individual-level survey data, and with this type of data

Table 12.8: **PROTEST POTENTIAL BY VALUE TYPE AMONG BRITISH STUDENTS***

Value Type:a	
Materialist	22%
Mixed	34
Postmaterialist	77

*Percentage scoring "3" or above on additive scale.

a. The originial four-item values index described in Chapter 8 was used here.

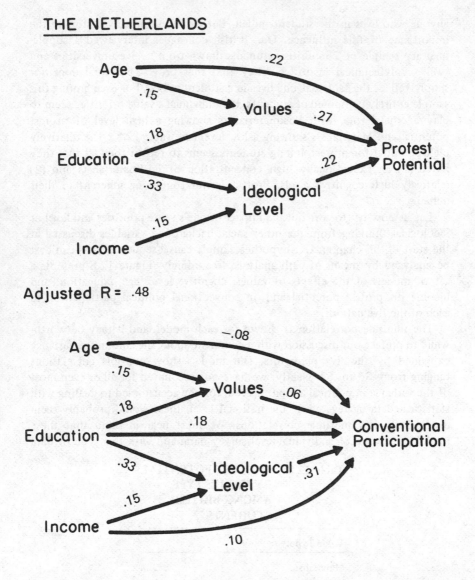

THE NETHERLANDS

Adjusted R = .48

Adjusted R = .46

Figure 12.8: PROTEST POTENTIAL AND CONVENTIONAL POLITICAL PARTICIPATION

BRITAIN

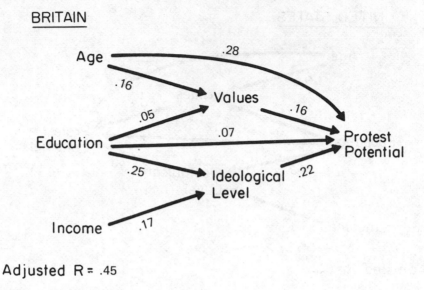

Adjusted R = .45

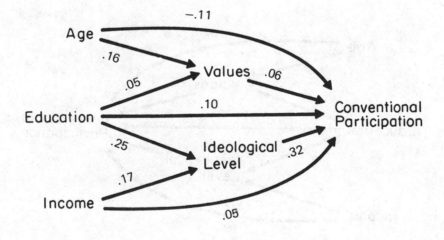

Adjusted R = .38

Figure 12.8: PROTEST POTENTIAL AND CONVENTIONAL POLITICAL PARTICIPATION (cont.)

UNITED STATES

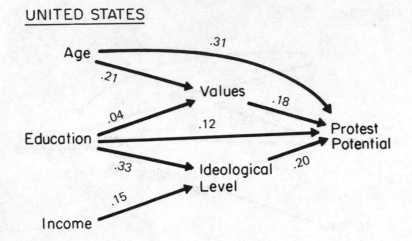

Adjusted R = .52

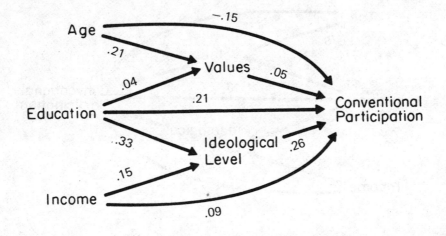

Adjusted R = .42

**Figure 12.8: PROTEST POTENTIAL AND CONVENTIONAL
POLITICAL PARTICIPATION (cont.)**

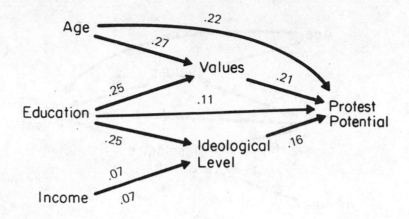

GERMANY

Adjusted R = .47

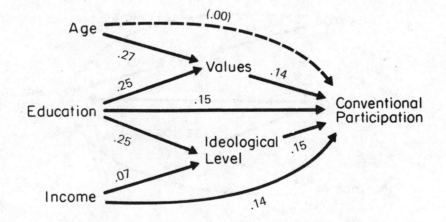

Adjusted R = .39

Figure 12.8: PROTEST POTENTIAL AND CONVENTIONAL POLITICAL PARTICIPATION (cont.)

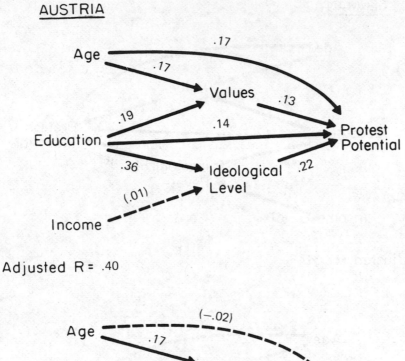

AUSTRIA

Adjusted R = .40

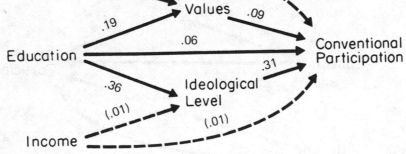

Adjusted R = .36

Figure 12.8: PROTEST POTENTIAL AND CONVENTIONAL POLITICAL PARTICIPATION (cont.)

the observed correlations are almost inevitably depressed by substantial amounts of measurement error. In aggregating to large groups, much of this error cancels out. In the preceding chapter, for example, we were able to explain 69 percent of the variance in value types with a single variable—aggregated to the nation level. At the individual level, however, one rarely explains a substantially higher proportion of the variance than has been done here unless one is examining connections between attitudes that are conceptually rather closely related. Since we have been exploring the linkages between one's propensities for action and background variables that bear no obvious relationship to the dependent variables, we view most of these multiple correlations as reasonably strong.

The overall pattern is quite similar across the five nations. In every case, one's age, value priorities, and level of ideological conceptualization have the greatest impact on protest potential; and one's level of ideological conceptualization is by far the most important factor governing Conventional Participation.

There is some cross-national variation, however. As hypothesized, age and values are the crucial factors behind protest potential in most settings, but ideological level also makes quite significant contributions; indeed, it plays the *most* important role in the Austrian case. Controlling for the effects of the other variables, values and age are of roughly equal importance: age has a direct linkage with protest potential, and one that passes from age to values to protest potential; and the Beta coefficients associated with the respective arrows to protest potential are of approximately equal strength. The direct path from age to protest potential sums up the impact of age per se, and might plausibly be interpreted as depicting the life cycle component of the age-protest relationship. The path from values to protest potential controls for life cycle effects; its strength, in a given country, indicates the degree to which Postmaterialists are disproportionately apt to engage in protest quite apart from the fact that they tend to be young. On the whole, life-cycle effects and value change seem to contribute in approximately equal measure to protest potential among Western publics. The impact of values is most pronounced in the Netherlands and Germany, while life cycle effects are strongest in the United States and Britain.

As the reader will note, the Beta coefficients between protest potential and age are positive in all five countries—reflecting the fact that the young have a greater propensity to protest. But these signs have a *negative* polarity in connection with conventional participation reflecting the fact that the young are *less* apt to engage in conventional political action. This helps explain the relatively weak linkages that we find between age and values and conventional participation. For Postmaterialists are relatively apt to engage in *both* types of political action—and they are substantially younger than those with Materialist values. Thus, the effects of age and value type reinforce each other in connection with protest potential, while they tend to cancel each other out in connection with conventional participation.

The linkage between education and political action seems to reflect the presence or absence of political *skills* above all. In regard to protest potential, ideological level—our indicator of cognitive skills—plays a major role, and in connection with conventional participation its importance is overwhelming. By contrast, the significance of education as an indicator of current affluence is small. One's current family income has virtually no impact on protest potential. Its Beta weights range from -.06 in Germany (indicating that the wealthier are slightly *less* apt to protest) to a high of .06 in Great Britain (where they have a slightly greater propensity to protest). This much is not unexpected. What is rather surprising, however, is the fact that income per se has only a modest impact on conventional participation in most settings (Germany being somewhat exceptional). Insofar as the direct linkage between education and political action can be taken to represent the effects of contacts and communications networks, one might conclude that these effects are moderately important in contributing to protest potential and rather substantial as an influence on conventional participation. As suggested earlier, cognitive and socioeconomic status-linked variables play the dominant role in shaping conventional political participation—but the advantages of a higher SES are more dependent on their linkage with greater cognitive skills than on their association with a higher income.

IMPLICATIONS

As we have seen, both life cycle and generational effects are present, particularly in connection with protest potential. The life cycle effects do not have any inherent long-term implications for political action: the normal process of population replacement would not necessarily bring any changes in mass behavior (although a gradual increase in the public's mean age would imply a slight decline in protest potential, coupled with a slight increase in conventional participation). But insofar as we are dealing with relatively fixed characteristics of a given generation, the process of population replacement *would* bring changes in mass political action. As relatively Postmaterialist younger age cohorts replace relatively Materialist ones in the adult electorate, we would anticipate a gradual rise in the public's propensity to employ "unconventional" techniques of political protest (and, of course, a change in what is conventional).

We would also anticipate a gradual but long-term increase in the Western public's capacity for conventional participation. For conventional participation is linked with educational and cognitive variables that tend to be irreversible characteristics of given adult cohorts. Insofar as higher education is simply an indicator that one is in the top 25 percent of the socioeconomic hierarchy, this would not necessarily imply long-term change. There will always be a top 25 percent, as well as a lowest quartile and two intermediate quartiles. But insofar as education indicates the presence of higher cognitive skills, it *does* imply change. For the educated and politically sophisticated will not, presumably, become less so as they mature. Even if we assume that the proportion of Western publics receiving higher education has now stopped rising, to remain permanently at its present level, the proportion of those with higher education among the younger age cohorts is so much higher than the proportion among the oldest cohorts that they are about to replace that the percentage of highly educated people in the electorate as a whole would continue to rise for at least two or three decades.

Thus there is reason to believe that the potential for both conventional and unconventional political action may be rising among Western publics. We stress the word "potential," because actual manifestations of political action are undoubtedly constrained by the institutions, events, and socioeconomic conditions of a given nation at a given time. We have made no attempt to deal with these aspects of the macropolitical context here, but sheer common sense indicates that they play a crucial role. Nevertheless, it seems safe to say that the processes of value change and of rising educational levels among Western publics seem to be increasing their *potential* for both conventional and unconventional forms of political action.

NOTES

1. See Lester Milbrath and M. Goel, *Political Participation,* Chicago: Rand McNally, 1976, chapter 5; and Norman Nie, Sidney Verba, and Jae-on Kim, "Political Participation and the Life Cycle," *Comparative Politics* 6 (April 1974), pp. 319-340; Verba and Nie, *Participation in America: Political Democracy and Social Equality,* New York: Harper & Row, 1972, chapter 9.

2. For example, see Angus Campbell et al., *The American Voter,* New York: John Wiley, 1960, chapter 6; Philip Converse and Georges Dupeux, "Politicization of the Electorate in France and the United States," in Angus Campbell et al., *Elections and the Political Order,* New York: John Wiley, 1967, cf., Ronald Inglehart and Avram Hochstein, "Alignment and Dealignment of the Electorate in France and the United States," *Comparative Political Studies* 5 (October 1972), pp. 343-372.

3. In this study, the following political parties were categorized as belonging to the "Left": Democratic Party (United States); Labour Party (Great Britain); Socialist Party (Austria); Socialist Party, Radical Party, Pacifist Socialist Party, Democrats, 1966 and Communist Party (Netherlands), and Social Democratic Party (Germany).

4. See Ronald Inglehart and Hans D. Klingemann, "Party Identification, Ideological Preference and the Left-Right Dimension Among Western Publics," in Ian Budge et al.

(eds.), *Party Identification and Beyond,* London and New York: John Wiley, 1975.

5. See Warren E. Miller and Teresa E. Levitin, *Leadership and Change: Presidential Elections from 1952 to 1976,* Cambridge, Mass.: Winthrop Publishers, 1976.

6. See Robert D. Putnam, "Studying Elite Political Culture: The Case of 'Ideology'," *American Political Science Review,* 65 (September 1971), pp. 651-681.

7. Political party preference was not included in these models because of its ambiguous and situation-specific role. It is worth mentioning, however, that additional sets of multivariate analyses were run in which political partisanship *was* included. As one would expect, those who identify with the Left show relatively high levels of Protest Potential; they also show somewhat lower levels of Repression Potential and, in some cases, higher levels of conventional participation. But political party preferences alone *cannot* account for the linkages shown in Figure 12.7. The impact of the other independent variables is reduced only slightly when we incorporate political party identification into the model.

Chapter 13

PERSONAL DISSATISFACTION

**SAMUEL H. BARNES, BARBARA G. FARAH,
and FELIX HEUNKS**

INTRODUCTION

Interest in the relationship between dissatisfaction and political behavior is at least as old as the serious study of politics. The basic assumptions undergirding this interest can be articulated quite succinctly. It is widely believed that a happy people give rise to a tranquil polity, that those who are dissatisfied are the source of public unrest, and that the roots of political violence are often to be found in individual frustration. These assumptions also include the belief that satisfaction and dissatisfaction derive from the presence or absence of a gap between an individual's value expectations and actual achievements; that this gap, or level of felt deprivation, is subjective and relative; and that consequently it is individual perceptions rather than objective conditions that matter.

As is the case with so many of our assumptions, these have been repeatedly subjected to anlysis and empirical testing without, however, theoretical or empirical closure having been achieved. It is not difficult to understand why this is true, for dissatisfaction is a multifaceted phenomenon with diverse interpretations. These diverse interpretations, in turn, make possible and probably inevitable widely differing approaches to problems of conceptualization and measurement. We have adopted an approach that is especially suitable to a cross-national study of individuals. Other ways of viewing the relationships studied in this chapter are of course available; but our design is the appropriate one for our theoretical interests, as it permits us to measure dissatisfaction at the individual level and to deal with deprivation as it is perceived by the individual. And with individual-level measurements we can deal with several thorny issues that recur in the study of dissatisfaction and deprivation, including the following: what is the relationship between objective socioeconomic conditions and feelings of deprivation? what is the impact of dissatisfaction and deprivation on varieties of political action, and especially protest potential? is there support for theories that emphasize change in actual or anticipated levels of satisfaction and deprivation as the origins of political protest? how do dissatisfaction and deprivation fare as explanations of protest when they are compared with the other variables that have been demonstrated in this study to be of prime importance, such as age, values, and ideological conceptualization? We have illuminating findings to present on all of these points. Before turning to these themes we will briefly discuss the theoretical background within which they are embedded and will present the measures that we have used in the study of personal dissatisfaction and deprivation.

THE CONCEPTUALIZATION AND MEASUREMENT OF PERSONAL DISSATISFACTION

The diversity of approaches to the analysis of dissatisfaction and deprivation merit a separate study. This is an important topic, rich in theory, speculation, and empirical findings. As a result, it is not easy to evaluate the research and writing in this area. Although the literature is voluminous, much that has been written is tangential to our interests.[1] A great deal of it derives from social-psychological experiments and research on small groups outside of "natural" political situations. Another, and more relevant, strand of research treats a substantial portion of the universe of political systems and utilizes socioeconomic data aggregated in a way that makes it difficult to generalize about individual behavior. A third research tradition focuses on the behavior of a limited number of individuals in a particular setting.

Although it is related to scientific concern for the relationship between frustration and aggression, the experimental literature is difficult to interpret in political terms. The relevance of findings from a laboratory setting from the everyday world of politics can be questioned, and the designs utilized in small group experiments seldom operationalize dissatisfaction and deprivation in a way that can be easily transferred to the study of national samples. However, research on the link between frustration and aggression—most of which is experimental in nature—provides us with an important clue as to what we might expect to find in studying deprivation and protest potential: frustration leads to aggression only some of the time, and only if there are facilitating attitudes present that support an aggressive response. The experimental literature alerts us to the complexity of the linkage between frustration and aggression.

The other two research traditions have been more directly relevant than the experimental one. Macrolevel research has been especially insightful about some political consequences of the frustration of expectations; it has given rise to a rich body of hypotheses, and some of the relationships uncovered have suggested that dissatisfaction is indeed a powerful variable for understanding political action. However, this body of data has two serious inadequacies as a guide to research among Western mass publics.

The first is that it uses socioeconomic data and does not specify the connection between the relationships observed at the aggregate level and individual behavior. In particular, socioeconomic data, of necessity, deal with *objective* measures of deprivation; they cannot reflect the *subjective* perceptions of individuals, which are the basis for feelings of relative deprivation.

A second inadequacy of these aggregate data studies is that it is unclear that patterns observable across the entire range of existing political systems should also exist within particular political systems or sets of systems. The thrust of the argument suggests that this similarity should exist, yet there is evidence that other similar multilevel phenomena do not in fact behave in the same way. For example, a relationship between socio-economic development and democratic political development has been demonstrated to exist by Lipset and Cutright.[2] But Neubauer found that beyond a "threshold," the relationship did not hold: "Some democratic countries that are highly developed socio-economically have high levels of democratic performance, whereas others rank quite low."[3] Similar discontinuities have been shown to exist concerning the relationship between urbanization and the level of organizational activity. The widely observed aggregate-level positive relationship has been demonstrated to be a function of the characteristics of individuals rather than of urban size, so that the level of organizational involvement of an individual with a particular set of characteristics is independent of size of community.[4] In countries as highly developed—and as similar—as the five we are treating, relationships that are found across a wider range of countries may not be detectable.

The third research tradition is more closely relevant to our substantive and methodological concerns. This very large group of studies seeks to understand the sources of protest behavior in Western societies. While this body of theory and data has been very useful to us, most of it focuses on particular groups, such as students or blacks, limited geographical areas, or particular incidents, and often in combination, such as student protesters in the University of Y in

1968. These studies are useful from a theoretical and methodological point of view. Yet, they tell us little about the societal distribution of the behaviors and attitudes studied, and they usually fail to place the particular events within a general theory of political action. While they tell us a great deal about protesters, they tell us little about the role of protest behavior in Western societies.

Our study was designed to overcome some of the inadequacies of these previous approaches. We have singled out a set of countries in which the patterns of political action are reasonably similar, in which the institutional bases of action fit the pattern of liberal democracies, and in which the levels of sophistication of mass publics are sufficiently high to make national surveys a viable instrument for gathering data. They all possess advanced industrial economic systems with complex institutions for channeling political activities, and all have been exposed, though in varying degrees, to the wave of protest activity that swept Western liberal democracies in the 1960s.

It is clear from previous research that the linkage process is crucial in relating personal dissatisfaction and political action.[5] We have not rested our research on the assumption that protest activity emerges fullblown from the subjective states of individuals. But we have concentrated our attention on individuals, and thus can only deal with aspects of linkage as they are reflected in individuals. Indeed, it is our recognition that extra-individual factors intervene that causes us to focus on protest potential, a psychological predisposition, rather than on protest behavior. We are aware that the relationship of dissatisfaction to actual behavior may sometimes differ from its relationship to another attitudinal variable such as protest potential, but our study shows that protest potential and actual behavior are strongly related.

At this point we need to be more specific about the particular approach to the study of dissatisfaction that we have followed. Our thinking about the relationship between dissatisfaction and political action has been greatly influenced by the concept of relative deprivation.[6] According to Runciman, relative deprivation may be broadly defined by saying "that A is relatively deprived of X when (i) he does not have X, (ii) he sees some other person or persons, which may include himself at some previous or expected time, as having X (whether or not this is or will be in fact the case), (iii) he wants X, and (iv) he sees it as feasible that he should have X. Possession of X may, of course, mean avoidance of or exemption from Y."[7] Runciman doubts the usefulness of the term "absolute deprivation," because the standards both of the observer and of the person deprived may be equally likely to vary. Morrison likewise disregards absolute deprivation and emphasizes another aspect of relative deprivation, namely "a special type of cognitive dissonance in which there develops the belief in a legitimate expectation and, simultaneously, the discrepant belief that there is high probability that the expectation will not be fulfilled," resulting in feelings of "injustice" or "inequity."[8] Gurr uses a similar definition of relative deprivation in a different phrasing: "a discrepancy between people's expectations about the goods and conditions of life to which they are justifiably entitled, on the one hand, and, on the other, their value capabilities—the degree to which they think they can attain these goods and conditions."[9]

Several types of relative deprivation are differentiated in the literature. Both Gurr and Morrison stress relative deprivation as a difference between what one believes to be one's just deserts and what one believes one actually receives, the perceived difference between justice and achievement. Runciman puts forward the difference between aspiration and actuality, where aspiration is symbolized by the level attained by reference groups or by the individual in the past or in the future. Still another way to conceptualize deprivation is the difference between actual attainment as perceived by the person and the best possible level.

We have adopted a combination of the "best possible" and the "just deserts" versions. In designing our study we sought measures of satisfaction that would be easy to administer cross-nationally, that would permit us to measure the gap between aspirations and achievements, and that would also make possible the analysis of the impact of change between present and future expectations. In the vast literature, many varieties of conceptualization and operationalization have been suggested. However, many of them have not been utilized with individual-level data, while others are weak on one or the other of our criteria. We settled on the measurement procedure developed by Cantril and widely used in studies in a variety of countries.[10] Its ease of administration and ready quantification seemed made to order for our needs.

Briefly, the Cantril measures rely on the respondents placing themselves on a self-anchoring scale that runs from zero to ten, along any dimension specified by the researcher. In our study, the precise wording of the question is as follows:

> First I'd like to ask you how you feel you and your family are doing these days. Number ten here at the top of the ladder represents the very best possible situation that you could imagine for yourself. And zero down here at the bottom represents the worst possible situation for you. Now, let's think first about the material side of your life today— the things you can buy and do—all the things that make up your material standard of living.
>
> (Interviewer: hand card to respondent)
>
> All things considered, how satisfied or dissatisfied are you overall with the material side of your life today?

After the respondent has indicated a position between zero and ten on the scale, the question is repeated as follows:

Where would you have put yourself five years ago? And where do you expect you might put yourself in five years' time? And—still thinking just about your material standards—what do you think is the right point on the scale for people like yourself? I mean, what level of material satisfaction do you feel that people like yourself are entitled to?

After the series about the material side of life, the entire battery is repeated as follows:

Now, let's think about your life as a whole. All things considered, how satisfied or dissatisfied are you overall with your life these days? Where do you put yourself on the scale?

The auxiliary questions are then posed for life as a whole.

With the results, it is possible to compute deprivation scores for the respondents; these are the difference between the sets of scores people give themselves. The literature on deprivation is not clear as to which sets of differences in scores, or which gaps, are the most salient. An obvious candidate is the gap between the present level and the level to which people feel entitled, and we pay particular attention to this. It is equally plausible to focus on the gap between the level to which people feel entitled and the level anticipated five years in the future. We also have examined this deprivation measure carefully. However, it turns out to be less useful than might have been expected because of the optimism of the young and the pessimism of the old. So we have placed the most emphasis on the gap between present levels of achievement and the levels to which people feel entitled, on both the material and life as a whole dimensions. Other measures of deprivation are also available, such as the past-present and present-future differences. We will also examine these and we will look at changes in expectations as well as the size of the gap, as there is a vast literature and some empirical findings on the impact of changing levels of expectations on political action.

In the remainder of this section we will present our findings on country and socioeconomic group differences in levels of dissatisfaction and deprivation. Not surprisingly, absolute levels of material and life as a whole satisfaction are rather similar across the five countries (see Table 13.1). "Entitlement" expectations are likewise similar across countries, with the result that material and life as a whole deprivation are roughly similar. The exception to this is the Netherlands—an extraordinarily satisfied country! The deprivation levels along both dimensions there are −.3 compared with −1.3 for the next least deprived countries (see Table 13.1).

Several points stand out in the data. Despite being the most satisfied people in the sample, the Dutch have the lowest aspiration levels of any of the countries studied. Dutch material satisfaction levels are far higher than

Table 13.1: NATIONAL DIFFERENCES IN DISSATISFACTION LEVELS*

	The Netherlands	Britain	United States	Germany	Austria
Material Satisfaction	7.6	6.6	6.9	6.7	6.6
Material Entitlement	7.8	8.4	8.3	8.0	7.9
Material Deprivation**	−0.2	−1.8	−1.4	−1.3	−1.3
Life as a Whole Satisfaction	7.6	7.3	7.4	7.1	7.1
Life Entitlement	7.9	8.4	8.6	8.3	8.2
Life Deprivation**	−0.3	−1.1	−1.2	−1.2	−1.0

*Figures are mean scores on 0−10 scale: 0 = low satisfaction and low deprivation.
**Deprivation scores are difference between actual and entitlement levels.

those of other countries. On the life as a whole dimension, on the one hand, the levels of satisfaction in other countries are as high as the Dutch; on the other hand, Dutch aspirations are considerably lower than those of other countries. Thus they are .2 of a point higher than Americans on satisfaction but .7 lower than Americans on mean aspiration levels, hence the greater feelings of deprivation in the United States. This combination of low dissatisfaction and low aspirations obviously results in low deprivation feelings in the Netherlands.

When we turn to the investigation of various subgroups within these populations, a striking phenomenon is observable in all countries: the feelings of satisfaction of various socioeconomic groups are roughly similar. Several cross-national analyses have documented this finding. In a study of well-being in Scandinavia, Allardt found that "within each country the overall satisfaction level tends to be surprisingly constant across categories defined by social characteristics."[11] Similar findings are reported by Inglehart utilizing data from European Community surveys in nine nations.[12] Social background variables including age, sex, income, occupation, education, religious denomination, church attendance, political party identification, political information, labor union membership, region, size of community in which the respondent lives, mother tongue, race, and value type did not predict much of the variance in satisfaction level. Another review by Yuchtman (Yaar) of findings in this area concluded that "the objective standing of individuals in their socioeconomic environment has a limited influence upon their subjective perceptions of their economic welfare, and probably upon other aspects of their psychological well-being."[13]

Finally, this is also the conclusion of Campbell, Converse, and Rodgers in their work on social indicators. They emphasize a person-environment fit model, in which people gradually adjust their aspirations to their evaluations of their current situation. Consequently, with time, people adjust so as to lessen or eliminate the gap between aspirations and achievements: "Alternatives that are progressively recognized as inaccessible lose their salience as reference points for criticisms of the present, and the poorly educated generally have a less rich store of such alternatives to work from in any event."[14] It is important to note that Campbell, Converse, and Rodgers differentiate between satisfaction and happiness. They found that old people become increasingly satisfied—that is, the gap between aspirations and present evaluations is narrowed—but they also become increasingly unhappy. Unfortunately, our study does not include separate measures of happiness.

Life cycle differences are an important key to the dynamics underlying youthful protest. According to Campbell, Converse, and Rodgers: "Indeed our most passive respondents are the relatively unhappy but relatively satisfied elderly, who seem resigned to their condition, and our most active ones are the happy but dissatisfied young."[15] And "the very young display both unusually high aspiration levels and an uncommon gap between these expectations and their evaluations of their current situations, in producing marked dissatisfaction with these situations."[16] They add that "the well-to-do young are, relative to early periods, uncommonly disgruntled."[17] Katz and his associates also found that the young were consistently less satisfied.[18]

Strumpel, following up on the argument concerning environmental fit, concluded that "age seems to be a proxy for realism. The options of the young become the constraints of the old, and they are perceived that way. Unattainable goals are abandoned or modified as time passes."[19]

Since the levels of dissatisfaction among socioeconomic groups do not vary much, it is obvious that the utility of social background variables for understanding personal dissatisfaction is severely limited. Summarizing the impact of a number of social background variables, Inglehart found that taken together they explain more than three times the percentage of the variance in left-right self-placement and in partisan identification than in overall life satisfaction.[20]

Our data support the conclusions of these other studies concerning the inadequacy of social background variables for understanding personal satisfaction. For example, differences between men and women on material and life as a whole deprivation are small; women are generally more satisfied but also have higher aspirations, so that the gap (deprivation) is fairly constant across countries (table not shown).

The impact of age is also minimal. The young are generally among the most dissatisfied on the material dimension. This is also true of the life as a whole dimension except in Germany and Austria, where the older generation exhibits greater dissatisfaction than the young. But the old in those two countries also exhibit lower levels of aspirations, so the deprivation levels are in the same general range in all age groups. The levels of deprivation—on both the material and life as a whole dimensions—among those fifty and older are substantially lower than for younger age groups only in the United States. And on this, as all other variables examined, the Dutch exhibit the smallest gap between aspirations and achievement.

Patterns are also roughly similar for different categories of educational achievement. In every country the best educated of the three educational groups is the most satisfied on the material dimension and in all cases except Austria on the life as a whole dimension as well. And even though their aspirations are often higher, the best educated group feels less deprivation than the others. Only life as a whole deprivation in Austria fails to fit the pattern. The low levels of deprivation felt by the Dutch at all educational levels are apparent here as well. However, the differences among the groups discussed here are small.

Our findings thus far can be summarized as follows: socioeconomic and national differences in dissatisfaction are small. Most socioeconomic differences are in the expected direction, with those higher in the stratification system more satisfied. However, these findings are irregular, and in any case group differences are small and patterns are not invariable. The clearest pattern is that of decline in levels of satisfaction with increasing age. This decline becomes more striking in our analyses, presented later in this chapter, of differences in optimism and pessimism for the future. The clearest implication of this analysis of levels of satisfaction is that studies of deprivation that focus on objective measures of well-being are inadequate insofar as they assume a close relationship between objective conditions and subjective evaluations of satisfaction and dissatisfaction.

PERSONAL DISSATISFACTION AND POLITICAL ACTION

The previous chapters of this volume have emphasized the complexity of the relationship between attitudes and political action. It is thus no surprise that the simple correlations between measures of dissatisfaction and protest potential are not very strong and do not reach statistical significance for entire populations (see Table 13.2). They are, however, generally in the expected direction, and significance is reached for some age categories in some countries (these tables not shown). In the Netherlands, for example, the

Table 13.2: PROTEST POTENTIAL AND DISSATISFACTION*

	The Netherlands	Britain	United States	Germany	Austria
Material Satisfaction	−.05	−.11	−.09	−.03	−.03
Life as a Whole Satisfaction	−.12	−.08	−.09	.02	.02
Material Deprivation	−.05	−.10	−.11	−.03	−.03
Life as a Whole Deprivation	−.06	−.07	−.12	−.03	−.03

*Measure is r.

relationships between protest potential and all four of the measures—material satisfaction and deprivation and life as a whole satisfaction and deprivation—are significant at the .01 level for those fifty years of age and over, but only for that age group. In the United States, both the deprivation measures and the life as a whole satisfaction measures correlate with protest potential at the .01 level of significance for those under thirty, while the material deprivation measure reaches that level for those thirty through forty-nine years of age. In Germany, the relationship between life as a whole deprivation and protest potential reaches the .01 level for those under thirty, while the same is true of the material satisfaction measure for those thirty through forty-nine. In Britain and Austria, on the other hand, none reaches that level of significance.

It is at the extremes that some of the conventional assumptions about the relationship between dissatisfaction and protest find support (see Table 13.3). If we collapse the levels of material satisfaction into five categories, the extremely satisfied and the extremely dissatisfied conform to expectations: those in the lowest category on material satisfaction are in every country higher on protest potential than those in the highest category, but those in the three middle categories seem to fit no clear patterns across the five countries. Life as a whole satisfaction is not as consistent as material satisfaction, as these same patterns exist for three of the countries, but not for Germany and Austria (table not shown).

Both of the deprivation measures are similar to the above two in their overall relationships with protest potential, though not as regular: in the Netherlands, Britain, and the United States, protest potential is highest among those highest on material deprivation and lowest among those who feel no deprivation at all; German and Austrian patterns are irregular (tables

Table 13.3: PROTEST POTENTIAL AND MATERIAL SATISFACTION

		Mean Protest Potential (0–7)				
Material Satisfaction		*The Netherlands*	*Britain*	*United States*	*Germany*	*Austria*
(Low)	1	3.8	1.9	2.8	2.0	1.6
	2	3.1	2.0	2.3	1.9	1.5
	3	2.7	2.2	2.7	2.0	1.6
	4	2.8	1.8	2.5	2.0	1.8
(High)	5	2.5	1.3	2.0	1.6	1.5

not shown). The results are somewhat less consistent for life as a whole deprivation. In every country except Austria protest potential is highest among those who feel most deprived on this dimension. For Britain and the United States the patterns are linear, with protest potential rising with dissatisfaction. The Netherlands has the phenomenon of high protest potential among those least deprived. Germany and Austria exhibit few differences among categories (table not shown).

Given the role that age has assumed in this volume, one final aspect of dissatisfaction and protest potential merits mention, and that is the greater impact of deprivation on the young. Relationships within national samples as a whole defy interpretation, but for the youngest age category the pattern is consistent: the deprived have a substantially higher protest potential than

Table 13.4: PROTEST POTENTIAL AND MATERIAL DEPRIVATION
(by age; mean protest potential [0-7])

Country		≤ 21	22-29	30-49	≥ 50
The Netherlands	Deprived	3.9	3.3	2.9	2.5
	Neither	3.1	3.2	3.0	1.7
	Privileged	3.1	3.1	3.3	2.1
Britain	Deprived	3.1	3.0	2.3	1.6
	Neither	2.7	1.8	1.9	1.3
	Privileged	2.4	2.9	1.8	1.2
United States	Deprived	3.6	3.2	2.7	1.8
	Neither	3.1	3.2	2.4	1.7
	Privileged	2.9	3.0	2.4	1.9
Germany	Deprived	3.2	3.0	2.1	1.6
	Neither	2.5	2.7	2.0	1.4
	Privileged	3.3	3.3	1.7	1.5
Austria	Deprived	2.3	1.8	1.7	1.3
	Neither	1.0	1.9	1.7	1.4
	Privileged	1.8	1.7	1.2	1.4

those who feel privileged or who feel that they have what they deserve (see Table 13.4). Only in Germany is this not the case. In that country it is the privileged in both younger age categories who have the highest protest potential. In Table 13.4 we have divided the 16 through 29 age group into those 16 through 21 and those 22 through 29, in order to demonstrate the greater protest potential of those who feel deprived in the very youngest group.

Detailed findings will not be presented for repressive potential and conventional participation. In all countries except Austria, repressive potential is highest among the most satisfied on the material and life as a whole dimensions. Deprivation levels reflect our now familiar pattern: in the same four countries, repressive potential is at its highest level among those who feel no discrepancy between aspirations and achievements. But nowhere are the relationships strong.

Conventional participation seems to be the most country-specific of our measures of political action. Conventional participation is highest in the Netherlands among those *least* satisfied and *most* satisfied on the material dimensions, while in the United States it is *lowest* among those two groups. In the other three countries rates of conventional participation are unrelated to levels of satisfaction. Life as a whole satisfaction is associated in exactly the same manner as material satisfaction except in Germany, where conventional participation increases monotonically with satisfaction. Our deprivation measures appear to be unrelated to conventional participation in any systematic manner.

The relationships described demonstrate that it is primarily extreme dissatisfaction and deprivation that are associated with higher levels of protest potential. Overall relationships are modest, and models of protest that assume linearity undoubtedly underestimate the impact of dissatisfaction and deprivation.

We close this analysis of personal dissatisfaction and political action with a brief presentation of the relationship between personal dissatisfaction and deprivation, on the one hand, and our typology of political actors, on the other. This typology, it should be recalled, combines scores on the protest potential and conventional participation indices, so that we separate out Inactives (low on both) from Activists (high on both) and Protesters (high only on protest potential), with Conformists (moderate on conventional and low on protest) and Reformers (high on conventional and moderate on protest) as mixed categories.

Results are interesting though hardly astounding (see Table 13.5). It is clear that the groups high on protest (Activists and Protesters) are generally, but not always, the least satisfied and most deprived, as was apparent in the discussion in the previous section. In a majority of countries it is the Activists

Table 13.5: SATISFACTION AND ACTION TYPOLOGY (figure is mean satisfaction)

	The Netherlands	Britain	United States	Germany	Austria
	Material Satisfaction				
Inactives	7.7	6.8	6.9	6.6	6.5
Conformists	7.7	6.9	7.1	6.9	6.9
Reformists	7.8	6.8	7.0	6.9	6.5
Activists	7.5	6.2	6.6	6.2	6.7
Protesters	7.4	6.4	6.7	6.6	6.9
	Life as a Whole Satisfaction				
Inactives	7.8	7.4	7.6	6.9	7.1
Conformists	8.0	7.7	7.5	7.2	7.3
Reformists	7.8	7.4	7.5	7.3	7.2
Activists	7.4	6.8	7.1	6.9	7.3
Protesters	7.6	7.2	7.3	7.1	7.4
	Material Deprivation				
Inactives	−.1	−1.6	−1.3	−1.2	−1.2
Conformists	−.3	−1.5	−1.2	−1.3	−1.0
Reformists	.0	−1.7	−1.2	−1.1	−1.3
Activists	−.4	−2.1	−1.8	−1.6	−1.5
Protesters	−.5	−2.1	−1.6	−1.3	−1.1
	Life as a Whole Deprivation				
Inactives	−.2	−1.3	−1.0	−1.2	−.9
Conformists	.0	−1.2	−1.1	−1.1	−1.0
Reformists	−.2	−1.2	−1.1	−1.0	−1.1
Activists	−.4	−1.8	−1.8	−1.5	−1.2
Protesters	−.3	−1.5	−1.3	−1.2	−1.0

NOTE: All scales are 0−10.

who deviate most from the others. This is especially apparent on the life as a whole deprivation measure, which is the sole instance of clarity across all of the countries: without exception, Activists feel greater deprivation than other action types. The material deprivation measure, on the other hand, shows the Protesters as the most highly deprived in some cases, surpassing the Activists in the Netherlands and equalling them in Britain. In Austria, however, Protesters feel less material deprivation than all except the Conformists, a finding for which we have no ready explanation other than the idiosyncratic nature of other Austrian results.

This section has demonstrated that in most simple correlations between a measure of dissatisfaction and protest potential the relationships are in the theoretically expected direction. In most cases they are weak, however, and dissatisfaction is not a significant contributor to protest potential except among the most dissatisfied within several age groups that vary from country to country.

The literature on dissatisfaction and deprivation suggests that these variables should be a major contributor to political unrest or, as we have operationalized it, protest potential. It is clear from the previous chapters in this volume that several other variables are very important contributors to protest potential. When we began our analysis of the relationship of dissatisfaction and deprivation and protest potential, we were interested in the strength of our dissatisfaction and deprivation measures compared with these other important contributors, especially age, Materialist/Postmaterialist values, and level of ideological conceptualization. Chapters 7 through 12 have documented the strong contribution that these variables make to protest potential, and the popular wisdom suggests that personal dissatisfaction and deprivation should parallel them in importance. However, if basic relationships between dissatisfaction and deprivation measures and protest potential are weak there is nothing to be gained by pursuing our original intention of evaluating the relative weight of these variables. The fact is that measures of dissatisfaction and deprivation are not closely related to protest potential; their inclusion in multiple regression analyses with age, values, and level of ideological conceptualization as additional independent variables merely renders clearer what is already obvious (table not shown).

Given the important role that various theories have assigned to personal dissatisfaction as a source of unrest, we will briefly discuss some explanations that may help account for the weak relationship. These explanations are both individual level and societal level in their origins. And there is also a methodological issue that must be mentioned before we turn to the individual and societal-level explanations.

It is possible that stronger relationships between dissatisfaction and protest potential would have emerged had we altered the wording of our question slightly. We followed the usage of *The Pattern of Human Concerns,* which defines the top of the ladder as the "best possible" level of achievement.[21] This formulation leaves the respondent free to determine what is the "best possible," so the referent obviously varies from person to person. Of course, this is not an incapacitating problem, since all personal evaluations are inevitably and properly subjective. But the "best possible" formulation exacerbates the basic problem as it can give rise to "pie-in-the-sky" standards of comparison with the present level of dissatisfaction. In a work not available at the time we designed our project, Muller suggested that a "just deserts" formulation achieves better results than the "best possible."[22] The "just deserts" version encourages the respondent to use his or her own conception of justice rather than "best possible" hopes which, for many people, may have little contact with reality or with their own behavior. It would not be surprising to find that feelings of justice denied have stronger behavioral consequences than feelings that things are not as good as they might be. Our operationalization of deprivation approaches the "just deserts" formulation in that we ask respondents to indicate the level on the ladder that they feel entitled to. The gap between that level and their actual level of achievement is our principal measure of deprivation. We do not believe that using the "best possible" level as the top of the ladder results in uninterpretable answers.[23] But it is possible that a "just deserts" formulation might have led to stronger relationships.

There is no reason to attribute our results solely to the wording of the question. There are other, entirely substantive, explanations for weak relationships. The most important we label the problem of translation: in order to have political importance, personal dissatisfaction must be translated into political terms, and many people are unable to carry out the translation process.

The fact is that much personal dissatisfaction has no tie at all to politics, while other aspects may be so marginally political in origin or solution that the tenuous linkage may not be made by respondents. For example, it is clear that satisfaction in many specific areas of activity sums up to overall satisfaction. This is well documented in the work of Campbell, Converse, and Rodgers.[24] Satisfaction with family life is one of the most important ingredients of satisfaction with one's quality of life. And social scientists know that family life is greatly affected by governmental activity in domains such as Aid to Dependent Children and other welfare areas, educational programs, and tax policy. But for individuals with marital problems it is probably rare that the action or inaction of government is viewed as the principal source of the problem, and the linkage of personal dissatisfaction of this sort with governmental outputs is probably rare. Of course, there will be some who will blame the government. Furthermore, it is to be expected that those who are more sophisticated about politics, whether from participation or cognitive development, or both, will be more likely to make the connection. It is people who lack personal resources, whether of time, money, or facilitating attitudes, who are least likely to carry out the translation process successfully.

Individual-level propensities to ignore politics can be greatly influenced by system-level phenomena. The most important, of course, concern the pattern of mobilization of the society. The presence of mass political parties such as the European communists and socialists, trade unions, church-related groups, and other types of organizations certainly makes it easier for individuals with given levels of dissatisfaction to relate their personal state of mind to what goes on in the political system. Some political organizations in fact devote great effort to the translation of personal dissatisfaction into political terms.

Opportunity is also important in the translation process. The visibility of protest behavior, a milieu that publicizes it in a positive light, and, especially, repeated demonstration that political activity of either a conventional or unconventional variety is efficacious in achieving goals undoubtedly increases greatly the likelihood of translation of personal dissatisfaction into protest potential.[25] As we pointed out in the introduction to this chapter, we focus on protest potential rather than actual protest behavior because we cannot study opportunity very well in national surveys of this kind. Moreover, we cannot treat the process of mobilization—the ways in which parties and organizations prod individuals into activity—in an adequate manner in this analysis. We know, however, that opportunity and mobilization are important intervening variables between dissatisfaction and action; our focus on protest potential minimizes but does not eliminate the impact of opportunity.[26]

Thus personal dissatisfaction may or may not lead to political action, depending on what goes on in the translation process. What goes on in that process is more proximate to action than the original dissatisfaction, and is therefore more powerful in predicting political action. Despite the weakness of relationships, it is difficult to dismiss entirely the relevance of dissatisfaction to political action. But it is clear that the former lies far back in the causal chain, that the translation process is crucial, and that other, more proximate, influences condition the extent and the form of political action.

We have seen that, for many possible reasons, absolute levels of dissatisfaction and deprivation are only weakly related to political action. In the next section we will examine the political consequences of changes in expectations concerning these two variables.

CHANGES IN EXPECTATIONS AND PROTEST POTENTIAL

The previous analysis has demonstrated inadequacies in the theory that inspired our inquiry. However, we have explored static versions of the theory; there are other formulations that focus on dynamic aspects of expectations. These versions emphasize the importance of changes in levels of satisfaction over time, of declining and rising expectations, and their resulting optimism or pessimism.

There are several possible ways of analyzing dynamic aspects of dissatisfaction and deprivation, and our data are especially appropriate for two of them. These are equated by James C. Davies with the names of Karl Marx and Alexis de Tocqueville.[27] According to Davies, Marx and de Tocqueville reached opposite conclusions concerning the patterns of changing expectations that should be associated with revolution, and Davies thought that he had discovered a way to reconcile the two. He argued that Marx had associated revolution with declining expectations—"increasing misery"—while de Tocqueville believed that revolution resulted from rising expectations that exceeded system capacity. Davies posited a J-curve relationship between changes in expectations and revolution, in which expectations rise over time along with achievement, followed by a downturn in achievement level that creates an intolerable gap between what people have come to expect and what they actually achieve.

We have measured levels of material satisfaction and life as a whole satisfaction for five years in the past, the present, and five years in the future. This gives us several possible patterns to examine in addition to the J-curve pattern. Following Grofman and Muller, we shall label the J-curve pattern the Rise-and-Drop pattern, meaning that expectations fall sharply following a rise.[28] These two authors suggest that "Just as the J-curve produces a high degree of dissatisfaction, so will a *reverse* J-curve produce a high degree of satisfaction."[29] This reverse J-curve is a Drop-and-Rise pattern, in which falling expectations are followed by rising expectations for the future. Another possible pattern is one of Decreasing expectations, in which there is a decline over both time periods of past-to-present and present-to-future or when one is stable and there is a decline in the other. The Increasing expectations pattern is the reverse of the Declining: there is either an increase in both periods or stability in one and an increase in the other. Finally, there are two stable patterns: one that is high in satisfaction and one that is low, labeled by Grofman and Muller, No-Change Gratification and No-Change Deprivation, respectively. Grofman and Muller utilized measures of satisfaction with work, income, housing, and children, so our measures of material and life as a whole satisfaction are not directly comparable. Moreover, our measure of protest potential is similar to but not identical with their index of "potential for political violence" or PPV. Nevertheless it is patterns that we seek, and our data are sufficiently similar to theirs for this purpose.

Grofman and Muller found that most of their Rise-and-Drop predictions—that respondents with rising expectations followed by falling expectations would be high on "potential for political violence"—were confirmed (their Confirmation Index—or CI—was .72). But their Drop-and-Rise predictions were incorrect (CI = .05), because a high percentage of the respondents in this latter category were high on their PPV index.[30] They consistently found that the two No-Change categories were lowest on PPV.

Our findings are consistent with their conclusions but are more striking in their implications for theory. For, with much larger samples, and in five countries, we found consistently that—contrary to theoretical assumptions—

Table 13.6: CHANGE IN EXPECTATIONS AND PROTEST POTENTIAL (percentage high on protest potential; high = 3 or more)

When Material Satisfaction Is:	Rise and Drop		Decreasing		No-Change Deprivation		No-Change Gratification		Increasing		Drop and Rise	
The Netherlands	50%	(99)	45%	(198)	43%	(7)	40%	(235)	51%	(394)	51%	(53)
Britain	17	(59)	30	(287)	29	(28)	23	(181)	34	(489)	40	(140)
United States	44	(62)	37	(254)	35	(23)	30	(185)	54	(688)	61	(214)
Germany	32	(223)	24	(565)	36	(67)	29	(261)	37	(721)	38	(113)
Austria	16	(149)	19	(282)	13	(53)	14	(125)	25	(398)	34	(53)
When Life as a Whole Satisfaction Is:	Rise and Drop		Decreasing		No-Change Deprivation		No-Change Gratification		Increasing		Drop and Rise	
The Netherlands	38%	(79)	48%	(145)	40%	(5)	41%	(325)	53%	(346)	58%	(72)
Britain	18	(60)	27	(189)	40	(25)	26	(308)	35	(455)	34	(119)
United States	26	(42)	33	(165)	33	(24)	39	(293)	57	(711)	56	(194)
Germany	30	(58)	25	(114)	23	(18)	32	(148)	38	(217)	39	(42)
Austria	26	(28)	14	(35)	20	(12)	17	(45)	26	(77)	29	(17)

NOTE: ( ) = number of cases.

those in the Drop-and-Rise category on material satisfaction had the highest protest potential; and usually had the highest protest potential for the life as a whole dimension as well (see Table 13.6). In every case, the Increasing expectations category was higher in protest potential than the Decreasing. But most important of all is the lack of support for the J-curve theory, for on the life as a whole dimension in the Netherlands, Britain, and the United States, the Rise-and-Drop category is the *lowest* of all on protest potential.[31] In Britain it is the lowest on the material satisfaction dimension as well. Thus our data provide no support for the J-curve as an explanation of political protest and, indeed, in three countries the results are completely opposite to the propositions inspired by the J-curve theory, at least for the life as a whole dimension of satisfaction.

There is still another dynamic pattern that merits investigation. It is apparent from this work of Grofman and Muller, and others,[32] that a principal distinction is between those whose expectations are stable and those that are changing. The former two authors refer to this phenomenon as the V-curve hypothesis: both those whose expectations are declining and those that are increasing have higher levels of protest potential than those whose expectations are stable. We have replicated their analyses in the five countries for both the material and life as a whole dimension. Using the categories in Table 13.6 we combined the Rise-and-Drop with the Decreasing category, placed the two No Change groups together, and merged the Drop-and-Rise with the Increasing to form the Decreasing, No Change, and Increasing categories in Table 13.7. Our results are similar to Grofman and Muller. In every case, it is those with rising expectations that have the highest protest potential (see Table 13.7)[33] In half of the cases those with stable expectations are the lowest, but in Germany and Austria it is those with decreasing expectations who are lowest on protest potential, and this is true of life as a whole expectations in the United States. These findings also hold within the

Table 13.7: CHANGES IN EXPECTATION AND PROTEST POTENTIAL (mean protest potential 0–7)

	The Netherlands		Britain		United States		Germany		Austria	
Material Expectations										
Decreasing	2.79	(297)	1.77	(346)	2.18	(316)	1.80	(718)	1.47	(431)
No Change	2.60	(242)	1.61	(209)	1.96	(208)	1.87	(318)	1.48	(178)
Increasing	3.02	(447)	2.22	(629)	2.83	(902)	2.30	(834)	1.87	(451)
Life as a Whole Expectations										
Decreasing	2.74	(224)	1.78	(249)	2.00	(207)	1.76	(653)	1.45	(350)
No Change	2.63	(330)	1.74	(333)	2.11	(317)	2.02	(541)	1.46	(323)
Increasing	3.10	(418)	2.23	(574)	2.88	(905)	2.33	(683)	2.02	(353)

NOTE: ( ) = number of cases.

low, middle, and high education groups. Only in the low- and middle-educated Dutch groups are the increasing expectations categories not the highest on protest potential (table not shown).

Up to this point we have concentrated on the level of protest potential within each category without regard for the number of respondents involved. By paying attention to the composition of the cells of the matrices we are able to map some of the nuances of the relationship between protest and changing expectations. When we examine the percentage of each national sample with Decreasing, No Change, and Increasing expectations, and especially as we look at the expectations of particular age and other groups in society, several important aspects of the relationship between protest potential and satisfaction stand out.

National differences in optimism are much more striking than the differences in the simple measures of satisfaction and deprivation. For example, almost twice as high a percentage of Germans and Austrians have Decreasing expectations as do Americans; in the former two countries the number with decreasing expectations is equal to those with rising expectations, while in the United States the optimists outnumber the pessimists three to one! The Netherlands and Britain fall in between (see Table 13.8). Only in the United States and Britain are those with rising expectations in the majority.

When we examine optimism and pessimism among various categories of activism, national differences continue to be evident (see Table 13.9). Except for the Inactives, there are insignificant differences in the rising expectations categories among the Dutch. The British and American patterns are essentially similar to one another, with optimism highest among Activists and Protesters. The German and Austrian patterns are likewise similar to one another: Activists are the most optimistic, with Protesters ranking second. The Activists are the most optimistic category in every country except Britain, and the difference between Activists and Protesters in that country is miniscule.

Table 13.8: CHANGE IN MATERIAL EXPECTATIONS

Expectations	The Netherlands	Britain	United States	Germany	Austria
Decreasing	30%	29%	22%	41%	41%
No Change	25	18	15	16	17
Increasing	45	53	63	43	42
	100	100	100	100	100

Division into age groups does not alter the overall findings concerning national differences. In every country, optimism declines with age within each category of the action typology (see Table 13.10). The relationship between age and expectations has been commented on earlier in this chapter, so our overall findings concerning changing expectations and age will consequently come as no surprise: the young in every country are much more likely than other groups to have rising expectations (see Table 13.11). National variations are of interest, however, for they demonstrate once again the large impact of country. In the United States the difference between the percentage declining and rising among those under thirty is unusually large, with British youth only slightly less optimistic. The Dutch are the least optimistic of all in the youngest group, though in all countries, that group is the most optimistic of the three. Among those fifty and over, national similarities outweigh the differences, with the percentage with declining expectations larger than that with rising expectations in every country except the United States, where even the old are more optimistic than pessimistic. It

Table 13.9: **ACTION TYPOLOGY AND CHANGE IN MATERIAL EXPECTATIONS (percentage of each type with each pattern)**

Action Typology	The Netherlands	Britain	United States	Germany	Austria
Inactives					
Decreasing	33%	33%	32%	46%	43%
No Change	33	21	28	20	22
Increasing	33	46	40	34	35
Conformists					
Decreasing	30	34	29	49	47
No Change	22	21	20	15	17
Increasing	48	45	51	36	36
Reformists					
Decreasing	25	28	21	41	40
No Change	29	17	12	14	13
Increasing	47	55	67	45	47
Activists					
Decreasing	29	24	16	26	27
No Change	20	15	10	12	16
Increasing	51	61	74	62	57
Protesters					
Decreasing	33	26	17	36	36
No Change	21	12	11	17	12
Increasing	46	62	72	47	52

is the 30 through 49 age category that demonstrates the greatest variation by country. The difference in this category between the United States, with only 7 percent with declining expectations, and Germany and Austria, with 40 percent and 41 percent, is especially striking.

When we examine protest potential within the sets of respondents' age categories, we find some reversals of the previously noted pattern of higher protest potential among those with rising expectations (table not shown). The pattern continues to hold for every age group in the United States and Austria, but the other three countries exhibit some reversals. In both Germany and the Netherlands, youth under thirty with declining expectations have the highest mean protest potential scores, while in Britain and the Netherlands among those 30-49 it is those with stable expectations who have the highest protest potential scores. But it should be noted that this declining expectations category is numerically considerably smaller than the rising one in all countries.

What conclusions can we draw that might shed light on the J-Curve and V-Curve hypotheses? It is clear that the major thrust of both hypotheses—that protest is associated with dissatisfaction and declining expectations—is

Table 13.10: MATERIAL SATISFACTION AND ACTION TYPOLOGY
(percent with Increasing material expectation, by age)

Action Typology	The Netherlands	Britain	United States	Germany	Austria
Inactives					
< 30	58%	71%	66%	60%	54%
30-49	50	72	50	41	43
⩾ 50	10	25	26	24	20
Conformists					
< 30	75	56	84	63	64
30-49	56	76	64	37	36
⩾ 50	32	28	37	27	30
Reformists					
< 30	58	78	81	59	69
30-49	42	63	79	47	48
⩾ 50	38	38	40	34	29
Activists					
< 30	58	81	78	71	71
30-49	53	60	74	59	60
⩾ 50	31	33	50	39	40
Protesters					
< 30	54	78	83	63	76
30-49	48	73	66	53	48
⩾ 50	25	29	47	29	26

blunted by our findings. In every case dealing with material satisfaction in national populations the highest protest potential is found among groups whose expectations are Increasing.

Before we reject the underlying theories about deprivation and revolution we must confront a simple fact: our data do not derive from revolutionary epochs or populations. It is consequently difficult to relate our findings to a revolutionary situation. Despite the unrest of the 1960s and 1970s, only a very small percentage of national populations exhibit support for extreme forms of unconventional activity. Our measure is of potential rather than behavior, and it includes activities that range from mild though unconventional forms of behavior to those that may be widely viewed as threatening public order. Our surveys have uncovered a surprisingly large body of persons who seem to be willing to engage in unorthodox activities, especially those of the milder variety: presumably, in bad times or difficult times or revolutionary times fewer people would have rising expectations and more would have declining ones. From our general knowledge of political behavior, we would expect those who are more participant—on either the conventional or unconventional dimensions, or both—to be the most sensitive to the cues of the times. It is possible that expectations of much of this active group would switch from optimism to pessimism. Undoubtedly, people high on protest would be included, and perhaps they would be among the first to change in outlook. The study of what is, cannot foretell with certainty what will be.

Table 13.11: CHANGE IN MATERIAL EXPECTATIONS (by age)

Age	The Netherlands		Britain		United States		Germany		Austria	
< 30										
Decreasing	27%	(93)	18%	(48)	12%	(53)	27%	(105)	23%	(49)
No Change	14	(50)	6	(17)	7	(30)	10	(40)	11	(23)
Increasing	59	(207)	76	(201)	81	(368)	63	(250)	66	(142)
Total	100	(350)	100	(266)	100	(451)	100	(395)	100	(214)
30–49										
Decreasing	27	(91)	20	(72)	7	(32)	40	(319)	41	(192)
No Change	24	(78)	12	(43)	13	(57)	13	(103)	14	(63)
Increasing	49	(162)	68	(253)	80	(353)	47	(376)	45	(209)
Total	100	(331)	100	(368)	100	(442)	100	(798)	100	(464)
⩾ 50										
Decreasing	39	(113)	43	(225)	36	(171)	49	(353)	50	(190)
No Change	35	(104)	27	(142)	26	(121)	23	(170)	24	(92)
Increasing	26	(78)	30	(158)	38	(180)	28	(208)	26	(100)
Total	100	(295)	100	(525)	100	(472)	100	(731)	100	(382)

But it is clear that declining expectations are a very poor predictor of protest potential at the present time.

Thus, the optimism of those high on protest potential is perhaps one of the most striking findings of our study. It is not lack of hope for a better future but—more likely—the expectation of it that is distinctive about this group. What would happen if expectations were to decline is an interesting—if speculative—question.

The contrast between the optimism of the citizens of the English-speaking democracies and the pessimism of the German-speaking ones, with the Dutch in between, merits comment. The contrast is heightened by the troublesome performance of the economies of the former two countries and the prosperity of Germany and Austria. Assuming that our findings are not the result of something inherent but unidentified in the English and German languages—an intriguing notion with no empirical basis whatsoever—one would expect good economic performance to lead to optimism, and poor performance to pessimism. One would assume a two-way process of translation at work—from the personal to the political realms and from the political to the personal. We have seen that personal dissatisfaction has little impact on political action; it seems equally true that economic prosperity has little impact on personal optimism and pessimism. Hence if the economic and political systems are working well, individuals may still be pessimistic. And the reverse is true as well: people may be predominantly optimistic in poorly functioning economic systems. Historical memories are long and resistant to modification. It seems that only an extended period—perhaps generations—can alter the pessimistic outlook engendered, presumably, by the traumas of the twentieth century in Central Europe. And it seems that personal optimism, once established, can survive several years of troubles at the level of the nation. This is further evidence that the relationship between personal feelings and politics is weak and the linkage complex.[34] Dissatisfactions that concern things political in a direct and obvious way are more promising as variables to account for political action, and we will turn to these subjects in the next chapter.

CONCLUSION

The vast literature on the relationship between personal dissatisfaction and political action has been a poor guide in our exploration of dissatisfaction. Most of the hypothesized relationships simply were very weak at the individual level. Apart from some politically important subgroups, the desperation of most of mankind seems to be quiet indeed.

It is not difficult to formulate reasons why this might be the case: most people lack the resources and the opportunity to pursue strenuous political activities, under normal circumstances, and this is particularly true of many who are dissatisfied. Our findings from these advanced industrial societies may thus be irrelevant for other societies or epochs of our five countries in which the politically competent are as likely as the incompetent to be dissatisfied. In our set of countries at the present time, however, competence and personal satisfaction tend to be found together, with some important exceptions.

But it is not only a question of competence: politics is a marginal activity for many people, and personal dissatisfaction is often blamed on one's personal inadequacies or on bad luck or on both. An increasing politicization of life may be observable everywhere, along with the tendency to blame society rather than one's self for one's fate; but politics as therapy is still in the experimental stage, practiced by a small but influential group who may—or may not—be setting a pattern for the future.[35]

NOTES

1. Among the vast number of relevant works we have found Ted Robert Gurr, *Why Men Rebel*, Princeton, N.J.: Princeton University Press, 1970; Charles Tilly, "Revolutions and Collective Violence," in F. I. Greenstein and N. W. Polsby (eds.), *Handbook of Political Science*, Vol. 3, Reading, Mass.: Addison-Wesley, 1975, pp. 483-555; and Douglas A. Hibbs, Jr., *Mass Political Violence: A Cross-National Causal Analysis*, New York: John Wiley, 1973, to be especially useful.

2. S.M. Lipset, "Some Social Requisites of Democracy: Economic Development and Political Legitimacy," *American Political Science Review*, 53 (March 1959), pp. 69-105; Philips Cutright, "National Political Development: Its Measurement and Social Correlates," in Nelson W. Polsby, Robert A. Dentler, and Paul A. Smith (eds.), *Politics and Social Life*, Boston, Mass.: Houghton Mifflin, 1963, pp. 569-582.

3. Deane E. Neubauer, "Some Conditions of Democracy," *American Political Science Review*, 61 (September 1972), pp. 928-959.

4. Norman H. Nie, G. Bingham Powell, and Kenneth Prewitt, "Social Structure and Political Participation," *American Political Science Review*, 63 (June and September 1969), pp. 361-378, 808-832.

5. Several scholars have dealt with the linkage process. In particular see Russell Dalton, *The Quality of Life and Political Satisfaction: An Analysis of European Mass Publics*, Ph.D. dissertation, University of Michigan, 1978, especially chapter 6; Daniel Katz, Barbara A. Gutek, Robert L. Kahn, and Eugenia Barton, *Bureaucratic Encounters: A Pilot Study in the Evaluation of Government Services*, Ann Arbor: Institute for Social Research, 1975; Richard A. Brody and Paul M. Sniderman, "From Life Space to Polling Place: The Relevance of Personal Concerns for Voting Behavior," *British Journal of Political Science*, 7 (July 1977), pp. 337-360; and Sniderman and Brody, "Coping: The Ethic of Self-Reliance," *American Journal of Political Science*, 21 (August 1977), pp. 501-522.

6. See especially W.G. Runciman, *Relative Deprivation and Social Justice*, Berkeley, Cal.: University of California Press, 1966, pp. 10, 250-251.

7. Ibid.

8. D.E. Morrison, "Some Notes Toward the Theory on Relative Deprivation, Social Movements, and Social Change," *American Behavioral Scientist*, 14 (May-June 1971), p. 682.

9. Gurr, *Why Men Rebel*, p. 596.

10. Hadley Cantril, *The Pattern of Human Concerns*, New Brunswick, N.J.: Rutgers University Press, 1965, p. 23.

11. Eric Allardt, "The Question of Interchangeability of Objective and Subjective Social Indicators of Well-Being." Paper presented to the 1976 Congress of the International Political Science Association, Edinburgh, August 16-21, p. 9.

12. Ronald Inglehart, *The Silent Revolution*, Princeton, N.J.: Princeton University Press, 1977, chapter 5. See also Russell Dalton, *The Quality of Life and Political Satisfaction*.

13. Ephraim Yuchtman (Yaar), "Effects of Psychosocial Psychological Factors on Subjective Economic Welfare," in Burkhard Strumpel (ed.), *Economic Means for Human Needs: Social Indicators of Well-being and Discontent*, Ann Arbor, Mich.: Institute for Social Research, 1976, p. 126.

14. Angus Campbell, Philip Converse, and Willard L. Rodgers, *The Quality of American Life: Perceptions, Evaluations, and Satisfactions*, New York: Russell Sage Foundation, 1976, p. 169.

15. Ibid., pp. 491-492.

16. Ibid., p. 180.

17. Ibid., p. 29.

18. Daniel Katz et al., *Bureaucratic Encounters*, p. 185.

19. Burkhard Strumpel, with the assistance of Richard T. Curtin and M. Susan Schwartz, in Strumpel (ed.), *Economic Means for Human Needs*, p. 26.

20. Inglehart, *The Silent Revolution*, p. 130, Table 5.3.

21. Hadley Cantril, *The Pattern of Human Concerns*. Cantril's measures have been widely accepted as a cross-nationally valid device for obtaining measures of deprivation. For example, Gurr, *Why Men Rebel;* Bernard N. Grofman and Edward N. Muller, "The Strange Case of Relative Gratification and Potential for Political Violence: The V-Curve Hypothesis," *American Political Science Review*, 57 (June 1973), pp. 514-539, especially p. 517.

22. Edward N. Muller, "Relative Deprivation and Aggressive Political Behavior." Paper prepared for delivery at the 1975 Annual Meeting of the American Political Science Association, San Francisco, September 2-5.

23. Grofman and Muller seem to take the same position: "we do conjecture that any of the particular results that we find for the Best Possible definition of the AD concept also will hold true for other microlevel achievement discrepancy measures that might be constructed," in "The Strange Case of Relative Gratification," p. 519.

24. Campbell et al., *The Quality of American Life*, p. 169.

25. Albert Bandura and Richard H. Walters, "the nature of the response to frustration will depend on the prior social training of the frustrated subject, or, more specifically, on the reinforcement and modeling procedures which he has previously experienced." *Social Learning and Personality Development*, New York: Holt, Rinehart & Winston, 1963, p. 159; quoted in Edward N. Muller, "A Test of a Partial Theory of Potential for Political Violence," *American Political Science Review*, 66 (September

1972), p. 929. Muller finds that belief that political violence has led to goal attainment in the past is directly related to potential for political violence. Ibid., p. 954. See also Muller, "A Model for Prediction of Participation in Collective Political Aggression." Paper prepared for delivery at the 1976 Congress of the International Political Science Association, Edinburgh, August 16-21.

26. Edward N. Muller and Thomas O. Jukam have demonstrated the importance of community (which is a prime example of an operational measure of opportunity and mobilization) on aggressive political behavior: "On the Meaning of Political Support," *American Political Science Review,* 71 (December 1977), pp. 1561-1595, especially pp. 1578-1580.

27. James C. Davies, "Toward a Theory of Revolution," *American Sociological Review,* 27 (February 1962), pp. 5-19.

28. Grofman and Muller, "The Strange Case of Relative Gratification," pp. 519-520. This article contains an excellent overview of the theories, hypotheses, and problems associated with changing expectations and protest potential.

29. Ibid., p. 520.

30. Ibid., p. 526.

31. A recent test of the J-curve theory and black urban unrest reached similar conclusions: "The results demonstrate that the J-curve theory is not a valid explanation of the riots." Abraham H. Miller, Louis H. Bolce, and Mark Halligan, "The J-Curve Theory and the Black Urban Riots: An Empirical Test of Progressive Relative Deprivation Theory," *American Political Science Review,* 71 (September 1977), pp. 964-982, especially p. 981.

32. Grofman and Muller, "The Strange Case of Relative Gratification."

33. We also used as another operationalization of change the difference between the present "entitlement" level and the expected future level. This measure seems to reflect the ambiguities of the entitlement version, as relationships with protest potential are weaker than the ones we report here.

34. If the linkage chain is long, relationships will be weak. For example, if the only linkage between two variables is through a third variable, and each correlates .5 with the third variable, the correlation between the first two would be .25.

35. Brody and Sniderman reach a similar conclusion: their findings argue "against suggestions of the privatization of politics and the attenuation of a civil outlook"; "From Life Space to Polling Place," p. 360.

Chapter 14
POLITICAL DISSATISFACTION

**BARBARA G. FARAH, SAMUEL H. BARNES,
and FELIX HEUNKS**

That citizens *evaluate their political order and that these evaluations* have action consequences are recurring themes in the literature on political participation. Evaluations affect both the stability and persistence of the polity. Positive evaluations are based in part on the belief that the political order is responsive to citizen demands. These demands, whether individual or collective in origin, are expected to result in governmental outputs. Most demands are articulated through regularized and legitimized channels. According to normative theories of democratic representation, people have issue priorities that are usually channeled through the electoral process, interest group activities, or direct communication with public officials. It is the responsibility of the elected officials to translate these demands into public policy; their performance is subsequently evaluated by the constituency and if rated positively, ceteris paribus, they continue to be supported. On the other hand, when performance is viewed negatively, either the electoral option of "voting the rascals out" or other methods are used to express dissatisfaction. In this manner citizens are able to exercise control over their elected officials and to express their policy preferences through regularized channels.

AUTHORS' NOTE: We would like to acknowledge the assistance of Kai Hildebrandt and Ethel D. Klein in this chapter.

It has been argued throughout this volume that citizens utilize a variety of means to influence the content of the public agenda. Most of the time the methods used are viewed as legitimate means of effecting changes in government policy performance. Yet the turmoil of the 1960s in most Western societies suggests that governments are no longer perceived to be effective or responsive to the needs of some segments of the population. For these groups, dissatisfaction is often manifested through protest behavior rather than conventional modes of political activity. For some observers the rise in protest activity signals growing disenchantment and brings into question the continued support and involvement of protesters in the democratic political order.

What has not been fully understood or explored is the relationship between the various forms of political dissatisfaction and protest. In this chapter we explore several dimensions of political dissatisfaction and their links to both conventional and unconventional political action. The political dissatisfaction concept is linked theoretically to Easton's model of system support.[1] It is citizen evaluation of political outcomes that determines the degree to which public authorities, governments, and political systems as wholes are supported by mass publics.

From the outset we draw a distinction between four dimensions of political dissatisfaction—support or opposition for the incumbent authorities, policy dissatisfaction, political responsiveness, and political efficacy. All four concepts will be developed and discussed in a later section. We begin with policy dissatisfaction and elaborate more fully on it because it is a concept that has not been widely treated empirically in this manner.[2]

The development of the measure of policy dissatisfaction draws upon a series of questions covering ten different issue domains of public policy and three different dimensions. The issue domains are the following:

Looking after old people
Guaranteeing equal rights for men and women
Seeing to it that everyone who wants a job can have one
Providing a good education
Providing good medical care
Providing adequate housing
Fighting pollution
Guaranteeing neighborhoods safe from crime
Providing equal rights for ethnic or racial minorities[3]
Trying to even out differences in wealth between people

For each of these the respondents were asked whether the issue was very important, important, not very important, or absolutely unimportant. Next, the respondent was asked "How much responsibility do you feel the government has for dealing with this problem?"[4] The response categories were an essential responsibility, an important responsibility, some responsibility, or no responsibility at all. Finally, the respondents were asked, "How well do you think the government has been doing in handling this problem?" The response categories were very good, good, bad, or very bad.

The list of issues is not meant to be exhaustive. We have tried to include sufficiently broad issues that would be relatively equivalent cross-nationally and that would be easily recognizable by large segments of the population. Moreover, many of these issues have already become part of people's issue agenda. Job security, educational opportunities, and medical care are cases in point. Yet the inclusion of these issues is particularly germane to a cross-national perspective because it allows us to determine the extent to which mass publics differ in their perceptions of the government's handling of issues that are an integral part of the public agenda in all countries.

Issue Agenda

Not all issues become part of the public agenda. Indeed, the number of issues that are personally important to an individual but are never slated for government action far outnumber those that eventually enter the public domain. In part this is due to the relatively recent history of government involvement in matters once considered to be the primary responsibility of the individual and not the state. Since the turn of the century, however, most of the European nations have relied on greater government involvement in the area of social welfare. The United States followed the European lead somewhat later in time and a bit more cautiously. This nation remains an anomaly among the others. Today, with little exception, the question of whether government should be involved in matters of individual well-being is moot. The majority of people in these advanced industrial societies have grown up to expect social security benefits, unemployment compensation, and medical care programs, to name just a few. Still other issue domains now command the attention of governments that extend well beyond the issues of social welfare. In the United States, for example, racial problems gained new impetus and led to government's vigorous action in the early 1960s.

Although government involvement in matters of common concern to most citizens is no longer flatly rejected, there is still considerable disagreement surrounding the question of how "big" should Big Government be, and this concern has had a differential impact in the five nations. The question of which issues should become part of the public agenda remains controversial.

The distinction drawn between issues that are on individuals' personal agendas and those that appear on the public agenda must be kept in mind. It is apparent from the above that our emphasis is on the latter. The issue agenda combines the two components, the one that taps the private domain and the other that focuses on the public arena. The private dimension consists of how important an issue or policy is to a particular person. While it is not necessarily the case that all important issues will appear on the public agenda, high issue salience leads rather than follows the assignment of responsibility to the government for the handling of that issue. It is the introduction of the second component, the recognition of need for government involvement in policy problem-solving, that brings the personal priorities into the public sphere and establishes the demands that citizens place on their governments.[5]

An inspection of the overall mean scores for all the issues on each of the two dimensions will illustrate these points. It is clear that the issues selected were considered to be generally highly important: for the United States the mean importance score is 3.4 while for the remaining four nations it is 3.5—based on a four-point scale, running from low to high importance—a difference that is statistically significant.[6] When we look at the overall mean score with regard to responsibility attributed to the government dimension, however, we discover more variation across the five nations. The Netherlands and Germany have the highest mean score, 3.3, while Britain and Austria follow close behind with a mean score of 3.2; only the United States deviates with the lowest mean score of 3.0 on government responsibility—these scores are also based on a four-point scale.

An issue agenda index was constructed by giving equal weights to the categories of the two components. That is, the highest score on the index was given to the respondents who indicated that the issue was both very important and an essential responsibility of the government. The lowest score on the scale included respondents who either felt the issue was not at all important, regardless of governmental responsibility, or that the government had no responsibility for the problem, regardless of importance. For each of the ten items, then, a five-point issue agenda index was constructed (1 = low, 5 = high).

The issue agenda indices are ordered from high to low according to the population mean on each issue in Table 14.1. Several aspects of the ordering of the issue agendas should be mentioned. First, no two nations have the same issue ordering on the ten items. Indeed, we would be hardpressed to explain complete congruence in agenda rankings among five nations as diverse politically, socially, and culturally as these. Yet there are items that appear in approximately the same place on all five national lists. This is borne out by the relatively high rank order correlations among the nations; the average Spearman rank order correlation coefficient is .72.[7] The most striking feature of this table is the dominance of the upper half of the rankings by social welfare or "bread and butter" issues—issues of traditional politics—while three issues of the "new politics" dealing with equality are consistently

Table 14.1: MEAN SCORE RANKINGS OF ISSUE AGENDAS

The Netherlands	Britain	United States	Germany	Austria
Education (4.5)	Medical care (4.6)	Education (4.1)	Crime control (4.6)	Crime control (4.5)
Medical care (4.3)	Education (4.4)	Crime control (4.1)	Medical care (4.4)	Medical care (4.4)
Housing (4.2)	Old age (4.3)	Old age (3.9)	Job security (4.3)	Job security (4.3)
Job security (4.1)	Housing (4.3)	Medical care (3.9)	Pollution (4.3)	Education (4.1)
Pollution (4.1)	Job security (4.2)	Pollution (3.7)	Education (4.2)	Pollution (4.1)
Crime control (4.1)	Crime control (4.1)	Job security (3.6)	Old age (4.1)	Old age (4.0)
Old age (4.0)	Pollution (4.0)	Minority equality (3.4)	Housing (3.7)	Housing (3.7)
Wealth equality (3.4)	Minority equality (2.8)	Housing (3.3)	Sex equality (3.2)	Wealth equality (3.1)
Sex equality (3.3)	Wealth equality (2.7)	Sex equality (3.0)	Wealth equality (3.1)	Sex equality (2.9)
Minority equality (2.9)	Sex equality (2.6)	Wealth equality (2.0)	Minority equality (2.7)	Minority equality (2.4)

at the bottom of each nation's rankings. The two other issues of the "new politics," pollution control and making neighborhoods safe from crime, either occupy a position midway in the lists of all nations (pollution), or else are ranked top priority in three countries (crime).

The dominance of the bread and butter issues on the agendas of all five nations is interpretable from several perspectives. First, issues as basic as guaranteeing job opportunities, housing, educational opportunities, and medical care have consumed much of the time and attention of mass publics and political elites for well over half a century; they have dominated the individual agendas—the demand structure—of most people as well. Second, with few exceptions, the complexities of advanced industrial societies no longer guarantee an individual seclusion from the ill-effects of societal-level conditions, such as inflation or wars. Both the need and the recognition of the need to rely on government to provide some basic protection against the impediments to a secure life and livelihood continue to promote and perpetu- ate a general preoccupation with material concerns.[8] In light of this, it is not too surprising to find that crime control and pollution protection have entered the top ranks of people's agenda. It may be that the sheer magnitude of these problems, coupled with the seriousness of their content, has encour- aged more reliance on government to effect a solution.

The three issues dealing with social equality do not rank as high as the other issue items on the agendas of mass publics. This may be largely a result of the relatively recent entry of two issues, sex equality and equality of racial or foreign minorities, into the political dialogue of Western democracies. Even in the case of the equal distribution of wealth issue, which is certainly not new to the agendas of Western societies, it appears that it has been recast in the political climate of the 1970s. Wealth equality is no longer seen as a class-based issue perpetuated by and for the working class, but rather ad- dresses the inequities of life opportunities which result from the existing stratification pattern.

These rankings do not mean that the problems of social inequality are not highly salient for certain groups. Not unexpectedly, we find that the Post- materialists consistently outdistance the other respondents in assigning a high priority to the question of social equality. Table 14.2 shows that across the five nations the Postmaterialists outdistance the Materialists in their ranking on these three issues of social equality.

Further, in the United States the question of racial equality receives a higher ranking among the blacks (mean score = 4.27) than among the rest of the population (mean score = 3.32). In the total American sample the racial equality issue ranks higher than the other two social equality agenda items, and even ranks above the housing issue. We suggest that the intensity of the civil rights movement in the 1960s coupled with the presence of a strong

Table 14.2: **DIFFERENCE IN MEAN SCORES BETWEEN POSTMATERIALISTS AND MATERIALISTS ON ISSUES OF SOCIAL EQUALITY**

		Sex Equality	Minority Equality	Wealth Equality
The Netherlands	Postmaterialists (9–10)	3.84	3.41	3.88
	Materialists (1–2)	3.02	2.38	2.89
Britain	Postmaterialists	3.16	3.58	3.15
	Materialists	2.41	2.59	2.31
United States	Postmaterialists	3.52	3.96	2.44
	Materialists	2.77	3.10	1.78
Germany	Postmaterialists	3.74	3.57	3.73
	Materialists	3.09	2.43	2.93
Austria	Postmaterialists	2.69*	3.00	3.67
	Materialists	2.88*	2.30	3.10

*Not significant at the .01 level.

black minority group in American society are responsible for increasing the awareness of a larger segment of the population of the problem of racial inequality and are affecting the overall agenda ordering of this issue. We might speculate further that as the women's movement gains momentum, it, too, will help focus more attention on the issue of sexual inequality, which, in turn, might increase its standing on the agendas of mass publics.

It is possible that the problems of social equality may never rank as high as the bread and butter items for the majority of the population for the simple reason that issues such as these have little immediate or measurable impact on the lives of most people. We suggest that while issues such as racial equality or equality for foreign workers, sexual equality, and redistribution of wealth may continue to win an increased number of supporters, they may never outdistance the rankings of the more fundamental issues of material well-being. For even among the Postmaterialists the concerns over jobs, educational opportunities, and medical care are shared universally with the rest of society.[9]

Despite the broad categorical distinctions that we have made from the agenda orderings between issues of social well-being and those of social equality, the responses are little more than idiosyncratic. Any structural similarities that might exist among particular issues cannot be determined from the rankings. Yet, from what we know from previous research, policy preferences do have dimensionality.[10] We would assume, therefore, that these issue agendas would also fall into predictable, patterned groupings.

To determine whether there is an underlying structure to the responses in the five nations, we relied on a multidimensional scaling technique (see the Technical Appendix). We found two similar cluster patterns in the responses of all five countries.[11] The individual well-being agenda subindex consists of four issues: jobs, education, medical care, and housing. Not only are these issues among those dominating the upper rankings of the agenda list, but they are also shown to be spatially proximate. Indeed, it is not surprising to find that these issues are at the core of traditional politics, and, as such, have been linked programmatically by the political parties for several decades. Social welfare legislation, after all, is multifaceted.

The second subindex contains the three social equality agenda items. Reducing the disadvantages of and giving equal rights and status to the poor, racial minorities, foreign workers, or women formed a clearly discernible cluster in each of the five nations. The common denominator of all three agenda items is the perceived disadvantage each of these groups has in the society as a whole. They are the "have-nots" among those who "have," the powerless surrounded by the powerful. While each issue has a separate constituency, it is apparent that there is an overlap in interests across the three domains. And as indicated above, the Postmaterialists champion them all.

The two issue subindices present some striking cross-national differences. It is clear that in every country it is the individual well-being items that rank higher on the agenda. Cross-national differences follow the ideologically based expectations of conventional wisdom, with socialist Britain scoring the highest on this subindex and the United States lowest. The gap between the individual well-being agenda mean and the social equality mean ranges from .9 in the United States to 1.0 in the Netherlands, 1.1 in Germany, 1.3 in Austria, and 1.7 in Britain (See Table 14.3). The discrepancy in the British agenda scores is worthy of pause. Britain's preoccupation with matters of

Table 14.3: MEAN COUNTRY SCORES ON ISSUE AGENDA SUBINDICES

	The Netherlands	Britain	United States	Germany	Austria
Individual Well-Being Agenda (1–5)	4.2	4.4	3.7	4.1	4.1
Social Equality Agenda (1–5)	3.2	2.7	2.8	3.0	2.8

material well-being is telling of the economic and social hardships it has had to endure during the past decade, a condition not reflected in the attitudes of the publics of the other postindustrial societies. It is also insightful from the point of view that other issues dealing more with Postmaterialist values are clearly placed substantially lower on the priority list.[12]

The issue agendas represent the demands that citizens make on their government. The existence of clearly defined issue agenda clusters is strong confirmation that mass publics have *common* expectations about policy priorities. Additionally, the two subindices affirm that there is multiple dimensionality to the issue agendas of most people, dimensions that incorporate both the concerns of traditional politics and the politics of Postmaterialism.

But what of governments' response to these policy demands? Are they being responsive to the demands that mass publics are making, as democratic theory suggests they should be? Or, are there issues that are being ignored or improperly handled by government? One major interest we have is determining whether or not there are items that are high on the public's issue agenda but are perceived as being handled poorly by the government. This discrepancy between policy expectations and citizens' evaluation of government performance is what we refer to as "policy dissatisfaction." We turn now to a consideration of the ways in which citizens evaluate governments' handling of their agenda priorities.

Government Performance

Readers will recall that respondents were asked to evaluate governments' performance on each of the ten issues. From the overall mean scores of the issue items on the performance dimension it is apparent that governments in these five nations are not rated highly in handling most policy agenda items. Austrians lead the other nations in expressing most satisfaction with government performance (2.8); Germans are least satisfied with their government's performance (2.5); respondents in the remaining three nations rate their governments between this range (2.6).

The Austrian government's high performance evaluation presents a marked contrast to that of the other nations. One explanation for this may be found in the uniqueness of the Austrian setting at this time. Unlike the other Western societies that faced political turmoil and social and economic disruption, Austria was the picture of peace and tranquility. Indeed, Austria seemed little affected by the major currents that swept across Europe and the United States. Under these circumstances it would be somewhat incongruous to expect the rating of government performance to be comparable to those received by the governments in other nations.

Whereas the issue agenda rankings displayed remarkable similarity across all five countries, no dominant pattern emerged on the performance dimension (Table 14.4). Even dimensional analysis on the performance domain failed to uncover any comparable clusters across the five nations. It is apparent that while mass publics in advanced industrial societies may have common policy demands, they are unlikely to assess government outputs in the same manner. Indeed, we would be hard pressed to explain similar evaluation patterns in light of the differences in political, social, and economic climates that prevailed in each nation during the period of this study. The recession did not have the same impact in all nations; nor did all countries have their Watergates.

The evaluation of government performance regarding the provision of jobs is an illustration in point. Whereas Germans and Austrians praised their governments' efforts in this area, in Britain and the Netherlands the evaluation was moderate, and in the United States it was judged most unfavorably. Several factors may account for the high performance evaluations in the former two countries. Unemployment was not a serious problem for either Germany or Austria. In Germany foreign workers have helped to alleviate a serious labor supply problem. This transient work force acts as a cushion during high unemployment situations. Another factor influencing the evaluations on this particular issue is related to the amount of protective legislation, especially in Germany and Austria, that already exists for the unemployed.

Two distinguishing features of advanced industrial societies are the relatively high levels of educational attainment and the availability of comprehensive medical services. All five nations have compulsory education for all children and rank among the highest in the world in terms of the number of people who receive advanced educational training. Low infant mortality and a long life span are but gross indicators of the advanced medical technology that is also provided to the mass publics of postindustrialism. From what we have already noted, educational opportunities and medical care are high on the agenda rankings in all five countries. The government's performance in these two areas is appraised positively in each country with only a few exceptions.

The low rankings on performance in the areas of crime control and pollution prevention among the five nations provide a striking contrast to the education and medical care issues evaluations. Crime and pollution are problems of advanced industrialization. They are issues that have emerged on the public agenda only recently and have attracted the attention of mass publics and won placement on the public agenda. From the relatively high placement of these items on the issue agendas in all five countries, it is evident that people were concerned and wanted their government to initiate some action. Yet the discrepancy between the expectations of citizens, on the one hand,

Table 14.4: RANKING OF ISSUE AGENDAS

The Netherlands	*Britain*	*United States*	*Germany*	*Austria*
EDUCATION	MEDICAL CARE	EDUCATION[a]	Crime control	Crime control
MEDICAL CARE	EDUCATION	Crime control[a]	MEDICAL CARE	MEDICAL CARE
HOUSING	Old age[a]	MEDICAL CARE[b]	Pollution[a]	JOB SECURITY
Pollution[a]	HOUSING[a]	Old age[b]	JOB SECURITY[a]	EDUCATION[a]
Crime control[a]	JOB SECURITY[b]	Pollution	EDUCATION	Pollution
JOB SECURITY[a]	Crime control[b]	JOB SECURITY	Old age	Old age
Old age	Pollution	Minorities equality	HOUSING	HOUSING
Wealth equality	Wealth equality	HOUSING	Sex equality	Wealth equality
Sex equality	Minorities equality	Sex equality	Wealth equality	Sex equality
Minorities equality	Sex equality	Wealth equality	Minorities equality	Minorities equality

RANKINGS ON GOVERNMENT PERFORMANCE

The Netherlands	*Britain*	*United States*	*Germany*	*Austria*
MEDICAL CARE	MEDICAL CARE	EDUCATION	MEDICAL CARE	JOB SECURITY
EDUCATION	EDUCATION	Sex equality	JOB SECURITY	EDUCATION
Old age	Old age	Minorities equality	EDUCATION	MEDICAL CARE
Sex equality	Minorities equality	MEDICAL CARE	Sex equality	Old age
JOB SECURITY	Crime control	HOUSING	Old age	Sex equality
HOUSING	JOB SECURITY	Pollution	Minorities equality	Minorities equality
Wealth equality	Sex equality	Old age	HOUSING	Crime control
Minorities equality	Pollution	JOB SECURITY	Crime control	HOUSING
Crime control	HOUSING	Crime control	Wealth equality	Wealth equality
Pollution	Wealth equality	Wealth equality	Pollution	Pollution

NOTE: a and b represent tied rankings
All capital letters and words are individual well-being items.
Entries in italics are social equality items.

[419]

and the dissatisfaction expressed toward government's handling of these problems, on the other, indicates that a time lag exists between public agenda-setting and government problem-solving.

As interesting as the individual country differences are on certain issues, our concern is to uncover common patterns in policy dissatisfaction among the five countries. In the next section we introduce our discrepancy measure—the discrepancy between issue priorities (expectations) and government performance (evaluations).

Policy Dissatisfaction

An index of policy dissatisfaction was constructed by combining the issue agenda score for each item with its corresponding performance score. When an issue was highly salient and the evaluation was good or very good, the resulting index rating was low dissatisfaction (1); high issue priority and a bad or very bad performance rating resulted in a high dissatisfaction index score (5). The middle scores in the index (2-4) consisted of most of the indifferent or low issue priorities ratings, whether government performance was scored good or bad (see the Technical Appendix for construction). The discrepancy index thus is an evaluation measure weighted by the priority ranking of the issue on the individual's policy agenda. An overall mean score for the ten individual policy dissatisfaction measures was computed to form the policy dissatisfaction index (PDI). In addition, two policy dissatisfaction subindices—individual well-being PDI and social equality PDI—were constructed to parallel the issue agenda subindices.

The mean PDI score varies from 2.5 in Austria to 2.9 in the United States and Germany, with Britain's mean of 2.7 and the Netherlands' of 2.8 in between. The high satisfaction level of the Austrians was anticipated from the high overall performance ratings and the high expectations the citizens had of their government to solve their problems. What is somewhat unexpected is the same score received by Germany and the United States, both in view of their considerably different political and economic situations, and also their posture toward government intervention in matters of social and economic well-being. We will see that these results have a particular interpretation.

The overall policy dissatisfaction index score represents the average level of policy dissatisfaction (see Table 14.5). The level of dissatisfaction between the two subindices differs. In dissecting the policy dissatisfaction index measure, however, we find that in the European countries the level of dissatisfaction on the social equality dimension is considerably greater than on the individual well-being issues. In the United States this distinction does not hold so that the overall PDI mean is not affected by the differential weights.

Table 14.5: AGENDA AND POLICY DISSATISFACTION INDEX [PDI]
(mean scores)

		The Netherlands	Britain	United States	Germany	Austria
Summary	Agenda	3.9	3.8	3.5	3.9	3.8
Indices	PDI	2.8	2.7	2.9	2.9	2.5
Individual	Agenda	4.2	4.4	3.7	4.1	4.1
Well-being	PDI	2.5	2.4	2.8	2.4	2.1
Social	Agenda	3.2	2.7	2.8	3.0	2.8
Equality	PDI	3.0	3.0	2.8	3.1	2.8

The European-American differences are further emphasized by a comparison of agenda and policy dissatisfaction scores. These show that the four European samples consistently score higher on the agenda items but at the same time exhibit considerable satisfaction with performance, while the gap between agenda and PDI scores is in every case much smaller for the Americans, among whom the concerned seem dissatisfied (see Table 14.5).

Policy Dissatisfaction and Its Antecedents

We indicated at the beginning of the chapter that the demand-oriented side of system evaluation has been little explored and virtually untested. If our measure of policy dissatisfaction taps this particular dimension, we could link it to the process that translates private needs into political action. Before we continue, however, we have to know more about the causes of policy dissatisfaction. Below we introduce a model used to present the common process and the relationships thought to generate a negative assessment of government policies. Our intention is to understand the conditions and circumstances that promote policy dissatisfaction in all five nations.[13]

Three competing interpretations of the sources of policy dissatisfaction are represented in the model shown in Figure 14.1. One is grounded in the concepts of relative deprivation, social inequity, and the Marxist notion of class cleavages. The second stems from the nature of contemporary value change and has been discussed by Inglehart in earlier chapters of the book. The third interpretation contends that policy dissatisfaction is the translation of a negative response to the electoral outcome by the opponents of the incumbent authorities. The model is divided into three parts with the lower section dominated by the components of the social inequity theory, the upper part occupied by the measures of the values dimension, and the middle section devoted to the electoral outcome variable. A discussion of the various components of the model will demonstrate the contribution that each is expected to make to a negative evaluation of government policy-making.

A repetitive observation running through modern historical thought in Western nations is that societies are basically hierarchical and the distribution of resources is unequal. One theoretical thread suggests that there are both objective conditions of an individual's life and subjective expectations that an individual has about his or her life's needs that lead the person to perceive inequities in the system.[14] Insofar as these evaluations of stratification in society are politicized, they will be reflected in the political attitudes and orientations of individuals. From this line of reasoning we would expect to find people low on the socioeconomic ladder likely to be dissatisfied with government policy performance because the political system is not perceived to be structured to protect their interests. Others would argue that it is not just an objective evaluation that leads to a negative assessment of government performance. Dissatisfaction is a result of a discrepancy between the individuals' perception of the quality of life they feel they are entitled to and what they perceive they and people like them are getting. Finally, it is possible that the perception of inequality in the system as a whole might cause some people to react negatively to policies that perpetuate the stratification and class cleavages in society.

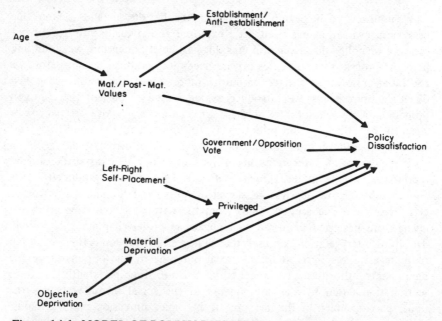

Figure 14.1: MODEL OF POLICY DISSATISFACTION

Three measures have been used to assess the impact of social inequity on policy dissatisfaction: an objective measure of an individual's position in the social hierarchy and two measures of perceived deprivation that differentiate between the individual as the referent and the society as the focal point. To measure the objective dimension of social inequity Treiman occupation prestige scores were used (see the Technical Appendix).[15] The prestige score reflected the relative position of an occupation in a socioeconomic hierarchical schema. We would anticipate from the theoretical discussion of this dimension that the socioeconomic status of an individual would have a direct impact on policy dissatisfaction. We would also suggest that the measure has an indirect effect on policy dissatisfaction insofar as the perception of individual well-being is a function of an individual's place in the social hierarchy. Both paths from Treiman prestige scores are diagrammed in the model.

To assess the relative deprivation dimension we used Cantril self-anchoring scales (described in the previous chapter). Here material deprivation was selected instead of the general life satisfaction measure since the former dealt more specifically with the socioeconomic component of an individual's life. Material deprivation measures the discrepancy between an individual's present material satisfaction level and the level one feels entitled to. In chapter 13 we found that material deprivation had little direct effect on political action. We suggest that in order for personal dissatisfaction to have an impact on political behavior it has to be cast in political terms. Policy dissatisfaction, we contend, is one of the ways in which politicization occurs. According to this formulation we would expect higher policy dissatisfaction for those with greater material deprivation scores. It is also possible that material deprivation has an indirect path to policy dissatisfaction. In this instance the inequity perceived for the society as a whole is at least partly based upon the treatment an individual feels he or she is receiving from the system.

The third path introduces the perception of social inequity into the model. The measure taps whether individuals acknowledge the existence of groups who receive either more or fewer rewards from the society than they deserve. According to the theoretical discussion of this path, people's perception of stratification in the society will lead to policy dissatisfaction. Identifying over- and underprivileged groups in society is seen as a function of a personal sense of being deprived by the system or else as an assessment of society in basically ideological terms. With respect to the latter, the left-right self-placement scale was used to determine the extent to which the ideological orientation of individuals influences their perception of societal inequity. A common assertion made is that leftists are more likely than rightists to view society as stratified.

A major theme of this volume has been to challenge the social stratification explanation as a source of discontent in advanced industrial societies. Inglehart has argued that it is the value orientations of people that are major determinants of policy dissatisfaction. Próponents of this approach posit that changes in societies of advanced industrialization have led to a shift in value priorities among some segments of the population. For these people, the traditional concern of fulfilling the basic material needs of an individual, which is at the core of theories of social stratification, is no longer in question. For the Postmaterialists the problem facing governments and societies is the need to improve the quality of life of all citizens. In one sense, the Postmaterialists have an expanded issue agenda: they, like the Materialists, are interested in the bread and butter issues, but, unlike their counterparts, are also concerned about matters involving social equality. A basic difference between the Postmaterialists and others in the society, however, is that the former seek goals not out of a sense of self-interest but rather for the sake of social justice and social equity. From this perspective it is possible to anticipate that the Postmaterialists would be dissatisfied with government policy performance. The Materialist/Postmaterialist measure, discussed in chapters 11 and 12, is used to evaluate the impact of this component on the evaluation of government performance.

From a somewhat different perspective, the value orientation of an individual may have only an indirect effect on policy dissatisfaction. In this case it is the value orientations of a person that lead to his or her identification with certain groups in society. This group identification is not perceived in terms of class or social stratification but rather in terms of shared values and value priorities. In this theoretical framework, groups are perceived to be supportive of the established order or are part of the elite-challenging counterculture movements. Our own measure of this group identification concept is based on a variable that delineates groups supportive of the establishment (small businessmen, military, police, unions, and civil servants) from those that oppose it (student protesters, the women's liberation movement, and disadvantaged groups) [see the Technical Appendix]. Our expectation would be that the individual's position on the side of or in opposition to the established forces in society would have a direct effect on policy evaluation.

As indicated above, both components of the value orientations side of the model have direct links to public policy dissatisfaction. We have also modeled the indirect path from the Materialist/Postmaterialist to the establishment/anti-establishment dimension. Both of these factors are influenced by yet another: age. It is the young, not yet burdened with the responsibilities of a job and family, who are more likely to be critical of the "establishment" and to identify with movements and causes that challenge the system. Age is also an indicator of generational differences, which link it to the differing value orientations of Materialists and Postmaterialists.

The final source of policy dissatisfaction is measured by whether or not the respondent had voted for the incumbent party in the previous parliamentary election (in the United States, the presidential candidate). The assumption made here is that it would be easier to blame the government for not doing an adequate job in certain issue areas if the party in power was not the one supported by the individual. Conversely, electoral support for the governing party could have a "halo effect" on the performance evaluation. By including this factor in the model we can determine the degree to which the process leading to negative policy evaluations is explained by dissatisfaction with the incumbent authorities.[16]

In order to evaluate the validity of the model we have used the ordinary least squares regression analysis technique. The unstandardized regression coefficients are reported in Figure 14.2. These coefficients are used because they allow us to compare the causal structures across the five sample populations and also provide a means of interpreting the contribution that each measure makes to policy dissatisfaction.[17] Let us begin by examining the impact of the three hypothesized sources of policy dissatisfaction on the model.

In assessing the contribution of the social stratification component, we find that the basic assumption of the theory is not borne out by the model. That is, the path leading from the objective measure of an individual's socioeconomic status to policy dissatisfaction is significant across four of the countries but in the opposite direction from what the theory would lead us to predict. The relationship between objective social stratification and material deprivation is also consistent across all nations, as indicated by similar slopes, but again in the wrong direction. Individuals of high socioeconomic status are more likely to perceive deprivation and to be discontented with governmental performance than people low on the stratification ladder. Britain is the only country in which the objective stratification measure has no impact on policy dissatisfaction.

In contrast to the objective side of the stratification model, the perceived stratification relationships did work in the predicted direction, and consistently in all five countries. Again, the slopes show remarkable similarity across the nations, thus suggesting that the translation of these perceptual measures of personal deprivation and societal stratification into policy dissatisfaction is virtually the same. Only in the Netherlands is the path from material deprivation to policy dissatisfaction statistically insignificant; for this country, at least, it is the perception of social inequality in the system as a whole that is converted into a negative evaluation of political outcomes.

When we look at the top half of the model—the values component—we find that the process outlining the conversion of value orientations into evaluations of government performance is upheld in all nations. With one

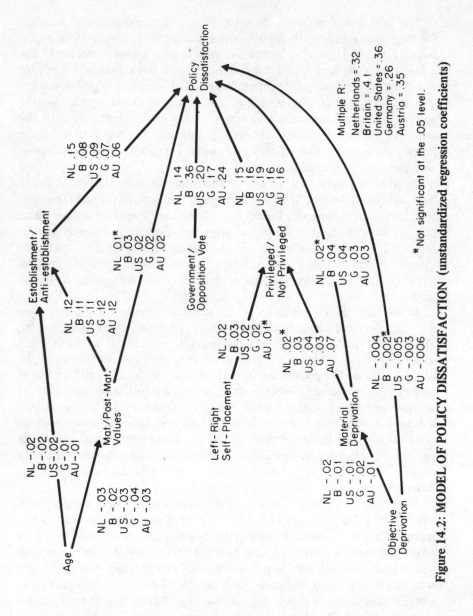

Figure 14.2: MODEL OF POLICY DISSATISFACTION (unstandardized regression coefficients)

exception, both direct paths in this component are significant. The establishment/anti-establishment factor dominates in its impact on policy dissatisfaction, and, in the Netherlands, in a very impressive way: the coefficient for this nation is nearly twice that of any other country.

It is gratifying to find that the dominant predictor in this component fits neatly with what conventional wisdom would have us believe about Dutch politics. The Netherlands has been called a consociational democracy because it is a fragmented society in which the various "zuilen," or pillars, accommodate one another in order to ensure a stable, effective government. According to Lijphart: "Dutch national consensus is weak and narrow, but it does contain the crucial component of a widely shared attitude that the existing system ought to be maintained and not be allowed to disintegrate."[18] System maintenance here means the maintenance of the existing cleavages and the current "establishment." Because the politics of accommodation favors the established groups, policy dissatisfaction manifests itself among individuals who oppose the old order.

In the case of the values orientation factor, the direct path to policy dissatisfaction is significant for all nations except the Netherlands. Its impact, however, is much less than that of the establishment/anti-establishment dimension. Insofar as the value priorities of an individual have a substantial effect on policy evaluation, it is indirectly through some form of group identification. A distal cause of both value orientations and establishment/anti-establishment feelings is age, which has virtually the same effect on both of these factors.

The final component of the model, the government/opposition dimension, proves to be another source of policy dissatisfaction. Similar to the stratification and values components, the incumbent authority dimension has a direct impact on how people assess what governments are doing for them. The one distinguishing feature about this relationship, however, is that there is greater variability among the coefficients across the five nations: the government/opposition measure has the least impact in the Netherlands and the greatest in Britain, with the other three countries falling in between. These findings pair nicely with what we know about the structure of the party systems in all five countries. At one end is the Netherlands, representing a multiparty system in which the governing coalition united Catholics, Protestants, and Socialists. The ideologically mixed government coupled with the shared responsibility for government decision-making among several parties makes it unrealistic to assume that the voters would be able to identify policy output with their own party.

In sharp contrast to the Dutch pattern is the British case in which the slope for the government/opposition dimension is considerably larger than for any other nation. It is also the case that is considered the clearest representation of a responsible party system. In this situation, government and opposition parties are clearly distinguished and formally charged with their specific duties and responsibilities. Focusing responsibility for poor performance on policy matters is, therefore, rather straightforward and, in fact, is an expected consequence of this form of parliamentary democracy. The ranking of the other three countries in terms of the scores also fits nicely into this responsibility dimension.

Thus far we have outlined the process by which various components affect policy dissatisfaction. We find that all components, save one, work in their predicted direction and function in a very similar fashion across the five nations. We now want to address the additional question of whether or not one component of policy dissatisfaction contributes more weight to the evaluation of government policies than the others. In the assessment of the importance of each component, standardized slope coefficients are used. The standardized coefficients take into account both the causal relationship between the independent and dependent variables, as indicated by the slope, and the variance and covariance among the independent and dependent variables. Each aspect of the variance/covariance structure can be a potential source of difference in the relative impact of the components.[19]

In the previous analysis we looked at each component in its disaggregated form and asked whether the relevant factors operated in a similar fashion across the five nations. Now we want to find summary measures that will assess the impact of each component on policy dissatisfaction. We derive our summary measures by forming a linear combination of the appropriate factors, weighting them by their slopes. To illustrate how we created our combined terms, we begin by setting up the basic regression equation. We will use the equation for Austria as our sample case.

	Constant	Perceived Stratification	Objective Stratification
Policy Dissatisfaction =	2.1	+ [.03 Mat. Dep. +.16 Priv/Not]	+ [−.01 Treiman]

	Value Orientations	Incumbency
	+ [.02 Mat/Post + .06 Est/Anti]	+ [.24 Govt/Opp]

The equation shows the clustering of variables into four components. The stratification component has been left decomposed into two dimensions, perceived stratification and objective stratification, because of the contradictory findings that are inherent in this domain. The summary measure of perceived stratification is a linear combination formed by multiplying material deprivation scores and privileged/not privileged scores by their respective slopes, .03 and .16 and then adding the products. The same procedure was used to construct the values orientation component. Once our summary terms were formed, we reestimated the regression equation for policy dissatisfaction using standardized coefficients so that we could assess the relative impact of the various components.

Table 14.6 presents the standardized coefficients for the equations for the five nations. While there are variations in terms of which component has the greatest impact across the nations, we find that with the exception of the Netherlands the major components—perceived stratification, value orientations, and incumbency—contribute relatively equally to policy dissatisfaction. In addition, objective stratification is the least important contributor to policy unrest in three countries. The only aberration in this pattern is the Netherlands in which we find one component—value orientations—clearly dominating all the others: the value score is substantially inflated while the scores for the other components are depressed. The emergence of the values component as the major source of policy dissatisfaction in the Netherlands adds further credence to our earlier discussion about the importance of the institutional pillars in Dutch society in shaping policy demands.

We conclude from our findings about the sources of policy dissatisfaction that the linkage between individual perspectives and the political system is highly complex. Displayed as a causal process, however, the translation of personal resources into political evaluations unveils a common underlying pattern across the five nations. In terms of the relative importance of one source of policy dissatisfaction over another, we found that with few exceptions each component contributes equally among these countries.

Dimensions of Political Dissatisfaction

In the theoretical discussions of conditions leading to political action a major consideration has been the way in which citizens evaluate the political system. The expectation is that these evaluations of the political system—whether positive or negative—have consequences for both the individual and the polity. Much of the research in this area has attempted to specify the impact of people's evaluations of governments and the consequences of these assessments for political action.

In beginning our discussion of evaluations we borrow from Easton's writing on system supports.[20] Easton distinguishes between the nature of support, whether diffuse or specific, and the objects or referents of support—the political community, the authorities, and the regime. Diffuse supports reflect a generalized assessment of whether or not the mechanism channeling political demands serves the long-term interests of the polity. Easton and Dennis write that they provide "a reservoir upon which a system typically draws in times of crises . . . when perceived benefits may recede to their

Table 14.6: COMPONENTS OF POLICY DISSATISFACTION

	Policy Dissatisfaction Index Score	Constant	Perceived Stratification	Objective Stratification	Values	Government/Opposition
The Netherlands	3.85	2.6	.48	-.29	.80	.26
Britain	4.30	2.0	.88	*	.70	.72
United States	4.14	2.5	.97	-.38	.65	.40
Germany	3.98	2.6	.78	-.29	.55	.34
Austria	3.28	2.1	.78	-.58	.50	.48

*Not significant.

lowest ebb."[21] People also respond to more specific policies, conditions, or events. These are generally based on short-term evaluations of government outputs and need not interfere with more generalized assessments.

Easton also distinguishes among referents of support. Incumbent authorities are the caretakers of the political order. As such, they may be affected by temporal forces and evaluations based on specific policy demands. The regime refers to the political order, its institutions, and the rules of the game. It relies for the most part on diffuse supports to sustain it during periods of disillusionment that may be fostered by succeeding sets of authorities. According to this conceptualization, however, very little can change or topple the regime in democratic societies without a constitutional restructuring. Yet, we know that regimes have changed, in content if not in form. The emergence of the New Deal in the United States and the Labor Party in Britain signaled a redirection of their respective regimes. We contend that the regime component has two dimensions—one is associated with the political institutions and one deals with its public philosophy, with the question of what the priorities of the nation *should* be. Included in the latter is an acceptance by the polity of the kinds of responsibilities that the government should assume for the well-being of its citizens. In this sense the content of this dimension may be very specific.[22]

In combination, the referents and types of political evaluation have differential impacts on the modes of political action that are pursued. We utilize three measures that reflect different configurations of the type and referent distinctions, as follows:

		Types of Political Evaluations	
		Specific	Diffuse
Referents of	Authority	Government/ Opposition	–
Political Evaluations	Regime	Policy Dissatisfaction	Responsiveness

The government/opposition measure, introduced earlier, combines specific evaluations with an authority referent. Accordingly, government outputs are assessed positively or negatively, depending upon whether an individual is supportive or opposed to the incumbent. Political responsiveness is a diffuse measure of evaluation of the regime. The stimuli used in this measure deal with basic institutions of the political system: the parties, the public officials, and the national government.[23] Responsiveness is an assessment of the openness of the political order and of the respondents' perceived effectiveness in influencing political decisions and decision makers. Policy dissatisfaction shares the specific component with the government/opposition measure insofar as the content of the measure is largely based on issues that make up the demand structure of the publics in the five nations. Yet it is also an evaluation of the regime because most of the issues in our measure are part of the prevailing public agenda and are not associated with one specific set of authorities or another. Instead, the public agenda might be regarded as the set of national priorities that are identified with the political order.

We round off the political evaluations dimension by introducing another measure—efficacy—which uses the individual rather than the political system as the referent.[24] This personal assessment of political capabilities taps the confidence of individuals in their ability to act politically. The measure uses two items from the Survey Research Center's political efficacy scale: "Voting is the only way that people like me can have any say about how the government runs things," and "Sometimes politics and government seem so complicated that a person like me cannot really understand what is going on." The internal efficacy dimension addresses the question of whether or not the individual feels capable of acting in the political system regardless of the political circumstances; in contrast, the responsiveness measure, which is the external dimension of the political efficacy measure, asks whether or not acting makes a difference.

In most of the literature dealing with system support the concept of trust in government plays a central role. Initially we had anticipated using a truncated two-item trust measure as an indicator of diffuse regime support.[25] However, after some preliminary analyses we discovered that our trust measure presented certain problems that could not be resolved in the context of our study. Perhaps most important was the fact that the referent in the trust measure was ambiguous. We found that trust was correlated with government/opposition, with policy dissatisfaction, and with the responsiveness measure as well, all at least at the .40 level. Rather than referring to the regime, as we would have anticipated from the early literature, it seemed to relate both to the regime and to the incumbent authorities. Indeed, these findings confirm much of what has been cited in the recent literature about the changing nature of the trust concept. Some scholars have argued that the referent is no longer the regime but rather the incumbent authorities.[26] Because our index is based on only two items, it is impossible to do an adequate testing of these competing hypotheses in the context of this study.

Since we want to be able to preserve the distinctions, both conceptual and analytical, among the various dimensions of evaluations, it is necessary for us to bypass the trust measure in favor of the responsiveness index. After all, the latter is conceptually linked to the trust measure insofar as both have been used to tap diffuse evaluations of the regime. In addition, responsiveness is not as highly correlated with the other dimensions of evaluations—government/opposition and policy dissatisfaction—as was the trust measure.[27]

Thus far we have emphasized the negative side of political evaluations. Political dissatisfaction, after all, assumes that the government or the authorities are receiving a poor evaluation for their performance. We will continue to stress political dissatisfaction, particularly as it relates to unconventional participation. But in the following discussion we address evaluations in general, both positive and negative.

Political Evaluations and Political Action

The basic premise of this chapter is that the way in which people evaluate the political system will affect their propensity to act in the political sphere. Additionally, it determines whether different types of political dissatisfaction will lead to different kinds of action. We develop a general model of political action in order to test these relationships. Here our interest is twofold. In the first place we want to establish the relationship between the various dimensions of political evaluations and political action. We are also interested in assessing the net effect of the evaluation component compared with other determinants of political activity. To handle these objectives we have included several measures that have figured prominently in this volume and that have consistently proved to be important factors in predisposing people to act politically. Postmaterialism and levels of ideological conceptualization have been linked directly to political action; age and education, two structural characteristics, have also been discussed as contributing factors. We expect all these components to have direct effects on political action.

We have shown, however, that political action has two faces, one conventional and the other unconventional. In the context of the general model that we will present, it is possible to determine whether the antecedents posited work differently for the two types of political action that are being explained. We begin by looking at the influence that the evaluation measures have on both conventional and unconventional participation. Next, we discuss the impact of the evaluations relative to other major determinants.

Conventional Participation. Normative theories of democratic representation expect ordinary citizens to play an active role in political affairs, to be aware of political decision-making, and to articulate their policy preferences. Although there is a sizeable discrepancy between what citizens *should* do and what they actually do in the political realm, for those who engage in political activity there is a sense that participating will make a difference. The underlying assumption here is that people who feel that the political system is responsive to their needs will show their support for the political order by participating in activities sanctioned by the regime. Feeling satisfied that they can influence decisions will make these individuals more likely to become involved in politics. Because conventional participation measures habitual behavior patterns rather than specific expectations about performance outputs, we would expect the referent of the evaluation to be the regime rather than the incumbent authorities.

Almond and Verba have argued that it is important in a democratic society to effect a balance between diffuse and specific evaluations of the political order.[28] Participation, they posited, should be a response to a general support for the norms of the political order and also to specific expectations that citizens have of their policy makers. Following this line of reasoning, we would assume that political responsiveness would have a positive impact on traditional forms of political action. Further, both policy dissatisfaction and the government/opposition measures would be expected to contribute to people's motivation to become involved in conventional political activity. The direction of the relationship for these two specific evaluations is somewhat harder to anticipate. It could be argued that satisfaction with the policies of the incumbent government would provide the incentive necessary to motivate some people to engage in political acts. It is also possible that a negative response to specific issues or policies of the government would lead citizens to participate. Depending upon which interpretation prevails, we would expect either a negative or a positive relationship between the specific evaluation measures and conventional participation, or no relationship if both interpretations apply to parts of the public.

In contrast to the interpretation that considers conventional participation as a direct response to citizens' assessment of the conditions of political order, another notion is that political activity flows from an evaluation of what an individual perceives he or she can do politically. Accordingly, the assessment of whether an individual can cope with the political environment will determine whether he or she will ultimately act upon it. In this sense, the internal efficacy index assesses a person's self-perceived ability to perform political acts and is devoid of any direct evaluation of the content of political activity. As such, highly efficacious citizens would engage in conventional modes of behavior because they feel competent as political actors.[29]

The remaining four factors—Postmaterialism, level of ideological conceptualization, age, and education—have already been discussed and their direct effects on political action have been modeled in chapter 12. We include them in our model in order to determine the relative impact of the evaluation component, controlling for these other influences.

Once again, we used ordinary least squares regression analysis to assess the contribution made by the eight measures included in the model. Since our major concern is with the evaluation component and the interplay among the four dimensions, we will focus our discussion of the findings on evaluations.

When we look at the results of our analysis presented in Table 14.7 we find that it is the evaluation of the regime that is prompting people to engage in conventional action. Furthermore, it is both the diffuse attachment to the regime and also the specific reference to the public agenda that leads people to participate in politics. However, it is clear that the diffuse dimension dominates; responsiveness is the only evaluation measure that relates to conventional participation consistently in the five countries. Although there is some variation in the magnitude of the slopes, the responsiveness dimension of political evaluation is statistically significant in the predicted direction in all countries. However, participation benefits the most from this factor in the United States and Austria and the least in the Netherlands and Britain, with Germany falling in between. The dominance of diffuse evaluations fits nicely with the theoretical expectation that habitual behavior represented by the conventional participation measures is a function of the citizen's satisfaction with the operating norms of the political order.

Where policy dissatisfaction does have an impact on conventional participation its effect is positive. This means that people participate when they perceive the government's handling of the issue agendas to be poor or inappropriate. While the influence of policy dissatisfaction on conventional participation is limited to two nations, the Netherlands and the United States,

Table 14.7: SLOPE COEFFICIENTS OF PREDICTORS OF CONVENTIONAL PARTICIPATION

	The Netherlands	Britain	United States	Germany	Austria
EVALUATIONS					
Government/Opposition	*	.18	.32	*	*
Policy Dissatisfaction	.16	*	.19	*	*
Responsiveness	.25	.29	.42	.33	.39
Internal Efficacy	.34	.23	*	.66	*
POSTMATERIALISM	*	.04	*	.09	.07
LEVELS OF IDEOLOGICAL CONCEPTUALIZATION	.34	.43	.40	.19	.48
EDUCATION	.33	.15	.45	.23	*
AGE	.01	.01	.01	*	.01
R^2	.23	.17	.19	.22	.17

*Not significant.

it nevertheless suggests that people in these polities who are disillusioned with the public agenda use conventional modes of action to redress their grievances.

People's evaluation of the incumbent authorities plays a role that is subordinate to their evaluation of the regime. Only in the United States and Britain are opponents of the incumbent authorities likely to be more politically involved; in the remaining three countries, orientation toward the authorities was not a factor in promoting conventional activity. We suspect, however, that the impact of the government/opposition measure really reflects the mobilization of leftist party voters when their parties are unsuccessful at the polls. In countries where government/opposition had no effect, leftist parties were represented in the governing coalition. Where leftist parties were not in power—the United States and Britain—there was a positive effect.

To test this proposition we substituted a left/right vote measure for the government/opposition factor. We assigned a left, center, or right label to the political parties and then assigned individuals a score on this scale in accordance with their party vote (see the Technical Appendix). We had hoped to find a negative relationship between left/right vote and conventional participation in Britain and the United States and no relationship in the remaining nations. These expectations are only partially borne out (results not shown). Having a conservative party in power does serve as a catalyst in the United States but not in Britain. Furthermore, voting for a party of the left in the Netherlands is a significant factor for conventional participation, which runs contrary to our expectations.

A nice counterpoint to the influence that system evaluation has on conventional participation is the impact of internal efficacy. In looking at whether or not an individual's self-perceived ability to deal with political objects is related to conventional participation, we find no consistent pattern across the nations. In those countries where efficacy is significant, the translation process varies widely. Germany stands out as one case where the influence of the individual's political competence is dramatically higher than in the other four countries. The influence of this dimension is two times greater than the impact of responsiveness.[30] It appears that in Germany traditional action is motivated by citizens' awareness of themselves as effective political actors; this awareness extends beyond acceptance of and satisfaction with the norms of the regime. The German public has been politicized. The passivity often attributed to the German population during the Third Reich and in the decades after (as in *The Civic Culture*) seems to have been replaced by a basic need of citizens to feel that they control their environment.

In sum, conventional participation is in part motivated by people's evaluation of the political order and in part by their assessment of themselves as political actors. Their evaluation of the incumbent authorities is only tangentially relevant to this form of activity. Although both diffuse and specific evaluations of the regime encourage citizens to engage in traditional forms of political action, it is clear that the former dominates in all five nations. Positive aspects of evaluations prevail over the negative ones in this action domain.

Protest Potential. In contrast to conventional participation, which is supposed to sustain the democratic process, unconventional activities—operationalized here as protest potential—are often seen as disruptive of both the regime and the incumbent office holders. To the extent that evaluations are important to this form of political activity, we want to know if the various components are weighted in the same manner across the two action domains.[31]

We have already found that satisfaction with the basic tenets of the political system predisposes citizens to engage in political action that is supportive of the regime. Diffuse evaluations, however, can be translated to effect quite the opposite results. Implicit in the system-stability model, which stresses a positive relationship between diffuse support and conventional participation, is the fear that people who perceive the system as being unresponsive provide a constituency that can be mobilized by counterelites to challenge the existing order. Because these people do not support the rules of the game and do not accept the legitimacy of the system, they are more likely to engage in activities neither supportive of nor approved by the established order.[32] According to this formulation, we would expect the relationship between the responsiveness measure and protest potential to be negative.

Protest potential is also associated with individuals who are opposed to the existing public agenda and who seek to bring about changes in the goals of the society. Protesting, after all, is goal-oriented and usually issue-specific. Petitions are signed to *stop a war,* to make an appeal for *lower taxes,* or to increase *social welfare benefits*; demonstrations are joined to publicize the *unfair treatment* of some groups in society and *to oppose an unpopular policy.* It is precisely because these people are apt to feel constrained and ineffectual using techniques that are identified, supported, and maintained by the status quo that they are more likely to step outside the regularized channels of action to express their demands. Under these circumstances the perception of the inadequate handling of the public agenda would lead to protest behavior or the readiness to protest. We would anticipate that a specific evaluation of the regime, as is involved in policy dissatisfaction, would have a positive impact on protest potential.

Protesting may also be directed toward the incumbent authorities for pursuing unpopular policies. For those individuals who have opposed the authorities in the electoral contest, there might be a greater willingness to use unconventional political methods to express their displeasure with decision makers. After all, they have seen the traditional modes work to their disadvantage in the choice of political elites. We would expect to find the opponents of the incumbent authorities more likely to engage in protest activities than their electoral supporters.

Perception of one's own capabilities is another crucial factor in determining whether an individual will defy the established modes of participation. Feeling capable of acting in a political setting should be as important if not more important for those contemplating protest action as for those engaging in conventional activity. People stepping outside the conventional sphere of political activity are seemingly more aware of themselves as competent political participants, able and willing to use methods that might be more effective than those traditionally used. We posit that internal efficacy will have a direct impact on protest potential.

Having expected a relationship between diffuse and specific evaluations of the regime and protest, we found, upon estimating the parameters, that the level of diffuse support does not enter into the decision to protest (see Table 14.8). Responsiveness was not related to protest potential in any of the five nations. People who felt the system was unresponsive did not provide a constituency for potential protesters. The fact that there is no relationship means that people who perceive the system as responsive are as likely to engage in protest as those who perceive the system as unresponsive. It is

Table 14.8: SLOPE COEFFICIENTS OF PREDICTORS OF PROTEST POTENTIAL

	The Netherlands	Britain	United States	Germany	Austria
EVALUATIONS					
Policy Dissatisfaction	.21	.27	.28	.20	.13
Responsiveness	*	*	*	*	*
Internal Efficacy	.28	.32	.19	.28	.18
LEFT/RIGHT VOTE	.50	.21	.30	.25	*
POSTMATERIALISM	.16	.10	.08	.11	.09
LEVELS OF IDEOLOGICAL CONCEPTUALIZATION	.27	.30	.21	.20	.24
EDUCATION	*	.19	.26	.12	.14
AGE	−.02	−.02	−.03	−.02	−.01
R^2	.30	.25	.33	.26	.17

*Not significant.

possible that this absence of a relationship reflects the cloaking of two different causal mechanisms: it may be that people who feel the system is highly responsive are not likely to protest because they are supportive of the system, while those who feel the system is not malleable are apathetic and are not engaged in either form of political action.

While assessments of the responsiveness of the political order are not determinants of protest potential, negative evaluations of the public agenda of the regime seem to predispose people to protest. In all five countries, policy dissatisfaction has an impact on protest potential. In a broad sense, then, protesting is a response to dissatisfaction with specific societal goals. Negative assessments of policy performance influence whether or not citizens contemplate nonconventional alternatives to political action. This pattern is consistent across all nations and the magnitudes of the slopes are fairly uniform except in Austria.

The relationship between the evaluation of the incumbent authorities and protest potential is not confirmed in all five nations (results not shown). While the magnitude of this incumbency measure is consistent across four of the five countries, with Austria showing no relationship at all, the direction changes. It appears that the relationship between government/opposition and protest potential is dependent upon whether or not a left or left-oriented party is in power. In those countries where there is a conservative regime this relationship is positive, while in countries where leftist parties are represented in the ruling coalition the relationship is negative.

Once again we suspect that upon substitution of our left/right vote measure we would find leftist voters are more likely to protest in the four nations where incumbency seems to be a factor. We initially estimated the equation with both government/opposition and left/right vote measures included. In no country was government/opposition significant. However, due to severe multicollinearity problems, left/right vote also was not significant in two of the five nations. When the government/opposition measure was omitted, the left/right vote became significant in the expected four countries. Leftist voters were most prone to protest in the Netherlands; the impact is somewhat less in the United States, Germany, and Britain. This illustrates that the propensity of leftist voters to pursue unconventional activity is independent of whether or not conservatives are in power.

We conclude that protest is not necessarily motivated by a dislike of the office holders per se. It is a general unfavorable reaction to the policy priorities of governments in these five nations, as indicated by the salience of policy dissatisfaction, that fosters this behavior. Challenging the issue agendas in postindustrial societies seems to entail the use of additional forms of behavior not necessarily sanctioned by the polity as a whole.

Feeling competent to perform in the political arena has implications for protest potential as well as for conventional activity. We find the relationship between internal efficacy and protest potential supported in all five countries, and in a fairly uniform manner. Furthermore, internal efficacy as a translation mechanism is more consistent when explaining protest potential than conventional participation. The ability to engage in political activities that extend beyond what is considered within the traditional norms of society seems to rest upon the self-confidence of an individual in defying the prescribed channels of participation.

Protest potential, then, like conventional participation, stems from an evaluation of the political regime as opposed to the transient authorities. Indeed, the authority dimension does not appear as a factor for protest potential and its impact on conventional behavior is limited to two countries. While the regime is the salient object of evaluation in both spheres of political action, the types of evaluation that are being made differ substantially from one domain to the other. The dominance of diffuse over specific evaluations in the conventional model confirms much of what we already know about the nature of traditional participation patterns in Western democratic societies. Traditional participation seems to be a demonstration of citizens' support for the political regime, its rules, and its institutions. In contrast, the emergence of specific evaluations in the protest domain sheds some new light on the meaning of protest in advanced industrial societies. Insofar as people's evaluations of the regime have an impact on protest activity it is apparent that what is being contested are the priorities that governments place on certain policies. People who seek to challenge the goal orientations of the regime show a willingness to expand their political repertory to include actions not necessarily sanctioned by the polity in order to effect the changes that they desire.

Evaluations in Two Political Action Domains

The final question that remains to be addressed concerns the contribution of the evaluation component in both political action domains relative to the other major determinants. Whereas in the preceding section we used unstandardized slope coefficients to compare the causal relationships among the various evaluation components across the five populations and across the two political action domains, we now employ standardized coefficients (Betas) to assess the impact of evaluations in the two models of political action. Since standardized coefficients are influenced by the variance-covariance structure among the variables, we would expect that a difference in the distribution of ideologues, Postmaterialists, or the politically dissatisfied from one population to the next would be reflected in the contribution these measures make to both forms of political activity.

In its decomposed form we have shown that the dimensions of evaluations—differentiated by type and referent—have influenced people's modes of political activity. Because we now want to ascertain the impact of evaluations as a whole, we need to create a summary measure that combines these dimensions. Replicating the technique used earlier, we form a linear combination of the appropriate factors that have been weighted by their slopes. In the case of conventional participation, all four dimensions of evaluations are present in the summary measure. For protest potential, however, the summary measure does not include the government/opposition element. Our prior analysis of the unstandardized coefficients led us to conclude that the authority referent did not serve as a motivating factor in pursuing unconventional activity; rather, it was whether the individuals supported a leftist party that played a significant role in encouraging protest. Our present analysis of the determinants of unconventional participation parallels the revised equation presented in Table 14.8. The left/right vote factor, while included in the equation, is not linked conceptually to the evaluation component.

In the conventional participation sphere we find that in four of the five countries the contribution of the evaluation component is outweighed only by the levels of ideological conceptualization measure; in Germany, the strongest predictor of people's involvement in conventional participation is evaluations (see Table 14.9). The prominent role played by ideological sophistication and evaluations in the conventional participation model is what we would expect, given the types of behavior involved. People must possess certain cognitive abilities and have some affect toward the political system in order to read about politics in newspapers, engage in community affairs,

Table 14.9: DETERMINANTS OF CONVENTIONAL PARTICIPATION (standardized slope coefficients)

	Evaluations	Post-materialism	Level of Ideological Conceptualization	Education	Age
The Netherlands	.22	.03*	.28	.13	.09
Britain	.15	.06	.31	.09	.11
United States	.16	.01*	.25	.18	.11
Germany	.31	.11	.12	.11	−.02*
Austria	.19	.08	.29	.04*	.04*

*Not significant at the .05 level.

convince other people to vote as they do, and write letters to public officials. The major predictor in our model, the level of ideological conceptualization, taps the cognitive ability of individuals to distinguish among political objects and then to make positive and negative assessments of these objects. The evaluations factor rests mainly on the individuals' perception of the responsiveness of the political order and also of themselves as competent political participants. Conventional participation requires skills, both cognitive and evaluative, that help to motivate individuals to be politically active and to sustain this involvement from one year to the next.

When we turn to protest potential yet another pattern unfolds. Ideological thinking and evaluations do not dominate in the protest sphere. Although these factors remained substantial contributors to protest potential, their influence in this domain is less dramatic than in the conventional arena. We find that age, Postmaterialism, and left/right vote surface as important contributors to people's predisposition to engage in protest activities. Almost without exception, the Beta values for age and Postmaterialism double or triple as we move from conventional to unconventional modes of action (see Table 14.10).

The sizeable impact of age, Postmaterialism, and left/right vote in the protest domain lends further confirmation to what has been pointed out in previous chapters about the nature of protest and the types of individuals who engage in this form of political action. Protest activity is very much oriented toward effecting change in society. Young people, unencumbered by the constraints of the established patterns of participation and also more prone to seek changes in the existing order, may use new political techniques to further their objectives. Advocates of Postmaterialism may also find conventional methods of political action biased in favor of maintaining the value priorities of the status quo and, therefore, would resort to unconventional forms of activity to effect the changes that are necessary. Furthermore, people who are change-oriented are supportive of the parties and politics of the political left. The connection between the political left and pro-change policy orientations can be traced to the history of industrialism and postindustrialism. Despite the shift in objectives and priorities of the pro-change groups in society from one historical period to the next, they have nevertheless remained associated with the Left or New Left.

The directionality of change that seems so important to protest potential may explain why the evaluation component, in general, and policy dissatisfaction, more specifically, do not play more dominant roles in the unconventional action domain. Since the policy dissatisfaction measure does not differentiate between conservatives and leftists, both of whom may be discontented with the public agenda, it is possible that some of the potential impact of this measure has been suppressed. That is, we would expect to find

Table 14.10: DETERMINANTS OF PROTEST POTENTIAL (standardized slope coefficients)

	Evaluations	Left/Right Vote	Post-materialism	Level of Ideological Conceptualization	Education	Age
The Netherlands	.11	-.25	.19	.20	.02*	-.18
Britain	.15	-.12	.11	.19	.09	-.25
United States	.16	-.17	.11	.17	.13	-.30
Germany	.16	-.15	.16	.16	.07	-.21
Austria	.12	.002*	.12	.21	.09	-.15

*Not significant at the .05 level.

conservatives who are dissatisfied with government's handling of policies to be less likely to engage in protest activities, but would anticipate that leftists would be more willing to resort to unconventional modes of action to redress their grievances. The potential interaction between policy dissatisfaction and ideological orientation remains speculative because its testing takes us beyond the scope of this chapter. The contribution of policy dissatisfaction to protest activity remains intact regardless of further conceptual elaborations of the measure.

The R^2 provides additional information with which we can assess how well our model fits reality. We find that our determinants of political action perform well in accounting for both forms of participation. In both instances we explain a respectable amount of variance, ranging from 17 percent to 23 percent on conventional participation and 17 percent to 33 percent on protest potential. The antecedents posited in the general model of political action proved to be applicable for both forms of participation, though the translation of several factors differed across the two domains. We found on the one hand that level of ideological conceptualization had a greater impact on conventional participation than on protest potential. On the other hand, factors equated with political and social change had stronger direct effects on unconventional activity than on the traditional modes of political behavior. One striking distinction made between protest potential and conventional participation surfaced when we looked at the types of evaluations people made. Conventional participation was largely a function of system responsiveness, or support for the rules of the game, while unconventional activity was attributable to unhappiness with the existing political agenda.

Conventional participation is a manifestation of support for the political order. It reflects a diffuse support for the rules of the game—a belief that the system is responsive to the needs of its citizens. The counterpart of support is dissent. The presence of dissent in democratic societies is often indicated by unconventional modes of action. The voicing of dissent through protest is attributed to a negative evaluation of specific policies pursued by the regime. It appears that insofar as support and dissent exist in contemporary societies citizens show a need to channel their responses to each in dramatically different directions. The expansion of people's political repertories, therefore, seems to reflect a more basic and general response to the exigencies of political life in more complex societies.

NOTES

1. David Easton deals with the impact of people's evaluations of the political system on system stability in *A Systems Analysis of Political Life*, New York: John Wiley, 1966.

2. Our thinking about the conceptualization and measurement of policy dissatisfaction has benefitted greatly from the pioneering developmental work of Lester Milbrath. We have borrowed freely from his work and wish to acknowledge our debt. See, in particular, Lester W. Milbrath, "The Nature of Political Beliefs and the Relationship of the Individual to the Government," *American Behavioral Scientist,* 12 (November-December, 1968), pp. 28-36; "A Paradigm for the Comparative Study of Local Politics," *Il Politico,* 36 (1971), pp. 5-35; *People and Government,* unpublished, State University of New York at Buffalo, 1971; and, with M. Goel, *Political Participation,* Chicago: Rand McNally, 1977.

For other treatments of this topic see: Arthur H. Miller, Warren E. Miller, Alden S. Raine, Thad A. Brown, "A Majority Party in Disarray: Policy Polarization in the 1972 Election," *American Political Science Review,* 70 (September 1976), pp. 753-778; Peter McDonough, Amaury De Souza, and Thomas R. Rochon, "Preferences, Priorities, and Impacts: Mass Attitudes Toward Birth Control and Other Issues in Brazil." Paper delivered at the Annual Meeting of the Midwest Political Science Association, Chicago, 1977.

3. The item related to foreign workers in the three continental countries.

4. Considerable effort was made to select a term that would be functionally equivalent in all five nations. In Britain "The Government" was used since it specified the governing party, which is responsible for administrative and legislative matters. The Dutch used the term *de regering,* which also identified the ruling coalition with the responsibility of legislative decision-making. In Germany and Austria a more generic term, *der Staat,* was introduced. *Die Regierung* was bypassed primarily because it was considered to have a partisan bias and was too transitory. Needless to say, this was potentially a deviation from the meaning of the term assigned by the other countries. As we will see below, there seems to have been no detectable bias introduced by the use of the term der Staat. In the United States, "the government" was the stimulus. Here, no clues were given to suggest whether federal, state, or local levels of government were being addressed. It was left entirely up to the respondent to decide the foci. Again, we have very little fear that this strategy introduced incongruities in interpretation.

5. See McDonough et al., "Preferences, Priorities, and Impacts," for a different operationalization of issue agenda.

6. Unless otherwise specified all reports of mean score differences are statistically significant.

7. We calculated the Spearman rank order correlations for all possible pairs of nations and then computed the average coefficient. See Hubert M. Blalock, *Social Statistics,* New York: McGraw-Hill, 1960, pp. 317-318.

8. The importance of what we have termed "bread and butter issues" has been discussed widely in the literature. See Hadley Cantril, *The Pattern of Human Concerns,* New Brunswick, N.J.: Rutgers University Press, 1965; Angus Campbell, Philip E. Converse, and Willard L. Rodgers, *The Quality of American Life: Perceptions, Evaluations, and Satisfactions,* New York: Russell Sage, 1976; Burkhard Strumpel (ed.), *Subjective Elements of Well-Being,* Paris: Organization for Economic Co-operation and Development, 1974. While Inglehart contends that issues of the new politics are becoming increasingly important for certain groups in postindustrial societies, he nevertheless emphasizes the centrality of the social welfare issues for these same people. See Ronald Inglehart, *The Silent Revolution,* Princeton: Princeton University Press, 1977.

9. With the exception of the three social equality issues and crime control there are no significant differences between Materialists and Postmaterialists. In the case of the crime issue, however, it was the Materialists who assigned a higher agenda priority to it,

but this is not surprising since concern for crime is a component of the instrument measuring values.

10. Arthur H. Miller et al., "A Majority Party in Disarray"; Gerald M. Pomper, "From Confusion to Clarity: Issues and American Voters, 1945-1968," *American Political Science Review*, 66 (June 1972), pp. 516-528; Kai Hildebrandt and Russell J. Dalton, "Die Neue Politik: Politischer Wandel oder Schoenwetterpolitik?" *Politische Vierteljahresschrift*, 18 (1977), pp. 230-256; in translation, in Klaus v. Beyme (ed.), *German Political Studies*, Beverly Hills and London: Sage Publications, 1976.

11. The three remaining issues, old age, crime, and pollution, did not appear consistently across the five nations in one of the two major clusters and, therefore, they were left out of the subindices.

12. Alan Marsh, "The 'Silent Revolution', Value Priorities and the Quality of Life in Britain," *American Political Science Review*, 69 (March 1975), pp. 21-30.

13. For a balanced discussion of various models suggested in the literature see Russell Dalton, "Quality of Life and Political Satisfaction," unpublished Ph.D. dissertation, University of Michigan, 1978.

14. Ted Robert Gurr, "A Causal Model of Civil Strife: A Comparative Analysis Using New Indices," I. K. Feierabend, R. L. Feierabend, and T. R. Gurr (eds.), *Anger, Violence and Politics: Theories and Research*, Englewood Cliffs, N.J.: Prentice-Hall, 1972, pp. 184-222; I. K. Feierabend and R. L. Feierabend, "Systemic Conditions of Political Aggression: An Application of Frustration-Aggression Theory," pp. 136-83.

15. Treiman prestige scores for occupation of head of the household were used in this analysis.

16. We find that the conceptual distinction that we draw in our policy dissatisfaction model is mirrored in the intercorrelation matrix for each nation. Nowhere is the correlation between pairs of items that belong to different components higher than .30.

17. The appropriateness of using unstandardized slope coefficients is discussed in Jae-on Kim and Charles W. Mueller, "Standardized and Unstandardized Coefficients in Causal Analysis," *Sociological Methods and Research*, 4 (May 1976), pp. 423-438.

18. Arend Lijphart, *The Politics of Accommodation: Pluralism and Democracy in the Netherlands*, Berkeley: University of California, 1975, p. 102.

19. Kim and Mueller detail the methodological and conceptual distinctions between the use of standardized and unstandardized slope coefficients, "Standardized and Unstandardized Coefficients in Causal Analysis."

20. David Easton, *The Political System*, New York: Alfred A. Knopf, 1953.

21. David Easton and Jack Dennis, "A Political Theory of Political Socialization," in Jack Dennis (ed.), *Socialization to Politics*, New York: John Wiley, 1973, p. 46.

22. Gamson also suggests that Easton's regime referent contains two dimensions: the political institutions of a regime and the public philosophy of a regime. William A. Gamson, *Power and Discontent*, Homewood, Ill.: Dorsey Press, 1968, pp. 50-51.

23. 1. I don't think that public officials care much about what people like me think.

    2. Generally speaking, those we elect to (Parliament) lose touch with the people pretty quickly.

    3. Parties are only interested in people's votes, but not in their opinions.

Response categories ranged from 1 = low responsiveness to 4 = high responsiveness. One missing data value was allowed (see Technical Appendix).

24. For a discussion of the internal and external components of the SRC efficacy measure, see George I. Balch, "Multiple Indicators in Survey Research: The Concept 'Sense of Political Efficacy'," *Political Methodology*, 1 (Spring 1974), pp. 1-44.

25. The two items included in our survey are:

Generally speaking, would you say that this country is run by a few big interests looking out for themselves or that it is run for the benefit of all the people?

How much do you trust the government to do what is right?

26. See the debate between Arthur H. Miller, "Political Issues and Trust in Government: 1964-1970," *American Political Science Review,* 68 (September 1974), pp. 951-972 and Jack Citrin, "Comment: The Political Relevance of Trust in Government," *American Political Science Review,* 68 (September 1974), pp. 973-988. The former author argues that the referent in the trust measure is the regime while the latter contends that what is being referenced is the incumbent authorities.

27. The intercorrelation between pairs of evaluation items shows a fairly moderate relationship in all nations. The strongest correlation exists between the responsiveness and efficacy items, ranging from .30 in the Netherlands to .54 in Germany, with the other three countries falling in between.

28. Gabriel A. Almond and Sidney Verba, *The Civic Culture,* Princeton: Princeton University Press, 1963, pp. 252-253.

29. For a discussion of the importance of internal efficacy to political action see Ada Finifter, "Dimensions of Political Alienation," *American Political Science Review,* 64 (June 1970), pp. 389-410; Edward N. Muller, "Behavioral Correlates of Political Support," *American Political Science Review,* 71 (June 1977), pp. 454-467.

30. The reader should note that we can make these comparisons because the metric is the same for both measures.

31. For a discussion of the problem of system support and evaluation in two action domains see: Edward N. Muller and Thomas O. Jukam, "On the Meaning of Political Support," *American Political Science Review,* 71 (December 1977), pp. 1561-1595.

32. Finifter discusses the possible action outcomes for individuals with different perceptions of system responsiveness, "Dimensions of Political Alienation."

Chapter 15

GENERATIONS AND FAMILIES
General Orientations

M. KENT JENNINGS, KLAUS R. ALLERBECK,
and LEOPOLD ROSENMAYR

INTRODUCTION

A key question in analyzing politics in advanced industrial societies is the rate and source of change across succeeding generations. Shifts in the center of behavioral and attitudinal gravity within a polity can have two origins. First, transformations and departures can take place across virtually all sociopolitical strata within an extant population. Such sweeping changes are often referred to as period or historical effects. A second source of change is population replacement. Older cohorts may not change, but their places are taken by cohorts socialized into a different set of values, attitudes, and behaviors. The first model predicates rapid shifts with attendant structural strains, though little intergenerational conflict. The second model predicates much more gradual change but one trumpeted by generational cleavages.[1] In the real as opposed to the abstract world, neither of these models is likely to be found in a pure state. Historical trends sweep up some people and not others; succeeding generations usually have some points of strong political resemblance. One of the challenges of studying an evolving form of society— such as the advanced industrial state—is to sort out the mix of these patterns of change and continuity.

The place of the nuclear family in this process is of special importance. Although the empirical evidence supporting a model of offspring replication of parental political characteristics is (appropriately) uneven, there is little doubt that in a variety of ways the family shapes and bends the political make-up of its children.[2] Sometimes, as in the classic case of rebellion, the family is a negative referent for the growing child. More often than not, however, children tend to enter adulthood looking more like than unlike their parents—though the similarity varies dramatically depending upon the political characteristic being considered. This happens through some rather direct processes—such as observational learning and reinforcement within the family—as well as through more indirect ways—such as the child's being part of the same sociopolitical milieu occupied by the parents. But the extent to which children reproduce the value orientations of their parents is conditioned by many factors, not the least of which are the availability of other socialization forces and the broad social movements which may be at large.[3] To understand fully the nature of how change and continuity are occurring in advanced industrial societies we need to look at what is going on within the crucible of the family.

From another perspective, theories seeking to explain system persistence tend to assign a prominent function to the socialization process. Socialization processes can serve to explain the persistence of systems in spite of continuous replacement of their members. Political socialization is designed to produce "diffuse system support" in children, as diffuse system support of the population is considered critical to system persistence. On the crucial importance of such general support "critical theorists" (like Habermas) tend to agree with functionalists (like Easton and Dennis)—the difference being one of language. The same construct of generalized support is labeled either "mass loyalty" or "diffuse system support."[4]

Plausible as it may be, the proposition that diffuse system support is a necessary condition of system persistence has not been tested. As Sears notes in his discussion: "To test the Easton-Dennis notions as a 'political theory' would require a range of values of the key outcome variable: persistence of the political system. However, Easton and Dennis' own data deal with only one value of it, viz., the state of the American political system of the mid-1960's."[5]

A "political" theory of political socialization—as opposed to a "psychological" theory—is, of course, rather demanding in terms of the data needed to support it. Systematic evidence supporting such a theory that links the microlevel (socialization processes) with the macrolevel (systemic outcomes) is hard to come by. Such evidence would have to be of an unusual kind. It would have to be valid information about processes and relations within families and other agencies of socialization. This would have to be available for several social and political systems. Both requirements go beyond what conventional survey research has to offer.

The most frequent source of information about families as socialization agencies, for instance, is reports by children or adolescents, or retrospective reports of adults about their youth. Methodological research suggests that the validity of such reports is questionable, at the very least.[6] If adolescent rebellion is the substantive question, adolescents' reports of their parents opinions are likely to be potentially biased, for instance. To enhance validity, information from several members of the same family is needed. Self-reports are necessary, not perceptions of other family members. This requires a study design that in the past was rarely realized in national studies. Cross-national, comparable data are necessary. If we are to explain system-level phenomena, variation at the system level is required. Support for the linkages of family processes and systemic outcomes would necessitate variation of both.

To help meet these requirements we gathered information from a subset of parent-adolescent pairs embedded within each country's sample.[7] The adolescents range in age from 16 to 20 years. One limitation of the pairs in terms of generalizability is that they are made up of parents and offspring living within the same household. For the younger adolescents, that contingency does not constitute a serious problem, but as they approach 20 years of age the likelihood of their having left the family domicile increases. Just how much bias this introduces into our analysis is uncertain.[8] In any event the availability of the pairs (Ns range from 173 to 257) for cross-national comparisons provides a rare opportunity to go beyond conventional cross-section designs.[9]

What we intend to do in this and the following chapter is to deal with many of the major themes forming the corpus of the analysis of the national cross-section samples. Because of their centrality to questions about political socialization and political change, some topics will receive more attention than others. In the present chapter we treat value orientations, political cognitions, and political satisfaction. These topics embrace many of the key independent and intervening variables associated with forms of political action, the focus of the succeeding chapter.

Procedures

Our task is three-fold. First we wish to look at aggregate similarity between the two generations and across the five countries. Other terms for such similarity are *group* correspondence, congruence, or concordance. Three main ways are used to show group correspondence. First are the marginal distributions on a given variable. These are often presented in the tables contained herein. Second, a summary expression of these distributions is the arithmetic mean. Third, and somewhat more complex, we have constructed a generation gap figure based on the cross-tabulation of parent versus offspring scores on the various measures. All such matrices, of course, have a main diagonal that indicates the perfect union of parent and offspring scores. Cells off this diagonal represent departures from perfect agreement. By subtracting the proportion of cases lying on one side of this diagonal from those on the other, we have a measure of the "gap" or difference between the generations represented by the pairs. Our convention (see Table 15.1) will be to affix either a "P" (parent) or "O" (offspring) next to the generation gap figure to indicate which generation is "higher" on or "has more of" the political value in question. For example, if a political conservatism scale runs from low to high—a generation gap figure of 15 percent—P would mean that the net difference between the generations was 15 percent, with the parents being more conservative. Usually this gap figure will parallel the results presented for each generational sample as a whole, but since missing data from either generation reduces the size of the pair Ns, occasional anomalies may appear. As a rule of thumb we will take differences of 10 percent or greater as indicative of a meaningful generation gap.

Our second major task is to look at within-family similarity across the five countries. *Pair* correspondence, congruity, and concordance, are other suitable terms. Here we are not interested in the generations as a whole, but rather in the degree to which parents appear to be socializing their offspring in their own likeness (whether through direct or indirect processes).[10] The simplest but somewhat deceiving method for estimating the concordance is to look at the exact agreement in the dyads as manifested by those cells along the main diagonal in the parent-by-offspring matrix. To help keep our terminology consistent, we subtract this proportion from 100% (i.e., the total corner percentage) in order to arrive at a lineage gap figure.[11] This figure may be compared with the generation gap figure. A further refinement is to determine the *ratio* of the generation gap to the lineage gap, what we shall call the adjusted (adj.) generation gap. This figure simply indicates how much of the generation gap potential was realized, given a certain lineage gap.[12]

These, then, are measures of *absolute* agreement. Responses of parents and children are treated as similar only if parent and child choose the same response category. A different approach to the measurement of similarity is the use of measures of association such as tau and gamma for ordinal or lambda for nominal-level data.[13] They are not measuring absolute agreement, but rather something like relative agreement. They express how accurately we can predict the child's response once we know the parent's (or vice versa). They reach the maximum value, 1, if we make predictions on this basis that are perfectly accurate—without making the assumption of identity of responses. To take a case in point: suppose all children were on some left-right continuum exactly one-standard deviation (or any other amount) to the left of their parents. Measures of association would indicate a perfect relationship,

1, in this case, whereas all measures based on absolute agreement would indicate perfect lack of agreement. Actual data, of course, never allow coefficients to reach their upper limits, but the extreme example illustrates that measures of association and measures of absolute agreement convey different pieces of information about pair data. For this reason, we report both types of measures.

We report two measures of association for ordinal data: tau-b and gamma. While both are similar, they differ in their treatment of tied ranks. For a given set of variables, gamma will usually be higher than tau-b, since ties have the result of reducing the tau-b value. As some ties may result from floor or ceiling effects (our response categories may not cover the whole attitude continuum), a sizeable difference of gamma and tau-b can point to such effects. This kind of difference, then, may protect us from interpreting a ceiling effect as lack of relative agreement. Partly because of its more conservative nature we will rely mostly on the tau-b correlation. As a rule of thumb we will consider tau-b correlations in the neighborhood of .25 or higher as signifying reasonably strong parent-child concordance.[14]

A third, more theoretical objective is to discuss the relationship of the socialization process to the nature and dimensions of generational discontinuity. How is the effectiveness of the socialization process related to the magnitude of the generation gap? Is the generation gap, if and where it exists, the result of a failure of socialization agencies? Does effective socialization as a microprocess produce the macrolevel outcome of stability?[15] Although we shall address these questions at least indirectly throughout our discussion, the fuller statement will be found at the conclusion of the following chapter.

We are not unmindful of the fact that we have static data for what are basically questions of a dynamic sort. The contemporary degree of continuity or discontinuity between the generations as age cohorts at our point in time is no guarantee of the juxtapositioning at a future time point. Similarly, the prevailing congruence between parents and offspring within the family is not necessarily a good predictor of what the future will bring. Life course, generational, and historical effects are all potential confounding as well as explanatory factors when it comes to looking at political change and continuity from our perspective.[16] Yet to avoid tackling difficult questions because of the lack of a perfect study design is shortsighted in the extreme, even assuming the possibility of such a perfect design. The middle-range strategy pursued in these two chapters is to speak confidently of existing states of relationships and to make informed inferences and speculations about the future, and occasionally about the past.

UNDERLYING VALUE ORIENTATIONS

Broad value dimensions are employed by individuals in trying to structure their political worlds. People do not confront each issue of the day, each new political candidate, each conflict de novo. Out of training, experience, and feedback certain broad postures tend to develop. As new phenomena cross the perceptual screen of the individual, these postures or value orientations can be drawn upon to make sense of the political world, to reduce the opportunity costs associated with trying to investigate thoroughly each new phenomenon, and to give a fix on preferences and behaviors. In this section we will take up four underlying dimensions which have been demonstrated to have such properties. One of the key questions asked about generational change and continuity is the extent to which such dimensions seem to be in a state of flux and the place of the family in this process. We cover four such overarching orientations in this section. They are all central elements in our study of advanced industrial societies.

Levels of Conceptual Thinking

A considerable amount of recent empirical research in European countries, as well as the present inquiry, and more informal observations, has supported the postulation about the presence and utility of the left-right dimension. If the left-right dimension does serve as a filtering mechanism, then it becomes important to know whether and how change is occurring across the generations. Shifts toward the left would presumably dictate one set of political consequences, whereas shifts toward the right would suggest another. A prior question which must be asked, however, is if people have an understanding of the dimension. Clearly, one cannot place oneself on the continuum or engage its properties without at least some minimal comprehension of what the dimension consists. Our first task, then, is to probe the recognition and understanding of the ideological dimension; after that we will examine the self-placement of the two generations.

An inspection of the distribution on ideological sophistication (Table 15.1) leaves little doubt that there is considerable variation across countries and some across generations. The low (1) category consists of those individuals who simply could not handle the concept of left-right. For them it had no meaning. Given the absence of left and right as popular concepts in the United States (where liberalism and conservatism are more common terms), it is not surprising to see the high incidence of pure nonideologues on this dimension. What is perhaps more surprising is that American youth are no more likely than their parents to be able to handle the concept. Even more surprising is the distance between British parents and adolescents. Contrary to what one might expect, British parents are much more familiar with the concept, a finding which may reflect the greater class-based cleavages associated with an earlier period of British politics. Finally, we may note the great facility with the dimension displayed by both generations in the Netherlands and Germany. By comparison, the other continental country—Austria—shows a striking lack of familiarity. Our task here is not so much to unravel the reasons for these cross-country variations as to point them out and to observe in particular the intergenerational patterns.

As already suggested by discussing only the pure nonideologues, the cross-generation patterns in the aggregate are similar across all countries except Britain. This similarity is reflected both in the mean scores and in the generation gap figures. That is, even though there is great cross-country variance, the cross-generation variance within a country is relatively small in four of the countries. Because one gains familiarity with politics through exposure and practice, we would ordinarily expect the older generation to have a more sophisticated understanding of politics. Therefore, the modest edge found for the parental generation in three of the countries, and the outright small edge for the offspring in Holland, may presage a greater degree of ideological sophistication as the younger generation matures. Only if the classical left-right continuum becomes clouded over with new dimensions (as is entirely possible), would we expect entry into the experience with the world of real politics to inhibit growth of ideological sophistication. To which may be added the fact that great numbers in the filial generation have yet to complete their education. More education would almost inevitably mean greater comprehension. The British case, however, suggests that the young would have a tremendous amount of catching up to do.

Turning from the aggregate patterns to the pair relationships, we find rather considerable cross-country similarity. Both the ordinal statistics and the lineage gap figures are proximate to each other, with Britain being something of an outlier. Although cross-national similarity prevails, it is obvious that no country meets our criterion of strong pair correspondence (tau-b = .25). Rather, there is a modest amount of putative intergenerational transmission from parent to child. What is interesting about this finding is that ideological sophistication is, in great part, a cognitively based orientation. In general such attributes are more readily "passed on" within the family than are attitudinal traits. There are both genetic and environmental forces influencing this congruence. It is, therefore, a bit unsettling to observe only modest parent-child concordance on this dimension.[17]

We have seen that some respondents in every country simply cannot cope with the left-right concept. Still others have a rather primitive understanding of it. Let us be generous, however, and assume that if respondents could at least locate themselves somewhere on the scale that the dimension has some

Table 15.1: UNDERSTANDING OF LEFT-RIGHT CONTINUUM

	The Netherlands		Britain		United States		Germany		Austria	
	Parents	Offspring	Parents	Offspring	Parents	Offspring	Parents	Offspring	Parents	Offspring
Understanding:										
Low 1	6%a	11%	18%	34%	30%	29%	7%	11%	26%	31%
2	23	20	17	22	14	18	9	13	14	29
3	4	2	12	12	18	18	2	4	6	8
4	20	14	35	18	2	2	30	22	21	18
5	19	14	9	6	11	6	22	21	15	9
High 6	27	38	9	8	26	27	32	30	18	14
$\overline{X}$	4.0	4.1	3.3	2.6	3.3	3.2	4.5	4.2	3.4	3.0
N	(233)	(233)	(173)	(173)	(244)	(244)	(257)	(257)	(212)	(212)
*Pair Relationships:*b										
tau-b	.22		.17		.21		.19		.20	
gamma	.28		.21		.26		.24		.24	
lineage gap	45%		56%		50%		40%		48%	
generation gapc	4%—O		24%—P		4%—P		6%—P		13%—P	
adj. "	.09		.43		.08		.15		.27	
N	(223)		(173)		(244)		(257)		(212)	

a. Percentages are based on a collapsing of the original eight-point scale. All missing data cases are in the "low" category.

b. Correlations are based on the original eight-point scale. Gap figures are based on treating cells directly adjacent to main diagonal as part of main diagonal in the 8 x 8 matrix.

c. The percentage entry shows the difference between the proportion on one side of the diagonal and that on the other side in the parent-offspring matrices. P = parents, O = offspring.

meaning for most of them. It then becomes a simple but intriguing operation to compare the generations in terms of their self-placement. The original ten-point scale has been collapsed into five categories to facilitate presentation (Table 15.2). It will be observed that here, as well as in succeeding tables, the Ns for each generation within a country will vary because of inapplicability and missing data and that the Ns for the pair relationships will almost invariably be lower than the N for either generation as a whole because the former is a joint function of the "inaps" and missing data from each generation when cross-tabulated.

Our theoretical expectations are that the parental generation would be more right-leaning than the younger generation. Everything we know about the social and political currents of the last decade, as well as the historic (but not universal) tendency of the younger generation to be more liberal than its predecessor at a given point in time, would lead us to expect that. Given this expectation, the results are uneven though explicable. In terms of mean values, the United States, the Netherlands, and Germany clearly support the expectation, whereas in Austria and Britain there is a dead heat between the generations. The picture becomes more uniform when we look at the generation gap figures derived from the pair analysis. Now parents in all countries are more often on the conservative side. Yet the differences are rather trivial in Britain and Austria, modest at best in the United States, and sizeable only in the Netherlands and Germany. Indeed, in the latter two countries, one detects what would often be construed to be a demonstrable gulf between the generations. The rising generation is rather spectacularly more leftist than its predecessor. Hence the implications about the political conflict between generations and the shape of the political future would seem to be much more dramatic in these two countries than in the remaining ones.

Before leaving the overall results, it is worth noting that in each country both generations have a normal curve, bell-shaped distribution, a distribution which also emerges when the full 10-point scale is employed. With but one exception (Dutch youth) the modal category is the middle one. Thus even though differences in proclivities exist, the tendency in each generation is more centrist than anything else. To that extent, we would expect a fair amount of continuing flexibility and a large, potentially mobilizable middle to persist in the various countries.

Turning to within family patterns, the results are quite checkered. Once having screened out all of those people who were not capable of handling the left-right scale, we might expect to find a rather generous amount of lineage similarity. Yet the ordinal relationships show a range from scarcely any congruence in the United States to reasonably strong ones in Britain, the Netherlands, and Austria. These ordinal statistics vary dramatically in the face of fairly narrow differences in terms of the lineage gap percentages. We have

Table 15.2: PLACEMENT ON LEFT-RIGHT CONTINUUM

	The Netherlands		Britain		United States		Germany		Austria	
	Parents	Offspring	Parents	Offspring	Parents	Offspring	Parents	Offspring	Parents	Offspring
Left-Right Placement:										
Left 1	8%	12%	12%	6%	3%	8%	2%	5%	6%	6%
2	18	36	21	22	12	22	19	32	17	19
3	32	32	38	47	54	42	45	43	40	42
4	30	17	21	24	20	22	28	16	29	22
Right 5	12	4	8	1	10	5	7	4	9	11
$\overline{X}$	3.2	2.7	2.9	2.9	3.2	2.9	3.2	2.8	3.2	3.2
N	(210)	(198)	(142)	(115)	(172)	(173)	(240)	(229)	(157)	(147)
Pair Relationships:[a]										
tau-b	.31		.24		.05		.17		.29	
gamma	.35		.28		.06		.20		.33	
lineage gap	57%		51%		56%		50%		47%	
generation gap	32%–P		2%–P		9%–P		21%–P		5%–P	
adj. "	.56		.04		.16		.42		.11	
N	(189)		(102)		(134)		(221)		(124)	

a. Correlations are based on the original ten-point scale. Gap figures are based on treating cells directly adjacent to main diagonal as part of main diagonal in the 10 x 10 matrix.

[458]

here ample evidence of what we warned about earlier, namely, absolute agreement (or disagreement) between parents and offspring is not necessarily a good indicator of overall congruence. Indeed, the country with the largest lineage gap (the Netherlands at 57 percent) actually has the highest concordance in terms of the more comprehensive ordinal statistics.

Underscoring the limitations of the lineage gap figures in another way is their relatively poor performance as predictors of the generation gap. For example, although Dutch and American figures are but one percentage point apart in terms of the lineage gap, they are dramatically different in terms of the generation gap. Finally, the adjusted generation gap figures are interesting because they show that out of all the intergenerational difference possible on the basis of within-family differences, only the Netherlands and Germany realized a large dividend. Which is to say that much of the lineage differences in the other countries resolved themselves in some adolescents becoming more liberal than their parents while others became more conservative.[18]

Party Attachment

In addition to and sometimes working hand in glove with left-right ideological thinking as a guiding orientation is that of party attachment. In light of the prominence of parties in our five countries and the constellation of characteristics associated in the voter's mind with them, it becomes important to examine the degree to which party attachment is changing across the generations and the direction in which any changes might be moving. Adding to the importance of this quest is the fact that the viability of the traditional party system in the "New Politics" of advanced industrial societies is by no means clear. We begin, then, with the question of whether there is attachment at all.

The sheer holding of a partisan preference is extremely variable across countries, but there is a similar cross-country pattern between the generations, as these figures show:

Attachment to a Party (% Yes)

The Netherlands		Britain		United States		Germany		Austria	
Parents	Off-spring	Parents	Off-spring	Parents	Off-spring	Parents	Off-spring	Parents	Off-spring
91%	50%	85%	54%	88%	77%	68%	46%	75%	50%

In each country a very sizeable majority of the parental generation declared itself as having a party to which it usually feels closest. Only in the United States is that true for the rising generation. The gulf between the generations is greatest in the Netherlands, least in the United States.

At first glance one is inclined to interpret this as clear evidence of generational shifting in the aggregate. That may well be, for there is evidence in some of the countries that new cohorts are not acquiring a partisan affiliation with the same dispatch as did previous cohorts.[19] However, it is also true that party attachment tends to be an attribute that expands over time. Without much if any opportunity to express their partisanship and without the accompanying opportunities for these expressions to become hardened into some sort of enduring preference, it is not difficult to imagine why adolescents are less partisan than their elders. It also seems to be true that socialization into partisanship as a family matter is carried out more successfully in some countries (e.g., the United States and Britain) than in other countries. Thus the most that one would want to say is that at this point there is a noticeable difference between the two generations and that the younger one has much catching up to do if partisanship is to mean the same for it as for the older one. If it does not close the gap, then we would expect the party systems and electoral outcomes to have even more slack and flexibility than they now have. By the same token, forces other than those represented by a "standing partisan commitment" would have more room for play in the system.

It is but a brief but important step to move from the question of sheer attachment to the question of the intensity of attachment. Although there are exceptions, the usual tendency is for the more strongly committed partisans (at any point in time) to be more faithful in their voting behavior and to be more participative in an electoral sense. If they waver they are more likely to return to the fold. The party faithfuls provide a more or less stable base that enables a party to ride out short-term losses and return with renewed strength. By the same token, the incapacity to develop a cadre of intense followers portends the eventual withering of the party—as witness the virtual demise of most of the new Dutch parties that sprang to life in the mid-1960s to early 1970s.

Results from the analysis of the intensity of attachment are of a piece with those presented above. Here we will present the data from the pair analysis only. Those without any attachment at all are scored lowest, while the three remaining categories range from feeling not very close, fairly close, or very close to the chosen party.

Intensity of Party Attachment (Low–High)

	The Netherlands	Britain	United States	Germany	Austria
tau-b	.08	.24	.15	.21	.23
gamma	.12	.35	.21	.30	.33
lineage gap	65%	72%	67%	60%	67%
generation gap	24%–P	50%–P	26%–P	24%–P	31%–P
adj. " "	.37	.69	.39	.40	.46
N	(221)	(173)	(232)	(251)	(212)

At the aggregate level (represented by the generation gap entries) it appears that the overall depth of commitment is much greater among parents than their offspring. That appearance is a bit deceptive, however, Once we remove all those respondents without any party attachment the differences between parents and children drop, though only in Germany does it come close to disappearing, and in Britain the differences remain substantial. What is happening, then, is that fewer of the young possess a party preference, but among those who do their intensity tends to converge toward the level possessed by their parents. The implication is that if more come to possess an identification during the course of time, they will resemble the older cohort. As we have pointed out, however, there are signs that secular shifts are working against the adoption of partisanship in at least some of these countries.

Moving to the intrafamilial level, the figures indicate that intensity is but weakly transmitted within the family. The ordinal statistics are modest at best, and the lineage gap is high. Moreover, there is a moderately high conversion rate of the lineage gap into a generation gap, as the adjusted figures reveal. Thus parents are doing a relatively poor job of socializing the young into the level of commitment possessed by them. Of somewhat greater interest is the question of the directionality and composition of the transmission, a question to which we now turn.

In any but the simplest of two-party systems it is difficult to array the parties on a single dimension, unless one wants to make simplifying assumptions about, for example, left versus nonleft, or confessional versus nonconfessional. Therefore, we will treat party preference as a nominal variable and use the appropriate statistics as well as percentage agreement scores to indicate the flow of partisan orientations across generations. In the interest of providing at least a crude indicator of net directional flow, however, we will also make a rough dichotomy between left and nonleft parties.

We will find it useful to approach these questions by successive steps. First, we take *all* responses, regardless of whether a party preference was expressed by either member of the pair. This procedure will provide an overall measure of the fidelity of the reproduction process within the family. Two measures will be used to depict the congruence. One is the lineage gap and the other is the lambda coefficient, a nominal-level statistic that (in its asymmetric form) shows how well categories of the dependent variable are predicted by the independent variable. In this case we wish to know how well offspring answers are predicted by parental preferences.

The absolute amount of disagreement is moderate to large across the countries, as these figures attest: Britain, 57%; United States, 40%; the Netherlands, 67%; Austria, 49%; and Germany, 52%. The corresponding lambda values are .14, .18, .18, .20, and .12, respectively. With its large number of parties it is almost inevitable that the Netherlands would register a large lineage difference. Considering the conservative nature of the lambda statistic, these values are not unimpressive. But we shall see momentarily that they dim when matched with parallel assessments in the religious domain. Inflating the lineage gap and depressing the lambda coefficients are the large numbers of adolescents with no preference.

After setting aside those respondents with no declared affiliation, we can then consider whether there are differences in the *tendance* of the two generations. To answer this question we have allocated preferences into a crude socialist (left), nonsocialist (nonleft) dichotomy in the full realization that some information is thereby lost, especially in the multidimensional Dutch party system. On the other hand the essential dichotomy is a widely recognized one and has also proven viable in the analysis of party systems and electoral behavior.[20]

Looking first at the aggregate distributions we encounter a rather unexpected finding: with the exception of the Netherlands, the profiles are remarkably similar for the generational samples within a country, as these figures show:

Preference for Socialist (Left) Parties

The Netherlands		Britain		United States		Germany		Austria	
Parents	Off-spring	Parents	Off-spring	Parents	Off-spring	Parents	Off-spring	Parents	Off-spring
37%	66%	54%	55%	62%	66%	44%	52%	51%	54%
N (198)	(164)	(146)	(94)	(214)	(182)	(171)	(117)	(144)	(94)

If the tides of the times may be said to be running in a more liberal direction, they are running with equal force for both generations. Of course party preference is but one instrument by which this drift may be symbolized. Yet to the degree that the general liberal/conservative division of the parties does capture those tendencies, it is clear that the upcoming generation is scarcely more left-leaning than its predecessor, save in the Netherlands. Within each major party there are liberal-conservative rifts, of course; these are not picked up with the sheer declaration of party preference. As our left-right analysis indicated, however, only in the Netherlands and Germany were the youth demonstrably more leftist than their parents. Strictly in terms of the broad picture, the party balance as such does not seem to be in the process of great change—for those having a party preference.

Based on our preceding analysis of the pair data, we know that—with the exception of the Netherlands—the concordance is high. Having now divided all preferences into a socialist versus nonsocialist dichotomy we can state the rank order relationships as well as the net directional flow (generational gap) within families. Contrary to many of our findings, in this case the high degree of group correspondence is generally echoed at the pair level also, as these figures illustrate:

Pair Relationships on Party Preference
(Left versus Nonleft)

	The Netherlands	Britain	United States	Germany	Austria
tau-b	.38	.65	.55	.53	.81
gamma	.77	.91	.86	.83	.98
lineage gap	37%	17%	21%	23%	9%
generation gap	29%–O	1%–O	4%–O	3%–O	1%–O
adj. " "	.78	.17	.19	.13	.11
N	(152)	(86)	(164)	(90)	(75)

Even in the Netherlands, where group correspondence is at best moderate, the pair correspondence is rather high. In the other countries, it reaches a level seldom found in this or any other investigations of the political socialization process. The generation gap entries simply reinforce the pattern found when taking each sample as a whole. What difference there is within the family tends to be counterbalanced by movements on the part of each generation in self-cancelling directions. Thus there is strong presumptive evidence for the transmission and maintenance of party cleavages within the family circle.[21]

Religious Orientations

Previous chapters have dealt with the political side of organized religion in a peripheral fashion. Here we take a close look because of its prominence in the socialization process and its enduring connection to the political world. Although advanced industrial societies are becoming increasingly secularized, the vestiges of religious cleavages are impressive indeed. One of the most successful predictors of party allegiance and voting in most Western European countries remains religious preference, however nominal that preference may be.[22] Many European parties are divided into the secular versus confessional based, and sometimes within the latter between Catholic and non-Catholic. Religious preference is still one of the social categories to which people most easily assign themselves. Moreover, religious institutions continue to be strongly evident in all countries. Nor should it be overlooked that many issues are shot through with religious overtones, the feminist movement (especially as represented on the abortion issue) being perhaps the most salient in the contemporary period. Finally, religion has traditionally been considered one of those domains most jealously guarded by the nuclear family. It has been peculiarly impervious to the unauthorized influence of outside agents.

When viewed simply in terms of a declared religious identification, the foregoing emphasis seems well put. In Germany and Austria all but 1% or less of both parents and offspring associated themselves with a religious body.[23] Of course that distribution comes about in part because children are literally born with a designated religion in those two countries. Nevertheless the fact that even the younger generation universally associates itself with a religion demonstrates strong nominal identification. Nor is the picture much different in the United States, where the legal situation is decidedly different. At least 95% of both generations classified themselves religiously. The same was true of Britain. Only in the Netherlands do we see serious inroads on the propensity toward self-identification. There 83% of the parents and 66% of the offspring classified themselves—still healthy majorities but some distance away from the other countries.

Given these lopsided marginal distributions it is not surprising to find that pair correspondence tends to run high. Taking the full array of answers (including no preference) the lineage gap exceeds 20% only in the Netherlands (22%) and Britain (31%). Figures in the latter two countries come from shifts among the young to no preference as well as to other religious preferences. Using the conservative asymmetric measure lambda to predict variance in offspring preferences on the basis of parental preferences the coefficients are: Germany, .83; United States, .65; the Netherlands, .65; Austria, .63; and Britain, .18. Only in the latter country is the prediction less than extremely powerful. With that partial exception we may conclude that religious identity continues to be quite successfully passed on from parent to child in these advanced industrial societies. To the extent that religious identity continues to influence the political process—as seems likely—we may expect a continuation in the upcoming generations.

A comparison of these figures with those constructed in the same way for partisan classification reveals that the latter reflect much less pair congruence. Religious preference is passed along much more successfully.

While religious identification alone provides individuals with a reference point from which to interpret incoming political stimuli, it has been demonstrated that the intensity of religious commitment adds an important qualifying element. The more intense the commitment the more likely will individuals exhibit the political tendencies associated with the religious preference.[24] Consequently, even though the younger generation may be following rather faithfully in the footsteps of their elders in terms of declared preference, their intensity may be considerably less. Indeed, that is what one would expect both from a life cycle perspective and from the trends of the time.

Two indicators of religious intensity support this line of thinking. One is behavioral, resting on the reported frequency of church attendance. Rather than present the full array of information, we will present only the pair relationships:

Church Attendance (Low–High)

	The Netherlands	Britain	United States	Germany	Austria
tau-b	.63	.42	.57	.58	.60
gamma	.79	.65	.70	.76	.76
lineage gap	44%	46%	49%	45%	47%
generation gap	23%–P	18%–P	5%–P	25%–P	2%–P
adj. " "	.52	.39	.10	.56	.04
N	(141)	(171)	(227)	(238)	(206)

We may use the generation gap figures to illustrate the nature of the overall aggregate differences; using the means for each generation separately reveals a similar pattern. As predicted, parents are more devout than their children in each country, but the range is quite large, with three countries having substantial margins and two relatively small differences. To the extent that church attendance taps intensity and is related to subsequent political attitudes and behaviors, we would expect to see a diminishing impact especially in Germany, the Netherlands, and Britain.

On the other hand, and of a piece with our notions about intrafamily patterns of religious socialization and control, the congruence between parent and offspring is exceedingly healthy. Even in Britain, with the lowest congruence, the coefficient is well beyond what we set as a minimal level of acceptance for strong pair correspondence. One very simple explanation for these high relationships is that church-going is typically a family affair, one over which the parents have a fair, though varying degree of control. Parents may not be able to enforce or indoctrinate a particular attitude; they are much more likely to be able to compel certain behavioral manifestations.

Again, the Netherlands and Germany, and Britain to a lesser extent, stand out as countries wherein the amount of lineage difference generates a large degree of generational difference. Despite the fact that the lineage gap is virtually identical across the five countries, the results in Austria and the United States are quite at variance with those for the other three countries. The differences at the family level are not transformed into differences at the larger aggregate level. In concrete terms this means that despite the tides of secularization, many offspring in these two countries profess to be more church-going than their parents.

Our supposition that behavioral rather than attitudinal correspondence is more readily achieved is strikingly illustrated if we turn to our second measure of intensity, namely, the professed degree of religiosity in response to the question, "Generally speaking, would you consider yourself very religious, somewhat religious, a little religious, not very religious?" The summary statistics follow:

Professed Religiosity (Low–High)

	The Netherlands	Britain	United States	Germany	Austria
tau-b	.34	.18	.31	.43	.26
gamma	.50	.27	.43	.64	.39
lineage gap	59%	68%	52%	49%	55%
generation gap	31%–P	35%–P	13%–P	32%–P	6%–P
adj. " "	.52	.51	.25	.65	.11
N	(215)	(168)	(238)	(232)	(211)

Aggregate differences are all higher than in the case of church attendance, sometimes appreciably so. Clearly the younger generation does not have the subjective fervor possessed by the older. And the degree to which this fervor is passed on within the family is markedly less than in the case of church attendance. Although all tau-b coefficients except for Britain remain above .25, they are still considerably lower than in the case of church attendance. The same applies to the simpler estimate as represented by the lineage gap figure.

Reviewing the three indicators of religious orientation, we can see a progressive decline as we move from broad classifications of self, through concrete behaviors over which parental control can be exerted, on to subjective feelings of religious attachment. From the more global, macro point of view the similar self-allocation of the generations into religious groupings suggests a persistence of religiously based cleavage structures, albeit there is cross-country variation on this count. But especially when turning to the intensity dimension, there is a strong suggestion of generational shifts, engendered in part by the inability of parents to induce successfully a self-perception of religiosity on the part of their children. If, as seems to be the case, intensity of commitment fuels the fires of religiously based cleavages, then the prospects would be for a weakening of the overall impact of religion. This would allow for the greater play of value systems based on something other than religious principles. It is to one such value system that we now turn.

The Spirit of Postmaterialism

The kinds of things people value in sociopolitical life are not necessarily summed up in traditional institutions and structures such as political parties and religious bodies nor in the classical left-right, liberal-conservative dimensions that have permeated Western societies for so long. People also develop value structures and apply them in a variety of other ways. When these structures or clusters begin to be represented in sizeable segments of the population, and when they seem to have political relevance, they become objects of inquiry for those interested in intergenerational change. More often than not the handmaiden of value structure change is population replacement rather than conversion. Overall population shifts become more probable as new cohorts enter the polity and old ones die out. At the same time some strata are more prone to change than are others.

One such value constellation dealt with in this study has come to be called Postmaterialism.[25] The availability of the two-generation data enables us to examine the incidence and rate of putative change in Postmaterialism across five countries. Variations by age, as reported in chapter 11, would lead us to predict distinctive generational patterns.

At the aggregate level these predictions are nicely borne out in Table 15.3. Leaving aside for the moment the question of internation modalities, in all countries save one—Britain—the offspring are more Postmaterialist than the parents. Both the mean figures and the generation gap percentages provide graphic evidence along those lines. Britain as the exception is fully consistent with previous analysis of cross-sectional data showing that the gap between age cohorts is less in Britain than in other European countries. Interestingly enough, the source of the British deviation lies much more in the relatively high level of Postmaterialism found among the parents (compared with parents in other countries) rather than in the low Postmaterialism of the offspring, whose scores compare favorably with their counterparts in other countries.

At the other extreme from Britain is Germany. The miracle of postwar recovery in Germany is a familiar story. Those youths represented in the German sample were born, at the earliest, in 1954. Their histories are of a radically different and less deprived nature than those of their parents. Indeed the German parents rank lowest among all parents in their espousal of Postmaterialist values. As the experiences borne by the parental generation become less and less prominent in the German populace it seems likely that the cross-national differences will diminish.

Accompanying the low group correspondence in all countries except Britain is the low level of pair correspondence. Commitment to Postmaterialism is but weakly a product of any direct or indirect transmission from parent to child. So weak, in fact, that the correspondence is actually negative in Britain. This is one of the very few instances in our entire analysis in which negative correlations are obtained. Not that the sheer lineage gap in Britain is appreciably greater than in other countries. Austria has a lower figure but a

Table 15.3: SUBSCRIPTION TO POSTMATERIALISM

	The Netherlands		Britain		United States		Germany		Austria	
	Parents	Offspring	Parents	Offspring	Parents	Offspring	Parents	Offspring	Parents	Offspring
Postmaterialism:										
Low 1	4%a	3%	4%	6%	13%	6%	26%	10%	21%	9%
2	32	10	24	21	32	19	42	19	37	32
3	26	21	36	28	28	22	22	22	12	19
4	27	32	26	36	19	33	8	26	27	28
High 5	12	33	10	9	9	20	2	23	3	13
X̄	3.1	3.8	3.2	3.2	2.8	3.4	2.2	3.3	2.7	3.1
N	(211)	(214)	(168)	(168)	(236)	(239)	(253)	(249)	(202)	(205)
Pair Relationships:b										
tau-b	.08		-.03		.13		.12		.15	
gamma	.09		-.03		.16		.15		.17	
lineage gap	64%		63%		70%		75%		57%	
generation gap		31%—O		3%—O		26%—O		52%—O		28%—O
adj. "	.48		.05		.37		.69		.49	
N	(207)		(164)		(231)		(246)		(197)	

a. Percentages are based on a collapsing of the original ten-point scale.
b. Correlations are based on the original ten-point index. Gap figures are based on treating cells directly adjacent to main diagonal as part of main diagonal in the 10 x 10 matrix.

higher tau-b statistic. Moreover, the Austrian lineage gap is transformed into a sizeable generation gap in contrast to no transformation in Britain.

On balance, of the four "global" value orientations surveyed in this section the greatest intergenerational shift is occurring in the Materialism/Post-materialism dimension—except for Britain. The same is pretty much true at the family level also. To the extent that Postmaterialism has true ideological properties, there are strong portents for the future. But the idealism and age-specific concerns of the adolescents may lead them away from Postma-terialism as they wind their way through the phases of the life course. By contrast, the anchorings and reinforcements available in the traditional domains of ideology, partisanship, and religion may actually result in greater durability among these latter orientations.

POLITICAL EXPECTATIONS AND SATISFACTION

The twentieth century has witnessed an increasing intervention of governments in the lives of individuals and institutions alike. Mixed forms of socialism and capitalism characterize the five countries included in our inquiry. Compared with the activities of a half century ago each country has been marked by drastic increases in government regulation and in providing services for society. As was demonstrated in chapter 14, basic differences do exist among individuals and across countries concerning the personal importance of various issue domains and the responsibility of governments in addressing those issue domains. The intersection of personal importance and government responsibility assignment results in what we have labeled "political agendas." Accompanying the variations in political agendas are variations regarding the effectiveness with which governments are implementing preferred values. The intersection of agenda placement and performance rating results in what we have called policy dissatisfaction.

In this section we examine on a cross-generational and cross-national basis two main themes: the issue agenda and the discrepancy between agenda priority and perceived performance.[26] Expectations about and evaluations of governmental implementation of preferred values, while a cornerstone of our larger inquiry, are relatively poorly understood in generational terms. Our present undertaking is, therefore, much more exploratory in nature than previous topics.

The Issue Agenda

We have little to guide us in hypothesizing about cross-generational comparisons. In contrast to the broad ideological values covered in the previous section and the instrumental values involved in evaluating protest behavior in the following chapter, there is neither good theory nor cue-giving signs from contemporary events to suggest the directionality of our hypothesis. That is, do we have good cause to expect that the younger generation will assign higher political priority to various problems than does the older generation? For those familiar with American politics the answer is only a probable yes, because "big government" and the welfare-state ideology in particular are still strongly resisted by various political leaders and segments of the mass public. The idea of government responsibility in these areas, being newer, probably falls more receptively on the less hardened ears of the young—even though both generations might assign equal personal importance to a given issue. For the European countries the question may be less problematic. With strong histories of a governmental role in a multitude of areas, especially those of public welfare and material security, it is unlikely that the kind of differences which might appear in the United States would also surface in the four European countries.

From one perspective the intergenerational comparisons (Table 15.4) converge with speculation. Only the United States presents a vivid contrast, and that is in accord with our thinking. Both the mean scores and the generation gap difference reveal that the younger generation is much more inclined to place a larger number of topics toward the top of the political agenda. Assuming that this contrast signifies a secular trend—as seems very probable—the forecast for the United States would be a citizenry increasingly committed to the notion of the modern, all-purpose state.

Shifting to the other countries, we find that the cross-generational differences are all in the opposite direction, the most outstanding example being the Netherlands. Although we would not want to make too much of these small to strong differences, the fact that they are there at all gives one pause. Does this represent a creeping disillusionment with the modern state apparatus in Western Europe? Probably not, because at least one or two of the tasks contained in the pool making up this index are especially sensitive to age-specific concerns. Medical care, for example, is an especially relevant concern for the middle-age group whereas for the younger (healthier) cohort it is less consequential. An examination of other individual items shows that at least part of the reason for the parental edge in these four countries comes from their giving the government greater responsibility in select and sometimes country-specific areas. It seems very likely that as the adolescents begin their progress through the life cycle that they will come to resemble their predecessors. Nevertheless, the implications of the European findings for the current scene should not be ignored. These implications are that the lines of age-related political cleavage do not rest on the younger generation's wanting

Table 15.4: OVERALL ISSUE AGENDA

	The Netherlands		Britain		United States		Germany		Austria	
	Parents	Offspring	Parents	Offspring	Parents	Offspring	Parents	Offspring	Parents	Offspring
Agenda Score:										
Low 1	14%a	26%	22%	28%	50%	36%	21%	24%	26%	36%
2	26	32	29	29	19	27	24	24	24	25
3	28	26	22	27	20	21	26	24	25	19
High 4	32	16	27	16	11	16	29	28	24	20
$\overline{X}$	2.8	2.3	2.5	2.3	1.9	2.2	2.6	2.6	2.5	2.2
N	(218)	(219)	(173)	(168)	(242)	(242)	(253)	(254)	(208)	(207)
Pair Relationships:										
tau-b	.23		.17		.08		.30		.34	
gamma	.31		.23		.11		.40		.44	
lineage gap	69%		73%		69%		60%		59%	
generation gap	27%–P		9%–P		16%–O		3%–P		14%–P	
adj. "	.39		.12		.23		.05		.24	
N	(217)		(168)		(241)		(250)		(205)	

a. All figures are based on a four-fold bracketing of the original mean index scores.

[471]

more government action. If anything, the parental generation might well be worried about the lesser role assigned by the filial generation.

Close inspection of the means and distributions across the five countries reveals that the source of the American cleavage lies primarily in the very conservative position taken by the parental generation. Although the American adolescents (along with the Austrians) do trail their peers in other countries, the discrepancy at the parental level is much greater. Here we can see the effects of the life histories experienced by the American versus the European parental generation. European parents have clearly become accustomed to the notion of governmental responsibility across a wide spectrum. The generation represented by the American parents has come much more slowly and with a different cultural heritage into that state of mind. Projecting into the future, always a hazardous matter, it seems likely that as population replacement moves the views epitomized by the parental generation out of the mass public the effect will be to bring American views more in line with those of Europe.

The level of pair correspondence varies from very modest to moderately strong. Austria and Germany have reasonably high pair correspondence, but Britain, with a level of group correspondence midway between that of Germany and Austria, has much lower pair congruence. Just why parents are more successful in passing on their orientations in Austria and Germany is difficult to fathom. One reason may lie especially in the longer existence of the social welfare system in those two countries. Perhaps positions have crystallized more, thus making them more susceptible to being passed on from parent to child.

Contained within the overall agenda measure are separate subindices, basically those of physical/material well-being and of social equality. The latter consists of the issue areas of guaranteeing equal rights for men and women, providing equal rights for ethnic and racial minorities, and evening out differences in wealth. To some degree these topics exemplify values associated with the "New Politics" of advanced industrial democracies rather than the "Old Politics" which revolve around materialism and class interests.

Once more, the rationales for informed hypotheses about intergenerational difference are not self-evident. Based on an assessment of contemporary events one would certainly expect the American adolescents to assign high political priority to this domain. Both the civil rights and womens' liberation movement have drawn disproportionate support from the young. Offhand, we would also expect the European youths to be more supportive on this dimension. In contrast to the public welfare area, with its long history, that of social equality is more recent and would seem to strike a more responsive chord among the young than the old—partly because egalitarianism is a constant refrain in the rhetoric of youthful protest.

Despite this line of reasoning, only in the United States and Germany is it supported, and even there the support is only modest. Adolescents assign a higher priority to social equality issues than do their elders, the generation gap being 16% in the United States and 12% in Germany. In the other countries the differences are trivial. Again the major reason for the gap in the United States lies more in the comparatively low scores of the American parents rather than in abnormally high ones among the adolescents.[27] Assuming no major life cycle shifts, we would expect the population replacement process to bring the Americans more in line with the Europeans. Much of the discrepancy between the generations in the United States comes from differences in the perceived responsibility of government to act in this domain, with the young investing much more responsibility than do their parents. In contrast, the generational dissonance in Germany springs more from the greater personal importance the young assign to this domain.

Lineage congruence in this area runs from low to modest, tau-b's ranging from .06 to .26, but the lack of congruence is translated into a demonstrable adjusted generation gap only in the United States (.23) and Germany (.20). It might have been thought that on the basis of social similarity alone (remembering that these pairs come from the same families) that there would be more concordance between parent and child. But here, as elsewhere in our findings, it must be concluded that the sources of political value orientations are multifarious. Nor should it be forgotten that we are dealing with rather "soft" measures for the most part and that the young, especially, are still in a malleable state.

Findings for the other major subagenda cluster, that of well-being, differ only moderately from those for social equality. Again the United States is the most deviant case, the young stressing well-being more than their elders (generation gap = 14%–0). Moreover, a separate examination looking only at the responsibility section of the agenda measure reveals that the distance between the two American generations therein is particularly wide (generation gap = 20%–0). At the other extreme, the gap in the Netherlands is 18%, but there the greater emphasis comes from the parents. Cross-generational differences are slight in the remaining countries.

Satisfaction with Government Performance

The issue agenda scores indicate the degree to which individuals feel that governmental rather than nongovernmental sources should be trying to enhance values of personal importance as represented by the functional areas presented to our respondents. One way of gauging the degree to which the agenda is being acted on is to ascertain the individual's assessment of government performance in those very same areas. We will first, then, briefly examine performance evaluations and then move on to an analysis focusing on the discrepancy between responsibility and evaluations. For present purposes we will employ the two domains of individual well-being and social equality.

When assessing the agenda in the area of well-being we found rather small differences between the generations except in the United States, where the difference was not only sizeable but in a different direction from that found in the European countries. A perusal of the performance ratings in this domain reveals a similar pattern. Although the cross-generational differences as indexed by the generation gap run from tiny to modest (12% edge for parents to 9% edge for offspring), it is intriguing that the United States once more stands out as a deviant case in terms of directionality. American youth give a more favorable nod to government delivery than do their parents, whereas the opposite is true across the ocean. Both generations in the United States have perceptibly lower mean scores than do their European counterparts. But even within this range of low evaluations the parents are more negative than their children. The malaise and disgruntlement said to characterize much of "middle America" may be reverberating through these evaluations. At the same time the European findings, though modest, are in the direction that one would ordinarily expect, namely, that youth would be less generous in their appraisals.

The pair correspondence, though variable, is reasonably impressive (.14 to .33). With the strong exception of Germany the parent-child congruity is higher in all countries than it is for the comparable dimension on the political agenda measure. The affective component introduced by performance ratings probably induces this higher level. Governments are often the target of good-bad evaluations in the home, and it seems likely that children pick up this valence.

Turning to the second domain, social equality, we find a continuation of the European pattern. Now the Americans follow suit, though just barely (parental margin of 3% versus a high of 22% in the Netherlands). In general, the performance scores are lower than those in the well-being domain across all countries and generations. Given that lower level, however, it is significant that the parental generation continues to feel the more positive. The edge is especially high in the Netherlands and Austria. In those two countries the lineage gap present within the family is converted into a sizeable gap across the generations as a whole (adjusted gap > .30). Pair correspondence, though positive, tends to run lower here than in the well-being domain.

Having given an overview of the evaluational dimension we can now take up the tantalizing question of what happens when performance is laid against expectations. The difference between agenda priority and performance defines the level of policy dissatisfaction. Another way of viewing the relationship is to say that the difference captures the subjective estimate of government output weighted by expectations. The lower the agreement between assigned responsibility and perceived performance the greater the feeling of positive governmental output.

Remembering that we are now moving into a contingent evaluational realm, our hypothesis about intergenerational comparisons are ostensibly more securely anchored. Since much of the past and continuing protest about the conduct of government has emanated from more youthful sources, one would expect discrepancy rates to be higher among them than among their parents. Not that the parental generation in these various countries has been completely quiescent. Dissatisfaction with governmental outputs, especially in the United States, has been voiced by the middle-aged as well as by the very young and very old. Nevertheless, the perceived failure of governments to live up to expectations seems to have been more characteristic of the young, among whom idealism tends to run high in any event.

Our first cut into the data utilizes all ten value areas, summed up as overall policy dissatisfaction (Table 15.5). The higher the score on the index the greater the dissatisfaction. Both the mean scores and the generation gap entries verify our speculation about the directionality of the findings in Europe. Clearly, the European milieu produces the classic, stereotypical view of youth dissatisfied with the status quo. This is the stuff of which challenges to contemporary leaders and institutions are made.

How, then, are we to account for the opposite findings in the United States? It will be recalled that American parents actually had lower expectations about governmental performance than did their offspring. On the other hand, the adolescents were more satisfied with the job the government was doing. In any event an *individual's* dissatisfaction score is a joint function of the two dimensions. The various intersections thereby provided allow for the sort of net drift observed in Table 15.5.

Nevertheless the findings are paradoxical when viewed in light of the widespread American youth movement beginning in the middle 1960s. On that basis one might well have expected the young rather than the middle aged to feel the more aggrieved. One obvious explanation for the seeming anomaly is that the issues that exercised the young were not primarily those represented by the values included in our instrument. War and peace (Vietnam), student power, and the like are not included (although three "social equality" items are). Middle-aged parents, by contrast, are acutely conscious of these values/tasks because they deal with them on a daily business. Ensuring job security, medical care, adequate housing, and safe neighborhoods, for example, are vital elements in their lives. It is on such issues that American parents find the government deficient—given certain levels of expectations.

Table 15.5: OVERALL POLICY DISSATISFACTION

	The Netherlands		Britain		United States		Germany		Austria	
	Parents	Offspring	Parents	Offspring	Parents	Offspring	Parents	Offspring	Parents	Offspring
Dissatisfaction Score:										
Low 1	27%a	15%	27%	18%	20%	24%	14%	11%	40%	30%
2	23	21	20	24	22	22	20	18	23	29
3	23	35	28	31	29	33	34	32	29	30
High 4	26	28	25	27	28	21	31	40	8	11
$\overline{X}$	2.5	2.8	2.5	2.7	2.6	2.5	2.8	3.0	2.0	2.2
N	(218)	(201)	(169)	(158)	(234)	(236)	(249)	(245)	(205)	(200)
Pair Relationships:										
tau-b	.13		.25		.02		.20		.17	
gamma	.17		.34		.07		.28		.24	
lineage gap	71%		66%		69%		61%		67%	
generation gap	12%–O		13%–O		8%–P		12%–O		12%–O	
adj. " "	.17		.20		.12		.20		.18	
N	(191)		(155)		(228)		(238)		(198)	

a. All figures are based on a four-fold bracketing of the original mean index scores.

In Europe the generally lower marks accorded the government by the young enter the dissatisfaction calculus to help produce noticeable though not overwhelming cross-generational differences. These differences suggest that the cutting edge of political change, or the demand for it, would come from the younger generations as they make their way into the adult political world. That assumes, of course, a conversion of perceived discrepancy into political action. It is difficult to make the reverse argument in the United States. Although the parental generation is by no means old, and is perhaps at the height of its political participation, it is nevertheless at the beginning of the downward slope on age. Moreover, it is not, as we shall see in the next chapter, a generation as given to the more unorthodox form of political expression as the upcoming generation. Consequently, it is not at all inconceivable that the parental generation will become increasingly bitter and dissatisfied.

Another country-specific pattern is intriguing. Both the Austrian parents and their offspring have the lowest levels of dissatisfaction across the five countries. Examining the internals of the tables making up this index indicates that this low dissatisfaction stems primarily from the high grades given the Austrian government on performance. Strictly in terms of subjective well-being in the governmental realm, the Austrians appear to be perpetuating the most positive pattern across the generations.

With the exception of the Netherlands the intrafamily concordance is moderately high (Table 15.5). The concordance figures are particularly impressive given the conglomerate nature of the index. This occurs despite a very high lineage gap (absolute disagreement) in all countries. Notice also that these gap figures have but a poor relationship to the ordinal statistics. What this means, of course, is that while the majority of pairs are not in absolute agreement, a good many of them are in proximate agreement. Their rank orders are similar. We suspect it is the evaluational component that makes congruence higher here than when dealing only with assigned responsibility. More general dispositions about government are tapped by this index and such dispositions are more likely to be the subject of the socialization process rather than such matters as the total scope of government activities.[28] Despite the rather high rate of absolute disagreement, only a modest amount of this is transformed into generational differences, with Austria having the high adjusted figure.

Since overall dissatisfaction embraces a variety of value domains, it will be useful to take a quick look at the two subsets treated previously, that is, well-being and social equality. The most general comment to make about a comparison between the two is that virtually all of the relationships are much more sharply drawn in the well-being domain. There are—save in Germany— greater aggregate differences as represented both by mean scores for the entire samples and the generation gap figures from the pairs. Simultaneously, however, the pair correspondence is appreciably higher in all countries except Germany. With respect to social equality the tau-b values for pairs range from −.03 in the United States (one of the rare negative signs found in the analysis) to .22 in Austria; the corresponding range on well-being is .12 to .29. Contrary to what might be expected, then, the "old issues" represented by the Materialist, well-being domain continue to provide a greater cleavage line than the "new issues" represented by the Postmaterialist, social equality domain. At the same time the greater salience and historical relevance of the well-being values make them generally more reproducible within the family.

Satisfaction with Political Processes

In the preceding sections we dealt with political satisfaction with respect to concrete areas of public policy. Obviously there is more to political satisfaction than policy outputs. Citizens are also concerned about such questions as representation, input into decision-making, conversion processes, the style of political leadership, whether the rules of the game are fair and are being followed, and so forth. Such questions are not directly inquired into by eliciting evaluations of government performance in specific policy areas. Therefore, we have utilized additional measures that address other dimensions of satisfaction in the realization that the outcomes of socialization and the nature of generational continuity and change should be observed in these dimensions as well. Two indicators will be used in this section.

Our first measure dealing with the processes and conduct of government is that of political trust, an index comprised of responses to two questions— whether the government is run for all or the benefit of a few, and whether the government can be trusted always, most of the time, some of the time, or never. Especially in the American context these indicators of trustworthiness have been used to signify the feelings people have about the authorities as well as more general feelings about the goodness of the political system.[29] Although the empirical evidence has not supported it, the popular impression is that in recent years the young have been less trusting than their elders.

Turning to the results from the pairs, we find both firm patterns and some mild surprises (Table 15.6). In the first place, congruence across the generations is high in all countries, as the mean values and the generation gap figures show. Whatever seeds of distrust may have been planted by the protest years and the revelations of skulduggery in most Western countries seem scarcely to have affected the generations in any differentiated way. Even in Germany and the Netherlands, where sharp schisms were noted with respect to some political orientations presented earlier in this chapter, a gap scarcely exists at all. And in the United States, where the political generation gap was (is) in part a matter of how much the authorities should or could be trusted, there is virtually no difference.

Although intergenerational similarity dominates within nations, marked dissimilarity exists across nations. Anchoring one end of this dissimilarity are the two Germanic countries. Upwards of one-half of each cohort in each country scores at the high end of the trust index (here collapsed into a trichotomy). Standing in sharp contrast are the Anglo-American countries, where nearly half of each cohort is at the low end of the trust measure. In the instance of the United States the low investment of trust reflects in part the deteriorating levels observed among virtually all segments of the populace since the mid-1960s. Trend data are not as handy for Great Britain, but the declining fortunes of that country, coupled with a number of national scandals, would seem to have exerted a toll comparable to that of the American case. At any rate, the crucial datum is that whatever importance political trust assumes for a given system it is a commodity shared in equally by two biologic generations.

Compared with the measures of dissatisfaction based on the intersection of agenda priority and performance evaluation (Table 15.5 above), the pair concordance on political trust is higher in every instance. Indeed, with the exception of the Americans, parents and their offspring display a moderately high level of similarity. There would seem to be two reasons for the within-family similarity. First, expressions of political trust tend to be related to partisanship. Adherents of the party in power traditionally exhibit higher levels of trust than do nonadherents. And since partisanship is one of the most successfully transmitted orientations, the moderate congruence on trust could easily be expected. A second possible explanation is that trust in the system is also a global orientation that would be displayed in a number of ways in the home. An accumulation of such cues could serve to orient the growing child in the direction upheld by the parents. Both of these explanations certainly help explain the European patterns, but the question remains as to why the American findings are deviant. Actually they are not deviant compared with other studies of American families, but they obviously depart from the European pattern. There is no ready explanation at hand, but one line of reasoning is plausible. The articulation between political trust and being an adherent of the ruling party is lower in the United States than in the other four countries. Thus the kind of constraint operating to promote concordance in European families would not be as operative in American families.

In some respects the findings dealing with our second measure, system responsiveness,[30] are the mirror image of those dealing with political dissatisfaction over policy outcomes. It was found that young people in the four European countries were less satisfied with policy outcomes than were their

Table 15.6: POLITICAL TRUST

	The Netherlands		Britain		United States		Germany		Austria	
	Parents	Offspring	Parents	Offspring	Parents	Offspring	Parents	Offspring	Parents	Offspring
Trust:										
Low 1	33%a	25%	48%	47%	49%	45%	22%	24%	16%	10%
2	30	38	32	29	28	33	26	30	33	38
High 3	36	37	20	23	23	22	52	46	51	52
$\overline{X}$	2.0	2.1	1.7	1.8	1.7	1.8	2.3	2.2	2.3	2.4
N	(190)	(195)	(154)	(137)	(233)	(227)	(220)	(216)	(186)	(192)
Pair Relationships:										
tau-b	.30		.43		.07		.27		.29	
gamma	.45		.62		.12		.42		.47	
lineage gap	53%		40%		59%		48%		49%	
generation gap	8%—O		2%—P		3%—O		4%—P		8%—O	
adj. ,, ,,	.14		.04		.06		.07		.16	
N	(171)		(127)		(218)		(194)		(171)	

a. All figures are based on a three-fold bracketing of the original mean index scores.

parents; the opposite prevailed in the United States. Curiously, the situation is reversed with respect to system responsiveness, as Table 15.7 demonstrates. In Europe the young are likely to feel that the system is more responsive, while in the United States it is the parents who feel that way. This shift stems partly from the extraordinarily high marks given by American parents versus European parents, though it should be noted that both American generations are at or very near the top of such marking across the five countries. But the fact remains that European youth are considerably less skeptical about the attention paid to ordinary people than are their elders. The contrast with the results for political trust are instructive because in that instance the generational differences were small or even slightly the reverse of those for responsiveness. Judging from these differences (as well as the only moderate intercorrelation of the two indices), the two measures are tapping somewhat separate aspects of satisfaction even within the realm of political process.

One reason the European findings seem counterintuitive is that so much of the academic and popular literature has focused on the American scene. Our images of youthful feelings about the responsiveness of the political system are correspondingly conditioned by that literature. As we see, the image is borne out in the United States, though not handsomely so. A likely explanation of the more benign outlook of European youth lies in their greater sense of political competence and skills. As we shall see in the next chapter young people on the continent also feel more politically efficacious than do their parents. In evaluating their own system's responsiveness these younger and better educated individuals may well be reflecting their views of the system's responsiveness to people like *themselves*. It is also likely that the younger generation is imbued with more of the popular democratic rhetoric, a rhetoric that emphasizes the importance of direct and responsive linkages between leaders and the led, rather than relying solely on the mechanical workings of the electoral system and indirect parliamentary democracy.

Of course it is possible that what we are observing among the European adolescents is simply an idealism and naivete that will soon pass as they enter the mainstream of their respective political systems and encounter the harsh realities of the political process. Perhaps the European youth are simply behind (in a relative sense) the less sanguine posture of the American youth. Weighing somewhat against that possibility is a set of comparisons from Table 15.7. A striking finding is the fact that the two European countries with the largest generation gap—the Netherlands and Austria have drastically different political environments. The politically uninhibited Dutch youth find their system remarkably responsive and the Dutch parents trail only the Americans in their positive evaluations. On the other hand, the Austrian youth are least generous in their praise and their elders are decidedly so. Yet the generation gaps are substantial in both countries, thereby suggesting that it is not the

Table 15.7: SYSTEM RESPONSIVENESS

	The Netherlands		Britain		United States		Germany		Austria	
	Parents	Offspring	Parents	Offspring	Parents	Offspring	Parents	Offspring	Parents	Offspring
Responsiveness:										
Low 1	18%[a]	13%	27%	23%	14%	18%	34%	26%	57%	36%
2	28	19	34	33	26	19	21	26	18	23
3	21	26	16	21	17	28	14	15	7	17
High 4	33	42	23	23	42	35	31	33	18	24
$\overline{X}$	2.7	3.0	2.3	2.4	2.9	2.8	2.4	2.6	1.9	2.3
N	(209)	(200)	(171)	(156)	(242)	(239)	(254)	(250)	(203)	(197)
Pair										
Relationships:										
tau-b	.21		.25		.06		.28		.14	
gamma	.29		.33		.09		.38		.20	
lineage gap	66%		66%		59%		60%		66%	
generation gap	16%—O		4%—O		10%—P		9%—O		24%—O	
adj. "	.24		.07		.16		.15		.36	
N	(190)		(154)		(236)		(247)		(192)	

a. All figures are based on a four-fold bracketing of the original mean index scores.

absolute climate of perceived responsiveness that leads to the more positive evaluations of the young across the European four.

Turning to pair correspondence, it is apparent that beliefs about system responsiveness are reproduced at varying rates across the five countries, as the ordinal statistics reveal. Only in the United States is the relationship at the trivial level, despite the fact that the lineage gap figure is actually lower in the United States than in the other nations. On the other hand, only Britain and Germany meet our criterion of tau-b $\geq$ .25. Congruence in general runs as high or higher than that found for policy satisfaction in the previous section. Thus the perspective of the young about general system responsiveness is neither more nor less conditioned by parental perspectives than in the case of policy areas. Within each the young evidently have a number of other influences acting upon them. A comparison with the concordance levels found for political trust shows that similarity tends to be higher for the latter, further underscoring our contention that trust is more conditioned by partisan dispositions within the family.

In this chapter we have surveyed the generations and families with respect to two main dimensions conditioning and guiding political action, namely, broad sets of sociopolitical value orientations and satisfaction with the policy content and conduct of governments. The connections between many of these topics and political action have been alluded to in the present chapter and spelled out in some detail in chapters treating the entire cross-section samples. Within the confines of this book we cannot address ourselves to these linkages. What we can do, however, is to turn our attention to those elements of political action that have figured prominently in the overall theme of our work. Thus the following chapter will continue in a vein parallel to the present one. A concluding statement in that chapter will address the meaning of and the questions raised by the findings reported in both chapters.

NOTES

1. The starting point for discussions of political generations remains (from the original 1928 work) that of Karl Mannheim, "The Problem of Generations" in P. Kecskemeti, ed., *Essays on the Sociology of Knowledge,* London: Routledge & Kegan Paul, 1952. A more biosocial orientation is that of T. Allen Lambert, "Generations and Change: Toward a Theory of Generations as a Force in Historical Process," *Youth and Society,* 4 (September 1972), pp. 21-46.

2. A number of anthologies and handbooks contain treatments of this subject. Recent efforts include Stanley Renshon, ed., *Handbook of Political Socialization: Theory and Research,* New York: Free Press, 1977; and David C. Schwartz and Sandra Kenyon Schwartz, eds., *New Directions in Political Socialization* (New York: Free Press, 1975).

3. One of the most comprehensive empirical treatments of familial and nonfamilial sources of socialization is M. Kent Jennings and Richard G. Niemi, *The Political Character of Adolescence,* Princeton: Princeton University Press, 1974.

4. Cf. Jürgen Habermas, *Legitimation Crisis,* Boston: Beacon Press, 1975. Translation of *"Legitimationsprobleme im Spätkapitalismus,"* Frankfurt: Suhrkamp, 1973; and David Easton and Jack Dennis, *Children in the Political System,* New York: McGraw-Hill, 1969.

5. David O. Sears, "Political Socialization" in Nelson Polsby and Fred Greenstein, eds., *Handbook of Political Science,* Vol. 2, Reading, Mass.: Addison-Wesley, 1975, p. 114.

6. Richard G. Niemi, *How Family Members Perceive Each Other,* New Haven: Yale University Press, 1974.

7. Sampling strategies and other details are presented in chapter 1 and in the Technical Appendix. Note that the resulting samples of "younger" and "older" generation are not strictly representative for either generation, due to the condition that a matching member of the other generation had to be included in the sample as well. Resulting distortions are rather mild, however, as comparisons with the respondents in the comparable age brackets in the overall cross-section samples indicated.

8. The possible bias is particularly great in the United States. Although, as note 7 implies, reassuring comparisons were made between the cross-section 16-20 year olds versus those selected as a result of having a parent who was interviewed, the cases available for comparison are not plentiful, especially in the United States. Another possible source of difficulty is the moderate overrepresentation of mothers in the German and American samples. Although this overrepresentation introduces some bias in specific results, the general contours remain very much the same—as we discovered by arbitrarily weighting the two samples so that mothers and fathers would have equal representation.

9. The incidence of the pair design is still rare in political research. Probably the most extensive use of the design is an American study, as reported in Jennings and Niemi, *The Political Character of Adolescence.* See also Kent L. Tedin, "Influence of Parents on the Political Attitudes of Adolescents," *American Political Science Review,* 68 (December 1974), pp. 1579-1592. For results from a small-scale cross-national investigation, see Jack Dennis and Donald J. McCrone, "Pre-Adult Development of Political Party Identification in Western Democracies," *Comparative Political Studies,* 3 (July 1970), pp. 115-136. A report on a national sample in West Germany is M. Kent Jennings and Rolf Jansen, "Die Jugendlichen in der Bundesrepublik: Der Wunsch nach Veränderung und Meinungsvielfalt in der Politik," *Politische Vierteljahresschrift,* 17 (No. 3, 1976), pp. 317-343. Two non-Western studies employing the pair design are Akira Kubota and Robert E. Ward, "Family Influence and Political Socialization in Japan," *Comparative Political Studies,* 3 (July 1970), pp. 11-46, and Joseph A. Massey, *Youth and Politics in Japan* (Lexington: Lexington Books, 1976). By the same token, cross-national designs are also rare. A small but stimulating exception is the work carried out by Joseph Adelson and his colleagues in the United States, Great Britain, and West Germany. See, inter alia, Judith Gallatin and Joseph Adelson, "Legal Guarantees of Individual Freedom: A Cross-National Study of the Development of Political Thought," *Journal of Social Issues,* 27 (November 1971), pp. 93-108. A study of younger subjects is Fred I. Greenstein, "The Benevolent Leader Revisited: Children's Images of Political Leaders in Three Democracies," *American Political Science Review,* 64 (December 1975), pp. 1371-1398.

10. For a more thorough discussion of these two different uses of pair data see Kent L. Tedin, "Influence of Parents on the Political Attitudes of Adolescents," *American Political Science Review*, 68 (December 1974), pp. 1579-1592; and M. Kent Jennings, "Analyzing Pairs in Cross-National Survey Research," *European Journal of Political Research*, 5 (June 1977), pp. 179-197.

11. In practice the use of large matrices means that a relatively high proportion of cells will lie off the diagonal, thus artificially inflating the lineage gap. Therefore, for matrices ⩾ 7 x 7 we have also treated cells lying in the immediate diagonals on either side of the main diagonal as being part of the main diagonal. Notes to the tables will indicate when this procedure was used. Although the effect is to decrease the lineage gap percentages, the effects are similar across all countries. This procedure can affect the generation gap figures also, but again in a relatively uniform way across countries.

12. An earlier application of these techniques is M. Kent Jennings, "The Variable Nature of Generational Conflict: Some Examples from West Germany," *Comparative Political Studies*, 9 (July 1976), pp. 171-188. A blocked analysis of variance approach to multigeneration comparisons is Vern L. Bengtson, "Generation and Family Effects in Value Socialization," *American Sociological Review*, 40 (June 1975), pp. 358-371.

13. On the use of multiple measures see Herbert F. Weisberg, "Models of Statistical Relationships," *American Political Science Review*, 68(December 1974), pp. 1638-1655; and Thomas P. Wilson, "Measures of Association for Bivariate Hypotheses" in Hubert M. Blalock, Jr., ed., *Measurement in the Social Sciences*, Chicago: Aldine, 1974.

14. All such figures are to some extent arbitrary. One guideline is that corresponding Pearsonian product moment correlation coefficients were nearly always sufficiently high to explain (when squared) 10% or more of the variance in the offspring scores.

15. It should be stressed that we are employing two conceptualizations of the term generation. One looks at generations from the biological, lineage point of view, the other from an age cohort point of view. An important point to bear in mind is that while we definitely have a two-generation study in the lineage sense, we cannot be quite so unequivocal in the cohort sense. Some violence can be done in the cohort sense simply within the 16-20 year age range of the youth. Even assuming that these youths do constitute a single cohort leaves us with the parental generation, where age has even more variance. Although the great majority of parents in each country falls within the 40-55 age range, that bracket in itself is very wide compared with that for the young generation. Thus the generation gap concept, strictly speaking, references aggregate differences between family (lineage, biologic) generations rather than age cohorts. On this point see Neal E. Cutler, "Generational Approaches to Political Socialization," *Youth and Society*, 8 (December 1976), pp. 175-207.

16. There is a growing literature on the statistical as well as theoretical and substantive problems involving these effects. See, e.g., Matilda White Riley, "Aging and Cohort Succession: Interpretations and Misinterpretations," *Public Opinion Quarterly*, 37 (Spring 1973), pp. 35-49; and Karen D. Mason et al., "Some Methodological Issues in Cohort Analysis of Archival Data," *American Sociological Review*, 38 (April 1973), pp. 242-258.

17. Very similar results were obtained using the measure known as "levels of ideological conceptualization in politics" (see chapter 8). Over the five countries the tau-b correlations ranged from .21 to .22, the gammas from .27 to .32. The parental generation scored higher than the younger generation in each country, with the generation gap figures running from a low in the Netherlands of 1% to a high in Britain of 25%.

18. Another, more complex measure of ideological orientation in politics that

measures direction left or right as well as level of conceptualization yields roughly similar results but with one important change. Again the parental skew is more toward the right than is that of the youths. And the smallest difference remains that in Britain. But in general the pair concordance is lower with this more cognitively based measure. Additionally, the large generation gap among the Dutch and the very sizeable tau-b pair relationship are both diminished.

19. The evidence is the most complete for the United States, but there are conflicting views about the point of inflection. Cf. Paul Abramson, "Generational Change and the Decline of Party Identification," *American Political Science Review,* 70 (June 1976), pp. 469-478; and Philip E. Converse, *The Dynamics of Party Support,* Beverly Hills: Sage, 1976.

20. This dichotomy was formed by combining the Center and Right parties described in the Technical Appendix and by leaving intact the Left parties. Perhaps the most intensive investigation of *tendance* among preadults is the work done by Annick Percheron in France. See her "Political Vocabulary and Ideological Proximity in French Children" in Jack Dennis, ed., *Socialization to Politics,* New York: John Wiley, 1973, pp. 211-230; *L'Universe politique des enfants,* Paris: Armand Colin, 1974; and "Ideological Proximity Among French Children: Problems of Definition and Measurement," *European Journal of Political Research,* 5 (March 1977), p. 53-81.

21. Comparisons will be drawn with pair correspondence on a variety of other sociopolitical groups in the following chapter.

22. Evidence along these lines is available from a number of sources. One of the most systematic is Richard Rose, ed., *Electoral Behavior: A Comparative Handbook,* New York: Free Press, 1974.

23. The religious identification question ran as follows: "Is your religious preference Protestant, Roman Catholic, Jewish, or something else?"

24. Rose, *Electoral Behavior.*

25. The concept, its measurement, and its meaning are put forth in chapter 11.

26. We follow here the thinking and measures outlined in chapter 14.

27. Thus the parental mean score was 2.2 compared with a parental range of 2.4 to 2.8 in the other countries; the youth mean was 2.7 compared with a youth range of 2.4 to 2.9.

28. Since dissatisfaction is conditioned by whether one's preferred party is in power—and since party preference is one of the more robust examples of pair correspondence—some portion of the pair correspondence on dissatisfaction is (strictly speaking) of a spurious nature.

29. The literature approaches the voluminous. For an interesting exchange of views, see Arthur H. Miller, "Political Issues and Trust in Government: 1964-1970," Jack Citrin, "Comment," and Miller, "Rejoinder," *American Political Science Review,* 68 (September 1974), pp. 951-1001.

30. The system responsiveness variable is discussed in chapter 14.

Chapter 16

GENERATIONS AND FAMILIES
Political Action

**KLAUS R. ALLERBECK, M. KENT JENNINGS,
and LEOPOLD ROSENMAYR**

One of the major elements of contention during protest periods is over how the political struggle shall be conducted. Protest behavior as such is nothing new. What does seem to be rather unusual, as argued in earlier chapters, is the degree to which unconventional behavior came to be adopted by large segments of sociopolitical strata not ordinarily associated with the more extreme forms of behavior. As noted before, during the past decade some elements with the most to gain eventually from a perpetuation of the status quo, for example, students and well-to-do liberals in the professions, were among the most prominent exponents of nonconventional behavior. At the same time it is clear that conventional methods did not pass out of existence. Moreover, protest techniques were often used to achieve a greater voice in the conventional decision-making mechanisms.

As of the time of this writing the more extreme forms of widespread protest are in abeyance, but there is little doubt that the political histories of most Western countries will vividly reflect the impact of the protest period. Moreover, the episodic outbursts of political violence (witness the German and Italian terrorists) as well as the continuing but more restrained forms of protest suggest that the residues of the so-called protest movement will have an enduring quality. Finally, the practice and acceptance of unconventional tactics seemed to be much more widely prevalent among the young; indeed much of the generational conflict had to do with the *methods* of bringing about change rather than the end goals in sight. In this chapter we shall approach the question of unconventionality and its relationship to conventionality in stages, beginning first with a consideration of sociopsychological orientations to political action and then moving on to more immediate indicators of action.

SUBJECTIVE ORIENTATIONS TO POLITICAL ACTION

In this portion we take up five major concepts: political efficacy, approval of protest behavior, views toward protest (and nonprotest) groups, the perceived effectiveness of protest behavior, and the degree of protest repression potential. With the exception of the first-named, these all deal very directly with normative orientations toward unconventional behavior and the political system. If behavior typically requires normative sanctioning, then this approach is well-taken. Normative orientations are often thought to be central elements of socialization within the family. On the other hand, conflicts in normative orientations often signal the cleavage point between the generations. Our materials are aptly suited to an examination of these two points.

Political Efficacy

Of all the sociopsychological preconditions of political action, political efficacy is perhaps the most salient to observers. Whether referred to as civic competence, subjective competence, perceived self-influence, or even estimated political self-worth, the concept of political efficacy has a powerful standing. A paucity of efficacious feelings is said to be injurious both to the health of a participatory democracy and, in some senses, to that of individual citizens within such a system. Although our measure of efficacy is both a system attribute as well as individual attribute, two of the three items comprising the measure lie in what is conventionally called the internal efficacy dimension.[1] Moreover, the third item is reasonably correlated with these two items. Political efficacy as a concept is distinguished from system responsiveness—treated in the previous chapter—by its greater emphasis on individual versus system attributes and by its role as a conditioner of participation, both conventional and nonconventional.

Before discussing the generational and pair correspondence patterns across the countries, the sharp contrasts in country-level tendencies should be noted (Table 16.1). At one end of the spectrum are the two Austrian cohorts. Each records the lowest scores on the efficacy measure—the parents by a tremendous margin. We see here an echo of the findings on the neighboring concept

Table 16.1: POLITICAL EFFICACY

	The Netherlands		Britain		United States		Germany		Austria	
	Parents	*Offspring*	*Parents*	*Offspring*	*Parents*	*Offspring*	*Parents*	*Offspring*	*Parents*	*Offspring*
Efficacy:										
Low 1	25%a	18%	19%	27%	15%	17%	44%	31%	66%	46%
2	25	26	37	28	22	20	22	20	21	19
3	28	20	22	22	22	20	10	18	9	18
High 4	22	37	22	23	41	43	24	32	5	18
$\overline{X}$	2.5	2.8	2.5	2.4	2.9	2.9	2.1	2.5	1.5	2.1
N	(222)	(215)	(171)	(166)	(243)	(242)	(256)	(255)	(207)	(202)
Pair Relationships:										
tau-b	.20		.06		.13		.24		.08	
gamma	.27		.08		.18		.33		.14	
lineage gap	67%		59%		67%		62%		63%	
generation gap	17%–O		1%–P		1%–O		18%–O		30%–O	
adj. "	.26		.02		.01		.28		.47	
N	(214)		(164)		(241)		(254)		(199)	

a. All figures are based on a four-fold bracketing of the original mean index scores.

of system responsiveness. Both Austrian generations see their government as having low responsiveness and their individual potential for influence as low in both an absolute and relative sense. If the results on satisfaction with policy outcomes are any guide, however, these low scores do not spill over into dissatisfaction with the policy performance of government.

The American case stands at the other extreme. Each cohort leads the field, the parents by an especially wide margin. The relatively high norm of efficaciousness in the United States is no new discovery, but its persistence in the face of the turmoil encountered from the mid-1960s onward is impressive. Adding to this impressiveness is the equally high absolute feelings on the part of each generation. Again, there is a parallel with the results for system responsiveness. To the extent that feelings of efficacy, on the one hand, and perceived system responsiveness, on the other hand, are preconditions for political action, the American cohorts would seem to be the best-positioned of all.

A comparison of the generations across all countries reveals a division between the Anglo-American pair and the continental trio. There is scarcely any intergenerational difference in the former but a substantial one in the latter. The young feel appreciably more efficacious, the outstanding case being that of Austria. Although the offspring scores are much lower than those in the remaining countries, the parents' scores are even more in arrears, thus leading to a noticeable generation gap and an adjusted gap almost equal to one-half of its potential. Differences are not as large in Germany and the Netherlands, but they are sufficient to suggest a rising level of potential activists in these countries.

Offhand, one would imagine that the development of political efficacy would be particularly vulnerable to home influence. Parents surely give cues about their feelings of civic competence, even—or perhaps especially—in apolitical homes. Some observers have gone so far as to suggest that such feelings are a basic part of one's psychological make-up. Is it not appropriate, then, to expect the developing child to take on some of these characteristics? Logical though the reasoning may be, the results are not strongly supportive. Only in Germany and the Netherlands do the tau-b correlations exceed .20. Germany continues to have some of the stronger pair relationships while at the same time displaying sizeable intergenerational differences. In this sense we are seeing a carry-over from the results of the previous chapter.

Legitimacy of Youthful Protest

Reflecting the heart of much debate about the place of youth in politics is the question of how they should express themselves. To some degree most polities expect the young to question the current state of affairs. According to popular beliefs, if one does not question the status quo before mature adulthood there is little likelihood that such questioning will ever occur. A countervailing expectation, though, is that questioning by the young must be evaluated by the more mature members of the society. In addition, the questioning must not go to extreme lengths, lest the fabric of society be rent apart. At least part of the division between age cohorts in the past decade had to do with the legitimacy of youthful protest, rather than the ultimate goals.

Our hypothesis about views on the legitimacy of youthful questioning is, not surprisingly, that adolescents will be more supportive than parents. The results from comparisons on a two-item index support the hypothesis in each country (Table 16.2).[2] Both the mean scores and the generation gap percentages demonstrate that the filial generation sees youthful protest as more legitimate. What is perhaps surprising about the results, however, is that the differences are not greater. Only in Germany would we say that anything approaching a massive difference emerges. Considering the radically different political histories undergone by the two German generations one might well expect the greatest difference there. A close inspection of the distributions shows that the generational gap in Germany is primarily a consequence of the less approving posture of the parental generation (compared with other countries) rather than an extraordinarily higher rate of approval among the youth.

An interesting paradox is presented if we move from the aggregate comparisons to the pair relationships. Despite the fact that the generations as a whole are further apart in Germany, the level of intrafamilial concordance is greatest in that country. Indeed, it is the only country in which parents appear to have their views incorporated by their offspring with much fidelity at all. On the other hand, the notion that adolescents and their parents are visibly at odds with each other is discounted by the fact that in no country are the relationships negative. One final point is worth noting. Only in Germany does the lineage gap within the family become converted into a high adjusted generation gap. This is a pattern that will be extended to additional countries in several succeeding findings. Somewhat contrary to the earlier arguments, these findings will suggest that whatever conflict does exist within the family in the protest arena has a tendency to be transformed into a polarized positioning.

Approval of Protest Tactics

As we have argued throughout this book, a variety of tactics is available for seeking desired outcomes in the polity. There is little contention about the legitimacy and political acceptability of most conventional, traditional modes, but heated controversy surrounds a number of the less conventional

Table 16.2: LEGITIMACY OF YOUTHFUL PROTEST

	The Netherlands		Britain		United States		Germany		Austria	
	Parents	Offspring	Parents	Offspring	Parents	Offspring	Parents	Offspring	Parents	Offspring
Legitimacy:										
Approve 1	16%a	26%	15%	23%	12%	20%	12%	32%	26%	28%
2	36	33	40	38	34	42	20	29	19	29
3	31	26	34	32	40	27	26	21	19	26
Disapprove 4	17	14	11	07	14	11	42	18	35	17
$\overline{X}$	2.5	2.3	2.4	2.0	2.6	2.3	3.0	2.2	2.6	2.3
N	(211)	(212)	(166)	(162)	(239)	(230)	(243)	(241)	(175)	(187)
Pair Relationships:										
tau-b	.11		.05		.13		.21		.06	
gamma	.16		.07		.19		.29		.08	
lineage gap	77%		66%		72%		73%		68%	
generation gap	13%—P		12%—P		17%—P		38%—P		13%—P	
adj. "	.17		.18		.24		.52		.19	
N	(201)		(156)		(225)		(232)		(164)	

a. All figures are based on a four-fold bracketing of the original mean index scores.

modes. In this section we will employ the protest approval scale in looking at the generations' normative orientations to protest behavior. We already know in terms of the cross-section analysis that there is a relationship between age and protest approval (chapter 4).

There are at least three reasons for expecting youth to be more favorably disposed toward protest behavior. In the first place, many of the more spectacular examples of protest behavior have been perpetrated by youth. To the extent that age identification and empathy affect evaluational mechanisms—as seems reasonable—we would expect youth to be more approving. A second reason is that young people have had little if any opportunity to engage in the more traditional forms of political behavior. Most of those in our samples, for example, have not been eligible to vote in a national election. Most of them are not tied into voluntary associations that engage in political lobbying. In short the political vehicles normally available to most mature members of the polity are simply not at hand for youths. A third reason for expecting greater approbation among the young is their seeming impatience. Elections occur relatively infrequently, the wheels of the bureaucracies grind slowly, and conventional ways of mobilizing support require time and patience. Coupled with impatience is a wariness about the utility of the standard mechanisms for effecting change in any event.

Turning to the results of our analysis (Table 16.3), we see that, as expected, the younger generation takes the more positive view of protest tactics. The pattern is clear and reasonably strong in all countries. Again, as on the previous measure, Germany stands at the extreme end in terms of the gulf between the generations. And again, the German situation develops in part because of the extreme scores of the parental generation, matched only by those in neighboring Austria. In fact the German youth have a clear lead only over the Austrian youth.

Looking at the within family relationships, we find an inconsistent pattern across countries. In two countries (United States and Austria) there is scarcely any overall concordance between parents and their offspring beyond what would be expected by chance, given the marginal distributions. Concordance is higher in Holland, and in Germany and Britain the tau-b coefficient approaches our magic criterion of .25. It is worth reiterating that the level of pair correspondence is, within outside limits, a rather poor guide to group correspondence. Britain and Germany exhibit the same pair correspondence, but stand at opposite extremes on the generation gap measure. By the same token, they are reasonably close on the simple lineage gap measure.

A sizeable proportion of the gap existing within the family is transformed into overall gaps between the generations. Without knowing the salience of the topic within families it is difficult to establish whether the within-family difference serves as the precipitating factor in swinging parents and children

Table 16.3: APPROVAL OF PROTEST TACTICS

	The Netherlands		Britain		United States		Germany		Austria	
	Parents	Offspring	Parents	Offspring	Parents	Offspring	Parents	Offspring	Parents	Offspring
Approval:										
Low 1	13%a	5%	26%	18%	19%	9%	36%	14%	38%	21%
2	34	20	33	27	33	23	32	24	38	38
3	18	20	20	23	31	26	23	27	14	16
High 4	35	55	21	32	16	42	8	34	10	26
$\overline{X}$	2.8	3.3	2.4	2.7	2.4	3.0	2.0	2.8	2.0	2.5
N	(214)	(217)	(171)	(163)	(237)	(235)	(252)	(248)	(177)	(180)
*Pair Relationships:*b										
tau-b	.18		.21		.16		.24		.06	
gamma	.21		.26		.20		.30		.08	
lineage gap	47%		39%		43%		45%		38%	
generation gap	18%—O		14%—O		22%—O		32%—O		20%—O	
adj. "	.38		.36		.51		.71		.53	
N	(209)		(161)		(228)		(246)		(157)	

a. These percentages are based on a collapsing of the original eight-category scale.

b. Correlations are based on the original scale. Gap figures are based on treating cells directly adjacent to main diagonal as part of the main diagonal in the 8 x 8 matrix.

in different directions. That is, discussion and conflict in the family may result in driving one or other part of the pair in the opposite direction or in reinforcing that tendency. Given the more conservative position of the parents and the place of parents as socialization agents, this swinging away is most often likely the offspring moving away from the parental position. In any event, out of all the generational differences that could emerge, given the internal cell distributions, a good deal does emerge. A comparison with tables in the previous chapter will show that comparable lineage gap figures often result in little or no generational gaps.

Evaluating Protest Groups

Another way of gauging the support for protest behavior is to ascertain the degree of approval awarded certain groups identified with protest actions. Groups serve as the vital connecting points between the individual and the state. During periods of wide-scale protest, attitudes toward the contesting groups serve to divide the populace. Respondents were asked to place groups on a scale running from 0 = very negative through 50 = neutral to 100 = very positive. In the United States a "thermometer" scale was used as the equivalent stimulus (see Technical Appendix).

Considering as favorable toward "student protestors" those young respondents who assigned values 50 and over, we obtain the following favorable percentages for the five countries: the Netherlands, 60%; Britain, 33%; United States, 41%; Germany, 38%; and Austria, 26%. We can summarize youth attitudes using the arithmetic means of the thermometer readings, thus taking into account the strength of positive and negative attitudes. All country means for "student protesters" are in the middle of the continuum, the Dutch mean being highest (58.9) and the Austrian being lowest (38.0).

In all countries young respondents are less favorably disposed toward explicitly revolutionary groups than toward student protesters. While the differences between countries seem substantial, these should not be overinterpreted. The magnitude of the differences may very well be explained by the difference in the meaning of "revolutionary groups"; while the translation in all three languages is rather literal, the connotations in these countries may be very different, ranging from the bombs of the "Rote Armee Fraktion" (or Baader-Meinhof group) in Germany to freely available white bicycles in the Netherlands.

The differences of the two generations within each country, however, can hardly be explained by differences of language. As we would expect, parents are less favorable regarding student movements than their children. The magnitude of the differences is not uniform in the five countries. On the 100-point scale parents are less favorable regarding student movements than are youths by about one standard deviation (based on the combined samples in each country) in Germany and the United States, about half a standard deviation in Austria and Britain, and about a third of a standard deviation in the Netherlands. Comparing across countries (Table 16.4), the parent means are all between 22 and 27, with the exception of Dutch parents (51.5).

The pattern for feelings about "revolutionary groups" is somewhat different. While we see parent-child aggregate differences in the same order of magnitude, we find them on a lower level, given the overwhelmingly negative responses of the parental generation. Parents seem to differ only in the degree of unfavorableness. The differences of generation means are largest in the United States (21), and in the 13-15 range (little more than half a standard deviation) in the other four countries.

Another movement for social change in these countries has been the movement for women's rights and greater equality of the sexes. As an indicator of support the interview schedule included a similar thermometer question about the *"women's liberation movement"* (WLM), using the appropriate national term to designate this—WLM in the United States and Britain, Dolle Minnas in the Netherlands, and the more descriptive term "Bewegungen zur Durchsetzung der Gleichberechtigung der Frau" in Germany and Austria—thus reflecting the less crystallized state of the modern women's movement in the latter two countries. Given the nationally different cognitive connotations, there is an obvious pitfall in comparing means across nations. Instead, we will focus on generational differences within the nations. Britain is the only country where the young appear less supportive of the WLM, the mean difference of parent and children's scores being −5. In Austria, there is scarcely any difference between the generations (+1). In the other three countries, the young generation is on average more favorable (United States, +6; Germany, +7; Netherlands, +11).

These evaluations of protest movements and actors can be juxtaposed against comparable evaluations made of established institutions and actors in the political system. For present purposes these include labor unions, the churches, police, and civil servants, and the major left and right parties in each country. As the bottom portion of Table 14.4 reveals, the results tend to be a slightly tarnished mirror image of those found for the protest movement. Although the disparities are not as striking, in general the parental generation accords higher marks than does the young generation to the established institutions. The differences are especially striking with respect to the clergy and to the police, the latter, of course, representing one of the prime symbols of the status quo. Even in the case of labor unions, which have more of a record on the side of challenging the established ways, the parental means are higher in two countries and significantly lower only in Germany.

Table 16.4: PARENT/CHILD RATINGS OF PROTEST GROUPS AND ESTABLISHED INSTITUTIONS: Means and Pair Correlations (r) of "Sympathy" Scores

	The Netherlands			Britain			United States			Germany			Austria		
	Parents	r	Offspring	Parents	r	Offspring	Parents	r	Offspring	Parents	r	Offspring	Parents	r	Offspring
	X̄		X̄	X̄		X̄	X̄		X̄	X̄		X̄	X̄		X̄
Protesting Students	51.5	(.20)	58.9	28.9	(.29)	43.2	27.0	(.21)	50.0	22.5	(.26)	46.3	23.0	(.32)	38.0
Revolutionary Groups	32.5	(.21)	46.5	18.6	(.14)	31.7	18.7	(.03)	39.0	10.4	(.23)	25.6	14.5	(.16)	27.0
Women's Liberation Movement	35.9	(.15)	47.1	43.0	(.25)	38.1	45.7	(.30)	51.8	56.8	(.51)	63.6	63.0	(.35)	64.0
Labor Unions	69.2	(.35)	65.9	53.8	(.38)	51.5	56.3	(.27)	57.6	57.1	(.39)	63.6	62.0	(.37)	63.0
Church-Clergy	66.9	(.33)	49.2	60.1	(.16)	50.4	81.3	(.27)	73.4	51.3	(.50)	38.9	66.8	(.33)	61.2
Police	77.0	(.13)	68.1	81.3	(.15)	71.9	79.2	(.17)	68.3	72.5	(.44)	60.4	74.8	(.25)	67.0
Civil Servants	61.4	(.30)	51.7	59.6	(.13)	53.0	66.0	(.09)	64.3	60.8	(.33)	53.4	63.2	(.29)	59.1
Major Left Party[a]	58.6	(.36)	55.8	57.5	(.36)	49.4	61.5	(.37)	57.9	54.1	(.49)	57.4	59.4	(.45)	57.0
Major Right Party[b]	45.6	(.16)	39.2	46.1	(.34)	41.6	50.7	(.27)	49.1	55.9	(.42)	46.5	56.4	(.44)	53.0
Establishmentarianism[c]	.39	(.24)	-.38	.34	(.19)	-.42	.46	(.29)	-.45	.44	(.33)	-.44	.30	(.20)	-.33

a. The Netherlands: PvdA; Great Britain: Labour; United States: Democrats; West Germany: SPD; Austria: SPO.
b. The Netherlands: VVD; Great Britain: Conservative Party; United States: Republicans; West Germany: CDU/CSU; Austria: OVP.
c. Entries are mean factor scores with a mean of 0. The higher the score the greater the positive feeling toward established groups and the greater the negative feeling toward protest groups (see Technical Appendix).

Thus the stereotype of generational conflict over the goodness of established institutions is at least moderately borne out by our findings. Moreover, the cross-country differences tend to be of a piece with other findings also. As is often the case, the generational differences tend to be among the highest in Germany and lowest in neighboring Austria. The generational cleavage structure permeating German politics simply has not taken hold in its less economically advanced neighbor. The Netherlands also exhibits significant intergenerational strains, especially with respect to religious institutions. We see in this instance a reflection of the drastic secularization and deconfessionalization process occurring in what was formerly a much more segmented, pillared society.

One way of summarizing the ratings applied to both the established and challenging groups is to employ the "establishmentarianism" scale based on a factor analysis of the individual ratings. This scale excludes only the parties as constituent parts of the factor scores assigned each respondent. By averaging these scores within each cohort we can obtain an overall impression of the distance between the two generations. The results are presented in the last row of Table 16.4.

One cannot view these figures without sensing a highly discernible gap between the generations in each country. Indeed the scores approach being direct opposites and depart considerably from the 0 midpoint established for the scale. Stated another way, the distance between the generations is almost a standard deviation unit (based on the pooled generations data in each country). To the extent that climates of opinion pave the way for political action of one sort or another, it is manifest that—barring dramatic alterations—the rising generation will provide a distinctly differently climate than its lineage predecessor.[3]

Notwithstanding the appreciable gulf between the generations at the aggregate level, the levels of correspondence between parent and child are, on the average, of moderate magnitude (Pearsonian r's presented in Table 16.4).[4] One reason for this is that well-known sociopolitical groups are tangible, easily cognized concepts. They are likely to be the objects of conversation in the home, family members may be at least nominal members of or be in interaction with members of various groups, and the mass media received in the home gives prominence and often makes judgements about the groups.

Among the groups evaluated by our respondents are some of the most salient throughout these countries. Even though the *absolute* ratings applied to the groups varied by generation, the *relative* ratings applied by generation representatives within family units are associated. Not that the correspondence is the same across all groups. Averaging the country scores (and excluding the establishmentarianism figure) shows that the four highest average correlations are not those applied to the protest groups. Rather, they are those given to the major left party (40.6), labor unions (35.2), the major right party (32.6), and the church (31.8). These are all highly visible, traditional institutions in the polity and are secondary groups toward which primary groups such as the family have traditionally had strong ties or feelings. As prominent objects and subjects of political action, they have the capacity for generating and then reinforcing intense loyalties. Thus the higher reproducibility of affect toward them within the family is explainable.

Just as the pair correlations tend to be higher among the very established traditional political institutions, so too are they higher among certain countries. By this time it comes as no surprise to note that the West German pairs are the most proximate to each (36.0) followed rather closely in this instance by the Austrian pairs (32.9). The other country pairs are well below these highs. Perhaps it is the relatively clear lines of social and political stratification in these two countries which lead to more familial homogeneity of group evaluations.

Effectiveness of Protest Behavior

A closely related question about protest actions concerns the perceived effectiveness of these actions to secure desired outcomes. As we saw in chapter 3, there is a positive linkage between approval of such behaviors and viewing them as potentially viable. Especially for the young this would seem to be a necessary association, given their greater endorsement of protest actions and their prominence in public manifestations of protest actions over the past decade. Still it remains to be seen whether at the absolute level the young exceed by a substantial margin their elders in viewing unconventional behavior as an effective political tactic. That would clearly be the direction of the hypothesis. The degree to which the young seem to be directly influenced by their own parents is, as we have come to see in a number of other respects, much more problematic.

As the figures in Table 16.5 show, the expected split between the generations is achieved. Mean differences are substantial in every country, and the generation gap decidedly favors the offspring generation in every country. Taking into account the fact that these younger cohorts have been socialized during a period when protest behavior was running at high tide in the Western democracies it is perhaps not surprising to observe this split. But the sheer presence of such activity was probably insufficient to instill a greater perception of effectiveness by the young. Rather, the fact that the various protests elicited reactions from the authorities would seem to have been pivotal. At times the reactions to demonstrations, sit-ins, and the like were repressive and unyielding in nature, at other times more accommodating and open, and at other times the authorities had to alter their behavior by dent of political pressure. The point is that the lessons and residues of the protest period have apparently settled down on the heirs of the period, the impressionable minds of the upcoming generation.

Whether this perceptual difference will persist is, of course, difficult to divine. If the belief that protest behavior is effective is never tested and reinforced in the cauldron of realpolitik, the belief may atrophy. A plausible case can also be made that the younger cohort is still filled with the romanticism attached to unconventional behavior and prefers to see it as effective. Assuming that the romanticism fades, the belief in the viability of protest may also fade. Nor is it inconceivable that age cohorts entering adolescence during the protest years still stand apart from upcoming generations not exposed to the intensity of these years. Such speculation does nothing to alter the presence of a sizeable generation gap as of the mid-1970s.[5] To the extent that each generation engages in politics, the potential set of tactics likely to be chosen for goal attainment will differ correspondingly.

Parents and their children resemble each other but modestly when it comes to evaluating protest effectiveness. While all relationships are more than trivial in magnitude, only Austria and Germany have correlations in the range suggesting a substantial transmission flow within the family. Unlike some of our modest findings, this one would seem to have a solid explanatory base in the political environment being experienced by the upcoming generation. As a deviant and "new" phenomenon, unconventional behavior would have many propagators, mediators, and models outside the nexus of the family. The developing child is likely to be very much influenced by these nonfamilial sources, especially in lieu of prior family-level cue-giving. A sizeable proportion of the high lineage gap figure (in percentage terms) is converted into a conflict between the generations, as shown by the adjusted generation gap figures.

Repression Potential

Our final normative orientation toward political action addresses the issue of how much tolerance should be extended to practitioners of the middle range forms of unconventionality. As the events of the past decade revealed, people have radically different ideas about how to handle unconventional behavior. These range from a rather passive acceptance and "wait them out" philosophy at one end to an active rejection and "stop at all costs" approach on the other end. It is often the handling of protest events that creates the drama and conflict rather than the issue or policy being contested. Rather than being simply an ad hoc evaluation of specific events crossing their perceptual screens, we may think of people's opinions on handling protests as

Table 16.5: EFFECTIVENESS OF PROTEST ACTIONS

	The Netherlands		Britain		United States		Germany		Austria	
	Parents	*Offspring*	*Parents*	*Offspring*	*Parents*	*Offspring*	*Parents*	*Offspring*	*Parents*	*Offspring*
Effectiveness:										
Low 1	47%[a]	21%	37%	18%	35%	20%	64%	35%	59%	41%
2	21	17	20	25	20	20	16	14	14	21
3	17	28	25	27	22	30	10	21	15	18
High 4	15	34	18	30	23	30	10	29	11	20
$\overline{X}$	2.0	2.7	2.2	2.7	2.3	2.7	1.7	2.4	1.8	2.2
N	(211)	(212)	(171)	(165)	(239)	(235)	(251)	(249)	(175)	(180)
Pair Relationships:										
tau-b	.13		.16		.14		.24		.24	
gamma	.18		.21		.19		.33		.34	
lineage gap	74%		72%		72%		62%		64%	
generation gap "	40%–O		22%–O		15%–O		18%–O		16%–O	
adj. "	.54		.31		.21		.28		.25	
N	(204)		(163)		(230)		(254)		(154)	

a. All figures are based on a four-fold bracketing of the original mean index scores.

tapping an underlying value structure about authority relationships in society, about systems of constraint, about the ways in which change should occur.

The repression potential scale (see chapter 3) serves as our indicator of this underlying value structure. People located at one end of the scale disapprove of virtually any attempt to repress or prevent the types of protest activities which served as stimuli in the interviews. At the other end are those who believe in the state using whatever constraints are necessary to control those same activities.

Our expectations about intergenerational differences on repression potential are of a piece with those concerning protest approval. Everything that has happened in the recent past and the findings of the present study (chapter 4) predict that the younger generation would be lower than their elders on repression potential. Especially because youth are frequently the targets of control agents in the protest settings, we might expect even more of a gulf between the generations.

The findings support the expectations (Table 16.6).[6] In each country the mean repression potential score is higher within the parental stratum as a whole and in each country the generation gap is described by parents having a plurality on the end of the scale. With the exception of the strikingly tolerant Dutch parents, parental scores across the countries are quite similar. There is more variance among the adolescent samples, ranging from the Dutch with very low repression potential to the Austrian and British with much higher modal tendencies. The contrast between the German and Austrian cases is especially compelling. Whereas the parental generation has an almost identical profile in the two countries, the adolescents differ substantially. It is as though the historical and contemporary forces molding the parents in these linguistically and historically related countries were parallel, whereas those affecting the upcoming generation were radically different. A review of the preceding two tables in this section will show a similar pattern. Indeed, one of the more illuminating cross-national findings to emerge out of our inquiry is the tendency toward cross-generational divergence in Germany versus that toward convergence in Austria.

Ranking equally high with Germany in terms of the generation gap is the United States. The echoes of the often-violent confrontations occurring in the late 1960s and early 1970s still reverberate within the United States and are amplified by occasional renewed outbreaks. Perhaps because the young often bore the brunt of physical sanctions, the American adolescents take a rather different stance than do their elders, a good many of whom are still convinced that firm resistance is the answer. Next to the United States the frequency and severity of protest confrontations were highest in Germany. It is probably no coincidence that the size of the generation gap is virtually identical in the two countries. To the degree that the repression potential

Table 16.6: REPRESSION POTENTIAL AGAINST PROTEST ACTIVITIES

	The Netherlands		Britain		United States		Germany		Austria	
	Parents	Offspring	Parents	Offspring	Parents	Offspring	Parents	Offspring	Parents	Offspring
Potential:										
Low 1	49%	56%	11%	21%	13%	42%	13%	41%	12%	17%
2	19	26	13	20	15	20	19	22	20	25
3	12	09	26	27	34	19	21	14	15	11
4	13	09	26	18	20	12	15	09	19	23
High 5	07	00	24	13	18	06	33	15	34	24
$\overline{X}$	2.1	1.7	3.4	2.8	3.2	2.2	3.3	2.3	3.4	3.1
N	(214)	(220)	(165)	(164)	(232)	(241)	(248)	(247)	(191)	(197)
Pair Relationships:[a]										
tau-b	.15		.13		.20		.25		.25	
gamma	.23		.17		.26		.33		.32	
lineage gap	58%		70%		76%		64%		74%	
generation gap	15%–P		25%–P		38%–P		43%–P		13%–P	
adj. "	.26		.36		.50		.67		.18	
N	(211)		(156)		(229)		(239)		(183)	

a. All figures are based on the original five-fold scale.

measure exemplifies the "law and order" theme, it is apparent that the basic conflict between the generations in both Germany and the United States remains unresolved.

The within-family analysis suggests that repression potential reflects a dimension of greater salience and transferability than that of protest approval and the legitimacy of youthful protest. Although the pair correspondence statistics are not overwhelming, they do run higher than those for the other two indicators. In part this difference would seem to be borne out of the fundamental aspects of individual versus state relationships embodied in the measure. The items used to form the scale are also very specific and concrete in content. In general we would expect to find higher pair correspondence on very salient and easily comprehensible issues. Still, the statistics belie the notion of strong lines of transmission between parent and child even on such a fundamental expression of instrumental values. With the exception of Austria, differences in orientation within the family were frequently transformed into overall generational difference.

THE REPERTORY OF POLITICAL ACTION

In all five countries the late 1960s and early 1970s saw a good deal of political and social activism among young people. The issues of the political and social movements of the time showed some similarities and many differences between countries. There was, however, a great deal of similarity in the means of activism. Rather than relying only on the established channels of the political system to make their demands, the young often preferred to make themselves heard by using less conventional means of political participation—some of them legal means that had not been in much use before, some barely legal, and some illegal. The level of such direct actions and unconventional political activity differed among the five countries for which we have data. At a superficial level it appears that youth and student movements had most impact and were most visible in West Germany and the United States, had less strength in the Netherlands, and were weakest in Britain and Austria. Our data will allow us to give some quantitative assessment of the accuracy of this evaluation. It is also clear from previous research that those movements by no means mobilized all young people, and that there were rather divided opinions among young people—the split between young people attending institutions of higher learning and their peers who had already joined the labor force being the most pronounced one.[7] In this section we take up four indicators of political action: actual performance of nontraditional activities, potential for protest behavior, levels of conventional participation, and the typology of political action.

Overt Nonconventional Behavior

Although we have argued that the repertory of political action includes the potential for action as well as the actual performances of such behaviors, there is no gainsaying the essence of the latter in terms of what directly affects political life. It was especially the manifestations of youthful dissatisfaction during the height of the protest movement that struck fear or admiration—depending upon their leanings—into the hearts of onlookers. These actions also made plausible the threats of continued protest. As a first step, then, we shall examine the frequency of protest behavior reported by our interviewees.

Survey data are notoriously weak devices for detecting the incidence of protest behavior on a national scale.[8] When evaluating the absolute level of unconventional participation it must also be kept in mind that many of our 16-20 year olds were too young to take part in protest actions during the movement's heyday. An older cohort would be necessary to make more relevant estimates of youthful engagement during the peak period. Consequently our particular cohort's participation rate undoubtedly underestimates the rate for the preceding cohort.

As expected, in all countries only a minority of the youths had participated in the activities associated with the protest movement. The qualified exception to this generalization is in the activity of signing petitions. We noted in chapter 3 that this activity is the "easiest" item in our various protest scales and that in at least two or three countries it scarcely qualifies as an unconventional act. Thus the frequency of petition signing—ranging from a high of 48% and 42% for American and German youth to a low of 27%, 24%, and 21% for British, Dutch, and Austrian youth—is understandably the highest of all activities within each country.

Turning to less frequent but more truly nonconventional modes, we find that attending lawful demonstrations was engaged in by 20% of the young in Germany, 13% in the United States, 12% in the Netherlands, 6% in Austria, and but 4% in Great Britain. This rank ordering corresponds to the more impressionistic descriptions of observers.

Demonstration turnout is but one indicator of movement participation, and one that tends to underestimate its strength, as it assumes that all people, no matter where they reside, had easy access to demonstrations. Another activity with mass participation was boycotting, designed to bring economic pressure to bear on targets of the movement. Calls for boycotting nonunion-picked lettuce and grapes issued by supporters of the United Farmworkers received wide publicity in the United States. Boycotts of South African goods in other countries were meant as a means of protest against apartheid policy. While we did not ascertain what goods our respondents boycotted specifically, and for which cause, we do have some quantitative estimates of how many young people participated in any boycott. The percentage is highest among American youth (15%), followed by German (9%) and Dutch youth (5%). The smallest percentages claiming to have participated in boycotts are found in the British (5%) and Austrian (3%) samples. Other more extreme actions were engaged in by no more than 5% of the youth. Although data from a cohort caught in the throes of a protest movement would probably yield a higher figure, it is nevertheless true that these more flagrant forms of protest are unlikely to be acted out by more than a fraction of any national population of youth.[9]

Because of the recency of the protest years and the prominence of the young in the movements, it is often assumed that the generation represented by their parents has had little, if any, experience along these lines. Yet, if only by reason of the parents' longer period of political maturity, one would question whether this is true. Even though the protest opportunity structure was perhaps not as lush for them as it has been for their children, the political histories of the five countries were rich enough during the ten years (the time span covered by the question) prior to field work to have offered multiple chances of protest display.

Surprisingly enough, the intergenerational results vary across the five countries. Of the ten action forms the young had the higher rate a majority of the time in the Netherlands, the United States, and Germany. By contrast, the parents held the edge more often in Britain and Austria. Why should three countries have patterns in accord with popular impressions whereas two do not? A full-fledged answer is clearly beyond our means at this stage, but an illustration will be instructive.

In Britain the parental advantage is especially noticeable in the domains of boycotts, legal demonstrations, and wildcat strikes. These are all long-established and occasionally practiced acts of defiance in Britain. They require no special impetus of a youth movement to trigger them. In the United States and the Netherlands the youths' greater frequencies are especially noticeable in some of the more esoteric and seldom-invoked practices such as painting slogans on walls, blocking traffic, doing physical or personal damage, and occupying factories. These acts, while certainly not completely novel in the two countries, were nevertheless not part of any ordinary stock of unconventional behavior. It would seem that the protest movement helped bring them more readily into the repertories of the young than the middle-aged.

Protest Potential

A basic contention of this book has been that the political repertory is not confined to activities that individuals have performed in the past. Rather, the activity pool consists also of actions known and understood by individuals that they would or might do under certain circumstances and to which they give normative approval. This reasoning lies at the base of the protest potential measure. Simply because only a minority of the populace ordinarily engages in protest action does not mean that under certain circumstances a larger number could not become involved. Nor does it mean that the political climate created by a diverse political repertory is the same as that fostered by a restricted one. An examination of our materials should shed light on the degree to which the widely heralded cleavage between the generations with respect to a propensity for protest action is actually present.

Certainly here is an instance in which the empirical data are in accordance with popular images, as adumbrated by the cross-section results (chapter 4). In every country and by substantial margins the young display a higher inclination toward protest behavior than do the middle-aged (Table 16.7). These are among the very highest divergencies observed in our entire analysis, an assessment applying to the mean score differences, the generation gap percentages, and the adjusted gap figures. Once more the generation gap is highest in Germany, but even Britain, with the smallest generational cleavage, registers a difference of 22%.

In view of the uniformly higher protest potential among the young, may we expect a continuation of such tendencies in the future? That is, to say the least, a difficult question to answer. The likelihood of protest activity is a joint product of the level of political dissatisfaction on the one hand and the costs and benefits associated with protest on the other. Dissatisfaction can remain high but protest low; similarly, it may not be costly to protest but since there is little dissatisfaction there is no incentive. Therefore, even if the current levels of protest potential persisted as the young move through the life cycle, there is no assurance that concrete behaviors would emerge or persist. At a minimum, however, we might say that the underlying structure would facilitate the expressions of protest. From either perspective the likelihood of unconventional behavior would be higher as the filial generation succeeds the parental one, ceteris paribus.

Despite the parallelism in cross-cohort differences, the absolute levels of protest potential differ rather dramatically among the nations. Based on the findings for the cross-section samples, it will come as no surprise that the two Austrian cohorts stand at the lowest end of the protest potential scale. Similarly, the ranking of the American and Dutch cohorts at the higher end parallels earlier findings. Perhaps most interesting is the relatively low level of protest potential among British youth, exceeded only by the quiescent young Austrians in their disavowal of unconventional inclinations. As with their

Table 16.7: PROTEST POTENTIAL

	The Netherlands		Britain		United States		Germany		Austria	
	Parents	Offspring	Parents	Offspring	Parents	Offspring	Parents	Offspring	Parents	Offspring
Protest:										
Low 1	29%a	13%	42%	27%	30%	12%	43%	18%	59%	35%
2	30	20	28	28	30	27	28	24	29	37
3	23	36	25	31	34	36	24	33	11	20
High 4	18	31	5	15	6	26	4	25	1	7
$\overline{X}$	2.3	2.8	1.9	2.3	2.2	2.8	1.9	2.6	1.5	2.0
N	(213)	(217)	(171)	(163)	(235)	(232)	(249)	(244)	(161)	(167)
Pair Relationships:										
tau-b	.10		.17		.19		.29		.20	
gamma	.14		.24		.26		.40		.31	
lineage gap	72%		68%		68%		67%		60%	
generation gap	33%—O		22%—O		36%—O		44%—O		30%—O	
adj. "	.45		.33		.53		.66		.50	
N	(208)		(161)		(223)		(240)		(139)	

a. All figures are based on a four-fold bracketing of the original eight-category scale.

parents, the British youth apparently feel that the traditional system is sufficiently flexible and open without having to make recourse to more unorthodox activities.

Whatever state of protest potential has been arrived at by the young is but modestly reflective of the orientations held by their parents. Only in Germany does the pair congruence become substantial. Given a relatively new phenomenon, the otherwise modest relationships are what one would predict.

Conventional Political Participation

Analysis of the national cross-section samples in our study revealed sizeable internation differences and important corollaries of political participation in the conventional mode. Of special interest was the way in which this mode combines with protest potential to form a political repertory. We will move on to a consideration of the repertory momentarily. Because of the predominance of the conventional over the unconventional—if for no other reason—it is advisable to examine initially the nature of aggregate and pair congruence in that domain.

Based on the treatment of the whole sample as well as what is known about participation over the life cycle, we would expect at the aggregate level to find higher parental than youth participation.[10] In all countries except the Netherlands that proves to be true, but there is an extraordinarily wide range in the generation gap (Table 16.8). Great Britain, the United States, and Austria, in that order, follow the traditional expectations that middle-aged people will be more participative than younger people. The very large gap in Britain is very much a function of the exceptionally low showing of British youth inasmuch as the British parents rank second only behind the Americans in their reported participation. Conversely, the still substantial distance between the American generations comes about largely because of the abnormally high level among the parents, over half of whom are in the highest bracket. Although the Austrian parents have the lowest mean participation rate, they still exceed by a considerable margin the even more depressed level among their children.

Germany, where the intergenerational difference is small, and the Netherlands, where no difference exists, provide the exceptions to the expected pattern. There are no ready explanations at hand for this departure from the expected. What is perhaps more intriguing is the question of whether the near parity possessed by the younger generation in these two countries portends a relatively higher rate of participation than the national norms (represented by the parents) as this cohort passes through its life course. That is, if the 16-20 year olds are already at a level close to that of the parental cohort—and given

Table 16.8: CONVENTIONAL POLITICAL PARTICIPATION

	The Netherlands		Britain		United States		Germany		Austria	
	Parents	Offspring	Parents	Offspring	Parents	Offspring	Parents	Offspring	Parents	Offspring
Participation:										
Low 1	30%a	34%	20%	51%	13%	24%	24%	34%	35%	49%
2	18	14	24	23	13	20	31	20	21	25
3	31	31	36	18	21	29	13	14	22	13
High 4	21	21	20	8	53	28	32	32	22	13
X̄	2.4	2.4	2.6	1.8	3.1	2.6	2.5	2.4	2.3	1.9
N	(223)	(222)	(172)	(173)	(244)	(241)	(257)	(257)	(212)	(211)
Pair Relationships:										
tau-b	.26		.18		.14		.16		.10	
gamma	.35		.26		.20		.22		.14	
lineage gap	64%		73%		67%		65%		72%	
generation gap	0%		44%—P		30%—P		6%—P		25%—P	
adj. ""	.01		.61		.45		.09		.35	
N	(222)		(172)		(241)		(257)		(211)	

a. All figures are based on a four-fold bracketing of the original eight-category scale.

the anticipated upward curve in participation with aging—then it would be reasonable to expect that by the time this cohort reaches its mid life stage it will be much more participative than the current parental cohort. The coming of age of the young German cohort during a period when participatory democracy was being increasingly stressed, versus the suppression of such modes during much of the preadult period of the parental cohort, suggests one possible reason for this line of development. The explanation in the Neterlands is much more problematic.

Surveying the lineage relationships, it is obvious that cohort discontinuities have little to do with family discontinuities. While it is true that the Netherlands, with the smallest generation gap, has the highest pair correspondence, it is also true that Britain, with the largest gap, has the second-highest pair correspondence. Beyond this point, it is also apparent that lineage correspondence is surprisingly modest. We say "surprisingly" because the expectation would be that behavioral predispositions might well be passed on more easily than attitudinal ones. In addition, there should be less "noise" in the measure of concrete behavioral acts and thus less deflation of any real correspondence between parent and child. The dyadic similarity is no greater than—and in many instances lesser than—that found for attitudinal dispositions.

The Action Repertory Typology

By combining the protest potential scale and the conventional participation scale we created a five-fold repertory typology of political action. Previous chapters have shown in some detail the corollaries and contingencies of the repertory types. Based on the findings reported by age (chapter 6) and what we have reported on the constituent parts of the typology in this chapter, we would expect to observe significant differences between the two generations. At the same time our expectations are also for only modest signs of lineage similarity. Because of the nominal variable nature of the typology, our mode of presentation will differ slightly from the customary pattern.

Let us first consider some overall patterns by country (Table 16.9). Britain and Austria stand out for having abnormally high proportions of *each* generation weighing in as Inactives (although German parents rank along with the British parents). Considering the parochial, subject orientations of the Austrians as we have observed them in this study, the fact that both generations emerge as the most Inactive is perhaps not surprising. Still, the fact that the young are very nearly as inactive as their parents must give one pause as to the future of a vital participatory democracy in Austria. However, the British case is in some ways even more puzzling for if ever a country

Table 16.9: POLITICAL ACTION REPERTORY

	The Netherlands		Britain		United States		Germany		Austria	
	Parents	Offspring	Parents	Offspring	Parents	Offspring	Parents	Offspring	Parents	Offspring
Repertory										
Inactives	14%	9%	26%	25%	8%	7%	27%	14%	36%	31%
		(5%–P)a		(1%–P)		(1%–P)		(13%–P)		(5%–P)
Conformists	15	4	15	2	22	5	16	4	23	4
		(9%–P)		(13%–P)		(17%–P)		(12%–P)		(19%–P)
Reformists	19	17	29	13	46	29	25	23	25	17
		(2%–P)		(16%–P)		(17%–P)		(2%–P)		(8%–P)
Activists	18	32	12	11	7	23	5	21	3	6
		(14%–O)		(1%–P)		(16%–O)		(16%–O)		(3%–O)
Protesters	34	38	17	48	17	36	27	37	13	42
		(4%–O)		(31%–O)		(19%–O)		(10%–O)		(29%–O)
N	(213)	(216)	(170)	(163)	(235)	(230)	(249)	(244)	(161)	(166)

a. Entries represent the difference between the parent and offspring percentages; "P" and "O" indicate parental and offspring advantage, respectively.

could be said to have a virile history of political action, it would be Britain. Yet a quarter of each generation scores very low on both the conventional and the protest potential scales (the Inactives cell).

Another country-specific finding of import is the very low proportion of Americans in the Inactive category. Again the fact that the young are equally low implies a perpetuation of the stereotypical American propensity toward activity rather than passivity. A final regularity across the generations is the high incidence of Protesters in the Netherlands. The Dutch young are clearly the most protest-oriented among the filial generations and the parents rank high among the parental generations. When placed in the context of the reknowned Dutch tolerance of diversity and the weak manifest action component of the Protester category, the high and similar proportion of the two Dutch generations suggests a continuation of the politics of accommodation in that country.

While particular modalities mark certain countries, the parallelism across countries is the more striking pattern. Examination of the first three rows of Table 16.9 demonstrates that in each country the parents hold the edge: they are more likely than the young to be Inactives, Conformists, and Reformists. By contrast, perusal of the last two rows demonstrates that with a single, slight exception (British Activists), it is the youth who hold the margin over their parents. Most often this is a decided edge, Britain and Austria offering the prime examples in the Protesters category and the Netherlands, the United States, and West Germany being the leading examples in the Activists category. Inasmuch as it is the degree of protest approval that most distinguishes the Activists and Protesters from the other three categories, it is patent that the two generations diverge most noticeably over the sanctioning of protest behavior. Whether that divergence will be reflected in the young cohort's continuing greater subscription to Activist and Protester modes of action remains to be seen. At this stage, however, the gulf looms large; it seems unlikely that it would wither away overnight.

The disparities between the generations at the aggregate level are matched by sizeable ones at the individual level. Presented below are the figures for the *overall* lineage gap and the gap for each of the five action types. The former is simply the percentage of parent-child pairs not falling into the same action cell. In evaluating the separate action type figures it should be remembered that these are not independent values, that is, the distributions and gap figures on any one or more action types help define the distributions and gap figures for the remaining ones. Still, the figures will be useful for comparative purposes.

Lineage Gaps on Action Types

	The Netherlands	Britain	United States	Germany	Austria
Overall	68%	71%	71%	66%	73%
Inactives	17	30	12	27	40
Conformists	16	15	24	17	25
Reformists	27	31	43	32	32
Activists	36	18	25	21	10
Protesters	41	47	38	36	47
N	(207)	(160)	(221)	(240)	(139)

Upwards of seven in ten parents and their offspring fell into different categories of the typology overall. Nor is there much difference across countries in the absolute size of the gap. Knowing the category of the parent is but a weak predictor of the child's category. In fact the highest reduction in prediction (based on the conservative, asymmetric lambda coefficient) is 6% for the Netherlands. Assuming that the measures are reliable and that there is substantial overtime stability, the development of youthful action orientations would seem to be but dimly affected by direct socialization processes such as observational learning and reinforcement in the home.

Shifting to the specific action types, we can determine the key sources of the overall discrepancy. In all countries the major gap lies in the Protesters category. A comparison of these figures with the difference figures in Table 16.9 (in parentheses) shows that not all of the lineage gulf is by any means a consequence of the young being Protesters while their parents are not. That is the strong drift, but there are plentiful examples in the opposite direction, especially in the Netherlands and Germany. The magnitude of the lineage differences vary substantially for the other action types.

CONCLUSION

In this and the previous chapter our discussion has focused on several aspects of political action. The data are rich in detail, and there is no simple way of summarizing all results in a few pages. Some features do stand out, though, and in conclusion we will address these common features and then go on to speculate about the meaning of our findings.

The Findings in Perspective

At the generational level our findings run from some rather dramatic cleavages to virtually imperceptible differences. With some noteworthy exceptions the filial generation emerges as considerably more "liberal" and less conventional than its predecessor. This is true, though with varying degrees, in the areas of left-right ideology, partisanship, religious orientations, postmaterialism, subscription to the legitimacy of youthful protest, the approval of protest tactics and groups, disapproval of repression techniques, and the propensity toward unconventional behavior. On the other hand, differences *tended* on the whole to be slight to modest on the subjects of the political agenda, policy dissatisfaction, and political trust. Curiously enough, then, in terms of day-to-day governmental concerns the intergenerational cleavage structure falls shy of that exposed on somewhat more global, age-specific, and passionate concerns. There is, of course, no guarantee that these divisions and lack of divisions are permanent, but they are suggestive about the future.

While cross-country similarities abound, it is also true that distinctiveness is also present. The contrast of the American case in the area of values and political satisfaction was cited at length. The relatively greater conservatism of the British and Austrian youth also stands out. The pronounced youth advantage in political efficacy and system responsiveness in three or four of the European countries is also worth noting. In many ways the overall generational cleavage is greatest in Germany, though each country has examples of sizeable conflict. At the same time, correspondence within familial dyads ran highest in Germany and, on balance, lowest in Britain. We are not prepared for a full-blown interpretation of the cross-country diferences, but it is patent that these are wrapped up in the recent political histories as well as the traditional cultures of each country.

The magnitude of the generation gap differs from country to country and from one orientation to another. However, even a large generation gap does not necessarily mean conflict within families; and familial conflict does not necessarily foster large generational conflicts. While measures of association that indicate the degree of harmony or conflict within families fluctuate over orientations and countries, being for the most part not of extraordinary magnitude, virtually all measures are positive. Knowing parents' political orientations allows one to make better predictions of their offsprings' orientation than one could without this knowledge. Similarity within the family is far more frequent than disagreement. These positive correlations do *not* mean that there is no political conflict at all on these issues between any of the parents and children we interviewed. It does mean that there are more children leaning in the same direction as their parents than there are children leaning in the opposite direction.

When student and youth movements reemerged in the second half of the 1960s, some observers and analysts were quick to suggest explanations that revived an old theme: generational conflict. Oedipal rebellion against parental authority was considered as the cause of these movements.[11] The family was seen as influential for the activities of their children; but it served as a negative referent according to such theories. Such explanations may have some plausibility. They link microlevel phenomena (rebellion in the family) and macrolevel outcomes (political conflict, opposition movements) in a way that differs only superficially from *political* theories of political socialization. The common aspect of both is this simple linkage of micro- and macrolevel. Rebellion in the family leads to a macrolevel conflict, as effective socialization is supposed to result in system persistence.

Plausible or not, generational conflict theories are quite incompatible with the unambiguous message of the cited results. The parent-child relationships in the five countries are remarkably similar. There are some differences in strength of the correlations, but within a limited range. All correlations are positive, indicating that agreement of adolescents with their parents is much more frequent than rebellion. It is clear that parents serve as positive referents much more frequently than as negative referents.

These results hold not only for the United States, but for Western and Central Europe as well. Their similarities show that the speculative literature suggesting very different frequencies of agreement and rebellion, due to assumed differences in family structure between the United States and Germany, for instance, is not supported by empirical data.[12] Nor are patterns of parent-child agreement limited to conventional political orientations and behavior. Parents and their children show about the same amount of agreement concerning the new protest movements and their tactics as for the "old politics"—in spite of claims by staunch supporters of those movements and their opposition that they were really "outside the system" and wanted no part in it.

Although it is beyond our present task to explore variations in the lineage and generational concordance across families, a few observations are in order. The modest to emphatic concordance rests in part on the very strong familial ties binding parents and their children. Contrary to much of the adolescent subculture and adolescent rebellion emphasis of a few years back, more recent thinking has reemphasized the integral place of parents in the lives of adolescents. This integral role facilitates the direct and indirect mechanisms whereby parents can influence their children.

Our data are very supportive in this regard. The young were asked (except in Britain) a series of open-ended questions about whom they felt closest to, whom they could most rely upon, and who understood them best. If their replies are divided between the three categories of parents, friends, and others, parents received a substantial majority in every instance. The majority was especially pronounced with respect to who could be best relied upon, where the proportion citing one or both parents was over 75% in each country. A cross-tabulation of responses to all three questions underscores the salience of parents. With three domains and three groupings of referents there are twenty-seven possible combinations. In Austria and Germany a majority named parents for *all three domains,* i.e., over half of the respondents designated the parent-parent-parent combination. Even though the proportion fell to about one-third in Holland and the United States, that was still far in excess of any of the other possible combinations. These strong affective and maintenance relationships can only serve to foster the potential socializing impact of parents.

Other data also support the primacy of the family. The adolescents were asked about their levels of agreement with their fathers and mothers (separately) in the four areas of politics, religion, sex, and study or work. Admittedly, these are subjective measures that may or may not be valid indicators of actual agreement. But they do denote the perceived state of harmony in the dyadic relationship, a condition that may be just as important—if not more so—than the actual concordance in terms of describing the tenor of familial relationships. In all countries solid to overwhelming majorities said they "agree completely" or "agree" with both their mothers and fathers in the domain of politics. The same held true in religion and study/ work. Only with respect to sex did the proportion fall below a majority, and even that was not true in Britain, Holland, and the United States. Moreover, for the three countries (Britain, Austria, and the United States) where identical questions were asked regarding friends, parents prevailed over friends in the domains of politics and religion. These figures clearly do not bespeak a state of high dyadic tension. Quite the contrary. Hence the context of the family is conducive to both direct and indirect socialization effects.

Concordance between parents and their children cannot, of course, be attributed exclusively to the influence the parents have on their child's attitude and behavior. We cannot exclude the possibility of "reverse socialization." We cannot ignore that both parents and children share common characteristics, such as the same location in the social structure—in terms of both the class structure and region. To some extent, parent-child agreement may be induced, or at least facilitated, by the operation of the same outside forces on both parents and children. The extent of this is difficult to assess. It is doubtful whether a decomposition of agreement in effects of parental influence and effects of influences from outside the family is indeed appropriate. The outcome of the socialization process may be the result of mutual reinforcement of parental influence and some outside influence operating in the same direction, the result depending on the degree of the agreement of both.[13]

One indication of similar outside forces operating and their limitations is given by the place of parents and children in the class structure, as they see it. Both parents and children were asked whether they considered themselves to be part of the working class, middle class, or upper middle class. There is a lot of agreement, as we would expect; 70% of the British, 47% of the American, 54% of the Austrian, 73% of the German, and 64% of the Dutch pairs agree on this self placement. (In terms of measures of association, Great Britain, gamma = .76, tau-b = .46; United States, gamma = .45, tau-b = .3; Austria, gamma = .53, tau-b = .28; Germany, gamma = .85, tau-b = .56; Netherlands, gamma = .68, tau-b = .44.)

The deviations are mostly caused by children who place themselves in a higher stratum than their parents. This deviation is probably not the failure of working-class parents to transmit "class-consciousness"; it likely reflects the expansion of the system of higher education. The child's class identification is to be considered the result of both parental social status *and* the child's own "track" in the school system.

Socialization and Political Change

Cross-section data such as ours do not inform us about the actual process of socialization. Such data do point to the results of these processes, however. Judging from these results, political socialization in the family appears to be about equally effective in the five countries. The extent and the nature of the "generation gap" in these five countries, on the other hand, seems to be very nation-specific. The "generation gap" appears to be most extensive in Germany and also the United States. The gap appears to be smaller in the Netherlands (where the parental generation takes a very liberal posture) and in Austria (where the adolescents appear quite moderate). There is hardly a gap in Britain.

Explanations of stability of systems in terms of efficient individual-level socialization, and explanations of conflict and change in terms of conflicts of individuals (such as rebellion of adolescents) imply that system-level and individual-level processes are somehow parallel. This type of explanation we can emphatically rule out of the basis of the data presented so far. The "generation gap," where it exists, cannot be explained as a result of processes within the family, be these adolescent rebellion or weakness of socialization. There are some differences in strength of the parent-child correlations, as we mentioned. But these differences between countries run counter to the aggregate differences.

How can we explain the aggregate gap, then? To suggest the "Zeitgeist" or to point to "social change" would provide hardly more than a verbal cover for our ignorance. A closer look at the processes within and between concrete social institutions would be more fruitful.

More than half a century ago Siegfried Bernfeld pointed out that youth is a stage in the course of individual development where the evaluative capacities of one's personality are accentuated.[14] Young people, then, are in a process of reevaluation of childhood values. The degree to which this potential for change is realized depends on the conditions of the "novel access" of the new cohorts to the existing culture, as Karl Mannheim elaborated in his classic study (1928) of the "Problem of Generations."[15]

Today, most important among those conditions of the "novel access" may be institutions such as the mass media, in particular those offering interpretations and definitions rather than just reporting events. The five countries differ a great deal in terms of the existence and strength of such media taking up and diffusing new ideologies concerning the image of and the transformation of society by recommending new ways of self-discovery and new liberties, and in the criticism of traditionalism and conservatism at large.

These forces of ideological transformation can and have to be studied when we turn to the institutions transmitting values to the new cohorts. While this is not the place for a detailed analysis, we are confident that such analysis would lead to stronger explanations not only of the aggregate differences between the generations but also of their differing magnitude in the five countries. To say that the sources of change are mostly outside the realm of the family does not mean that they cannot be studied empirically as well. As our current data on social relations and institutions focus on families, however, we are constrained to identify only where the sources of change are *not* located, in spite of much literature and speculation to the contrary.

What, then, is the proper role of socialization theories for explanations of stability and of political and social systems? It appears clear that the functioning of socialization as a microlevel process is *not* sufficient as an explanation of stability of systems. Nor do macrolevel conflict and change imply that socialization processes are not functioning properly on the microlevel. The process of political socialization in the family does insure, it seems, that substantial aggregate changes can take place with a minimum amount of interpersonal conflict within the family. Well-functioning socialization processes do not necessarily rule out such substantial aggregate differences.[16] The assumption that they necessarily have to do just that is as wrong empirically as it is logically false.

Comparative data such as ours point to the shortcomings of simple linkage theories. We have demonstrated in these chapters that there are only modest differences between the five countries in terms of the effectiveness of the socialization agency "family." The microlevel process within families appears almost invariant. Nevertheless, there are very substantial differences between nations in the magnitude of the aggregate differences between the generations. The task ahead is to develop more adequate theories that can account for those aggregate similarities and differences. Such theories would have to specify the institutional framework that provides the linkages between the individual and the societal level. While we cannot elaborate such theories here, it should be clear that such theories can be consistent with the accumulated evidence only if they avoid the assumption of perfect integration of societies and polities. Instead of postulated overintegration, the possibility of "loose coupling" of institutions would have to be incorporated into such theories.

Our analysis has focused mainly on one direction of the micro-macro linkage: does the microlevel process of socialization explain macrolevel phenomena like political protest and generation gaps? The answer was that it does not. The question, however, contained at least one silent assumption: mass attitudes are treated as if they were a macrolevel outcome. The assumption may be justified if mass attitudes and attitude changes (through cohort replacement, for instance) were effective constraints on the political system and its institutions.

If this were true, our results would be strong evidence against political theories of political socialization since political socialization in the family, effective as it is, does not necessarily produce "mass loyalty" or "diffuse system support," which is considered crucial for "system persistence." The data, however, do not simply disprove political theories of political socialization, be these of functionalist or "critical theory" persuasion. The seemingly paradoxical results call for a different type of theory. This type of theory has to specify the linkages between individuals, institutions, and the political system in a less simplistic fashion. It would be inconsistent with this view to see mass attitude changes as imposing tight constraints on the political system. The degree to which the "generation gap," where it exists, will have an impact on the political system depends largely on the nature of political institutions, other lines of cleavage, age distributions, and the like.

Such less simplistic specifications of linkages between system components do not reduce the importance of the empirical and theoretical study of processes of political socialization in times of stability or change. We have demonstrated how salient political socialization in the family is as a determinant of political attitudes and behavior. The concept of political socialization loses whatever analytic power it has, however, if it is used as an unmediated cause of macrooutcomes. Our potential for understanding macrooutcomes will be enhanced if we abstain from searching for individual attributes as immediate explanations.

NOTES

1. See George I. Balch, "Multiple Indicators in Survey Research: The Concept 'Sense of Efficacy'," *Political Methodology,* 1 (Spring 1974), pp. 1-44.
2. The index is described in the Technical Appendix.

3. Here, as elsewhere, we are admittedly on slippery ground in extrapolating into the future of the filial cohort. Recent work indicates, however, that cohorts tend not to become more conservative in an absolute sense as they age; rather they *tend* to become conservative relative to the upcoming cohorts. That is, they "conserve" their early-crystallized orientations. See David Butler and Donald Stokes, *Political Change in Britain,* New York: St. Martin's Press, 1971; and Norval E. Glenn, "Aging and Conservatism," *Annals of the American Academy of Political and Social Sciences,* CDXV (September 1974), pp. 176-186.

4. Product moment correlations are being used due to the inherently interval-level quality of the thermometer ratings.

5. On this and other possible scenarios involving the generation gap see the typological analysis by Vern L. Bengtson, "The Generation Gap: A Review and Typology of Social Psychological Perspectives," *Youth and Society,* 2 (September 1970), pp. 7-32.

6. An interesting case has been made that parents often try to socialize their children into new, adaptive orientations even though the parents themselves are not capable of (or do not want to) reform their own value orientations. See Alex Inkeles, "Social Change and Social Character: The Role of Parental Mediation," *Journal of Social Issues,* 11 (1955), pp. 12-23.

7. Regarding the German experience, see Max Kaase, "Die politische Mobilisierung von Studenten in der BRD," in K. R. Allerbeck and L. Rosenmayr, eds., *Aufstand der Jugend? Neue Aspekte der Jugendsoziologie,* Munich, Juventa, 1971, and "Demokratische Einstellungen in der Bundesrepublik Deutschland" in Rudolf Wildenmann, ed., *Sozialwissenschaftliches Jahrbuch für Politik,* Vol. 2, Munich: Olzog, 1971. The significance of the student role qua role is advanced in K. R. Allerbeck, "Some Structural Conditions for Youth and Student Movements," *International Social Science Journal,* 24 (1972), pp. 257-270. For a discussion of concept and variable specification in studying youth phenomena see Leopold Rosenmayr, "Introduction: New Theoretical Approaches to the Sociological Study of Young People," *International Social Science Journal,* 24 (1972), pp. 216-256.

8. In part this is due to the frequent concentration of such behavior by area and by demographic strata (including age).

9. A recent American study uncovered what is one of the highest frequencies reported in a national survey. Upon reinterviewing a sample of 1965 high school seniors in the year 1973, it was discovered that 16% claimed to have taken part in a "demonstration, protest march, or sit-in" during the interim. Their parents reported a rate of only 2%. In accordance with our speculations, the incidence of unconventional activity rose from 5% among those youths who had not gone to college, 15% for those who had experienced *some* college, and 29% for those with college degrees. Of course, these relatively high figures among the latter are precisely where we would expect the highest concentration. These data are taken from the "Socialization Panel Study," Center for Political Studies, University of Michigan.

10. Actually, the evidence is ambiguous and complex. As noted in chapter 6 there is no consistent pattern by age across countries. This may be due to the inclusion of some relatively passive activities in the scale that young people can take part in quite easily. Rising levels of education may also be offsetting the normal middle-age advantage. The controversy on aging and participation in the United States centers in part on whether the lower socioeconomic status of older cohorts "artificially" lowers their participation. See, inter alia, Norval Glenn and Michael Grimes, "Aging, Voting, and Political Interest," *American Sociological Review,* 33 (August 1968), pp. 563-575; Michael Hout and David Knoke, "Change in Voter Turnout, 1952-72," *Public Opinion Quarterly,* 39 (Spring

1975), pp. 52-68. At the cross-national level see Norman Nie, Sidney Verba, and Jae-on Kim, "Participation and the Life Cycle," *Comparative Politics* 6 (April 1974), pp. 319-340.

11. The most extensive statement of this type of explanation is Lewis Feuer, *The Conflict of Generations,* New York: Basic Books, 1969.

12. For different statements about the relation of family structure and likelihood of generational conflict, in Europe and the United States, see Erik Erikson, *Childhood and Society,* New York: W. Q. Norton, 1963; Robert E. Lane, *Political Ideology: Why the American Common Man Believes What He Does,* New York: Free Press, 1962; and Bertran Schaffner, *Fatherland,* New York, 1949.

13. This question has been addressed most directly in M. Kent Jennings and Richard G. Niemi, *The Political Character of Adolescence,* Princeton: Princeton University Press, 1974, especially chapters 6-9.

14. For an introduction to Bernfeld's theory of development, see Leopold Rosenmayr, *Geschichte der Jugendforschung in Osterreich,* Wien, 1962.

15. Karl Mannheim, "The Problem of Generations" in P. Kecskemeti, ed., *Essays on the Sociology of Knowledge,* London: Routledge & Kegan Paul, 1952.

16. If this appears to be counterintuitive, simple correlation and regression models may make this matter clearer, if not intuitively obvious. We can represent the relationship of parent and child attitude by a linear regression equation of the form

$$Y_i = a + b X_i + e_i$$

where Y_i is the attitude measure of the child and X_i the measure for the parent in the ith pair. The strength of the relationship of the two measures is indicated by the correlation coefficient r (a useful measure for the degree to which parent attitudes constrain their children's attitudes). A "perfect" correlation, +1, does not mean that both attitudes are identical. It is quite compatible with a nonzero intercept (a) in the regression model. Aggregate differences such as those discussed in these two chapters would have to appear as nonzero intercepts in this kind of regression model.

PART V: CONCLUSION

Chapter 17

IN CONCLUSION
The Future of Political Protest in Western Democracies

MAX KAASE and SAMUEL H. BARNES

*P*olitical protest has a rich past and a vigorous present in the five Western democracies that we have studied. Does it have a future? We believe that it does. And the wealth of our empirical data base permits us to contribute important insights into the likely role of protest in these advanced industrial societies. In this conclusion we will articulate what we see as the probable consequences for political action of economic, social, and political changes taking place today in Western democracies.

There are numerous scenarios for the likely evolution of Western democracies. One is voiced by the Marxist "critical school," mainly European, which predicts that the basic contradictions between the economic and political systems in bourgeois Western democracies are such that a breakdown of advanced capitalist societies is inevitable because of decreasing political legitimacy. Whether or not this breakdown is, or should be, of a revolutionary type, and what comes "after the revolution," are hardly matters of agreement among the proponents of this creed.[1] These predictions are emphatically contradicted by our data: we find no evidence of an imminent breakdown of these Western democracies because of a declining legitimacy.

Another scenario posits demands for greatly increased participation in decision-making in many areas of life, with resulting strains, as the theme of the future. This theme, which was developed by Huntington and Bell in speculative writing in the early 1970s, finds strong reinforcement in our study. Political competence, particularly among the young, has broadened

[523]

considerably through the incorporation into the political repertory of activities that were rare as properties of democratic mass publics even twenty years ago.

Analysis of parent-child pairs as well as cross-sectional data testify to the extent to which this new political repertory is a characteristic of youth that is reinforced by increasing levels of formal education, which is one of the most powerful predictors of unconventional political involvement. *We interpret this increase in potential for protest to be a lasting characteristic of democratic mass publics and not just a sudden surge in political involvement bound to fade away as time goes by.* Of course, we are aware of the potential bias introduced into our argument by tacitly assuming that we are mostly dealing with generational changes and not with life cycle phenomena. To complicate things more, we cannot safely exclude the possibility of a substantial period effect contaminating our findings. Nevertheless, based on our analyses we believe that we are indeed facing a generational impact that will be increasingly apparent as the well-educated young march down the corridors of time. There are good reasons why we believe this to be true.

First, the dependence of unconventional political behavior on education, cognitive skills, and Postmaterialism—well-documented in our analysis—displays too much of a structural component, and therefore permanence, to be considered just a fad of the young. While our political action measures have not been employed in any longitudinal study, our analyses of emerging Postmaterialism in this book and elsewhere[2] as well as our analyses of levels of political conceptualization, testify strongly to this point.

A second supporting notion stems from the logic of the repertory concept as we have developed and employed it. This concept assumes that abilities acquired through vicarious learning and reinforced through perceptions of positive reward will not be easily extinguished from the political action repertory even if stimuli for concrete direct action should be low at times.

A third, more subtle, point pertains to the parent-child pairs. While the respective lineage and generation gap figures for protest potential are among the highest found anywhere in the whole set of parent-child analyses, there is no indication that these differences are actually translated into generational conflict. Thus the strong reliance of the young on direct action tactics certainly cannot be regarded as an instance of Oedipal rebellion against parents, in which case they would likely fade as the young grow up.

Finally, analyses of an independent study carried out in Germany and not reported in this book, which employed broadly the same instruments as the cross-national study, testify to the extent to which protest potential is related to a measure of prodemocratic attitudes.[3]

What then are the implications of our findings for the political process in democratic societies of the future? As Huntington phrased the question,

"Postindustrial Politics: How Benign Will It Be?"[4]

While the emphasis of our arguments, in correspondence with our data base, will be on the individual properties of mass publics, we are not unmindful of relevant organizational and systemic factors. One such factor is the mass media. Advanced industrial societies are deeply influenced by the development of electronic mass communication, and television in particular. Research dealing with these phenomena has been strongly—and in our opinion too strongly—influenced by the stimulus-response paradigm, which seeks to explain short-term impacts of mass media communication. Only recently have political scientists begun to inquire more systematically into the long-term effects of the media on, for example, the world view of citizens, their trust of political institutions, and the like.[5] Scholarly observers were agreed much earlier on the role the media play in the success of direct action tactics;[6] more recently, the media's importance in the calculus of anxiety and terror by terrorists has been stressed.[7] Furthermore, we have not even begun to explore potential consequences of new mass communication developments such as cable television, direct satellite television, television-newspapers, and interactive communication systems for use in the home. Their impact has not yet been widely felt.

Huntington has reminded us that the political institutions of contemporary Western societies "still bear the imprint of the eighteenth century."[8] Huntington, along with other observers, also claims that the existing institutions of political involvement—such as parties, interest groups, associations, and the mechanism of elections—are no longer adequate to handle the quest for broadening participation.[9] Single-issue political movements and demands for industrial democracy (worker codetermination) are but two developments signaling potential trends.[10] Clearly these developments have not yet been fully absorbed by conventional political institutions.

Many such organizational and systemic factors will undoubtedly shape the future political process in advanced industrial societies. But what about the essence of politics? Of course, we do not argue that, after some imminent Armageddon, there lies the land of peace and eternal consensus. Rather, it seems obvious that politics will remain conflict-ridden as before. But the conflicts will take on new dimensions. Analyses presented in this book and elsewhere suggest that future politics will be increasingly Postmaterialist politics. Let us emphasize again that Postmaterialism does not imply that material values are not relevant; they will continue to be so. The point is that Postmaterialist values become *relatively* more important, and here is where we see potential sources of strain for postindustrial societies.

This is so for a variety of reasons. Postmaterialist values refer primarily to the substantive values of democracy and not, as when Materialist values were dominant, to the instrumental, procedural elements of the democratic process. The legitimacy basis of Postmaterialism is firmly imbued in the democratic creed. This is particularly relevant because Postmaterialists in sheer numbers—as we have demonstrated—still hold a minority position in contemporary postindustrial societies. They make up for their small numbers not only—as just indicated—because they argue and act in accordance with basic democratic values, but also because Postmaterialists are politically skillful, knowledgeable about the game of politics, and highly efficacious. Thus they will obviously be among the first to translate political dissatisfaction into remedial political action. We have discovered substantial potential for such processes in our analyses.

Taking these characteristics of Postmaterialism for granted, why should politics be less benign than present politics, as Huntington presumes. Huntington argues that it is the structure of ideology, values, and participation, exactly as we have analyzed it in this book, that is at odds with the tasks of good, efficient government.[11] This seems to be a point well-taken, particularly when one reflects—as Bell does—on the potential hedonism and irrationality in postindustrial politics. In addition, we must stress again the problems arising from the questionable legitimacy basis of uninstitutionalized, direct action groups. Because of their upwardly biased social composition, direct action groups do not even out, but in fact accelerate, differences in sociopolitical resources. Proponents of direct action tactics have, of course, recognized this dilemma; depending on their ideological home, they substantiate their claims either through the Marxist, elitist notion of the "false consciousness" of the noncommittal masses or through reference to the altruistic nature of their motives.

Huntington sees but one saving grace for the future: there may not be much of a postindustrial society after all, if the educational revolution comes to a grinding halt and expectations of continuing growth are frustrated through energy and environmental crises as well as through uncertainties in technological development and supply of raw materials.[12] These are, of course, factors that lie beyond our empirical reach. We therefore asked ourselves whether our study could provide enlightenment as to whether assumptions concerning the hedonism and irrationality of postindustrial politics are justified or not. Needless to say, we cannot come close to achieving the methodological elegance of the new political economy in the analysis of rational behavior. Rather, we are interested in finding a plausible and intelligible "rule of thumb" to assess how "benign" postindustrial political participation really was at the time of our study.

Figure 17.1 indicates one way of solving this problem. This figure displays the relationship as we conceptualize it between political action and political involvement. Political involvement is used here as a synthetic term conceptually reflecting the dimensions of both political motivation and understand-

Political Action

		No	Yes
	No	Political Apathy	Expressive Political Action
Political Involvement	Yes	Political Detachment	Instrumental Political Action

Figure 17.1: CONCEPTUAL REPRESENTATION OF MODES OF POLITICAL INVOLVEMENT

ing.[13] Our contention is that combining political action and political involvement will offer a clue regarding the balance of rational/instrumental versus expressive political styles in the five countries we have studied. As a first step, respondents' subjective political interest was used as an operationalization of political involvement, and whether or not the respondent was active at all was adopted as an operationalization of political action.

We decided to use political motivation and not the "levels of ideological conceptualization" measure because the former is more equivalent cross-nationally, whereas the latter reflects specific conditions of the political culture and institutional structures of the five societies.[14] (Table 17.1 shows how the apathy/detachment and instrumental/expressive balance in the five countries looks.)

Our primary concern is not with the apathy/detachment balance, because we can easily imagine circumstances in which an individual is interested in politics without necessarily wanting to engage in political action. What we are very interested in, however, is the balance between expressive and instrumental political styles found in our five countries. Expressive political style as an *orientation toward political action without political motivation* is, as we

Inactives

		Yes	No
	Not at all interested / Not much interested	Political Apathy	Expressive Political Action
Subjective Political Interest	Somewhat interested / Very much interested	Political Detachment	Instrumental Political Action

Figure 17.2: OPERATIONAL REPRESENTATION OF MODES OF POLITICAL INVOLVEMENT

Table 17.1: EMPIRICAL BALANCE BETWEEN MODES OF POLITICAL INVOLVEMENT

Political Style	The Netherlands	Britain	United States	Germany	Austria
Political Apathy	13%	23%	8%	16%	25%
Political Detachment	5	7	5	11	10
Expressive Political Action	29	32	22	19	18
Instrumental Political Action	53	38	65	54	47
Total	100	100	100	100	100
(N=)	(1136)	(1378)	(1605)	(2203)	(1264)

see it, a style that is highly disruptive if put into action. That is because an expressive political style undermines the basis for rational decision-making by hindering rational interchanges between authorities and partisans.

It is in this sense that the balance of expressive versus instrumental political action becomes highly relevant *at the level of the political system.* While we are cautious not to commit the individualistic fallacy—that is, generalizing from individual to system properties—we nevertheless maintain that the collective character of political action and its increasing facilitation through processes we have discussed before have a direct bearing on the quality of political life in advanced industrial societies.

Without any adequate benchmark from the past, it is not easy to evaluate results. In no country does the expressive mode exceed one-third of the adult population; everywhere, instrumental political orientations clearly dominate. Nevertheless, in sheer numbers the expressive mode indeed makes an impressive showing, even if one recalls that most of those in the category will hardly go beyond demonstrations and boycotts if they get involved in political action at all. We will forego further speculation about these matters until we have looked at the instrumental/expressive balance for each of the four action types. This analysis should provide us with a better understanding of the meaning of this balance.

We want to point out, before presenting the data, that the particular way of operationalizing the ratio between instrumental and expressive action does not a priori bias the coin in favor of any of the four types. If nothing were already known about the types, it would not be unreasonable to expect the instrumental/expressive ratio to be roughly equal for all four types. But this is, of course, not what we find.

Table 17.2 gives the percentage point ratios of instrumental over expressive style for the four action types. The following example should help to clarify the procedure. The entry of 3.44 for the Conformists in the Netherlands is obtained by dividing the percentage of instrumental Conformists, that is, Conformists with at least some interest in politics (77.7 percent), by the percentage of expressive Conformists, that is, Conformists with practically no interest in politics (22.3 percent).[15]

These data reveal a surprising and gratifying uniformity across countries, in that all ratios increase from Conformists through Reformists to Activists; and the balance is always tipped most toward an expressive political style with the Protesters. This is an intriguing result and has great relevance for the question we started out to answer: the relevance of direct action techniques for the "darker side of postindustrial society."[16] We recall that Reformists and Activists are both highly involved in conventional, and medium to highly involved in unconventional political participation. Even if the degree of instrumentalism suggests a higher mark for the Activists—who, we have to remember, are small in number—the data justify an assessment for both types that their proximity to conventional as well as unconventional political means conveys an overwhelmingly rational approach to politics. There can be no question that their use of direct action techniques is politically motivated.

Turning now to the Conformists, their political style is also predominantly instrumental even if the balance is not as striking as in the case of the Reformists and Activists. But here it has to be kept in mind that for them expressive involvement, as we have defined it, means political participation without political interest, but only participation in *conventional* politics. In this sense the expressive political style of the Conformists really is traditional,

Table 17.2: **RATIO OF INSTRUMENTAL OVER EXPRESSIVE POLITICAL STYLES**

Political Action Repertory Types	The Netherlands	Britain	United States	Germany	Austria
Conformists	3.45	1.64	3.94	3.82	3.27
Reformists	5.25	2.51	5.77	6.93	7.04
Activists	7.00	3.08	7.94	7.00	8.83
Protesters	0.53	0.29	0.69	1.20	0.81
All Four Types	1.83	1.19	3.00	2.84	2.61

ritualistic political participation. It emphasizes means, not ends, and clearly reflects the fact that many Conformists are in the "slow-down" phase of their political life cycle.

Finally, there are the Protesters, that is, those respondents who showed no inclination to conventional political participation whatsoever, but were involved in unconventional political action.[17] Surely, the point has to be made again that only in rare circumstances does the unconventional side of the typology reflect actual past behavior rather than behavioral readiness in the repertory sense. But even with this reservation in mind the data very clearly indicate a prevalence of expressive political style.

How do we interpret these results? First, we would like to point out that we do not want to overemphasize the aspect of sheer numbers, that is, the absolute size of the Protesters group. For instance, procedures of measurement and indicator construction, as we have pointed out in chapter 5, are such that many Protesters would reside in the Inactives category had we used a more behaviorally oriented protest potential scale. But, whatever the numbers, the fact remains that even a differently constructed protest potential scale we tried out did not tip the Protesters' balance in favor of a more instrumental outlook. Thus, we are bound to conclude, as Huntington and Bell had speculated, that protesting does indeed contain an element of hedonism and irresponsibility, probably reflecting youth and its fads. Obviously, such a protest is not primarily and unequivocally directed against particular aspects of most of the political systems. Germany marks a partial exception: highly educated female Protesters in that country are indeed instrumentally oriented and shun, as we phrased it in chapter 6, "the grey-suited male-dominated world of 'politics'." But in most countries the goals of protest are ambiguous.

If the results of these analyses are valid, then the future holds problems indeed. Since concrete political action only unfolds as a dynamic interaction between partisans and political authorities, authorities face the difficult task of reacting to similar political acts without knowing whether they are of the instrumental or expressive kind. Thus, if used unwisely coercive actions taken by the state may lead to a delegitimization rather than to a stabilization of the political system.

Consequently, the quest for increased political participation in democratic societies should not overlook the potential problems stemming from unconventional political involvement. Surely, Postmaterialists may have reason to be dissatisfied with institutions that still mirror the past. In addition, political elites in power usually do very little on their own account to institutionalize access to positions of influence by others. In this sense, rational use of direct political action techniques is a lever for motivating new elites to achieve political outcomes otherwise unachievable. But we do not argue that unconventional political action is the only way to obtain such outcomes. Rather, we believe that the participatory potential we have found to exist needs to be channeled into new political institutions aimed at broadening the basis of the democratic decision-making process[18] and the same time establishing a legitimate basis for these decisions.

Undoubtedly, elite positions in the future will become less and less permanent, hierarchical, and encompassing; contrary to C. W. Mill's expectations, the existing elite structure will become increasingly diverse and pluralistic. We hold this to be desirable for a democratic society. Furthermore, we are not frightened by the claim that decision-making will become more and more difficult because of broadened participation by citizens. This may well be true, but the old efficiency argument does not suffice in democratic politics; it has to be qualified and balanced by bringing in the consensus or legitimacy dimension as well. In fact, it appears entirely conceivable that citizens will be willing to engage in prolonged decision-making and to accept political outcomes not to their liking if their own involvement satisfied their self-realization needs and persuades them of the legitimacy of that outcome.

SUMMARY

Our research started from the observation that conflict will probably be an integral part of Western politics in the future. Analyses presented from our study in five Western democracies support the contention that a new political cleavage is presently emerging, crystallizing around a Materialist/Postmaterialist dimension. This cleavage in part dominates but does not replace older, more traditional class and religious cleavage lines: this conclusion can be seen in the way the "New Politics" theme is cutting across established party dimensions.[19] One element of the "New Politics" is a strong emphasis on broadening opportunities for political participation beyond the established sphere of electoral politics, which integrates to a large extent conventional and unconventional politics.

The "New Politics" creates severe dilemmas for political parties and the process of representation. As we have seen in chapter 14, most people are concerned primarily with bread-and-butter issues, and conventional politics deals more or less satisfactorily with these demands. But a minority places social equality issues first, and these issues are much more difficult to deal with and—particularly important—much less amenable to the compromising that is possible with economic issues. Moreover, this minority is a passionate minority that feels much more strongly about these issues than does the majority that focuses on bread-and-butter matters. And the minority is a highly educated, efficacious, and participating minority. Thus the parties, needing to win votes in elections, respond to majority demands; minorities are encouraged by circumstances to resort to unconventional forms of action that authorities cannot easily ignore. The result is a structurally based propensity toward protest activity in advanced industrial societies, as it is difficult for parties to respond to publics with widely differing values and goals. The parties are primarily oriented toward electoral politics, which disadvantages minorities. Protest is the great equalizer, the political action that weights intensity as well as sheer numbers.

What then is our answer to the question of how benign postindustrial politics will be? We have until now accepted the concept of "benign politics" without asking what concrete meaning it is supposed to convey. It must be stressed that Huntington himself does not clarify the point. His arguments are compatible with the conclusion that he equates benign politics with the maintenance of the existing political order. We find this concept deficient: clearly, politics will become more difficult for political authorities who have to put up with less apathetic and less deferential mass publics. But the increasing emphasis on participation, information feedback, and control of administrative decision-making is in no way part of a new, more ideological belief system aimed at overcoming the liberal democratic order. Quite the contrary: under a functionalist perspective these developments can very well be regarded as one possible response to ossified political structures that need to be cracked in order to accommodate and facilitate peaceful sociopolitical change. The Black Movement and Women's Liberation Movement in the United States are but two examples of what we have in mind.

The protest and direct action *potential* we have discovered must, of course, not be mistaken for action itself. For this potential to be mobilized, additional factors have to come into play. That one of these facilitating conditions is contextual stimulation and availability has been empirically demonstrated by Converse and Pierce.[20] We have already pointed out the important role we believe the mass media play in this process.[21] And, needless to say, political action as instrumental action will continue to require organization. The difference from traditional patterns of interest groups is that technological developments have facilitated tremendously the process of establishing ad hoc groups and single issue movements.

One of the consequences that follows from these arguments is that the present middle-class and youth bias of the direct action repertory need not necessarily continue. Political learning is an ongoing process, and here again the role of the mass media comes to the fore. Action groups as the "Bürgerin-itiativen" in Germany or the "Gray Panthers" in the United States may still have a middle-class bias in their leadership necessary for effective interaction with authorities, but they may increasingly be able to mobilize citizens from all strata of society.

Institutional reactions to such mobilization abound. Whereas American political institutions have generally been more flexible than their European counterparts, decentralization is an issue taken up by political leaders in such a traditionally centralized country as France. Citizen involvement in local planning is now taken for granted in countries such as Britain and even Germany where administrations have notoriously overlooked the role citizens could potentially play in rationalizing and legitimizing political outcomes.

The instrumental approach exhibited by substantial portions of the mass publics in the five democracies does not, we contend, warrant speculations that postindustrial politics will be "less benign" than industrial politics. But they will be different. Direct action politics, as we have stressed before, will raise problems of legitimacy and of representation; institutionalization is the answer to these potential threats. In addition, the enlarged political repertory will undoubtedly lead to much faster politicization of perceived deprivations, thereby maintaining the chance for direct, uninstitutionalized political actions to surface. But these, too, need not be malign, in particular since there is overwhelming rejection of violence against persons and things in the countries we have studied.

Thus what remains as a cause of concern is the potential for expressive political action in the future. Expressive acts devoid of political essence and, in the worst case, inextricably intertwined with instrumental political action, are bound to threaten the orderly, rational conduct of politics. If this were indeed to become a dominant political style, then Max Horkheimer's vision of postindustrial as totalitarian politics would be bound to materialize.[22] However, the empirical evidence we have unfolded makes this a very unlikely turn of events.

Our conclusions concerning the future of protest must be qualified. Several factors may limit their applicability even beyond the normal reservations that must be made about predictions in any area involving human behavior. That is, people learn, and populations seem to learn through time, so that present propensities may change as a result of changing expectations as well as changing conditions. Our generalizations about human behavior in politics are time bound, but we cannot specify the temporal boundaries in advance. Value change is an ongoing process; it will not stop with Postmaterialism. Socioeconomic structures will change, as will political structures. Thus one major qualification concerning our conclusions is simply that we cannot expect relationships to remain the same indefinitely.

But there is another qualification that emerges from the nature of our findings about protest. That is that a substantial percentage of the Protesters, who are so high on expressive rather than instrumental political action, may be transitory in that category. The Protesters are young and female compared with other groups. We know that conventional participation increases with age. Much conventional participation is electoral in nature, and hence the opportunity for involvement is tied to the electoral cycle. Many of the young have not lived through an electoral cycle. In addition, interest in politics increases with age—at least through middle age. The majority of women in the Protesters category in four of the countries undoubtedly reflects in part the domination of conventional politics by men, and this situation may change rapidly with the expansion of educational and employment opportunities for women as well as their growing political mobilization. Thus many of the Protesters may eventually become Activists.

A final qualification concerns the size of the Protester group. Our study was carried out at a time when the postwar baby boom was evident in the size of the youngest cohort. In the future, there will be fewer people in the age group from which Protesters were most heavily recruited at the time of our study. This demographic change may alter the atmosphere of the educated young in addition to reducing their numbers, in that it is probably much easier to socialize a smaller cohort into conventional politics than it was the huge numbers of young people of the 1960s and early 1970s. Indeed, the importance for protest potential of the sheer size of the cohort entering adulthood at the time of our study is undoubtedly great, though impossible to specify precisely.

Protest has waxed and waned in the histories of our five countries. We believe that the recent wave has expanded the repertory of political actions of those who lived through it, and we expect this expanded range of political actions to remain part of the potential repertory of those who have acquired these resources. How widely used they will be, and whether or not younger cohorts now arriving on the scene will develop the same repertory of actions, are topics for further investigation.

NOTES

1. Robert A. Dahl, *After the Revolution*, New Haven: Yale University Press, 1970.

2. Ronald Inglehart, *The Silent Revolution: Changing Values and Political Styles Among Western Publics*, Princeton: Princeton University Press, 1977.

3. Max Kaase, "Demokratische Einstellungen in der Bundesrepublik Deutschland," in Rudolf Wildenmann et al. (ed.), *Sozialwissenschaftliches Jahrbuch fuer Politik*, Band 2, Munich: Olzog Verlag, 1971, pp. 119ff.

4. Samuel P. Huntington, "Postindustrial Politics: How Benign Will It Be?" *Comparative Politics*, 6 (January 1974), pp. 163-191.

5. Such questions have been raised by Michael J. Robinson, "Public Affairs Television and the Growth of Political Malaise. The Case of 'The Selling of the Pentagon'," *American Political Science Review*, 70 (June 1976), pp. 409ff. Robinson's argument is challenged, but also partially supported by a content analysis of American newspapers in

the context of the 1972 presidential election. See Arthur H. Miller, Edie N. Goldenberg, and Lutz Erbring, "Typeset Politics: Impact of Newspapers on Public Confidence." Forthcoming in *American Political Science Review,* 73 (June 1979). The argument of the potential long-term impact of mass media communication is substantially stressed by Robinson's reformulation of the "two-step flow of communication" hypotheses. See John P. Robinson, "Interpersonal Influence in Election Campaigns: Two Step-Flow Hypotheses," *Public Opinion Quarterly,* 40 (Fall 1976), pp. 304ff.

6. Gladys Ethel Lang and Kurt Lang, "Some Pertinent Questions on Collective Violence and the News Media," *Journal of Social Issues,* 28 (Winter 1976), pp. 93ff.

7. Franz Wördemann, *Terrorismus,* Munich: Piper-Verlag, 1977, in particular the chapter on "Technologie und Terrorismus."

8. Samuel P. Huntington, "Postindustrial Politics: How Benign Will It Be?" p. 190.

9. Ibid., pp. 175ff.

10. Udo Bermbach, "On Civic Initiative Groups," in Max Kaase and Klaus von Beyme (eds.), *German Political Studies,* Vol. 3, Beverly Hills: Sage, 1978, pp. 227ff.

11. Samuel P. Huntington, "Postindustrial Politics: How Benign Will It Be?" p. 190.

12. Ibid.

13. We are well aware of the fact that the two concepts require an analytical approach that looks precisely at the relationship between the two and their relationship to precipitating factors like education. This approach has been followed in substantive detail in chapter 9 of the book.

14. This consideration is particularly relevant for the United States. The "levels of conceptualization" measure as an indicator of cognitive stock is based on the open-ended questions not only on the good and bad sides of the major left and right system parties, but also on the understanding of the meaning of Left and Right. These latter concepts, however, are not part of the everyday political discussion in the United States, as they are in the European countries. Since in this analysis we aim at maximum comparability across countries, we decided that, despite its well-known shortcomings, the subjective interest in politics measure corresponded more closely to the theoretical basis of our argument than the level of conceptualization measure. In passing, however, it may be noted that the basic structure of the results remains unchanged even if that latter measure is adopted for this analysis.

15. Cases with missing data on either variable were excluded from this analysis.

16. Samuel P. Huntington, "Postindustrial Politics: How Benign Will It Be?" p. 190.

17. It is important to recall here the way the typology was constructed. The Protesters are not differentiated with respect to those who were only willing to resort to demonstrations and boycotts and those going beyond these activities. This differentiation is contained in Figure 5.1 in chapter 5 as types Va and Vb. The relevant point is that the empirical ratio between the two is roughly 4:1. See the Technical Appendix for the detailed information.

18. For one example of such a new institution see Peter C. Dienel, *Die Planungszelle,* Opladen: Westdeutscher Verlag, 1977.

19. See Warren E. Miller and Teresa E. Levitin, *Leadership and Change: The New Politics and the American Electorate,* Cambridge: Winthrop Publishers, 1976. For an interesting example of the way the "New Politics" theme permeates the German party system see Kai Hildebrandt and Russell J. Dalton, "The New Politics: Political Change or Sunshine Politics," in Max Kaase and Klaus von Beyme (eds.), *German Political Studies,* pp. 69ff.

20. Philip E. Converse and Roy Pierce, "Die Mai-Unruhen in Frankreich—Ausmass und Konsequenzen," in Klaus R. Allerbeck and Leopold Rosenmayr (eds.), *Aufstand der*

Jugend? Munich: Juventa-Verlag, 1971, pp. 108ff. Further evidence is plentiful with respect to the evolution of the student movement.

21. The diffusion of external stimuli is also an important problem in cross-national research as Adam Przeworski and Henry Teune point out in *The Logic of Comparative Social Inquiry,* New York: John Wiley, 1970, pp. 51ff.

22. Quoted in *Der Spiegel,* 26 (1973), pp. 95ff.

TECHNICAL APPENDIX

SAMUEL EVANS and KAI HILDEBRANDT

INTRODUCTION

An implicit assumption of all empirical research is that analyses can be validated through replication. The purpose of this Technical Appendix is to explain the procedures followed in constructing the variables used in this volume. While in some cases the justification of certain scaling techniques is offered, the general intent is to provide explication rather than to champion the cause of specific methodologies. The theoretical foundations of these constructed variables are found in the appropriate analysis chapters and will not be repeated here except as necessary for explanation of construction procedures.

Questions, responses, and frequency distributions will be presented here where necessary to understand the construction of variables. Frequencies in this Technical Appendix refer to unweighted cross-sections, and all Ns are actual numbers of respondents. Most of these variables will be recreated in the data sets to be distributed by the Zentralarchiv fuer empirische Sozialforschung and the Inter-university Consortium for Political and Social Research. Minor discrepancies between the frequencies shown in this Technical Appendix and those distributed by the archives may result from subsequent archival processing. More precise details on the parent-child pair samples are presented in chapters 15 and 16. The variable construction techniques are generally the same for both the cross-sectional and pairs data sets.

PROGRAM AND SCALING TECHNIQUES

Thé data manipulation for the construction of these variables was performed using the OSIRIS III series of computer programs for social science data management.[1] Where appropriate, an explanation of the OSIRIS options used in constructing variables will be given in discussing scaling techniques so that these measures may be reconstructed with other software packages. In addition, OSIRIS III documentation should be consulted for further elaboration and details of program functions. Two types of indices—Guttman scales and mean scores—were used often enough to warrant a brief general explanation here.

Guttman Scales

Guttman scaling was used in constructing many of the political action measures. The basic assumption behind Guttman scaling is that the items are unidimensional and cumulative, that is, one is unlikely to score a positive response on items ordered at the high end of the scale unless one has responded positively to all previous items. Items used in the scale must be (made) dichotomous. The ordering of items is established from the frequency of positive responses for each item (ordering the items from those with the most to those with the fewest positive responses). The relative "difficulty" of many scale items was found to be country-specific, indicating different "meanings" for different behaviors. Consequently, the ordering of items for all Guttman scales was done on a country-by-country basis. The specific orderings are indicated below for each scale.

Once the ordering has been established, respondents are assigned scale scores equal to their number of positive responses (assuming no errors or missing data are encountered). For example, on a ten-item scale possible scores would range from zero (no positive responses) to ten (positive responses on all items). An example of a four-item scale would be:

		Item 1	Item 2	Item 3	Item 4
	0	No	No	No	No
	1	Yes	No	No	No
Guttman	2	Yes	Yes	No	No
Score	3	Yes	Yes	Yes	No
	4	Yes	Yes	Yes	Yes

If a respondent has missing data on one or more items, the scale score depends on the options specified in the OSIRIS program. If there are more missing items than allowed, the respondent is assigned a missing data value for the scale. If fewer than the specified number of missing data are encountered, missing data items are recoded to the response that would require the minimum change in the scale. For example, if a respondent had item scores of: missing data (MD), Y, Y, N on a four-item scale, the MD is assumed to be a positive response and a score of 3 is assigned the respondent.

An error occurs if the item scores for a respondent do not conform to the unidimensionality assumption of the scale, i.e., a negative response is followed by a positive response on the next item. When a specified limit on the number of errors for any respondent is exceeded, the respondent receives a missing data value for the scale. If fewer than the specified limit of errors occurs, the Guttman score that requires the minimum number of changes to produce an error-free pattern is assigned. For example: Y, N, N, Y on a four-item scale would be scored as 1, requiring only a change in the fourth item to produce an error-free pattern of Y, N, N, N.

It is possible, both with missing data and with errors, that there is no unique score, i.e., several outcomes are possible with the same minimum number of changes. For example: Y, Y, MD, N could be scored as Y, Y, Y, N for a score of 3, or Y, Y, N, N for a score of 2. Likewise, Y, N, Y, N could be scored as 1 (Y, N, N, N) with one change or as 3 (Y, Y, Y, N) with one change. In constructing the Guttman scales the median of a respondent's possible scores was used to resolve such ties. If, for example, scores of 1, 3, and 4 were possible, 3 (the median) would be assigned to the case. If the number of nonunique scores is even, the mean of the scores rounded to the nearest whole number is assigned.

Guttman scaling yields a coefficient of reproducibility that measures the accuracy of the scale, i.e., the degree to which the scaled items fit the assumption of unidimensionality. The formula for the coefficient of reproducibility is:

$$CR = 1.0 - \frac{\text{total number of errors in the scale}}{\text{number of cases scored} \times \text{number of items in the scale}}$$

A coefficient of reproducibility of .9 or greater is generally considered acceptable.[2] Since the commonly employed coefficient of reproducibility has been found to be a liberal measure, we also present for each scale the percentage of scored cases that could be assigned unique scores.

Mean Scores

Attitudes such as political responsiveness and efficacy, which did not fulfill the conditions of the Guttman scale (cumulativeness and order), were constructed as mean scores on all items in the scale. Mean scores do not assume dimensionality but give equal weight to each item. Items to be included in an index were generally decided on the basis of previous research, prior theoretical considerations, dimensional analysis, or some combination of these criteria. All items used to construct a mean score were recoded to conform in direction and scale. A maximum number of permissible missing data was specified for each respondent. If that maximum was not exceeded, mean scores were computed across all items with valid data. Mean score indices were sometimes divided into more comprehensive categories for tabular presentation in analysis chapters.

The following descriptions and explanations of the derived measures are presented in groups and roughly follow the order of presentation in the analysis chapters.

POLITICAL ACTION MEASURES

In order to explore as fully as possible the major focus of this research, the surveys measured responses to an extensive list of conventional and unconventional political behaviors. There were questions about actual activity in both areas; respondents were also asked whether or not they approved of protest activities and felt them to be effective. In addition, a battery of questions gauged attitudes toward the repression of protest.

Because the raw measures presented almost an overload of information, scaling methods were employed to extract patterns of responses in order to facilitate both comprehension and presentation. In some instances, individual items had to be disregarded in the construction of scales, usually because they were too severely skewed. While the emphasis in this Technical Appendix—as throughout this volume—is on the resulting scales of political activity, each measure in this following section is preceded by a table displaying the full array of item-by-country marginals from which the summary measure was extracted.

Conventional Political Participation

The conventional political participation scale was constructed to reflect the repertory of conventional political behavior. Guttman scale scores were generated using the following information:

(1) frequency of reading about politics in newspapers
(2) frequency of discussing politics with other people
(3) frequency of convincing friends to vote the same as you

Table TA. 1: FREQUENCY OF CONVENTIONAL POLITICAL PARTICIPATION*

	Often	Sometimes	Rarely	Never	Missing Data**	(=100%)
The Netherlands						
Read about politics in papers	35%	29%	20%	16%	(0)%	
Discuss politics with friends	17	35	27	21	(0)	
Convince friends to vote as self	3	7	12	77	(1)	
Work to solve community problems	5	13	16	66	(1)	
Attend political meetings	1	5	8	85	(1)	
Contact officials or politicians	5	8	13	73	(1)	
Campaign for candidate	1	2	6	90	(1)	
Britain						
Read about politics in papers	36	30	19	15	(1)	
Discuss politics with friends	16	30	23	30	(1)	
Convince friends to vote as self	3	6	8	82	(1)	
Work to solve community problems	4	13	13	69	(2)	
Attend political meetings	2	7	12	78	(2)	
Contact officials or politicians	2	9	13	74	(2)	
Campaign for candidate	1	3	3	91	(2)	
United States						
Read about politics in papers	47	27	17	8	(1)	
Discuss politics with friends	27	37	24	11	(1)	
Convince friends to vote as self	6	13	21	59	(1)	
Work to solve community problems	8	28	25	38	(1)	
Attend political meetings	3	15	25	57	(1)	
Contact officials or politicians	4	23	24	48	(1)	
Campaign for candidate	2	12	15	70	(0)	

Table TA. 1: FREQUENCY OF CONVENTIONAL POLITICAL PARTICIPATION* (cont.)

	Often	Sometimes	Rarely	Never	Missing Data**	(=100%)
Germany						
Read about politics in papers	46%	27%	19%	8%	(0)%	(=100%)
Discuss politics with friends	13	30	31	26	(1)	
Convince friends to vote as self	7	16	23	54	(1)	
Work to solve community problems	4	10	21	64	(1)	
Attend political meetings	5	17	24	52	(1)	
Contact officials or politicians	3	8	16	72	(1)	
Campaign for candidate	2	6	13	78	(1)	
Austria						
Read about politics in papers	30	28	22	19	(0)	
Discuss politics with friends	13	32	31	25	(0)	
Convince friends to vote as self	5	12	14	69	(1)	
Work to solve community problems	4	10	12	73	(1)	
Attend political meetings	5	13	20	61	(1)	
Contact officials or politicians	2	10	16	72	(1)	
Campaign for candidate	2	3	7	87	(1)	

*Percentages in this table add row-wise to 100 percent. Rounding errors are possible. The percentages are based on the full samples in each country. Ns are: The Netherlands: 1201; Britain: 1483; United States: 1719; Germany: 2307; Austria: 1584.
**Missing data includes don't know and not ascertained.

(4) frequency of working with other people in this community to try to solve some local problem
(5) frequency of attending political meeting or rally
(6) frequency of contacting officials or politicians
(7) frequency of spending time working for a political party or candidate

The response categories for all of these variables were (1) often, (2) sometimes, (3) seldom, and (4) never. Because Guttman scaling requires dichotomies, questions 1 to 6 were recoded as follows: 1 and 2 = 1 (yes) and 3 and 4 = 3 (no). The low frequency of campaigns and campaign activity prompted us to recode question 7 as 1 to 3 = 1 (yes) and 4 = 3 (no). Two missing data and three errors were allowed before a case was coded as missing. As indicated above, the item-orderings were established separately for each country and are as follows:

									CR	% Unique
The Netherlands	1,	2,	4,	6,	3,	7,	5		.95	85.6
Britain	1,	2,	4,	6,	3,	5,	7		.95	87.3
United States	1,	2,	4,	7,	6,	3,	5		.91	75.0
Germany	1,	2,	3,	5,	7,	4,	6		.94	86.9
Austria	1,	2,	5,	3,	4,	7,	6		.94	84.8

The response range for the conventional political participation scale was 0 to 7, where 0 = no conventional participation and 1 to 7 define the participation repertory according to the above ordering. The marginal frequencies for this variable are:

Scale Score

	0	1	2	3	4	5	6	7	MD
The	350	250	360	101	55	24	12	42	7
Netherlands	29.3	20.9	30.2	8.5	4.6	2.0	1.0	3.5	
Britain	407	372	448	98	53	23	17	42	23
	28.0	25.4	30.6	6.7	3.6	1.6	1.2	2.9	
United	282	302	407	213	152	134	119	104	6
States	16.5	17.6	23.8	12.4	8.9	7.8	6.9	6.1	
Germany	533	726	380	214	117	92	98	135	12
	23.2	31.6	16.6	9.3	5.1	4.0	4.3	5.9	
Austria	541	357	343	115	62	42	35	82	7
	34.3	22.6	21.7	7.3	3.9	2.7	2.2	5.2	

Protest Attitudes and Behaviors

Protest Approval The protest approval scale was constructed to gauge approval of different kinds of protest activity. It was created from evaluations

Table TA. 2: APPROVAL OF UNCONVENTIONAL POLITICAL BEHAVIORS*

	Approve Very Much	Approve	Disapprove	Disapprove Very Much	Missing Data	(=100%)
The Netherlands						
Petitions	44%	48%	3%	1%	(3)%	(=100%)
Lawful demonstrations	30	50	12	5	(3)	
Boycotts	9	33	38	13	(7)	
Rent strikes	5	26	45	19	(5)	
Unofficial strikes	3	17	50	24	(6)	
Occupying buildings	7	35	36	18	(5)	
Blocking traffic	4	18	45	30	(3)	
Painting slogans	2	9	47	39	(3)	
Damaging property	0	1	24	72	(2)	
Personal violence	1	1	25	73	(2)	
Britain						
Petitions	24	58	10	3	(5)	
Lawful demonstrations	13	52	22	7	(5)	
Boycotts	5	30	39	15	(11)	
Rent strikes	4	19	48	23	(7)	
Unofficial strikes	2	11	45	38	(4)	
Occupying buildings	2	12	41	39	(6)	
Blocking traffic	1	13	44	38	(4)	
Painting slogans	1	1	31	65	(2)	
Damaging property	1	0	21	76	(2)	
Personal violence	1	1	18	79	(2)	

[544]

Table TA. 2: APPROVAL OF UNCONVENTIONAL POLITICAL BEHAVIORS* (cont.)

	Approve Very Much	Approve	Disapprove	Disapprove Very Much	Missing Data	(=100%)
United States						
Petitions	47%	42%	5%	2%	(4)%	(=100%)
Lawful demonstrations	26	47	16	8	(4)	
Boycotts	13	39	27	13	(9)	
Rent strikes	4	16	40	37	(4)	
Unofficial strikes	1	12	40	31	(15)	
Occupying buildings	2	13	39	40	(6)	
Blocking traffic	1	6	40	50	(2)	
Painting slogans	1	3	34	59	(3)	
Damaging property	0	1	17	81	(2)	
Personal violence	1	1	17	80	(1)	
Germany						
Petitions	43	39	8	7	(4)	
Lawful demonstrations	23	39	19	17	(3)	
Boycotts	11	25	29	30	(6)	
Rent strikes	3	10	30	52	(5)	
Unofficial strikes	1	8	25	63	(3)	
Occupying buildings	1	5	23	68	(4)	
Blocking traffic	2	10	29	56	(3)	
Painting slogans	1	6	22	67	(3)	
Damaging property	0	1	10	87	(2)	
Personal violence	1	2	12	84	(2)	

Table TA.2: APPROVAL OF UNCONVENTIONAL POLITICAL BEHAVIORS* (cont.)

	Approve Very Much	Approve	Disapprove	Disapprove Very Much	Missing Data	(=100%)
Austria						
Petitions	52%	30%	5%	6%	(7)%	
Lawful demonstrations	24	34	16	18	(8)	
Boycotts	7	15	21	32	(24)	
Rent strikes	4	9	22	45	(20)	
Unofficial strikes	1	6	21	60	(12)	
Occupying buildings	1	5	22	57	(15)	
Blocking traffic	4	13	25	48	(10)	
Painting slogans	1	6	20	65	(8)	
Damaging property	1	1	8	83	(7)	
Personal violence	1	2	9	80	(8)	

*Percentages in this table add row-wise to 100 percent. Rounding errors are possible. The percentages are based on the full sample in each country. Ns are: The Netherlands: 1201; Britain: 1483; United States: 1719; Germany: 2307; Austria: 1584. In Austria, respondents could also choose "(5) it depends"; this was coded as missing data for the construction of the index.

of seven types of protest behavior. The types of behavior considered were (1) signing petitions, (2) joining in boycotts, (3) attending lawful demonstrations, (4) refusing to pay rent or taxes, (5) joining in wildcat strikes, (6) occupying buildings, and (7) blocking traffic. In each case the response categories were (1) strongly approve, (2) approve, (3) disapprove, and (4) strongly disapprove. The responses were dichotomized into approval (1 or 2) and disapproval (3 or 4). Two missing data items and three errors were allowed before a case was coded as missing. The following item-ordering was established:

								CR	% Unique
The Netherlands	1,	3,	2,	6,	4,	7,	5	.93	76.4
Britain	1,	3,	2,	4,	6,	7,	5	.93	76.5
United States	1,	3,	2,	4,	5,	6,	7	.96	78.8
Germany	1,	3,	2,	4,	7,	5,	6	.96	83.4
Austria	1,	3,	2,	7,	4,	5,	6	.95	75.2

The range of the protest approval scale runs from 0 to 7 with 0 = no approval and 1 to 7 conforming to the above order. The frequencies for each country are:

	Scale Score								
	0	1	2	3	4	5	6	7	MD
The	29	140	324	204	140	121	105	97	41
Netherlands	2.5	12.1	27.9	17.6	12.1	10.4	9.1	8.4	
Britain	139	246	441	288	123	68	51	53	74
	9.9	17.5	31.3	20.4	8.7	4.8	3.6	3.8	
United	85	264	413	455	201	97	60	68	76
States	5.2	16.1	25.1	27.7	12.2	5.9	3.7	4.1	
Germany	280	440	734	463	125	67	51	73	74
	12.5	19.7	32.9	20.7	5.6	3.0	2.3	3.3	
Austria	140	322	458	213	116	56	36	22	221
	10.3	23.6	33.6	15.6	8.5	4.1	2.6	1.6	

Protest Activity The protest activity scale measures whether or not the respondents had ever engaged in various forms of protest behavior or were inclined to do so. For each of the seven activities mentioned above, respondents were asked whether they (1) had done, (2) would do, (3) might do, or (4) would never do such a thing. The responses were dichotomized into (1 and 2) = positive and (3 and 4) = negative. Again, nation-specific ordering was

Table TA. 3: BEHAVORIAL INTENTIONS TOWARD UNCONVENTIONAL POLITICAL BEHAVIORS*

	21%	54%	13%	9%	(3%)	(=100%)
The Netherlands						
Petitions	21	54	13	9	(3)	
Lawful demonstrations	7	39	22	29	(2)	
Boycotts	5	27	22	41	(6)	
Rent strikes	3	23	25	46	(3)	
Unofficial strikes	2	14	17	64	(4)	
Occupying buildings	2	23	19	54	(3)	
Blocking traffic	1	13	15	68	(3)	
Painting slogans	2	5	8	82	(3)	
Damaging property	1	1	3	93	(2)	
Personal violence	0	2	4	91	(3)	
Britain						
Petitions	22	31	22	21	(4)	
Lawful demonstrations	6	25	24	42	(4)	
Boycotts	5	17	23	47	(7)	
Rent strikes	2	10	20	65	(4)	
Unofficial strikes	5	7	15	69	(3)	
Occupying buildings	1	6	13	77	(3)	
Blocking traffic	1	7	15	74	(2)	
Painting slogans	0	1	2	95	(2)	
Damaging property	1	1	2	95	(2)	
Personal violence	0	1	4	93	(2)	
United States						
Petitions	58	20	13	6	(3)	
Lawful demonstrations	11	28	29	28	(4)	
Boycotts	15	20	27	31	(8)	
Rent strikes	2	8	22	65	(3)	
Unofficial strikes	2	5	21	59	(14)	
Occupying buildings	2	5	17	71	(6)	

Table TA. 3: BEHAVORIAL INTENTIONS TOWARD UNCONVENTIONAL POLITICAL BEHAVIORS* (cont.)

	Have Done	Would Do	Might Do	Would Never Do	Missing Data
Blocking traffic	1	2	15	79	(2)
Painting slogans	1	1	7	88	(3)
Damaging property	1	0	3	94	(2)
Personal violence	1	0	5	92	(2)
Germany					
Petitions	31	40	13	14	(2)
Lawful demonstrations	9	33	24	33	(2)
Boycotts	4	24	23	45	(4)
Rent strikes	1	8	21	67	(5)
Unofficial strikes	1	6	16	75	(3)
Occupying buildings	0	4	13	80	(3)
Blocking traffic	2	8	17	71	(2)
Painting slogans	1	4	11	82	(3)
Damaging property	0	1	3	95	(2)
Personal violence	0	1	5	93	(2)
Austria					
Petitions	34	31	10	14	(12)
Lawful demonstrations	6	21	17	43	(12)
Boycotts	2	12	15	46	(25)
Rent strikes	1	5	11	61	(23)
Unofficial strikes	1	3	11	71	(15)
Occupying buildings	0	2	8	72	(17)
Blocking traffic	1	5	14	68	(12)
Painting slogans	1	1	5	82	(12)
Damaging property	0	1	2	86	(12)
Personal violence	0	1	3	84	(12)

*Percentages in this table add row-wise to 100 percent. Rounding errors are possible. The percentages are based on the full sample in each country. Ns are: The Netherlands: 1201; Britain: 1483; United States: 1719; Germany: 2307; Austria: 1584.

used in constructing Guttman scales with two missing data and three errors allowed. The ordering for each country is as follows:

								CR	% Unique
The Netherlands	1,	3,	2,	4,	6,	5,	7	.92	78.6
Britain	1,	3,	2,	5,	4,	7,	6	.95	86.1
United States	1,	3,	2,	4,	5,	6,	7	.96	84.2
Germany	1,	3,	2,	7,	4,	5,	6	.96	84.6
Austria	1,	3,	2,	7,	4,	5,	6	.97	83.1

The response range for the protest activity scale runs from 0 to 7 with 0 = never done any and 1 to 7 = conforming to the above order. The marginal frequencies for each nation are:

	0	*1*	*2*	*3*	*4*	*5*	*6*	*7*	*MD*
The	207	320	226	125	107	74	53	58	31
Netherlands	17.7	27.4	19.3	10.7	9.1	6.3	4.5	5.0	
Britain	587	325	223	140	60	43	21	35	49
	40.9	22.7	15.5	9.7	4.2	3.0	1.5	2.4	
United	306	524	325	312	94	34	14	34	76
States	18.6	31.9	19.8	19.0	5.7	2.1	.9	2.1	
Germany	592	559	558	319	110	36	43	32	58
	26.3	24.9	24.8	14.2	4.9	1.6	1.9	1.4	
Austria	349	498	291	100	58	12	10	13	253
	26.2	37.4	21.9	7.5	4.4	.9	.8	1.0	

Protest Effectiveness. This variable is a mean index constructed to obtain a measure of the respondent's perception of the overall effectiveness of unconventional forms of political participation. Evaluations regarding the effectiveness of petitioning were deleted because the overwhelming majority of respondents felt that this frequent and familiar activity was effective. This left six of the protest items for the scale: (1) boycotts, (2) lawful demonstrations, (3) refusal to pay rent or taxes, (4) wildcat strikes, (5) occupying buildings, and (6) blocking traffic. Analysis of these items indicated that they were not cumulative and Guttman scaling was thus inappropriate. Instead, a mean score across all six items was computed.

The response categories for the original items in this index were (1) not at all effective, (2) not very effective, (3) somewhat effective, and (4) very effective. Up to two missing responses were allowed for a nonmissing score on the index. The mean scores in this index run from 1 (low effectiveness) to 4

Table TA. 4: EFFECTIVENESS OF UNCONVENTIONAL POLITICAL BEHAVIORS*

	Very Effective	Somewhat Effective	Not Very Effective	Not at All Effective	Missing Data	(=100%)
The Netherlands						
Petitions	21%	51%	19%	4%	(5)%	
Lawful demonstrations	17	46	23	9	(5)	
Boycotts	12	34	27	18	(9)	
Rent strikes	7	23	33	32	(6)	
Unofficial strikes	3	17	39	35	(6)	
Occupying buildings	14	35	24	22	(5)	
Blocking traffic	4	17	33	42	(3)	
Painting slogans	1	7	29	57	(6)	
Damaging property	1	2	13	80	(4)	
Personal violence	1	3	13	80	(4)	
Britain						
Petitions	15	55	20	4	(5)	
Lawful demonstrations	10	48	26	11	(5)	
Boycotts	7	37	34	13	(9)	
Rent strikes	6	20	37	31	(6)	
Unofficial strikes	9	31	33	22	(5)	
Occupying buildings	4	23	30	37	(6)	
Blocking traffic	5	24	31	35	(5)	
Painting slogans	2	3	23	69	(4)	
Damaging property	4	6	18	69	(4)	
Personal violence	4	7	17	68	(4)	

Table TA. 4: EFFECTIVENESS OF UNCONVENTIONAL POLITICAL BEHAVIORS* (cont.)

	Very Effective	Somewhat Effective	Not Very Effective	Not at All Effective	Missing Data	(=100%)
United States						
Petitions	31%	52%	10%	3%	(5%)	(=100%)
Lawful demonstrations	16	51	19	7	(6)	
Boycotts	16	47	20	9	(9)	
Rent strikes	6	18	35	36	(5)	
Unofficial strikes	6	30	28	20	(16)	
Occupying buildings	5	26	31	31	(7)	
Blocking traffic	4	18	35	40	(4)	
Painting slogans	2	7	26	61	(5)	
Damaging property	3	6	19	68	(4)	
Personal violence	4	7	21	65	(3)	
Germany						
Petitions	22	39	26	10	(3)	
Lawful demonstrations	17	38	27	14	(3)	
Boycotts	12	27	28	26	(6)	
Rent strikes	4	10	27	53	(6)	
Unofficial strikes	5	15	27	49	(5)	
Occupying buildings	4	13	25	54	(5)	
Blocking traffic	5	15	29	47	(4)	
Painting slogans	1	7	26	62	(4)	
Damaging property	2	3	13	78	(4)	
Personal violence	3	5	14	75	(4)	

Table TA.4: EFFECTIVENESS OF UNCONVENTIONAL POLITICAL BEHAVIORS* (cont.)

	Very Effective	Somewhat Effective	Not Very Effective	Not at All Effective	Missing Data
Austria					
Petitions	32	41	12	6	(8)
Lawful demonstrations	4	9	20	45	(22)
Boycotts	12	21	19	23	(26)
Rent strikes	4	9	20	45	(22)
Unofficial strikes	4	14	24	45	(12)
Occupying buildings	6	16	22	40	(17)
Blocking traffic	8	19	25	37	(11)
Painting slogans	2	9	23	57	(10)
Damaging property	3	4	12	71	(10)
Personal violence	4	7	14	65	(10)

*Percentages in this table add row-wise to 100 percent. Rounding errors are possible. The percentages are based on the full sample in each country. Ns are: The Netherlands: 1201; Britain: 1493; United States: 1719; Germany: 2307; Austria: 1584.

(high effectiveness). Descriptive statistics for the protest effectiveness index are as follows:

	Mean	Std. Dev.	Total N	% Missing
The Netherlands	2.22	.604	1201	4.75
Britain	2.20	.574	1483	4.59
United States	2.28	.600	1719	5.24
Germany	1.95	.631	2307	4.54
Austria	2.03	.659	1584	14.15*

*In Austria, respondents could also choose (5) "It depends"; this was coded as missing data for the construction of the index.

Protest Potential The protest potential measure combines the evaluative and action aspects of protest behavior that were described above (see also chapter 4). Actual protest activity is not as frequent as approval of such behavior; unconventional behavior often requires the stimulus of specific situations. Consequently, both participation in and approval of protest were used for the construction of a less skewed summary measure of protest potential. For each of the seven types of protest an intermediate variable of potential participation was constructed according to the following scheme:

	Approval			
Participation	Strongly Approve	Approve	Disapprove	Strongly Disapprove
Have done	Yes	Yes	No	No
Would do	Yes	Yes	No	No
Might do	Yes	Yes	No	No
Never do	No	No	No	No

Missing data on either the approval or participation variables and "It depends" responses on either of the two components resulted in missing data for an intermediate variable. The seven resulting measures of potential participation were then subjected to Guttman scaling procedures, with two missing data and three errors allowed. The scale orderings were:

								CR	% Unique
The Netherlands	1,	3,	2,	6,	4,	7,	5	.94	78.5
Britain	1,	3,	2,	4,	7,	6,	5	.95	81.4
United States	1,	3,	2,	4,	6,	5,	7	.96	80.5
Germany	1,	3,	2,	4,	7,	5,	6	.97	84.1
Austria	1,	3,	2,	7,	4,	5,	6	.97	79.5

The protest potential scale runs from 0 to 7, with 0 = no approval and 1 to 7 conforming to the ordering listed above. The marginal frequencies for each country are:

	0	1	2	3	4	5	6	7	MD
The	101	234	291	174	120	83	76	70	52
Netherlands	8.8	20.4	25.3	15.1	10.4	7.2	6.6	6.1	
Britain	325	313	345	206	90	47	28	44	85
	23.2	22.4	24.7	14.7	6.4	3.4	2.0	3.1	
United	142	340	385	428	135	91	50	44	104
States	8.8	21.1	23.8	26.5	8.4	5.6	3.1	2.7	
Germany	418	470	653	415	101	60	39	56	95
	18.9	21.2	29.5	18.8	4.6	2.7	1.8	2.5	
Austria	263	423	327	142	65	27	13	7	317
	20.8	33.4	25.8	11.2	5.1	2.1	1.0	.6	

Repression Potential

The repression potential scale taps the respondent's approval of repressive government action against those who engage in protest behavior. The four items used in constructing this scale were:

(1) The police using force against demonstrators who disregard police
(2) The courts giving severe sentences to protesters
(3) The government passing a law to forbid all public protest demonstrations
(4) The government using troops to break strikes

The response categories for all four items were (1) strongly approve, (2) approve, (3) disapprove, (4) strongly disapprove. These were dichotomized into approval (1-2) and disapproval (3-4) categories, and the nation-specific ordering was used in constructing Guttman scales. One missing data point and one error in the scale were allowed before the case was coded as missing. The ordering for each nation was as follows:

					CR	% Unique
The Netherlands	2,	1,	4,	3	.94	82.6
Britain	2,	1,	4,	3	.95	80.7
United States	1,	2,	4,	3	.95	82.7
Germany	2,	3,	1,	4	.93	79.8
Austria	2,	3,	4,	1	.91	78.8

Table TA. 5: APPROVAL OF POLITICAL REPRESSION

	Approve Very Much	Approve	Disapprove	Disapprove Very Much	Missing Data	(=100%)
The Netherlands						
Courts Giving Severe Sentences	6%	30%	51%	8%	(4)%	(=100%)
Police Using Force Against Demonstrators	5	30	49	12	(5)	
Troops Breaking Strikes	2	18	46	28	(6)	
Government Forbids All Demonstrations	1	10	57	29	(3)	
Britain						
Courts Giving Severe Sentences	23	54	16	1	(6)	
Police Using Force Against Demonstrators	14	54	23	3	(6)	
Troops Breaking Strikes	7	36	29	19	(10)	
Government Forbids All Demonstrations	4	20	49	20	(7)	
United States						
Courts Giving Severe Sentences	21	46	24	5	(4)	
Police Using Force Against Demonstrators	19	49	21	6	(5)	
Troops Breaking Strikes	6	29	38	20	(7)	
Government Forbids All Demonstrations	6	18	45	28	(3)	
Germany						
Courts Giving Severe Sentences	33	42	17	6	(2)	
Police Using Force Against Demonstrators	18	29	34	16	(2)	
Troops Breaking Strikes	11	25	30	29	(4)	
Government Forbids All Demonstrations	19	33	28	17	(3)	
Austria						
Courts Giving Severe Sentences	26	36	24	6	(8)	
Police Using Force Against Demonstrators	15	24	29	24	(7)	
Troops Breaking Strikes	20	23	18	29	(9)	
Government Forbids All Demonstrations	30	30	20	13	(7)	

The range of the new scale runs from 0 to 4, with 0 = no approval and 1 to 4 for approval corresponding to the above ordering. The marginal frequencies for each nation on the repression potential scale are:

	Scale Scores					
	0	*1*	*2*	*3*	*4*	*MD*
The	539	258	145	137	56	66
Netherlands	47.5	22.7	12.8	12.1	4.9	
Britain	160	210	387	370	256	100
	11.6	15.2	28.0	26.8	18.5	
United	299	260	459	324	295	82
States	18.3	15.9	28.0	19.8	18.0	
Germany	410	401	405	408	580	103
	18.6	18.2	18.4	18.5	26.3	
Austria	242	294	201	308	399	140
	16.7	20.3	13.9	21.3	27.7	

Participation Typologies

Typology of Political Participation Several participation measures combining the protest potential and conventional participation measures were also created. The first of these was a typology of political participation constructed by cross-tabulating both participation measures and collapsing categories according to the following scheme:

		Conventional Political Participation								
		0 (low)	1	2 (medium)	3	4	5	6	7 (high)	MD
0 (low)		1	1	2	2	3	3	3	3	MD
1		1	1	2	2	3	3	3	3	MD
2 (medium)		7	7	4	4	5	5	5	5	MD
3		7	7	4	4	5	5	5	5	MD
4		9	9	8	8	6	6	6	6	MD
5		9	9	8	8	6	6	6	6	MD
6 (high)		9	9	8	8	6	·6	6	6	MD
7		9	9	8	8	6	6	6	6	MD
MD		MD	MD	MD	MD	MD	MD	MD	MD	MD

Protest Potential (row label at left)

The resulting nine-point participation typology has the following categories:

Typology Code	Protest Potential	Conventional Participation
1	Low	Low
2	Low	Medium
3	Low	High
4	Medium	Medium
5	Medium	High
6	High	High
7	Medium	Low
8	High	Medium
9	High	Low

The frequencies for this typology are:

	1	2	3	4	5	6	7	8	9	MD
The Netherlands	205	108	19	181	46	59	236	162	128	57
	17.9	9.4	1.7	15.8	4.0	5.2	20.6	14.2	11.2	
Britain	418	187	27	235	69	37	244	105	67	94
	30.1	13.4	1.9	16.9	5.0	2.7	17.6	7.5	4.8	
United States	199	175	107	304	276	110	232	122	88	106
	12.3	10.8	6.6	18.8	17.1	6.8	14.4	7.6	5.5	
Germany	587	202	96	302	241	98	524	78	79	100
	26.6	9.2	4.3	13.7	10.9	4.4	23.7	3.5	3.6	
Austria	442	173	70	168	96	25	204	50	37	319
	34.9	13.7	5.5	13.3	7.6	2.0	16.1	4.0	2.9	

Political Action Typology This nine-point scale was further collapsed into the five-point political action typology that was the focus of chapter 5. Respondents were categorized by participation type as follows:

	New Codes	Codes from Nine-Point Typology
(1)	Inactives	1
(2)	Conformists	2, 3
(3)	Reformists	4, 5
(4)	Activists	6, 8
(5)	Protesters	7, 9

The marginal frequencies for the political action typology are:

	1	2	3	4	5	MD
The	205	127	227	221	364	57
Netherlands	17.9	11.1	19.8	19.3	31.8	
Britain	418	214	304	142	311	94
	30.1	15.4	21.9	10.2	22.4	
United	199	282	580	232	320	106
States	12.3	17.5	36.0	14.4	19.8	
Germany	587	298	543	176	603	100
	26.6	13.5	24.6	8.0	27.3	
Austria	442	243	264	75	241	319
	34.9	19.2	20.9	5.9	19.1	

MEASURES OF IDEOLOGICAL ORIENTATION AND THINKING

This series of variables was designed to measure the respondents' ability to evaluate politics or political symbols in conceptual or ideological terms. In some of these variables the left-right dimension is used to distinguish between the attitudes of those with the same capacity for conceptualization but with different ideological leanings.

These variables were based on the responses to several open-ended questions about the meaning of "right" and "left" and what the respondents liked and disliked about the main left and right political parties. Responses to these open-ended questions were coded according to the criteria discussed below. These variables contain no missing data. A respondent's inability to answer was taken as a sign of low levels of conceptual ability with regard to politics. Although refusals to answer may be politically motivated, there is no way to distinguish them from the inability to reply.

Active Use of an Ideological Mode of Thought in Politics

This variable was designed to measure the degree to which the respondent uses ideological terms in evaluating political parties.[3] Political parties were chosen because they are highly visible and recognizable. In order to achieve cross-national equivalence, the largest nonextreme left and right parties in each nation were used for the national surveys:

Nation	Left Party	Right Party
The Netherlands	Labour Party (PvdA)	Liberal Party (VVD)
Britain	Labour Party	Conservative Party
United States	Democratic Party	Republican Party
Germany	Social Democratic Party (SPD)	Christian Democratic Union, Christian Socialist Union (CDU/CSU)
Austria	Social Democratic Party (SPO)	Peoples Party (OVP)

Respondents were asked about the good and bad points of each party. Answers were coded according to five broad conceptual categories: (1) ideological concepts (liberal, conservative, and so on), (2) social group concepts, (3) "nature of our times" concepts (referencing specific policies and government competence), (4) those related to particular politicians, and (5) affective evaluations not using political concepts (e.g., "good," "bad," "right," "wrong," and so forth). A maximum of three responses was coded for *each* conceptual group.

The resulting classification is described in greater detail in chapter 8. The categories are as follows:

(1) Ideologues
(2) Near ideologues
(3) Nonideological conceptualizers
(4) Noncognizers

Sometimes categories (3) and (4) are combined as nonideologues.
This procedure yielded the following distribution of conceptual thinking:

	Ideologues	Near Ideologues	Nonideological Conceptualizers	Non-cognizers
The Netherlands	105	327	436	333
	8.7	27.2	36.3	27.7
Britain	55	254	910	264
	3.7	17.1	61.4	17.8
United States	124	226	1138	231
	7.2	13.1	66.2	13.4
Germany	174	603	1382	148
	7.5	26.1	59.9	6.4
Austria	61	238	1013	272
	3.9	15.0	64.0	17.2

Recognition and Understanding of an Ideological Mode of Thought in Politics

Only a small portion of the population may be considered to be ideologues in the restricted sense of active usage of ideological concepts to evaluate specific political objects such as political parties. However, a larger proportion of the population is able to recognize ideological concepts such as "left" and "right." The present variable was constructed in order to measure passive ideological knowledge.

Two questions were used to construct this variable. Respondents were first required to place themselves on a left-right scale. This question demanded that the respondents recognize a political symbol with ideological meaning. The second question asked the respondent to elaborate on the substantive meaning of these symbols.

The constructed variable (recognition and understanding of an ideological mode of thought in politics) was based on the responses to these two questions. If the respondents could not place themselves on the left-right scale, they were given a code value of 8 (no recognition of the dimension). The remaining seven codes were based on whether the respondents explained one or both of the dimensions (left and right) in terms of the following four categories: (1) ideological understanding, (2) a group-related understanding (including political parties), (3) an idiosyncratic understanding, and (4) false understanding. Although multiple responses to the open-ended question could be given, only the highest level was used in coding this variable. Therefore, the response codes and their descriptions are as follows:

1 Both left and right understood in terms of ideology
2 Left or right understood in terms of ideology
3 Both left and right understood in terms of political parties and social groups
4 Left or right understood in terms of political parties and social groups
5 Idiosyncratic or affective understanding of both left and right
6 Idiosyncratic or affective understanding of left or right
7 Wrong or no understanding of left and right
8 No recognition of the left-right dimension

The frequency distribution for this variable is:

	1	2	3	4	5	6	7	8
The	324	251	190	45	23	9	243	116
Netherlands	27.0	20.9	15.8	3.7	1.9	.7	20.2	9.7
Britain	171	174	412	36	130	13	275	272
	11.5	11.7	27.8	2.4	8.8	.9	18.5	18.3

United States	410	173	15	23	215	64	262	557
	23.9	10.1	.9	1.3	12.5	3.7	15.2	32.4
Germany	699	599	484	69	50	7	218	181
	30.3	26.0	21.0	3.0	2.2	.3	9.4	7.8
Austria	341	281	230	58	59	14	207	394
	21.5	17.7	14.5	3.7	3.7	.9	13.1	24.9

This eight-category variable was collapsed into a four-category variable. Respondents were categorized as follows:

	Codes from Eight-Category Variable
1. Both left *and* right understood in terms of ideology	1
2. Left *or* right understood in terms of ideology	2
3. Nonideological understanding of left and/or right	3–6
4. False understanding or no recognition of left and right	7, 8

The distributions for this variable are:

	1	*2*	*3*	*4*
The Netherlands	324	251	267	359
	27.0	20.9	22.2	29.9
Britain	171	174	591	547
	11.5	11.7	39.9	36.9
United States	410	173	317	819
	23.9	10.1	18.4	47.6
Germany	699	599	610	399
	30.3	26.0	26.4	17.3
Austria	341	281	361	601
	21.5	17.7	22.8	37.9

Levels of Ideological Conceptualization

The above two variables represent what are referred to as the active and passive dimensions of ideological thinking. To arrive at a measure of overall ideological understanding, the two variables were combined as follows:

Passive Dimension

(Variable: Recognition and Understanding of an Ideological Mode of Thought in Politics)

	1	2	3	4
1	1	2	3	4
2	2	3	4	4
3	3	4	5	5
4	4	4	5	6

Active Dimension

(Variable: Active Use of an Ideological Mode of Thought in Politics)

The levels of ideological conceptualization measure has six categories: the ideologues are coded in the top four categories (1 = high level ideologues, 4 = very low level ideologues), the nonideologues in category 5, and the noncognizers in category 6.

Two collapsed versions of this variable were created. The four-category version is given below. The three-category version combines high and middle levels.

New Code	Six-Category Variable
1. High level ideologues	1
2. Middle level ideologues	2
3. Low and very low level ideologues	3, 4
4. Nonideologues and noncognizers	5, 6

The marginal frequencies for these two variables are:

	Six-Category Variable						Four-Category Variable			
	1	*2*	*3*	*4*	*5*	*6*	*1*	*2*	*3*	*4*
The	62	141	210	301	277	210	62	141	511	487
Netherlands	5.2	11.7	17.5	25.1	23.1	17.5	5.2	11.7	42.5	40.5
Britain	22	88	137	246	808	182	22	88	383	990
	1.5	5.9	9.2	16.6	54.5	12.3	1.5	5.9	25.8	66.8
United	88	104	246	273	839	169	88	104	519	1008
States	5.1	6.1	14.3	15.9	48.8	9.8	5.1	6.1	30.2	58.6

Germany	86	264	578	619	681	79	86	264	1197	760
	3.7	11.4	25.1	26.8	29.5	3.4	3.7	11.4	51.9	32.9
Austria	36	89	266	348	666	179	36	89	614	845
	2.3	5.6	16.8	22.0	42.0	11.3	2.3	5.6	38.8	53.3

MATERIALIST/POSTMATERIALIST VALUE ORIENTATIONS

The index of Materialist/Postmaterialist value orientations follows earlier work of Inglehart[4] and is based upon two sets of questions. The first of these asked respondents to choose the two most important of the following possible political goals (Postmaterialist items are starred):

1 Maintain order in the country
2 Give people more say in the decisions of government*
3 Fight rising prices
4 Protect freedom of speech*

Second, respondents were asked to choose the three most important and the three least important political goals from the following list (again, Postmaterialist items are starred):

5 Maintain a high rate of economic growth
6 Make sure the country has strong defense forces
7 Give people more say in how things are decided at work and in the community*
8 Maintain a stable economy
9 Fight against crime
10 Move toward a friendlier, less impersonal society*
11 Move toward a society where ideas are more important than money*

The Materialist/Postmaterialist value index was based on responses to the first or second most important goals in the two-item set and the first, second, or third in the seven-item set, while allowing for one of the five items to contain missing data.

For the ten-point values index the number of the important *Postmaterialist* goals mentioned was combined with the number of the important *Materialist* goals as follows:

Number of Materialist Issues Mentioned as Important

		0	1	2	3	4	5
Number of Post-materialist Issues Mentioned as Important	0	MD	MD	MD	MD	2	1
	1	MD	MD	MD	4	3	
	2	MD	MD	6	5		
	3	MD	8	7			
	4	10	9				
	5	10					

The range of the Materialist/Postmaterialist scale runs from 1 to 10 with 1 = Materialist and 10 = Postmaterialist.

The marginal frequencies for this variable are:

	Materialist								Postmaterialist		
	1	*2*	*3*	*4*	*5*	*6*	*7*	*8*	*9*	*10*	*MD*
The	27	41	147	110	247	110	220	48	117	71	63
Netherlands	2.2	3.4	12.2	9.2	20.6	9.2	18.3	4.0	9.7	5.9	5.2
Britain	93	58	274	125	408	143	206	40	54	15	67
	6.3	3.9	18.5	8.4	27.5	9.6	12.9	2.7	3.6	1.0	4.5
United	193	31	434	90	433	86	243	37	86	38	48
States	11.2	1.8	25.2	5.2	25.2	5.0	14.1	2.2	5.0	2.2	2.8
Germany	431	186	629	150	476	82	172	33	68	36	44
	18.7	8.1	27.3	6.5	20.6	3.6	7.5	1.4	2.9	1.6	1.9
Austria	118	216	271	288	255	186	86	40	13	14	97
	7.4	13.6	17.1	18.2	16.1	11.7	5.4	2.5	.8	.9	6.1

A collapsed four-point version of this Materialist/Postmaterialist value index was created based on the ten-point version as follows:

10-point codes		4-point codes
1–3	=	1 = Materialist
4–5	=	2
6–7	=	3
8–10	=	4 = Postmaterialist

The frequencies for the four-point version are:

	Materialist		Postmaterialist		
	1	*2*	*3*	*4*	*MD*
The Netherlands	215	357	330	236	63
	17.9	29.7	27.5	19.7	5.2
Britain	425	533	349	109	67
	28.7	35.9	23.5	7.3	4.5
United States	658	523	329	161	48
	38.3	30.4	19.1	9.4	2.8
Germany	1246	626	254	137	44
	54.0	27.1	11.0	5.9	1.9
Austria	605	543	272	67	97
	38.2	34.3	17.2	4.2	6.1

PERSONAL SATISFACTION AND DEPRIVATION

To assess respondents' personal satisfaction with their lives, satisfaction scales based on Cantril's self-anchoring ladders were used. Respondents were asked to evaluate how they felt about the material side of their lives on a scale from zero (completely dissatisfied) to ten (completely satisfied), and how satisfied they were with their lives in general. Four questions were asked for each of these two dimensions:

(1) *Present satisfaction:* "All things considered, how satisfied or dissatisfied are you overall with the material side of your life (or your life as a whole) these days?"

(2) *Past satisfaction:* "Where would you have put yourself five years ago?" (on these two dimensions)

(3) *Future satisfaction:* "Where do you expect you might put yourself in five years' time?" (on the two dimensions)

(4) *Normative satisfaction:* "What level of (material or overall) satisfaction do you feel that people like yourself are entitled to?"

The differences between the various satisfaction questions were used to construct measures of relative deprivation. The principal measure of relative *material deprivation* was constructed by subtracting normative material satisfaction from present material satisfaction. Similarly, the principal measure of relative *life deprivation* was derived by subtracting normative life satisfaction from present life satisfaction. The results were two integer scales ranging from −10 (high deprivation) to +10 (negative deprivation or oversatisfaction). As might be expected, most respondents fell into the −10 to zero range. The frequency distributions for these two variables are presented in Table TA. 6.

Table TA. 6: FREQUENCIES ON MATERIAL AND LIFE DEPRIVATION

Material Deprivation	-10	-9	-8	-7	-6	-5	-4	-3	-2	-1	0	1	2	3	4	5	6	7	8	9	10	MD
The Netherlands	3	0	0	4	4	11	12	50	98	181	489	117	75	25	5	5	2	1	0	0	1	118
	.3			.4	.4	1.0	1.1	4.6	9.0	16.7	45.2	10.8	6.9	2.3	.5	.5	.2	.1			.1	
Britain	8	4	12	14	36	88	104	185	248	157	405	48	21	14	4	6	0	0	0	0	1	127
	.6	.4	.9	1.0	2.6	6.4	7.7	13.7	18.3	11.6	29.9	3.6	1.5	1.0	.3	.4					.1	
United States	10	7	10	22	27	93	95	155	248	204	511	92	59	27	10	5	1	0	1	0	0	142
	.6	.4	.6	1.4	1.7	5.9	6.0	9.8	15.7	12.9	32.4	5.8	3.7	1.7	.6	.3	.1		.1			
Germany	6	1	5	14	25	74	87	253	397	371	821	60	43	16	6	2	0	0	2	1	0	123
	.3	.0	.2	.6	1.1	3.4	4.0	11.6	18.2	17.0	37.6	2.7	2.0	.7	.3	.1			.1	.0		
Austria	1	1	4	7	25	61	63	165	249	202	598	39	25	13	5	3	0	1	0	0	0	122
	.1	.1	.3	.5	1.7	4.2	4.3	11.3	17.0	13.8	40.9	2.7	1.7	.9	.3	.2		.1				

Life Deprivation	-10	-9	-8	-7	-6	-5	-4	-3	-2	-1	0	1	2	3	4	5	6	7	8	9	10	MD
The Netherlands	2	1	1	4	0	12	18	45	82	166	475	144	61	17	9	1	0	1	2	0	0	160
	.2	.1	.1	.4		1.2	1.7	4.3	7.9	15.9	45.6	13.8	5.9	1.6	.9	.1		.1	.2			
Britain	6	2	7	14	21	62	66	143	219	222	499	61	24	10	3	2	0	1	0	0	0	123
	.4	.1	.5	1.0	1.5	4.6	4.8	10.5	16.1	16.3	36.6	4.5	1.8	.7	.2	.1		.1				
United States	9	3	10	20	20	71	84	147	220	259	527	104	50	21	7	1	1	0	0	2	0	163
	.6	.2	.6	1.3	1.3	4.6	5.4	9.4	14.1	16.6	33.9	6.7	3.2	1.3	.4	.1	.1			.1		
Germany	4	1	10	11	22	69	89	177	342	402	857	71	45	9	6	1	0	0	0	0	0	191
	.2	.0	.5	.5	1.0	3.3	4.2	8.4	16.2	19.0	40.5	3.4	2.1	.4	.3	.0						
Austria	0	1	9	11	17	31	53	108	191	269	667	38	29	6	2	2	0	0	0	0	0	151
	.1	.1	.6	.8	1.2	2.2	3.7	7.5	13.3	18.8	46.5	2.6	2.0	.4	.1	.1						

ISSUE AGENDA AND POLICY DISSATISFACTION

The respondents were asked to consider the following list of issues facing society:

1 Looking after old people
2 Guaranteeing equal rights for men and women
3 Seeing to it that everyone who wants a job can have one
4 Providing a good education
5 Providing good medical care
6 Providing adequate housing
7 Fighting pollution
8 Guaranteeing neighborhoods safe from crime
9 Providing equal rights for ethnic or racial minorities (in Germany, Austria, and the Netherlands: "for guest [foreign] workers")
10 Trying to even out differences in wealth between people

Three dimensions of feelings on these issues were explored with the questions:

A. "How important is this issue in your own view?"
   (1) Very important
   (2) Important
   (3) Not very important
   (4) Absolutely unimportant
B. "How much responsibility does government in general (in Germany and Austria, 'the state') have toward this problem?"
   (1) An essential responsibility
   (2) An important responsibility
   (3) Some responsibility
   (4) No responsibility at all
C. "How well do you think government has been doing in handling the problem?"
   (1) Very good
   (2) Good
   (3) Bad
   (4) Very bad

For each issue, an issue agenda variable and a policy dissatisfaction variable were created. In addition, several summary measures were constructed: (1) the mean scores for the three dimensions described above (importance, responsibility, and performance); (2) the mean agenda score across all ten issues; (3) two agenda subindices; (4) the policy dissatisfaction mean index (PDI) across all ten issues; and (5) two policy-dissatisfaction subindices.

Table TA. 7: MEAN SCORES ON ISSUE AGENDAS AND POLICY DISSATISFACTION

Variable	The Netherlands		Britain		United States		Germany		Austria	
	Mean	% Missing	Mean	% Missing	Mean	% Missing	Mean	% Missing	Mean	% Missing
Issue Importance	3.53	1.5	3.51	3.6	3.44	1.6	3.50	0.8	3.49	2.0
Issue Responsibility	3.32	2.6	3.23	4.6	3.00	2.6	3.33	0.9	3.23	2.8
Issue Performance	2.60	10.8	2.63	9.3	2.55	7.8	2.53	2.9	2.80	4.2
Agenda Mean (overall)	3.89	2.6	3.80	4.7	3.52	2.9	3.87	1.3	3.76	2.8
Individual Well-Being Agenda Mean	4.25	2.0	4.37	1.8	3.73	2.0	4.14	0.6	4.14	2.2
Social Equality Agenda Mean	3.20	3.1	2.68	5.3	2.82	2.6	3.05	1.4	2.79	3.1
Political Dissatisfaction Index (PDI) [overall]	2.78	11.3	2.69	9.6	2.88	8.4	2.89	3.3	2.51	4.2
Individual Well-Being PDI	2.47	6.4	2.45	3.8	2.78	5.3	2.43	1.3	2.07	2.6
Social Equality PDI	3.02	9.5	3.03	10.3	2.85	6.2	3.09	3.6	2.82	6.7

Mean Scores on Ten Issues for Importance, Government Responsibility, and Government Performance

In order to gauge the average evaluation a respondent gave to these dimensions, three summary scores were created by taking the mean value over the ten issues for each of the three domains (importance, responsibility, and performance). Two missing data were allowed in the construction of each scale. The original scores were reversed, and the mean scores now run from 1 = low/bad to 4 = high/good. Table TA. 7 presents descriptive measures and missing data information for this and the following summary issue agenda and policy dissatisfaction indices.

Political Issue Agenda

A measure was constructed to reflect the perceived position on the public agenda for each issue. The perceived personal importance and the government's responsibility for the ten issue areas were combined according to the following recode scheme:

			Importance (Very Important)		(Not at All)	
			1	2	3	4	MD
Responsibility	(An essential responsibility)	1	5	4	3	2	MD
		2	4	3	2	1	MD
		3	3	2	1	1	MD
	(Not a responsibility)	4	2	1	1	1	MD
		MD	MD	MD	MD	MD	MD

The resulting agenda measures ranged from 1 = low on the agenda to 5 = high on the agenda; missing data on either the responsibility or the importance variable resulted in missing data for the combined measure.

Agenda Mean

To summarize the combined private and public importance of these issues, a mean agenda score over all ten issues was calculated. Two missing data were allowed. The mean score runs from 1 = low on the agenda to 5 = high on the agenda.

Agenda Subindices

Because the entire range of issues described above was so heterogeneous, more homogeneous subsets of these issues were desired. While substantive groupings could be suggested a priori, it was decided to determine which issues would cluster empirically in each of the countries. For this purpose, multidimensional scaling was used, a dimensional technique that requires no more than ordinal level data.

Based on a correlation matrix (pairwise deletion of missing data) of potential scale items, multidimensional scaling established a geometric representation of the association between items by maximizing the correspondence between the order of the size of correlations and the order of corresponding distances in the resulting space.

> The program starts with an initial configuration [here, a principal comparative solution usually eliminating the first factor], and iterates (using a procedure of the "steepest descent" type) over successive trial configurations, each time comparing the rank order of the corresponding measure in the data. A "badness of fit" measure (stress coefficient) is computed after each iteration and the configuration is rearranged accordingly to improve the fit to the data, until, ideally, the rank order of distances in the configuration is perfectly monotonic with the rank order of dissimilarities given by the data; in that case, the "stress" will be zero.[5]

The iteration procedure was stopped when successive iterations reduced the stress values insignificantly.

As a result of multidimensional scaling analysis two clusters were defined consistently across the five nations. Mean scores ranging from 1 to 5 were computed across the items in each of the clusters. One missing data value was allowed in the construction of each subindex.

The following issues were used to construct each of the measures:

A. *Individual Well-Being Agenda* Mean:
   1 Jobs agenda
   2 Education agenda
   3 Medical agenda
   4 Housing agenda

B. *Social Equality Agenda* Mean:
   1 Sex equality agenda

2 Minority equality agenda
3 Equal wealth agenda

Three issues—old age, pollution, and crime—did not cluster consistently in all nations and were therefore not included in these subindices.

Policy Dissatisfaction Indices (PDI)

In order to create a measure of policy dissatisfaction for each of the issues described above, the dimension of government performances was combined with the agenda measure for each of the ten issues. Note from the recode table below that the "performance" dimension is critical in determining whether or not the respondent feels politically dissatisfied, while the agenda serves as a weighting factor.

Agenda		Government Performance: 1 (Very Good)	2	3	4 (Bad)	MD
(Low)	1	3	3	3	3	MD
	2	3	3	3	3	MD
	3	2	2	4	4	MD
	4	1	2	4	5	MD
(High)	5	1	1	5	5	MD
	MD	MD	MD	MD	MD	MD

Policy Dissatisfaction Mean

To tap the general level of policy dissatisfaction across all issues a summary score was created for the policy dissatisfaction items. The mean was computed over the ten items with two missing data values allowed. The resulting mean scores run from 1 = low to 5 = high policy dissatisfaction.

Policy Dissatisfaction Subindices

Following the grouping of issues into the agenda subindices, the policy dissatisfaction measures for the same subgroups of issues were combined into policy dissatisfaction subindices. Because the agenda subindices are seen as defining the domains of human concerns, and because satisfaction on a specific issue depends upon governmental performance, the grouping of the agenda items was given priority over possible independent groupings of the policy dissatisfaction measures. Indeed, multidimensional scaling analyses of the latter items produced no common solution, but reflected instead the successes and priorities of the various national governments.

The mean scores were constructed with one missing data value allowed, and range from 1 = low policy dissatisfaction to 5 = high policy dissatisfaction. See above for the specific issues that were combined to form the *individual well-being* and the *social equality policy dissatisfaction* means.

ATTITUDES TOWARD THE POLITICAL SYSTEM

Several well-known concepts were operationalized by combining individual questions. These variables were constructed as means rather than as additive indices to prevent the loss of information due to missing data. In subsequent analyses these variables were often collapsed into a few discrete categories. Cutting points for these recodes were chosen to approximate quartile or quintile distributions based on either the national or the combined cross-national marginals. Table TA. 8 presents descriptive measures and missing data information for all of these mean indices.

Efficacy Indices

Two indices were created from responses to the following three statements:

(1) People like me have no say in what government does.
(2) Voting is the only way that people like me can have any say about how the government runs things.
(3) Sometimes politics and government seem so complicated that a person like me cannot really understand what is going on.

One efficacy index is based on all three items. For this scale one missing data value was allowed.

To extract a more homogeneous internal efficacy measure, item 1 was excluded from the second mean index. For this scale complete responses on both items were required. Responses on these questions ranged from 1 = agree strongly (low efficacy) to 4 = disagree strongly (high efficacy) so that the range on the mean indices ran from 1 = low efficacy to 4 = high efficacy.

Table TA. 8: MEAN SCORES ON EFFICACY, RESPONSIVENESS, AND POLITICAL TRUST

Variable	The Netherlands		Britain		United States		Germany		Austria	
	Mean	% Missing	Mean	% Missing	Mean	% Missing	Mean	% Missing	Mean	% Missing
Efficacy (3-item)	2.18	1.8	2.12	3.0	2.30	1.2	2.02	1.1	1.73	4.2
Efficacy (2-item)	1.90	5.7	1.85	5.2	1.94	2.6	1.80	3.4	1.55	7.8
System Responsiveness Index	2.26	8.6	2.13	5.0	2.24	3.0	2.09	2.6	1.89	5.9
Political Trust	2.59	16.2	2.36	17.9	2.08	9.0	2.83	13.7	2.95	11.0

System Responsiveness Index

This is a mean index constructed from responses to the following three statements:

(1) I don't think that public officials care much about what people like me think.
(2) Generally speaking, those we elect to (Parliament) lose touch with the people pretty quickly.
(3) Parties are only interested in people's votes, but not in their opinions.

Response categories were the same as in the above discussion, resulting in an index ranging from 1 = low responsiveness to 4 = high responsiveness. One missing data value was allowed.

Political Trust Index

This is a mean index constructed from the following items:

(1) Generally speaking, would you say that this country is run by a few big interests looking out for themselves or that it is run for the benefit of all the people?
  1 For a few big interests
  4 For all the people
(2) How much do you trust the government to do what is right?
  1 Almost never
  2 Only some of the time
  3 Most of the time
  4 Just about always

The resulting index has the range 1 = low political trust, 4 = high political trust. Missing data on either item resulted in missing data for the index, as did responses of "for no one" to the first item (Austria only).

PARTISAN PREFERENCE VARIABLES

Vote for Left, Center, or Right Parties

The respondents' reported vote was recoded to indicate whether or not they voted for a left, center, or right party. In the United States the respondents' vote for president was used in the construction of this variable. Those who did not vote, who voted for parties that could not be classified, who did not know which party they voted for, or who refused to answer received a missing data code. The classification of parties follows the scheme suggested by Inglehart and Klingemann.[6]

	Left	Center	Right
The Netherlands	Labour Party (PVDA) Democrats '66 (D '66) Pacifist Socialist (PSP) Radical Party (PPR) Communist Party (CPN)	Democratic Socialist '70 (DS '70)	Catholic Peoples Party (KVP) Liberals (VVD) Anti-Revolutionary Party (ARP) Christian Historical Union (CHU) Christian Democratic Appeal (CDA) Farmer's Party (BP) GPV, SGP, RKPN, DMP, NMP
Britain	Labour Party Communist Party	Liberal Party Welsh Nationalist Scottish Nationalist	Conservative Party
United States	Democrat (McGovern)		Republican (Nixon) American Independence Party (Wallace)
Germany	Social Democratic Party (SPD) German Communist Party (DKP)	Free Democratic Party (FDP)	Christian Democratic Union (CDU/CSU) National Democratic Party (NPD)
Austria	Socialist Party (SPO) Communist Party (KPO)	Free Democratic Party (FPO)	Austrian Peoples Party (OVP)

The marginal frequencies are as follows:

	Left	Center	Right	MD
The Netherlands	372 43.2	25 2.9	464 53.9	340
Britain	470 47.0	69 6.9	460 46.0	484
United States	371 33.4	0	739 66.6	609
Germany	806 43.5	217 11.7	829 44.8	455
Austria	672 55.2	55 4.5	490 40.3	367

Party Preference Left-Right

This measure differs from the preceding variable, left-right party vote, in that it is based on partisan preferences rather than on voting intentions. In every country (except the United States), the question was asked, "Which political party do you usually feel closest to?" In the United States respondents were asked, "Do you usually think of yourself as a Republican, a Democrat, an Independent, or what?" followed by prompting to elicit the strength of partisanship. The recoding into left, center, or right partisanship follows the same pattern as above; however, the United States was coded as follows:

(1) Left	Strong Democrat	
	Not very strong Democrat	
	Independent closer to Democrats	
(2) Right	Strong Republican	
	Not very strong Republican	
	Independent closer to Republican	
(9) Missing Data	Independent, other, etc.	

The marginals are as follows:

	Left	Center	Right	MD
The Netherlands	460	11	493	237
	47.7	1.1	51.1	
Britain	555	171	474	285
	46.3	14.3	39.5	
United States	897	0	474	348
	65.4		34.6	
Germany	666	114	731	796
	44.1	7.5	48.4	
Austria	577	33	425	549
	55.7	3.2	41.1	

Voting for Government or Opposition Parties

The respondents' reported vote was also recoded to indicate whether they voted for a party that formed the government or was part of the governing coalition in that country, or whether they voted for another party. In the United States, the respondents' vote for president was used in the construction of this variable. Those who did not vote, who did not know which party they voted for, or who refused to answer received a missing data code. The coding scheme was as follows (for complete party names consult the left-center-right voting index description, above):

	Government	Opposition
The Netherlands	PVDA	VVD
	KVP	CHU
	ARP	CPN
	D '66	DS '70
	PPR	SGP
		GPV
		BP
		PSP
		RKPN
		DMP
		NMP
Britain	Conservative	Labour
		Liberal
		Welsh National
		Scottish National
		~ Communist
United States	Republican	Democrat
	(Nixon)	(McGovern)
Germany	SPD	CDU/CSU
	FDP	NPD
		DKP
Austria	SPO	OVP
		FPO
		KPO

The marginal frequencies are as follows:

	Govt.	Opp.	MD
The Netherlands	540	321	340
	62.7	37.3	
Britain	460	539	484
	46.0	54.0	
United States	726	384	609
	66.2	33.8	
Germany	1014	838	455
	54.8	45.2	
Austria	667	550	368
	54.8	45.2	

Government/Opposition Party Preference

This measure parallels the government/opposition vote index, except that it is based on the respondents' party preferences rather than on reported vote (see also "Party Preference Left-Right" above). Again, the United States coding differed from that of the other countries:

(1) Government	Independent/no preference, but closer to Republican	
	Not very strong Republican	
	Strong Republican	
(2) Opposition	Strong Democrat	
	Not very strong Democrat	
	Independent/no preference, but closer to Democratic	
(3) Missing Data	Independent, other, etc.	

The marginal frequencies for this variable are:

	Govt.	Opp.	MD
The Netherlands	535	429	237
	55.5	44.5	
Britain	474	726	285
	39.5	60.5	
United States	474	897	348
	34.6	65.4	
Germany	771	740	796
	51.0	49.0	
Austria	573	462	549
	55.4	44.6	

Strength of Party Attachment

This variable constructs a measure of the respondents' reported closeness to a political party. In order to be consistent across countries, only respondents who spontaneously named the party to which they felt close were included in codes 1 to 3 of this partisan strength measure. British and Dutch respondents were shown a list of parties if they could not spontaneously name a party they felt close to. Respondents from these two countries were coded 4 (no party preference) on this variable even if they did choose a party from the list presented to them, because this second chance was not available to respondents in the other countries. Subject to these constraints, the strength of party attachment variable is a recode of responses to the question, "Would you say you feel very close fairly close, or not very close to that party?" with the original responses coded as follows:

	New Codes	The Netherlands, Britain United States	Germany, Austria
	1	Very close	Very strong
	2	Fairly close	Fairly strong
	3	Not very close, don't know, refused	Moderate, fairly weak, weak, don't know, refused
	4	No spontaneous party preference (all countries)	
	MD	NA	

The frequencies for this variable are as follows:

	Very Close	Fairly Close	Not Very Close, DK, Refused	No Spontaneous Party Preference	MD
The Netherlands	113	471	400	209	8
	9.5	39.5	33.5	17.5	
Britain	216	626	351	283	7
	14.6	42.5	23.7	19.1	
United States	227	680	479	303	30
	13.4	40.3	28.4	17.9	
Germany	209	588	701	794	15
	9.1	25.7	30.6	34.6	
Austria	220	353	465	546	0
	13.9	22.3	29.3	34.5	

OTHER SOCIAL AND POLITICAL ATTITUDES

Attitudes Toward Young People

This is a mean index created from responses to the following statements:

(1) Young people should always question the present state of affairs.
(2) We should not be too upset if young people sometimes break the law when protesting against what they consider unjust.

The response categories ranged from 1 = agree strongly to 4 = disagree strongly, resulting in an index that ranges from 1 = youth should *not* question or protest to 4 = youth should question and protest. No missing data were allowed. The mean scores for this measure are as follows:

	Mean	% Missing
The Netherlands	2.25	7.3
Britain	2.25	7.1
United States	2.27	5.9
Germany	2.54	8.0
Austria	2.36	19.1

Factor Scores: Establishment and Partisanship Dimensions

The objective of these measures was to develop indices of "old politics" and "new politics" positions based on the respondents' affect toward various social groups. Respondents were asked to place the groups on a scale running from 0 = very negative through 50 = neutral to 100 = very positive. (In the United States a "thermometer" scale was used as the equivalent stimulus.) Such scale ratings usually exhibit a general "response tendency," i.e., a tendency for individuals to use only a narrow range of the scale. For example, one respondent might consider "50" a poor rating and therefore use primarily the 50-100 range. In contrast, another may consider 50 a high rating and therefore use the 0-50 range in evaluating the various social groups.

To remove this "response tendency" the average rating across all groups was computed for each respondent. This was seen as the reference standard actually used by each respondent. Each respondent's mean score was then subtracted from the scale rating of each group. Thus for each respondent some groups are evaluated more negatively than the respondent's mean while other groups are evaluated more positively.

These adjusted scale ratings were then factor analyzed, and factor scores were constructed. The entire procedure was as follows:

(1) A respondent's mean score across all groups was computed. (Six missing data values were allowed before a missing data code was assigned on this variable.) The groups used were:

A.	Unions	G.	Student protesters
B.	Left party	H.	Right party
C.	Clergy	I.	Minorities
D.	Big business	J.	Women's liberation
E.	Police	K.	Revolutionaries
F.	Civil servants	L.	Small business

(2) The intergroup mean was subtracted from each scale rating.
(3) A Pearson correlation matrix using pair-wise deletion of missing data was computed separately for each nation.
(4) The correlation matrices were used as the bases of principal components analyses in each country. Only two dimensions were extracted and a varimax rotation was used. The first two dimensions

Table TA. 9: FACTOR MATRIX FOR FIVE NATIONS

Ratings for:	The Netherlands		Britain		United States		Germany		Austria	
	Partisan	Est./ Anti-Est.	Partisan	Est./ Anti-Est.	Partisan	Est./ Anti-Est.	Partisan	Est./ Anti-Est.	Partisan	Est./ Anti-Est.
Unions	.66	.32	.75	-.08	.58	.03	.64	-.19	.71	.15
Major Left Party	.75	.02	.80	.00	.70	-.01	.75	-.17	.81	.11
Clergy	-.52	.39	-.04	.51	-.09	.59	-.67	.08	-.64	.23
Big Business	-.59	.31	-.54	.16	-.37	.39	-.63	.13	-.39	.07
Police	-.07	.69	-.13	.61	-.12	.72	-.01	.76	-.07	.65
Civil Servants	.10	.54	-.11	.37	.30	.46	-.04	.57	.08	.57
Student Protesters	.41	-.45	-.03	-.70	-.02	-.76	.25	-.71	.15	-.71
Major Right Party	-.78	-.01	-.76	.18	-.74	.18	-.81	.17	-.82	-.03
Minorities	-.03	-.31	.06	-.19	.07	-.24	.10	-.19	-.12	-.37
Women's Liberation	.28	-.68	.09	-.44	.03	-.57	.41	.02	-.29	-.08
Revolutionaries	.26	-.69	.00	-.67	-.04	-.71	.06	-.71	.20	-.67
Small Business	-.34	.18	-.29	.37	-.23	.37	-.09	.48	-.22	.25

appear to represent an old politics and a new politics factor in each nation.

(5) These varimax rotated factor structures were used to compute factor scores for two factors. The resulting factor scores are standardized with a mean of 0 and a standard deviation of 1. Where necessary the polarity of a dimension was reversed to make the score consistent cross-nationally.

Table TA. 9 presents the factor matrix on which the computation of the factor scores were based. On the *partisan dimension,* positive (high) scores signify pro-left attitudes, while negative (low) scores mean right partisan leanings.

Partisan Dimension

	Minimum	*Maximum*	*% Missing*
The Netherlands	−3.71	3.56	10.1
Britain	−2.53	2.73	9.0
United States	−4.35	3.68	4.7
Germany	−3.05	3.16	1.3
Austria	−2.80	2.86	9.7

On the *anti-establishment/establishment dimension,* negative (low) scores result from anti-establishment feelings while positive (high) scores signify pro-establishment attitudes.

Anti-establishment/Establishment Dimension

	Minimum	*Maximum*	*% Missing*
The Netherlands	−4.33	3.31	10.1
Britain	−5.19	2.29	9.0
United States	−4.91	2.43	4.7
Germany	−4.65	2.46	1.3
Austria	−4.58	2.61	9.7

Perception of Group Privilege

This variable was created to measure the degree to which respondents perceived the existence of privileged and underprivileged groups in society. The variable was constructed from two questions:

(1) Do you think there are any groups of people who are getting more rewards than they deserve or which have an unduly privileged position in our society?

(2) Do you think there are any groups who are getting a poor deal from society, not getting rewards or basic rights they deserve?

Response categories were 1 = Yes, 2 = It depends, 3 = No.
The perception of group privilege measure was constructed according to the following recode table:

Perception of Privileged Groups

		Yes	Depends	No
Perception of Underprivileged Groups	Yes	1	2	2
	Depends	2	2	2
	No	2	2	3

Missing data on either question resulted in missing data for this constructed variable. The frequencies for this variable are:

	1	*2*	*3*	*MD*
The Netherlands	847	223	27	104
	70.5	18.6	2.2	8.7
Britain	951	286	92	154
	64.1	19.3	6.2	10.4
United States	1029	379	96	215
	59.9	22.0	5.6	12.5
Germany	1216	485	211	395
	52.7	21.0	9.1	17.1
Austria	724	461	132	267
	45.7	29.1	8.3	16.9

DEMOGRAPHIC CODES

Education

The development of a standard cross-national education code proved to be challenging since educational systems vary dramatically, especially between Europe and the United States. Unresolved differences within the group as to what the functional equivalence in educational attainment is across these five nations resulted in the construction and subsequent use of two different education measures. The first variable described (respondent's education) was used in chapters 11-14 and the second variable (years of educational experience) was employed in chapters 2-10. A careful review of the categorization of the types of school for each variable (Tables TA. 10 and TA. 11) will illustrate the ways in which the two education measures differ.

The two education measures are quite similar since they are derived from the same original information. In correlational analyses involving the two different education measures the results will show few differences. However, when education is used as a categorical variable, the varying definitions of education levels will result in substantive differences. The two measures themselves correlate as follows:

	The Netherlands	Britain	United States	Germany	Austria
Kendall's tau-b	.72	.80	.80	.81	.81
Pearson's r	.76	.92	.85	.93	.92

Respondent's Education A five category education variable was constructed from the school or college last attended and the last year completed. The recodes used in the construction of this variable are presented in Table TA. 10. The variable was sometimes collapsed as follows:

	Basic Level	Lower Level	Middle Level and Higher
The Netherlands	1–2	3	4–5
Britain	1	2	3–5
United States	1–3	4	5
Germany	1	2	3–5
Austria	1	2	3–5

The marginals for these two variables are:

	Five-category						Three-category			
	1	2	3	4	5	MD	1	2	3	MD
The Netherlands	230	185	513	179	94	0	415	513	273	0
	19.2	15.4	42.7	14.9	7.8		34.6	42.7	22.7	
Britain	535	443	130	277	78	20	535	443	485	20
	36.5	30.3	8.9	18.9	5.3		36.5	30.3	33.1	
United States	80	256	283	531	561	8	619	531	561	8
	4.7	15.0	16.5	31.0	32.8		36.2	31.0	32.8	
Germany	1101	496	441	123	127	19	1101	496	691	19
	48.1	21.7	19.3	5.4	5.6		48.1	21.7	30.2	
Austria	825	306	314	100	38	1	825	306	452	1
	52.1	19.3	19.8	6.3	2.4		52.1	19.3	28.5	

Years of Educational Experience The second measure of educational experience was constructed from the same variables but according to different criteria. Table TA. 11 presents the recodes used to construct this variable. The marginals for this variable are:

	1	2	3	MD
The Netherlands	928	179	94	0
	77.3	14.9	7.8	
Britain	979	381	78	47
	68.1	26.5	5.4	
United States	477	903	331	8
	27.9	52.8	19.3	
Germany	1597	565	126	19
	69.8	24.7	5.5	
Austria	1132	414	38	0
	71.4	26.1	2.4	

Occupational Prestige Score

In order to arrive at a cross-nationally comparable occupational status measure we relied on the work of Donald J. Treiman, who has created a standard international occupational prestige scale. His measure assigns prestige scores to the International Labor Organization's occupational code categories on the basis of the empirical assessment of occupational prestige in sixty countries. For details of the scale construction and a further elaboration of the theoretical and empirical attributes of this measure, see Donald J. Treiman, *Occupational Prestige in Comparative Perspective* (New York: Academic Press, 1977).

The index ranges from 1 = low prestige occupation to 92 = high prestige occupation.

Table TA. 10: DESCRIPTION OF RESPONDENTS' EDUCATION

Education Code and Label	The Netherlands	Britain	United States	Germany	Austria
1. Basic Level	Elementary or Primary School or less (Basisnivo)	Elementary/Primary School or less	Less than 7th grade completed	Elementary/Primary School or less (Volksschule mit oder ohne Abschluss)	Elementary/Primary School or less (Pflichtschule ohne Lehre)
2. Lower Level	Less than 3 years secondary school or lower occupational course (Lager nivo)	Secondary Modern School	Less than 10th grade completed	Occupational Training School (Berufsschule)	Occupational Training School (Pflichtschule mit Lehre)
3. Extended Lower Level	3 or 4 years secondary education or lower middle occupational education (Uitgebreid Lager nivo)	Technical School or Technical College	Did not receive High School diploma	Middle School or Occupational Training School completed (Mittlere Reife, Realschulabschluss, sonstige Berufsfach- oder Fachschule)	Middle School (incomplete) or Occupational Training School (Mittelschule ohne Matura Fachschule, Handelsschule)
4. Middle Level	5 or 6 years secondary education or Middle occupational education (Middelbaar nivo)	Comprehensive or Grammar School completed, Public School, Commercial or technical training	Completed High School and noncollege training	Academic Secondary School or Technical School completion, still in school (Abitur, Technikerschule, oder in Ausbildung, unter 20 Jahren)	Middle School completion (Matura)
5. Higher than Middle Level	Semi-high and higher occupational study, postsecondary academic study (Semi-hoger nivo, Hoger nivo)	College or University, teachers training	Post-High School education (college, university, professional)	Any postsecondary training or studies (Ingenieurschule Studenten, Universität, Hochschule, Lehrerbildung)	College, University, Professional/post-secondary studies (Abgeschlossene Hochschule)

Table TA. 11: DESCRIPTION OF YEARS OF EDUCATIONAL EXPERIENCE*

Education Code and Label	The Netherlands	Britain	United States	Germany	Austria
1. Compulsory Education Level	Basisnivo Lager nivo Uitgebreid Lager nivo	Elementary/Primary School Secondary Modern School	1-10 grades	Berufsschule Volksschule ohne Abschluss Volksschule mit Abschluss	Pflichtschule ohne Lehre Pflichtschule mit Lehre
2. Middle and Further Schooling	Middelbaar nivo	Commercial Training Vocational Training Technical School Technical College Comprehensive School Grammer School Public School	11-14 grades	Schüler (in Ausbildung, unter 20 Jahren) Sonstige Berufsfach- oder Fachschule Technikerschule Mittlere Reife, Realschulabschluss Abitur	Fachschule, Handelsschule Mittelschule ohne Matura Matura
3. Higher Education	Semi-hoger nivo Hoger nivo	Polytechnic and Art College Teacher Training University Post University Institute	15-17 grades or more	Ingenieurschule Studenten (in Ausbildung, 20 Jahre und älter) Universität, Hochschule, auch Lehrerbildung	Abgeschlossene Hochschule

*For English language equivalents see Table TA. 10.

[588]

SAMPLING AND FIELDWORK

In order to make the data valid and comparable, national multistage probability samples were used to select a representative cross-section of the population 16 years of age and over in the five countries. In each country, small geographical areas or administrative units were selected *at random* from all such areas or administrative units. This first stage yields a probability sample of "primary sampling units" (PSUs). Sampling in this stage was *stratified* by using available census and other official statistical data on variables such as population, urbanization, voting returns, religion, and so on. Details of this procedure were nation specific and followed established procedures of survey research in each country. The procedures ensure that in all nations the selected PSUs are indeed a representative selection of all possible PSUs. The number of PSUs varies between 63 in the Netherlands and 560 in Germany.

Within each PSU, a prespecified number of *households* (or dwelling units) were selected at random. This sample of households was drawn from official registration data in continental Europe. In Britain, the Electoral Register was used to sample *addresses* (*not* electors!). In the United States, a controlled random selection process was used to select dwelling units within the PSU.

In each household the interviewers listed all members of age 16 and above (in Austria, people above 70 years were excluded) in a prespecified order by sex and age. The selection of the respondent within each household followed the procedure described by Leslie Kish.[7] Selection tables were attached to the face sheet of each interview schedule. These tables tell interviewers which person is to be interviewed from the listing.

The sampling procedure yields representative random samples of the total population in the same age categories. The procedure does contain a very slight household size bias (except in Britain, where the probability of selection of a household depends on the number of electors in it). Analysis shows that this correction did not alter the results to an appreciable degree. Thus results reported in this volume are based on the unweighted data.

In practice, not all people selected in this fashion can actually be interviewed. Some potential respondents cannot be reached, in spite of three or more attempts to contact them. Some are not available during the time period of field work. Some refuse to be interviewed. Completion rates varied between 64 percent (Austria) and 77 percent (Britain). The achieved completion rates correspond to the results obtained in good survey practice in the five countries.

Sampling and field work were performed by ISR's Survey Research Center in the United States, Mary Agar Fieldwork, in Britain, Gesellschaft fuer

---

NOTE: This section was prepared by Klaus R. Allerbeck.

Table TA. 12: SAMPLING INFORMATION

	The Netherlands	Britain	United States	Germany	Austria
Number of Primary Sampling Units	63	120	74	560	208
Size of Sample	1800	2345	2429	3195	2493
Number of Realized Interviews	1201	1802*	1719	2307	1584
Completion Rate	67%	77%	71%	72%	64%
Pair Sample Size	223	173	244	257	212
Date of Fieldwork	March 1974= August 1974	November 1973= February 1974	June 1974= September 1974	February 1974= May 1974	April 1974= September 1974

*In Britain, PSUs with a large percentage of middle-class households were oversampled. For this volume, these excess respondents were removed by a random process so that weighting would not be necessary. The interviews utilized in Britain (reflecting a representative national sample) total 1483.

Angewandte Sozialpsychologie (GETAS), in Germany, the Institut fuer empirische Sozialforschung (IFES) in Austria, and the Sociological Institute of the University of Tilburg in the Netherlands.

The basic data of the sampling process are assembled in summary fashion in Table TA. 12. As a check on the actual representation of the population, results of the study were compared with available census data on variables such as sex, marital status, age, education, region, religion, and so on. These comparisons yielded results that were considered satisfactory. Deviations were mostly very small and within the limits of normal sampling error.

The parent-child pair sample. The samples of parent-child pairs were drawn in the following way. Whenever there was a 16 through 20 year old and a parent in the household, in addition to the respondent selected by the above defined procedure, an interview was conducted with the respective other member of the pair. If there was a choice, an objective procedure was used for selection. Exact response rates for the pair samples cannot be determined, as we do not know the household composition of those households where no interview or household listing could be obtained in the first place. Completion rates of those additional interviews, to the extent to which these could be determined, tend to be in the order of magnitude of the completion rates for the cross-section or somewhat higher.

On the computation of sampling error. In order to compute confidence intervals or to establish the statistical significance of results, estimates of the sampling error of the respective parameter are required. For multistage samples, estimates based on formulas for simple random sampling would be misleading. An occasionally used rule of thumb is to multiply the sampling error appropriate for a simple random sample of equal size with $\sqrt{2}$. More appropriate procedures require the computation of the "design effect" (Kish) of the sample. In order to allow its calculation, which takes a good deal of computational effort and requires use of a computer, the PSU identification is part of each data set.

Additional information. Technical descriptions of sampling procedure, interviewer characteristics, comparisons of sample estimates, and known population characteristics have been deposited with the Zentralarchiv fuer empirische Sozialforschung in Cologne.

NOTES

1. For specific program information see OSIRIS III, Volume I, *System and Program Description,* developed by the Center for Political Studies, the Inter-university Consortium for Political and Social Research, and the Survey Research Center of the Institute for Social Research (Ann Arbor: University of Michigan, 1973).

2. Ibid., pp. 665-75; and Delbert Miller, *Handbook of Research Design and Social Measurement* (New York: David McKay, 1970), pp. 91-94; and Clyde H. Coombs, *A Theory of Data* (New York: John Wiley, 1964), chapter 11.

3. The conceptual and technical aspects of the construction of this set of variables are the work of Hans D. Klingemann and are considered more completely in his chapter 8 of this volume, and in his *Ideologisches Denken in der Bevölkerung Westlicher Industriegesellschaften,* Habilitationsschrift, Mannheim, 1977. A summary is included here to ensure completeness of this section.

4. Ronald Inglehart, *The Silent Revolution* (Princeton: Princeton University Press, 1977).

5. OSIRIS III, Volume I, p. 616.

6. Ronald Inglehart and Hans D. Klingemann, "Party Identification, Ideological Preference, and the Left-Right Dimension Among Western Mass Publics," in Ian Budge, Ivor Crewe, and Dennis Farlie (eds.), *Party Identification and Beyond* (New York: John Wiley, 1976), pp. 243-273.

7. Leslie Kish, "A Procedure for Objective Respondent Selection Within the Household," *Journal of the American Statistical Association,* 44 (September 1949), pp. 380-387.

LIST OF PUBLICATIONS

Klaus R. Allerbeck, "Beziehungen zwischen Jugenlichen und Eltern (-generation)," in Helge Pross (ed.), *Familie-wohin?* Reinbek: Rowohlt Verlag, 1979.

Klaus R. Allerbeck, *Demokratisierung und sozialer Wandel in der BRD. Sekundaranalyse von Umfragen 1953-1974,* Opladen: Westdeutscher Verlag, 1976.

Klaus R. Allerbeck, "Political Generations: Some Reflections on the Concept and its Application to the German Case," *European Journal of Political Research* 5 (June, 1977), pp. 119-134.

Anselm Eder, *Jugend, Ideologie und Protest,* Vienna, 1977 (dissertation).

Felix J. Heunks, *Nederlanders en hun Samenleving,* with a summary in English, Amsterdam: APA Holland University Press, 1979.

Felix J. Heunks, "Politieke Participatie," in M. Van Schendelen (ed.), *Kernthema's van de Politicologie,* Meppel/Amsterdam: Boom, 1976, pp. 98-122.

Felix J. Heunks, "Vervreemding onderzocht," *Mens en Maatschappij* 52 (2), 1977, pp. 172-205.

Ronald Inglehart, "Politische Konsequenzen von materialistischen und post-materialistischen Prioritäten," in Helmut Klages and Peter Kmieciak (eds.), *Wertwandel und gesellschaftlicher Wandel,* Frankfurt: Campus Verlag, 1979.

M. Kent Jennings, "Analyzing Pairs in Cross-National Survey Research," *European Journal of Political Research* 5 (June, 1977), pp. 179-197.

M. Kent Jennings and Barbara G. Farah, "Continuities in Comparative

Research Strategies: The Mannheim Data Confrontation Seminar." *Social Science Information,* 16 (2), 1977, pp. 231-249.

Max Kaase and Hans D. Klingemann, "Politische Ideologie und Politische Beteiligung," *Mannheimer Berichte,* Mannheim: Universitaet, 11 (December 1975), pp. 326ff.

Max Kaase, "Political Ideology, Dissatisfaction and Protest: A Micro Theory of Unconventional Political Behavior," in Klaus von Beyme (ed.), *German Political Studies,* Band 2, Beverly Hills and London: Sage Publications, 1976, pp. 7ff.

Max Kaase, "Bedingungen unkonventionellen politischen Verhaltens in der Bundesrepublik Deutschland," in Peter Graf Kielmannsegg (ed.), *Legitimationsprobleme politischer Systeme,* 7. Sonderheft der Politischen Vierteljahresschrift, Opladen: Westdeutscher Verlag, 1976, pp. 179ff.

Max Kaase, "Strukturen politischer Beteiligung," in Rudolf Wildenmann (ed.), *Form und Erfahrung,* Festschrift fuer Ferdinand A. Hermens, Berlin: Duncker and Humblot, 1977, pp. 129ff.

Hans D. Klingemann, *Ideologisches Denken in der Bevolkerung westlicher Industriegesellschaften,* Habilitationsschrift, Mannheim, 1977.

Alan Marsh, "Explorations in Unorthodox Political Behavior: A Scale to Measure 'Protest Potential'," *European Journal of Political Research,* 2 (June 1974), pp. 107ff.

Alan Marsh, *Protest and Political Consciousness,* Beverly Hills and London: Sage Publications, 1977.

Alan Marsh, "The New Matrix of Political Action," *Futures,* 11 (April, 1979).

David K. Matheson, *Ideology, Political Action and the Finnish Working Class: A Survey Study of Political Behavior,* Commentationes Scientiarum Socialium, Helsinki: Societas Scientiarum Fennica 1979.

Pertti Pesonen and Risto Sänkiaho, *Kansalaiset ja känsanvaltä: Suomalaisten kasityksia poliittisesta toiminnasta,* Helsinki: Werner Söderström Osakeyhtiö, 1979.

Leopold Rosenmayr (ed.), *Determinanten politischer Beteiligung* (with contributions by Anselm Eder, Inga Findl, Kathleen Stoffl, and Elfi Urbas), Wien: Verlag für Geschichte und Politik, 1979.

Leopold Rosenmayr and Anselm Eder, *Politische Aktivität und Lebensalter,* Wien: Verlag für Geschichte und Politik, 1979.

Giacomo Sani and Giovanni Sartori, "Frammentazione, polarizzazione, e cleavages: democrazie facili e difficili," *Rivista italiana di scienza politica,* 8 (December 1978), pp. 339-361.

ABOUT THE AUTHORS

Klaus R. Allerbeck is Professor of Sociology at the University of Bielefeld. He received his doctorate from the University of Cologne. He was a Research Associate at the Zentralarchiv fuer empirische Sozialforschung (1970-1972) and Assistant Professor of Sociology at Harvard University (1972-1976). Along with numerous articles, he has published *Datenverarbeitung in der empirischen Sozialforschung, Soziologie radikaler Studentenbewegungen, Demokratisierung und sozialer Wandel in der Bundesrepublik* and, with Leopold Rosenmayr, *Einfuehrung in die Jugendsoziologie*.

Samuel H. Barnes is Chairman and Professor of Political Science and Program Director, Center for Political Studies, the University of Michigan. He received B.A. and M.A. degrees from Tulane University and a Ph.D. from Duke University. He was a Fulbright scholar at the Institut des Sciences Politiques in Paris (1956-1957) and a Fulbright visiting professor at the Universities of Florence (1962-1963) and Rome (1967-1968). His publications include *Party Democracy* and *Representation in Italy*.

Barbara G. Farah is Research Associate at the Center for Political Studies, the Institute for Social Research, and Lecturer in the Department of Political Science, the University of Michigan. She has been involved in research on political representation in West Germany, a study of presidential nominating conventional delegates, and a cross-national study of gender roles.

Felix Heunks graduated from the Faculty of Social Sciences of the Catholic University at Tilburg; he obtained his doctor's degree in the same faculty with a thesis entitled *Alienatie en stemgedrag (Alienation and Voting Behavior*, with a summary in English). After an initial period as researcher in rural sociology he is now Research Fellow at Tilburg. He is mainly engaged in political-sociological investigations, and in training graduate students in research.

Ronald Inglehart is Professor of Political Science and Faculty Associate in the Center for Political Studies at the University of Michigan. He has taught at the Universities of Geneva and Mannheim and since 1970 has participated in the design and analysis of the European Community's nine-nation public opinion surveys. His book, *The Silent Revolution: Changing Values and Political Styles Among Western Publics,* has appeared in English, German, and Japanese editions.

M. Kent Jennings is Professor of Political Science and Program Director, Center for Political Studies, the University of Michigan. He received a B.A. from the University of Redlands and a Ph.D. from the University of North Carolina. He is the author or coauthor of *Community Influentials, The Image of the Federal Service, Governing American Schools,* and *The Political Character of Adolescence.*

Max Kaase is Professor of Political Science at the University of Mannheim and Executive Director of the Zentrum fuer Umfragen, Methoden und Analysen, an academic social science research institute based in Mannheim. He received his doctorate from the University of Cologne. Among his publications are *Die Wechselwaehler* (ed.), *Wahlsoziologie heute,* and, with Klaus von Beyme (eds.), *Elections and Parties.* He has spent extended periods of time in the United States doing research at, among others, the University of Michigan, the University of Iowa, and the State Universities of New York at Buffalo and Stony Brook.

Hans D. Klingemann is Privatdozent fuer Sociologie at the University of Mannheim, and Deputy Acting Director of the Zentrum fuer Umfragen, Methoden und Analysen, Mannheim. He has taught Sociology and Political Science at the Universities of Cologne, Bonn, Tubingen, and Mannheim. Among his publications are *Bestimmungruende. der Wahlentscheidung* and, with Franz Urban Pappi, *Politischer Radikalismus.*

Alan Marsh is Principal Social Survey Officer with the Office of Population Censuses and Surveys in London. He received his B.A. from the School of African and Asian Studies, University of Sussex and his Ph.D. in Social Psychology from the London School of Economics and Political Science. In the period 1974-1975 he was a Ford Foundation West European Scholar at the University of Michigan and prior to that worked on the Political Action project with the British Social Science Research Council's Survey Unit in London. Among his publications are *Protest and Political Consciousness.* He has also published widely in the field of race relations.

Leopold Rosenmayr is Professor of Sociology at the University of Vienna and Director of the L. Boltzmann Institute of Research on Age Groups and the Life Course. He has studied philosophy and sociology in Vienna and Paris and was Rockefeller Fellow at Harvard University and guest professor at Fordham University. His main work is in the areas of family relations, youth sociology, and social gerontology. His publications include *Familien-beziehungen und Freizeitgewohnheiten jugendlicher Arbeiter, Jugend* and *Familie-Alter,* Vols. 6 and 7 of R. Konig (ed.), *Handbuch der empirischen Sozialforschung,* and, with Hilde Rosenmayr, *Der alte Mensch in der Gesellschaft.*

INDEX OF NAMES

SUBJECT INDEX